D1327598

THE BOOK OF ACTS IN ITS
FIRST CENTURY SETTING

Bruce W. Winter

Series Editor

I. Howard Marshall • David Gill

Consulting Editors

Papyrus fragment, part of P91, is one of the oldest
surviving fragments of the book of Acts

Courtesy of Macquarie University, Sydney, Australia

THE BOOK OF ACTS IN ITS
FIRST CENTURY SETTING

VOLUME 1

The Book of Acts in Its
Ancient Literary Setting

Edited by

Bruce W. Winter and Andrew D. Clarke

WILLIAM B. EERDMANS PUBLISHING COMPANY
GRAND RAPIDS, MICHIGAN

THE PATERNOSTER PRESS
CARLISLE

Copyright © 1993 by Wm. B. Eerdmans Publishing Company
255 Jefferson Ave. S.E., Grand Rapids, Michigan 49503

First published 1993 jointly
in the United States by
Wm. B. Eerdmans Publishing Company
and in the U.K. by
The Paternoster Press,
P.O. Box 300, Carlisle, Cumbria CA3 0QS

Eerdmans ISBN 0-8028-2433-1

British Library Cataloguing in Publication Data

Book of Acts in Its Ancient Literary Setting. —
(Book of Acts in Its First Century Setting Series)
I. Clarke, Andrew D.   II. Winter, Bruce W.   III. Series.
226
ISBN 0-85364-563-9

TABLE OF CONTENTS

LIST OF CONTRIBUTORS

Dr. Loveday Alexander is a Lecturer in New Testament, Department of Biblical Studies, University of Sheffield. She holds her doctorate from Oxford University where she read classics and ancient history as an undergraduate and has published *The Preface to Luke's Gospel: Literary Convention and Social Context in Acts 1:1-4 and Acts 1:1* (1993) and edited *Images of Empire: the Roman Empire in Jewish, Christian and Greco-Roman Sources* (1991). She has chaired the Luke-Acts and the The Social World of New Testament Texts seminars of the annual British New Testament Conferences.

Professor Richard Bauckham holds the chair of New Testament Studies, St Mary's College, University of St. Andrews, Scotland and has recently published *Jude and the Relatives of Jesus in the Early Church* (1990), *The Theology of the Book of Revelation* (1993) and *The Climax of Prophecy: Studies on the Book of Revelation* (1993). He read history as an undergraduate at Cambridge University where he subsequently obtained his doctorate.

Dr. Conrad Gempf undertook his first degree at Gordon College and his MTS at Boston University. His doctoral work at Aberdeen University was on 'Historical and Literary Appropriateness in the Mission Speeches in Acts' and subsequently he completed and edited the late Dr. Colin Hemer's manscript *The Book of Acts in the Setting of Hellenistic History* (1989) before taking up the position of Lecturer in New Testament Studies at LBC Centre for Undergraduate and Postgraduate Theological Studies, London.

Mr. Peter Head is Lecturer in New Testament, Oak Hill College, London. He holds a Bachelor of Theology from the Australian College of Theology and a M.A. in Biblical Hermeneutics from LBC Centre for Undergraduate and Postgraduate Theological Studies, London. He has published articles in the field of textual criticism and is co-authoring a book on *Method in New Testament Textual Criticism from 1500 to 1850* with Dr. P. Satterthwaite.

Dr. T.W. Hillard is Lecturer in Ancient History, School of History, Philosophy and Politics, Macquarie University with special interests in history and historiography of republican Rome as well as classical Greek history and underwater archaeology. He obtained his doctorate at Macquarie University.

Professor I. Howard Marshall holds the chair of New Testament Exegesis, King's College, Aberdeen University where he read classics and divinity as an undergraduate. He has written extensively on Luke and Acts with a commentary on the Greek Text of Luke (1978) and on the English text of Acts (1980) *Luke: Theologian and Historian* (ed. 3, 1988) and *The Acts of the Apostles: New Testament Guides* (1992).

Dr. Alanna Nobbs is Senior Lecturer in Ancient History, School of History, Philosophy and Politics, Macquarie University, Sydney who publishes in the field of Graeco-Roman Historiography in late antiquity and the early Byzantine period. She undertook her doctoral studies in Latin at the University of Syndey.

Mr. Darryl Palmer, who holds an M.A. from Melbourne, B.D. from Drew and a Th.M. from Harvard, is Senior Lecturer in Classics, University of Newcastle, Newcastle, Australia. His central research interest is in early Christianity and the Graeco-Roman world on which he has published numerous articles.

Dr. David Peterson is Head of the Department of Ministry, Moore Theological College, and Lecturer in Divinity, University of Sydney. He has published *Hebrews and Perfection* (1982) and *Engaging with God: a Biblical Theology of Worship* (1992). He is a graduate of Sydney and London Universities and obtained his doctorate from Manchester University.

Dr. Brian S. Rosner is a graduate of Sydney University and Dallas Theological Seminary and completed his doctoral studies at Cambridge University. He is currently Lecturer in New Testament, University of Aberdeen and has published on the influence of the OT on the NT. His dissertation on Paul, Scripture and Ethics is in the process of publication.

Dr. Philip E. Satterthwaite read Hebrew and Aramaic at Cambridge University after graduating in classics at Oxford University. He secured his doctorate in OT at Manchester University and was a Lecturer in Classics, University of Transkei, South Africa. He is completing work on rhetoric in the Early Church Fathers. He holds a Tyndale House fellowship and is an Affliated Lecturer, Faculty of Oriental Studies, University of Cambridge.

Dr. S. Scott Spencer is Associate Professor of Religion, Wingate College, North Carolina. He is a history graduate, University of Texas and his doctorate was secured from Durham University. His book *The Portrait of Philip in Acts: A Study of Roles and Relations* was published in 1992.

Dr. David Wenham is a graduate of Cambridge University where he read theology; he obtained his doctorate from Manchester University. He is a Lecturer in New Testament, Wycliffe Hall, Oxford and a member of the Theological Faculty, Oxford University. He has published recently on *The Parables of Jesus: Pictures of Revolution* (1989) and is at present undertaking a major work on Jesus and Paul.

Dr. Bruce W. Winter read politics and biblical studies at the University of Queensland and obtained his doctorate at Macquarie University, Sydney. He is Warden, Tyndale House, Cambridge and a member of the Divinity Faculty, Cambridge University. His interests lie on the intersection of the New Testament with the Graeco-Roman world. His book on Philo and Paul and the first century sophistic movement is being published in 1994.

PREFACE

This is the first volume in a proposed six part series which will look at the Book of Acts. The intention is to place it in its first-century setting as far as extant evidence permits. To do this a multifaceted approach is required because the Acts of the Apostles belongs in literary, regional, cultural, ideological and theological settings of the early Roman Empire. Hence the volumes will cover Acts in its various settings: its ancient literary setting (edd. A.D. Clarke and B.W. Winter), the Graeco-Roman world (edd. D. Gill and C. Gempf), Roman custodial practice in relation to Paul's imprisonment (B. Rapske), Palestine (ed. R. Bauckham), Diaspora Judaism (I. Levinskaya) and finally its place in early Christian theology (edd. I.H. Marshall and D. Peterson).

Nineteenth-century studies in Acts were largely taken up with historical questions. The Tübingen School of F.C. Baur and his successors took a somewhat negative view. A more positive one was adopted by W.M. Ramsay who investigated especially the Roman world in which Paul worked and used it to throw light on his career as recorded in Acts and on his letter to the Galatians.[1]

This phase of study was summed up in the first volume of a massive work entitled *The Beginnings of Christianity* in 1920. The five volumes which constituted Part I of an intended project were to be prolegomena to a history of the rise of early Christianity. In fact, only this preliminary study of Acts was to be completed, with the last

---

[1]See especially W.M. Ramsay, *St. Paul the Traveller and the Roman Citizen* (London: Hodder & Stoughton, 1895); *A Historical Commentary on St. Paul's Epistle to the Galatians* (London: Hodder & Stoughton, 1899).

volume appearing in 1933.[2] It would be true to say that the approach
was historical rather than theological, provided that the reference of
these terms is carefully defined. The authors were interested not so
much in the theology expressed by the author of Acts as in the
historical value of Acts as a source for research into the theology of
the early church which (it was assumed) was reflected in the book.
Thus, while theological questions were not overlooked, the theology
in question was not that of Luke, and the work had a historical aim,
namely, to open up the way for a discriminating use of Acts in the
historical reconstruction of the life and theological development of
the early church.

Some 25 years later saw the appearance of a commentary on
Acts by E. Haenchen which set the mood for a new phase of study.[3]
For Haenchen the key question was 'What was Luke trying to do?', as
he opened up the way for a consideration of Acts as a literary
composition intended to promote the interests of its author. The
study of the redaction history of Acts had begun, and a generation of
scholars were to be occupied with the study of Luke as a theologian.[4]

The progress of academic study is sometimes compared to the
oscillations of a pendulum from one extreme to another. There is
something to be learned from scholars at both ends of the arc, and
also those at the new periphery of subsequent swings of the pendulum, for it is impossible for the pendulum to go back to precisely
where it was before or for scholars to ignore its sweeps.

The literary and theological questions raised by Haenchen and
those who followed his approach may be said to be at one end of the
arc of scholarship. They are clearly important and fruitful, and no
Lukan scholar would want to bypass or ignore them. But equally it
can be argued that any exclusive attachment to them does not place

---

[2]Volume 1 'The Jewish, Gentile and Christian Backgrounds'; Volume 2
authorship; Volume 3 the question of the original text of Acts; Volume 4 a full
Acts commentary by K. Lake and H.J. Cadbury; and Volume 5 additional,
detailed notes on a host of issues.

[3]E. Haenchen, *Die Apostelgeschichte* (KEK; Göttingen: Vandenhoeck und
Ruprecht, 1956; ed. 7, 1977); E.T., *Acts* (Oxford: Basil Blackwell, 1971).

[4]H. Conzelmann, *Die Apostelgeschichte* (HNT; Tübingen: J.C.B. Mohr, 1963; ed. 2,
1972). E.T., *Acts* (Hermeneia; Philadelphia: Fortress Press, 1987). To Conzelmann
is generally assigned the credit for initiating the study of Luke as a theologian in
Die Mitte der Zeit. Studien zur Theologie des Lukas (Tübingen: J.C.B. Mohr, 1954,
1964); E.T., *The Theology of St Luke* (London: Faber, 1960), although he was in fact
anticipated by N.B. Stonehouse, *The Witness of Luke to Christ* (London: Tyndale
Press, 1951), a work that failed to make much of an impact on critical scholarship.

Acts as fully as it should in its first-century environment. The cultural and historical interests of scholars at the other end of the arc also have recently re-emerged—but because of the pendulum swing are fruitfully being done so in new ways in the light of literary and theological studies.[5]

An international group of ancient historians and New Testament scholars from Australia, the United States of America, Canada and Russia as well as the United Kingdom gathered in Cambridge for a consultation on this project at the end of March 1993. This proved to be a stimulating experience as new approaches were tried and knowledge was shared across the disciplines. Of the chapters in this first volume some nine were discussed at the consultation, and the remaer were commissioned as a result of our meeting together. Other contributions will find their way into subsequent volumes.

In this cross-disciplinary gathering historians of antiquity felt that there needs to be a much more rigorous approach by biblical scholars to the study of aspects of the ancient world which impinge on the New Testament. That involved taking note of the on-going discussions of ancient literary sources and their genre when relating them to Acts. Measured deliberations of epigraphists and papyrologists on the ever expanding body of newly discovered inscriptions and papyri can be shown to be as important as actual citations of that material in studies on Acts. Furthermore from time to time there are significant shifts in the way aspects of the ancient world are interpreted. For example there are changed perceptions of Roman Greece and Asia Minor by classical historians which have a significant bearing on the picture of life in the geographic crescent where much of the recorded activities of early Christianity took place.[6] Acts studies need to take note of these.

---

[5]M. Hengel, *Zur urchristlichen Geschichtsschreibung* (Stuttgart: Calwer Verlag, 1979); E.T., *Acts and the History of Earliest Christianity* (London: SCM Press, 1979) in particular has brought his great knowledge of the ancient world to bear on the understanding of the New Testament; G. Lüdemann, *Das frühe Christentum nach den Traditionen der Apostelgeschichte. Ein Kommentar* (Göttingen: Vandenhoeck und Ruprecht, 1987); E.T., *Early Christianity according to the Traditions in Acts: A Commentary* (London: SCM Press, 1989) has concentrated attention on the difficult task of disentangling redaction and tradition and evaluating the claims of the latter to have a historical basis.
[6]S. Mitchell, *Anatolia. Land, Men, and Gods in Asia Minor.* Vol. 1: *The Celts and the Impact of Roman Rule*; Vol. 2: *The Rise of the Church* (Oxford: OUP, 1993).

However, the days have gone when it was possible for a New Testament scholar to keep abreast of the most recent discussion of primary sources and interpretative trends on the early Roman empire as well as the prolific work being done on Acts. There are ancient historians who are keen to work alongside scholars of Acts in order to come together in a beneficial partnership or συγκοινωνία. They can help place the Book of Acts more confidently in particular first-century settings. And the traffic has proved to be not all one way as Acts illustrates or complements aspects of life in the first century for historians. The consultation in Cambridge clearly illustrated this.

Special thanks must be given to Dr. Andrew Clarke for the production of camera ready copy, to Heather Richardson who typed manuscripts on the computer and Nicole Beale, Orlando Saer, Lyn and Elizabeth Winter who worked so hard on the indexes of this first volume.

Finally, we have been greatly encouraged by the enthusiasm of Bill Eerdmans Jr., the President of Wm. Eerdmans Publishing Company for this project and Paternoster Press for their ready partnership in this venture. It is anticipated that the remaining five volumes will be published within the next two years.

David W.J. Gill
I. Howard Marshall
Bruce W. Winter

September, 1993

CHAPTER 1

ACTS AND THE ANCIENT HISTORICAL MONOGRAPH

Darryl W. Palmer

Summary

In modern study the phrase 'historical monograph' is applied to ancient Greek and Roman writings which deal with a limited issue or period and which may also be limited in length. In ancient discussion Polybius contrasts the historical monograph with his universal history. Sallust writes Roman history 'selectively'. Cicero's letters reveal his concept of various features of the historical monograph Some Hellenistic Jewish writings correspond to the same pattern. Acts is not a romance (Pervo), an 'apologetic history' (Sterling) or a technical treatise (Alexander). In its length, scope, focus and internal features, Acts is a short historical monograph

I. Introduction

In recent years considerable attention has been given to the classification of New Testament writings according to standard

Greek and Roman literary genres.[1] The issue of the genre of the Acts of the Apostles continues to be discussed. Some scholars have been particularly concerned to treat the Gospel of Luke and Acts as a single literary work. Even so, views of the combined work have varied. R. Maddox saw Luke-Acts as 'to some extent shaped by the style and technique of Greek historiography'; but 'the best analogies for Luke's work are the historical works of the Old Testament, and perhaps post-Old Testament Jewish histories such as I Maccabees'. The genre of Luke-Acts is designated 'theological history'.[2] Most recently, G.E. Sterling has proposed that in the Hellenistic period there existed a type of history whose narratives 'relate the story of a particular people by deliberately hellenizing their native traditions'. According to Sterling: 'This is precisely what Luke-Acts does'. And for the genre he uses the term 'apologetic historiography'.[3] L.C.A. Alexander's investigation of the Lukan prefaces led her to understand Luke-Acts against the background of technical treatises. She sees 'Luke as a writer set firmly within the context of the scientific tradition. . .The scientific tradition provides the matrix within which we can explore both the social and literary aspects of Luke's work, both the man himself and the nature of his writings'.[4] C.H. Talbert interpreted Luke-Acts as a mixture of two sub-types of Graeco-Roman biography.[5]

However, biography has more usually been considered as an appropriate genre for the Gospel of Luke along with other gospels,

---

[1]D. Aune's study, *The New Testament in its Literary Environment* (Philadelphia: Westminster, 1987) examines the major genres of the NT writings and their constituent oral and literary forms against their Jewish, Greek and Roman background. Concise bibliographies give a good indication of modern scholarship.

[2]R. Maddox, *The Purpose of Luke-Acts* (Edinburgh: T. & T. Clark, 1982) 16.

[3]G.E. Sterling, *Historiography and Self-Definition. Josephos, Luke-Acts and Apologetic Historiography* (Leiden: Brill, 1992) 374.

[4]L.C.A. Alexander, 'Luke's preface in the context of Greek preface-writing', *NovT* 28 (1986) 48-74 at 70. Cf. her Oxford D.Phil. thesis, *Luke-Acts in its contemporary setting, with special reference to the prefaces (Luke 1.1-4 and Acts 1.1)*; this has now been revised as a book, *The Preface to Luke's Gospel. Literary convention and social context in Luke 1.1-4 and Acts 1.1* (Cambridge: Cambridge University Press, 1993). For criticisms (based on her article and thesis), see S.E. Porter, 'Thucydides 1.22.1 and speeches in Acts: is there a Thucydidean view?', *NovT* 32 (1990) 121-142 at 125-126; Sterling, *Historiography*, 340.

[5]C.H. Talbert, *What is a Gospel? The Genre of the Canonical Gospels* (Philadelphia: Fortress, 1977) 134. For criticisms, see Aune, *Literary Environment*, 79; Sterling, *Historiography*, 319-320.

and apart from Acts. It is only because Aune is not willing to separate Luke from Acts, that he cannot accept Luke as a biography.[6] But it seems better to allow 'that Luke and Acts are themselves different in type, even when we grant their essential unity and continuity'.[7] Acts, when considered separately from Luke, has most commonly been regarded as a historical writing.[8] And, in particular, several recent scholars have canvassed the category of historical monograph.[9] One other view must also be acknowledged. R. Pervo has emphasised the entertaining dimension of the adventurous episodes of Acts.[10] His study caused him to class Acts among the historical novels of antiquity.[11] His discussion deserves a more extensive response than can be attempted here. In brief, it is hardly possible to distinguish history, and particularly the historical monograph, from the novel on the basis of the entertainment value of the two genres. As Gabba has said in the context of his treatment of historical monographs, biographies and anthologies: 'in the same climate of paradoxographical [i.e., anthological] literature the "novel" is born and develops; the novel in antiquity is in fact a form of history'.[12]

---

[6]'By itself, Luke could (like Mark, Matthew, and John) be classified as a type of ancient biography. But Luke. . .was subordinated to a larger literary structure. Luke does not belong to a type of ancient biography for it belongs with Acts, and Acts cannot be forced into a biographical mold.' Aune, *Literary Environment*, 77. Similarly Sterling, *Historiography*, 339.

[7]C.J. Hemer, *The Book of Acts in the Setting of Hellenistic History* (Tübingen: Mohr/Siebeck, 1989) 33. Cf. Aune, *Literary Environment*, 77: 'Luke is commonly regarded as a "gospel" because of obvious similarities to the other Gospels, and Acts is widely categorized as "history". . .'

[8]So Sterling, *Historiography*, 317-318 with references in nn. 36-37.

[9]H. Conzelmann, *Acts of the Apostles* (Philadelphia: Fortress, 1987; 1st German ed. 1963) xl; E. Plümacher, 'Die Apostelgeschichte als historische Monographie', in J. Kremer (ed.), *Les Actes des Apôtres. Traditions, rédaction, théologie* (Gembloux: Duculot, 1979) 457-466; *idem*, 'Neues Testament und hellenistische Form. Zur literarischen Gattung der lukanischen Schriften', *Theologia Viatorum* 14 (1977-78) 109-123; M. Hengel, *Acts and the History of Earliest Christianity* (London: SCM, 1979) 14, 36; G. Schneider, *Die Apostelgeschichte* (2 vols.; Freiburg: Herder, 1980-82) 1.123: K. Berger, 'Hellenistische Gattungen in Neuen Testament', *ANRW* II.25.2 (1984) 1031-1432 at 1275, 1280-81; cf. G. Schille, *Die Apostelgeschichte des Lukas* (Berlin: Evangelische Verlaganstalt, 1984) 66.

[10]R. Pervo, *Profit with Delight. The Literary Genre of the Acts of the Apostles* (Philadelphia: Fortress, 1987) 11

[11]Pervo, *Profit*, 137-138.

[12]E. Gabba, 'Literature', Chapter 1 in M. Crawford (ed.), *Sources for Ancient History* (Cambridge: Cambridge University Press, 1983) 15. For brief criticisms of Pervo, see Aune, *Literary Environment*, 80; Sterling, *Historiography*, 320.

II. The Term 'Historical Monograph'

The phrase 'historical monograph' is a modern one with some basis in ancient terminology. In modern discussion the phrase is commonly applied to ancient historical writings which deal with a limited issue or period without regard to the length of the books themselves. Thus 'Sallust's first two works' have been described as 'monographs concerned with limited themes of special interest'.[13] Again, the task of the potential writer of a historical monograph has been expressed as 'the interpretation of a special period'.[14] Such a concept, when applied to the available evidence, means that 'Thucydides of Athens. . .is the historian of the Peloponnesian War and therefore the creator of the historical monograph'.[15] (Thucydides's incomplete work comprises eight books.)

On the other hand, the term 'monograph' may be used to designate ancient historical writings limited in length as well as scope. Thus Sallust's *Bellum Catilinae* and *Bellum Iugurthinum* are frequently referred to as monographs in order to distinguish them from the fragments of his *Historiae* in at least five books.[16] Goodyear allows that Sallust may be criticised, 'in his *Catiline* at least, for the disproportionate bulk of introductory matter in a comparatively short composition'.[17] And Paul remarks on 'an apparently puzzling feature of the monograph. In a work dealing ostensibly with the conspiracy, the amount of space allotted to the speeches of Caesar and Cato, and the comparison between them, may seem excessive; is

---

[13]F.R.D. Goodyear, 'Sallust', in E.J. Kenney with W.V. Clausen (eds.), *The Cambridge History of Classical Literature, Vol. 2: Latin Literature* (Cambridge: Cambridge University Press, 1982) 268-280 at 268.

[14]A.H. McDonald, 'The Roman Historians', in M. Platnauer (ed.), *Fifty Years of Classical Scholarship* (Oxford: Blackwell, 1954) 391.

[15]H. Bengtson, *Introduction to Ancient History* (Berkeley: University of California Press, 1970) 90. Cf. C.W. Fornara, *The Nature of History in Ancient Greece and Rome* (Berkeley: University of California Press, 1983) 32: 'The war monograph implicit in Herodotus emerged perfected at Thucydides' hands'. A. Momigliano ('Greek historiography', *History and Theory* 17 [1978] 1-28 at 10-11) also refers to the 'Thucydidean monograph'. Cf. also Dionysius of Halicarnassus, *On Thucydides* 6-7.

[16]E.g., McDonald, 'Roman Historians', 391; Fornara, *Nature*, 67; A.J. Woodman, *Rhetoric in Classical Historiography* (Sydney: Croom Helm, 1988) 117; so also W. Steidle, *Sallusts Historische Monographien* (Wiesbaden: Steiner, 1958) as in his title.

[17]Goodyear, 'Sallust', 270.

the internal balance of the work not thereby endangered?'[18] Or as Syme with characteristic succinctness put it: 'a monograph, demanding concentration, entailed omissions'.[19]

But even in the case of Sallust's writings, the issues of length and scope become somewhat confused. Sallust's monograph on the Jugurthine war deals with the years 118 to 105 B.C. with some sketching of earlier background. The extant fragments of the *Historiae* cover only the period 78 to 67 B.C., although some scholars postulate that Sallust intended to carry his treatment further.[20] Sallust is recognised as the first Roman historian to use the form of the monograph, since it was introduced to Latin historiography by Coelius Antipater after 121 B.C.[21] But Coelius wrote on the Second Punic War (218-201 B.C.) in *seven* books.

An ancient historical monograph in the narrower sense (i.e., limited in both scope and length) consists of a single book or volume. However, a single volume may not always have been contained in one scroll. Sallust's monographs each comprise a single volume, but one is nearly twice the length of the other. The Gospel of Luke and Acts are each close to the normal maximum length for a Greek Scroll. Sallust's *Bellum Catilinae* would have fitted comfortably on one scroll; but the *Bellum Iugurthinum*, being too long for a single scroll, would probably have been accommodated on two scrolls shorter than the average length.[22]

III. Polybius's Views

In ancient discussion, Polybius (2nd century B.C.) firmly distinguished his own 'universal' history from the 'monographs' of

---

[18]G.M. Paul, 'Sallust', in T.A. Dorey (ed.), *Latin Historians* (New York: Basic Books, 1966) 85-113 at 94.

[19]R. Syme, *Sallust* (Berkeley: University of California Press, 1964) 69.

[20]Syme proposes 51 or 50 B.C., but is not enthusiastic about Bonnet's suggestion of 40 B.C.; see Syme, *Sallust*, 192 with n. 54. Cf. Woodman, *Rhetoric*, 117. W. Allen Jr. drew attention to 'a confusion in the modern usage of the word "monograph"' in his article, 'The unity of the Sallustian corpus', *CJ* 61 (1966) 268-269 at 269 n. 5.

[21]See McDonald, 'Roman Historians', 391; Steidle, *Historische Monographien*, 1; A.D. Leeman, *Orationis Ratio* (Amsterdam: Hakkert, 1963) 74; Bengtson, *Introduction*, 94.

[22]See F.G. Kenyon, *Books and Readers in Ancient Greece and Rome* (2nd ed.; Oxford: Clarendon, 1951).

other historians. In this polemical context he did not maintain a consistent concept of universal history.[23] And his remarks about monographs bear different emphases in various passages. In designating the monograph Polybius uses the phrases ἐπὶ μέρους or, more often, κατὰ μέρος (literally, 'in part') in a range of grammatical constructions. The latter phrase also has other uses in Polybius ('in particular'; 'in detail'). Conversely, the phrases are not yet used in Herodotus, Thucydides or Xenophon with reference to the historical monograph; nor are they subsequently so used in Diodorus Siculus, Dionysius of Halicarnassus, Josephus or Dio Cassius. In discussing the merits of general history (τὰς κοινὰς ἱστορίας, D.S. 1.1.1.), Diodorus merely mentions in passing the majority of historians who 'described the separate wars of a single nation or city' (ἑνὸς ἔθνους ἢ μιᾶς πόλεως αὐτοτελεῖς πολέμους ἀνέγραψαν, D.S. 1.3.2).

The phrase ἐπὶ μέρους is used only twice in Polybius. In both occurrences it is used adjectivally (between article and noun) in connexion with 'particular histories'. In 3.31-32 Polybius has a historiographical digression, of which at least part belongs to a second edition. The closing phrase of this passage refers to 'particular compositions' (τῶν ἐπὶ μέρους συντάξεων, 3.32.10), by which Polybius means historical writings concerned with particular wars (πολέμους, 3.32.8). His own work now stands complete at forty books (3.32.2); but the particular histories, about which he complains, are many times as long (πολλαπλασίους, 3.32.4). Thus, according to Polybius, a 'monograph' may be much longer than a 'universal history'. Within a short historiographical digression at 7.7.6-8 Polybius mentions 'those who describe particular actions' (οἱ τὰς ἐπὶ μέρους γράφοντες πράξεις, 7.7.6). These writers, he claims, both expand their subjects (7.7.1) and inflate their importance (7.7.6). The accounts of the fall of Hieronymus (7.7.1), taken as examples, are multi-volume monographs (τὰς βύβλους, 7.7.7).

The majority of occurrences of the phrase κατὰ μέρος, when used to denote particular histories, is adjectival. The phrase may qualify either the *subject-matter* of history or the historical *writing* itself. There is reference, on the one hand, to wars (πόλεμοι, 1.4.3) or actions (πράξεις, 1.4.3; 9.44.2; 16.14.1); and on the other hand, to history (ἱστορία, 1.4.7, 10; 8.2.2 pl.) or compositions (συντάξεις, 8.2.5). The several examples of the phrase in 1.4 occur within Polybius's

---

[23]K. Sacks, *Polybius on the Writing of History* (Berkeley: University of California Press, 1981) Chapter 3, 'The Genre: Universal History'.

historiographical introduction to his whole work (1.1-4). In this section Polybius indicates his own reasons for undertaking his task, including the claim that none of his contemporaries has written a universal history (1.4.2). But only by so doing can one gain a synoptic view of the whole and the interrelation of its parts—something which is not possible on the basis of particular histories (1.4.6, 7, 10-11). Polybius himself does not mention the names of any authors of particular histories in 1.4; 8.1-2; or the fragmentary 9.44. At 16.14 he begins a digression criticising the 'particular' historians Zeno and Antisthenes of Rhodes. Zeno probably wrote in fifteen books; the scope and length of Antisthenes's work are unknown.[24]

In two contexts which have already been considered, Polybius also uses the phrase κατὰ μέρος adverbially. Literally, he refers to 'those particularly writing histories' (τῶν κατὰ μέρος γραφόντων τὰς ἱστορίας, 1.4-6) and 'the compositions of those writing particularly' (τὰς τῶν κατὰ μέρος γραφόντων συντάξεις, 3.32.3). In both cases, a paraphrase referring to 'particular histories' is desirable in English. On one occasion Polybius constructs a noun phrase denoting 'the composition of particular (histories)' (τῆς τῶν κατὰ μέρος συντάξεως, 8.2.11). Here, at the end of the introduction to Book 8, the phrase is strongly contrasted with 'universal and general history' (τῆς καθολικῆς καὶ κοινῆς ἱστορίας).

In another historiographical digression at 29.12, Polybius repeats his criticisms of 'particular' historians on the grounds that they expand their treatment and exaggerate the importance of their subjects (cf. 7.7). In this context the monograph is indicated by reference to its 'single and unitary subject-matter' (ἁπλᾶς καὶ μονοειδεῖς...ὑποθέσεις, 29.12.2).[25] Since Polybius complains about 'the multitude of the books' (τῷ πλήθει τῶν βύβλων), it is clear that he envisages multi-volume monographs as at 3.32 and 7.7. Polybius had previously used the term 'unitary' in the historiographical introduction to Book 9. There, however, it designates the unitary nature of his own universal history (9.1.2). For, unlike nearly all other writers, who deal with every branch (μέρος) of history, Polybius avoids not only mythology but also accounts of colonisation,

---

[24]See F.W. Walbank, *A Historical Commentary on Polybius* (3 vols.; Oxford: Clarendon, 1957-79) 2.517-518.

[25]The terms ἁπλοῦς and μονοειδής seem to be largely synonymous, and the expression therefore pleonastic. Their combination may have been idiomatic (as in 'times and seasons'); cf. 6.10.6.

foundation of cities and family relationships; instead, he concentrates solely on 'the actions of nations, cities and rulers' (τὰς πράξεις τῶν ἐθνῶν καὶ πόλεων καὶ δυναστῶν, 9.1.4).[26] In summary, Polybius frequently distinguishes between universal history and particular history or monograph. Monographs deal with a particular issue within a limited period. However, they may adopt a wider perspective and are generally even longer than Polybius's universal history.

IV. Sallust's Theory and Practice

After a political and military career of mixed success and failure, Sallust (c. 86-c. 35 B.C.) resolved that the rest of his life should be spent far from public affairs (*Cat.* 4.1). More specifically, he says 'I decided to write an account of the actions of the Roman people selectively, as each (topic) seemed worthy of record'.[27] The reference to 'actions' (*res gestae*) corresponds to the Greek πράξεις, and became standard in Latin historiography.[28] The motif of what is worthy of record is also traditional.[29] If the term 'selectively' (*carptim*) alludes to the monograph, that would follow the pattern of Polybius's discussions. The term is indeed frequently understood in this sense.[30] Ramsey, for example, explains the term as meaning 'in monographs or separate essays on a limited period rather than a continuous history of R. from the foundation'.[31] And Woodman actually paraphrases Sallust's Latin: 'I decided to write an historical monograph on a Roman theme'.[32]

---

[26]The only other occurrence of μονοειδής in Polybius is at 6.10.6, where he mentions that Lycurgus did not make his constitution 'single nor unitary'.
[27]*statui res gestas populi Romani carptim, ut quaeque memoria digna uidebantur, perscribere, Cat.* 4.2. *quaeque* (n. pl.) suggests 'each group (of events)'.
[28]E.g., Asel. *hist.* 1; Hirt. *Gal.* 8. pr. 2; Caes. *Civ.* 2.32.5; 3.106.3; Sal. *Hist.* 1.1; Liv. *pr.* 1.
[29]Th. 1.1.1. (ἀξιολογώτατος); X. *HG* 4.8.1. (ἀξιομνημόνευτος); Plb. 1.2.1 (ἐλλογιμώτατος), 2 (τῆς παραβολῆς ἄξιος καὶ συγκρίσεως); D.S. 1.6.1. (ἀκοῆς ἄξιος); 1.3.6 (εἰς μνήμην παραδεδομένος); cf. Liv. 21.1.1 (*maxime omnium memorabile*).
[30]E.g., P. McGushin, *C. Sallustius Crispus Bellum Catilinae. A Commentary* (Leiden: Brill, 1977) 9, 55; Steidle, *Historische Monographien*, 1; cf. Goodyear, 'Sallust', 273.
[31]J.T. Ramsey (ed.), *Sallust's 'Bellum Catilinae'* (Chico, CA: Scholars Press, 1984) 68. Cf. Syme, *Sallust*, 56: 'Sallust announces that he will take certain portions of Roman history, selectively...'
[32]Woodman, *Rhetoric*, 73.

There are difficulties in the interpretation of this Sallustian passage in addition to, but not unconnected with, the significance of *carptim*. In the prologues of both his monograps Sallust develops a scheme of ability, excellence, achievement and glory. The scheme is applicable not only to mankind in general as distinct from the animals, but also to historians in particular as well as to men of action. Sallust uses the idiomatic phrase *res gestae* only in the prologues (twice in each monograph) and once in the early digression outlining the previous history of Rome in *Cat.* 5.9-13.5.[33] In *Cat.* 3.2 Sallust anticipates 4.2 by speaking of the difficulty of the historian's task in writing an account of 'actions' (*arduom uidetur res gestas scribere*). In *Cat.* 8.2 he acknowledges the impressive and magnificent nature of the 'actions' of the Athenians (*Atheniensium res gestae*). The phrase *memoria rerum gestarum* is used twice in *Iug.* 4, but in slightly different senses in each occurrence. The 'recording' of actions is particularly useful (*Iug.* 4.1); while the 'memory' of actions kindled in the hearts of outstanding men a flame which was not extinguished until their excellence equalled the fame and glory of their ancestors (*Iug.* 4.6). These instances of the phrase *res gestae* have just been translated in a neutral way as 'actions'. But the Sallustian contexts suggest rather the more positive significance of 'achievements'.

This point should be kept in mind when the sequence of thought in *Cat.* 4.2-3 is considered. 'I decided to write an account of the actions (achievements) of the Roman people, selectively. . .Therefore I shall briefly describe the conspiracy of Catiline as truthfully as I can. . .' However, the conspiracy of Catiline is not an 'achievement' of the Roman people in the sense that Sallust has established for *res gestae*. Rather, as Sallust immediately proceeds to say, it is a deed, or even misdeed, which is especially memorable by reason of the unprecedented nature of the crime and the threat.[34] Nor does Sallust go on to write a series of 'selective' monographs: only the *Bellum Iugurthinum*, then the *Historiae*. And for the topic of his second monograph, Sallust goes backwards in time. Moreover, despite the similarity of the prologues of the two monographs, there is no equivalent of *carptim* in the *Bellum Iugurthinum*. On the other

---

[33] *res in Africa gestas* (*Iug.* 30.1) is not quite the same idiom.
[34] *nam id facinus in primis ego memorabile existumo sceleris atque periculi nouitate, Cat.* 4.4. The pejorative sense of *facinus* is usual in Sallust, when the term lacks a descriptive adjective; see Ramsey, *'Bellum Catilinae'*, 63, 69 (on 2.9; 4.4).

hand, despite the relatively short digressions at *Iug.* 17-19 (geographical) and 41-42 (political), there is in that writing nothing of the scope or length of the so-called archaeology and the central digression of the *Bellum Catilinae*. It is in general remarkable how much of the material of the *Bellum Catilinae* is not actually narrative of the conspiracy. And in particular, if this writing is intended to focus selectively on the limited period of the conspiracy itself, it is noticeable that the outline of the earlier history of Rome occupies some eight chapters (*Cat.* 5.9-13.5) and is continued by the political digression at *Cat.* 36.4-39.5.[35]

Sallust is fond of adverbs ending with -*im*, an archaising feature. In extant Latin literature, *carptim* first occurs at *Cat.* 4.2; and it is used only here in Sallust's extant writings. Its position in the word order of this sentence is emphatic. McGushin claims that the term is employed 'in the same sense as is used by Pliny, *Ep.* 8.4.7; Tacitus [*sic*], *Hist.* 4.46.4'.[36] But neither these nor the other classical examples are much help in elucidating Sallust's meaning. Tacitus refers to people who were 'dismissed for a fault, but separately (*carptim*) and individually'. Pliny uses the adverb almost as a noun, to refer to 'selections' from a draft history of the Dacian war. Closer to Sallust's usage is Pliny *Paneg.* 25.1: 'it would be more respectful to leave things unspoken and implicit in our hearts, than to run through (the emperor's actions) selectively and briefly' (*carptim breuiterque*). The last quotation at least involves a selection of historical events to be included in a literary composition.[37]

According to some scholars, Sallust understood the Catilinarian conspiracy as symptomatic of the decline of Rome.[38] This view fits

---

[35]'In this discussion of the contemporary political situation, S. continues with and brings up to date his earlier picture of Rome (chs. 11-13). . .', (McGushin, *Commentary*, 200).

[36]McGushin, *Commentary*, 55.

[37]The other classical instances of *carptim* between Sallust and Suetonius (indicated by computer search) are Liv. 22.16.2; 28.25.10; 44.41.7; Colum. 9.15.12; Plin. *Nat.* 18.362; Plin. *Ep.* 6.22.2; 8.14.16; Suet. *Dom.* 9.3.

[38]Paul, 'Sallust', 92, 93; Woodman, *Rhetoric*, 125; cf. Hemer, *Acts*, 89 with n. 83. The *Bellum Iugurthinum* has recently been interpreted in a similar way: see D.S. Levene, 'Sallust's *Jugurtha*: an "historical fragment"', *JRS* 82 (1992) 53-70. Referring to the programmatic statement at *Iug.* 5.1-2, he writes: 'we see it now against the background of a large-scale Roman decline, and we are prepared for the idea that the important thing about the Jugurthine War is the way in which it relates to the past and future decline' (56); cf. 59: 'I showed above that the philosophical preface was so set up as to give us a moral theme in general, then

quite well with Sallust's use of the term *carptim*. For Sallust does not merely select a period of Roman history for treatment in a monograph. And the Latin *carptim* is not simply an equivalent of the Greek κατὰ μέρος. Rather, Sallust portrays the history of the Roman people by means of a survey (the 'archaeology') combined with a particular example (Catiline and his conspiracy) which symbolises the whole. In this way Sallust 'gives an account of the actions of the Roman people selectively': *res gestas populi Romani carptim. . .perscribere, Cat.* 4.2.[39] The account contains a warning relevant at the time of composition some twenty years after the main events described. The selective focus of the writing is appropriate to a monograph. The promise that the topic will be dealt with 'briefly' (*paucis, Cat.* 4.3) is fulfilled, and justifies the designation of the writing as a short historical monograph. In the prologue to the *Bellum Iugurthinum*, Sallust mentions neither brevity nor selectivity. And, although he does not repeat an outline history of Rome, his second work grows longer than the first. However, it too qualifies as a short historical monograph.

V. Cicero's Concept

It is a familiar irony that the monograph, which Cicero (106-43 B.C.) wanted written about his own glorious role in the *suppression* of the Catilinarian conspiracy, did not appear during his lifetime. Sallust probably composed or published his monograph soon after the death of Cicero. The focus of attention is not upon Cicero or any other hero, but upon the culprit Catiline. Cicero had no specific *term* for the historical monograph; but his correspondence provides evidence for his *concept* of various features of the genre.

On 15 March 60 B.C. Cicero sent to Atticus a 'sketch' (*commentarius*, sg.) of his consulship in Greek.[40] At that stage he was

---

to show the decline of Rome as a specific instance of that general theme, and finally to set the work against the background of Roman decline'.

[39]This understanding of Sallust's use of *carptim* bears comparison with Levene's study of the *Bellum Iugurthinum* as 'a deliberate fragment: a work that is notionally complete, in that it is written and presented as something finished and whole, but which at the same time draws the reader's attention in a more or less systematic fashion to the fact that it is incomplete; it shows itself to be only part of the whole'. Levene, 'Sallust's *Jugurtha*', 53; cf. 65, 66.

[40]*commentarium consulatus mei Graece compositum misi ad te.* Cic. *Att.* 1.19.10.

also thinking of producing a Latin version of it.[41] In a letter written at some time after 12 May 60 B.C., he refers to this writing as a 'book' (*liber*).[42] On 1 June 60 B.C. He received from Atticus an equivalent sketch, which Atticus had composed in Greek.[43] Cicero had apparently sent another copy of his own composition to Posidonius; this he designates by the Greek title ὑπόμνημα ('memorandum', 'note', 'draft').[44] The ostensible purpose was that Posidonius should work up Cicero's material into something more elaborate and polished. But Posidonius had by now replied that he was deterred from, rather than stimulated to, such a task.[45] Cicero had in fact done a thoroughly cosmetic job already: 'Now my book has used up Isocrates' entire perfume-cabinet along with all the little scent-boxes of his pupils, and some of Aristotle's rouge as well. . .I shouldn't have dared send it to you except after leisurely and fastidious revision'.[46]

Nearly five years later Cicero was still trying to persuade someone to write a laudatory account of his consulship. Lucceius was approaching the end of the composition of his 'History of the Italian and Civil Wars'. He is asked by Cicero whether he would prefer to include the latter's involvement with the rest of the events, or to 'separate the civil conspiracy from the wars with enemies and foreigners'. Cicero's analogies for separate treatment are Greek: Callisthenes, *Phocian War*; Timaeus, *War of Pyrrhus*; Polybius, *Numantine War*.[47] It is possible that Callisthenes's work consisted of

---

[41]*Latinum si perfecero, ad te mittam.* Cic *Att.* 1.19.10.

[42]*de meis scriptis misi ad te Graece perfectum consulatum meum. eum librum L. Cossinio dedi.* Cic. *Att.* 1.20.6; likewise 2.1.1.

[43]*commentarium consulatus mei Graece scriptum reddidit.* Cic. *Att.* 2.1.1.

[44]Cic. *Att.* 2.1.2.

[45]Cic. *Att.* 2.1.2.

[46]*meus autem liber totum Isocrati myrothecium atque omnis eius discipulorum arculas ac non nihil etiam Aristotelia pigmenta consumpsit. . .quem tibi ego non essem ausus mittere nisi eum lente ac fastidiose probauissem.* Cic. *Att.* 2.1.1 (tr. D.R. Shackleton Bailey).

[47]Cic. *Fam.* 5.12.2; cf. 5.12.6. In the case of Callisthenes, most editors adopt *Phocicum* for the manuscript reading *Troicum*. The validity of Cicero's examples is uncertain. '. . .Polybius' special work on the war is not elsewhere recorded. . .The fact may be that *none* of the three special works covered a period dealt with in their authors' general histories (Timaeus' case being in doubt). . .' D.R. Shackleton Bailey (ed.), *Cicero: Epistulae ad Familiares* (2 vols.; Cambridge: Cambridge University Press, 1977) 1.320.

only one book;[48] but likely that Timaeus's contained more.[49] Cicero envisages that Lucceius will concentrate on one theme and one person.[50] But the desired scope of the monograph has now been expanded: 'For from the beginning of the conspiracy up to our return it seems to me a volume of moderate size could be composed'.[51] Shackleton Bailey comments that the use of *corpus* ('volume') is 'exceptional of a single *liber*'.[52] But perhaps Cicero is leaving it open, whether there should be one book or more, especially in view of the expanded scope of the proposed monograph. Instead of the one year of his consulship, Cicero is probably thinking of a period from December 66 B.C. to 57 B.C.[53] Cicero concludes his letter to Lucceius by hoping for a positive reply, and by offering to draft notes on all the events. These notes (*commentarii*) would presumably differ little from the sketch (*commentarius, liber, ὑπόμνημα*), which Cicero had composed some years earlier.[54]

In short, Cicero has a concept of a historical writing of limited length and scope. His various designations for it are modest: sketch, book, memorandum, volume (*commentarius, liber, ὑπόμνημα, corpus*). Even for the same topic, the scope is variable (one year, or eight to nine years). Greek analogies confirm Cicero's concept, even if his actual examples are not entirely apt. Such a work requires concentration on one theme and, in Cicero's case, one person. And, although his ostensible rough draft is sufficiently polished to deter others,[55] Cicero nevertheless wants someone else to attempt the task.

---

[48]ὥς φησι Καλλισθένης ἐν τῷ περὶ τοῦ ἱεροῦ πολέμου, Ath. (= Athenaeus, *Deipnosophists*) 13.560C.

[49]ἐν τοῖς περὶ Πύρρου, Plb. 12.4b.1.

[50]*si uno in argumento unaque in persona mens tua tota versabitur*, Cic. *Fam.* 5.12.2.

[51]*a principio enim coniurationis usque ad reditum nostrum uidetur mihi modicum quoddam corpus confici posse.* Cic. *Fam.* 5.12.4.

[52]Shackleton Bailey, *Cicero: Epistulae ad Familiares*, 1.320.

[53]For Cicero's own early dating of the beginning of Catiline's plots, see Asc. *Tog.* 92; Cic. *Catil.* 1.15; *Mur.* 81; *Sul.* 11-12. Exiled in 58 B.C., Cicero was recalled in the following year and arrived in Rome on 4 September 57 B.C.

[54]*conficiam commentarios rerum omnium*, Cic. *Fam.* 5.12.10. Cf. Cic. *Att.* 4.11.2 (26 June 55 B.C.): *tu Lucceio nostrum librum dabis*; also *Att.* 4.9.2 (27 April 55 B.C.), where Atticus already appeared as intermediary between Cicero and Lucceius.

[55]Cf., with regard to Caesar's *Commentarii*, Cicero's own remark (*Brut.* 262) and Hirt. *Gal.* 8.pr.4.

VI. Fragmentary Evidence

If Jewish writings are excluded, no single-volume historical monographs in Greek or Latin survive from the period before Sallust. The same may be said for the period between Sallust and the composition of Acts. Testimonia and fragments of lost writings leave it uncertain whether such monographs once existed. After treating the three examples from Cic. *Fam.* 5.12.2, Plümacher mentions three more 'instructive' instances.[56] Of these, however, Philinus wrote on the First Punic War in at least two books;[57] the length of Dellius's writing on the Parthian War of 36-35 B.C. is unknown;[58] so too is that of Crito on Trajan's Dacian War.[59] Walbank, commenting on Polybius's introductory remarks about general and particular histories, mentions fourteen 'examples of such contemporary writers of particular histories'.[60] For some of these works the evidence indicates more than one book; for others the evidence is unclear. In one case it is possible that the writing comprised a single volume: Baton of Sinope is quoted ἐν τῷ περὶ τῆς τοῦ Ἱερονύμου τυραννίδος.[61] Interpretation of the length of the work depends on what noun is to be understood with the article τῷ. And if βιβλίῳ is to be understood, it depends whether that term refers to a single book of a multi-volume work, or to a multi-volume work as a whole. The word may have either meaning. At any rate, this sample of the fragmentary evidence indicates that prior to Sallust single-volume historical monograps were rare, if they existed at all.[62] It is equally clear that both short and long monographs of Greek and Roman tradition regularly dealt with wars.

---

[56]Plümacher, 'Apostelgeschichte', 462 and n. 27, with reference to F. Jacoby, *Die Fragmente der Griechischen Historiker*, Nr. 106-226: Spezialgeschichten und Monographien.

[57]Polybius refers to the second book at 1.15.1; 3.26.5.

[58]The testimonium in Strabo 11.13.3 actually has ἀδέλφιος Δέλλιος is Casaubon's emendation. Cf. Plu. *Ant.* 59.4: Δέλλιος ὁ ἱστορικός.

[59]The phrase ἐν τοῖς Γετικοῖς occurs several times in the testimonia (*FGH* Nr. 200), but leaves the number of books unclear.

[60]Walbank, *Commentary*, 1, 44 on Plb. 1.4.3, with cross reference to 42 on Plb. 1.3.2.

[61]Testimonium from Ath. 6.251E.

[62]As previously noted, Sallust's only known Latin predecessor, Coelius Antipater, wrote on the Second Punic War in seven books.

VII. 'Apologetic Historiography'

Sterling (*Historiography*; see n. 3 above) sets out to find a genre for Luke-Acts. Genre is to be defined by an analysis of 'the content, form, and function of a text' (p. 14).

> The application of this genre model uncovered the presence of apologetic historiography. . .Using the model it became evident that there was a group of texts which all told the story of a particular group of people (content) by recasting native texts into a mold more palatable in the Greco-Roman world (form). All of the authors were natives or 'insiders' who related the story of their own group in an effort to offer a self-definition of that group (function). . .The works are therefore apologetic, but may be either directly or indirectly apologetic depending upon the primary audience. (pp. 16-17).

Sterling attempts to trace the development of Greek ethnography from its origins to the time of Josephus and Luke. Major early writers, Hecataeus of Miletus and Herodotus, were both Greeks who travelled in foreign parts. Later, Hecataeus of Abdera and Megasthenes were Greeks who lived in the lands which they described. In the next stage, native writers gave an account of their land and culture. Examples of such writings are the *Babyloniaca* of Berossus and the *Aegyptiaca* of Manethon. 'The largest literary corpus which we have that reflects the attempt of an ethnic group to present its own story within the Hellenistic world is Jewish' (p. 137). The fragmentary Hellenistic Jewish historians Demetrius, Artapanus, pseudo-Eupolemus and Eupolemus are treated. 'The works served to give the Jewish people a new identity in a new world' (pp. 224-25).

But the main Hellenistic Jewish historian is Josephus. It is not the contemporary history of the *Jewish War* which serves Sterling's purpose, but the *Jewish Antiquities*. 'Josephos' programmatic statements make it clear that he considers *BJ* and *AJ* to belong to two different historiographical traditions'; it is the latter which 'stands in a Near Eastern tradition of historiography which emphasizes native traditions' (p. 245). In short:

> At its core the *Antiquitates* offers a self-definition of Judaism in historical terms. It presented Judaism to the Greek world in a bid to overturn misconceptions and to establish a more favourable image. It presented Judaism to the Roman world with the hope that the favourable status Judaism had enjoyed would continue unabated.

Finally it presented Judaism to the Jews themselves in the form Josephus thought would best serve as the basis for a reconstructed Judaism.

      Josephus consciously placed himself and his work in the category of Oriental historiography, i.e. apologetic historiography. (p. 308).

Sterling regards Luke and Acts as belonging to a single work and therefore to the same genre, history (p. 339). 'It is the story of Christianity, i.e., of a people. In this sense it is reminiscent of historical works which relate the story of a particular people' (p. 349). Luke-Acts is regarded as indebted to LXX in language, concept of history and some literary forms (p. 363). Concluding his discussion of Septuagintal influence, Sterling writes:

> More important than this is the realization that our author conceived of his work as the *continuation* of the LXX. His deliberate composition in Septuagintal Greek and the conviction that his story was the fulfillment of the promises of the OT imply that as a continuation, Luke-Acts represents *sacred narrative*. (p. 363).

These conclusions seem to go beyond the evidence of Sterling's preceding discussion. However, both points are picked up again, when Sterling compares Luke-Acts with Josephus.

> Both authors attempted to tell the story of a given people through the rewriting of texts from within their group. Technically they differed in scope: Josephos retold the entire story; the author of Luke-Acts was a continuator. Yet in another way they both agree: both tell the story of their people from the beginning point of their records. More importantly they both emphasize the antiquity of their movement: Josephos through a chronological reckoning and Luke-Acts by insisting that Christianity was not new, but a continuation. Linked to their use and understanding of the LXX is their conviction that their narratives are sacred history. (pp. 368-69).

In Sterling's view the function of Luke-Acts was 'to define Christianity in terms of Rome (politically innocent), Judaism (a continuation), and itself (*traditio apostolica*)' (p. 386).

      Sterling's extensive treatment (310 pages) of the classical and Hellenistic background of the postulated genre of 'apologetic historiography' may be accepted for the sake of the discussion. (Questions might be raised about his definition of the genre; in particular, it might be asked whether the apologetic purpose is constitutive of this genre and limited to it). As indicated in the Introduction to this chapter and in Section IX, it does not seem necessary or desirable to regard Luke and Acts as belonging to a single work or a single genre. Christianity as portrayed in Acts is not a foreign country and Christians are not an ethnic group. It is not clear that Luke intended to write a continuation of the Greek Jewish Bible or 'sacred narrative' in the sense of scripture. The parallel between the *Jewish Antiquities* of Josephus and Luke-Acts is forced, when it is claimed that 'both tell the story of their people from the beginning point of their records' (p. 368). And the antiquity of Christianity (from Luke's point of view) can only be maintained by claiming that 'Christianity was not new, but a continuation' of Judaism (p. 369). (This is a separate point from the concept of Luke-Acts as a 'continuation' of LXX.)

The issue of self-definition has been prominent in recent sociological study of early Christianity and its Jewish matrix.[63] For the most part, self-definition is an implicit function of writings which have some other ostensible purpose. Acts may have the implicit function of defining Christianity as Sterling suggests (p. 386), but its ostensible function is to give a selective account of mission to Jews and Gentiles from Jerusalem to Rome.[64] Definition of Judaism is at least more explicit in Josephus, *Jewish Antiquities*, than definition of Christianity in Acts.

Sterling is attempting to trace the development of a genre, not to provide a series of exact parallels to the book of Acts. It is difficult to assess the length and scope of some of the fragmentary writings which he considers. Other writings do not match Acts in one respect or the other. The Greek Megasthenes wrote on India in three or four books; the natives Berossus and Manethon wrote on Babylonia and Egypt respectively in three books each. The fragmentary Hellenistic Jewish writers generally covered a broader scope than Acts: Demetrius (Adam to Ptolemy IV), Artapanus (Adam to Moses), Eupolemus (Adam to 158/7 B.C.). Compared with Acts, the *Jewish Antiquities* of Josephus is far more extensive both in length and in

---

[63]In general, see E.P. Sanders etc., *Jewish and Christian Self-Definition* (3 vols.; Philadelphia: Fortress, 1980-82); and for a similar approach to Luke-Acts in particular, P.F. Esler, *Community and Gospel in Luke-Acts* (Cambridge: Cambridge University Press, 1987).
[64]See D.W. Palmer, 'Mission to Jews and Gentiles in the last episode of Acts', *RTR* 52 (1993) 62-73.

scope: it treats the period from creation to the Jewish war in twenty books.

The question of the historical monograph receives very little attention in Sterling's treatment. The distinction between monograph and universal history as discussed by Polybius and Diodorus Siculus is briefly noted (pp. 5, 7). Among Hellenistic Jewish writings, 2 Maccabees is excluded from consideration on the grounds that it 'belongs to a different literary genre of historiography since it covers a period of only twenty or so years' (p. 141, n. 19). However, within the last two pages of his text, Sterling expresses the issue more positively. 'In particular I think II Maccabees might prove to be an important work to compare with Luke-Acts.' 'I would not place II Macc. in the category of apologetic historiography since its scope is too narrow, but do think it shares a number of historiographical concerns with Luke-Acts' (p. 387 with n. 380). Certainly, both the length and the scope of 2 Maccabees are comparable to Acts and appropriate to a short historical monograph. Sterling is primarily concerned to place Luke-Acts in the general area of historiography, when he acknowledges the views of modern scholars, who regard Acts as belonging to 'the *Gattung* of history' (p. 317) or as being specifically a historical monograph (p. 318). Sterling rejects this classification. However, while Acts may be allowed an implicit function of apology or self-definition, its length, scope, focus and formal features fit the pattern of a short historical monograph.

VIII. Hellenistic Jewish Historiography

Both the Gospel of Luke and Acts reflect the author's knowledge of the Greek Jewish Bible. The influence of 'biblical history' on Acts will be treated in another chapter of this volume. In the present section of this chapter it is not intended to consider fragmentary Hellenistic Jewish historiography, but only those works which survive as complete books. In effect, this means the three 'apocryphal' writings, 1 Esdras and 1 and 2 Maccabees.

There are many uncertainties about the nature and aims of 1 Esdras. It may be assumed that it derives from a period towards the middle of the second century B.C. Although its original language is uncertain, the extant work is Greek. If the present length of the work is deliberate rather than accidental (cf. 9:55), it is about two thirds of the length of Acts. It is, therefore, of a possible length for a short historical monograph. Although its chronology is confused, the book covers a period of more than 200 years from 622 to the late fifth or early fourth century B.C. The evidence so far considered indicates that this is an abnormally long period for a short historical monograph. However, the extent of the period covered may be determined by the selective focus on a particular theme. 'The fact that the work presents a picture of the continuity between the old and the new temples may indicate that it was designed to play some role in the polemics of the second century between the Jerusalem temple and its rivals. . .'[65] The book begins almost as abruptly as it ends: it has no prologue. The form of the whole is narrative of past events. Included in the narrative are speeches of various types (3:18-24; 4:2-12, 14-32, 43-46; 8:74-90, Ezra's prayer-sermon), quoted letters (2:17-24, 26-29; 6:8-22; 8:9-24) and decrees whether oral or written or both (2:3-7; 6:24-26, record of a decree; cf. report of the king's letters of instruction in 4:47-57). In short, the writing is a single volume of limited length and unitary focus, although it covers (selectively) an extended period; and it contains narrative, speeches and quoted letters and decrees, but has no prologue. It thus has many, but not all, of the features of the short historical monograph as conceived by Cicero and Sallust. Its religious subject-matter anticipates the Acts of the Apostles.

It is generally agreed that the Greek text of 1 Maccabees is derived from a lost Hebrew original. The book was probably written at about the beginning of the first century B.C. It is somewhat longer than Acts (about 20 per cent or more), but shorter than Sallust's *Bellum Iugurthinum*. The work deals with the four decades of the events leading up to the Maccabean revolt and the subsequent campaigns (175-134 B.C.). The lengthy first chapter serves as an introduction to the book by treating the historical background (Alexander the Great, the Successors and Antiochus Epiphanes); but there is no prologue as such. 'The style is soberly narrative after the manner of Old Testament historical writing.'[66] The book contains numerous shorter and longer speeches, including those of Judas and Jonathan before battle (3:18-22, 58-60; 4:8-11; 9:44-46), the farewell

---

[65]H.W. Attridge in *Jewish Writings of the Second Temple Period* (ed. M.E. Stone; Assen: Van Gorcum, 1984) 160.

[66]E. Schürer, *The History of the Jewish People in the Age of Jesus Christ (175 B.C. - A.D. 135)* (rev. and ed. G. Vermes, F. Millar, M. Goodman; Edinburgh: T. & T. Clark, 1986) III.1.181.

speech of Mattathias (2:49-68), the address of Jewish envoys to the Roman senate (8:20-32), the exhortation of Simon to the people in Jerusalem (13:3-6) and others (2:7-13, 17-18, 19-22; 6:10-13, 22-27, 57-59; 9:29-30; 12:44-45; 15:33-35; 16:2-3). Quoted letters are also frequent (1:44-49 and 50, indirect then direct speech; 5:10-13; 8:31-32; 10:18-20, 25-45; 11:30-37, 57; 12:5-18, 20-23; 13:36-40; 14:20-23; 15:2-9, 16-21). There are further reports of messages (7:27; 10:52-54, 55-56, 70-73; 11:9-10, 42-43; 13:15-16; 15:28-31), presumably oral except in the case of 11:57; and references to letters not quoted (1:41; 10:3, 7, 59; 11:22; 12:2, 4; 16:18). The book is thus a single volume of limited length, covers a limited period and has a clear focus on the Maccabean campaigns. It has an introductory chapter but no prologue; and its narrative contains speeches and quoted letters. By giving so much attention to the *wars* of the Maccabees, the book shares the usual subject-matter of short and long monographs of the Greek and Roman tradition. At the same time, the religious perspective of the writer and of the main Jewish participants in his account corresponds rather to earlier Jewish historiography and, again, anticipates Acts.

The underlying source of 2 Maccabees is the five-volume Greek history composed by Jason of Cyrene. The body of the writing (2:19 to the end) identifies itself as an epitome of this earlier work (2:23, 26, 28). The summariser has succeeded in producing a single volume comparable in length to Acts. It covers a period of at least fifteen years from a point within the reign of Seleucus IV (187-175 B.C.) to 161 B.C. Compared with 1 Maccabees, it begins at an earlier stage of the events leading up to the Maccabean revolt and stops at the earlier point of Judas's victory over the Seleucid general Nicanor. It is possible that the epitome was composed in 124/3 B.C., the date mentioned in the first letter prefixed to the body of the writing (1:1-9); however, later dates prior to 63 B.C. have also been suggested. The former date would make 2 Maccabees earlier than 1 Maccabees.

While the early chapters of 2 Maccabees reveal internal Jewish rivalries, the main emphasis is on oppressive Hellenisation by the Seleucid rulers of Syria. The withdrawal of Judas Maccabaeus and his companions is briefly reported at 5:27. However, the account of oppression then continues a little further (6:1-11), until the writer makes an explicit theological digression (6:12-17). There follow the martyrdom accounts of the elderly Eleazar (6:18-31) and of the seven brothers and their mother (7:1-42). The rest of the book is primarily concerned with the campaigns of Judas; an editorial conclusion rounds off the book (15:37-39). The arrangement of the contents is somewhat uneven. And the writer has certain thematic interests, such as temple purity[67] and resurrection as a reward for martyrs who die obedient to the law. But these factors do not upset the overall chronological structure: Syrian oppression reaches a peak in the martyrdoms, but is overturned by the successful campaigns of Judas. The work may thus be regarded as having a consistent focus.

The letters prefixed to the body of 2 Maccabees at 1:1-2:18 are clearly secondary, whatever the date of their addition. If these are detached, the writing begins with a prologue (2:19-32). The narrative of past events contains speeches and quoted letters. After the speeches of Eleazar (6:24-28, 30), six of the seven brothers make brief speeches before their martyrdoms within the passage 7:2-19; there follow speeches of their mother (7:22-23, 27-29) and their youngest brother (7:30-38). The only other directly reported speech is that of Alcimus to king Demetrius (14:6-10); cf. 14:33 (oath); 14:35-36 and 15:22-24 (prayers). But the two exhortations of Judas are reported basically in indirect speech (8:16-20; 15:8-16). Letters are quoted at 9:19-27; 11:16-21, 22-26, 27-33, 34-38.

In summary, 2 Maccabees is a single volume of moderate length covering a limited period and having a consistent focus. Apart from the prefixed letters, it contains a prologue, narrative, speeches, quoted letters and an editorial conclusion. The subject-matter of religious wars corresponds to the content of 1 Maccabees. And the inclusion of the martyrdom accounts more specifically anticipates the martyrdom of Stephen in Acts 7.

IX. The Genre of Acts in the Light of its Preface

In her recent book (*Preface*; see n. 4 above), Loveday Alexander is primarily concerned to establish the social context of writer and readers in the light of the implications of the Lukan prefaces. The following discussion is restricted to the direct and indirect relevance of some of the author's investigations for the genre of Acts. Alexander makes a strong case for the view that the preface of the Gospel of Luke is most similar to the prefaces of a wide range of technical treatises. The preface of Acts receives only limited and subordinate treatment (pp. 142-46). Only the first verse of Acts is

---

[67]See esp. R. Doran, *Temple Propaganda: The Purpose and Character of 2 Maccabees* (Washington: Catholic Biblical Association, 1981).

regarded as constituting its preface. It is acknowledged that the
'opening words recall the recapitulations found in many scientific
and other texts' (p. 143, emphasis added). And it is claimed that 'Luke
is only unusual in that he fails to complete the summary with a
description of the contents of the current work: his τὸν μὲν πρῶτον
λόγον is left without its expected νῦν δέ and we plunge directly into
the narrative' (p. 143).

However, there are three types of prologue which might be
used by Hellenistic Greek writers for sequential books: (1)
retrospective summary of preceding book(s) and prospective
summary of current book; (2) retrospective summary only; (3)
prospective summary only. The second type appears in the disputed
prologues of Xenophon's *Anabasis* (at 2.1.1; 3.1.1; 4.1.1-4; 5.1.1; 7.1.1;
of Hellenistic date?), in Josephus's *Jewish Antiquities* (at 8.1; 13.1) and
in Herodian's *History of the Empire* (at 3.1.1; 4.1.1; 5.1.1; 6.1.1; 7.1.1;
8.1.1; early third century A.D.). Polybius has a prospective summary
(type 3) of his whole work within the general introduction in Book 1
(at 1.3.1-2). There is a good example of retrospective and prospective
summary (type 1) at 4.1.1-4. In a more complex example at 3.1.1-3 he
refers back to the prospective summary of Book 1 and the reasons
there given for the writing of Books 1 and 2, and then gives a
prospective summary for Book 3 (type 1). At first sight, the beginning
of Book 2 also appears to contain a preface of the first type: 'In the
preceding book we made clear. . .But now we shall attempt in a
summary manner (κεφαλαιωδῶς) to show the events following
these. . .' (2.1.1-4). But here the term 'in a summary manner' refers to
the sketchy treatment used throughout Books 1 and 2. Hence this
preface is more appropriately regarded as belonging to the second
type. The preface of Acts also appears to belong to this type.

It is, therefore, hardly 'unusual' that Luke has no prospective
summary at the beginning of Acts. Other Greek historical writers
may also 'plunge directly into the narrative' after a retrospective
summary. Moreover, Luke's τὸν μὲν πρῶτον λόγον does not
necessarily expect a following νῦν δέ. Since classical times mevn
solitarium had been used especially with some form of πρῶτος. And
there was 'a tendency. . .to open a work, or part of a work, with μέν,
with or without an expressed or implied antithesis, perhaps in order
to mitigate the harshness of the inevitable asyndeton'.[68] On the other
hand, the use of μέν and δέ at the beginning of a book is not confined

---

[68]J.D. Denniston, *The Greek Particles* (corrected ed.; Oxford: Clarendon, 1966) 382.

to the first type of preface with retrospective and prospective summary. All the passages cited above from (pseudo-) Xenophon, Josephus and Herodian have a μέv. . .δέ structure; and all have only a retrospective summary before moving straight into the narrative. If the Xenophontic prefaces are not authentic, then an editor has in each case prefixed a μέv-sentence to a book which originally began with a δέ-sentence. But such an editor must have regarded the resulting structure as acceptable to readers.

Alexander states:

> The practice of beginning each new book with a recapitulation is foreign to classical Greek and Roman historians (see above ch. 3). Some Hellenistic historians do use recapitulations, but only at specific points and for specific purposes. (p. 143; n. 47 follows).

At this point Acts 1:1 is under discussion. And the implication is that Acts is unlike classical Greek and Roman histories, since it does have a recapitulatory preface. However, it is generally acknowledged that the Hellenistic Greek Ephorus began the practice of dividing his own work into individual books. The 'fifth-century classics, Herodotus and Thucydides' (Alexander's main examples in ch. 3: p. 23) did not yet make such divisions, as Alexander herself notes (p. 25). The 'classical Greek' historians thus did not have the opportunity of 'beginning each new book with a recapitulation', since their works were not divided into books. Hellenistic Greek writers, especially historians, used recapitulation in prefaces both of type 1 and of type 2. The writers include Polybius, Diodorus Siculus, Philo, Josephus and Eusebius for type 1 as well as (pseudo-)Xenophon, Polybius, Josephus and Herodian for type 2.[69]

It does not seem appropriate to regard the preface of Acts as ending in the midst of a sentence at the end of Acts 1:1 (pp. 142-46). Moreover, the ostensibly retrospective summary is complicated by Luke's use of two ascension accounts. Thus the summary extending from the beginning of Jesus's ministry to his ascension (Acts 1:1-2) not only looks back to Luke 24 but also points forward to Acts 1:9-11. And in Acts 1:3-8 Luke continues to summarise post-resurrection appearances and teaching of Jesus. Corresponding to the tension between retrospective and prospective summary, the initial 'I'-style

---

[69]See D.W. Palmer, 'The literary background of Acts 1.1-14', *NTS* 33 (1987) 427-438; V. Larranaga, *L'Ascension de Notre Seigneur dans le Nouveau Testament* (Rome: Institut Biblique Pontificale, 1938) 322-23 summarising his preceding analysis.

(Acts 1:1) gives way to reported speech of Jesus (1:4), which is converted to direct speech by the end of the same verse. Luke has deliberately blurred the transition from prologue to narrative.[70]

In the opening words of Acts the writer speaks in the first person (singular). Alexander cites parallels (singular and plural) only from technical writers (pp. 144-45). Earlier, it had been mentioned that self-designation of the author in the third person was 'a feature of many kinds of literature in the early period. . ., was adopted by Herodotus and Thucydides and remained a recognizable characteristic of historical writing long after it had disappeared in other genres. . .' (p. 24). On the other-hand, it is said that in later literature the 'archaic third-person form and the position in the opening words were not. . .generally retained. . .' (p. 26). The implication of the former statement is that Acts does not fit the pattern of historical prefaces, whereas the latter statement suggests that it does. At any rate, in some examples of historical prefaces of type 2 (noted above) the author does speak in the first person (plural): Plb. 2.1.1; J. *AJ* 8.1; 13.1; Hdn. 7.1.1; cf. J. *Ap.* 2.1 (singular).

As the title indicates, the preface of Luke's gospel is Alexander's primary concern. There is some ambivalence as to whether, and to what extent, this preface applies to Acts as well as to the gospel (pp. 2, n. 1; 206). This ambivalence is carried over to the issue of the genre of Luke and Acts (pp. 3, 9, 200, 206). It seems that Alexander would like to resolve this ambivalence in the following way: the prefaces of Luke and Acts are most similar to those of technical treatises; ancient biographies may be regarded as part of the technical tradition (pp. 202-04); Luke and even Acts may be regarded as biographical; and the 'parallel with scientific literature. . .could be sought not in content or form but in literary praxis' (p. 205), in the transmission of tradition. This scheme illustrates one of the main problems with Alexander's thesis: the discrepancy between the technical features of the Lukan preface and the biographical and historical content of Luke and Acts.

Alexander herself prefers the view 'that Luke's two works should be regarded as two parts of a single whole' (p. 2, n. 1); and she regards this view as having 'predominance' (p. 206). However it is acknowledged that two major commentators, Haenchen and Conzelmann, see Luke 1:1-4 as applying only to the gospel (*ibid.*). The retrospective preface of Acts might seem to confirm Alexander's

---

[70]See Palmer, 'Literary background', 427-28.

view. However, in the prefaces of scientific treatises 'we find regularly a certain amount of information about. . .the relationship of the book to others by the same author' (p. 49). Furthermore:

> not all recapitulations signal a close literary unity of the type presupposed in current study of Luke-Acts. The critic who finds a unitary conception in the texts themselves may indeed find confirmation for this unity in the two prefaces. But it needs also to be stated clearly that the critic who finds that the two works, while complementing each other, are none the less very different in conception, need not find the prefaces a stumbling-block. The connection between two successive works of a corpus linked by recapitulations is not always as tight as we might expect. (p. 146).

Alexander's documentation for this point is limited to technical treatises (p. 49 and preceding pages). However, cross reference to other writings within an author's corpus occurs elsewhere. Philo's treatise *On Dreams* 1.1 refers back to 'the writing before this' (not extant) on a different class of dreams. His *Life of Joseph* 1 states: 'Since I have described the lives of these three,. . .I will carry on the series by describing a fourth life, that of the statesman'. Mixing genres, Philo writes in *On the Decalogue* 1: 'Having related in the preceding treatises the lives of those whom Moses judged to be men of wisdom,. . .I shall now proceed in due course to give full descriptions of the written laws'. *On the Special Laws* 1.1 refers back to 'the preceding treatise', *On the Decalogue*. Cf. *On the Virtues* 1; *That every good man is free* 1, referring back to 'the former treatise' (not extant) on the opposite theme (noted by Alexander in another connexion, p. 158); *On the Contemplative Life* 1, referring to previous discussion of Essenes. At the beginning of his *Antiquities* (1.4), Josephus refers back to his *Jewish War*; and at the beginning of his writing *Against Apion* (1.1), he refers back to the *Antiquities*. Towards the end of his *Life* (412), Josephus refers the reader to his *Jewish War* for certain episodes. These writings are not narrowly 'historical'; but they are not 'technical' or 'scientific' either. The recapitulatory preface of Acts does not necessarily imply that Luke is writing the second volume of a single work. It does not necessarily imply that Acts belongs to the scientific tradition. And it does not necessarily imply that Acts must be of the same genre as the Gospel of Luke.

To a large extent Alexander's study consists of a comparison of formal features of Lukan and scientific prefaces. Perhaps the most significant functional topic within this discussion is the issue of tradition. In scientific prefaces, received 'tradition' is one of the components of the 'author's qualifications' (esp. pp. 82-85). But such authorial claims imply that the main content of their books will be an account of the received tradition (e.g., p. 82). In the gospel preface (Lk. 1:2), the author claims to be the recipient of tradition (pp. 116-117). And the content of both Luke and Acts may be regarded as an account of traditional material (pp. 203-06). This analysis appears to provide a strong double parallel between Luke-Acts and technical treatises. On the other hand, there seems to be a substantial difference between the empirical tradition of technical expertise in crafts and the written or oral traditions about Jesus and the apostolic figures of Acts. The formal parallel between the mention of tradition in Lukan and scientific prefaces remains. But the larger parallel between the content of scientific treatises and Luke-Acts is not so compelling after all. Consequently the grounds for viewing Acts in the context of technical treatises rather than historiography are weakened.

X. Conclusion

The comments of Polybius provide some basis for the use of the term 'particular history' or 'historical monograph'. However, Polybius was thinking of multi-volume works, which might be even longer than his own universal history. Sallust's remarks about selectivity and brevity give an indication of his concept of the genre. Cicero's discussions of the length, scope and focus of a possible monograph also help to define this type of writing. The fragmentary evidence for numerous Greek monographs and one in Latin confirms the existence of the genre, but does not give a picture of what an individual example looked like. Apart from Jewish writings, for an extant short monograph from the period prior to Acts it is necessary to look to Sallust.[71] His works conform to the theoretical requirements for a short monograph: they each comprise a single volume, cover a limited historical period, and focus on one theme

---

[71]Apart from the question of date (98 A.D.?), the one-volume works of Tacitus do not provide appropriate analogies. The *Germania* is an ethnographic treatise; the *Agricola* is a biography, but also contains an ethnographic digression (10-12) and two balanced speeches (30-34) in the manner of a historical monograph.

and, to a significant extent, on one person.[72] And the constituent literary components of the *Bellum Catilinae* include a prologue (1-4), narrative, speeches (20, 51, 52, 58), and a quoted 'despatch' (*mandata*, 33) and two 'letters' (*litterae*, 35; 44.5).[73] The *Bellum Iugurthinum* not only has the same major components, but also quotes in direct speech the 'gist' (*sententia*) of two 'letters' (*litterae*, 9.1-2; 24.1-10).

The Hellenistic Jewish historical writings, 1 Esdras and 1 and 2 Maccabees, correspond in many of their features to the theory and practice of Cicero and Sallust. They are each of an acceptable length for a single volume. 1 and 2 Maccabees have an appropriate chronological scope. 1 Esdras covers an unusually extensive period, but this may be due to the author's focus on the particular theme of 'the continuity between the old and the new temples' (n. 66 above). Indeed, all three writings have a unitary focus on their chosen theme. Only 2 Maccabees has a proper prologue. Narrative of past events is the basic method of all three writings. And they all contain speeches and quoted letters. Like Greek and Roman monographs, 1 and 2 Maccabees are largely concerned with wars. However, they also have a religious perspective, which is noticeably lacking at least in Sallust. This perspective is shared with 1 Esdras and with 'biblical history'. The three Hellenistic Jewish writings are earlier than Cicero and Sallust. But they perhaps point to the Graeco-Roman heritage which lies behind Cicero and Sallust on the one hand and to the milieu of 'biblical history' on the other. Indeed, they provide a link between this double background in the past and the future composition of Acts.

In addition to the formal features which have already been considered, these Hellenistic Jewish writings also tend to focus on one main figure, or at least on one at a time. By comparison with the canonical material to which it is related, 1 Esdras plays down the role of Nehemiah largely by omission. The result is to give greater prominence to Ezra; and this is reinforced by the more elevated

---

[72]Catiline, in the one case; the Numidian Jugurtha tends to be balanced by the Roman Marius in the latter part of the second monograph.

[73]The prologues of both *Cat.* and *Iug.* are untypical for historical writings. 'Sallust. . .was not merely unusual but possibly unique. And what makes his case even odder is that he knew perfectly well how he ought to have begun an historical work. In both 'Bellum Catilinae' and 'Bellum Iugurthinum' the traditional formulae do eventually make their appearance. . .' C.D. Earl, 'Prologue form in ancient historiography', *ANRW* I.2 (1972) 842-856 at 846.

designation of Ezra in 1 Esdras.[74] In 1 Maccabees there is a fairly
strict division between the periods of leadership of Judas (3:1-9:22),
Jonathan (9:23-12:53), Simon (13:1-16:17) and John (16:18-24); see
especially 9:22: 'The rest of the history of Judas, his wars, exploits and
achievements—all these were so numerous that they have not been
written down' (NEB). Because of the date at which the author has
chosen to end his account, Judas is the sole Maccabean leader in 2
Maccabees.

Among Roman writers, it was Cicero who raised the issue of
concentration on one person in a monograph (*Fam.* 5.12.2; n. 50
above); and Cicero was thinking of himself. Sallust made Catiline the
main personal focus of attention in his monograph on the
Catilinarian conspiracy. With regard to the *Bellum Iugurthinum*,
Levene allows a greater variation of focus among different figures.
'. . .I shall examine how the leading characters, Jugurtha, Metellus,
Marius, and Sulla, fit into the work. . .the chief object in Sallust's
portrayal of these four characters, is to show them linked to one
another in a single chain of personal and general moral
degeneration.'[75] This understanding of 'leading characters. . .linked
to one another in a single chain' would make the *Bellum Iugurthinum*
a closer parallel for Acts than the *Bellum Catilinae*. For, in contrast
with his Gospel, Luke does not concentrate on one individual
throughout Acts. But he does tend to portray one missionary leader
at a time (Peter, Stephen, Philip, Paul) in the service of the main
theme.[76]

The Acts of the Apostles consists of a single volume of
moderate length. It covers a limited historical period of some thirty
years. Its geographical scope is not universal, but restricted by its
theme. There is a consistent focus, at least from the author's point of
view, on the one issue of the progress of the Christian mission. And
Luke tends to portray one leading figure at a time in the service of
this theme. The literary components of Acts include a prologue,
narrative, speeches and quoted letters (15:23-29; 23:26-30). Even the

---

[74]For example, 'in 1 Esd 9:40, 49 he is referred to as "high priest", *archiereus*,
whereas in the parallel passages in Nehemiah he is called "the scribe" (8:1) and
"the scribe, the priest" (8:9)', J.M. Myers, *I and II Esdras. Introduction, Translation
and Commentary* (Garden City, N.Y.: Doubleday, 1986) 9.
[75]Levene, 'Sallust's *Jugurtha*', 59; cf. n. 73 above.
[76]The constant prominence of the Holy Spirit in Acts does not provide a human
actor analogous to Catiline or Jugurtha; and only emphasises how secular
Sallust's approach is.

survey of salvation history (Acts 7:2-53), though presented not in narrative but in a speech, bears comparison with the 'archaeology' of Sallust (*Cat.* 5.9-13.5).[77] The history of an incipient religious movement is an unprecedented subject for an ancient monograph. But the way has been prepared by the religious content of the Hellenistic Jewish historical monographs. And the combination of length, scope, focus and internal literary features indicates that Acts deserves consideration as a short historical monograph.[78]

It may indeed be part of the approach of Acts to present a 'succession of interesting, "action-packed" stories'.[79] That would align Acts with the dramataic sort of historical monograph, which Cicero had in mind.[80] But it would not mean that Acts is a romantic rather than a historical writing. 'Ancient historians achieved *delectatio* by using subject-matter which was guaranteed to interest their audience. . .'[81] Even Polybius, in supporting the merits of universal history, believes that the reader should 'derive from history at the same time both profit and delight'.[82]

---

[77]Sallust's own predecessor is Thucydides (1.2-21).

[78]It is an unsatisfactory use of terminology, when Aune refers to Herodotus as the writer of a historical monograph and to Luke-Acts as general history (*Literary Environment*, 87, 138-140).

[79]Pervo, *Profit*, 12.

[80]Cic. *Fam.* 5.12.5; quoted by Pervo, *Profit*, 6.

[81]A.J. Woodman, 'Theory and practice in ancient historiography', *Bulletin of the Council of University Classics Departments* 7 (1978) 6-8 at 7.

[82]ἅμα καὶ τὸ χρήσιμον καὶ τὸ τερπνὸν ἐκ τῆς ἱστορίας ἀναλαβεῖν, Plb. 1.4.11; similarly 3.31.13, with the verbs τέρπειν and ὠφελεῖν.

CHAPTER 2

ACTS AND ANCIENT
INTELLECTUAL BIOGRAPHY

L.C.A. Alexander

Denn so ist es, Herr: dem Sokrates gaben sie ein Gift zu trinken, und
unsern Herrn Christus schlugen sie an das Kreuz!
Theodor Storm, Der Schimmelreiter

Summary

Charles Talbert's suggested comparison between Luke-Acts and the Lives *of the*
Philosophers *of Diogenes Laertius has a number of points of potential significance for*
the reader of Acts. At the narrative level, however, the comparison shows up as many
differences as similarities, and it is hard to believe that any work of this type could have
been Luke's literary model. To make the comparison work at the level of the literary text,
we have to assume that the tradition behind Diogenes (on which Luke also drew, on this
hypothesis) was radically different from the Lives he presents; but this does not appear to
have been the case. However the school traditions lying behind the literary texts are of
great significance for Acts, and the last section of this paper argues that the Pauline
narrative is continuously informed and shaped by the template provided by the
biographical tradition relating to Socrates.

I. Introduction

It is now almost twenty years since Charles Talbert put forward the brilliant proposal that the clue to the two-fold structure of Luke-Acts was to be found in the compendium of philosophic biography which goes under the name of Diogenes Laertius' *Lives of the Philosophers*. Not that Diogenes Laertius could be in any direct sense Luke's literary model—the probable date of the compendium is the early third century A.D.[1]—but he attests to a long tradition of writing up the lives of great teachers, and to an interest in the 'succession' by which a particular tradition was passed on and developed from the founding teacher to a series of disciples. Diogenes Laertius cites a variety of sources, the bulk of them dating from the hellenistic period, i.e. III - I B.C.:[2] and it is among these sources, Talbert postulates, that the model for Luke's two-volume work is to be found:[3]

> The similarities between the lives of the founders of philosophical schools presented by Laertius and Luke-Acts are remarkable. First of all, as to *content*. . .Luke-Acts, as well as Diogenes Laertius. . .has for its contents (a) the life of a founder of a religious community, (b) a list or narrative of the founder's successors and selected other disciples, and (c) a summary of the doctrine of the community. In the second place, in *form* Luke-Acts, like Diogenes Laertius' *Lives*, has the life of a founder as the first structural unit, followed by a second, namely, the narrative of successors and selected other

---

[1]See the discussion in J. Mejer, *Diogenes Laertius and his Hellenistic Sources* (Hermes Einzelschriften 40; Wiesbaden: Franz Steiner, 1978). Diogenes' citation of secondary sources like Favorinus makes a late second century date the earliest possible.

[2]On the hellenistic substance of Diogenes' work, cf. R.D. Hicks, *Diogenes Laertius* (Loeb Classical Library; 1925) xxxii: 'scarcely any allusion is made to the changes of the three centuries from 100 BC to AD 200'. For more recent discussion of Diogenes' sources, see Mejer, *op. cit.* and B.A. Desbordes, *Introduction à Diogène Laërce. Exposition de l'Altertumswissenschaft servant de préliminaires critiques à une lecture de l'oeuvre* (Doctoral Thesis; Utrecht: Onderwijs Media Institut, 1990) vols. I & II.

[3]Charles H. Talbert, *Literary Patterns, Theological Themes and the Genre of Luke-Acts* (SBLMS 20; Missoula: Scholars Press, 1974); *idem, What is a Gospel?* (Philadelphia: Fortress Press, 1977); *idem*, 'Biographies of philosophers and rulers as instruments of religious propaganda in Mediterranean antiquity', *ANRW* II.16.2 (1978) 1619-1651; *idem*, 'Biography, Ancient', *ABD* I (New York: Doubleday, 1992) 745-49.

disciples. . .There is furthermore a similarity of *purpose* between Luke-Acts and the Lives of philosophers following this pattern, whether they be collections or individual Lives. Both are concerned to say where the true tradition is to be found in the present. . .[T]he conclusion seems inescapable. Luke-Acts, just as Diogenes Laertius, derived the pattern for his work, (a) + (b), from the widespread use of it since pre-Christian times in portraying the lives of certain philosophers. If so, then Luke-Acts, to some extent, must be regarded as belonging to the genre of Greco-Roman biography, in particular, to that type of biography which dealt with the lives of philosophers and their successors. ([1974] 125-34).

Most of the recently-revived interest in ancient biography has been centred, naturally enough, on the Gospels,[4] and most readers would probably concur with Aune's bald statement that Luke 'does not belong to a type of ancient biography for it belongs with Acts, and Acts cannot be forced into a biographical mold'.[5] However, I believe that the reader of Acts has much to learn from the study of ancient biography; and Talbert's proposal makes a good starting-point in a number of ways.

First of all, the 'succession' structure deals precisely and neatly with Aune's problem of the structure of Luke's double work (and incidentally enables us to avoid the potentially ridiculous situation in which Matthew, Mark and John may be regarded as biographies but Luke may not). This does not entail trying to 'force Acts into a biographical mold', but it does mean taking seriously the extent to which the narrative of Acts is structured around a series of individual apostles, and in particular the extent to which one story-line, that of Paul, progressively dominates from his first, low-key introduction at 7:58. Paul is in fact the sole hero of the narrative from chapter 13 to chapter 28, i.e. for more than half the book, and Acts conveys far

---

[4]The revival of interest in biography among students of the NT is exemplified by the reprint in 1970 of Clyde Weber Votaw's classic study, 'The Gospels and Contemporary Biographies in the Greco-Roman World', *American Journal of Theology* 19 (1915) 45-73 & 217-49; (repr. Facet Books, Biblical Series 27; Philadelphia: Fortress Press, 1970). For more recent studies see: R.A. Burridge, *What are the Gospels?* (SNTSMS 70; Cambridge: Cambridge University Press, 1992); K. Berger, 'Hellenistische Gattungen im Neuen Testament', *ANRW* II.25.2 (1984) 1034-1380, esp. 1231-45.

[5]David E. Aune, *The New Testament in its Literary Environment* (Cambridge: James Clarke & Co., 1988) 77. Cf. Burridge, *op. cit.*, 243-7.

more information about Paul than about any other apostle.[6] Indeed this is one of the difficulties in classifying Acts as a 'history of the church' or even as 'The Acts of the Apostles': it is too lop-sided to sit comfortably with either title. Acts is not just a biography of Paul, but it *contains* a Pauline biography in the same way that the books of Samuel contain the Davidic 'succession narrative', or Genesis contains the story of Joseph—and this storyline can be studied in exactly the same way. But Talbert's hypothesis also alerts us to look at the way in which the Pauline story-line is embedded in the larger narrative, particularly at the way in which relationships with the other apostles are handled.

Secondly, Talbert's proposal encourages us to focus on a particular area of ancient biography. Ancient biography is a notoriously confusing field to understand, especially since it never attained the status of the genres recognised by classical rhetoric.[7] But there is a lot to be said for limiting our explorations to an area which may be loosely defined as 'intellectual biography', i.e. biography of individuals distinguished for their prowess in the intellectual field (philosophers, poets, dramatists, doctors) rather than in the political or military arena (kings, statesmen, generals). This gives us the initial advantage of limiting the field to Greek texts, since the bulk of

---

[6]Paul plays a major role in every episode from 13:4 to the end of Acts, except 18:24-28 (Apollos). The Jerusalem conference (15:1-29) is not a real exception: Paul is still the hero here, Peter a secondary character. Burridge points out, *op. cit.*, 246, that Paul is named in 14.5% of the sentences in Acts, a higher proportion than any other human character (Peter scores 6%). For comparison, analysis of an acknowledged biography like Tacitus' *Agricola* reveals that the hero figures as the subject of 18.1% of the verbs. A similar analysis of Paul in Acts would be well worth while.

[7]Burridge, *op. cit.* provides a helpful recent discussion with bibliography. Major general studies (where more specialist bibliography may be found) include F. Leo, *Die griechisch-römische Biographie nach ihrer literarischen Form* (Leipzig: Teubner, 1901); D.R. Stuart, *Epochs of Greek and Roman Biography* (Berkeley: University of California Press, 1928); A. Momigliano, *The Development of Greek Biography*, now available in a new expanded edition (Cambridge, Mass.: Harvard University Press, 1993); originally published as *The Development of Greek Biography* and *Second Thoughts on Greek Biography*, both 1971; Albrecht Dihle, *Studien zur griechischen Biographie* (Göttingen: Vandenhoeck & Ruprecht, 1956); *idem, Die Entstehung der historischen Biographie* (Sitzungsberichte der Heidelberger Akademie der Wissenschaften, phil.-hist. Klasse 1986/3; Heidelberg: Carl Winter, 1987).

political biography dates from the Roman period.[8] It also limits the field to the central core of undisputed biographical writing from the hellenistic age, which, as Gigon has pointed out, was largely confined to literary and philosophical heroes and hence to the sphere of private rather than public life.[9] This is clearly the sphere to which Paul belongs, and indeed the most obvious parallels are with the biographical material connected with philosophical teachers. However, philosophical biography is in many ways only a sub-group of intellectual biography, and although it is an important sub-group which may well prove to have unique features, it shares many formal features with the larger group.

Within this broader field, to restrict our lines of investigation to the philosophical 'succession-literature' highlighted by Talbert would be too narrow, especially since most examples of the genre are lost; and in fact Talbert himself points to a number of other aspects of philosophical biography which are potentially illuminating for the reader of Acts. In his major *ANRW* article he suggested a five-fold classification of biography according to social function:

A: To provide the readers with a pattern to copy.
B: To dispel a false image and provide a true one to follow.
C: To discredit by exposé.
D: To indicate where the true succession is to be found.
E: To validate and/or provide a hermeneutical key to a teacher's doctrine.[10]

---

[8]It has even been suggested that political biography properly so called did not exist before Cornelius Nepos—though this is largely a matter of definition (J. Geiger, *Cornelius Nepos and Ancient Political Biography* [Historia Einzelschriften 47; Wiesbaden/Stuttgart: Franz Steiner, 1985]).

[9]O. Gigon, 'Biographie. A. Griechische Biographie', *Lexikon der Alten Welt*, 469-71. The major collection of literary biography is A. Westermann (ed.), *Biographi Graeci Minores* (Braunschweig: 1845; repr. Amsterdam: Hakkert, 1964).

[10]Talbert, *Literary Patterns, Theological Themes and the Genre of Luke-Acts*, 1620-23. The usefulness of this typology has not been universally accepted. Talbert himself excludes a whole class of biography which he calls 'non-didactic' (*ibid.*, 1620), and the attempt to provide a single grid of social functions to account for the whole range of biographies of 'philosophers and rulers' incurs the charge of over-simplification: cf. Dihle, *op. cit.*, 8. But we are only concerned here with the philosophical side of the grid, and in order to pursue the parallel with Acts we only need to establish that there were *some* ancient biographies with some of these functions.

Besides Type D, the interest in the 'succession' of a great teacher's disciples which we have already mentioned, two of these indicate areas of interest in the ancient biographical tradition which are of particular significance for the reader of Acts.

(i) Type E: the 'hermeneutical key'. The description of biography as providing a 'hermeneutical key' to the teacher's doctrine underlines the fact that many intellectual biographies are ancillary to an independent and pre-existent body of writings. To put it more logically, much intellectual biography takes its starting point from the fact that its subject is independently known as an author; that is why he or she gets written about in the first place.[11] In this respect, as I have suggested on another occasion, 'Talbert's model works better for Acts than for the Gospel. Luke's account of Paul's missionary activities could well be seen as a biographical/hagiographical appendage to the corpus of genuine and deutero-Pauline epistles, put together as an accompaniment to this pre-existent body of Pauline teaching. Acts would in fact make a lot of sense as the product of a "Pauline school" which was also indulging in the typical "school" activities of collecting a corpus of letters and expanding it along lines deemed to express the master's thought in changing circumstances'.[12]

(ii) Type A: the teacher as *exemplum*. The idea that the lifestyle (*bios*) of great teachers is as important in the education of their students as their sayings or writings is well attested in antiquity: Seneca provides a good example from the first century:

> Cleanthes would never have been the image of Zeno if he had merely heard him lecture; he lived with him, studied his private life, watched him to see if he lived in accordance with his own principle. Plato, Aristotle and a host of other philosophers all destined to take different paths, derived more from Socrates' character than from his words. It was not Epicurus' school but living under the same roof as

---

[11]See especially Janet Fairweather, 'Fiction in the biographies of ancient writers', *Ancient Society* 4 (1974) 231-75; Mary Lefkowitz, *The Lives of the Greek Poets* (London: Duckworth, 1981).

[12]Loveday Alexander, *The Preface to Luke's Gospel* (SNTSMS 78; Cambridge: Cambridge University Press, 1993) 203-204.

Epicurus that turned Metrodorus, Hermarchus and Polyaenus into great men.[13]

Lucian's *Life of Demonax* provides a classic expression of this ideal in the form of biography:

> It is now fitting to tell of Demonax for two reasons—that he may be retained in memory by men of culture as far as I can bring it about, and that young men of good instincts who aspire to philosophy may not have to shape themselves by ancient precedents alone, but may be able to set themselves a pattern [κανών] from our modern world and to copy [ζηλοῦν] that man, the best of all philosophers whom I know about. (Lucian, *Demonax* 2, LCL).

Here the Life exists not to provide information ancillary to a pre-existent body of writings but to act as a 'template' for the readers to pattern their own lives on.[14] The importance of this function in ancient biography is widely recognised, especially among students of the biography of the later Empire, both pagan and Christian.[15] Reading Acts along these lines would encourage us to explore the ways in which Paul is presented as a pattern for imitation, a narrative extension of the process already visible in the epistolary corpus by which, in Conzelmann's words, 'with Paul's death not only his teaching but also the image of his work becomes the content of the tradition'.[16]

Talbert's hypothesis offers the further potential of anchoring the literary comparison to a specific social context, that of the hellenistic schools. In the 1974 study cited in n. 3, he explicitly associates the collection and maintenance of the lives of philosophers and their disciples with the interests of the schools as communities. 'The most striking similarity. . .is that between the function of Luke-Acts and the individual lives of philosophers with an (a) + (b) pattern. Both are cult documents intended to be read and used within the community which produced them and in the interests of its

---

[13]Seneca, *Ep.* VI.5, tr. Campbell (*Seneca: Letters from a Stoic* [Harmondsworth: Penguin Books, 1969] 40).

[14]I am indebted to Susie Orbach, writing in 'The Guardian' on 27th March 1993, for this useful term.

[15]Cf. e.g. P. Rousseau, *Ascetics, Authority and the Church in the Age of Jerome and Cassian* (Oxford: Oxford University Press, 1978) 11-18, 68-74; Patricia Cox, *Biography in Late Antiquity* (Berkeley: University of California Press, 1983) *passim*.

[16]Conzelmann, 'Luke's place in the development of early Christianity', in L. Keck and J.L. Martyn (eds.), *Studies in Luke-Acts* (London: SPCK, 1968) 307.

ongoing life' ([1974] 134). The commitment of discipleship (whatever the formal setting) is presupposed even more strongly where the biography also has the function of setting forth the sage as a pattern to imitate. The possibility of using the hellenistic schools (philosophical and other) to provide a social model for the early church is one which has aroused increasing interest over the years.[17] Especially in connection with the collection and publication of the Pauline letters,[18] it suggests a much needed concrete setting for a whole range of 'deutero-Pauline' literary activities (collecting and editing of genuine letters, production of pseudepigrapha, biographical narration), all of which can be paralleled among philosophers (Socrates, Plato, Epicurus), and in other technical traditions.[19] But only a detailed comparison can reveal how well the analogy works in practice.

The 'school' context also ties in with my own long-term investigation of the conventions employed in the Lukan preface, which led me to the conclusion that the web of expectations set up by the highly conventional language of the preface would lead the

---

[17]Cf. Wayne Meeks, *The First Urban Christians* (Yale University Press, 1983) 75-84. A.D. Nock, *Conversion* (Oxford, 1933). E.A. Judge, 'The early Christians as a scholastic community', *Journal of Religious History* 1 (1960) 4-15, 125-37. I have pursued this interest at great length (and suggested other parallels) in 'The Living Voice: Scepticism towards the Written Word in Early Christian and in Greco-Roman Texts', in D.J.A. Clines, S.E. Fowl & S.E. Porter (eds.), *The Bible in Three Dimensions* (Sheffield: Sheffield Academic Press, 1990); *eadem*, 'Schools, Hellenistic', in *Anchor Bible Dictionary* V (New York: Doubleday, 1992) 1005-11; *eadem*, 'Paul and the Hellenistic Schools: the Evidence of Galen', to be published in Troels Engberg-Pedersen (ed.), *Paul in his Hellenistic Context* (Philadelphia: Fortress Press, Spring 1994).

[18]H. Conzelmann, 'Paulus und die Weisheit', *NTS* 12 (1965) 231-44 (esp. 233); 'Luke's place in the development of early Christianity', in L. Keck and J.L. Martyn (eds.), *Studies in Luke-Acts* (London: SPCK, 1968) 298-316 (esp. 307-8). Cf. among more recent examples Mark Kiley, *Colossians as Pseudepigraphy* (Sheffield: JSOT, 1986) 91ff.; but the term tends to be used with little if any attention to its precise social significance. Cf. Alexander, *The Preface to Luke's Gospel*, 204 & n. 29. Alan Culpepper's useful study *The Johannine School* (SBLDS 26; Missoula: Scholars Press, 1975) was precipitated by a similar lack of precision in Johannine studies.

[19]Wesley D. Smith, *Hippocrates: Pseudepigraphic Writings* (Studies in Ancient Medicine 2; Leiden: Brill, 1990); Jody Rubin Pinault, *Hippocratic Lives and Legends* (Studies in Ancient Medicine 4; Leiden: Brill, 1992). Pinault suggests (*op. cit.*, 33) that the composition of the Life of Hippocrates was closely linked with the publication of the Letters, which themselves constituted a kind of 'novella in letters' (Smith, *op. cit.*, 20).

ancient reader to expect, not a work of historiography in the classic mould of Thucydides, Polybius or Josephus, but a technical treatise emanating (at whatever remove) from some kind of 'school' setting.[20] In fact Diogenes Laertius, though he did not figure in the original study because of his date, does contain a brief preface which parallels many of the features found in the technical prefaces which formed the subject of this study,[21] and thus falls broadly within the same literary category. Putting Acts in this context would also provide one possible solution to a literary problem raised by the Lukan preface. At the surface level, its most obvious message is that the author is promising to act as a faithful conduit for traditional material.[22] This is easy to understand for the Gospel, less so for Acts: recent scholarship has on the whole been reluctant to assign a large rôle to tradition in the composition of Acts (although the possibility has received new attention latterly in the work of Jervell and Lüdemann).[23] Looking at the rôle played by biographical traditions in the hellenistic schools could help us to a better understanding not only of the function of such traditions but also of their shaping: how they are structured and what is narrated. Finally, note that my use of the term 'hellenistic' should not be taken to imply a sharp distinction between 'Hellenism' and 'Judaism'. Many of the questions asked here about the role of biography in the hellenistic schools could also be asked of the rabbinic academies—and in fact I believe that a true appreciation of the social model of the 'school' as a tool for understanding early Christianity will only arise from a 'compare and contrast' exercise setting early Christian social structures alongside both hellenistic and rabbinic 'schools'. Only limitations of space prevent my pursuing the parallel here.

---

[20]Alexander, *The Preface to Luke's Gospel*, 200-210.

[21]The beginning of the work is lost, but the account of Plato's thought is introduced at 3.47 with a classic prefatorial passage addressed to Diogenes' unnamed (female) dedicatee. Note the following parallels (refs. to Alexander, *The Preface to Luke's Gospel*: use of φιλο- compounds in dedication (100); opening reference to dedicatee's disposition (74); author's decision as main verb (70); contents of book as object to main verb (71-3); modesty about presentation (99); purpose clause as final element in long dedicatory sentence (74-5).

[22]Alexander, *The Preface to Luke's Gospel*, 201-202, 207.

[23]J. Jervell, 'The problem of traditions in Acts', *Studia Theologica* 16 (1962) 25-41, repr. as pp. 19-39 of *Luke and the People of God: A New Look at Luke-Acts* (Minneapolis: Augsburg, 1962); Gerd Lüdemann, *Early Christianity According to the Traditions in Acts* (London: SCM, 1989).

II. Luke-Acts and Diogenes Laertius: A Narrative Comparison

The parallel between Diogenes Laertius (DL) and Luke-Acts (LA), then, is one which for many reasons I would like to make work. The problem is that the closer we look at the comparison in literary terms, the more obvious it seems that DL is a 'bad fit', at any rate for Acts. The most obvious difficulty for the comparison is that Diogenes Laertius dates from the early third century A.D. and is therefore too late to act in any direct sense as a literary model for Luke-Acts. Talbert's comparison is not between Luke-Acts and Diogenes Laertius but between Luke-Acts and Diogenes' sources: 'Luke-Acts, just as Diogenes Laertius, derived the pattern for his work. . .from the widespread use of it since pre-Christian times in portraying the lives of certain philosophers'.[24] There is nothing wrong with this procedure in principle, since Diogenes quotes a large number of sources, most of them from the hellenistic period; but it has had the effect of diverting attention away from the text of Diogenes to a body of material which survives, if at all, only in the form of epitomes and quotations, for many of which Diogenes himself is our best witness. Scholars have recently begun to question the consensus view on Diogenes' sources: no-one doubts that they existed, but the difficulty of determining their precise form and extent has probably been underestimated.[25] For our purposes, this concern to get 'behind' Diogenes has masked a number of obvious differences between the two texts at the level of the narrative. Only by giving full weight to the comparison at this surface level can we begin to appreciate the achievement of the author of Acts in shaping one of early Christianity's most important bodies of story.

1. The narrative agenda

The first question to ask is a simple one: what is narrated? What do Luke on the one hand, and DL on the other, think that their readers should be told? For simplicity's sake, I use here a list of the typical

---

[24]Talbert, *Literary Patterns, Theological Themes and the Genre of Luke-Acts*, 134.
[25]See especially Mejer, *op. cit.* and Desbordes, *op. cit.*

features of DL's lives cited by Ingemar Düring.[26] Düring stresses that not all items always appear: if the information was not available, DL did not include it. But the list is a useful indicator of the kinds of information that DL wanted to convey to his readers: and it cannot be solely dependent on the amount of material available to DL from his sources, for there are some cases, like Xenophon and Socrates, where we know that DL had far more information available about the character from literary sources than is given here.

1.   Origin, pedigree (*genos)*
2.   Relation to a philosophic school; scholarchate, διαδοχή
3.   Education
4.   Character, often illustrated by anecdotes and apophthegms
5.   Important events of life
6.   Anecdotic account of his death, usually followed by an epigram
7.   ἀκμή (i.e. period when the philosopher 'flourished') and related chronological data
8.   Works (list of book-titles)
9.   Doctrines
10. Particular documents, wills, letters
11. Homonyms (other people of the same name)

A tabular summary will show how this works out in practice (using Düring's example of the Aristotle biography in Diogenes): see Table I. It will readily be observed that the order of topics is not preserved even in this example ('Character', and even 'events of life' actually come after 'death' in this case), but it is widely agreed that the order varies widely in Diogenes. What is important, and is generally agreed, is that the list represents fairly the narrative range of Diogenes' Lives; a cursory read confirms the constant recurrence of most of these items, even though not all of them occur in any one Life, and even though there might be better ways of classifying the material.

It is clear that Diogenes had very little information on many of his minor philosophers, and that (not surprisingly) the fullest Lives are those of the founders of schools. It is also clear that some information was available for certain schools only: e.g. the wills figure mostly in the Lives of the major Peripatetics. 'Education' does not figure in the Life of Aristotle, and is hard to distinguish in general

[26] I. Düring, *Aristotle in the Ancient Biographical Tradition* (Acta Universitatis Gothoburgensis: Göteborgs Universitets Årsskrift LXIII/2; 1957) 77-8.

from item (2): but many of the Lives contain a short note on the occupation of the philosopher before he or she entered the philosophic life, and some at least of these traditions may have the function of pointing up a contrast with the philosophic life.[27] The list of Works figures in almost every Life, but the major section on Doctrines tends to be attached to the founders of major schools.

Table I: Narrative Topics in Diogenes Laertius

	ARISTOTLE (D.L. bk. V)	PAUL (Acts)
1. *Genos* (origin, pedigree)	5.1	22:2f, 28; 21:37, 39f.; 23:6, 34
2. School (scholarchate, διαδοχή)	5.2	*ch. 9?*
3. Education	. . .	22:3; 23:6; 26:4f.
4. Character (anecdotes and apophthegms)	5.17-21	. . .
5. Events of life	5.3-11	chs. 13-19
6. Death (epigram)	5.6 5.6	chs. 20-28 . . .
7. Chronology (ἀκμή)	5.6, 9-10	11:28; 12:18
8. Works	5.21-27	. . .
9. Doctrines	5.28-34	speeches?
10. Documents (wills, letters)	5.7-8; 5.11-16	speeches? 20:18-35
11. Homonyms	5.35	. . .

Note: chapter nos. in DL do not match NT verses in length. Each chapter represents around 12 lines of Greek.

Even at a quick glance, it is evident that there are similarities and differences here. On the one hand, under '*Genos*' DL includes information about city of origin, parentage (if known) and family

---

[27]O. Gigon, 'Antike Erzählungen über die Berufung zur Philosophie', *Museum Helveticum* 3 (1946) 1-21 (esp. 2-3).

connections; like Acts (and unlike Luke's Gospel) he rarely shows any interest in birth stories, miraculous or otherwise. On the other hand Acts never makes any explicit remarks about Paul's character, and the anecdotal material which is used to illustrate character in DL (and there is a lot of this) is not easy to parallel in the Pauline tradition. Paul's story is much less anecdotal than that of Jesus, as a comparison between Luke's Gospel and Acts makes clear. The other major gap is 'Works': notoriously, Luke never mentions Paul's letters, and scholarship has often worked on the assumption that he did not know them. If he did not, then another possible parallel is removed: for the easiest way to parallel the 'Doctrines' section in DL is to think of Acts as a biographical introduction to the Epistles, which would then represent the 'Doctrines' of the apostle. But if Luke did know the Epistles, then (on the Diogenes model) we would expect him to mention them. The Pauline speeches in Acts might in theory be thought of as an equivalent: but that brings us up against another difficulty, which deserves a separate section.

2. Narrative mode

If it is not easy to argue for a good match between Acts and Diogenes at the level of agenda—i.e. in terms of topics covered—it becomes downright difficult when we turn our attention to the mode of the narrative, i.e. not just to *what* is told (informational content) but to *how* it is told. This means paying attention to a number of concrete factors which affect the structure of the narrative in significant ways.

1. *Genos*. This is always the first item of information in Diogenes, conveyed directly by the narrator in the opening words. The subject of the Life is normally the grammatical subject of the first sentence. In Acts the meagre information we are given about Paul's origins (and it does not include the names of his parents, as is normal in Diogenes) is conveyed indirectly, at a late stage in the story, and comes from the lips of Paul himself. It is often said that 'Luke tells us that Paul was a Roman citizen': in fact Luke the narrator does not 'tell' us this, but allows his character Paul to tell us instead.

2. *School affiliations*. This is normally conveyed along with the opening information about name and parentage in Diogenes, and clearly forms one of the major organising principles of the collection. More

information may be given in the second paragraph. In the case of
Paul, there is no difficulty with Talbert's suggestion that this *idea* of
maintaining the correct 'succession' of the 'living voice' can be
paralleled in Paul's struggles with the Jerusalem apostles and that the
same kind of concern lies behind Paul's concept of his own
apostleship (cf. esp. Gal. 1-2). The problem is with the *expression* of
the idea in Luke's narrative. Where Diogenes is direct and
unambiguous, Luke is indirect and ambivalent. On the one hand
Paul's commission from the resurrected Jesus (the basis for Paul's
own Christian affiliation in Gal. 1) is narrated fully no less than three
times, once in the narrator's words (ch. 9) and twice in Paul's. As
Ronald Witherup has pointed out recently, this certainly indicates
that the episode is important for Luke's narrative.[28] On the other
hand, though, Luke (notoriously) differs from Paul in making it
appear that Paul had some contact with the Jerusalem apostles soon
after his conversion (9:27), which some have seen as an attempt to
imply dependence on Jerusalem (this thought underlies Talbert's
view of Acts as 'succession narrative'). But in fact Luke carefully
refrains from saying that Paul received any teaching from the
apostles at this or at any point: if he does want to convey some kind
of 'succession', he does it in an indirect and allusive fashion very
different from that of Diogenes.[29]

3. *Education.* Again, this information in Acts is conveyed indirectly by
the character Paul, not directly by the narrator. But, as we have seen,
this item does not figure large in Diogenes' agenda: as in Acts, there
is little or no trace of the theme of 'childhood brilliance' associated
with more romantic biography. What we find in Acts, as in the
Epistles, is rather a contrast, not between Paul the Pharisee and Paul
the Christian but between the persecutor and the follower of Jesus.[30]
A number of philosophical biographies similarly stress the dramatic
nature of the first encounter with philosophy (which may well be

---

[28]Ronald D. Witherup, 'Cornelius over and over and over again: "Functional
Redundancy" in the Acts of the Apostles', *JSNT* 49 (1993) 45-66.
[29]Talbert is aware of this difficulty: cf. 'Biography, Ancient', *ABD* I, 749: LA
'shares with certain biographies a concern to say where the true tradition is in the
present, even if his sense of the radical difference between apostolic and post
apostolic times caused him to eschew use of the typical succession vocabulary'.
[30]Acts 7:58-8:1, 9:1-2; Gal. 1:13-14, Phil. 3:6, 1 Cor. 15:9-10.

structured as a 'conversion') and the previous unsuitability of the subject to the philosophic life.[31]

4. *Character*. We have already mentioned the obvious formal differences (one of the major difficulties in the way of reading *any* biblical narrative in terms of Graeco-Roman biography) that Diogenes describes the *ethos* of his characters directly, and then cites a number of anecdotes to prove the point, whereas Luke conveys it indirectly through the story itself. It is of course an important question in itself to what extent the biblical writers share the modern novelist's preoccupation with 'character', but all that concerns us immediately is the formal difference.

5. *Events of Life*. In fact this item on the agenda is hard to distinguish from (4), and it might be better to say simply that Diogenes tends to fill a section of his Lives with disconnected anecdotes, some illustrative of character and some filling out of the life story of the hero. In many cases, this information was clearly very meagre: but it is worth noting that it seems to have formed a relatively unimportant part of the agenda even when more information could easily have been put in: Xenophon, for example, gets only a very short narrative section here, despite the fact that his own writings provided plenty of information for the biographer (DL II.48-59). Paul's life, by contrast, is given full and detailed narrative treatment in Acts. The difference is visible at every level. Where Diogenes uses the curtly-formulated anecdote as the raw material for his narrative, Luke uses fully-narrated episodes, packed with irrelevant detail of the sort the *chria*-form was designed to eliminate. Like the Gospel writers, but to a much greater degree, Luke provides a connected narrative in Acts with full travel details to cement the link between one episode and another. This is 'thick' narrative if anything is: the contrast could hardly be greater with Diogenes' brief summary statements.[32]

6. *Death*. Diogenes appears to have had an interest in death scenes, which may be traced back to the hellenistic biographical tradition. But his accounts (often multiple) of the deaths of his philosophers are

---

[31]Cf. Gigon, *op. cit.*; Nock, *op. cit.*, ch. XI. The most dramatic 'conversion' story in DL is that of Polemo, IV.16.

[32]The Aristotelian anecdotes in DL V.17-21 take up about 3 lines of Greek each. The total allotted to 'events of life' in V.3-11 (a generous estimate including non-narrative excurses) is 99 lines. By contrast, Acts 14 (3 episodes plus a travel summary) takes 63 lines.

formulated in the same curt and factual fashion as the rest of his
narrative, and treated with a disarming mixture of irony and
Schadenfreude. Socrates' death is narrated with the reverence we
would expect of the prototypical martyr of the philosophic tradition,
but other philosophers die from a variety of undignified causes: gout,
a broken finger, and falling over a chamber pot are in turn drily
narrated and celebrated with the little epigrams composed (as he
proudly tells us) by Diogenes himself.[33] Luke, by contrast,
notoriously does not narrate the death of his hero at all, so strictly
speaking this item should not appear under Acts. On the other hand,
as Robert Maddox points out, the trial and impending death of Paul
dominate the last few chapters of the book to a remarkable degree.
The trial and journey to Rome occupy slightly more narrative space
than the mission, and account for 'some 23.5% of the text of Acts and
12% of the whole of Luke-Acts' (a proportion comparable with the
narrative time devoted to the passion of Jesus in the Gospel). If we
take the Pauline narrative alone and include chapter 20, the point at
which it is clearly established that Paul is to die (20:25), Paul's 'death'
takes up more than half the time devoted to his story.[34] This is an
important structural point to which we shall return.

7. *Chronology*. As one would expect in such a compendious collection,
chronology, relative and absolute, is important to Diogenes and
usually gets a direct statement to itself.[35] It is much less important to
Luke: the Gospel begins with a proper comparative dating (3:1-2), but
Acts contains no parallel to this. External dating criteria, like the
death of Herod or the expulsion of the Jews by Claudius, are
mentioned as part of the narrative, not allotted separate statements of
their own. Relative chronology is notoriously vague in Acts.

8. *Works* and 9. *Doctrines*. Both these have already been mentioned:
again, even if we admit the speeches or the letters as an equivalent to
these items in the Diogenes *Lives*, there is no formal parallel to the
method of their introduction. Direct speech in Diogenes is limited to
the apophthegms (one-liners) or to the hymns, poems and letters
which are sometimes quoted. Doctrine is summarised by Diogenes in

---

[33]DL V.68. (Lycon); VII.28 (Zeno); IV.14-15 (Xenocrates). On the death theme and
Diogenes' epigrams cf. Mejer, *op. cit.*, 46-50.
[34]Robert Maddox, *The Purpose of Luke-Acts* (Göttingen: Vandenhoeck & Ruprecht,
1982) 66-7.
[35]DL frequently cites the *Chronica* of Apollodorus: e.g. V.9. Cf. Mejer, *op. cit.*, 34.

his own voice, not expressed in direct speech placed on the lips of the philosophers themselves. And the listing of titles of books is an important part of the agenda.[36]

10. *Documents.* The wills quoted by Diogenes occur chiefly, as already stated, in the Peripatetic *Lives*; other documents, like letters, are occasionally included (e.g. Epicurus).[37] It is tempting to read Paul's farewell speech in Acts 20:18-35 as some kind of 'Testament', but this does not make it a formal parallel to the Testament of Aristotle: the wills quoted by Diogenes are real ones, legal documents concerned with the disposition of property and family arrangements, not ideological constructs like those of the biblical tradition. Conversely, the documents quoted by Luke (such as the letter of Claudius Lysias in Acts 23:26-30) form part of the narrative.[38]

11. *Homonyms.* Acts offers no parallel to this rather odd feature of Diogenes' compendium. It clearly derives from one of the many hellenistic sources he quotes, and expresses well the concern for cataloguing which dominates so much of this literature.[39]

It may be seen from this analysis that even where there are parallels in content between Acts and the Lives of Diogenes Laertius, detailed examination at the level of narrative mode points up as many contrasts as similarities. Acts uses full narrative where Diogenes makes summary statements; Acts uses indirect narrative (information conveyed by the characters) and indirect characterisation where Diogenes always gives the bare facts; episodes from the life of the hero are structured in a completely different way. Acts gives us 'thick' narrative where Diogenes gives us 'thin'. It may in fact be doubted whether Diogenes' story can be dignified with the name 'narrative' at all: it might be better to say that Luke tells his story in 'narrative mode' while Diogenes' is much closer to the 'analytical

---

[36]Some lives consist of little more than a list of titles, e.g. Simon the Shoemaker (II.122), Cebes (II.125), although not all philosophers were known as authors, e.g. Hipparchia (VI.96-98). The list can run to several pages, e.g. Theophrastus (V.42-50).
[37]Epicurus: will X.16-21; letters X.22, 35-83, 84-116. Cf. the exchange of letters and decree cited in VII.7-9, 10-12 (Zeno).
[38]So, rightly, H.J. Cadbury, *The Making of Luke-Acts* (N.Y.: Macmillan, 1927) 190-199.
[39]On Demetrius of Magnesia, whom DL cites as his source for the homonyms, cf. Mejer, *op. cit.*, 38-39.

mode'.[40] Luke speaks throughout with the unified voice of a narrator. Diogenes' work, by contrast, contains a strong authorial presence which repeatedly draws attention to a plurality of narrators, some anonymous ('they say'), others named.[41] From the formal perspective, what is interesting is not the identification of these 'sources' but Diogenes' attitude to them. He repeatedly draws attention to their existence, sometimes quoting chapter and verse (correctly). This maintains a constant distance between the implied author and what he narrates and creates a sense of detachment which is increased on the not infrequent occasions where Diogenes points out a conflict in his sources.[42] Luke makes use of a similar authorial voice in his prefaces (Lk. 1:1-4, Acts 1:1), but that voice never intrudes itself into the narrative. Even the 'we-passages', I would argue, do not constitute a breach in the narrative framework of Acts: the narrator there simply (and oddly) becomes a temporary character in his own narrative, but there is no consciousness of a plurality of narrators, much less of conflicting narratives, such as there is in Diogenes.

---

[40]'Mode': I borrow the term from John Douglas Minyard, *Mode and Value in the De Rerum Natura* (Hermes Einzelschriften 39; Wiesbaden: Franz Steiner, 1978) ch. 4. Of the narrative mode he says (pp. 90-91): 'Narrative works are concerned with the sequential ordering of topics, not with the hierarchies of logical relations (as in analytical works). . .They spend their energies on the development of an appropriate rhythm and verbal design, associative connections, the recollection or intimation of earlier events by later ones, the qualities of feeling which can be incorporated in a recreation of an incident or particular description, and the stabilization of attitudes and perspectives through a variety of incidents. The narrator does not assert logically testable propositions, he does not argue a case, and the narrative voice is not pluralized so that the incidents are seen from different points of view. The order is sequential (whether progressive or paratactic), and the narrative voice is unitary. Unity in the whole is founded upon the stabilization in style, incident, perspective and narrative voice.' The 'analytical' mode, by contrast is described on pp. 89-90: 'Works in the analytical mode try to create an order based upon logical relationships in an effort to explain a process of reasoning or aspect of reality. They strive for logic in argument, the clear statement of testable propositions, and the systematic analysis of public proofs. . .'
[41]Cf. Desbordes, *op. cit.*, vol. I, ii: 'le moi-narrateur ne peut renvoyer à aucun fait biographique réel'.
[42]Conflicting sources: e.g. VII.28 (Zeno's age at death); V.2 (different reasons for name 'Peripatetic').

III. Behind Diogenes Laertius: Biography in the Hellenistic Schools

It is clear from this comparison that, while Luke and Diogenes Laertius share a certain number of narrative concerns, they differ considerably in their manner of expression. One response to this is to stress the catholicity of the genre, as do both Talbert and Burridge in different ways;[43] but this is to lessen the usefulness of the genre-description as a distinctive, and has the effect of blurring precisely those details of presentation which constitute the individuality of one kind of story-telling over against another. If we are to use the category of intellectual biography in any way to assist our understanding and appreciation of the narrative of Acts, it is worth persisting with the comparison; but it is clear that we must move behind Diogenes himself to the hellenistic biographical tradition on which he drew.

The comparison between Luke and DL tacitly assumes this move, as we saw earlier; but it also assumes that the tradition which underlies Diogenes' work was different in significant ways from the collection as we have it now. This assumption is in tune with recent scholarship on Diogenes which has begun to stress his own contribution as an author, in contrast with an earlier scholarship which saw him simply as a compiler; the epigrams, the doxographical sections, and perhaps other elements of the overall structure of the work should probably be credited to Diogenes himself.[44] Moreover there is evidence from the papyri that some earlier biographical narration was less compressed than that of Diogenes.[45] But there is a limit to what can be discovered about the narrative mode of lost or fragmentary sources, since it is precisely the surface structure that tends to disappear in the process of epitomising

---

[43]Talbert, 'Biography, Ancient', *ABD* I, distinguishes the 'essential' from the 'accidental' in ancient biography; Burridge, *op. cit.* draws up an intentionally wide list of constitutive features.

[44]See especially the work of Mejer, *op. cit.* and Desbordes, *op. cit.*, with further references there.

[45]The biography of the Epicurean Philonides found at Herculaneum (P. Herc. 1044) is in a tantalisingly fragmentary state, but it looks to have contained real narrative, not just disconnected anecdotes: see Italo Gallo, *Frammenti Biografici da Papiri* vol. II (Roma: Ateno & Bizarri, 1980) 55-95. The Ptolemaic 'Life and Apophthegms of Socrates' contained in P. Hibeh 182 includes a fuller form of the story told at DL II.34; structurally, however, this is little more than a collection of anecdotes with some doxography (Gallo, *op. cit.*, 177-199).

and excerpting;[46] and there does seem to be a constantly recurring pattern of biographical *topoi* very similar to that of Diogenes' Lives both among his sources and in other forms of intellectual biography.[47]

To conduct a thorough survey of narrative agenda and narrative mode in all the biographies which can be dated before the second century A.D. is outside the scope of this paper. But it is necessary for the comparison with Acts to understand something of the nature of the hellenistic tradition, and for these purposes the question of function is crucial. We began by selecting three possible functions for biography among those put forward by Talbert's hypothesis which could be useful for understanding Acts. Two at least of these, the 'succession' type and the 'exemplary' type, presuppose a stance of commitment to one particular school or teacher; and the hypothesis of a 'school' setting also depends on such a stance.[48] But it is precisely this sense of commitment which is absent from Diogenes Laertius at the level of narrative mode;[49] and indeed it is hard to see how a compendium which narrates the lives of philosophers from all the competing schools of Greek philosophy could serve the interests of any one school in this way. Diogenes himself is described by Ingemar Düring as 'an erudite amateur, isolated and without personal connections with the contemporary schools of learning'[50]—and as we have seen, this estimate is borne out by a detailed study of Diogenes' work. But the very act of compilation distances the biographer from commitment to any one teacher. To make the paradigm work, we have to assume that behind

---

[46]The publication in 1912 of a papyrus containing Satyrus' biography of Euripides (using a totally unexpected dialogue form) revealed how fragmentary our knowledge is and how dangerous it is to make assumptions on the basis of negative evidence: cf. Momigliano, *op. cit.*, 115.

[47]Cf. Mejer, *op. cit.*, 92-93. Compare the *Life of Hippocrates* attributed (probably correctly) to Soranus (Pinault, *op. cit.*, 7-8), which is different from the Lives of DL but not markedly so.

[48]Cf. Talbert, *Literary Patterns, Theological Themes and the Genre of Luke-Acts*, 134 ('cult document') and 'Biographies of philosophers and rulers as instruments of religious propaganda in Mediterranean antiquity', 1626, 'Do any Greco-Roman biographies arise out of, presuppose, or function in the interests of religious/worshipping communities?'

[49]As a colleague observed at a seminar conducted on DL, 'He doesn't appear to like any of these guys very much'.

[50]Düring, *op. cit.*, 469.

a collection like Diogenes' lie a number of single Lives (and successions), originating in the different schools.

This is where our first problem lies, for most of the committed, individual Lives cited by Talbert are post-Christian in date (*Secundus*, Lucian's *Demonax*), some of them substantially so (Philostratus, Porphyry). For pre-Christian *Lives* we are reliant largely on citations and allusions in later authors, or on biographical remains (mostly fragmentary) in the papyri. Clearly there is a need for a thoroughgoing study of all the evidence here: but, it seems clear from the evidence we do have (and from Diogenes Laertius himself) that single, committed Lives of the type posited by Talbert would be the exception rather than the rule in the hellenistic biographical tradition.

The *Successions of Sotion*, one of Diogenes' most important predecessors, dating from the mid second century B.C., traced 'the roster of teachers and pupils in a continuous series from the earliest times down to his own day': like Diogenes' work, this seems to have been an even-handed, disinterested study of all the philosophical schools.[51] Fraser argues that Sotion drew most of the substance for his work from 'a more elaborate work by Theophrastus': 'Such "successions" were already known in outline to Plato and Aristotle and were much elaborated by Theophrastus, from whom apparently Sotion extracted the biographical and discarded the purely philosophical elements'.[52] The writing up of 'successions' may thus be seen as part of the Peripatetic interest in drawing up a universal history of the intellectual life.[53] 'Successions' devoted to the work of a single school were 'apparently far less popular'; Mejer cites eight known examples, of which two are from Plutarch and two from Galen.[54]

Diogenes' other major predecessor, Hermippus of Smyrna, was contemporary with or slightly earlier than Sotion. His work was even wider in scope: 'Hermippus' *Lives* contained biographies of eminent men, arranged according to their field of activity: of the Seven Wise Men, of distinguished lawgivers, philosophers and others. The *Lives* thus supplemented the largely bibliographical information to be found in Callimachus' *Pinakes*'.[55] Hermippus (whose work is

---

[51]P.M. Fraser, *Ptolemaic Alexandria* (Oxford: Clarendon Press, 1970) vol. I, 453. On Sotion and the 'Succession' literature in general, see Mejer, *op. cit.*, 40-42, 62-74.
[52]Fraser, *op. cit.*, 469.
[53]Cf. Momigliano, *op. cit.*, 119 on 'The Peripatetic interest in historical research'.
[54]Mejer, *op. cit.*, 74-75.
[55]Fraser, *op. cit.*, vol. I, 781. Cf. also Mejer, *op. cit.*, 32-34, 90-93.

described by Fraser as 'unreliable and scandalous')[56] seems to owe less to the ideals of philosophical *imitatio* than to the bibliographical labours of Callimachus, engaged in cataloguing the Alexandrian library: it is a type of biography which has been aptly called 'pinacographic'. Again, this kind of biography seems to have been compilatory in origin: Satyrus' more elaborate *Lives of the Tragedians*, of which only the *Life of Euripides* survives, was also a compilation, and the tradition continues down to the *Lives of the Poets* and other so-called 'minor biographers'.[57] It is this fact that leads Mejer to the conclusion, 'It is in fact difficult to find any difference between biographies of philosophers and those of other types of personalities except perhaps that the former contained more apophthegms and anecdotes involving sayings. That there was little or no difference is also indicated by the fact that the more prolific authors of biographies were not philosophers. . .Thus, we have no reason to assume that the motivation for writing biographies of philosophers was any different from the general motive of Hellenistic biography, sc. the wish to depict a famous personality's ἦθος and πράξεις'.[58] Even among the biographers who can more properly be assigned to the Peripatetic school, with its interest in the moral qualities associated with the philosophic life, much of the material of which we have evidence seems to be compilatory and comparative rather than individual.[59] The typical title is περὶ βίων, not βίος τοῦ δεῖνου: *On the Tyrants of Sicily, On the Socratics, On Poetry and Poets*: the whole is seen by Stuart as a subdivision of the hellenistic impulse to 'polymathy'.[60] Such material could be used in the polemics between the different schools, but its character was in many ways anything but philosophical:

> Hellenistic biography was far more elaborately erudite than any previous biographical composition. It was also far more curious about details, anecdotes, witticisms and eccentricities. In so far as it supported one philosophy against another and helped its readers to understand writers and artists, it can be said to have pursued professional aims. . .But. . .men did not write biographies because they were philosophically-minded or because they were engaged in some kind of intellectual or political controversy. The educated man

---

[56]Fraser, *op. cit.*, vol. I, 453.
[57]Cf. works listed in n. 9 and n. 11 above.
[58]Mejer, *op. cit.*, 93. Cf. Momigliano, *op. cit.*, 84.
[59]Cf. especially D.R. Stuart, *op. cit.*, ch. V.
[60]Stuart, *op. cit.*, 129.

of the Hellenistic world was curious about the lives of famous people.[61]

There is, then, little evidence to support the assumption that Diogenes Laertius put his collection together from a number of originally separate, single biographies originating in the different schools. What seems to lie behind Diogenes (as is in fact perfectly clear from his own allusions to his sources) are more compilations, showing all the variety of interests of hellenistic erudition. Some of the material must go back to the archives of the individual schools: letters and wills fall most obviously into this category. Some is drawn directly from known literary sources (Xenophon, Plato). Chronological notices go back to the bible of hellenistic chronology, Apollodorus' *Chronica*; the lists of 'Homonyms' which close every Life come, as Diogenes tells us himself, from a treatise on 'Men of the Same Name'. The gossipy notes about the bisexual love-lives of the philosophers may go back in some cases to a polemic source like Aristoxenus' hostile biography of Socrates,[62] but Diogenes himself ascribes them to a treatise 'On the Luxury of the Ancients' which must have made fruity reading. It is no wonder that, at a seminar which I conducted recently on Diogenes, one participant suggested that his work looks like 'a kind of coffee-table book, with just the information that the educated person needs to know': this character must be seen in large part as an accurate reflection of the hellenistic biographical tradition on which he drew.

So the origins of the 'heroic' biography of the philosopher seem as elusive as those of the so-called 'aretalogy of the divine sage' which in many ways it resembles.[63] Behind the encyclopaedic compilations of the early Empire lie, for the most part, not individual Lives but more series and collections. Behind them, and feeding into this literary activity at every stage, seem to be the real hard currency of biography in the hellenistic schools: sequences and catalogues, floating anecdotes and sayings, a name attached to a teacher, a name or an anecdote attached to a doctrine or discovery, archival collections of letters or wills. The process may be illustrated briefly by looking at the meagre biographical information preserved by the tradition about Hippocrates of Chios, not the famous doctor but a

---

[61]Momigliano, *op. cit.*, 119-120.
[62]Stuart, *op. cit.*, 132-54.
[63]See on this especially Cox, *op. cit.*, 30-44.

mathematician of the fifth century B.C. of whom virtually nothing is known and of whom no 'Life' was ever written.

Björnbo in the *RE* article which bears his name,[64] argues that the biographical tradition about this Hippocrates rests on three pieces of evidence:

a) a notice in Proclus, believed to go back to Eudemus, which places H. in a chronological sequence: 'After Pythagoras. . .came Anaxagoras and Oinopides, who was younger than Anaxagoras. . .and after them Hippocrates of Chios, who discovered the quadrature of the moon, and Theodorus. . .'

b) Aristotle, *Meteor*. I.342b35ff.: 'Hippocrates of Chios and his disciples held views similar to this'.

c) Aristotle, *Eth. Eud*. VIII.2.5 1247a17-20: <do men succeed because of wisdom? no:> 'for example, Hippocrates was skilled in geometry but was thought to be stupid and unwise in other matters, and it is said that on a voyage owing to foolishness he lost a great deal of money taken from him by the collectors of the two-per-cent duty at Byzantium'.

Here we have three isolated biographical details, linked (a) to chronological sequence, (b) to a particular scientific hypothesis, and (c) to an ethical point. The last belongs clearly to a well-known class of anecdotes on the foolishness of philosophers and mathematicians, of a type which Jaeger calls the 'absentminded astronomer'.[65] The three illustrate neatly, albeit at a very early stage of the tradition, the three major loci for biographical interest in the hellenistic schools: sequencing and chronology; doxography/bibliography; and ethics. In the last, which clearly alludes to a fuller narrative whose details may have been already lost when Aristotle cited the example, we have a type of moral paradigm expressed in the form of a biographical anecdote. This particular topos seems to express popular sentiment of a mildly (though generally affectionately) anti-philosophical flavour, but there is a related group, going back to the fifth century, which 'owe their coinage entirely to men of a different class, men who were

---

[64]*RE* VIII.2 (1913) 1781-1801, art. 'Hippokrates (14)'.
[65]Werner Jaeger, *Aristotle: Fundamentals of the History of his Development* (2nd ed.; tr. R. Robinson; Oxford: Clarendon Press, 1948) Appendix II, 426-61, 'On the Origin and Cycle of the Philosophic Ideal of Life'.

themselves full of the *ethos* of what was later called the "theoretic life", and made themselves a sort of symbol for it in the striking utterances of the wise men of old'.[66] It is here that we come closest to the biography of the sage as a paradigm for the philosophic life, but this function inheres in the isolated anecdote: there is no biography as such. We are of course largely dependent on literary sources, some of which in the later period are biographical, for the preservation of most of these 'floating' anecdotes; but the evidence of the papyri, as well as the existence of unattached anecdotes like this, confirms that they also circulated independently.[67]

In terms of the 'development' of intellectual biography, then, what we seem to have is not the expected progression

Anecdote—Life—Collected Lives

but one which misses out the middle stage:

Anecdote—. . .—collection

—but the collection may just as well be a series of anecdotes (*Chriae*) or a series on a topic as a collection of *bioi*. When and why this pattern changed to encourage the composition of individual Lives remains a mystery. It would be a mistake to take it as an inevitable development: the rabbinic school tradition, with an essentially similar repertoire of catalogues and anecdotes, never developed individual biography.[68] Whatever the explanation, it seems to be the fact that the crucial steps were taken in a number of adjacent areas at around the turn of the eras: Andronicus' *Life of Aristotle* (perhaps),[69] the Epicurean *Life of Philonides* (P. Herc. 1044), Philo's *Vita Mosis*, the Gospels and Acts, and then the second-century examples like *Secundus the Silent Philosopher* and Lucian. Perhaps we should remember Ben Perry's famous warning about looking for the 'development' of the novel: 'The first romance was deliberately

---

[66]Jaeger (cited in previous note) 428.

[67]Cf. Gallo, *op. cit.*, vol. II, 221, 229-30, 317, 331-33, 345, 351, 363, 371, 385-86.

[68]P.S. Alexander, 'Rabbinic biography and the biography of Jesus: A survey of the evidence', in C.M. Tuckett (ed.), *Synoptic Studies* (Sheffield: JSOT Press, 1984) 19-50.

[69]On Andronicus, see esp. Düring, *op. cit.*, 413-467. D. argues that Andronicus' work was not in fact a biography of Aristotle but a kind of 'catalogue raisonné' in which biographical data were used to determine the chronology and authenticity of the texts discussed.

planned and written by an individual author, its inventor. He conceived it on a Tuesday afternoon in July'.[70]

IV. The Genre of Acts

It is time to return to Acts, and ask how this material may help us to read Luke's composition. On the face of it, intellectual biography in the hellenistic period fails to provide a clear literary model for Acts, at least if by that we mean a full biography committed to an individual school and describing the teacher's life in such a way as to provide a moral paradigm for imitation. Biographical texts of this kind, widespread as they are in the period of late antiquity, seem to have been far from typical of the hellenistic tradition. But if we broaden our definition of biography to include not only the fully-fledged biographical texts but also the underlying traditions and patterns of thought, it is not difficult to see many points of interest for Acts.

The hellenistic school tradition offers clear evidence of biographical interest clustering around three foci: chronology and succession; doxography and bibliography; and the paradigm of the sage. This interest is expressed in biographical anecdotes and notices which circulate independently and may be combined in a variety of different 'collections'. I would suggest that the existence of these varied foci of biographical concern is of considerable interest to students of Acts. In all the years of debate about the existence or non-existence of 'sources' or 'traditions' behind the narrative of Acts, few have paused to ask what kind of social context might provide a matrix for the production or preservation of such material. It seems to me that the hellenistic school tradition provides just such a social matrix whose value has yet to be exploited for Acts. Parallels worth exploring include: the preservation of isolated anecdotes about famous teachers; the interest (as Talbert rightly saw) in the arrangement of disparate teachers into a 'succession'; concern for chronology and sequence; and the tendency to extract biographical details from a writer's works (especially letters) in default of external biographical information. And this interest was not limited to the philosophical schools; the preservation of the prefatorial letters of

---

[70]B.E. Perry, *The Ancient Romances* (Berkeley: University of California Press, 1967) 175.

Archimedes and Apollonius of Perge, the Hippocratic pseudepigrapha and the Lives which they apparently inspired, and the
bibliographical 'autobiographies' of Galen suggest that similar
interests, if less frenetically expressed, existed in mathematical and
medical circles.[71] As we argued above, the very fact that all this
'historical' activity was going on in the schools has relevance for the
genre of Acts, which does not fit easily into the patterns of political
historiography.

In this final section I would like to explore one particular
template from the repertoire of hellenistic philosophical biography
which I think did exert some influence on the structuring of Luke's
Pauline narrative, and that is the hugely—perhaps uniquely—
influential paradigm of Socrates. Socrates, though he figures as one
philosopher among others in Diogenes Laertius, is actually in a rather
different position from most of the subjects of philosophical
biography. Historians of the genre dispute whether or not the
Socratic writings of Plato and Xenophon are to be classified as
'biography'.[72] What is important for our purposes, however, is that
what lies behind the tradition, in this case, is not a series of
disconnected anecdotes or doxographical notices, but a substantial
body of written texts operating on a level of literary complexity
which Diogenes Laertius lacks. Here, as nowhere else in the
hellenistic biographical tradition, are detailed narrative and first-
person discourse; even if we discount the bulk of the Platonic
dialogues,[73] Xenophon's less ambitious *Memorabilia* describe Socratic
encounters with far more detail than the curtly-formulated *chriae* of
Diogenes Laertius. Moreover, we know that this was not a fossilised
literary tradition. Socratic anecdotes (not derived from Plato or
Xenophon) are almost as common as *chriae* relating to the Cynic
Diogenes of Sinope; Diogenes Laertius knows some of them, and
some are collected in P. Hibeh 182.[74] A vigorous letter-writing
activity clustered around the fourth-century sage and his disciples,
probably dating from the Augustan age.[75] Socrates is cited as a moral

---

[71]For Hippocrates, cf. n. 19 above. Galen's two short treatises, *De libris propriis*
and *De ordine librorum suorum* may be found in vol. II of the *Scripta Minora* in the
Teubner edition (Kühn, vol. XIX).
[72]Momigliano, *op. cit.*, 17.
[73]As ancient scholars seem on the whole to have done: DL II.45.
[74]Cf. nn. 67 & 45 above.
[75]A.J. Malherbe (ed.), *The Cynic Epistles* (SBLSBS 12; Missoula; Scholars Press,
1977) 2.

paradigm by first-century writers like Seneca, Dio Chrysostom and Epictetus. And, perhaps most significant for us, episodes from his life (and even more, his death) provided a template for describing the lives of others in a number of texts dating from the first century and the beginning of the second.[76]

1. *The divine call*. The story of Paul's 'call' occupies a prime position at the beginning of his biography in Acts (ch. 9), and its twofold repetition in chapters 22 and 26 keeps it at the forefront of the readers' attention.[77] Similarly, Socrates' mission begins with an oracle from Delphi (Plato, *Apol.* 20e-22a) which inspires his mission and which he regards in the light of a military commission: 'the God gave me a station, as I believed and understood, with orders to spend my life in philosophy and in examining myself and others' (Plato, *Apol.* 28e, LCL; cf. Epictetus I.9). This oracle figures prominently in Diogenes Laertius' account, where it is described as 'universally known' (II.37, Yonge); it also provided a template for a number of other 'call' stories attached to the lives of philosophers.[78] Note that the primary literary expression of this call is in the first-person *apologia* in which Socrates, on trial for his life, defends his own obedience to the divine message: compare Paul's dual first-person account of his call in his own *apologia*, Acts 22 and 26.

2. *The mission*. Paul's divine call points directly to his mission, which forms the central section of his biography (Acts 13-19). For Socrates, too, the Chaerephon-oracle is the beginning of a lifelong commitment: 'therefore I am still even now going about and searching and investigating at the God's behest anyone, whether citizen or foreigner. . .and by reason of this occupation I have no leisure to attend to any of the affairs of the state worth mentioning, or of my own, but am in vast poverty on account of my service to the God' (Plato, *Apol.* 23b LCL; cf. DL II.21-22). Dio Chrysostom models his own mission on Socrates' in the *De Fuga* (*Or.* XIII). Like Socrates', Dio's mission begins with an inquiry to the oracle (422R, 243.1-12

---

[76]The data are collected in Klaus Döring, *Exemplum Socratis: Studien zur Sokratesnachwirkung in der kynisch-stoischen Popularphilosophie der frühen Christentum* (Hermes Einzelschriften 42; Wiesbaden: Franz Steiner, 1979). See also A. Ronconi, 'Exitus illustrium virorum', *Reallexikon für Antike und Christentum* (Stuttgart: Hiersemann, 1966) vol. VI, cols. 1258-68.

[77]Cf. n. 28 above.

[78]Cf. Gigon, *op. cit.*

Teubner); unlike Socrates', it involves travel 'until you come to the farthest part of the earth' (243.10-11), an Odyssean lifestyle only bearable under direct orders from God (243.12-17).[79] The detailed rationale of this mission is presented as 'some ancient discourse, said to be by a certain Socrates, which he never ceased proclaiming, shouting and raising his voice everywhere and before everybody, both in the palaestras and in the Lyceum and before the law courts and in the market-place, like a *deus ex machina*, as somebody said' (244.17-22).[80]

3. *The daimonion*. One of the charges against Socrates is that of 'introducing new gods (καινὰ δαιμόνια) which the city does not believe in' (Plato, *Apol.* 24b, DL II.40). The charge arises out of Socrates' claim to receive divine guidance at every step from his own *daimonion* (Xenophon, *Mem.* I.2-5; DL II.32). The identity of this *daimonion* was receiving renewed attention at the end of the first century; Socrates was also acquiring an enhanced mantic reputation as a 'prophet'.[81] Paul too experienced direct divine guidance at perplexing moments (e.g. 16:6-10), and was accused (in Athens) of introducing new gods (ξενὰ δαιμόνια: Acts 17:18). Luke's choice of words is interesting here. This is the only occasion in the New Testament where δαιμόνια is used in a non-pejorative sense: by implication, the word refers to 'Jesus and the resurrection', and the charge is never denied.[82] Note also that in Diogenes Laertius the Areopagus is regularly the scene for the trial of a philosopher.[83]

4. *Tribulations*. The mission is described by Socrates as involving 'herculean' labours. The Hercules metaphor is expanded in the Cynic tradition, but others know of extensive catalogues of Socrates' 'labours': commentators have long suspected that this kind of list provided the model for Paul's own catalogue of his labours in 2

---

[79]DL II.22 seems to presuppose a pattern of the philosophic life which does involve travel (ἀποδημία): Socrates did not travel, but most philosophers did.
[80]Cf. also Epictetus III.i.19-20, III.xxi.19, I.xii.3 (S. paired with Odysseus), III.xxii.26.
[81]Plutarch, *De genio Socratis* (Moral, 575b-598f.); Döring, *op. cit.*, 11-12.
[82]Socratic allusions in Acts 17 are suggested tentatively by Hans Dieter Betz, *Der Apostel Paulus und die sokratische Tradition* (Beiträge zur historischen Theologie 45; Tübingen: Siebeck-Mohr, 1972) 38 and n. 182; more decisively Karl Olav Sandnes, 'Paul and Socrates: the Aim of Paul's Areopagus Speech', *JSNT* 50 (1993) 13-26.
[83]Trials on the Areopagus: DL II.101, II.116, VII.169.

Corinthians 10-13.[84] Seneca, *Ep.* 104.27-8 provides a good example of such a catalogue:

> If, however, you desire a pattern (*exemplum*), take Socrates, a long-suffering old man, who was sea-tossed amid every hardship and yet was unconquered both by poverty (which his troubles at home made more burdensome) and by toil (*laboribus*), including the drudgery of military service. (LCL).[85]

Socrates is not the only example cited, however. Like Lucian *(Demonax 2)*, Seneca feels the need to present an *exemplum* nearer home, so he follows the catalogue of Socrates' troubles with a parallel list of Cato's who, 'just as much as Socrates, declared allegiance to liberty in the midst of slavery' (§§ 29-33). The fact that the actual circumstances of the two lives were quite different does not affect the parallel.

5. *Persecution*. For Socrates, obedience to the divine call is accompanied from the start by hostility and persecution from his fellow-citizens (Plato, *Apol.* 22e-23a); in fact much of the *Apology is* an expansion on this theme. Diogenes Laertius links the two directly:

> very often, while arguing and discussing points that arose, he was treated with great violence and beaten, and pulled about, and laughed at and ridiculed by the multitude. But he bore all this with great equanimity. So that once, when he had been kicked and buffeted about, and had borne it all patiently, and some one expressed his surprise, he said, 'Suppose an ass had kicked me, would you have had me bring an action against him?' (DL II.21, tr. Yonge).

The link is made even more explicitly in Acts, where the apostle's call is to persecution as much as to mission (9:16; 22:18; 26:17) and the narrative devotes as much time to the former as to the latter.

6. *Trial*. The culmination of years of hostility, and the focal point of the Socrates tradition, is the trial which leads to his death: the accidents of literary history mean that a disproportionate amount of

---

[84]Cf. Betz, *op. cit., passim.*

[85]Note that Gummere (LCL translator) implies a metaphorical shipwreck even for this most landlocked of sages: *iactare* is often cited in the context of a storm at sea, cf. C.T. Lewis and C. Short, *A Latin Dictionary* (Oxford: Clarendon Press, 1879) sv.

Socratic biography takes the form of *apologia*, i.e. his own defence speech spoken in the first person. For Paul, too, the series of trials which brings Acts to an end takes up an apparently disproportionate amount of narrative space (below), and involves a substantial amount of first-person *apologia*. Note here again Luke's choice of words: ἀπολογία and its cognate verb occur seven times in this context, more than anywhere else in the New Testament. Socrates was of course the philosophical martyr *par excellence*, the prototype of a long line of sages confronting tyrants: 'the first philosopher who was condemned to death and executed' (DL II.20 tr. Yonge) but not the last. Epictetus is particularly fond of citing Socrates as a paradigm for courageous opposition to tyranny.[86] John Darr in a recent book draws attention to Luke's casting of Herod Agrippa in the 'tyrant' role in the Gospel accounts of the trial of Jesus: there are several contenders for this role in Acts, but there can be no doubt that the part of the philosophic hero falls pre-eminently to Paul.[87]

7. *Prison*. 'When we read Acts as a whole, rather than selectively, it is Paul the prisoner even more than Paul the missionary whom we are meant to remember.'[88] As the dramatic setting for two of Plato's most famous dialogues, prison inevitably figures just as large in the biography of Socrates.[89] Two linked motifs are relevant here. Socrates, like Paul, sings hymns in prison: this minor detail of Plato's account (*Phaedo* 60d) is mentioned by Diogenes Laertius (II.42) who cites the actual words of the hymn in question. In Epictetus' hands, however, the episode becomes not an opportunity for pedantry but a pattern of philosophic constancy:

> A platform and a prison is each a place, the one high (ὑψηλός), the other low (ταπεινός); but your moral purpose can be kept the same, if you wish to keep it the same, in either place. And then we shall be emulating (ζηλωταί) Socrates, when we are able to write paeans in prison. (II.vi.27, cf. IV.iv.23).

---

[86]Cf. I.xix.6 ('Who becomes a zealous follower of yours [ζηλωτής] as [men did] of Socrates?'), I.xxix.16ff., 29; II.ii.8ff., 15ff.; II.v.18-19; II.xiii.24; IV.i.123 (parallel with Helvidius); IV.vii.28.

[87]John A. Darr, *On Character Building: the reader and the rhetoric of characterization in Luke-Acts* (Westminster: John Knox Press, 1992) ch. 6; cf. Ronconi, *op. cit., RAC* VI.1264 on the death of Herod in Acts 12:23.

[88]Maddox, *op. cit.*, 67; cf. Richard Pervo, *Profit with Delight* (Philadelphia: Fortress Press, 1987) on the prominence of prison scenes in Acts.

[89]Esp. Epictetus: e.g. I.i.23-24, I.iv.24, I.xii.23.

The theme may be a development of a longer passage in the *Phaedo*, where Socrates compares his deathbed discourses with the songs of the swans who 'when they feel that they are to die, sing most and best in their joy that they are to go to the God whose servants they are' (84e-85b). A Socratic reading of Acts suggests that we might see Paul's determination to carry on 'preaching and teaching' in his Roman prison (Acts 28:23-30) in the same light.

8. *Death*. The Socratic paradigm was, above all, a paradigm for facing death: in Seneca's words (*Ep.* 104.22) Socrates 'will show you how to die if it be necessary'. Epictetus makes the point countless times: Socrates' conviction that his accusers 'may kill me, but they cannot harm me' is cited on several occasions in the *Discourses* and is the motto chosen to close the *Enchiridion* (53.4).[90] His death, moreover, was explicitly paralleled with those of contemporary martyrs among the Stoic opposition under Nero and Domitian: with Helvidius Priscus (Epict. IV.i.123), with Cato and other Roman heroes of an earlier age (Seneca *Ep.* 98.12, 104.27-33). Seneca himself seems to have consciously modelled his own death on that of Socrates, and it seems clear that Tacitus' written account of the episode has the Socratic paradigm in view, following the precedent of Thrasea Paetus, Junius Rusticus and other Stoic biographers who patterned their subjects' deaths on that of their most famous predecessor.[91]

What about Acts? As we have seen, the last nine chapters of Acts are structured around an event which is never narrated directly, Paul's impending death. In Maddox's words, 'Since we have on other grounds every reason to judge that Luke composes with a careful eye to the dramatic movement and balance of his work, we may regard this long, final section as intended by the author to carry an emphasis and to form at least in some degree the goal and climax of his composition'.[92] A Socratic reading of Acts may provide at least a partial explanation for this remarkable structure. Chapters 20 and 21 play a crucial role here: the renewed insistence on Paul's readiness to face 'imprisonment and afflictions' (20:22-24), repeated prophecies of

---

[90]Döring, *op. cit.*, 45 and following.
[91]Oswyn Murray, 'The "Quinquennium Neronis" and the Stoics', *Historia* 14 (1965) 41-61; Miriam Griffin, *Seneca: A Philosopher in Politics* (Oxford: Clarendon Press, 1976) ch. 11; Ronconi, *art. cit.*
[92]Maddox, *op. cit.*, 66.

disaster (20:23; 21:10-11)[93] and the tearful farewells (20:36-37; 21:5; 21:12-13) which do nothing to break Paul's resolve (21:13-14). Note the sudden appearance of 'wives and children' in 21:5, and the implied inclusion of the daughters of Philip among 'the people there' in 21:12: this is very much a 'women's scene' in Socratic tradition, based on the removal of the weeping Xanthippe in *Phaedo* 60a and Socrates' refusal to be swayed by the claims of wife and children (*Crito* 45cd). The fact that this is a 'we-section' increases the Socratic effect (the narrative of the *Phaedo* is also in the first person plural): the final scene (21:12-14) strongly recalls the weeping of Socrates' friends in *Phaedo* 65-67, and his words of acceptance to Crito: 'if this is the will of the gods, so let it be'.[94]

V. Conclusion

The Socratic paradigm which I have sketched here does not exist in this form in any known biography of Socrates. It is not a 'genre' or a 'literary model' so much as a narrative pattern familiar to a wide range of writers in the first century A.D., and used by them in a wide variety of styles and literary *Gattungen*. In these texts and others like them we can see the life of Socrates being used as a template for describing crucial events in their own lives or in the lives of more immediate heroes, particularly by those writers concerned with chronicling the deaths of philosophers who had faced martyrdom under Nero and Domitian. In the words of a modern novelist, 'Most people like to fit themselves into a story they already know; it makes them feel a bigger part of life than they are'.[95] I would suggest that this Socratic paradigm was available to Luke's readers and offered them the possibility of fitting Paul's story—and by implication their own—into 'a story they already knew', one which could work alongside the paradigm of the prophet which Luke employs to such good effect in the Gospel and in the first half of Acts. In Storm's words, 'so *ist* es, Herr'; that's how it *is*, this story from the past tells us something about our own lives: 'dem Sokrates gaben sie ein Gift zu trinken, und unsern Herrn Christus schlugen sie an das Kreuz!'.

---

[93]Note Diogenes Laertius relates a tale of a *magus* coming to Athens from Syria and foretelling Socrates' violent death (II.45).

[94]*Crito* 43d, cited by Epictetus, *Ench.* 53.3 and elsewhere, cf. Döring, *op. cit.*, 45.

[95]Amanda Cross, *No Word from Winifred* (London: Virago, 1987) 30.

CHAPTER 3

ACTS AND BIBLICAL HISTORY

Brian S. Rosner

Summary

A look at Acts and the Old Testament accounts for many features of Acts. There is evidence that in writing Acts, Luke used biblical language and models. Acts and the Old Testament have many themes in common, share certain literary techniques and subscribe to the same theological understanding of history. The Jewish Scriptures exerted a profound influence upon not only the theology of Acts, as is widely recognised, but also upon its character as a piece of literature. This finding sheds light upon the genre and purpose of the book.

I. Introduction

The Old Testament is of central importance to the book of Acts. In the words of C.K. Barrett, 'Luke's use of the Old Testament [in Acts] is co-extensive with most of the aims and interests that he has incorporated in his book'.[1]

---

[1] C.K. Barrett, 'Luke-Acts', *Scripture Citing Scripture: Essays in Honour of Barnabas Lindars* (Cambridge: CUP, 1988) 243. Cf. *Luke the Historian in Recent Study*

Acts cites the Jewish Scriptures[2] some thirty-five times.[3] However, the debt of Acts to the Old Testament extends well beyond the many quotations and allusions which pepper the document. Scholars have recognised the influence of the Bible on Luke's language, literary techniques, narrative style and employment of various themes.

Luke's dependence upon the Scriptures in Acts has been used to study a number of subjects, such as Christology,[4] the problem of the Western text, the relation between Acts and Josephus, the medical terminology in Acts,[5] the question of Paul in Acts and Paul in his

---

(London: Epworth Press, 1961) 15: 'no New Testament writer is more clearly aware of the importance of the Old Testament'.

[2] Scholars are divided on the question of whether the 'Jewish Scriptures' in New Testament times comprised those books currently printed in the Hebrew Bible (i.e. the Old Testament). Some argue for a three-stage canonisation theory (the Law, c. 400 B.C.; the Prophets, c. 200 B.C.; and the hagiographa, c. 90 A.D. at Jabneh [Jamnia]; see *inter alia* A.C. Sundberg, *The Old Testament and the Early Church* (London, 1964); and J. Barton, *The Oracles of God* (London: Darton, Longman and Todd, 1986) who believes that the Prophets were also unsettled in NT times. However, there is good evidence that the Old Testament canon was effectively closed before the New Testament was written. The notion of a certain number of books forming a fixed collection at an early date is supported, in particular, by Josephus, *Against Apion* 1.38-42 and 2 Esdras (= 4 Ezra) 14:44-46. See E. Earle Ellis, 'The Old Testament Canon in the Early Church', in M. Mulder (ed.), *Mikra: Text, Translation, Reading and Interpretation of the Hebrew Bible in Ancient Judaism and Early Christianity* (Assen: Van Gorcum, 1988) 653-90 = Ch. 1 of *The Old Testament in Early Christianity: Canon and Interpretation in the Light of Modern Research* (WUNT 54; Tübingen: J.C.B. Mohr [Paul Siebeck], 1991); and especially R.T. Beckwith, *The Old Testament Canon of the New Testament Church and its Background in Early Judaism* (Reading: SPCK, 1985) for a full and convincing treatment. Barton reviews Beckwith in *Theology* 90 (1987) 63-65, labelling it an 'apologetic for fundamentalism'. Beckwith returns the compliment in *VT* 41 (1991) 385-95. His criticisms are more substantive concluding that Barton 'misrepresents part of the evidence and fails to do justice to the rest of it' (p. 395).

[3] See G.L. Archer and G.C. Chirichigno, *Old Testament Quotations in the New Testament* (Chicago: Moody Press, 1983).

[4] E.g. Darrell L. Bock, *Proclamation from Prophecy and Pattern: Lukan Old Testament Christology* (Sheffield: JSOT, 1987).

[5] See W.K.L. Clarke, 'The Use of the Septuagint in Acts', in F.J. Foakes Jackson and Kirsopp Lake (eds.), *The Beginnings of Christianity: Part 1. The Acts of the Apostles* (London: Macmillan, 1922) 80-84.

letters,[6] and Luke's theology of fulfilment.[7] It even has relevance to setting the date of Acts according to C.H. Dodd and J.C. O'Neill.[8]

The interest of this chapter is in the question of whether the close relation of Acts to the Scriptures can tell us anything about the genre of Acts. In particular can it help us to answer the question, did Luke intend to write history? Determining the genre of a literary work is obviously an important step in assessing its value as a historical source. For example, R.I. Pervo believes that Acts should be identified with ancient romances,[9] and M. Dibelius that the author of Acts wrote short stories (*Novellen*).[10] Such views naturally lead to scepticism about the historical intent of Acts.

The question of the genre of Acts is usually approached by looking for a contemporary precedent, some analogous work from the first century.[11] There is of course legitimacy to this search and it has shed some light on Luke's compositional strategy (see the chapter by D. Palmer). Nonetheless, a case can be made for considering the Scriptures as a possible point of comparison. It was not unheard of in the ancient world to model a piece of writing on a much earlier work or author.[12] Furthermore, the Jewish Scriptures, especially in Greek translation, were in fact first century literature in a vital sense: not written but widely read in the first century. Finally, as a candidate for Luke's literary model, the Scriptures have a distinct advantage over contemporary works. The many Biblical quotations in Acts prove that Luke not only knew the Scriptures but was positively inclined towards them.[13]

---

[6]F.F. Bruce, 'Paul's use of the Old Testament in Acts', in Gerald F. Hawthorne and Otto Betz (eds.), *Tradition and Interpretation in the New Testament* (Grand Rapids: Eerdmans, 1987) 71-79.

[7]See the following chapter by David Peterson.

[8]J.C. O'Neill, *The Theology of Acts in its Historical Setting* (London: SPCK, 1961) 3, 166; C.H. Dodd, 'The Fall of Jerusalem and "the Abomination of Desolation"', *JTS* 37 (1947) 47-54.

[9]R.I. Pervo, *Profit with Delight: The Literary Genre of the Acts of the Apostles* (Philadelphia: Fortress, 1987).

[10]M. Dibelius, *Studies in the Acts of the Apostles* (ET; London, 1956) 4.

[11]See e.g. Colin Hemer, *The Book of Acts in the Setting of Hellenistic History* (Tübingen: J.C.B. Mohr [Paul Siebeck], 1989) 33ff. The Old Testament is strangely absent from his list; and Gregory E. Sterling, *Historiography and Self Definition: Josephos, Luke-Acts and Apologetic Historiography* (Leiden: Brill, 1992).

[12]See discussion of mimēsis in section II.

[13]The only other quoted author or work is the Cretan poet Epimenides (Acts 17:28).

This chapter argues that Acts is consciously modelled on the accounts of history found in the Old Testament. A look at Acts and the Scriptures urges the conclusion that Luke did intend to write history, biblical history. In writing Acts, Luke used biblical language, themes, models and literary techniques. Most importantly, his very concept of history seems to derive from the Bible. Much of the work on the influence of the Old Testament in Luke-Acts has concentrated on the Deuteronomistic history. However, there is no reason to limit the present enquiry to one segment of the Jewish Scriptures. 'Biblical history' is used as a label for the historical books of the Old Testament in general (which share certain features; see sections II-VI).

II. Language

It is widely recognised that much of the language of Acts, its idioms and syntax, has a certain Semitic colouring. Clear examples of Hebraisms include ἐγένετο δέ ('and it came to pass'), ἐν τῷ with the infinitive (e.g. 2:1), συνέθετο συλλαβεῖν (e.g. 12:3) and ἀποκριθεὶς . . .εἶπεν (e.g. 8:24).[14] It remains a question of some debate whether such features are mainly due to translation, underlying sources, the influence of oral synagogue Greek,[15] or an imitation of the language of the LXX. Then there is the task of distinguishing Hebraisms, due to translation from Hebrew or the influence of the LXX, from Aramaisms, which may be put down to Aramaic sources.[16] All of this is complicated by the fact that people were operating in a bilingual, if not trilingual environment.

The issues are very complex. While precise answers stated with certainty may not be possible there is much to be said for the view of H.F.D. Sparks that the presence of Semitisms in Acts is usually due to

---

[14]For summaries of the data see E. Haenchen, *Acts of the Apostles* (Oxford: Blackwell, 1971) 73-77, and for Luke's gospel, Joseph A. Fitzmyer, *The Gospel According to Luke, I-IX: Introduction, Translation and Notes* (Garden City: Doubleday, 1981) 114ff.

[15]Cf. Fred L. Horton, 'Reflections on the Semitisms of Luke-Acts', in Charles H. Talbert (ed.), *Perspectives on Luke-Acts* (Edinburgh: T. & T. Clark, 1978) 1-23.

[16]Aramaisms have been detected mainly in 1:1-5:16; 9:31-11:18 and parts of chs. 12 and 15. As Bruce states, *The Acts of the Apostles: The Greek Text with Introduction and Commentary* (ed 3; Grand Rapids: Eerdmans, 1990) 69: 'in those parts where Luke's sources of information are most likely to have been Aramaic, in their original form at least'. See J. de Zwaan, 'The Use of the Greek Language in Acts', *Beginnings of Christianity*, 1.2, 44-64.

the influence of the LXX.[17] Not unlike the impact of the AV/KJV on the style of many English writers since 1611, in composing Acts Luke has used 'biblical' idiom. Eckhard Plümacher has compared Luke's imitation of LXX language and style, especially in the speeches, with classical mimēsis[18] and sees it as consistent with his general archaising tendencies.[19] Luke, he believes, adopts the common practice in the hellenistic world of imitating literary models. He chose to give his work, 'a biblical atmosphere' (to use J.A. Emerton's words).[20]

A strong challenge to this explanation was mounted by Max Wilcox in his book, *The Semitisms of Acts*, in which he argues that while some Semitisms are explicable as Lukan Septuagintalisms, most examples can only be explained on some theory of Aramaic and Hebrew sources underlying the composition.[21] Wilcox's work was the subject of an extended review by J.A. Emerton.[22] Emerton has successfully disputed (to my mind) Wilcox's two main points: that there are quotations of the Old Testament in Acts (in seventeen verses) which differ so markedly from the LXX so as to suggest sources which contained quotations originally in Hebrew or Aramaic; and that there are Semitisms in Acts which cannot be explained as Septuagintalisms.

Raymond A. Martin's work discounts the influence of the LXX less than Wilcox does.[23] He focuses on the positioning of conjunctions, prepositions and articles and argues, perhaps more convincingly than Wilcox, that while one cannot ignore septuagintal influence upon certain phrases in Acts some Semitic syntactical features point to Semitic sources. In any case the dispute focuses on the number and not the presence of Septuagintalisms in Acts.

One question remains. Why is it that not all parts of Acts are equally septuagintal? Most, though not all, of the Semitisms are

---

[17]H.F.D. Sparks, 'The Semitisms of Acts', *JTS* (1950) 16-28. Cf. F.F. Bruce, *The Acts of the Apostles*, 68: 'Hebraisms [in Acts] are most likely due to LXX influence'.
[18]Eckhard Plümacher, *Lukas als hellenistischer Schriftsteller: Studien zur Apostelgeschichte* (SUNT 9; Göttingen: Vandenhoeck & Ruprecht, 1972) esp. 50-64. He cites both Greek and Latin examples.
[19]Plümacher, *Lukas*, 72-78; e.g. christological titles such as παῖς and ὁ ἅγιος καὶ δίκαιος.
[20]Emerton, 'Review of Max Wilcox', *The Semitisms of Acts*', *JSS* 13 (1968) 285.
[21]Wilcox, *The Semitisms of Acts* (Oxford: Clarendon Press, 1965).
[22]Emerton, *JSS* 13 (1968) 282-97.
[23]Martin, *Syntactical Evidence of Semitic Sources in Greek Documents* (SBL 3; Cambridge, Massachusetts: Society of Biblical Literature, 1974).

found in chapters 1-15. The uneven spread may be due to Luke's 'historical as well as to his dramatic sense'.[24] Sparks has observed that the Septuagintalisms in Luke-Acts are at their thickest in Luke 1-2, the advent of the Messiah, 'to all intents and purposes an Old Testament scene'.[25] Likewise the first part of Acts, being set in Palestine, receives a more Semitic stamp than the second. For Paul's journeys the Septuagintalisms, while not disappearing, are less prevalent.

III. Themes

With the hellenistic background in view Darryl W. Palmer rightly concludes that despite the many points of contact between Acts and ancient Greek historiography, 'the subject-matter [of Acts] is unprecedented'.[26] On the other hand, many of the concerns of Acts bear a close relation to the Old Testament. In the following chapter David Peterson notes the substantial overlap of subject-matter between Acts and the Old Testament and conceives of the connection in terms of promise/prophecy and fulfilment. Other topics which do not fit this pattern also bear mention. W. Ward Gasque has noted that the centre of the story in both Luke and Acts is the focus of much of the Old Testament story, Jerusalem. Whereas the flow of the gospel is toward Jerusalem, the movement in Acts is away from the city (cf. 1:8), although Jerusalem is never far from view in Acts (see chs. 1-7; 15; 18:22; 19:21; 20:6; 21:11-14; 21:17-23:22; 25:1-3; 26:10, 20). For Luke the city of Jerusalem and its temple are representative of Israel. Gasque draws out the likely significance of Luke's interest in Jerusalem: 'Jerusalem provides a bridge between Israel and the church, and thus a link between what a later generation of Christians were to refer to as the Old Testament and the New'.[27] The basically

---

[24]Sparks, 'The Semitisms of Acts', 27.
[25]Sparks, 'The Semitisms of Acts', 270.
[26]Palmer, 'Acts and the Historical Monograph', *TynB* 43 (1992) 373.
[27]Gasque, 'A Fruitful Field: Recent Study of the Acts of the Apostles', *Int* 42 (1988) 121. Cf. P. Rolland, 'L'organisation du Livre des Actes et de l'ensemble de l'oeuvre de Luc', *Biblica* 65 (1984) 81-86; F.D. Weinert, 'The Meaning of the Temple in Luke-Acts', *Bib Theol Bull* 11 (1981) 85-89.

positive attitude of Acts to the Jewish people and the Law[28] may be seen in a similar light.[29]

J.T. Sanders has, on the other hand, described Luke's portrayal of the Jews as critical, even anti-Semitic.[30] Perhaps Acts takes up Old Testament themes, but in a negative fashion? Sanders' judgement is too severe. He exaggerates Luke's hostility to Jews. Certain Jewish characters are excluded from his analysis—the prophets Anna and Simeon (Acts 2:25, 36), the synagogue-leader Jairus (Acts 8:41), and the poor widow (Acts 21:2)—all of whom are portrayed in positive terms. Sanders also plays down the missionary successes among Jews in Acts. If the same standards were applied many of the Hebrew prophets would be branded anti-Jewish.

IV. Models

Scholars have suggested that in composing various episodes in Acts Luke followed patterns based on the Old Testament. David P. Moessner contends that Luke presents Paul in Acts 19:21-28:31 in 'the prophetic mold à la Jesus the Deuteronomistic Prophet like Moses'.[31] He also sees Peter and Stephen as playing a similar role.[32] Evaluation of these assertions would take us too far afield, for Moessner's theory is based on the argument that in the central chapters of the Gospel of Luke Jesus is portrayed as a prophet like Moses who is rejected by the people and journeys through the wilderness to the promised land.[33]

---

[28]Cf. I.H. Marshall, *An Introduction to Acts* (Sheffield: JSOT Press, 1992) 46: 'Throughout Acts Luke seizes the opportunity to show all who may read it that the Christian faith and witness are not contrary to the laws and true interests of Judaism.' Cf. S.G. Wilson, *Luke and the Law* (SNTSMS 50; Cambridge: CUP, 1983).
[29]Perhaps it also reveals Luke's concern for positive Jewish-gentile Christian relations.
[30]Sanders, *The Jews in Luke-Acts* (Philadelphia: Fortress, 1987).
[31]Moessner, *Lord of the Banquet: The Literary and Theological Significance of the Lukan Travel Narrative* (Minneapolis: Fortress, 1989) 299. F. Scott Spencer, *The Portrait of Philip in Acts: a Study of Roles and Relations* (Sheffield: JSOT, 1992) sees Philip in Acts in a similar light
[32]Moessner, *Lord of the Banquet*, 296-307.
[33]Suffice it to say that the book has received some very positive reviews. E.g. Robert B. Sloan, *Theologische Zeitschrift* 47 (1991) 368: 'The brilliance and compelling force of Moessner's proposal marks. . .a significant milestone in Lukan studies'.

On more sure ground we may table the view that Luke modelled Paul's conversion on certain Old Testament patterns. Gerhard Lohfink points to Acts 9:4b-6 as an appearance conversation which has analogies in the Old Testament (e.g. Gn. 31:11-13; 46:2f.; Ex. 3:2-10).[34] This form has three parts: (1) address or call; (2) answer with question; and (3) introduction with charge. A complementary view is that of K. Stendahl, J. Munck and A.F. Segal who compare Luke's account of Paul's conversion to the call of the Old Testament prophets; Acts 9 recalls the vivid experiences of Isaiah, Jeremiah and, especially, Ezekiel. When Ezekiel beheld the glory of God he reports, 'I fell upon my face, and I heard the voice of one that spoke (Ezk. 1:28). Then the Lord said: "Stand upon your feet, and I will speak with you. . .I send you to the people of Israel"' (2:1). Both Paul (according to Acts) and Ezekiel received a revelation, heard a voice and fell to the ground.[35] The striking difference is that Paul's charge is to go to the Gentiles and not only to the Jews.

Old Testament antecedents for other scenes in Acts have also been suggested. In a study examining both the Jewish and Graeco-Roman milieu of Acts 1, D.W. Palmer argues that the farewell scene and the ascension employ a number of typical features of earlier Biblical and Jewish models.[36] W.K.L. Clarke suggested that the meeting of Philip with the Ethiopian eunuch in Acts 8 echoes verses in Zephaniah and other Old Testament texts.[37] D. Daube claims that Acts 6 was written with Moses appointing judges in Exodus 18/ Deuteronomy 1 in mind.[38] The narrative of Acts 27:1ff. is perhaps another example of this kind of modelling. F.F. Bruce asserts that the

---

[34]Lohfink, 'Eine alttestamentliche Darstellungsform für Gotteserscheinungen in den Damaskusgerichten (Apg 9;22;26)', *BZ* 9 (1965) 246-57.

[35]See J. Munck, *Paul and the Salvation of Mankind* (London: SCM, 1959) 24-30; K. Stendahl, *Paul among Jews and Gentiles* (London: SCM, 1977) 7-23; Alan F. Segal, *Paul the Convert: The Apostolate and Apostasy of Saul the Pharisee* (New Haven/London: Yale University Press, 1990) 9-11.

[36]Palmer, 'The Literary Background of Acts 1:1-14', *NTS* 33 (1987) 427-38. Cf. M.D. Goulder, *Type and History in Acts* (London: SPCK, 1964) 149 who considers that 'the Old Testament has had a governing hand in the formation of the story of the ascension in Acts 1'.

[37]Clarke, 'The Use of the Septuagint in Acts', 101. The parallels are as follows: Acts 8:26 - Zp. 2:4; Acts 8:27 - Zp. 2:11-12; 3:10 (cf. Ps. 67:32; Is. 41:3); Acts 8:39 - Zp. 3:4 (cf. 1 Ki. 43:12; 2 Ki. 2:16; Ezk. 3:12; 8:3).

[38]Daube, 'A Reform in Acts and its Models', in Robert Hamerton-Kelly and Robin Scroggs (eds.), *Jews, Greeks and Christians: Religious Cultures in Late Antiquity: Essays in Honor of William David Davies* (Leiden: E.J. Brill, 1976) 151-63.

account of the shipwreck 'shows some dependence on the Septuagint account of Jonah's abortive Mediterranean voyage (Jonah 1, 4ff.)'.[39]

What was Luke's purpose in employing such models for his narratives? It may be possible to suggest different purposes on a case by case basis. For example, connecting Paul's conversion with the call of Old Testament prophets might serve to enhance his status, especially in the eyes of Jewish Christians. However, there may have been a more overriding goal in mind.

James L. Kugel describes a literary phenomenon of late Biblical (Old Testament) historiography and many post-biblical writings whereby 'the present is encouraged to become part of biblical history. . .by describing current events, from as it were, the Bible's perspective'.[40] The extension of biblical history to the present can be illustrated from the book of Esther. Kugel explains:

> It [Esther] recounts the entertaining tale of a wicked courtier's overthrow and the salvation of the Jews in such a way as to make it sound like the great events of the past—particularly the story of Joseph in Pharaoh's court on which some of its language is modelled.

Sangra Berg's study of the motifs, themes and structure of Esther concurs with Kugel's comments. She describes the Joseph story as constituting 'Esther's literary model'.[41] It is possible that Luke's use of biblical models is designed to produce a similar effect. Coupled with his use of deliberate Septuagintalisms such modelling would suggest Luke intends to create a 'biblical effect' for those readers of Acts familiar with the Bible.

What implications do the influence of Old Testament models on Acts carry for the historical value of Acts? M.D. Goulder concludes that Luke's resort to such models betrays his lack of historical information. Goulder laments:

> Sometimes, especially in the early chapters [of Acts], we may be driven to think that he has inferred the detailed course of divine

---

[39]Bruce, 'The Acts of the Apostles', *ANRW* II.25.3 (1988) 2578.

[40]James L. Kugel, *Early Biblical Interpretation* (Philadelphia: Westminster Press, 1986) 47-48. Kugel speaks of these works '"biblicizing" recent events'.

[41]Sandra Berg, *The Book of Esther: Motifs, Themes and Structure* (Missoula: Scholars Press, 1979) 186. On the stories of Joseph, Daniel and Esther and the genre of the Jew in the court of the foreign king see Lawrence M. Wills, *The Jew in the Court of the Foreign King* (Minneapolis: Fortress, 1990).

action from the scriptures where we should have preferred him to rely on the evidence of personal testimony.[42]

In fact, Goulder believes that where no type from the Old Testament or the life of Jesus can be seen in Acts, there Luke is writing history: 'where there are no types Acts is intended to be factual'.[43]

In answer to Goulder, it is important to note a distinction between the selection of data and the invention of data to fit into a pattern. The Old Testament may simply have influenced Luke's choice of material and the way it is presented.[44] It does not necessarily follow that to write with a purpose and with selectivity one must not be writing with serious historical intention. As Bruce states, 'a writer may be at one and the same time a sound historian and a capable theologician'.[45]

Paul's conversion serves as a case in point. Is Luke's account largely unhistorical due to its highly stylised presentation? Its essential historicity may be established with reference to Paul's letters. Gerd Lüdemann points out that Acts and Paul are in basic agreement concerning the event, including the christophany and the proximity to Damascus.[46] Even more decisive against the possibility that Luke fabricated his account of Paul's conversion with Old Testament materials in mind is the observation of Segal that Paul also appears to make the connection between his conversion and the call of Ezekiel.[47] Paul associates the term 'glory' with Christ (Phil. 3:21; 1 Cor. 2:8; Rom. 6:4; 9:23; Phil. 4:19; Eph. 1:18; 3:16; Col. 1:27) and speaks of 'the glory of the Lord' (2 Cor. 3:16-4:6) in the places where he describes his own conversion. Being transformed into 'the image of Christ' (Rom. 8:29; 1 Cor. 15:49) also recalls the language of Ezekiel

---

[42]Goulder, *Type and History in Acts*, 146. Cf. W.K.L. Clarke, 'The Use of the Septuagint in Acts', 100: 'If [in Acts] we find descriptions of events moulded to any serious extent on the LXX, the character of a conscientious historian claimed in the prologue to the gospel is considerably impaired'.

[43]Goulder, *Type and History in Acts*, 181. Cf., 173, 'When facts were remote and hard to come by it was natural for St. Luke to lean more heavily upon the inspiration that the cycle of Christian life or the scriptures provided'.

[44]Clarke puts a similar question, 'The Use of the Septuagint in Acts', 101: the question is 'whether this [modelling] is merely a natural colouring of the narrative by Old Testament language, or whether the facts themselves have been put together out of hints contained in the Old Testament'.

[45]Bruce, 'The Acts of the Apostles', 2600.

[46]Gerd Lüdemann, *Early Christianity according to the Traditions in Acts: A Commentary* (ET; London: SCM, 1989; orig. German 1987) 114-15.

[47]Segal, *Paul the Convert*, 110.

('the appearance of the likeness of the Glory of the Lord'; Ezk. 1:28; cf. Acts 22:11 where Paul's blindness is due to 'the glory of that light').

We might also consider Acts 27. F.F. Bruce does not doubt Luke's accuracy in Acts 27 despite the possible parallel with Jonah. He notes the impressive knowledge of ancient seamanship which the chapter shows[48] and the genuineness of the details of the ship and the route. The fact that the account is given in the first person plural, constituting one of the so-called 'we' sections, suggests to Bruce that it is based on 'personal recollection'.[49]

V. Literary Techniques

Many scholars assume that the literary techniques of Acts are hellenistic in origin. It is possible that Greek traditions of writing history may themselves be indebted to early ancient Near Eastern models, the milieu of the Old Testament. It is not necessary to treat Graeco-Roman and Biblical/Jewish models for Acts as strict alternatives. Both undoubtedly exercised some influence. Do these techniques also have parallels in the Old Testament?[50]

A number of literary techniques characterise Old Testament historical works, especially, though not exclusively, the so-called

---

[48]Cf. H.J. Holtzmann, *Handcommentar zum Neuen Testament* (Freiburg im Breisgau, 1889) 421.

[49]Bruce, 'The Acts of the Apostles', 2578. Another view of the we-passages which also gives credence to the historicity of the material they narrate is that of Jürgen Wehnert, *Die Wir-Passagen der Apostelgeschichte: Ein lukanisches Stilmittel aus jüdischer Tradition* (GTA 40; Göttingen: Vandenhoeck & Ruprecht, 1989). He contends that Luke was influenced by first person narration in certain Old Testament and Jewish literature which were designed to guarantee the historical reliability of the portrayal of events (see section III). Wehnert suggests that in the case of Acts the actual eyewitness informant (the 'we') was Silas, a conjecture which has little warrant.

[50]Sections III and IV build upon the work of Daryl Schmidt, 'The Historiography of Acts: Deuteronomistic or Hellenistic?', *SBL Seminar Papers* (Atlanta: Scholars Press, 1985) 417-27; and Sterling, *Historiography*, 354-63. Another author who associates Luke's method in Acts with the historical works of the Old Testament is Arnold Ehrhardt, *The Framework of the New Testament Stories* (Manchester: Manchester University Press, 1964) 65-66.

Deuteronomistic history (Dt. - 2 Ki.).[51] Many of these same devices are used in Acts.

First, the repetition of a set formula or pattern as a connective is used for example in 1 and 2 Kings to move from one king to another (see 1 Ki. 14:19-20, 31; 15:8, 24, etc.). A similar device may be seen in Acts in the series of summary statements, which, although not identical, all report the progress of the church (6:7; 9:31; 12:24; 16:5; 19:20; 28:31).

Secondly, in Old Testament historical works speeches by major figures or editorial comments are used to introduce or sum up the theme of a unit or to serve as a transition to the next unit. This practice strikes an obvious chord with the many speeches and prayers in Acts. A specific example is the prayer in Acts 4:24-30, which interprets the course of events in similar fashion to 1 Kings 8:22-53.[52]

Thirdly, the periodisation of history, with the dovetailing of eras and themes is another widespread technique. Van Seters finds three such periods in the Deuteronomistic history based upon 1 Samuel 8:8; 10:18-19; 12:6ff.: the exodus and conquest, the age of the judges and the rise of the monarchy.[53] Students of Luke-Acts have often noted a periodisation of history. Conzelmann divided Luke-Acts into the three periods of Israel, Jesus and the church.[54] C.H. Talbert discovered four stages involving the law and the prophets, Jesus, the apostolic age, and the post-apostolic age.[55] A simple promise (the Old Testament)—fulfilment (Jesus in Luke and the church in Acts) schema is certainly apparent.

A fourth technique of Old Testament historiography is the writing of a narrative through a series of main characters, which is the case with Acts. Martin Hengel argues that 'the model for the

---

[51]See John Van Seters, *In Search of History: Historiography in the Ancient World and the Origins of Biblical History* (New Haven and London: Yale University Press, 1983) 321 and 358; G. von Rad, *Studies in Deuteronomy* (London: SCM, 1953) 77-78; and Moshe Weinfeld, *Deuteronomy and the Deuteronomic School* (Oxford: Clarendon, 1972) 320-59.

[52]Sterling, *Historiography*, 353.

[53]Van Seters, *In Search of History*, 276. Genesis to Numbers could similarly be divided into four periods of time: Adam, Noah, Abraham and Moses.

[54]H. Conzelmann, *The Theology of St. Luke* (ET; London: Faber, 1960) 12-15, 149-51.

[55]Talbert, *Literary Patterns, Theological Themes and the Genre of Luke-Acts* (Missoula: Scholars Press, 1974) 103-17.

collection and literary presentation' of the materals we find in the gospels and Acts is:

> the account of history to be found in the Old Testament and Judaism, which to a large degree are composed of 'biographical' sections. . .One common feature of most of these biographical complexes of Old Testament and Jewish tradition is that they are composed of individual narratives which contain particular striking scenes or anecdotes.[56]

This is the case, for example, in Genesis with the patriarchs (Abraham, Jacob and Joseph), Exodus to Deuteronomy with Moses, in the conquest with Joshua, and with David and Elijah-Elisha in the books of Samuel and Kings. It is also the case with Acts which, although traditionally entitled 'the Acts the Apostles', would be more accurately, if less attractively, headed, 'Certain Acts of Certain Apostles'.[57] Acts largely concentrates its attention upon Peter and Paul, with Stephen and Philip occupying important asides.

Caution must be exercised in assessing the significance of these common features. As Van Seters states, such literary devices were widely used both in the ancient near East generally and in early Greek prose,[58] not to mention Greek historiography contemporary with Luke. For example, several of the devices go back as far as Herodotus. Nonetheless, overlap with the Old Testament should not be ignored.

The so called we-passages in Acts, first person narration, represents a stylistic device which has received a number of explanations.[59] Recent work by Jürgen Wehnert sees a Biblical/ Jewish background to Luke's procedure. There are examples in biblical (e.g. Isaiah, Jeremiah, Hosea) and post-biblical (e.g. 3 Ezra, Tobit, 1 Enoch) texts of a narrative personality alternating between first and third person speech. For example, Daniel 6:29-10:1, Wehnert believes, is an exact analogy for the structure of Acts 16:8-18.[60] Both

---

[56]Martin Hengel, *Acts and the History of Earliest Christianity* (ET; London: SCM, 1979; orig. German 1979) 30-31.

[57]Cf. R.N. Longenecker, 'The Acts of the Apostles', in Frank E. Gaebelein (ed.), *The Expositors Bible Commentary* 9 (Grand Rapids: Zondervan, 1981) 214: In Acts, 'like the historiography of the Old Testament, there is a tracing of the activity of God in various historical events as viewed from a particular perspective'.

[58]Van Seters, *In Search of History*, 358.

[59]See Jürgen Wehnert, *Die Wir-Passagen*, 47-124 for a *Forschungsbericht*.

[60]Wehnert, *Die Wir-Passagen*, 154-58.

texts begin in the third person (Dn. 6:29/Acts 16:8); introduce the report of a vision (7:1-28a/16:9); switch to the first person (7:28b-9:27/16:10-17); and then return to the authorial perspective (10:1/16:18ff.).[61] Wehnert concludes that the we-passages in Acts are a deliberate imitation of biblical style. As attractive as this conclusion is to the thesis of this chapter, it is not without difficulties. The length and content of the model from Daniel does not fit very will with Acts 16. Furthermore, the alleged Jewish examples of first person narration do not use the plural form. Further work on the device in non-Jewish Graeco-Roman literary sources is needed to see if the parallels Wehnert has adduced are in fact distinctive.

VI. Theological Understanding of History

A final and crucial area of Luke's indebtedness to the Old Testament in Acts is the presuppositions which seem to underly his conception of history. Gregory Sterling asks the question, how have the historical works of the Old Testament influenced Acts? His contention is that 'first and foremost they have provided the author with his understanding of what history is'.[62]

The notion of God's control of human history is basic to all of the Old Testament. Genesis to Numbers is on one level God's working out of the promises made to Abraham and his descendants. The Deuteronomistic history is held together theologically by the conviction that God blesses the righteous and punishes the wicked, defined in terms of covenant relationship (e.g. Dt. 28; Jos. 1:12-18; Judg. 2:10-23; 2 Sa. 7:5-15; 1 Ki. 15:3-4). The Chronicler's history stresses God's sovereign acts of election[63] as determining the progress of events. The idea of a personal and sovereign God who purposes to fulfil his covenant promises for his people and metes out punishment for moral failure (common to the Old Testament and Acts) is to be distinguished from that of fate in Greek historiography where judgement is more capricious and individualistic.

---

[61]The several citations of and allusions to Daniel in Luke-Acts confirm Luke's familiarity with the book.
[62]Sterling, *Historiography*, 357-58.
[63]Cf. election of David to be king, 1 Ch. 28:4; 2 Ch. 6:6; of Solomon to build the temple, 1 Ch. 28:5-6, 10; 29:1; of Jerusalem, 2 Ch. 6:6, 34, 38; 12:13; 33:7; of the temple to be the place where God's name would dwell, 2 Ch. 7:12, 16; 33:7; of the tribe of Levi to serve before the Ark, 1 Ch. 15:2.

Like the Jewish Scriptures, Acts subscribes to a theological understanding of history.[64] Certain key terms make this apparent.[65] These include: (1) ἡ βουλὴ τοῦ θεοῦ ('the will/counsel of God')—2:23; 4:28; 13:36; 20:27; cf. also 5:36-37). Luke would have concurred with Isaiah 46:10: 'declaring the end from the beginning and from ancient times not yet done, [God says] "My counsel (LXX: βουλὴ) shall stand, and I will accomplish all my purpose"'. (2) θέλημα ('will') is a related term—see 13:22; 21:14; 22:14 with reference to the divine will. (3) δεῖ ('it is necessary') occurs 22 times in Acts (101 times in the whole New Testament; 6 in Mark; 8 in Matthew; 18 in Luke). It refers in Luke-Acts not to a compulsion because of fate (a common notion in Greek thought) but to 'divine necessity which propels historical events'.[66] For Luke these events are the life and death of Jesus (Lk. 2:49; 4:43; 9:22; 13:33; 17:25; 22:37; 24:7, 26, 44; Acts 3:21) and the course of Paul's life (Acts 19:21; 23:11; 27:24, 26). Three verbs denote God's direction of history in Acts: (4) ὁρίζω ('appoint in advance/ foreordain')—2:23; 10:42; 17:31. (5) προορίζω ('predestine')—4:28. (6) προοράω ('foresee')—2:31. As Gasque observes, 'Acts lays great stress on the foreknowledge, will, purpose and plan of God'.[67] The Lord of history is never caught off guard, but is bringing his purposes to climax in Christ.

Key events in Acts are narrated as the action of God. It is God and Jesus who pour out the Spirit in chapters 2, 8 and 10 (see 10:47; 11:17; 15:8 which make this clear). The movements of the missionaries are directed by the Spirit of God (see 16:6-7). As in the Old Testament angels operate to execute God's will, so in Acts angels open prison doors to free apostles (5:19), give Philip directions (8:26), appear in a vision to Cornelius (10:30), wake and lead Peter out of prison (12:7-10), kill Herod Antipas (12:23) and protect Paul at sea (27:23).

The notion of God directing the affairs of humanity to bring about His will comes through most clearly in the theme of fulfilment (see D. Peterson's chapter). Even at this point Acts is comparable to the Old Testament historical works. From Genesis 12 onwards the

---

[64]I.H. Marshall, *Luke: Historian and Theologian* (Exeter: Paternoster, 1970) 56, believes that the concept of a divine plan in Luke-Acts comes from the Old Testament.

[65]On these terms see H. Conzelmann, *The Theology of St. Luke*, 151-54; J. Fitzmyer, *The Gospel According to Luke*, 1:170-81.

[66]Sterling, *Historiography*, 358.

[67]Gasque, 'Fruitful Field', 124.

Pentateuch is about the way God's promises to Abraham are fulfilled. In the Deuteronomistic history the pattern of prophecy and fulfilment is especially prominent.[68] Moses' speech in Deuteronomy 28, for example, paints with a broad brush a picture of the history of the nation in advance.[69]

VII. Conclusion

A look at Acts and the Old Testament accounts for many features of Acts. The Semitic cast of the book is best explained in terms of the linguistic influence of the LXX, that is, the use of deliberate Septuagintalisms. Many of the themes of Acts, including its preoccupation with Jerusalem, the Jews and the Law of Moses are Old Testament concerns. Some of its episodes are subtly patterned on Old Testament models. Acts has in common with Old Testament history certain literary techniques. Finally, both Acts and the Old Testament hold to a theological understanding of history in which God is in control of human affairs. These links are all the more impressive when it is noted that they involve different levels of the composition of Acts: the Old Testament appears to have influenced the language, form, content and presuppositions of Acts. In conjunction with the fact that Luke certainly knew and respected the Old Testament,[70] and that many of these points of contact seem to be intentional and not simply unwitting or coincidental, we may conclude that the Jewish Scriptures exerted a profound influence upon not only the theology of the book of Acts, as is widely recognised, but also upon its character as a piece of literature.[71]

---

[68]Van Seters, *In Search of History*, 358.

[69]See further 1 Ki. 8:24; 22:38; 2 Ki. 1:17; 7:17-20; 9:36-37, 15:12; 17:23.

[70]Cf. C.K. Barrett, *Luke the Historian*, 19: 'that Luke was familiar with the Old Testament and its manner of writing history, is beyond question'.

[71]The hypothesis that Luke imitated biblical Greek, incorporated biblical themes, employed biblical models and wrote with biblical historiography in mind envisages a sophistication and high level of literary artistry on Luke's part. Such an assessment is not out of keeping with Lukan scholarship. F.F. Bruce, 'Paul and the Old Testament in Acts', expresses such an opinion when he asserts, 77, that there is reason to believe that Luke wrote from the outset with both the gospel and Acts in mind (Luke and Acts are parallel in many ways). Cf. I.H. Marshall, *An Introduction to Acts*, 24: 'There is general agreement that Luke was a careful writer'. Marshall claims, for instance, that the repetition of phrases and words

Did Luke intend to write history? The fact that Acts has so many features in common with Old Testament historical works strongly suggests that Luke was writing what he conceived to be a historical work. The conclusion that Luke wrote as a historian does not of course settle the question of whether he was a reliable writer. That would depend on the state of his sources, the soundness of his historical judgement, and so on.[72] Nonetheless, this finding has implications for a number of issues in the study of Acts, including the genre and purpose of the book.[73]

Is it possible that Luke saw himself as writing Scripture? This is certainly not normally claimed for the New Testament documents.[74] Nonetheless, several authors have suggested this for Acts (with less evidence before them than has been assembled in this chapter). Gregory Sterling states:

> Our author conceived of his work as the *continuation* of the LXX. His deliberate composition in Septuagintal Greek and the conviction that his story was the fulfillment of the promises of the OT imply that as a continuation, Luke-Acts represents *sacred narrative* (italics original).[75]

Ward Gasque concurs:

> The narratives of. . .the birth of the church [Acts] are marked by the revival of the gift of prophecy, brought about by the coming of the Spirit upon individuals, and thus suggest that the time of silence in Israel is now ended and that it is time for the story of redemption to be resumed. These observations lead most writers to conclude that

---

suggests that 'Luke is in a way *cross-referencing his material*, so that readers of any one section will be reminded of material elsewhere' (italics original; 25).

[72]On these matters see Hemer, *The Book of Acts*.

[73]Since it is widely held that Luke-Acts is a single literary work (R. Maddox, *The Purpose of Luke-Acts* [Edinburgh: T. & T. Clark, 1982] ably defends the view that Luke 1:1-4 covers the contents of both the Gospel and Acts) the findings of this chapter ought to be considered in the light of Luke's gospel, a work described by John Drury as 'a renaissance of Old Testament story-telling' (Drury, *Tradition and Design*, 80). Unfortunately space forbids this exercise.

[74]The consensus view is stated by Carson, Morris and Moo, *An Introduction to the New Testament* (Grand Rapids: Zondervan, 1992) 231: 'the abiding religious significance, in the sense of canonical, authoritative documents, was the product of later decision rather than intention at the time of writing'.

[75]Sterling, *Historiography*, 363.

the author is continuing the story of Israel where it left off. That is to say, he is intending to write *biblical narrative* (italics original).[76]

It is certainly true that Luke viewed the Old Testament as a book which pointed forward and was in some sense incomplete. Acts deals with the big unresolved themes of the Old Testament: the messianic hopes and apocalyptic expectations; the question of what has happened and will happen to Israel; and the issue of how God is fulfilling his covenant promises.

Whether or not Luke saw himself as writing Scripture, the evidence of this chapter indicates that Acts is integrally related to the Scriptures regarded by Jews as normative and not simply a document brought into an artificial relation with the Old Testament by the later Christian Church.

This leads to the subject of the purpose of Acts. In setting out to report the events of the past to provide a foundation for the faith and its extension Acts is reminiscent of the books of Samuel and Kings and of the Chronicles which reflect upon sacred history for the benefit of their respective communities. As in Acts the question in these Old Testament books is one of continuity with the past: What is our relationship to the Israel of old? What has God done with his covenant promises?

The material rehearsed in this chapter suggests that Luke in Acts is not merely concerned to draw a link between the time of Jesus and the time of the early church, as is commonly noticed, but also between the time of Israel and the time of Jesus and His church. Acts insists that the God who was at work in the history of his ancient people, Israel, bringing them salvation, is the same God who is at work in the church.

---

[76]Gasque, 'A Fruitful Field', 120. Cf. H. Grundman, *Das Evangelium nach Lukas* (Berlin, 1959) 23, who contends that in his gospel Luke wrote holy history, as sacred as the Old Testament itself.

CHAPTER 4

THE MOTIF OF FULFILMENT
AND THE PURPOSE OF LUKE-ACTS

David Peterson

Summary

With the motif of fulfilment, the author of Luke-Acts proclaims and explains the accomplishment of God's purposes in the life and ministry of Jesus and the earliest Christians. This perspective would have appealed alike to Jewish and Gentile readers in the first century. The belief was widespread that a divine necessity controls human history and that history fulfils certain oracles. Luke's focus is on the fulfilment of prophecies from the Old Testament as well as prophecies from contemporary figures such as Jesus and Paul or angelic messengers. By this means, he shows Christian readers how to interpret the events he records, to draw out the implications appropriately, and to make a confident appeal to their contemporaries.

Even the casual reader of Luke-Acts must notice the extent to which the author employs fulfilment terminology throughout his narrative and focuses on how the divine plan of salvation is being realised. Many of the references to the fulfilment of Scripture or the accomplishment of significant events in God's plan occur in special Lukan material in the Gospel or in Lukan additions to the common material. Having generated certain expectations in his first volume, Luke has various means of demonstrating the reality of fulfilment in the speeches and events that he records in Acts. But how can a study of this motif lead us to a better understanding of the Book of Acts in its first century setting?

Luke's interest in this theme is part of a wider emphasis on the divine control or guidance of sacred history, a perspective particularly familiar to those who knew the Jewish Scriptures. Indeed, as Brian Rosner has argued, Luke seems to have modelled his work to some extent on the historical books of the Old Testament. There, 'past history is regarded as expressing the purpose of God, and future history is the object of prophecy by men with an insight into the intentions of God'.[1] But in Mediterranean antiquity more generally the belief was also widespread that a divine necessity controls human history. Providence was a central theme in Hellenistic historiography, where it often had an apologetic or religious application.[2] The concept of history's fulfilling oracles, whether written or oral, was also common in Hellenistic literature. So,

> whether Luke's community was composed of former Jews or pagans—or both—his original readers would have found no surprises in the theme of history's course being determined by the fulfilment of oracles/prophecies.[3]

In this study, a brief survey of the linguistic data will be followed by an analysis of some of the more significant expressions in their literary and theological context. This will involve a progressive discussion of the way in which Luke understands Scripture to have been fulfilled. Considerable attention is paid to the teaching of Luke's Gospel on the understanding that this is essential

---

[1] I.H. Marshall, *Luke: Historian and Theologian* (Exeter: Paternoster, 1970) 104-5.

[2] J.T. Squires, *The Plan of God in Luke-Acts* (SNTSMS 76; Cambridge: CUP, 1993) 36, argues that stylistically Luke's work is more like the histories of Diodorus Siculus and Dionysius of Halicarnassus, whose references to providence are relatively scarce. But as far as substantive matter is concerned, Luke's work is more like that of Flavius Josephus.

[3] C.H. Talbert, 'The Fulfillment of Prophecy in Luke-Acts', *Reading Luke: A Literary and Theological Commentary on the Third Gospel* (New York: Crossroads, 1989) 234-240 (238). Cf. his 'Promise and Fulfillment in Lukan Theology', in C.H. Talbert (ed.), *Luke-Acts: New Perspectives from the Society of Biblical Literature Seminar* (New York: Crossroads, 1984) 91-103.

for interpreting the Acts of the Apostles. It will be shown that Luke's use of the Old Testament is not confined to a simple proof-from-prophecy or promise-and-fulfilment schema. A concluding section will consider Luke's purpose in highlighting this theme and the effect that his presentation might have had on readers from Gentile as well as Jewish backgrounds.

I. The Language of Fulfilment

πληρόω is the most commonly used word in this semantic field. It is found 9 times in Luke's Gospel and 16 times in the Acts of the Apostles.[4] Fundamentally, it expresses the notion of *filling*, either in a literal (Lk. 3:5; Acts 5:28), or figurative sense, so that Luke can describe people being filled with particular qualities or emotions (Lk. 2:40; Acts 2:28; 5:3; 13:52) or being filled with the Holy Spirit (Acts 13:52).[5] For our purpose, the most interesting usage is in connection with the filling up or *completion* of certain periods of time (Lk. 21:24; Acts 7:23, 30; 9:23; 24:27) or of certain events and activities (Lk. 7:1; 9:31; 22:16; Acts 12:25; 13:25; 14:26; 19:21). Most important of all is Luke's reference to the completion or *fulfilment* of divine revelation in the person and work of Jesus and in the experience of those associated with him (Lk. 1:20; 4:21; 24:44; Acts 1:16; 3:18; 13:27).

The compound συμπληρόω has a more limited use. Apart from a reference to the filling of a boat with water (Lk. 8:23), this verb marks the completion or fulfilment of two critical moments of salvation history in Luke 9:51 and Acts 2:1. The compound ἐκπληρόω is found only in Acts 13:33, where it functions as a further means of expressing the notion that God's promises in Scripture have been fulfilled (cf. ἐκπλήρωσις in Acts 21:26). Another common term for 'filling' in Luke-Acts is πίμπλημι which, together with the compound ἐμπίμπλημι, is found 15 times in the Gospel and 5 times in Acts. The usage parallels that of πληρόω with respect to filling in a physical sense (Lk. 1:53; 5:7; 6:25) as well as filling with certain emotions or

---

[4]My statistics are derived from K. Aland, *Vollständige Konkordanz zum griechischen Neuen Testament* (Berlin/New York: de Gruyter, 1978-1983). Matthew uses this verb 16 times, Mark 3 times and John 15 times. Luke-Acts uses it more extensively than any other New Testament writing.

[5]Cf. Acts 2:2. The related adjective πλήρης is mostly applied to those who are 'full of the Holy Spirit' or some particular grace (Lk. 4:1; Acts 6:3, 5, 8; 7:55; 9:36; 11:24; contrast Acts 13:10; 19:28).

qualities (Lk. 4:28; 5:26; 6:11; Acts 3:10; 5:17; 13:45; 14:17; 19:29) or with the Holy Spirit (Lk. 1:15, 41, 67; Acts 2:4; 4:8, 31; 9:17; 13:9).[6] However, πιμπλήμι is only once employed with reference to the fulfilment of Scripture (Lk. 21:22).

Although πιμπλήμι is occasionally used to describe the fulfilment or completion of periods of time (Lk. 1:23, 57; 2:6, 21, 22), it is not used for the accomplishment of events or activities. Luke reserves several other verbs for that purpose, namely τελέω (Lk. 2:39; 12:50), συντελέω (Lk. 4:2, 13; Acts 21:27), ἐκτελέω (Lk. 14:29, 30), ἀποτελέω (Lk. 13:32), τελειόω (Lk. 2:43; 13:32; Acts 20:24) and πληροφορέω (Lk. 1:1). τελέω is also used in connection with the fulfilment of Scripture (Lk. 18:31; 22:37; Acts 13:29) and τελείωσις is similarly applied to the fulfilment of divine revelation (Lk. 1:45).[7]

Some further linguistic observations are relevant to this study. Luke-Acts contains a number of references to the *plan* or *will of God*. βουλή is the term used in Luke 7:30; Acts 2:23; 4:28; 5:38-9; 13:36; 20:27; and θέλημα in Luke 11:2; 22:42; Acts 21:14; 22:14 (cf. Acts 1:7). Other expressions speak of God's having predetermined the things that have taken place (Lk. 22:22; Acts 10:42; 17:31; 22:14; 26:16). The note of God's sovereignty and of the fulfilment of his plan of salvation is further stressed by the extensive use of δεῖ or ἔδει ('it is/was necessary') in Luke 2:49; 4:43; 9:22; 13:33; 17:25; 19:5; 21:9; 22:37; 24:7, 26, 44; Acts 1:16, 21; 3:21; 4:12; 5:29; 9:6, 16; 14:22; 15:5; 16:30; 17:3; 19:21; 20:35; 23:11; 24:19; 25:10; 27:24.[8] Again, Luke regularly uses γραφή in the singular or the plural (Lk. 4:21; 24:27, 32, 45; Acts 1:16; 8:32, 35; 17:2, 11; 18:24, 28) and the verb γράφω (Lk. 2:23; 3:4; 4:4, 8, 10, 17; 7:27; 10:26; 18:31; 19:46; 20:17, 28; 21:22; 22:37; 24:44, 46; Acts 1:20; 7:42; 13:29, 33; 15:15; 23:5; 24:14) with reference to the Scriptures. These passages show how much the events of his

---

[6]The stem of πιμπλήμι is the same as that of πληρόω and the verbs agree in sense. Cf. G. Delling, *TDNT* 6:128.

[7]G. Delling (*TDNT* 6:292) suggests that πληρόω is 'parallel in use but not synonymous by origin or specific content' with τελέω in the NT. Cf. Jn. 19:28, 30; Rev. 17:17. It is arguable that the τελ- words in such contexts suggest that the ultimate goal or intended end of divine revelation is reached in the events recorded.

[8]The adjective ἀναγκαῖον ('necessary') is similarly employed in Acts 13:46. J.T. Squires, *The Plan of God*, 1-10, sets out more fully the evidence for Luke's view of a divine plan and surveys the way scholars have interpreted this. C.H. Talbert, 'Promise and Fulfillment', 94, points out that 'the divine *dei*, which expresses the will of God, refers not only to the course of holy history. . .but also to God's expectations for human behavior'.

narrative are to be understood and interpreted in the light of the Old Testament and its expectations.

II. The Pattern of Fulfilment

1. The Gospel of Luke

The Gospel begins with a preface in the style of Hellenistic literary prologues, making an impressive opening statement that is briefly echoed in the introduction to the Acts of the Apostles. Debate continues about the particular literary tradition with which this prologue is to be identified, but 'Luke is evidently claiming some relationship between his own work and published literary, and especially, historical works of his day'.[9] The secular style of the preface has often been noted, but the absolute use of ὁ λόγος ('the word') and the employment of πληροφορέω in the expression τῶν πεπληροφορημένων ἐν ἡμῖν πραγμάτων are pointers to the way Luke views his subject matter. With Fitzmyer, we should go beyond the bland translation 'the things which have been accomplished among us' (RSV) and render the phrase 'the events that have come to fulfilment among us'.[10] The events in question are those of the ministry of Jesus and of the early church, set within the framework of contemporary Roman and Palestinian history, but related as well to the divine plan of salvation. Thus the motif of fulfilment is signalled from the beginning of Luke's work.

Fulfilment terms are extensively used in the infancy narratives (Lk. 1:20, 23, 45, 57; 2:6, 21, 22, 39, 43), where Luke introduces some of the main themes of his Gospel. Here there is a transition from the story of Israel to the story of Jesus, with godly characters proclaiming the realisation of Israel's hopes with the birth of John the Baptist and Jesus the Messiah.[11] Angelic revelations (1:11-20, 26-37; 2:9-14)

---

[9]J. Nolland, *Luke 1-9:20* (WBC 35A; Waco: Word, 1989) 5. Nolland provides a helpful guide to the scholarly literature and the issues involved in this debate (3-12). More extensively, cf. L.C.A. Alexander, *Luke to Theophilus: The Lucan Preface in Context* (SNTSMS; Cambridge: CUP, 1993).

[10]J.A. Fitzmyer, *The Gospel According to Luke (I-IX)* (AB 28; Garden City: Doubleday, 1981) 292-3. So also NIV. Note Fitzmyer's discussion of the alternatives.

[11]Cf. R.E. Brown, *The Birth of the Messiah* (London: Chapman, 1977) 242-3. Brown compares the role of Acts 1-2 in relation to the rest of Acts with the role of Luke

combine with prophetic declarations by those 'filled with the Holy Spirit' (1:41-5, [1:46-55], 1:67-79; 2:25-35, [2:36-8]) to explain the significance of the great events to follow. These chapters parallel in some respects the Spirit-inspired interpretation of Jesus and his ministry found in the speeches of Acts. In a variety of ways, Luke 1-2 uses Old Testament prophecy to proclaim the messiahship of Jesus, but not in the manner of a simple 'proof from prophecy' apologetic.[12]

Two critical references show how God is speaking directly to his people again, confirming the promises of the prophets and requiring absolute trust in his words. Zechariah is rebuked by the angel because he did not believe the good news about the birth of a son and the special ministry that God would give him.[13] We are assured that the words of the angel, which are particularly inspired by the prophecy of Malachi, will indeed be 'fulfilled in their time' (1:20, πληρωθήσονται εἰς τὸν καιρὸν αὐτῶν). In due course, when he is filled with the Holy Spirit, Zechariah himself endorses these promises and reveals something more of the link between the Baptist and the Messiah in God's redemptive plan (1:67-79). By way of contrast, Elizabeth blesses Mary, 'who believed that there would be a fulfilment of what was spoken to her from the Lord' (1:45, τελείωσις τοῖς λελαλημένοις αὐτῇ παρὰ κυρίου). That word was again mediated by the angel Gabriel. Mary herself goes on to proclaim that the conception of her child is the sign of God's intention to fulfil his saving purposes for Israel (1:46-55).

Within this framework of thought, the time for the Baptist's birth is solemnly announced (1:57, ἐπλήσθη ὁ χρόνος τοῦ τεκεῖν αὐτήν) and then the time for the Messiah's birth is declared in similar terms (2:6). The verb πίμπλημι could simply denote the completion of the time of pregnancy here, 'but in the Lukan narrative, which makes so much of fulfilment, the overtone is unmistakable'.[14] 'The time to give birth' in both cases is a significant moment in the accomplishment of God's saving plan, as previously announced and explained by divine revelation. The expression ὅτε ἐπλήσθησαν (αἱ) ἡμέραι ('when the

---

1-2 in introducing the main characters of the Gospel and pointing to their significance.

[12]Cf. D.L. Bock, *Proclamation from Prophecy and Pattern: Lucan Old Testament Christology* (JSNTS 12; Sheffield: JSOT, 1987) 55-90.

[13]If there is any conscious patterning of the narrative in Lk. 1:18-23 on the portrayal of Gabriel as the revealer of eschatological mysteries in Dn. 8-12 it is to give full weight and significance to the revelation received by Zechariah.

[14]J.A. Fitzmyer, *Luke (I-IX)*, 373.

days were fulfilled'), which introduces 2:21 and 2:22, simply means that the time set for these activities had been 'filled up'. However, this clause functions to link these verses with 2:6 and suggests that everything took place in accordance with God's will (cf. 1:23 [ἐπλήσθησαν]; 2:39 [ἐτέλεσαν]).

Jesus' public ministry is introduced with the note that he came into Galilee 'in the power of the Spirit' and taught in their synagogues (4:14-15). Luke then illustrates that synagogue ministry and the responses that it generated in Nazareth and Capernaum (4:16-44). The Nazareth scene appears to have been brought forward by the evangelist (cf. Mk. 6:1-6=Mt. 13:53-8) to highlight important features of the ministry of Jesus from the beginning. Most significantly for our purposes, Luke's account records the reading of Isaiah 61:1-2 (augmented with a phrase from Is. 58:6) and the declaration 'Today this scripture has been fulfilled in your hearing' (Lk. 4:21, πεπλήρωται). At the very least this points to Jesus as the eschatological prophet, who brings liberty to captive and oppressed Israel.[15] This announcement corresponds to the proclamation of Jesus in Mark 1:15 (πεπλήρωται ὁ καιρὸς καὶ ἤγγικεν ἡ βασιλεία τοῦ Θεοῦ), but with a more explicitly christological focus. In Luke's narrative, even before the phrase 'the kingdom of God' appears on his lips (Lk. 4:43),

> Jesus has proclaimed that he and his preaching are the fulfilment of something mentioned in the Scriptures of old associated with God's salvation. In his person and his preaching he inaugurates the year of God's favour spoken of in Isaiah 61:1-2.[16]

For readers of the Third Gospel, an indication that Jesus is the one who fulfils the Isaianic prophecy has already been given in affirmations about his anointing with the Spirit at his baptism (3:21-2; cf. 4:1, 14; Acts 10:38). Further confirmation is given with another allusion to Isaiah 61 in the response of Jesus to the disciples of John the Baptist in Luke 7:18-23. This summarises and explains the activity

---

[15]It is likely that Jesus' 'anointing' in Luke-Acts is to be understood as both prophetic-Mosaic and royal-Davidic (cf. D.L. Tiede, *Prophecy and History in Luke-Acts* [Philadelphia: Fortress, 1980] 46). Is. 61 also seems to incorporate aspects of the ministry of the Servant of the Lord in its portrait of the eschatological prophet. Ultimately, the concepts of prophet, Messiah and Servant of the Lord merge in Luke's presentation of Jesus. Cf. D.L. Bock, *Proclamation*, 105-111.

[16]J.A. Fitzmyer, *Luke (I-IX)*, 153. For the use of Jubilee year language to image eschatological salvation cf. J. Nolland, *Luke 1-9:20*, 197-8.

of Jesus in the intervening chapters. Luke 4:16-30 becomes a paradigm of what Jesus says and does and of the opposition he receives, culminating in his crucifixion. Rejection of his gracious words by his own people, with a demand for confirmatory signs, leads to his departure and the suggestion that he might find a better reception amongst the Gentiles. At this level the passage also becomes a paradigm of the mission of his disciples as portrayed in Acts (cf. Acts 13:44-52; 28:23-8).

As in the other Synoptic Gospels, Jesus' Galilean ministry is climaxed by the revelation that he is the Son of man who must 'suffer many things, and be rejected by the elders and chief priests and scribes, and be killed, and on the third day be raised' (Lk. 9:21=Mk. 8:31=Mt. 16:21). Even more explicitly than in the other Gospels, the transfiguration of Jesus is then a revelation of the glory that awaits him, beyond his predicted suffering and death (Lk. 9:28-36=Mk. 9:2-8=Mt. 17:1-8).[17] Confirmation of his true identity and of the need to go on listening to his extraordinary teaching is given by the voice from heaven (Lk. 9:35). Into this common material, however, Luke inserts an important interpretive clause. Jesus was speaking with Moses and Elijah about 'his departure which he was about to accomplish at Jerusalem' (9:31, τὴν ἔξοδον αὐτοῦ ἥν ἤμελλεν πληροῦν ἐν Ἱερουσαλήμ). At the most basic level, his 'departure' would refer to his death, since ἔξοδος is so used in Wisdom 3:2; 7:6; 2 Peter 1:15. Yet Jesus' heavenly 'ascension' is also to be accomplished at Jerusalem (Lk. 9:51, ἀναλήμψις; cf. Acts 1:2, 11, 22) and so a number of writers have argued that his ἔξοδος means 'his entire transit to the Father ending in the ascension'.[18]

An *event*, rather than a prophecy, is to be accomplished or fulfilled according to Luke 9:31 (cf. Jesus' 'baptism' in 12:50; the Passover in 22:16). But it is clear from what follows that such events are foreordained in God's salvific plan, to be fulfilled as Scripture directs and as Jesus himself outlines (e.g., Lk. 18:31; 22:37; 24:25-7, 44-6). The idea that Jerusalem is the city of destiny for Jesus is taken up again in 9:51. There the so-called 'travel narrative' begins in a sonorous way: 'when the days drew near for him to be received up

---

[17]The word δόξα appears in Lk. 9:31, 32, but not in the parallel accounts. Cf. Lk. 24:26 where 'glory' is the status of the risen Christ and 2 Pet. 1:17.

[18]J.A. Fitzmyer, *Luke (I-IX)*, 800. In a conversation with Moses and Elijah, the use of ἔξοδος must surely imply that these events are to be an act of salvation for Israel, paralleling the exodus conducted by Moses. Cf. J. Mánek, 'The New Exodus in the Books of Luke', *NovT* 2 (1955) 8-23.

(ἐγένετο δὲ ἐν τῷ συμπληροῦσθαι τὰς ἡμέρας τῆς ἀναλήμψεως αὐτοῦ), he set his face to go to Jerusalem'. The Lukan expression ἐν τῷ συμπληροῦσθαι τὰς ἡμέρας for the 'filling up of days' means that 'the days leading to his "taking up" were being fulfilled':[19] God's plan of salvation through Jesus was moving to a new stage of realisation. The end of the Gospel and the beginning of Acts show how it all happened.

Four times in Luke-Acts the verb τελέω is associated with the idea that Jesus is the consummator of redemptive history. In the most detailed passion prediction of all Jesus insists that 'everything that is written of the Son of man by the prophets will be accomplished' (Lk. 18:31, τελεσθήσεται). The passive often points to the activity of God, but in this context stress is also laid on what Jesus will endure at human hands (vv. 32-3). Even the details of Jesus' betrayal and suffering are considered to be a fulfilment of what is written in Scripture (cf. Lk. 22:22, 37; Acts 1:20; 2:23; 3:17-18; 4:24-8). Nevertheless, Jesus' willing acceptance of the divine plan and his determination to do what is required of him is revealed in a passage like Luke 12:50. There the approaching ordeal is described as 'a baptism with which to be baptised', and Jesus is 'constrained' or 'distressed' until his work 'is accomplished' (ἕως ὅτου τελεσθῇ). In the upper room he tells the disciples in most emphatic terms that 'this scripture (Is. 53:12) must be fulfilled in me' (Lk. 22:37, τοῦτο τὸ γεγραμμένον δεῖ τελεσθῆναι ἐν ἐμοί), for 'what is written about me has its fulfilment' (τὸ περὶ ἐμοῦ τέλος ἔχει).[20] The same perspective is found in the sermon at Pisidian Antioch, where Paul proclaims that those living in Jerusalem and their rulers 'fulfilled all that was

---

[19]I.H. Marshall, *The Gospel of Luke A Commentary on the Greek Text* (NIGTC; Exeter: Paternoster, 1978) 405. Cf. Acts 2:1 (συμπληρόω) and Lk. 1:23; 2:6, 21, 22; 21:22 (πιμπλήμι). Marshall notes that although the noun ἀναλήμψις could simply mean 'death', the corresponding verb is used both of death and of being taken up into heaven (Acts 1:2, 11, 22; Mk. 16:19; 1 Tim. 3:16). The primary reference in Lk. 9:51 is probably to the death of Jesus, 'but it is hard to resist the impression that there is also an allusion to Jesus' being "taken up" or "taken back" to God in the ascension' (*Ibid.*).

[20]The expression τέλος ἔχει in Lk. 22:37 shows why the verb τελέω is so appropriate in such contexts: the intention is to convey the notion that the Old Testament reaches its τέλος in the person and work of Jesus the Messiah. I am not persuaded by the argument of I.H. Marshall, *The Gospel of Luke*, 826, and others that τὸ περὶ ἐμοῦ τέλος ἔχει means 'my life's work is at an end'.

written of (Jesus)' (Acts 13:29, ἐτέλεσαν πάντα περὶ αὐτοῦ γεγραμμένα).[21]

Jesus' prediction of the fall of Jerusalem (Lk. 21:20-4) contains two interesting references to fulfilment, which are not found in the Synoptic parallels. 'Days of vengeance' are about to come upon Jerusalem, 'to fulfil all that is written' (v. 22, τοῦ πλησθῆναι πάντα τὰ γεγραμμένα). This judgement on the city and its people will continue 'until the times of the Gentiles are fulfilled' (v. 24, ἄχρι οὗ πληρωθῶσιν καιροὶ ἐθνῶν). Whether this is a rewrite of Mark or material drawn from another tradition of Jesus' teaching, it contains themes and emphases that are particularly important for Luke. The wording of the passage alludes to a number of Old Testament contexts, suggesting a comparison with an earlier judgement upon the city at the hands of the Babylonians.[22] The fulfilment implied is thus a repetition of Israel's previous experience, though now in an eschatological context. Nevertheless, even the period of Gentile domination over the city has a limit, namely the fulfilment of an allotted time, here called 'the times of the Gentiles'. This period will give way to the coming of the Son of man (Lk. 21:25-8).

In Luke 22:16 Jesus proclaims that the Passover meal is to be 'fulfilled in the kingdom of God' (πληρωθῇ). Since the Passover 'gathers up into itself a large number of various strands of covenant-promise',[23] to speak of its full realisation in the kingdom of God is to imply that the whole framework of thought and activity associated with the Passover finds its full and final expression in the End time. The meaning can hardly be that the Passover finds its fulfilment in what is later called 'the Lord's Supper' (cf. 1 Cor. 11:20). The referent must be the messianic banquet of Old Testament prophecy (cf. Is. 25:6-7: Lk. 22:29-30), representing the fellowship of God's new

---

[21]Lk. 13:32 applies the language of completion to the *person* of Jesus. The verb τελειοῦμαι alludes to Jesus' death, as does ἀπολέσθαι (v. 33). However, since resurrection and ascension are so intimately connected with Jesus' suffering and death in Luke's presentation, we may conclude that 'death as crowned by victory' is implied in the perfecting of Jesus here (cf. V. Taylor, *Jesus and his Sacrifice* [London/New York: Macmillan, 1959] 169).

[22]I.H. Marshall, *The Gospel of Luke*, 771-4. The fulfilment presumably also involves the carrying into effect of specific threats such as 1 Ki. 9:6-9; Je. 6:1-8; Dn. 9:26; Mi. 3:12.

[23]C.F.D. Moule, 'Fulfilment-Words in the New Testament: Use and Abuse', *NTS* 14 (1967-8) 318. Moule considers this an example of fulfilment in the most profound sense: 'all the promise and hope attaching to all that is epitomised in the Bible by God's covenant with his people' (294).

creation, secured for believers by Jesus' redemptive death. Put another way, the Passover had a typological significance and what it represented was to be 'fulfilled' by means of Jesus' sacrifice, inaugurating 'the New Covenant' (Lk. 22:20).

The concluding references to the fulfilment of Scripture in the Third Gospel continue to highlight the necessity of Jesus' suffering and prepare for the teaching of Acts. Both volumes are concerned to show that Jesus' rejection and suffering was not an accident of history but part of the plan of God, as revealed in specific passages such as Isaiah 53 (cf. Lk. 22:37; Acts 8:26-35),[24] and in the Old Testament more generally (cf. Acts 2:23; 3:18; 17:3; 26:22-3). Although the disciples on the road to Emmaus regarded Jesus as 'a prophet mighty in deed and word', who might 'redeem Israel' (Lk. 24:19-21; cf. Acts 7:22), he goes on to expand their understanding, revealing himself as the suffering Messiah, of whom Moses and all the prophets had written (vv. 25-7). Later, he tells the eleven apostles that *everything* written about him 'in the law of Moses and the prophets and the psalms must be fulfilled' (Lk. 24:44, δεῖ πληρωθῆναι). In both of these passages the Old Testament canon as a whole is in view. There are many strands of Scripture that have to be linked together for a full understanding of Jesus and his ministry. Nevertheless, it is clear from what follows that the need for the Christ to suffer and be raised from the dead is once again at the heart of what Jesus was teaching them (24:45-6).

These parallel incidents in Luke 24 leave the reader with the impression that a global view of the Old Testament and its promises is necessary for understanding the eschatological plan and purpose of God. Far from disqualifying Jesus as the Messiah of Israel and saviour of all, his death and resurrection make it possible for repentance and forgiveness of sins to be 'preached in his name to all nations, beginning from Jerusalem' (Lk. 24:46-7). With this last clause, the mission that is committed to the disciples is also related to the

---

[24]V. Taylor, *Jesus and his Sacrifice*, 193-4 and R.T. France, *Jesus and the Old Testament* (London: Tyndale, 1971) 114-116, argue that this reflects the mind of Jesus and is not the early church's attempt to produce scriptural justification for the offence of the cross. *Contra* J.A. Fitzmyer, *Luke (X-XXIV)*, 1432, it is arbitrary to say that Luke uses the Servant motif as part of a 'humiliation-exaltation' theme without reference to it in a vicarious sense. The whole of Is. 53 conveys the latter sense and it is more reasonable to assume that Is. 53:12 is being used as a reference to that whole context of thought rather than atomistically. Cf. D.L. Bock, *Proclamation*, 137-9.

fulfilment of Scripture.[25] The unfolding of events in Luke's second volume is thus meant to be viewed against the background of Old Testament expectations and Jesus' own predictions.

2. *The Acts of the Apostles*

The opening verses of Acts recapitulate the emphases of Luke 24 and outline what is to follow. Resurrection appearances are the context in which Jesus teaches the apostles and commissions them, reassuring them that they will soon be 'baptised with the Holy Spirit' (Acts 1:1-5). The central theme of Jesus' teaching continues to be 'the kingdom of God' (e.g., Lk. 4:43; 11:20; 17:20-1; 22:16, 18, 29-30), but with a new emphasis. From the parallel account in Luke 24:25-7, 44-9 it is clear that Jesus was teaching his disciples how to interpret his death and resurrection in the light of Scripture, demonstrating how these events are at the heart of God's plan for Israel and the nations. In so doing he was outlining for them how to understand the Scriptures christologically and in terms of 'the kingdom of God', a short-hand way of referring to Israel's hope for a decisive manifestation of God's rule in human history.[26] This theme remains at the heart of the apostolic preaching in Acts (e.g., 8:12; 19:8; 28:23, 31), where 'preaching the kingdom' (20:25) is actually equated at one point with declaring 'the whole counsel' or plan of God (20:27, πᾶσαν τὴν βουλὴν τοῦ Θεοῦ). Preaching the kingdom is also a matter of preaching Jesus and his resurrection within the framework of biblical prophecy (cf. Acts 2:14-36; 13:16-41; 20:20-1; 28:31).[27]

---

[25]On the syntax of the Greek here and the scriptural basis for this world-wide mission cf. I.H. Marshall, *The Gospel of Luke*, 906.

[26]Against those who doubt the historicity of this post-resurrection teaching by Jesus, C.H. Dodd (*According to the Scriptures: The Sub-Structure of New Testament Theology* [London: Nisbet, 1952] 109-110) points to the need for a creative mind like that of Jesus to account for the beginning of the most original and fruitful process of rethinking the Old Testament that we find in the pages of the New Testament.

[27]C.H. Dodd (*The Apostolic Preaching and its Developments* [London: Hodder, 1936] 46-7), rightly observes that, from the point of view of the apostolic speeches in Acts, 'the Kingdom of God is conceived as coming in the events of the life, death, and resurrection of Jesus, and *to proclaim these facts, in their proper setting*, is to preach the gospel of the Kingdom of God'. Luke implies in Acts 1:3/Lk. 24:44-47 that Jesus gave these facts their 'proper setting' in terms of OT Scripture, to show

Acts 1:6-8 suggests that God's sovereignty, which was decisively manifested through the death and resurrection of Jesus, would further be demonstrated through the preaching of the gospel and the bringing of men and women from all nations under God's rule by the power of his Spirit. The phrase 'to the end of the earth', which is so critical in Jesus' commissioning of the apostles in 1:8 (ἕως ἐσχάτου τῆς γῆς), appears to be an allusion to Isaiah 49:6 (cf. Lk. 2:29-32). This text is actually quoted by Paul in Acts 13:47 as a justification for his pattern of preaching to the Jews first and then turning to the Gentiles. Thus it is implied in Acts that there are aspects of the ministry of the Servant of the Lord that must be carried out by the disciples of Jesus. His 'fulfilment' of the Servant's role in his death and resurrection does not exhaust the meaning and application of the Servant Songs for the messianic era. Acts 1:8 is a prediction of the way the divine plan will be fulfilled through the witness of the apostles. The rest of the book shows how that happened, first in Jerusalem (chapters 2-7), then in all Judea and Samaria (chapters 8-11), and notionally 'to the ends of the earth' (chapters 13-28). In other words, the selection of events in Acts illustrates the beginning of the fulfilment of Jesus' foundational promise.

Peter is the first to use the actual language of fulfilment in Acts, asserting that 'the scripture had to be fulfilled, which the Holy Spirit spoke beforehand by the mouth of David concerning Judas who was guide to those who arrested Jesus' (1:16, ἔδει πληρωθῆναι). The passage in view is Psalm 69:25 (LXX 68:26), which is introduced after a description of the fate of Judas with the words 'for it is written' (γέγραπται, 1:20). Psalm 109:8 (LXX 108:8) is then added to this, as a scriptural justification for the election of another apostle to take the place of Judas. This has been described as a midrashic treatment of Scripture: 'what has been said of false companions and wicked men generally applies, *a minore ad majorem*, specifically to Judas, the one who proved himself uniquely false and evil'.[28] However, a degree of typology must be allowed here too, since both psalms are attributed specifically to David and the Holy Spirit is said to have made these

---

the apostles how to proclaim the kingdom appropriately, in the light of 'the things which have been accomplished among us'.

[28]R.N. Longenecker, *Biblical Exegesis in the Apostolic Period* (Grand Rapids: Eerdmans, 1975) 97. Midrashic interpretation in Jewish exegesis is explained on pp. 32-8. He later notes that the 'correspondence in history' factor gives the treatment in Acts 1:20 'a pesher flavor as well' (100).

things known in advance of their ultimate expression in the life of the Messiah.

> As the things said of David or the righteous sufferer in the psalms were interpreted by Christians with reference to Jesus, so the enemies of David or the righteous sufferer could be seen as foreshadowing the enemies of Jesus.[29]

Acts 2:1 announces the arrival of another great moment in the outworking of God's saving plan with the expression ἐν τῷ συμπληροῦσθαι τὴν ἡμέραν τῆς πεντηκοστῆς (lit. 'when the day of Pentecost was being fulfilled'). συμπληροῦσθαι is used to indicate the 'filling up' of a period of time in Luke 9:51, but here it signifies the actual coming of the appointed day.[30] The theological importance of this particular Pentecost was anticipated in Jesus' teaching about 'the promise of the Father' and being 'baptised with the Holy Spirit' (Acts 1:4-5). In the flow of the narrative, what happens is clearly a fulfilment of Jesus' prediction as well as a fulfilment of Old Testament prophecy. The full import of the event is developed in Peter's sermon, which begins with the assertion that 'this is what was spoken by the prophet Joel' (Acts 2:16).

What follows in Acts 2 has been called 'a pesher interpretation of Scripture', because Peter is identifying a portion of the Old Testament as pertinent to the Messianic Age and explicating it 'in accordance with the tradition and principles of Christ'.[31] But the issue is more complicated than that. Most importantly, the sermon goes on to link the fulfilment of Joel 2:28-32 (LXX 3:1-5) with the resurrection

---

[29]F.F. Bruce, *The Acts of the Apostles: The Greek Text with Introduction and Commentary* (3rd ed.; Grand Rapids/Leicester: Eerdmans/Apollos, 1990) 110. Cf. D.J. Moo, 'The Problem of Sensus Plenior', in D.A. Carson & J.D. Woodbridge (eds.), *Hermeneutics, Authority and Canon* (Grand Rapids: Zondervan, 1986) 179-211, for a discussion of the 'appropriation techniques' of the NT writers, as they interpreted and applied OT texts.

[30]'In both cases the fulfilment of a time is emphasised because the days in question bring the fulfilment of prophecy' (R.C. Tannehill, *The Narrative Unity of Luke-Acts*, Vol 2 [Minneapolis: Fortress, 1990] 26).

[31]R.N. Longenecker, *Biblical Exegesis*, 99-100. The 'pesher' technique is particularly associated with the DSS, where Scripture was interpreted as having its imminent, eschatological fulfilment in the life and personalities of the sect (Longenecker, 38-45). NT preachers and writers certainly shared a sense of eschatological completion and the desire to apply Scripture to contemporary history. But they differed significantly from the Qumran sectarians in their understanding and use of the OT.

and ascension of Christ (2:22-36), using citations from Psalms 16:8-11 and 110:1 to develop the argument. Jesus is the one who has poured out the promised Holy Spirit (v. 33) and he is 'the Lord' upon whom Israel must call for salvation in the coming judgement of 'the day of the Lord' (v. 36; cf. Joel 2:32). Luke sees the Scripture fulfilled in terms of certain particular prophecies and in terms of the re-introduction and fulfilment of Old Testament 'patterns' that point to the presence of God's eschatological salvation in Jesus.[32] Old Testament Scripture is used to proclaim the true significance of Jesus and what he has accomplished. Peter's call for repentance and baptism in the name of Jesus carries with it the promises of the New Covenant: forgiveness of sins and reception of the gift of the Holy Spirit (2:38; cf. Je. 31:34; Ezk. 36:25-7). With this proclamation, the fulfilment of Jesus' mission plan commences in Jerusalem (cf. Lk. 24:47; Acts 1:8).

Peter's Pentecost discourse is foundational in Acts because it interprets that great event in the light of Scripture, Jesus' own teaching and his heavenly exaltation. Moreover, it makes a theological statement which explains 'the subsequent acts of the apostles in the missionary endeavours of the new community that will grow into the Christian church familiar to Luke and his contemporaries'.[33] In later speeches there is little mention of the Spirit (though cf. 11:15-18; 15:8-9) and nothing basically is added to what has already been taught in Acts 2. However, the theology of the Spirit developed in that chapter dominates the entire book. Moreover, 'extensions' of the Pentecostal event are recorded in 8:14-17; 10:44-6; 19:1-6, aimed at meeting special needs and marking the progress of the gospel to the ends of the earth. Given the programmatic nature of the sermon in Acts 2, there is an implicit statement of fulfilment every time Luke outlines such events. Joel's prophecy continues to be fulfilled or implemented as the message of salvation is proclaimed and received in a variety of contexts.

Peter's sermon in the temple precincts (3:12-26) makes another significant claim about the fulfilment of Scripture. 'What God foretold by the mouth of all the prophets, that his Christ should suffer, he thus fulfilled' (v. 18, ἐπλήρωσεν οὕτως). The reference is to

---

[32]Cf. D.L. Bock, *Proclamation*, 155-187, 277-9.
[33]R.F. Zehnle, *Peter's Pentecost Discourse Tradition and Lukan Reinterpretation in Peter's Speeches of Acts 2 and 3* (SBLMS 15; Nashville/New York: Abingdon, 1971) 131.

the denial of Jesus as 'the Holy and Righteous One' by the rulers and people of Jerusalem, when they handed him over to Pilate to be killed and asked for a murderer to be released in his place (vv. 13-15, 17). What is implied by the claim of v. 18 is that the pattern of Christ's rejection and suffering is to be found in many parts of the prophetic Scriptures. '*All* the prophets' may be hyperbolic (cf. 3:24; 10:43). But, following the lead of Jesus himself, passages from a variety of Old Testament books were taken by the earliest Christians as typological or prophetical of the sufferings of the Messiah. An example of this is found in the prayer of the disciples in Acts 4:24-8. Psalm 2:1-2, in which the Holy Spirit is said to have spoken 'by the mouth of our father David', is taken as a prediction of the rejection of the Messiah by 'Herod and Pontius Pilate, with the Gentiles and the peoples of Israel'.[34] It was all part of the 'plan' (v. 28, βουλή), which God had predestined to take place and which he had revealed in advance in the Scriptures.

The sermon in Acts 3:11-26 also introduces a factor that is important in later speeches to Jewish audiences. Peter presents a theological overview of Israel's history, beginning with the declaration of God's saving purpose to Abraham (3:25, citing Gn. 12:3; 22:18; cf. Lk. 1:55). The testimony of the prophets from Moses onward was that God's ultimate plan for Israel and the nations would be fulfilled in the raising up of a particular individual, here identified as a prophet like Moses (3:22-4, citing Dt. 18:15-16). In Stephen's speech the picture is filled out, especially in connection with the role of Moses and the bearing his story has on the rejection of Jesus and his representatives in the Messianic era (7:1-53). Sacred history is used to make sense of present-day events.

> Just as the Christology of Acts is made intelligible through the use of the OT, so this principle of interpretation is used at the time when the author takes up the problem he has begun through Chapters 1-5: Jewish rebelliousness towards the word of God.[35]

---

[34]Note the messianic use of Ps. 2 in Psalms Solomon 17:26. Ps. 2:7 is a prominent early Christian *testimonium* for Jesus' messianic dignity and divine sonship (e.g., Lk. 3:22 par; Acts 13:33; Heb. 1:5; 5:5). Once this application had been established, other parts of the psalm were interpreted with reference to him (cf. F.F. Bruce, *The Acts of the Apostles*, 157).

[35]J. Kilgallen, *The Stephen Speech: A Literary and Redactional Study of Acts 7, 2-52* (AnB 67; Rome: Biblical Institute, 1976) 111. Note how fulfilment language is used to mark the completion of certain significant periods of time in Moses' life

In short, Scripture is used in a polemical way, against Jewish opponents of the gospel, as well as in a positive way, to expound the significance of Jesus and his saving work.

Paul's sermon in the synagogue at Pisidian Antioch offers another survey of salvation history (13:16-41). More attention is paid to David and God's promise to maintain the Davidic kingship, bringing to Israel from his posterity 'a Saviour, Jesus, as promised' (vv. 22-3, 32-7; cf. Lk. 1:32-3; Acts 2:25-36). In the argument of this sermon three synonymous fulfilment terms are employed. Those who lived in Jerusalem and their rulers did not understand 'the utterances of the prophets which are read every sabbath' and 'fulfilled these' by condemning Jesus (v. 27, ἐπλήρωσεν). 'When they had fulfilled all that was written of him, they took him down from the tree, and laid him in a tomb' (v. 29, ἐτέλεσαν). But, because of the resurrection of Jesus, Paul can bring the good news to Jews everywhere that 'what God promised to the fathers, this he has fulfilled to us their children by raising Jesus' (v. 33, ἐκπλήρωκεν). Here we find a familiar emphasis on the fulfilment of prophecy in the rejection of Jesus by his people and the details of his suffering. However, a broader interest in the way biblical theology reaches its climax in Jesus is revealed in the pattern of the sermon as a whole and in the particular reference to the fulfilment of 'what God promised to the fathers' in the resurrection of the Messiah.[36]

This critical example of Paul's diaspora preaching ends with a quotation from Habakkuk 1:5, warning the synagogue audience not to be counted amongst the scoffers, who reject the deeds of God with unbelief and so perish (13:40-1). The next sabbath, when some of the Jews contradict Paul and revile him, he indicates his intention to turn to the Gentiles, using Isaiah 49:6 as the scriptural justification for this move (13:44-7; cf. 18:6). In Acts 13, therefore, we see the fulfilment of prophecy motif used to highlight two key issues in Luke's presentation: God's age-old intentions concerning *the death and resurrection of the Messiah* and his plan to bring *salvation to the Gentiles*.

(vv. 23, 30; cf. 9:23; 21:26; 24:27). Even though the OT is the light by which Stephen reads Jewish opposition to the gospel, a simple promise-fulfilment schema is not used here. Behaviour in the present is *like* the scriptural examples cited.

[36]Quotations from Ps. 2:7, Is. 55:3 and Ps. 16:10 are drawn in to support this argument about the theological significance of Jesus' resurrection (Acts 13:33-7). Cf. D.L. Bock, *Proclamation*, 240-259.

Scripture quotations and affirmations of fulfilment are largely confined to the early chapters of Acts and to encounters with Jewish audiences.[37] Nevertheless, the claim that Israel's hopes are fulfilled in the resurrection of the Messiah becomes a dominant note in Paul's trial speeches (23:6; 24:14-15; 26:22-3). Here Paul's defence of his call and missionary activity is also part of Luke's wider apology for the Gentile mission. Furthermore, Paul himself appears as a prophet in Acts 20:22-5, 28-30; 27:10, 21-6, and various aspects of the narrative are used to show the fulfilment of these predictions.[38] Once again the effect is to show how everything occurred in accordance with God's plan. The final scene is of Paul testifying to Jews in Rome of the kingdom of God and 'trying to convince them about Jesus both from the law of Moses and from the prophets' (28:23). Isaiah 6:9-10 is quoted as applicable to many of the Jews encountered by him in the accomplishment of his ministry and as reason enough for taking the word of salvation to the Gentiles (28:24-8). So Luke's work ends where it began, with a declaration of the fulfilment of Scripture in the events he records (cf. Lk. 1:32-3, 46-55, 68-79; 2:29-32). Above all, 'he sees the world-wide extension of the gospel as the fulfilment of God's self-revelation progressively imparted in earlier days through mighty work and prophetic word, as recorded in the Hebrew scriptures'.[39]

III. Luke's Purpose in Highlighting the Theme of Fulfilment

Luke's interest in the fulfilment of prophecy is part of a wider concern to demonstrate God's sovereign outworking of his plan for the salvation of Jews and Gentiles, in the face of an imminent, universal and final judgement. Divine promises and warnings are expressed in quotations from Scripture or by living prophets such as John the Baptist, Jesus himself, some of the figures in the opening

---

[37]Note the table of quotations given by R.N. Longenecker, *Biblical Exegesis*, 86-7. The quotation of Am. 9:11-12 in Acts 15:14-18 is used to establish an ecclesiology in the light of God's mighty work amongst the Gentiles. Cf. D.L. Bock, *Proclamation*, 277-8 for an explanation of why Luke's attempt to develop Christology from the OT stops at Acts 13.

[38]J.T. Squires, *The Plan of God*, 151-3.

[39]F.F. Bruce, *The Acts of the Apostles*, 63-4. Cf. H. Flender, *St. Luke: Theologian of Redemptive History* (ET; London: SPCK, 1967); O. Cullmann, *Salvation in History* (ET; London: SCM, 1967).

chapters of the Gospel, together with preachers and prophets in the book of Acts. Almost always, contemporary revelations are a development or expansion of ancient scriptural promises or themes. Heavenly beings are another source of divine revelation, as in Luke 1-2 or Acts 27:23-4. In particular, 'the two crucial events of Luke's history, namely the passion of Jesus and the mission to the Gentiles, are each authorised and guided by prophecies given in both written and oral forms'.[40]

J.A. Fitzmyer rightly observes:

> Luke has a clear awareness that a new era of human history has begun in the birth, ministry, death and resurrection of Jesus. He does not express it in the same way as does Matthew (e.g., with formula quotations), but time after time he calls attention to fulfilment. Those allusions imply at least as much concern with the inbreaking of a new age as do the Matthean citations.[41]

First and foremost, the Old Testament is used in Luke-Acts to expound an appropriate Christology. Jesus' place in God's plans for Israel and the nations, in fulfilment of his covenant promises to Abraham, also comes to the forefront. Scripture is used to explain what God is doing in the world, as Luke records the triumphant progress of the gospel in the face of much opposition and rejection. Eschatology, soteriology and ecclesiology are all developed in the light of Old Testament revelation. Scripture provides a theological perspective for understanding the activities and events that Luke records. All this would have been vital for Christian readers, however well instructed, to enable them to interpret and proclaim the great gospel events and to draw out the implications appropriately. The renewal of prophecy itself, within the compass of contemporaneous events, was a sign that they lived within the orbit of divine promise, as beneficiaries of God's End-time blessings.

At a number of points throughout this essay I have expressed agreement with the thesis of D.L. Bock that when Luke used the Old Testament to expound Christology, he was not primarily engaged in a defensive apologetic but proclaiming the true significance of Jesus and his work. Yet Bock himself suggests that Luke was writing

---

[40]J.T. Squires, *The Plan of God*, 154. For a summary of different sources of divine revelation in Luke-Acts, cf. C.H. Talbert, 'Promise and Fulfillment', 94-5.
[41]J.A. Fitzmyer, *Luke (I-IX)*, 175.

for anyone in the church suffering doubt and who, as a struggling believer, sees in the persecution of the church the possible judgement of God either for attributing to Jesus a position that is not rightfully his or for extending the offer of salvation directly to those who formerly were regarded as being outside the promise of God.[42]

Apart from his Christological interests, Luke uses the Old Testament to justify the mission to the Gentiles and to account for and challenge the opposition experienced by Jesus and his followers. So an apologetic dimension to Luke-Acts cannot be discounted, even if Luke is writing specifically for Christians. His approach would have had considerable force for those engaged in debates with Jews or those like Paul, who had to defend Christianity before Gentile authorities in the light of Jewish charges.

But how would Luke's emphasis on God's sovereignty and the fulfilment of prophecy have impressed those outside specifically Christian circles? What would they have considered that Luke was attempting to achieve? Pagans and Hellenistic Jews alike thought of history as unfolding according to a divine necessity or compulsion. C.H. Talbert cites Polybius I.4.1-2 and Josephus, *Antiquities* 10.8.2-33, 42, as two obvious examples. J.T. Squires more extensively explores the parallels between Luke's work and Hellenistic histories. Both scholars argue that Luke's approach would have had considerable appeal to those familiar with this approach to historiography. The concept of history's fulfilling oracles, whether written or oral, was a particular feature of this genre. Talbert draws attention to Lucian's *Alexander the False Prophet*, which shows how a new religion could emerge as a result of one oral and two written prophecies. And Apuleius' *Golden Ass* records how one Lucius was initiated into the Isis cult after receiving an oracle from the goddess which he followed exactly and experienced 'salvation'. In these pagan examples, the fulfilment of oracles legitimated the religious authority of the person to whom the prophecy referred or of the god who gave it. Squires shows how the histories of Diodorus and Dionysius are marked by numerous acknowledgements of the divine guidance of human

---

[42]D.L. Bock, *Proclamation*, 277. He goes on to show how doubts could have arisen both for converts from Judaism and converts from the Gentile world. Persecution had come because of 'the church's high christology'. But Luke shows how 'that christology is the ground for the church's justified universal mission' (278). For a discussion of Luke's use of Scripture parenetically, to instruct about Christian life in the world, cf. C.H. Talbert, 'Promise and Fulfillment', 95-6.

affairs by means of inspired oracular pronouncements. Josephus demonstrates how 'a basically Jewish perspective on prophecy can be presented in a thoroughly hellenistic manner without damage to either point of view'.[43]

In the Hellenistic age it was also common for a people to try to trace its own origins back to the remotest antiquity (e.g., Josephus, *Against Apion* 2.152; Diodorus, 1.44.4; 1.96.2). So it is likely that Luke emphasised the Old Testament roots of Christianity and the fulfilment of Scripture in the events that he records for more than religious reasons. His approach would have given Greek-speaking Christians the chance to appeal to an argument from antiquity, allowing them to feel 'not the least bit inferior to pagans with their cultural and religious claims allegedly rooted in antiquity'.[44] At one level, therefore, the theme of the fulfilment of prophecy is 'a legitimation device' in the Lukan narrative, just as it was in Mediterranean antiquity generally. In a social context where such matters were considered important, it offered Christians a confident basis from which to address their contemporaries.

Squires concludes that Luke's work is a kind of cultural 'translation', an attempt to explain and defend Christianity to hellenised Christians. Various techniques familiar to educated readers from contemporary histories are embedded into the story of Luke-Acts to show how the gospel related to their thought-world. Luke's appeal is to 'insiders', using the categories provided by 'outsiders'. Although the primary audience for which Luke writes is the Christian community, his apologetic method offered Christians a 'missionary tool', to assist them in evangelism. Even the prominence of the Hebrew Scriptures and the insistently Jewish practices of Jesus and the earliest Christians in Luke-Acts 'reinforce the notion (essential in the hellenistic context) that Christianity was "no mere novelty", but was able to claim a long antiquity in Israel'.[45] Luke's attempt to outline the continuity between Christians and Israel and between the events of Jesus' career and Old Testament prophecies was an important aspect of his response to criticisms of Christianity that may have been made, both by Jews and by pagans.

---

[43]J.T. Squires, *The Plan of God*, 129.
[44]C.H. Talbert, 'The Fulfilment of Prophecy', 240.
[45]J.T. Squires, *The Plan of God*, 191. Note the way Squires (192-4) develops the argument that Luke's apology was directed to hellenised Christians.

These brief remarks about Luke's purpose must be read in the light of the complex debate that continues about this issue. No attempt has been made to survey and critique the range of scholarly opinion that exists on this topic. However, my survey of Luke's use of the fulfilment motif confirms me in the view that his two volumes were written primarily as a work of edification for a Christian audience, rather than as a direct apology for unbelievers.[46] Nevertheless, Talbert and Squires have helpfully exposed the apologetic potential of Luke's approach for Christians in the first-century Hellenistic world. As they debated with their contemporaries, Luke's readers would have been encouraged to claim that God was truly at work in their movement, fulfilling his ultimate saving purposes for the nations.

---

[46]For a survey of opinions about the purpose of Luke-Acts, leading to the conclusion that it is a work of edification addressed to a Christian audience, cf. R. Maddox, *The Purpose of Luke-Acts* (Edinburgh: Clark, 1982).

CHAPTER 5

THE *ACTS OF PAUL* AS A SEQUEL TO ACTS

Richard Bauckham

Summary

It is argued that the Acts of Paul *was a narrative at the final period of Paul's life, after the end of Acts. The author used 2 Timothy, 1 and 2 Corinthians and 1 Clement, as sources of information which he developed with historical imagination in the manner of ancient Jewish exegesis and some ancient biography. The genre of the* Acts of Paul *is not the novel, but resembles the novelistic biography. With the other apocryphal Acts it constitutes a new genre or subgenre, the acts of an apostle, which, while influenced by the Lukan Acts, is both more biographical and more fictional than Acts.*

When discussions of the genre of the Acts of the Apostles make no reference to the apocryphal Acts, it is because they are indebted to a strong tradition of scholarship which has sharply distinguished the genre of the apocryphal Acts from that of the canonical Acts. However, one recent proposal as to the genre of Acts attacks this consensus, stresses the similarity between Luke's work and the apocryphal Acts, and proposes that they belong to the same genre.[1] Furthermore, the lively and productive interest in the apocryphal Acts in recent years, especially in Swiss[2] and American[3] scholarship, makes it timely to address the question of the genre of the apocryphal Acts afresh.

The five oldest apocryphal Acts (the *Acts of Andrew*, the *Acts of John*, the *Acts of Paul*, the *Acts of Peter*, and the *Acts of Thomas*) have much in common, but recent work has also stressed the significant differences and the individuality of each. Since all too many discussions of the relationship between the apocryphal Acts and the canonical Acts have been based on hazardous generalisations about the apocryphal Acts as a corpus of literature, it seems likely that progress is now more likely to be made by taking the space to investigate the specific features of one of these works. For this purpose, the *Acts of Paul* has been chosen as the one which exhibits the most similarities to the canonical Acts.[4]

---

[1]R.I. Pervo, *Profit with Delight* (Philadelphia: Fortress Press, 1987).

[2]E.g. the works of F. Bovon, E. Junod, J.-D. Kaestli, J.-M. Prieur, W. Rordorf, to which references are made in notes below. These scholars are responsible for the volumes of new critical editions (with full introductory studies and commentary) of the apocryphal Acts which have appeared and are to appear in the CCSA series.

[3]E.g. the works of D.R. MacDonald, S.L. Davies, V. Burrus, to which references are made in notes below. Volume 38 (1986) of the journal *Semeia* brings the Swiss and American scholars into interaction with each other.

[4]We have no complete text of the *Acts of Paul*, only a series of sections and fragments of the work, which together provide us with a large part, but not all of the contents of the original work. There is as yet no complete critical edition of the texts, though one is to appear (ed. W. Rordorf) in the *Corpus Christianorum Series Apocryphorum*. The surviving evidence for the text is explained and the various texts are given in translation (quotations given below usually follow this translation) in W. Schneemelcher, 'Acts of Paul', in W. Schneemelcher (ed.), R. McL. Wilson tr., *New Testament Apocrypha*, vol. 2 (revised edition; Cambridge: James Clarke/Louisville: Westminster/John Knox Press, 1992) 213-270. The only way to make accurate references to the *Acts of Paul* is to refer to the various sections and papyri, for which I use the abbreviations used by Schneemelcher:

AThe = Acts of Paul and Thecla (references are to the numbered sections of this text)

MP = Martyrdom of Paul (references are to the numbered sections of this text)

3 Cor. = the correspondence between Paul and the Corinthians (chapter and verse numbers)

PH = Hamburg Papyrus (references are to pages)

PHeid = Heidelberg Coptic Papyrus (references are to pages)

PRy = John Rylands Library Coptic fragment

PG = Genf Coptic Papyrus.

The *Acts of Paul* is a narrative about Paul. To determine *what kind* of a narrative about Paul it is—how its author conceived it and expected it to be read—it is essential to determine its relationship to other literature by or about Paul, in particular the Acts of the Apostles and the Pauline corpus of letters. This is not easily done. Two of the most puzzling aspects of the *Acts of Paul* are its relationships to the Acts of the Apostles and to the Pastoral Epistles, or rather, to put the point more precisely, its apparently complete lack of relationship to the account of Paul in the Acts of the Apostles and its evidently close relationship to information about Paul in the Pastorals, especially 2 Timothy. These two puzzles have received a variety of proposed solutions, but they have usually been treated separately. In what follows I shall argue that there is essentially a single solution to both puzzles. I shall offer a thesis about the *Acts of Paul* which will explain both its lack of relationship to the Acts of the Apostles and its close relationship to 2 Timothy. The solution will also involve two other—much less discussed—literary relationships: to 1 *Clement* and to Paul's Corinthian correspondence. This discussion will also illuminate the way in which the *Acts of Paul* uses its sources to construct a narrative about Paul, and will generate some new insights with which, finally, to look afresh at the question of genre.

I. The *Acts of Paul* and the Acts of the Apostles

In a general sense the *Acts of Paul* resembles that part of the Lukan Acts which recounts Paul's missionary journeys. It takes the form of a travel narrative, within which Paul's activities in each place he visits are recounted in an essentially episodic manner. Paul's travels cover much the same geographical area as they do in the Lukan Acts, and, as in the Lukan Acts, they end in Rome. The contents of the episodes are in many ways similar to those of the Lukan Acts: Paul preaches to unbelievers, teaches believers, performs miracles, encounters opposition from Jews and pagans, is arrested, imprisoned and comes close to death. There are differences of emphasis—in the *Acts of Paul*, at least in the extant portions of the text, the Jews are far less prominent than they are in the Acts of the Apostles, there is more emphasis on Paul's teaching of Christians and less on his evangelisation of unbelievers, the miraculous is rather more prominent, particular episodes tend to be narrated at greater length—and some kinds of content which cannot be paralleled in the Lukan Acts, such as the inclusion of correspondence (a letter from the Corinthian church to Paul and Paul's reply: so-called '3 Corinthians') and the account of Paul's martyrdom which concludes the *Acts of Paul*. But the general similarities are sufficiently strong and obvious for the lack of *specific* parallels to be striking and in need of explanation.

In the first place, the itinerary Paul follows in the *Acts of Paul* cannot be correlated with that in the Acts of the Apostles. The incomplete state of our texts of the *Acts of Paul* makes it impossible to know the complete itinerary, but there are two sequences of places of which we can be virtually certain. These are: (1) Pisidian Antioch[5] - Iconium - Antioch - Myra - Sidon - Tyre; and (2) Smyrna - Ephesus - Philippi - Corinth - Rome.[6] What preceded the first of these sequences is unknown, though it seems that it cannot have been very extensive.[7] Some very small fragments, referring to events in Damascus and Jerusalem,[8] are usually thought to come from the lost beginning of the work, on the assumption that the fragment about Damascus refers to Paul's conversion, after which he visited Jerusalem. However, the reference to Paul's conversion is quite dubious (as we shall see later), and these fragments may well belong

---

[5]On the question whether Pisidian or Syrian Antioch is meant, see W.M. Ramsay, *The Church in the Roman Empire before A.D. 170* (London: Hodder & Stoughton, 1903) 390-391; Schneemelcher, 'Acts of Paul', 219-220.

[6]W. Rordorf, 'Nochmals: Paulusakten und Pastoralbriefe', in G.F. Hawthorne and O. Betz (eds.), *Tradition and Interpretation in the New Testament* (E.E. Ellis FS; Grand Rapids: Eerdmans/Tübingen: Mohr [Siebeck], 1987) 323-324, argues that Schmidt's (generally accepted) reconstruction of the sequence Ephesus - Philippi - Corinth is mistaken, and that there was more than one visit to Philippi in the original text of the *Acts of Paul*. He postulates that Paul's departure for Macedonia at the end of the Ephesus episode (PH 5) was followed by further travels before the visit to Philippi (to which PHeid 41-42, 44; PH 6 refer) which immediately preceded his visit to Corinth. However, Rordorf's reasons are not convincing (cf. Schneemelcher, 'Acts of Paul', 227). The reason he regards as the weightiest—that Paul's journey to Rome in the *Acts of Paul* is so different from that in the Lukan Acts that it must represent a second journey to Rome which occurred subsequent to Acts 28—is a correct observation, but is better seen as a reason for regarding the whole of the narrative of the *Acts of Paul* as subsequent to Acts 28: see below.

[7]Schneemelcher, 'Acts of Paul', 220.

[8]See C. Schmidt, ΠΡΑΞΕΙΣ ΠΑΨΛΟΨ: *Acta Pauli: Nach dem Papyrus der Hamburger Staats- und Universitäts-Bibliothek* (Glüchstadt/Hamburg: J.J. Augustin, 1936) 117-118; Schneemelcher, 'Acts of Paul', 218, 237-238.

in the missing portion of the text between the two sequences. This gap in the extant itinerary probably also included a visit to Crete, since the much later *Acts of Titus* recounts a visit of Paul and Titus to Crete (chapter 5).[9] Since everything else about Paul in the *Acts of Titus* certainly derives either from the canonical Acts or from the *Acts of Paul*, it is likely that the narrative about Crete derives from the latter.[10] So it may be that, in the original text of the *Acts of Paul*, Paul travelled from Tyre (at the end of the first extant sequence) to Damascus and Jerusalem, and then sailed (probably from Caesarea)[11] to Crete and, by a route we can only conjecture, reached Smyrna.

The majority of places in this itinerary are also visited by Paul in the canonical Acts, but the itinerary itself in each case is quite different. No sequences of more than two places correspond.[12] Moreover, the second striking difference is that not a single specific incident occurs in both works. There are some resemblances, but no identity. At Antioch in Pisidia, according to the *Acts of Paul*, Paul encounters such opposition that he is driven from the city and its region (PHeid 5-6), as in Acts 13:50, but the events which lead to this are quite different in each case. At Ephesus, according to the *Acts of Paul*, Paul again encounters severe opposition from the people of the city (PG; PH 1), as he does in Acts 19:23-31, and the specific mention of the goldsmiths (PH 1) can be compared with the role of Demetrius the silversmith and his fellow-artisans in Acts 19:24-27. But there the resemblance ends. Whereas in the Lukan Acts Paul is not even arrested, in the *Acts of Paul* the governor puts him in prison and has him thrown to the wild animals in the amphitheatre (PH 1-5). At Philippi, according to the *Acts of Paul*, Paul is imprisoned, as he is in Acts 16:16-40, but the reasons for his imprisonment (3 Cor. 2:2) and the events which lead to his release (PHeid 41-42, 44) are entirely different. During the final part of Paul's journey, according to the

---

[9]Text in F. Halkin, 'La légende crétoise de saint Tite', *Analecta Bollandiana* 79 (1961) 247-248.

[10]Schmidt, *ΠΡΑΞΕΙΣ ΠΑΨΛΟΨ*, 115-117; W. Rordorf, 'In welchem Verhältnis stehen die apokryphen Paulus-akten zur kanonischen Apostelgeschichte und den Pastoralbriefen?' in T. Baarda, A. Hilhorst, G.P. Luttikhuizen and A.S. van der Woude (eds.), *Text and Testimony* (A.F.J. Klijn FS; Kampen: J.H. Kok, 1988) 240-241. The mere information that Paul and Titus visited Crete could, of course, be known from the canonical Letter to Titus, but not the *Acts of Titus'* account of what happened there.

[11]For Caesarea, see R. Kasser, 'Acta Pauli 1959', *RHPR* 40 (1960) 50 n. 16, 51 n. 61.

[12]For Antioch - Iconium, cf. Acts 13:14-14:5; for Damascus - Jerusalem, cf. Acts 9:8-29; for Ephesus - Philippi, cf. Acts 19:1-20:2.

Acts of Paul, Paul knows that he is travelling to his death, and Christian prophets, inspired by the Spirit, prophesy what is going to happen to him (PH 6-7). There is here a general resemblance to the Lukan Acts (cf. Acts 20:22-24; 21:10-14, though in Acts Paul's death is not predicted), but the specific persons and circumstances differ. Finally, perhaps the most striking resemblance is that both works tell a story of a young man who sits on a windowsill while Paul is speaking to a Christian meeting, falls from the window, is taken for dead, but returns to life. However, in Acts 20:9-12 this happens at Troas to a man called Eutychus, whereas in the *Acts of Paul* it happens in Rome to Patroclus, Nero's cupbearer (MP 1).

Thirdly, there is almost no correlation between the persons who appear in the *Acts of Paul* and those who appear in the Acts of the Apostles. The only persons who appear both in Luke's account of Paul's missionary travels and in the account in the *Acts of Paul* are Aquila and Priscilla. It is interesting, as possible minor evidence that the author of the latter knew the Lukan Acts, that he uses the form of Priscilla's name that is used in Acts, rather than the form (Prisca) which is used throughout the Pauline letters (including 2 Timothy). But the information that the church in Ephesus met in their house (PG) must derive from 1 Corinthians 16:19 rather than from Acts, and so the coincidence with Acts is not impressive. Simon Magus, who encounters Peter in Samaria in Acts 8:9-24, also appears, along with Cleobius,[13] as a purveyor of Gnostic teaching in the Corinthian church in the *Acts of Paul* (3 Cor. 1:2), but Simon was a figure well-known, independently of Acts, in the second-century church. Recalling his visit to Damascus at the time of his conversion, Paul, in the *Acts of Paul* (PG), refers to Judas, the brother of the Lord. Probably this is the Judas of Acts 9:11, who has been secondarily identified with the Lord's brother of that name. Finally, 'Barsabas Justus of the flat feet' appears, as a Christian who was one of Nero's chief men, in the *Acts of Paul*'s account of the events in Rome which lead up to Paul's martyrdom (MP 2). Whether he is intended to be identical with the Joseph or Justus Barsabbas who appears in Acts 1:23 as one of the disciples nominated to replace Judas Iscariot among the twelve seems rather doubtful, and there is something to be said for the

---

[13]Cleobius was also a figure already known to readers of the *Acts of Paul*. He is mentioned by Hegesippus (*ap.* Eusebius, *Hist. Eccl.* 4.22.5), in a list of founders of heresies, along with Simon and Dositheus. See also *Apost. Const.* 6.8.1; 6.10.1, which may be dependent on the *Acts of Paul*.

suggestion that the *Acts of Paul* is here dependent rather on the tradition about Justus Barsabbas which Papias recorded (*ap.* Eusebius, *Hist. Eccles.* 3.39.9).[14] Given the very large number of named persons who appear in the *Acts of Paul* and in Luke's account of Paul's missionary journeys, the almost complete absence of persons common to both is quite remarkable.[15]

Thus the *Acts of Paul* appears to tell a quite different story from that told in the canonical Acts, albeit one with some resemblances to the latter. If the author knew the canonical Acts, then it would seem that he chose to ignore Luke's account of Paul and to write an alternative version of Paul's missionary career.[16] Perhaps he knew local traditions about Paul which he wished to preserve and which he preferred to Luke's account. However, in this case one would not expect such a *total* lack of correspondence with the Lukan Acts. One would expect that from time to time some information from the Lukan Acts might inform his account. Alternatively, perhaps the author knew and respected Acts, but was deliberately writing a kind of historical novel about Paul. With the freedom of a writer of fiction he felt no responsibility to the historical evidence, and even, we might suppose, deliberately avoided mixing history (Luke's account) with his own fiction. This might be plausible were it not for the fact that, while ignoring Acts, he does not ignore the Pauline letters. As we shall see, while virtually nothing he writes corresponds with Acts, much of what he writes corresponds with information in the Corinthian and Pastoral letters. This difference is not explained by the hypothesis that he was writing fiction.

---

[14]D.R. MacDonald, *The Legend and the Apostle: The Battle for Paul in Story and Canon* (Philadelphia: Westminster Press, 1983) 24-25.

[15]Since Luke appears in the *Acts of Paul* (MP 1, 7), he could be said to be common to the two works, if he is taken to be the author of the 'we' passages of Acts. It is unlikely that the Eutychus who appears in the *Acts of Paul* as a deacon of the church of Corinth (3 Cor. 2:1) is intended to be the same person as the Eutychus of Acts 20:9, or that the Theophilus who appears in the *Acts of Paul* as a presbyter of the church of Corinth (3 Cor. 1:1) is intended to be the same person as the dedicatee of the Acts of the Apostles (1:1).

[16]This is the view of W. Schneemelcher, 'Die Apostelgeschichte des Lukas und die Acta Pauli', in W. Eltester and F.H. Kettler (eds.), *Apophoreta* (E. Haenchen FS; BZNW 30; Berlin: Topelmann, 1964) 236-250; *idem*, 'Acts of Paul', 232-233. Although he finds no conclusive evidence that the author of the *Acts of Paul* knew Acts, he dates the former at a time (late second century) when it is very unlikely that he would not have done.

Is it possible, then, that the author of the *Acts of Paul* did not know Acts? There are a small number of cases of verbally identical or closely similar phrases in the two works,[17] which are probably most easily explicable as reminiscences of Acts by the author of the *Acts of Paul*. But they are not sufficient to prove dependence, and so it is possible for Rordorf to argue that Acts was not known to the author of the *Acts of Paul*.[18] By dating the *Acts of Paul* around the middle of the second century and the Acts of the Apostles in the first half of the second century, he can regard this as credible. Resemblances such as the two stories of Eutychus in Acts and Patroclus in the *Acts of Paul* he attributes to common early tradition, which had already taken divergent forms before being used by the two authors. Rordorf regards the close resemblances between the *Acts of Paul* and the Pastorals as also due not to literary dependence but to independent use of common tradition. But if, as I shall argue in the next section, the *Acts of Paul* is dependent on the Pastorals, then it might be that the author of the *Acts of Paul*, knowing the Pauline letters (including the Pastorals) but not knowing any written narrative account of Paul's missionary travels, constructed an account of Paul's travels solely on the basis of information he found in the Pauline letters, along with some local traditions. Most places which can be known from the Pauline letters to have been visited by Paul occur in the itinerary of the *Acts of Paul*, and it would not be difficult to postulate a visit to Thessalonica—the most obvious omission—in the missing portion of the text.

This is a possible explanation of the apparent lack of relationship between the *Acts of Paul* and the Acts of the Apostles. It depends on dating the former early enough and the latter late enough for ignorance of the Acts of the Apostles by the author of the *Acts of Paul* to be plausible. However, I wish to propose an alternative explanation, which coheres better with other evidence still to be adduced. This is that the *Acts of Paul* was intended as a sequel to the Lukan Acts, continuing the story of Paul's life up to his martyrdom. In other words, the missionary journey it describes is to be dated after the end of Luke's narrative. In the next section I shall argue that

---

[17]Most of these are discussed by Schneemelcher, 'Apostelgeschichte', 242-244, but to his list should certainly be added the address 'Men, brothers' (used twice in PG, as in Acts 15:7, 13; cf. also *Acts of Peter* [*Act. Verc.* 2, 17]), and perhaps also the phrase ἀγγέλου πρόσωπον (AThe 3; cf. Acts 6:15).
[18]Rordorf, 'Verhältnis', 227-237.

the relationship between the *Acts of Paul* and the Pastorals is best explained by this hypothesis. But there are two considerations which can be adduced in its support immediately.

In the first place, as far as the extant texts of the *Acts of Paul* allow us to tell, Paul is not represented as working as a pioneer missionary establishing churches for the first time in the places he visits.[19] Churches already exist in Iconium (though it is not impossible that this had been founded by Titus, who seems to have been in Iconium prior to Paul's arrival: AThe 2-3), Perga and other parts of Pisidia and Pamphylia (PHeid 35). Moreover, Paul's visits to Ephesus and Corinth, as recounted in the *Acts of Paul*, are certainly not his first to those places. He already knows the Christians he meets in the house of Aquila and Priscilla on his arrival in Ephesus (PG). The apocryphal correspondence between Paul and the Corinthians, included in the *Acts of Paul*[20] prior to the visit by Paul to Corinth which it reports, refers to Paul's establishment of the church in Corinth on an earlier visit (3 Cor. 1:4-6; 3:4). Of course, it is possible to postulate earlier visits to these places in the lost portions of the *Acts of Paul*, but it is easier to suppose that the *Acts of Paul* presupposes Luke's narrative of Paul's pioneer missionary work and intends to describe a journey devoted primarily to revisiting the churches Paul had founded at an earlier time.

A second indication that the narrative of the *Acts of Paul* is intended to follow that of the Lukan Acts can be found in the *Acts of Paul*'s relationship to 1 Clement. During Paul's visit to Corinth in the *Acts of Paul* Cleobius prophesies his coming martyrdom in Rome:

---

[19]This is noted, as a major difference between Acts and the *Acts of Paul*, by Schneemelcher, 'Apostelgeschichte', 246-247; *idem*, 'Acts of Paul', 232, but he fails to recognise its significance.

[20]It is disputed whether this correspondence was composed by the author of the *Acts of Paul* for its context in his work (so D. Guthrie, 'Acts and Epistles in Apocryphal Writings', in W.W. Gasque and R.P. Martin (eds.), *Apostolic History and the Gospel* [F.F. Bruce FS; Exeter: Paternoster, 1970] 339), or whether it already existed independently and was incorporated by him in his work (so A.F.J. Klijn, 'The Apocryphal Correspondence between Paul and the Corinthians', *VC* 17 [1963] 10-16; M. Testuz, 'La correspondence apocryphe de saint Paul et des Corinthiens', in A. Descamps (ed.), *Littérature et Théologie Pauliniennes* [RechBib 5; Louvain: Desclée de Brouwer, 1960] 221-222; Schneemelcher, 'Acts of Paul', 228-229, changing his previous view). I think the former view is the more probable, but in any case it is clear that the correspondence formed part of the *Acts of Paul* as designed by its author. In particular, the resemblances between Paul's letter to Corinth (3 Cor. 3) and his preaching on arrival in Italy (PH 8) should be noted.

'now Paul must fulfil all his assignment, and go up to the <. . .> of death <. . .> in great instruction and knowledge and sowing of the word, and must suffer envy (ζηλωθέντα) and depart out of the world' (PH 6). The attribution of Paul's death to envy—explained as the envy of the devil—recurs in the narrative that leads to Paul's martyrdom (MP 1). This theme must result from dependence on 1 Clement 5:5, where in the context of a whole section devoted to examples of suffering and death caused by envy (ζῆλος), Paul's sufferings culminating in his martyrdom are attributed to envy (διὰ ζῆλον καὶ ἔριν). However, if the author of the *Acts of Paul* used this passage about Paul in 1 Clement as a source, he will also have noticed that Clement's catalogue of Paul's sufferings includes the information that 'he was seven times in bonds' (ἑπτάκις δεσμὰ φορέσας).[21] As it happens there are only three occasions in the Acts of the Apostles on which Paul is said to have been bound in chains: in Philippi (16:23-26: δεσμά), Jerusalem and Caesarea (21:33: δεθῆναι ἁλύσεσι), and Rome (28:20: ἅλυσιν). But the *Acts of Paul* records another four such occasions: in Iconium (AThe 17-18: δεσμά), Ephesus (PH 3: δεσμά), Philippi (3 Cor. 3:35: δεσμά; cf. 2:2; 3:1), and Rome (MP 3: δεδέμενος).[22] Moreover, it seems clear that in doing so he had Clement's summary of Paul's sufferings in mind, since certainly on three of these four occasions—and probably also on the fourth—it is envy (ζῆλος) that leads to Paul's bondage and sufferings. The envy of Demas and Hermogenes (AThe 4: ἐζήλωσαν) and the envy of Thamyris (AThe 15: πλησθεὶς ζήλου) lead to Paul's imprisonment at Iconium (AThe 17-18).[23] Envy resulting from Paul's conversion of many to Christian faith leads to his arrest and imprisonment in Ephesus (PG), where the jealousy (ζηλοῖν) of Diophantes, because his wife is spending all her time with Paul, helps to ensure that Paul is thrown to the animals in the stadium (PH 2). In Rome it is the devil's envy of the love of the brethren which causes Patroclus' death (MP 1) and hence Paul's bondage and martyrdom. The account of what led to Paul's imprisonment at

---

[21]For a suggestion as to the way in which Clement arrived at this number, see J.D. Quinn, '"Seven Times he Wore Chains" (1 Clem 5.6)', *JBL* 97 (1978) 574-576.
[22]In view of my argument below that the author of the *Acts of Paul* thought 2 Timothy was written during this Roman imprisonment, note also 2 Tim. 1:16; 2:9.
[23]They also lead to Thecla's condemnation to be burned to death (AThe 20-22). So the author of the *Acts of Paul* may at this point have been thinking not only of 1 Clem 5:6 but also of 1 Clem 6:2 (where ζῆλος is said to be responsible for the persecution of women who suffered terrible and unholy tortures).

Philippi is lost, but since it was 'because of Stratonice, the wife of Apollophanes' (3 Cor. 2:2), it is a reasonable guess that the ζῆλος of Apollophanes was involved.

Therefore it seems very probable that the author of the *Acts of Paul*, reading 1 Clement and Acts, concluded that there must have been four more occasions after the end of Acts when Paul was put in fetters, and set out to record them.[24] This may already suggest that he meant, not only to complete the story of Paul which Acts left incomplete, but also to utilise, in doing so, whatever information he could find about Paul's life subsequent to Acts 28. As we shall see, he also found such information in some of the Pauline letters.

One reason why most scholars have not considered the possibility that the whole narrative of the *Acts of Paul* was intended to follow Luke's narrative in Acts is no doubt the belief that the *Acts of Paul* began with an account of Paul's conversion in Damascus. This is certainly not proved by Paul's speech at Ephesus in which he recalls his conversion in Damascus and immediately subsequent events (PG). This speech contains no indication that the events in question had already been narrated at an earlier point in the *Acts of Paul*.[25] It is entirely self-explanatory as it stands. However, there is also the Rylands Coptic fragment, which seems to come from the *Acts of Paul*,[26] though this cannot be regarded as entirely certain, and certainly records a visit of Paul to Damascus. Paul was told by speakers who cannot be identified in the fragmentary state of the text to go to Damascus and then to Jerusalem. Hearing this Paul 'went with great joy to Damascus', where he found (presumably either the Christian or the Jewish) community observing a fast. A reference to 'your fathers' may indicate that Paul was then represented as preaching to Jews or to Jewish Christians.[27] But despite Schmidt's confidence that the context of this fragment was a narrative of Paul's conversion parallel to Acts 9,[28] in fact it contains nothing which

---

[24]Another possible case of dependence on this section of 1 Clement is in PH 6, where the curious (and unfortunately fragmentary) references to David and Nabal might have been inspired by 1 Clem 4:13.

[25]Thus Schneemelcher, 'Acts of Paul', 218, is mistaken in using this passage to reconstruct the contents of the beginning of the *Acts of Paul*.

[26]Schmidt, *ΠΡΑΞΕΙΣ ΠΑΨΛΟΨ*, 118.

[27]Translation in Schmidt, *ΠΡΑΞΕΙΣ ΠΑΨΛΟΨ*, 117-118. The Coptic text has not been published.

[28]Schmidt, *ΠΡΑΞΕΙΣ ΠΑΨΛΟΨ*, 117-118; followed by Schneemelcher, 'Acts of Paul', 218, 237.

corresponds at all closely to the way in which Paul's conversion and related events are recorded in Acts, Galatians or the *Acts of Paul* itself (in Paul's recollection at Ephesus: PG). There seems no reason why the fragment should not refer to later visits of Paul to Damascus and Jerusalem. It may as easily be placed in the missing portion of the itinerary between Tyre and Smyrna as in the lost opening section of the *Acts of Paul*.[29]

II. The *Acts of Paul* and the Pastoral Epistles

That there is a close relationship between the *Acts of Paul* and the Pastorals has often been remarked and has been variously explained. Comparisons of the *Acts of Paul* with the Pastorals have usually been with the Pastorals treated as a whole, but for our argument it will be important to note that most points of contact are specifically with 2 Timothy.

With regard to Paul's itinerary, of course the Pastorals do not provide an itinerary, but they do refer to a number of places in such a way as to state or imply that Paul had been there. The places so mentioned in 2 Timothy are Rome (1:17), Ephesus (1:18), (Pisidian) Antioch, Iconium, Lystra (3:11), Troas (4:13), Corinth and Miletus (4:20), while 1 Timothy adds Macedonia (1:3) and Titus adds Crete (1:5) and Nicopolis (3:12). This list of eleven places includes six of the thirteen places which were certainly on Paul's itinerary in the *Acts of Paul* (Antioch, Iconium, Ephesus, Macedonia [Philippi], Corinth, Rome) while a seventh (Crete) was very probably, as we have seen, visited by Paul (along with Titus, as in Tit. 1:5) in the missing part of the itinerary of the *Acts of Paul* between Tyre and Smyrna. It would not be difficult to postulate visits to the remaining four places in missing parts of the text of the *Acts of Paul*: Lystra in the opening section immediately before Antioch, Miletus and Nicopolis in the gap between Tyre and Smyrna, Troas on the way from Ephesus to Philippi. But whether all or only most of the places to which the Pastorals refer occurred in Paul's itinerary in the *Acts of Paul*, it would make sense to think that the author of the *Acts of Paul*, like

---

[29]On my hypothesis the beginning of the lost opening section will no doubt have recorded Paul's release from captivity in Rome and his journey to Asia Minor. This would have been sufficient to fill the text missing from the beginning of the Heidelberg papyrus.

many readers of the Pastorals down the centuries, found that the references to places and events in them (especially in 2 Timothy and Titus) did not correspond to Luke's account of Paul's missionary travels and concluded that they must refer to a period after the end of Acts, which he himself set out to describe in such a way as to account for these references in the Pastorals.

The evidence of persons common to the *Acts of Paul* and the Pastorals (or rather, in this case, 2 Timothy alone) points in the same direction, and contrasts strikingly with the lack of such evidence in the case of the *Acts of Paul* and the Acts of the Apostles. There are seven persons who not only appear by name in both the *Acts of Paul* and 2 Timothy, but have common characteristics in both works: Aquila and Priscilla, Demas and Hermogenes, Onesiphorus, Luke and Titus. Of these, Aquila and Priscilla, found in Ephesus in both works (PG; 2 Tim. 4:19), are the least significant, since, as we have already noticed, the information in the *Acts of Paul* that the church in Ephesus met in their house more probably derives from 1 Corinthians 16:9. Demas and Hermogenes appear in the *Acts of Paul* as disciples of Paul who, in Iconium, reject and oppose him (AThe 1, 4, 11-16). Demas, while he does appear also in Colossians 4:4 and Philemon 24, appears as an unfaithful companion of Paul in the New Testament only in 2 Timothy 4:10, while Hermogenes is mentioned, uniquely in the New Testament, in 2 Timothy 1:15, as one of those in Asia who had turned away from Paul. Onesiphorus, whose wife and two children are named (AThe 3), repeatedly mentioned (AThe 23, 26) and twice described as his 'household' (οἶκος: AThe 4, 23) in the *Acts of Paul*, appears in the New Testament only in 2 Timothy (1:16-18; 4:19), where also repeated reference is made to his 'household' (οἶκος: 1:16; 4:19). In the *Acts of Paul*, Paul, on his arrival in Rome, finds Luke and Titus there awaiting him. Luke is said to have come from Gaul and Titus from Dalmatia (MP 1); they remain in Rome until after Paul's martyrdom (MP 7). Titus, who is never mentioned in Acts, does appear in Galatians and 2 Corinthians, as well as in Titus, but only in 2 Timothy is he associated with Dalmatia (4:10) in a context in which reference is then immediately made also to Luke, as present with Paul in Rome (4:11; for Luke in Rome, cf. also Col. 4:15; Phlm. 24).[30]

---

[30]It is unlikely that Eubulus, a presbyter of the church at Corinth (3 Cor. 1:1), should be identified with the Eubulus who is located in Rome by 2 Tim. 4:21. MacDonald, *Legend*, 60, supposes that 'Alexander the coppersmith' (2 Tim. 4:15-

Again, this evidence would seem to be explicable on the assumption that the author of the *Acts of Paul* intended to tell Paul's story after the end of the Lukan Acts. He therefore refrained from drawing characters in his story from Acts, but drew a number of them from 2 Timothy, since he believed that the events to which 2 Timothy alludes must have occurred after the end of Acts. At this point we may also mention the evidence that he drew on 1 and 2 Corinthians. Since it is not easy to fit the events and travels to which Paul alludes in these letters into the narrative of Acts, especially if one assumes that Luke would not have omitted significant events and movements from his narrative, the author of the *Acts of Paul*, I suggest, thought that the two Corinthian letters must have been written during Paul's travels after his release from his first Roman captivity, i.e. during the same period to which 2 Timothy and Titus refer. People and events from 1 and 2 Corinthians therefore occur in the narrative of the *Acts of Paul*. Stephanas (1 Cor. 1:16; 16:15, 17), who appears to be prominent in the leadership of the church of Corinth at the time of the writing of 1 Corinthians, appears in the *Acts of Paul* as presiding presbyter or bishop of the church in Corinth (3 Cor. 1:1). Because 1 Corinthians refers to 'Aquila and Prisca,

---

16) is the same person as Alexander, one of the chief men of the city of Antioch, who, in the *Acts of Paul*, fell in love with Thecla, was repulsed by her, brought her before the governor and had her condemned to the wild animals in the amphitheatre (AThe 26-36). But this is unlikely. It is hardly true that Alexander in the *Acts of Paul* 'opposes Paul' (MacDonald, *Legend*, 60) or his message (2 Tim. 4:16) or did Paul great harm (2 Tim. 4:15); his animosity is confined to Thecla. As we shall see below, the author of the *Acts of Paul*, by calling Hermogenes 'the coppersmith' (AThe 1), probably intended to identify Hermogenes (2 Tim. 1:15) with Alexander the coppersmith (2 Tim. 4:15).

It is very likely that the account of Paul's visit to Smyrna in chapter 2 of the *Life of Polycarp* attributed to Pionius derives from the lost section of the *Acts of Paul* in which Paul visited Smyrna immediately before his visit to Ephesus (cf. the beginning of PG). The chronological note that he arrived 'in the days of unleavened bread', and the information that he instructed the Christians there about Passover and Pentecost, accords with the narrative of the *Acts of Paul*, in which it is at the time of Pentecost that Paul arrives in Ephesus. In that case, another coincidence with 2 Timothy with regard to the names of persons can be added, for 'in Smyrna Paul went to visit Strateas, who had been his hearer in Pamphylia, being a son of Eunice the daughter of Lois', and finds the church meeting in his house (*Life of Polycarp* 2). (Strateas the son of Lois is also named in *Apost. Const.* 7.46, perhaps also in dependence on the *Acts of Paul*, as second bishop of Smyrna.) Strateas was therefore the brother of Timothy (as the author of the *Life of Polycarp* points out), whose grandmother Lois and mother Eunice are named only in 2 Tim. 1:5.

together with the church in their house' (16:19), in the *Acts of Paul* the Corinthian church meets in the house of Aquila and Priscilla (PG). The fact that, according to the *Acts of Paul*, Titus had evidently preceded Paul in Iconium (AThe 2), may be due to the role which Titus appears to play in 2 Corinthians, being sent by Paul ahead of him to places Paul himself intends to visit later (2 Cor. 8:16-18, 23-24; 12:18; cf. 2:13). Finally, as far as persons are concerned, the information in the *Acts of Paul* that a Corinthian Christian had been baptised by Peter (PH 7) is no doubt based on 1 Corinthians 1:12-17.

In the *Acts of Paul* Paul visits the church in Ephesus at the time of Pentecost (PG; PH 1), is there condemned to death by the governor, thrown to the wild animals in the amphitheatre, but, escaping this very serious threat to his life (PH 1-5), sails for Macedonia (PH 5), where he visits Philippi, is imprisoned there and, while in prison, receives and replies to a letter from the church in Corinth (3 Cor). Escaping from forced labour in Philippi, he goes on to Corinth (PHeid 41-42, 44, 43, 51-52; PH 6-7). Much of this itinerary and the events which occur correspond closely to information in 1 and 2 Corinthians, in which Paul writes that he intends to stay in Ephesus until Pentecost (1 Cor. 16:8), that he fought with wild animals in Ephesus (1 Cor. 15:32) and that in Asia he underwent an experience in which he despaired of life and thought he had received the sentence of death, but was rescued by God (2 Cor. 1:8-10), and that he intends to go to Macedonia and then to Corinth (1 Cor. 16:5-6; cf. 2 Cor. 2:13; 7:5; 9:2; 12:14).[31] It is noteworthy that this intended visit to Corinth is to be his third visit (2 Cor. 12:14): the author of the *Acts of Paul* may well have counted two visits to Corinth in the narrative of the Lukan Acts (18:1-17; 20:2-3) and intended himself to record this subsequent, third visit. He surely also intended '3 Corinthians', written 'in affliction', when Paul, having received the distressing news from Corinth, had begun 'to shed many tears and to mourn', lamenting that 'sorrow after sorrow comes upon me' (3 Cor. 2:2-5), to be the letter which Paul in 2 Corinthians said he had written 'out of much distress and anguish of heart and with many tears' (2 Cor. 2:4). The practice of filling an observable gap in an authentic

---

[31]Paul's visit to Philippi in the *Acts of Paul* was probably also intended as a fulfilment of his intention expressed in Phil. 1:26, which, if understood to have been written from Rome, would have to refer to a visit to Philippi after Paul's release from his first period of captivity in Rome, i.e. after Acts 28.

correspondence by writing a pseudepigraphical letter is an attested ancient literary practice.[32]

Finally, in support of the view that the author of the *Acts of Paul* read both 2 Timothy and the Corinthian letters as referring to the same period of Paul's life, we may notice that the central incident in the story he tells about Paul in the amphitheatre at Ephesus is an encounter with a lion. He has connected 1 Corinthians 15:32 ('I fought with wild animals at Ephesus') with 2 Timothy 4:17 ('I was rescued from the lion's mouth') as referring to the same event.[33]

However, my argument that the Pastorals—or at least 2 Timothy and Titus—were used by the author of the *Acts of Paul* as a source from which to reconstruct events in the final period of Paul's life needs to be defended in the face of a quite different hypothesis about the relationship between the *Acts of Paul* and the Pastorals. This is the thesis of D.R. MacDonald in his short, but ingeniously and persuasively argued book, *The Legend and the Apostle*.[34] MacDonald is one of a group of American scholars who have given special attention to features of the apocryphal Acts which might be described as socially radical.[35] In particular, the women who are often prominent in the apocryphal Acts are emancipated from the patriarchal structures of society by refusing to marry, or (if widows) remaining

---

[32]For example, Plato's seventh and twelfth letters refer to letters by Archytas. Fictitious letters purporting to be these letters of Archytas were therefore composed, and are quoted as genuine by Diogenes Laertius. Compare also the apocryphal Pauline *Letter to the Laodiceans*, intended as the missing letter to which Col. 4:16 refers.

[33]Probably Paul's 'defence' (2 Tim. 4:16) is his speech before the governor in Ephesus in PH 1.

[34]D.R. MacDonald, *The Legend and the Apostle: The Battle for Paul in Story and Canon* (Philadelphia: Westminster Press, 1983).

[35]See also S.L. Davies, *The Revolt of the Widows: The Social World of the Apocryphal Acts* (New York: Winston/Seabury, 1980); V. Burrus, 'Chastity as Autonomy: Women in the Stories of the Apocryphal Acts', *Semeia* 38 (1986) 101-117 (with response by J.-D. Kaestli: 119-131, and response to Kaestli by Burrus: 133-135); V. Burrus, *Chastity as Autonomy: Women in the Stories of the Apocryphal Acts* (Lewiston/Queenston: Mellen, 1987); cf. also J.-D. Kaestli, 'Les Actes Apocryphes et la Reconstitution de l'Histoire des Femmes dans le Christianisme Ancien', *Foi et Vie* 88 (1989) 71-79. Cf. the rather sweeping criticism by L.C. Boughton, 'From Pious Legend to Feminist Fantasy: Distinguishing Hagiographical License from Apostolic Practice in the *Acts of Paul/Acts of Thecla*', *JR* 71 (1991) 362-384, though much of her argument is devoted to denying that the story of Thecla has historical value as evidence of practice in the apostolic period and that the *Acts of Paul* or its story of Thecla was accorded authoritative status in the church.

unmarried, or (if married) refusing to cohabit with their husbands, in consequence of the apostles' preaching of sexual continence, which is a prominent feature of the ascetic ideal of the Christian life promoted in the apocryphal Acts, including the *Acts of Paul*. In the *Acts of Paul* there is, in particular, the story of Thecla, who refuses marriage, is twice condemned to death in consequence of her determination to remain celibate, adopts male dress, and is commissioned by Paul to work as a Christian missionary, teaching the word of God. By contrast with S.L. Davies, who considers that the *Acts of Paul* must have been written by a woman,[36] MacDonald accepts Tertullian's statement (*De bapt.* 17.5) that its author was a male presbyter, but postulates Christian women storytellers as the source of the oral legends which he argues have been incorporated in the *Acts of Paul*.[37] By identifying features of oral storytelling in major narratives of the *Acts of Paul*,[38] he is able to argue that its author depended on oral traditions which were also known to the author of the Pastorals. Although the *Acts of Paul* was written later than the Pastorals, it is not dependent on them. Rather the author of the Pastorals knew the same oral legends about Paul which were being told by groups of socially radical Christian women and were later incorporated in the *Acts of Paul*.

Three aspects of MacDonald's view of the relationship between the *Acts of Paul* and the Pastorals are important for the present discussion. In the first place, he points out the persons common to the *Acts of Paul* and the Pastorals, but also that there are differences in the information about them in the two works. For example, in the *Acts of Paul* the pair of disciples who turn against Paul are called Demas and Hermogenes the coppersmith (AThe 1), whereas in 2 Timothy it is not Hermogenes but another opponent of Paul, Alexander, who is called the coppersmith (2 Tim. 4:14). In the *Acts of Paul* Demas and Hermogenes are credited with the doctrine that the resurrection has already taken place (AThe 14), whereas in 2 Timothy this view is attributed rather to Hymenaeus and Philetus (2 Tim. 2:18). In the *Acts*

---

[36]Davies, *Revolt*, 105-109; cf. his argument that Tertullian, *De bapt.* 17.5 is not referring to the *Acts of Paul* but to some other apocryphal work: 'Women, Tertullian and the *Acts of Paul'*, *Semeia* 38 (1986) 139-143, with response by T.W. MacKay: 145-149.

[37]MacDonald, *Legend*, chapter 2. With regard to the Thecla story in particular, this argument is accepted by W. Rordorf, 'Tradition and Composition in the *Acts of Thecla:* The State of the Question', *Semeia* 38 (1986) 43-52.

[38]MacDonald, *Legend*, chapter 1.

of Paul, when Paul arrives in Rome he finds waiting for him Luke from Gaul and Titus from Dalmatia, whereas 2 Timothy 4:10-11 reads: 'Crescens has gone to Galatia [or Gaul], Titus to Dalmatia. Only Luke is with me'. Such combinations of resemblance and difference MacDonald argues are best understood as the kinds of variation that arise in oral tradition.[39]

Secondly, as well as the coincidences of personal names, MacDonald holds that the Pastorals also allude to episodes which are recounted at length in the *Acts of Paul*. Behind the reference in 2 Timothy 3:11 to persecutions Paul experienced in Antioch, Iconium and Lystra, lie the stories about Paul and Thecla which the *Acts of Paul* locate in Iconium and Antioch. Similarly, 2 Timothy 4:16-18 alludes to the story of Paul's experience at Ephesus in the *Acts of Paul*, which is one of those MacDonald shows to have features of oral storytelling.[40] Thus whereas I have proposed that such texts in 2 Timothy were the basis from which the author of the *Acts of Paul* developed some of his stories, MacDonald argues that these texts presuppose the stories which were later recorded in the *Acts of Paul*.

Thirdly, MacDonald holds that the Pastorals, in alluding to the same body of oral legends about Paul as the *Acts of Paul* preserve, had a polemical purpose.[41] The Pastorals portray a socially conservative Paul in order to counter the socially radical Paul of the legends. This contrast between the social attitude of the two bodies of literature is certainly real, even if MacDonald tends to exaggerate it, and it is especially striking in relation to women. 1 Timothy forbids women to teach (2:12), but the *Acts of Paul* portrays Thecla as commissioned by Paul to teach the word of God (AThe 41). The Paul of 1 Timothy would have younger widows marry and bear children (5:14), whereas the Paul of the *Acts of Paul* inspires Thecla to remain unmarried (AThe 5-10). In Titus Paul requires women to submit to their husbands (2:5), but in the *Acts of Paul* he encourages virgins not to marry and married women to refuse to cohabit with their husbands (AThe 5-6, 9; probably 3 Cor. 2:1). The false teachers who, according to 1 Timothy 4:3, forbid marriage and demand abstinence from foods, sound suspiciously like the Paul of the *Acts of Paul*, who

---

[39]MacDonald, *Legend*, 59-60, 62, 65. He also points out differences as well as resemblances in the information about Onesiphorus (60). See also Rordorf, 'Verhältnis', 237-241.
[40]MacDonald, *Legend*, 61.
[41]MacDonald, *Legend*, chapter 3.

not only discourages marriage but also uses water instead of wine in the eucharist (PH 4) and seems to be a vegetarian (AThe 25).[42] MacDonald rightly points out that the ascetic teaching of the *Acts of Paul* is not presented polemically, as though it were deliberately countering the different image of Paul to be found in the Pastorals, as R.A. Lipsius and J. Rohde thought.[43] The Pastorals, on the other hand, clearly are polemical. MacDonald suggests that, when Paul urges Timothy to 'have nothing to do with unholy myths of the kind old women tell' (1 Tim. 4:7: τοὺς δὲ βεβήλους καὶ γραώδεις παραιτοῦ), the author of the Pastorals is actually referring to the Pauline legends propagated by groups of liberated Christian women.[44] On the basis of this thesis about the *Acts of Paul* and the Pastorals, MacDonald develops the broader argument that in the post-Pauline period the Pauline tradition bifurcated and produced two opposing images of Paul: the socially radical Paul of the legends behind the *Acts of Paul* and the socially conservative Paul of the Pastorals.[45]

This fascinating thesis does explain a major feature of the *Acts of Paul*: that, despite its many contacts with 2 Timothy, its teaching on sexual asceticism is inspired by 1 Corinthians 7[46] rather than the Pastorals, and seems to run counter to the Pastorals' strong emphasis on the institution of marriage. It might, however, be more accurate to say that the *Acts of Paul* opposes sexual relations in marriage, rather than marriage itself.[47] Christians married to fellow-Christians— Onesiphorus and Lectra (AThe 2, 23), Thrasymachus and Aline, Cleon and Chrysa (PHeid 35), Aquila and Priscilla (PG)—appear in the *Acts of Paul* with no indication that they should not be married, presumably because these husbands 'have wives as if they had them not' (AThe 5). Not the patriarchal structure of marriage as such, but unconverted husbands or fiancés who will insist on conjugal relations are the problem. This point does not remove the contrast with the Pastorals, but it puts the contrast in a significantly different

---

[42]However, the point may only be that this was a cheap meal (cf. AThe 23).

[43]MacDonald, *Legend*, 63.

[44]MacDonald, *Legend*, 14, 58-59.

[45]MacDonald, *Legend*, chapter 4.

[46]Note the allusion to 1 Cor. 7:29 in AThe 5.

[47]On the other hand, Y. Tissot, 'Encratisme et Actes apocryphes', in F. Bovon *et al.*, *Les Actes Apocryphes des Apôtres* (Geneva: Labor et Fides, 1981) 115-116, probably underestimates the encratite tendency of the *Acts of Paul*. To the evidence for this should be added the story of the lion, who, after being baptised by Paul, met a lioness, but 'did not yield himself to her' (PG).

form. The difference is important because it becomes possible to see that, supposing the author of the *Acts of Paul* knew the Pastorals, he would have found 1 Timothy inconsistent with his views, but not 2 Timothy (which contains nothing relevant to this matter) or necessarily Titus. He could have read Titus 2:4-6 consistently with his belief in sexual abstinence within Christian marriage. The exhortations to young married women to be self-controlled and chaste (σώφρονας, ἁγνάς) and to young men to exercise self-control (σωφρονεῖν) could easily be interpreted in this encratite way. 1 Timothy, on the other hand, is in clear contradiction of the views of the *Acts of Paul* (especially 1 Tim. 2:11-15; 4:3; 5:14). But we should not suppose that an ancient writer had to think of the Pastoral letters as an indissoluble group of three. It was possible to discriminate among the Pastorals. Tatian, a contemporary of the author of the *Acts of Paul*, who held similar views on sexuality, seems to have rejected 1 Timothy but to have accepted Titus.[48] The author of the *Acts of Paul* may have accepted and used 2 Timothy and Titus as authentically Pauline, but have ignored or rejected 1 Timothy. In fact, virtually all the points of correspondence between the *Acts of Paul* and the Pastorals—in places, names and circumstantial information—are in fact between the *Acts of Paul*, on the one hand, and 2 Timothy and Titus on the other.[49] There is therefore no need to postulate a polemical relationship between the *Acts of Paul* and the Pastorals.

However, the question remains whether the correspondences between the *Acts of Paul*, on the one hand, and 2 Timothy and Titus, on the other, are better explained by MacDonald's thesis of common oral tradition, which is also the position of Rordorf,[50] or by the view which the majority of scholars have taken: that the author of the *Acts*

---

[48]Cf. Jerome, *in ep. ad Tit. praef.*, in Tatian, *Oratio ad Graecos and Fragments*, M. Whittaker (ed.) (Oxford: Clarendon Press, 1982) 82.

[49]1 Tim. 1:3 provides no information about Paul's itinerary which the author of the *Acts of Paul* could not also have derived from 2 Tim. 1:18; 1 Cor. 15:32; 16:5-6; 2 Cor. 2:13. The possibility that the phrase ὁ βασιλεὺς τῶν αἰώνων (MP 2, twice) is a reminiscence of 1 Tim. 1:17 is not great, since the phrase was a standard divine title (cf. Tob. 13:6, 10; 1 Clem 61:2; Rev. 15:3; *Acts of Andrew* [Pap. Utrecht 1, p. 15 line 23]; M. Dibelius and H. Conzelmann, *The Pastoral Epistles* [tr. P. Buttolph and A. Yarbro; Hermeneia; Philadelphia: Fortress, 1972] 30), and is used here in the *Acts of Paul* to contrast Christ's eternal kingship with Nero's temporal rule.

[50]Rordorf, 'Verhältnis', 237-241; 'Nochmals'. In the latter essay he takes the view that the *Acts of Paul* and the Pastorals independently preserve authentic traditions about the last period of Paul's life.

of Paul used these two Pastoral letters as a source.[51] The parallel with the way he has used 1 and 2 Corinthians, which we have already noticed, supports the latter view. But there are also two specific points of correspondence between the *Acts of Paul* and 2 Timothy which are much more easily explained by literary dependence than by common oral tradition.

The first is the relationship between 2 Timothy 4:17 and the story of Paul's encounter with the lion at Ephesus (PG; PH 4-5). Most commentators on 2 Timothy have understood the statement, 'I was rescued from the lion's mouth' (2 Tim. 4:17) to be metaphorical.[52] There is good reason for doing so, since the words (ἐρρύσθην ἐκ στόματος λέοντος) are a verbally exact echo of Psalm 22:20-21 (LXX 21:20-21: ῥῦσαι ἀπὸ ῥομφαίας τὴν ψυχήν μου. . .σῶσων με ἐκ στόματος λέοντος), where the imagery is unmistakably metaphorical. MacDonald ignores the allusion to the psalm and makes no reference to the possibility of a metaphorical sense in 2 Timothy 4:17, but in the light of the allusion it seems most likely, not that 2 Timothy alludes to the story told in the *Acts of Paul*, but that the story stands in an exegetical relationship to the text of 2 Timothy. The author of the *Acts of Paul* has treated 2 Timothy 4:17 in the way that Jewish exegetes were accustomed to treating the Old Testament. Finding an apparent reference to an episode in Paul's life which was not actually recounted in the text, he supplied an imaginative story to account for the reference.[53] His literal understanding of a metaphorical expression can be paralleled in other examples of Jewish and Christian exegesis, in which biblical metaphors are taken literally and sometimes become the source of a story.[54] With this phenomenon Hilhorst also makes a comparison of particular interest in the context of our present discussion: he refers to Lefkowitz's study of the

---

[51]For those who take this view, see MacDonald, *Legend*, 62-64, and 115 n. 27.

[52]E.g. Dibelius and Conzelmann, *Pastoral Epistles*, 124; J.N.D. Kelly, *A Commentary on the Pastoral Epistles* (BNTC; London: A. & C. Black, 1963) 219; G.W. Knight III, *The Pastoral Epistles* (NIGTC; Grand Rapids: Eerdmans/Carlisle: Paternoster, 1992) 471.

[53]The story borrows its central motif from the popular story of Androcles and the lion: see MacDonald, *Legend*, 21-23.

[54]A. Hilhorst, 'Biblical Metaphors Taken Literally', in T. Baarda, A. Hilhorst, G.P. Luttikhuizen and A.S. van der Woude (eds.), *Text and Testimony* (A.F.J. Klijn FS; Kampen: J.H. Kok, 1988) 123-129, considers some examples, including this one. Note also ApAbr 8.4-6 (discussed below), which creates a story partly on the basis of understanding Abraham's 'father's house' (Gn. 12:1) to be the building in which they lived.

ancient Greek lives of the poets, in which she showed that much of
the biographical material in these lives results from misinterpreting
passages in poetry by or about these poets, often by taking
metaphorical references literally.[55] For example, Pindar's reference to
his song as 'like a bee' (*Pyth.* 10.45) resulted in an anecdote in which a
bee builds a honeycomb in his mouth.[56] A similar example with
reference to a prose writer is the story that Lucian was killed by dogs:
it seems to be based on his own statement, 'I was almost torn apart
by Cynics as Actaeon was by dogs or his cousin Pentheus was by
women' (*Peregr.* 2).[57] It seems that the author of the *Acts of Paul* used
an established method of deriving biographical information about his
subject from the available texts, which can be paralleled both in
Jewish and Christian exegesis of scripture and in hellenistic
biography.

He also followed Jewish exegetical practice in interpreting
several texts in connection with each other. Evidently and very
naturally, he related 2 Timothy 4:17 to 1 Corinthians 15:32 as
referring to the same event,[58] and took the latter text as literally as the
former.[59] Moreover, he probably noticed the rather close verbal

---

[55]Hilhorst, 'Biblical Metaphors', 129-131, referring to M.R. Lefkowitz, *The Lives of the Greek Poets* (London: Duckworth, 1981).
[56]Lefkowitz, *Lives*, 59, 155-156. Note also the story of Hesiod's death, developed from a line of his poetry: Lefkowitz, *Lives*, 4.
[57]Lefkowitz, *Lives*, 90 n. 12 (quoted by Hilhorst, 'Biblical Metaphors', 130). The story is related to a similar one about Euripides (Lefkowitz, *Lives*, 90), just as the story of Paul and the lion reflects the story of Androcles and the lion.
[58]Note the words, 'O God of the man who fought with the beasts!' (ὁ τοῦ ἀνθρώπου θεὸς τοῦ θηριομαχήσαντος) (PH 5); cf. 1 Cor. 15:32: κατὰ ἄνθρωπον ἐθηριομάχησα.
[59]Whether Paul's reference to fighting with wild animals (1 Cor. 15:32) was actually meant metaphorically or literally is debated: the majority of commentators think it is metaphorical, but there are also scholars who take it literally: e.g. C.R. Bowen, 'I fought with Beasts at Ephesus', *JBL* 42 (1923) 59-68; G.S. Duncan, *St. Paul's Ephesian Ministry* (London: Hodder & Stoughton, 1929) 126-131; M. Carrez, 'Note sur les événements d'Éphèse et l'appel de Paul à sa citoyenneté romaine', in *À Cause de l'Évangile: Études sur les Synoptiques et les Actes* (J. Dupont FS; LD 123; Paris: Éditions du Cerf, 1985) 776-777.
Rordorf, 'Verhältnis', 234, accepts that 1 Cor. 15:32 is the source of the story of Paul in the amphitheatre in Ephesus in the *Acts of Paul*, but he does not deal with 2 Tim. 4:17. MacDonald, *Legend*, 23; *idem*, 'A Conjectural Emendation of 1 Cor. 15:31-32: or the Case of the Misplaced Lion Fight', *HTR* 73 (1980) 265-276, thinks the story of Paul's encounter with the lion was already circulating at the time of the writing of 1 Corinthians, was believed by the Corinthians but dismissed by Paul in 1 Cor. 15:32. This thesis, which involves postulating an

parallel between 2 Timothy 4:17-18 (ἐρρύσθην. . .ῥύσεταί με) and 2 Corinthians 1:10 (ἐρρύσατο ἡμᾶς καὶ ῥύσεται), and used the Jewish exegetical principle of *gezerâ shawâ* (according to which passages in which the same words occur may be used to interpret each other) to refer 2 Corinthians 1:8-10 also to the same event.[60] It is possible that a story based on these references in the Pauline letters originated in the first place in oral storytelling,[61] but the features of oral style which MacDonald finds in the story do not necessarily require this. A writer familiar with oral storytelling, perhaps himself a practitioner of it, is likely to employ features of oral style when composing a story in writing.[62]

A second instance where an exegetical relationship of the *Acts of Paul* to 2 Timothy is more plausible than common use of oral traditions is the reference both works make to the false teaching that the resurrection has already taken place (2 Tim. 2:18: τὴν ἀνάστασιν ἤδη γεγονέναι). In the *Acts of Paul* this teaching is related to the story of Paul and Thecla. Thamyris, Thecla's fiancé whom she has spurned in favour of remaining unmarried, gets into conversation with Demas and Hermogenes, Paul's companions who have turned against him. They explain that Paul teaches that remaining celibate is a condition

---

interpolation in 1 Cor. 15:31, is 'too complicated to be convincing' (Hilhorst, 'Biblical Metaphors', 129 n. 21).

[60] I think it is also quite possible that, in telling stories in which both Thecla (AThe 27-37) and Paul are condemned to the wild animals but protected from them, the author of the *Acts of Paul* had in mind Ignatius, *Rom.* 5.2: 'I long for the wild animals that have been prepared for me. . .I will even entice them to devour me promptly, not as has happened to some whom they have not touched through fear (τινῶν δειλαινόμενα οὐχ ἥψαντο)'. Compare the governor's words to Thecla, 'not one of the beasts touched you', and Thecla's own words, 'not one of the beasts touched me (οὐδὲ ἕν τῶν θηρίων ἥψατό μου)' (AThe 37). The theme is also found in the *Letter of the Churches of Vienne and Lyons*, which remarkably uses of the martyr Blandina almost exactly the words used of Thecla in AThe 37: μηδενὸς ἀψαμένου τότε τῶν θηρίων αὐτῆς (*ap.* Eusebius, *Hist. Eccl.* 5.1.42). Is this evidence of the influence of the *Acts of Paul* on the *Letter*? See also Gregory of Tours, *Life of Andrew* 18 (reflecting the ancient *Acts of Andrew*), where Andrew is untouched by the wild animals released against him in the arena, including a bull, which 'did not touch Andrew' (*Andream non attigit*).

[61] A judgement on this will depend in part on whether the reference to the story by Hippolytus, *In Dan.* 3.29 is judged to be a reference to the *Acts of Paul*. Whether his statement that the lion fell at Paul's feet and licked him corresponds precisely to the text of the *Acts of Paul*, it is impossible to be sure, owing to the fragmentary state of PH 4 at this point (see Schmidt, ΠΡΑΞΕΙΣ ΠΑΨΛΟΨ, 38), but it is certainly plausible as a reminiscence of the text (and cf. AThe 28, 33; PG).

[62] Cf. J.-D. Kaestli, 'Response', *Semeia* 38 (1986) 129.

of participation in the resurrection to come (AThe 12). Opposing
Paul's teaching, Demas and Hermogenes interpret the resurrection in
a way which, so far from requiring abstinence from marriage,
positively requires marriage: 'we shall teach you concerning the
resurrection which he says is to come, that it has already taken place
(ἤν λέγει οὗτος ἀνάστασιν γενέσθαι, ὅτι ἤδη γέγονεν) in the children
we have' (AThe 14).[63] Whereas the reference to this false teaching in 2
Timothy can be readily understood as alluding to an actual current
view—a spiritualised view of the resurrection as taking place in
present experience—this is not the case with the *Acts of Paul*. That
resurrection takes place in begetting children is surely not a view
which was being propounded by Christian teachers, but is rather an
ingenious interpretation of the meaning of 2 Timothy 2:18 occasioned
by a desire to situate this teaching in the context of the story of Paul
and Thecla. Moreover, the attribution of this teaching to Demas and
Hermogenes (to whom it is not attributed in 2 Timothy) can be
understood as a consequence of the description of Demas as 'in love
with the present world' (2 Tim. 4:10). Since he is in love with the
present world, resurrection in the next world is of no use to him and
so he claims that it takes place in this world through the thoroughly
this-worldly activity of begetting children. That Demas's love of the
present world is in view in this passage of the *Acts of Paul* is also
shown by the fact that Thamyris buys the advice of Demas and
Hermogenes with lavish provision of money and food and wine
(AThe 11, 13). All this is most easily understood if 2 Timothy 2:18 is
the original version of the statement that the resurrection has already
taken place, while the story in the *Acts of Paul* is exegesis of it.[64]

---

[63]The following clause—'and that we are risen again in that we have come to
know the true God'—is an alternative explanation of the notion that the
resurrection has already taken place. It fits the context less well than the first
explanation, and is lacking in the Syriac and Latin versions, and so it may not be
original.

[64]A few other possible examples of dependence by the *Acts of Paul* on the text of
2 Timothy may be mentioned here, although they would carry no great weight
alone: the reference to Demas and Hermogenes quarrelling (AThe 11: εἰς ἑαυτοὺς
μαχομένος) may reflect 2 Tim. 2:23-24 (μάχας, μάχεσθαι); PH 6 ('except the Lord
grant me power [δυναμίν]') may depend on 2 Tim. 1:8; the extensive use, in the
section following Paul's arrival in Italy, of the military metaphor of Christians as
'soldiers of Christ' (στρατιῶται Χριστοῦ) in the army of Christ their king (PH 8;
MP 2-4) may be inspired by 2 Tim. 2:3-4; 4:18 (cf. also *Acts of Peter*: Martyrdom 7);
the curious incident of the milk at Paul's execution (MP 5) may be an attempt at
literal interpretation of the metaphor in 2 Tim. 4:6.

If these examples count against MacDonald's theory of common oral tradition, then another explanation must be found for the fact that there are differences as well as resemblances in the information about persons in 2 Timothy and the *Acts of Paul*. Since the author of the *Acts of Paul* appears to have worked quite closely with the text of 2 Timothy, it is not very plausible to invoke mere carelessness or failure of memory. Instead, the explanation must be sought in deliberate exegesis of 2 Timothy by the author of the *Acts of Paul*.

We shall take, as a first example, the case of Demas and Hermogenes. In 2 Timothy there are three pairs of apostate disciples or false teachers:

| 2 Tim. 1:15 | Phygelus | and | **Hermogenes** |
| | *turned away from me* | | |

| 2 Tim. 2:17 | Hymenaeus | and | Philetus |
| | *swerved from the truth by claiming the resurrection has already* | | |

taken place

2 Tim. 4:10, 14	**Demas**	(and)	Alexander **the coppersmith**
	Demas, in love with the present world, has deserted me		
	Alexander did me much harm, strongly opposed our message		

(The third pair is not strictly a pair in the text of 2 Timothy, where Demas and Alexander are separated by three verses, but they are the two persons in the passage of whom derogatory things are said.) The author of the *Acts of Paul* seems to have identified the first and third of these pairs. By calling his pair of false disciples 'Demas and Hermogenes the coppersmith' (AThe 1) he deliberately rolls the two pairs into one. No doubt his basis for doing so is that what is said about Phygelus and Hermogenes—that they turned away from Paul—is equivalent to what is said of Demas—that he deserted Paul. As we have seen, the author of the *Acts of Paul* has also attributed to Demas and Hermogenes the teaching which in 2 Timothy is attributed to the second of the three pairs: Hymenaeus and Philetus. Again, this is explicable. Alexander the coppersmith is said to have strongly opposed Paul's message (2 Tim. 4:15), and so (the author of the *Acts of Paul* probably reasoned) he must have taught the only item of false teaching to which 2 Timothy refers: that the resurrection is already past. Moreover, we have already suggested that this teaching is appropriately attributed to Demas, who is said to have been 'in love with the present world' (2 Tim. 4:10). Perhaps the author of the *Acts of Paul* simply thought it appropriate that Demas and Hermogenes should have taught the same false teaching as Hymenaeus and Philetus did. More likely, he identified them with Hymenaeus and Philetus, thus rolling all three pairs into one.[65] Two comments can be made in support of the plausibility of this as his exegetical procedure. In the first place, collapsing the three pairs into one is effective storytelling technique. It enables a story to be told about them. Secondly, it is an instance of a kind of exegetical technique which was common in Jewish exegesis. Scriptural characters who seem to the modern reader to be quite distinct persons could be exegetically identified on the basis of some kind of exegetical link made between them. Probably the best known example is the identification of Phinehas and Elijah,[66] based on the fact that both were notable for their zeal for God (Nu. 25:10-13; 1 Kgs. 19:10, 14).

In a second case, that of Titus and Luke, the author of the *Acts of Paul* may have found a difficulty in the text of 2 Timothy and deliberately corrected it. 2 Timothy 4:10 could seem to parallel Titus with Demas, as though Titus, like Demas, had defected. The author of the *Acts of Paul*, naturally unhappy with this implication, read the text to mean that Titus had been to Dalmatia, but was now with Paul in Rome. To avoid the parallel between Demas and Titus, he created a parallel between Titus and the one disciple who, according to 2 Timothy 4:11, certainly was faithful to Paul at the end: 'There were awaiting Paul at Rome Luke from Gaul and Titus from Dalmatia' (MP 1). If this seems more like contradiction of 2 Timothy than exegesis of 2 Timothy, we should remember that Jewish exegesis was quite capable of effectively correcting the clear meaning of the Hebrew text of the Old Testament when that meaning was unacceptable.[67]

---

[65]This reduction of all Paul's opponents in 2 Timothy to a single pair might owe something to 2 Tim. 3:8, where the false teachers are compared with Jannes and Jambres, who opposed Moses.

[66]See R. Hayward, 'Phinehas—the same is Elijah: The Origins of a Rabbinic Tradition', *JJS* 29 (1978) 22-34; M. Hengel, *The Zealots* (tr. D. Smith; Edinburgh: T. & T. Clark, 1989) 162-168. The earliest extant instance seems to be LAB 48.1.

[67]A readily intelligible example is Dt. 26:5, where, in order to avoid the implication that Abraham was a Gentile (Aramaean), the LXX reads the text not as, 'An Aramean was my father', but as, 'My father left Syria' (see further D.I. Brewer, *Techniques and Assumptions in Jewish Exegesis before 70 C.E.* [TSAJ 30; Tübingen: Mohr (Siebeck), 1992] 178). An instructive example, because it is hard

III. The Sources and Composition of the *Acts of Paul*

In this section we shall summarise our findings with regard to the way in which the author of the *Acts of Paul* made use of earlier literature by and about Paul, and add some further observations on the way in which he composed his narrative. Comparisons with other literature will be made in the course of this discussion, but the aim is not yet to discuss explicitly the genre of the *Acts of Paul*, but to prepare the way for a discussion of genre in the next section.

The author of the *Acts of Paul* knew the Acts of the Apostles and the Pauline letters, and from his reading of the latter he concluded that the story of Paul in Acts was incomplete, not only because it did not record his martyrdom, but also because, after the events recorded in Acts, Paul engaged in further missionary travels in the eastern Mediterranean before returning to Rome and suffering martyrdom. He conceived his work, therefore, as a kind of sequel to Acts, continuing the story of Paul's missionary career and ending with his martyrdom.

As sources for his narrative he used, in the first place, those Pauline letters which he understood to have been written in this period of Paul's life (1 and 2 Corinthians, 2 Timothy, Titus) and which therefore supplied him with references to places visited by Paul, persons associated with Paul, and events of Paul's life in this period. He also made careful use of Clement's brief summary of Paul's sufferings (1 Clem 5:5-7). His use of these sources shows that he was concerned to conform his account as far as possible to what could be learned from sources which he would certainly have regarded as good historical sources. However, these sources as such supplied only rather minimal facts, such as that Paul was persecuted in Antioch, Iconium and Lystra (2 Tim. 3:11) or that he was in bonds four times during the period covered by the *Acts of Paul*. They did not provide the stories the author required in order to give a narrative account of the final period of Paul's life. In part, therefore, his work consists of stories which he, a skilled storyteller, has created to account for the references in his textual sources. His story of Paul's

---

to see the reason for it, is LAB 31.3, where the statement that Sisera fled on his horse appears to contradict the repeated information in the biblical text that he fled on foot (Judg. 4:15, 17). But many examples from works of the genre of 'rewritten Bible' (Jubilees, Genesis Apocryphon, LAB, Josephus' *Antiquities*) could be given to show that such exegetes did not hesitate to interpret the biblical text in such a way as in effect to correct it.

experiences at Ephesus, for example, must have seemed to him the kind of thing that must have happened to account for what Paul says in 1 Corinthians 15:32; 2 Corinthians 1:8-10 and 2 Timothy 4:16-18.

This kind of creative exegesis can be paralleled, as we have already noticed, both in hellenistic biography and in Jewish scriptural exegesis. Ancient biographers of writers, faced with a dearth of biographical information about their subjects, were often reduced to making fanciful deductions from allusions in the subject's own writings, sometimes creating a whole story on the basis of a brief reference.[68] Similarly, ancient Jewish exegetes frequently engaged in creative storytelling to explain features of the biblical text or to satisfy curiosity about biblical characters. To give a minor example, in order to account for the fact that, in Numbers 22:6, Balak appears to be already acquainted with the efficacy of Balaam's curse, Pseudo-Philo, LAB 18.2 creates a brief story of Balaam's activity prior to his appearance in the biblical narrative. This is not inventive storytelling for its own sake, but a kind of imaginative historical conjecture. A better known example, which provides a good parallel to the story of Paul in the amphitheatre at Ephesus, is the various stories of Abraham's escape from the fire. Jewish exegetes read אור in Genesis 11:28, 31; 15:7 as 'fire' rather than 'Ur.' Interpreting Genesis 11:28 in this way ('Haran died. . .in the fire of the Chaldeans'), Jubilees 12:12-14 tells a story in which Abraham set fire to the house of the idols, his brother Haran rushed in to rescue the idols and perished in the fire (see also Tg. Ps.-Jon. Gen. 11:28). In the Apocalypse of Abraham the story concerns Abraham's escape from the fire (Gen. 15:7): just as Abraham obeys God's command to leave his 'father's house' (Gen. 12:1, understood literally), fire from heaven burns up Terah's house and everything in it, including Terah himself (8:4-6). The most elaborate story occurs in LAB 6, in which Abraham is miraculously rescued by God from a great fiery furnace (cf. Gen. 15:7, which Tg. Ps.-Jon. 15:7 reads as, 'I am the LORD who brought you out of the furnace of fire of the Chaldeans'). Other versions of this story occur in later Jewish literature (Gen. Rab. 38:13; 44:13; b. Pes. 118a; b. 'Erub. 53a; Tg. Ps.-Jon. Gen. 11:28; Sefer ha-Yashar 6-9).[69] The variety of

[68]See especially Lefkowitz, *Lives*.

[69]On the stories of Abraham and the fire, see G. Vermes, *Scripture and Tradition in Judaism* (SPB 4; Leiden: Brill, 1961) 68-75; R. Bauckham, 'The *Liber Antiquitatum Biblicarum* of Pseudo-Philo and the Gospels as "Midrash"', in R.T. France and D. Wenham (eds.), *Gospel Perspectives III: Studies in Midrash and Historiography* (Sheffield: JSOT Press, 1983) 41-43.

stories created to explain the same texts may indicate that they were not taken too literally, but understood as exercises in historical imagination.

A story of this kind is not necessarily created *ex nihilo*. Other stories would provide models and motifs.[70] Thus the most popular story of Abraham and the fire was in part inspired by the story of the three young men in the fiery furnace in Daniel 3, from which it borrowed major motifs. Similarly, in constructing a story of Paul at Ephesus to explain the Pauline allusions, the author of the *Acts of Paul* modelled his story on the popular folktale of Androcles and the lion.[71] In his depiction of the events that lead to Paul's arrest and condemnation to the wild animals (PG; PH 1), he was also inspired by Acts 19:23-27, though without creating simply a duplicate of Luke's account. Finally, prompted by Clement's apparent attribution of Paul's bondage to 'jealousy' (1 Clem 5:5-6), he has worked in a subplot about the proconsul's wife Artemilla and his freedman's wife Eubula, who are baptised by Paul and arouse their husbands' anger by their devotion to him (PH 2-5). This subplot is a version of a motif common in the apocryphal Acts (cf. the story of Maximilla and Iphidama in the *Acts of Andrew*, and the story of Xanthippe in the *Acts of Peter*).

We have noticed a number of examples of the way the author of the *Acts of Paul* employs exegetical practices that belong in the tradition of Jewish exegesis of Scripture and characterise the literature known as the 'rewritten Bible.' Another example occurs in Paul's reminiscence of his conversion, in which he refers to 'the blessed Judas, the brother of the Lord' (PG). The Judas in whose house Paul stayed in Damascus, according to Acts 9:11, has here been identified with the Lord's brother of the same name. The identification has enabled the author of the *Acts of Paul* to suppose that Judas the Lord's brother must have introduced Paul into the community of Christian believers in Damascus, and so to expand and elaborate the information given in Acts about Paul's introduction into

---

[70]See also n. 57 above.

[71]MacDonald, *Legend*, 21-23. (In the early part of the story of Paul and the lion [PG], note also the allusion to Is. 11:6-7 and the explicit reference to Daniel in the lion's den.) There is nothing anomalous about this use of a folktale motif. Such motifs frequently occur in Jewish extra-biblical stories about biblical characters. For the use of folktales in Greek novels, see G. Anderson, *Ancient Fiction: The Novel in the Graeco-Roman World* (London/Sydney: Croom Helm/Totowa, New Jersey: Barnes & Noble, 1984) chapter 11.

Christian faith. It is an example of the regular Jewish exegetical practice of illuminating the identity of obscure biblical characters by identifying them with better-known characters who bore the same or similar names.[72] The same practice with regard to New Testament characters is well evidenced in second-century Christian literature.[73]

Of course, not all stories about Paul in the *Acts of Paul* are very closely related to the information the author derived from the Pauline letters and 1 Clement, though a surprisingly large number of them are in fact attached to the framework provided by these sources. Some of the others (like the story of Artemilla and Eubula already mentioned) are variations on narrative models provided by other works about apostles. Thus, the story of Patroclus (MP 1) is inspired by Luke's story of Eutychus (Acts 20:7-12), while the vision Paul has, on his way to Rome, of Jesus informing him that he is to be crucified again (PH 7) is modelled on the famous 'Quo vadis?' story in the *Acts of Peter (Act. Verc.* 35).[74] This kind of repetition of narrative motifs and patterns seems artificial to modern readers. Such stories tend to lose their credibility when we recognise their resemblance to others. But this is a modern reaction. The use of familiar motifs and patterns is constant in all forms of ancient narrative literature.[75] Ancient readers must have felt that, for example, the story of Patroclus was

---

[72]E.g. Joel the son of Samuel (1 Sa. 8:2) was identified with Joel the prophet (Num. Rab. 10:5); Jobab (Gn. 36:33; 1 Ch. 1:44) was identified with Job (LXX Job 42:17c-d; TJob 1:1; Aristeas the Exegete, *ap.* Eusebius, *Praep. Evang.* 9.25.1-3); Amoz the father of Isaiah was identified with Amos the prophet (AscIsa 1:2; 4:22).

[73]See R. Bauckham, 'Papias and Polycrates on the Origin of the Fourth Gospel', *JTS* 44 (1993) 30-31, 42-43.

[74]Since Peter dies by crucifixion but Paul does not, it is clear that the story was originally told of Peter, not Paul. This may be the result of literary dependence by the *Acts of Paul* on the *Acts of Peter*, or it may be that the story about Peter was known prior to its incorporation in the *Acts of Peter*. That there is a literary relationship between the *Acts of Paul* and the *Acts of Peter* seems clear from other evidence, but the direction of dependence is not easy to establish: I am inclined to think that the *Acts of Paul* is dependent on the original form of the *Acts of Peter* (from which it borrowed the 'Quo vadis?' story), but that the *Acts of Peter* in its later redacted form, as we have it in the Vercelli Acts, is in turn dependent on the *Acts of Paul*. The 'Quo vadis?' story may well have originated as exegesis of Jn. 13:36-37: see R. Bauckham, 'The Martyrdom of Peter in Early Christian Literature', *ANRW* II.26.1 (1992) 579.

[75]Note the interesting remarks, with reference to novels, made by J.R. Morgan, 'History, Romance, and Realism in the *Aithiopika* of Heliodorus', *Classical Antiquity* 1 (1982) 263-264 (cf. 248 for examples of the phenomenon he discusses).

the kind of thing that might have happened to Paul precisely because this kind of event was familiar from Luke's story of Eutychus. Even the story of Paul and the lion probably gained rather than lost credibility through its resemblance to the well-known folktale.[76] The more stories of miracles of resurrection performed by apostles the readers had heard, the more they would expect such stories and not be surprised by their frequency in the *Acts of Paul*. This is not to say that such stories would necessarily be accepted as historical fact, but rather that they would be credible at least as exercises in historical imagination (realistic, if not real).

The story of Thecla is of special interest because it is the only part of the *Acts of Paul* in which a character other than Paul takes centre-stage and because it bears a very close relationship to the themes of the Greek novels that tell the story of two lovers (such as Chariton's *Chaereas and Callirhoe,* and Xenophon's *Ephesiaca).* To some extent, the story of Artemilla and Eubula (PH 2-5), like other stories in the apocryphal Acts of women who forsake their husbands or deny conjugal rights to their husbands in order to follow the apostle's teaching, also employs an erotic theme reminiscent of the Greek novels and was probably intended to appeal to readers, especially women, who enjoyed such literature. But the theme of chastity is not explicitly developed in the story of Artemilla and Eubula, as it is in the story of Thecla, while the latter has so many resemblances to the Greek novel[77] that it must really be regarded as a deliberate small-scale equivalent to such a novel. Thecla, like the heroines of the novels, is a beautiful young girl who preserves her chastity and remains faithful to her beloved through trials and dangers in which she comes close to death but experiences divine deliverance. Thamyris and Alexander are unwanted suitors such as appear in the novels. Unlike the heroines of the novels, of course, Thecla's chastity is not temporary, but permanent, and represents her total devotion to God. But her devotion to God is also devotion to his apostle Paul, and the author does not hesitate to depict this devotion in terms which, while not intended to be sexual, parallel the erotic (cf. AThe 8-10, 18-19). As in the case of the heroes and heroines of the novels, the plot partly turns on the separation of Paul and Thecla, her search for

---

[76]Note how Hippolytus, *In Dan.* 3.29, argues for the credibility of the story of Daniel in the lions' den from the fact that it resembles the story of Paul and the lion (in whatever form he knew this story).

[77]See especially T. Hägg, *The Novel in Antiquity* (Oxford: Blackwell, 1983) 160.

and reunion with him (AThe 21-25, 40-41). Thecla's offer to cut her hair short in order to follow Paul wherever he goes (AThe 25) and her adoption of male dress when she travels in search of Paul (AThe 40) may not be signs of her liberation from patriarchal structures, as MacDonald[78] and others interpret them, so much as echoes of the novelistic theme of a woman travelling in male disguise to escape detection.[79] The wealthy upper-class circles in which the story takes place, including the historical figure of the emperor's relative Tryphaena,[80] are also consonant with the character of the Greek novels. It seems clear that the story of Thecla has been directly modelled on the themes of the Greek erotic novel,[81] both in order to entertain a readership similar to that enjoyed by the novels,[82] but also in order to express the author's message of sexual continence for the sake of devotion to God in an attractively symbolic way.[83]

A historical basis for the story of Thecla, which has often been postulated,[84] need not be entirely denied, but it is unlikely to be much more substantial than the kind of basis in exegesis of the Pauline letters which the author had for other stories. That Thecla was a historical person, a disciple of Paul who engaged in missionary work in Seleucia (AThe 43), is probably all that the author of the *Acts*

---

[78]MacDonald, *Legend*, 19-20.

[79]Cf. Xenophon, *Ephesiaca*, 5.1.4-8, quoted in Hägg, *Novel*, 25.

[80]For Tryphaena see Ramsay, *Church*, 382-389: she was queen of Pontus and a relative of the emperor Claudius. If her appearance in the story rests on an identification of her with the Tryphaena of Rom. 16:12, then either this identification was taken over by the author of the *Acts of Paul* from earlier tradition or else he did not notice that his chronology would put Paul's reference to her in Romans before her conversion to Christianity in the story of Thecla.

[81]See J.-D. Kaestli, 'Les principales orientations de la recherche sur les Actes apocryphes', in Bovon, *Les Actes Apocryphes*, 66-67, for the direct dependence of the erotic motifs in the apocryphal Acts on the Greek novels, against the thesis of R. Söder, for whom the relationship was indirect.

[82]Cf. Hägg, *Novel*, 161. Hägg's work is notable for its attempt to characterise the readership of the novels (chapter 3: 'The Social Background and the First Readers of the Novel'), and has interesting implications for the readership of the apocryphal Acts.

[83]An instructive parallel is the way in which the theme of romantic love, which featured in the secular literature and culture of twelfth-century Europe, was used, especially by Bernard of Clairvaux, as an image of monastic devotion to and mystical union with God: J. Leclercq, *Monks and Love in Twelfth-century France* (Oxford: Clarendon Press, 1979).

[84]See the survey of scholarship in Rordorf, 'Tradition and Composition', 46-47.

of Paul knew from oral tradition.[85] Since he evidently lived in Asia Minor (Tertullian, *De bapt.* 17), he may have made use of some other local traditions about Paul, but there is very little to indicate this.[86]

If the erotic element in the *Acts of Paul*, especially the story of Thecla, is due to the influence of the novel, the same should not be said of the theme of travel, by which the whole narrative is structured as an account of Paul's travels. Because travel is prominent in some, though not all, of the apocryphal Acts and is equally prominent in most, though not all, of the Greek erotic novels, it has often been regarded as a novelistic feature of the apocryphal Acts.[87] But the function of travel is quite different in the *Acts of Paul* from its function in the novels,[88] where it serves the plot by separating the lovers.[89] Paul's travels in the *Acts of Paul* are those of an apostle charged with a mission of evangelism and care of his churches, and there is no need to look for their model elsewhere than in the Lukan Acts. It is noteworthy that apostolic travels are more prominent in the *Acts of Paul* than in any other of the oldest group of apocryphal Acts, with the exception of the *Acts of Andrew* (insofar as it is possible to reconstruct the original form of this work).[90] In the original *Acts of Peter*, it seems that Peter made only one journey: from Jerusalem to Rome. In the *Acts of Thomas*, there are only a few brief and unspecific notes of travel: they do not structure the whole narrative as the references to travel do in the *Acts of Paul*. Travel is

---

[85]Boughton, 'Pious Legend', 381-382, is even more sceptical, but her suggestion that Thecla was actually an early second-century martyr is very insecure. That Thecla was actually a contemporary of Paul might receive some support from the fact that queen Tryphaena was in fact a historical contemporary of Paul, though her connection with Thecla is likely to be fanciful.

[86]The traditional prison of Paul at Ephesus (Duncan, *St. Paul's Ephesian Ministry*, 70) may be evidence of a local tradition, but the tradition could be dependent on the *Acts of Paul*, like later local traditions about Thecla.

[87]Pervo, *Profit*, 50-57, chapter 5, applies the same judgement to the Lukan Acts, but travel and adventure cannot be regarded as constitutive of the genre of the novel or uniquely characteristic of novels. Cf. G.E. Sterling, *Historiography and Self-Definition: Josephos, Luke-Acts and Apologetic Historiography* (NovTSup 64; Leiden: Brill, 1992) 320.

[88]For this issue in relation to the apocryphal Acts in general, see Kaestli, 'Les principales orientations', 64; D.E. Aune, *The New Testament in its Literary Environment* (Cambridge: James Clarke, 1987) 152.

[89]Nor are the travels in Philostratus' *Life of Apollonius*, or the Alexander romance of Pseudo-Callisthenes, really comparable.

[90]For the reconstruction of the *Acts of Andrew*, see J.-M. Prieur, *Acta Andreae* (CCSA 5-6; Turnhout: Brepols, 1989).

more important in the *Acts of John*,[91] but the apostle stays for much of the work in Ephesus: he is not so constantly on the move as Paul is in the *Acts of Paul*. The difference is explained simply by the fact that the author of the *Acts of Paul* has modelled the form of his narrative on Luke's accounts of Paul's travels. In this sense the structure of the *Acts of Paul* derives from its character as a sequel to the canonical Acts. It follows Luke's model of an episodic narrative structured by travel notices,[92] and diverges only at the end of the story, in its account of Paul's martyrdom and the events which immediately follow.

A feature unique to the *Acts of Paul* among the extant texts of the apocryphal Acts is its inclusion of a physical description of Paul (AThe 3).[93] Such descriptions were a standard feature of Greek and Roman biography.[94] They are often conventional to some degree, reflecting the theories of physiognomics, which were popular in the second century[95] and understood physical features as revelatory of

---

[91]E. Junod and J.-D. Kaestli, *Acta Johannis* (CCSA 1-2; Turnhout: Brepols, 1983) 683 (and cf. 533 n. 1), are not certain whether this feature of the *Acts of John* is modelled on the Acts of the Apostles. I am more inclined than they to think that both it and the 'we' style that accompanies it (uniquely among the early apocryphal Acts: Junod and Kaestli, *Acta Johannis*, 530-533) are indebted to Acts, but certainly the *Acts of John* as a whole bears much less resemblance to Acts than the *Acts of Paul* does.

[92]Attempts to distinguish the episodic structure of the apocryphal Acts from that of the Lukan Acts, such as Aune, *New Testament*, 152-153, are much too apt to generalise about the apocryphal Acts. In the case of the *Acts of Paul*, Aune's distinction is not valid: if the Lukan Acts 'has chronological movement towards a goal, the proclamation of the gospel in Rome', this movement appears in the narrative of Paul's travels only in the final stages, just as it does in the *Acts of Paul*, where the movement is towards both proclamation of the Gospel and martyrdom in Rome (PH 6-7).

[93]Since we do not have the earliest sections of the *Acts of Peter*, the *Acts of Andrew* or the *Acts of John*, we cannot be sure that such descriptions did not occur in them (though one might have expected such a description in *Acts of John* 27, had the author wished to provide one).

[94]E.C. Evans, 'Roman Descriptions of Personal Appearance in History and Biography', *Harvard Studies in Classical Philology* 46 (1935) 43-84; *idem*, *Physiognomics in the Ancient World* (Transactions of the American Philosophical Society 59/5; Philadelphia: American Philosophical Society, 1969) 50-58. They are also found in fiction: Evans, *Physiognomics*, 73 and n. 51. Note also the physical description of Moses (in a notably biographical treatment of Moses) by Artapanus, *ap.* Eusebius, *Praep. Evang.* 9.27.37.

[95]E.C. Evans, 'The Study of Physiognomy in the Second Century A.D.', *Transactions and Proceedings of the American Philological Association* 72 (1941) 96-108.

character and aptitudes. Suetonius' physical descriptions of the emperors, for example, are determined as much by physiognomical theory as by the actual appearances of the emperors, even when these were readily available in the form of statues and images on coins.[96] The description of Paul is to a large extent conventional (and certainly not unflattering, as it appears to modern readers):[97] bowleggedness and meeting eyebrows were admired, the hooked nose was a sign of magnanimity, and a moderately small stature indicated quickness of intelligence (since the blood flowed more quickly around a small area and more quickly reached the heart, the seat of intelligence).[98] Only the bald head is surprising, and might reflect an historical reminiscence.[99]

Finally, the accounts of Paul's teaching in the *Acts of Paul* are to a significant extent inspired by the Pauline letters, to which there are verbal allusions.[100] Of course, they also reflect the author's own theology. His Paulinism is an idiosyncratic interpretation of Paul, but it is clear that he made a genuine attempt to attribute Pauline themes and language to his Paul. Paul's speeches in Acts are less obviously reflected, but it may be that Paul's address to the Philippian church (PH 6) was inspired, in a general way, by Paul's address to the Ephesian elders (especially Acts 20:18-24), and that the pattern of Paul's sermon on arrival in Italy (PH 8; PHeid 79-80), in recalling both the Old Testament history of Israel and the ministry of Jesus, was modelled on Acts 13:16-41.

IV. The Genre of the *Acts of Paul*

Discussions of the genre of the apocryphal Acts have in the past worked with two concepts: the aretalogy and the novel (or romance). There are serious problems with defining both of these as genres of

---

[96]P. Cox, *Biography in Late Antiquity: A Quest for the Holy Man* (Berkeley/Los Angeles/London: University of California Press, 1983) 14-15; but cf. also Evans, 'Roman Descriptions', 63.

[97]R.M. Grant, 'The Description of Paul in the Acts of Paul and Thecla', *VC* 36 (1982) 1-4; and especially A.J. Malherbe, 'A Physical Description of Paul', *HTR* 79 (1986) 170-175.

[98]Evans, *Physiognomics*, 10.

[99]Malherbe, 'A Physical Description', 175.

[100]The subject deserves a fuller discussion than is possible here. There are also, of course, allusions to other New Testament writings.

literature in which the apocryphal Acts can be included.[101] The problems can be illustrated by the facts that Reitzenstein, who classified the apocryphal Acts as popular religious aretalogies, did so by postulating a genre which has not been transmitted in pure form except in the case of the apocryphal Acts;[102] that Rosa Söder, who very influentially placed the apocryphal Acts within a very broadly defined category of novelistic literature, also saw them as to some extent *sui generis*, derived from a popular tradition of tales of adventure, miracles and love, which also influenced the Greek novel but has not been preserved;[103] and, finally, that Richard Pervo, in his attempt to classify apocryphal and canonical Acts alike as historical novels, defines the novel so broadly as to include any kind of narrative fiction (including works which mix history with fiction).[104] In all these cases, we seem really to be left with the recognition that, while the apocryphal Acts resemble various kinds of contemporary literature in various ways, they are also not quite like anything else. It is therefore not surprising that most recent discussions have tended to consider the apocryphal Acts a new genre or subgenre (given the fluidity of the concept of genre, this difference is not necessarily real) of literature, indebted to a variety of literary models, including perhaps the Acts of the Apostles.[105] There is also a tendency to stress the differences between the various apocryphal Acts, in reaction against the tendency, in discussions of genre, to offer generalisations about the apocryphal Acts which are not in fact true of particular Acts.[106] These developments, while understandable and necessary, are scarcely a satisfactory conclusion to the discussion of genre, since, unless the new (sub)genre is more precisely specified and its relationship to existing genres defined, we are left without the

---

[101]Kaestli, 'Les principales orientations', 57-67, is now the best account of the history of discussion of the genre of the apocryphal Acts, along with acute criticism of the proposals which have been made.

[102]Kaestli, 'Les principales orientations', 61.

[103]Kaestli, 'Les principales orientations', 62.

[104]Pervo, *Profit*, 105 (his definition of the ancient novel), 109 (the apocryphal Acts are 'missionary novels'), 122 ('"historical novel" is an adequate characterization' of the apocryphal Acts). For criticism, see Aune, *New Testament*, 153; Sterling, *Historiography*, 320.

[105]Kaestli, 'Les principales orientations', 67; W. Schneemelcher, 'Second and Third Century Acts of Apostles: Introduction', in Schneemelcher, *New Testament Apocrypha*, 80; Aune, *New Testament*, 153; Prieur, *Acta Andreae*, 403-404; Hägg, *Novel*, 161.

[106]Junod and Kaestli, *Acta Johannis*, 682-684.

interpretative help which the concept of genre should provide: i.e. some insight into the kind of expectations the first readers would have had as to the kind of literature they were reading and the functions it would perform for them.

In the light of this current state of discussion, we shall proceed, not by defining a genre in which to include the apocryphal Acts in general or the *Acts of Paul* in particular, but by comparing the *Acts of Paul* in particular with those categories of ancient literature to which it bears some clear relationship. We begin with the Acts of the Apostles, since our previous discussion has shown that the *Acts of Paul* stands in a very definite, intentional relationship to the Lukan Acts. It continues the story of Paul which Acts leaves unfinished. In consequence, its overall structure—an episodic travel-narrative—is modelled on the accounts of Paul's missionary travels in Acts, and to some extent the kinds of content given to each episode also follow the model of Acts. The fact that some episodes (such as the 'romance' of Paul and Thecla or the correspondence between Paul and the Corinthians) do not conform to the model of Acts does not negate the observation that the overall framework is modelled on Acts, and does not in itself suffice to distinguish the genre of the *Acts of Paul* from that of Acts.[107] Nor does the contention that the *Acts of Paul* lacks the theological (salvation-historical) conception which governs Luke's work[108] necessarily indicate a difference of genre, provided that the *Acts of Paul* has its own salvation-historical perspective, which it certainly does have.

However, there are generically significant differences from Acts. In the first place, the *Acts of Paul* has a more biographical character than the Acts of the Apostles, though the point needs to be put rather carefully if it is not to be misleading. Despite Luke's virtually exclusive concentration on the story of Paul in the second half of Acts, the fact that he ends his story at the point he does demonstrates that his interest in Paul was subordinated to a non-

---

[107]Hence C. Schmidt's proposal to explain the genre of the apocryphal Acts as imitative of Acts is not in fact, in the case of the *Acts of Paul*, refuted by the arguments which have been all but universally held to have disposed of it (see Kaestli, 'Les principales orientations', 60).

[108]W. Schneemelcher, 'Second and Third century Acts of Apostles: Introduction', in W. Schneemelcher (ed.), R. McL. Wilson tr., *New Testament Apocrypha*, vol. 2 (London: Lutterworth, 1965) 170-173 (this section on the relationship of the apocryphal Acts to the Lukan Acts has been omitted in the most recent edition); cf. the trenchant criticism in Pervo, *Profit*, 123-125.

biographical concept of his work as a whole. However, his own work stimulated an interest in the individual stories of the major apostles who feature in Acts which, when combined with the strongly biographical interests of the age, made it difficult for second-century Christians to understand why he did not continue these stories. The author of the Muratorian canon wondered why Luke did not go on to record events which he knew (perhaps from the *Acts of Peter*) occurred not long after the end of Acts—Paul's journey to Spain and the martyrdom of Peter—and could only conclude that Luke confined himself to recording events of which he was an eyewitness. The author of the *Acts of Paul* shared this biographical concern which made Acts seem unfinished because it did not continue the story of Paul as far as his death. His inclusion of a physical description of Paul (AThe 3) is the feature which most obviously aligns his work with Graeco-Roman biography in a way which is not true of Acts.

Of course, the *Acts of Paul* is not a biography of Paul, since it covers only the final short period of Paul's life, and so its title, whether or not original, uses the term πράξεις, but not βίος.[109] Moreover, the biographical interest should not be taken to imply a shift of interest away from the purpose of God in salvation-history to Paul considered in himself as a so-called θεῖος ἀνήρ or holy man.[110] The interest in Paul is solely in Paul as apostle—or 'servant of God,' the preferred title in the *Acts of Paul* (AThe 4; PHeid 31; PH 6, 7; PHeid 28)—sent by God to accomplish his plan (οἰκονομία) (PG; cf. PH 4, 6, 7). It is the saving activity of God through Paul's preaching and miracles that is the concern of the *Acts of Paul*, but from this perspective Paul's story has its own special significance in the purpose of God. In this way the *Acts of Paul* participates, in its own way, in the trend towards the biographical that characterises both serious historiography and other forms of historical writing in this period.[111] While to some degree it could be said that the Lukan Acts

---

[109]Contrast the title of Pseudo-Callisthenes' work: Βίος καὶ πράξεις Ἀλεξάνδρου τοῦ Μακεδόνος.
[110]This misleading implication is suggested, of the apocryphal Acts in general, by, among others, Schneemelcher, 'Second and Third century Acts of Apostles: Introduction', in W. Schneemelcher, *New Testament Apocrypha*, vol. 2, 174; Aune, *New Testament*, 146.
[111]A. Momigliano, *The Development of Greek Biography* (Cambridge, Massachusetts: Harvard University Press, 1971) 93-100; Aune, *New Testament*, 30; Hägg, *Novel*, chapter 5.

already participate in this trend, the closer relationship of the *Acts of Paul* to biography represents a shift of generic identity.

Secondly, there is the question of historiography and fiction. Aune follows the generic distinction that has commonly been made when he says that, 'The author of the canonical Acts presents his work as *history*, while it is clear that the authors of the apocryphal acts were basically writing fiction'.[112] Even those who regard the Lukan Acts as highly tendentious or inaccurate history have still sharply distinguished its genre, as some kind of historiography, from that of the apocryphal Acts, as some kind of fiction. Only recently has Pervo dissolved all distinction in classifying the Lukan Acts and the apocryphal Acts alike as a historical novels.[113] However, our present discussion of the *Acts of Paul* requires us to reopen the question, not of the genre of the Lukan Acts, but of the relation of the *Acts of Paul* to historiography. The author of the *Acts of Paul* appears far from simply indifferent to historical reality. He uses what sources were available to him, and, meagre though these were, squeezes all the information he can out of them before allowing his creative imagination to take over. If his talents were for storytelling rather than historical judgement or analysis, the same could be said of many ancient historians. This is not to suggest that we can put his work in the same category as Luke's. His sources and methods, as we have described them, are quite different from Luke's, on any showing. But the difference—though surely a generic difference—is not between historiography and simple fiction. It is a difference between a form of historiography which, for all that its conventions allowed more licence for the use of imagination than modern historiographical conventions, nevertheless depended extensively on plausibly reliable sources, and a form of writing about historical persons and events which, while not neglecting historical sources, made liberal use of imagination. In fact, there were a great many ancient works of the latter type, with greatly varying admixtures of history and fiction. But it does not help very much to classify them all as 'historical novels'. It will be more useful to draw attention to some specific categories of them which can be related to the *Acts of Paul.*

We must begin with the novel (or romance) proper, i.e. the erotic novel which tells the story of two lovers who remain faithful to each other through separations, trials and dangerous adventures,

---

[112] Aune, *New Testament*, 152.
[113] Pervo, *Profit*, chapter 5.

before arriving at a happy and final reunion. This is a genre which can be quite easily and strictly defined,[114] and in a field where genre definition is difficult we should be glad of that fact and not confuse issues by claiming that other works of imaginative prose narrative are much the same as those which indubitably belong to this genre. That there was, as van Uytfanghe felicitously puts it, 'symbiosis' between the novel and the biography is true,[115] but it does not make biographies novels. The novel, defined in this sense, was pure fiction, but it often posed as historiography, owing to the fact that narrative prose fiction derived in some sense (whether by evolution or creative decision is disputed) from historical writing. The pose was no doubt transparent, but it was to some extent intrinsic to the genre, and was carefully cultivated by some novelists, such as Heliodorus.[116] It is the extreme case that alerts us to the fact that the boundaries between historiography and fiction in ancient literature are not simple.

The *Acts of Paul* is not a novel. Apart from any other considerations, novels relate 'the adventures or experiences of one or more individuals in their private capacities and from the viewpoint of their private interests and emotions',[117] whereas Paul in the *Acts of Paul* is a public figure, fulfilling a mission from God which belongs to God's purpose for the world and affects whole populations of cities and regions. But the *Acts of Paul* contains, in the story of Paul and Thecla, a section imitative of the novel genre. We have already discussed why this borrowing of themes from the novel, which seems to have been at the height of its popularity at the time when the *Acts of Paul* was written, should have been made. When we make strict comparison with the erotic novel proper, instead of absorbing both the apocryphal Acts and the novel proper in a much broader and less defined category of so-called novelistic or romantic literature, it is easy to see both that the *Acts of Paul* is not itself a novel

---

[114]The central texts of the corpus of literature so defined are listed, e.g., in B.P. Reardon, *The Form of the Greek Romance* (Princeton, New Jersey: Princeton University Press, 1991) 4-5. No writers on this subject seem to have much difficulty in so describing the common features of these texts as to make it clear that they constitute a distinctive genre.

[115]M. van Uytfanghe, 'L'hagiographie: un "genre" chrétien ou antique tardif?', *Analecta Bollandiana* 111 (1993) 146.

[116]See especially Morgan, 'History, Romance, and Realism'.

[117]B.E. Perry, *The Ancient Romances* (Berkeley/Los Angeles: University of California Press, 1967) 45.

and that one section of it is deliberately imitative of the novel.[118] The general themes of travel and adventure, though they are characteristic of the novel, are by no means unique to it, and in the *Acts of Paul* derive from the work's sources for the life of Paul, especially Acts. But the erotic themes of the story of Paul and Thecla are distinctive of the novel, whereas they have no parallel in the Lukan Acts.[119] This relationship with the novel therefore enables us to understand one point at which the *Acts of Paul* departs from the model provided by Acts.

We have noticed the extent to which the *Acts of Paul* employs techniques of creative exegesis characteristic of Jewish exegetical literature. This suggests that the relationship between the apocryphal Acts and that considerable body of Jewish literature which either retells the biblical story with all manner of creative expansions (e.g. Jubilees, Pseudo-Philo's *Liber Antiquitatum Biblicarum*, Artapanus) or tells largely extra-biblical stories about biblical characters (e.g. Joseph and Aseneth, Jannes and Jambres, 4 Baruch) deserves more attention than it has received. Much of this literature was read by Christians who did not regard it as canonical. It could well have suggested how the writings of the emerging New Testament canon could also be extended (e.g. *Acts of Paul, Acts of Peter)* or supplemented (e.g. *Acts of John, Acts of Andrew)* by extra-canonical stories about apostles.[120] Some of these Jewish works use exegesis of the biblical text as the starting-point and stimulus for exercises in historical imagination, others are more purely fictional.

Finally, the affinities between the *Acts of Paul* and biography, already noticed, make it important to observe that, as Momigliano comments,

---

[118]For a similar distinction with regard to the apocryphal Acts in general, see Kaestli, 'Les principales orientations', 65-67.

[119]Against Pervo, *Profit,* 127-128, the 'erotic' themes in the apocryphal Acts do constitute a significant distinction from the Lukan Acts (Acts 17:1-15, cited by Pervo, 182, n. 81, constitutes no sort of a parallel to the kinds of difficulties—e.g. with jealous husbands—that the apostles' women converts create for them in the apocryphal Acts), but he is right that this distinction as such is not a generic difference.

[120]This suggests a different relationship between the apocryphal Acts and the New Testament canon from that proposed by F. Bovon, 'La vie des apôtres: traditions bibliques et narrations apocryphes', in Bovon, *Les Actes Apocryphes,* 149-150.

The borderline between fiction and reality was thinner in biography than in ordinary historiography. What readers expected in biography was probably different from what they expected in political history. They wanted information about the education, the love affairs, and the character of their heroes. But these things are less easily documented than wars and political reforms. If biographers wanted to keep their public, they had to resort to fiction.[121]

We have already noticed that this is true of the lives of the Greek poets. Momigliano's comment needs qualification in the sense that some biographies were as scrupulously historical as the best ancient historiography.[122] Indeed, one can perhaps speak of the emergence, by the time of writing of the *Acts of Paul*, of two genres of biography: the historical, which remained close to good historical method, and the (for want of a better word) novelistic, which, while using sources, allowed more or less freedom to creative imagination.[123] It is instructive to compare the works of a younger contemporary of the author of the *Acts of Paul*, Philostratus. His *Lives of the Sophists*, dependent on oral sources, no doubt share the limitations of the sources, but in these Philostratus does not indulge in free invention.[124] Quite different is his *Life of Apollonius of Tyana*. Here the point where novelistic creativity takes over from history is impossible to determine, and scholars differ over whether even Philostratus' supposed source, Damis, is a novelistic invention.[125]

---

[121]Momigliano, *Development*, 56-57; cf. G. Anderson, *Philostratus: Biography and Belles Lettres in the Third Century A.D.* (London/Sydney/Dover, New Hampshire: Croom Helm, 1986) 227-228. Unfortunately I have not been able to see J.A. Fairweather, 'Fiction in the Biographies of Ancient Writers', *Ancient Society* 5 (1974) 231-275.

[122]C.B.R. Pelling, 'Truth and Fiction in Plutarch's *Lives*', in D.A. Russell (ed.), *Antonine Literature* (Oxford: Clarendon Press, 1990) 19-52, shows that Plutarch exercises no greater freedom with his material than most historians did.

[123]The latter is what Reardon, *Form*, 5, calls 'romantic biography', distinguishing it from the novel (romance) proper. He traces it from Xenophon's *Cyropaedia*, through the various forms of the Alexander-romance, to Apollonius' *Life of Philostratus*.

[124]See S. Swain, 'The Reliability of Philostratus' *Lives of the Sophists*', *Classical Antiquity* 10 (1991) 148-163.

[125]Anderson, *Philostratus*, chapters 7-12, defends the authenticity of Damis and tends to a maximal view of the historical material in the *Life*, though he is far from denying the novelistic element, while E.L. Bowie, 'Apollonius of Tyana: Tradition and Reality', *ANRW* II.16.2 (1978) 1663-1667, treats 'the invention of Damis' as 'conscious evocation of a novelistic tone and setting' (1663).

It is also instructive to notice how difficult scholars find it to classify the *Life of Apollonius* generically. Lo Cascio concludes that it is a combination of biography with the novel, the ὑπομνήματα, the panegyric and the aretalogy.[126] Reardon places it midway between biography and the novel, tending to the latter.[127] Raising the alternative of biography or novel, Anderson claims that, 'Philostratus likes to have it both ways, and does not have to exert himself very hard to produce an overlap between the genres'.[128] However, instead of confusing the genre with that of the novel proper, it would be better to say that this example of novelistic biography borrows themes from the novel proper, just as the *Acts of Paul* does. The way in which erotic subplots are included in the story of the ascetic Apollonius, presumably to appeal to the same kind of readership as enjoyed the novels,[129] is parallel to, though not the same as the way erotic themes are introduced into the *Acts of Paul* and the other apocryphal Acts. The semi-fictional or novelistic biography can be influenced by the novel proper, but it is not this influence that makes it semi-fictional. It is in any case a semi-fictional genre, novelistic in its own way.

The *Life of Apollonius*, written probably a few decades later than the *Acts of Paul*, tells the story of a first-century philosopher in a way which is based in history but is also freely imaginative. Another example, perhaps more nearly contemporary with the *Acts of Paul*, is the *Life of Secundus the Philosopher*.[130] Secundus, put to death by Hadrian for keeping to his vow of silence in defiance of the emperor's command to speak, also lived at roughly the same chronological remove from his biography as Paul did from the *Acts of Paul*.[131] The plainly novelistic story told to explain his vow of silence is plausibly understood as 'a romantic and sensational story' woven around the historical fact of the philosopher's silence, which would

[126]F. Lo Cascio, *La forma letteraria della Vita di Apollonio Tianeo* (Palermo, 1974), summarised in van Uytfanghe, 'L'hagiographie', 147 n. 44.

[127]B.P. Reardon, *Courants littéraires grecs des IIe et IIIe·siècles après J.-C.* (Paris, 1971) 10, quoted in Anderson, *Philostratus*, 236 n.1.

[128]Anderson, *Philostratus*, 229. He goes on to find that the closest links are with 'the classic example of romanticised biography, Xenophon's *Cyropaedia*, (231).

[129]Anderson, *Philostratus*, 230.

[130]B.E. Perry, *Secundus the Silent Philosopher* (Philological Monographs 23; Ithaca, New York: Cornell University Press for the American Philological Association, 1964).

[131]On the identity of Secundus, see the differing views of Perry, *Secundus*, 2-3; Anderson, *Philostratus*, 233-234.

no doubt have been actually connected with Pythagorean asceticism.[132] We are here in the same realm of stories developed to explain minimal historical facts as we are in the *Acts of Paul*. That Secundus is portrayed, like Paul, as a martyr also illustrates how at this period stories of heroic deaths for philosophical or religious principle appealed to both pagans and Christians.

In summarising Lo Cascio's view of the genre of the *Life of Apollonius*, I used the word aretalogy, which has not infrequently been applied to the *Life of Apollonius*. When the immense confusion which was caused by the ways in which the concept of aretalogy has been used in twentieth-century scholarship has been dispelled,[133] what the application of this concept to the apocryphal Acts really amounts to is the suggestion of a comparison with those lives of the philosophers which portray them as θεῖοι ἄνδρες, exercising miraculous powers. This was a type of philosophical biography which was only just beginning to be written at the time of the *Acts of Paul*,[134] and which includes the *Life of Apollonius*.[135] There is a general sense in which the Paul of the *Acts of Paul* might be perceived as comparable with such philosophers, though there do not appear to be, as there are in some cases in other apocryphal Acts,[136] specific borrowings of motifs from the lives of the philosophers. (It is tempting to connect the scene when Paul, after his martyrdom, appears to Nero to prove that 'I am not dead, but alive in my God' [MP 6, cf. 4] with Apollonius' appearance after his death to prove the immortality of the soul [*Life of Apollonius* 8.31]. The motif can be found elsewhere,[137] but it is suggestive that Paul appears to Nero when 'many philosophers' were with him.)

---

[132]Perry, *Secundus*, 8.

[133]Representative examples of the now widespread recognition that the term has been much abused, especially in supposedly labelling a genre, are Cox, *Biography*, 46-51; van Uytfanghe, 'L'hagiographie', 141-143.

[134]Van Uytfanghe, 'L'hagiographie', 153-154.

[135]On these biographies, see especially R. Goulet, 'Les Vies de philosophes dans l'Antiquité tardive et leur portée mystérique', in Bovon, *Les Actes Apocryphes*, 161-208, and on the comparison with the apocryphal Acts, see E. Junod, 'Les Vies de philosophes et les Actes apocryphes: un dessein similaires?', in *ibid.*, 209-219.

[136]Junod and Kaestli, *Acta Johannis*, 448-452, 537-541.

[137]See, e.g., R. MacMullen, *Enemies of the Roman Order* (Cambridge, Massachusetts: Harvard University Press, 1966) 96.

However, the Paul of the *Acts of Paul* is no θεῖος ανήρ.[138] There is no interest in him as a model for imitation, but only his missionary function as bringing a message of salvation from God. His miracles—certainly more plentiful and more remarkable than those of Paul in the Lukan Acts—demonstrate and attest his message. His power is from God, not inherent in him (PHeid 31; PH 6). He is 'the servant of God' to whom 'great deeds' are 'granted' for the salvation of people and the praise of God (PH 6). So it is misleading to speak of the *Acts of Paul* as aretalogical. The resemblance to the lives of the philosophers is a broad similarity of genre, not a specific similarity of subject-matter.

From this survey of similarities with other types of literature, it is instructive to observe how features of the *Acts of Paul*—its biographical interest in Paul, its use of erotic (or pseudo-erotic) narrative motifs, its delight in both miraculous escapes and miraculous deeds, its account of Paul's martyrdom—relate to the literary currents precisely of the second half of the second century in which it originated and to those genres of literature which were either reaching the height of their popularity at that time or becoming popular for the first time: the erotic novel, biographical works in general, the novelistic biography and in particular the life of the philosopher as θεῖος ανήρ, martyrology (emerging both as an element in biography and as a distinct genre). These relationships help us to see how an author, intending to continue Luke's story of Paul and modelling himself on Luke's narrative of Paul, was also subject to a variety of contemporary literary influences which account for the differences between the Lukan Acts and his own *Acts of Paul*. The physical description of Paul does not make the *Acts of Paul* a biography. The use of erotic motifs does not make it a novel. But such elements have taken their place in a work hospitable to influence from a variety of genres. Such hospitality, it should be noticed, is characteristic of the genre we have called novelistic biography.

I suggest that three major generic influences have contributed to the emergence of a new genre or subgenre. First, the Acts of the Apostles has significantly determined the form, structure and content of the *Acts of Paul*. Because it is a sequel to Acts, the *Acts of Paul* deals only with the last part of Paul's life, it is structured as an episodic travel-narrative, many of its episodes parallel the kinds of content the

---

[138]On the apocryphal Acts generally, the same point is made by Junod, 'Les Vies de philosophes', 214-215, 217-218.

Acts narrative of Paul's travels contains, and its presentation of Paul is informed by a salvation-historical theological perspective which, while not the same as Luke's, parallels Luke's. Secondly, Jewish literature of the kind often called 'rewritten Bible' has provided a model—as well as exegetical methods—for the use of scriptural texts as starting-points for developing non-scriptural narratives about a scriptural character. Thirdly, the novelistic biography provides a quite flexible genre in which genuine interest in history and freedom for historical imagination are not in tension but go naturally together. Its very flexibility makes it hospitable to borrowings of all kinds from other forms of literature, such as the erotic novel, and the *Acts of Paul* shares this hospitality. All three of these generic precedents would have helped to determine the first readers' understanding of the kind of work they were reading when they read the *Acts of Paul*—no doubt in varying degrees according to their own literary experience.

The result is a work of novelistic biographical character (not strictly a biography) suited to telling the story of a particular kind of historical figure: the Christian apostle. We may regard this as a new genre alongside the novelistic biography or as a subgenre of the novelistic biography.[139]

This conclusion cannot, of course, stand without some reference to the other apocryphal Acts. Despite the individuality of each of the five oldest apocryphal Acts, which recent discussion has stressed and which the present discussion would tend to confirm, nevertheless the similarities are so obvious that any conclusion that the *Acts of Paul* represents a new genre or subgenre which is not that to which the other apocryphal Acts also belong would be hard to defend. The issue is greatly complicated, however, by the fact that we cannot in the present state of research be at all sure either of the chronological order in which the apocryphal Acts were written or of the literary relationships between them. Thus we do not know which authors were composing according to a genre already established for them by the other apocryphal Acts they knew. However, I would suggest, as an heuristic aid to further study of the apocryphal Acts in comparison with one another, that the same three major generic influences that determined the genre of the *Acts of Paul* have gone into the making of the other apocryphal Acts, though in considerably varying degrees and not in every case directly. Thus it may be that,

---

[139]This is more or less how the apocryphal Acts are treated by Reardon, *Form*, 5; cf. Hägg, *Novel*, 160-161.

although the *Acts of Thomas* was not significantly modelled on the Acts of the Apostles, it was written according to a genre of which earlier examples, known to the author of the *Acts of Thomas*, had been influenced by Acts.

There is no doubt that the *Acts of Paul* resembles the Acts of the Apostles more closely than any other of the apocryphal Acts, at least in their extant texts. (How far the lost early section of the *Acts of Peter*, set in Jerusalem, resembled the early chapters of Acts, or whether the beginning of the *Acts of John* was set in Jerusalem and had links with Acts, we cannot know.) Its specific characteristic of being a sequel to the story told in Acts applies to one other text: the *Acts of Peter*, not in its original form, which seems to have told Peter's story from Pentecost onwards, but in its (probably third-century) redacted form as we have it in the Vercelli Acts.[140] There the story begins with Paul's release from captivity in Rome and departure for Spain, prior to Peter's arrival in Rome: an opening clearly designed to link the text to the end of Acts.[141] Of course, we could not expect the *Acts of Andrew* or the *Acts of Thomas* to be written as sequels to Acts. But there is one important way in which the Lukan Acts has determined the genre of all the apocryphal Acts. Though most, not being sequels to Acts but more like narratives parallel to Acts, cover much more of an apostle's life than the *Acts of Paul* does, none, so far as we know, begins the narrative before the resurrection. The genre of the acts of an apostle is defined as the narrative of the missionary activity of an apostle subsequent to the ministry, death and resurrection of Jesus. In telling the story of a single apostle as far as his martyrdom (or, in the unique case of John, death) they manifest the biographical interest which is intrinsic to the genre. But in excluding narration of the life of the apostle before and during the ministry of Jesus, the genre has been determined by the literary division of salvation-history represented by Luke's two volumes and reinforced by the second-century classification of Luke's Gospel with other Gospels and consequent treatment of Acts as a fully separate work. This is what decisively prevents us from simply classifying the apocryphal Acts as novelistic biography and requires that we assign them to a distinct

---

[140]For the original and secondary versions of the *Acts of Peter*, see G. Poupon, 'Les "Actes de Pierre" at leur remainement', *ANRW* II.25.6 (1988) 4363-4383; R. Bauckham, 'Martyrdom of Peter', 579.

[141]Perhaps this opening section of the Vercelli Acts is dependent on the lost opening of the *Acts of Paul*. Note that in chapter 2 Paul celebrates a eucharist with water instead of wine, as he does in the *Acts of Paul* (PH 4).

category, the acts of an apostle, whose structure is importantly determined by the Christian concept of the role of an apostle in salvation-history.

The apocryphal Acts are neither as different from Acts as the mainstream of scholarship has supposed nor as similar to Acts as Pervo has argued. The new genre to which they belong has been decisively influenced by Acts, but is both more biographical and more fictional. Their differences from Acts have much to do with the popular literary currents of the late second and early third centuries in which they originated.

CHAPTER 6

ACTS AND SUBSEQUENT ECCLESIASTICAL HISTORIES

Alanna Nobbs

Summary

Eusebius in the preface to his Ecclesiastical History *claims originality for his attempt to write a narrative history of the church from the time of Jesus. His major themes are set out in his introduction, and pursued throughout the work. Though he is clearly familiar with Acts, both as Scripture and as a source for the writing of the history the church in the early apostolic period, he does not consciously model his history of the church upon Acts. Nevertheless, the themes he selects and his interpretation of how God works in history are in many ways close to Acts. His successors in the genre follow the same line.*

The book of Acts provides us with a narrative and literary history of the early days of the Christian Church covering a period of almost thirty years from the ascension of Christ up until Paul's ministry in Rome. Eusebius of Caesarea (c. 263 to c. 340) was closely familiar with the book of Acts, which he cites in his *Ecclesiastical History* alone no fewer than 85 times.[1] Yet the claims for originality made in the preface to his *Ecclesiastical History* seem to suggest that he saw himself as writing the first narrative and literary history of the church. The present paper will examine the view of the genre of ecclesiastical history taken by Eusebius and his successors, with the aim of determining the influence of Acts upon subsequent ecclesiastical histories. In the present case the scope will be restricted mainly to Eusebius but with some reference to Socrates, Sozomen, Theodoret and Philostorgius, i.e. those ecclesiastical historians who wrote in Greek in the fifth century, to an extent in continuation and imitation of Eusebius' work.[2]

First, it is necessary to look more closely at Eusebius' claim, and then to compare his theme, as he defines it, with that of the book of Acts. By the early fourth century,[3] Eusebius was looking back on roughly 300 years of history from his starting point 'the first dispensation (οἰκονομία) of God concerning our Saviour and Lord Jesus Christ' (H.E. 1.1.2). Given this time span, he had to be selective about which themes he would choose to pursue and these are clearly defined in his opening words (H.E. 1.1.1) as:

(i)   the succession of the holy apostles;
(ii)   the number and nature of the transactions recorded in the history of the church;
(iii)   those who were distinguished as leaders of the church in the most notable provinces;
(iv)   those who were ambassadors of God in speech or writing;
(v)   an enumeration of heretics;
(vi)   the fate of the Jewish nation;
(vii)   an account of persecutions and martyrdoms.

Eusebius had devoted considerable preparation to this task by drawing up extensive chronological lists compiled from the 'scattered memoirs' (H.E. 1.1.4) of earlier writers. Nevertheless, he

---

[1] *Biblia Patristica: index des citations et allusions bibliques dans la littérature patristique*, vol. 4 (Paris, 1975) 278-285.
[2] On this genre, see A. Momigliano, 'Pagan and Christian Historiography in the Fourth Century', in *idem* (ed.), *The Conflict between Paganism and Christianity in the Fourth Century* (Oxford, 1963) 79-99; R.A. Markus, 'Church History and the Early Church Historians', *Studies in Church History* 2 (1975) 1-17.
[3] The date of composition of the various editions of the H.E. is much disputed. See T.D. Barnes, *Constantine and Eusebius* (London, 1981). Recently A. Louth, 'The date of Eusebius' Historia Ecclesiastica', *JTS* 41 (1990) 111-123.

claims to have been the first to have put together such material in a connected narrative. Comparing himself to a traveller on an untrodden path, he says he is the first to enter on this undertaking (ὑπόθεσις, H.E. 1.1.3). This is amplified at 1.1.5, where he claims that the task is necessary because he is unaware of any ecclesiastical writer who has up until this time paid attention to this type of writing. It is important to be clear about the exact terms of his claim. It is a detailed narrative history of the church which is the novel aspect.[4]

Eusebius then launches directly into his subject, beginning (H.E. 1.1.7) with the dispensation of God and the two-fold nature of Christ, a topic of violent controversy between Athanasians and Arians.[5]

Eusebius' preface, it will be noted, makes no allusion to the book of Acts and yet he was certainly not ignorant of its contents. This is revealed not only in the citations of Acts throughout the *Ecclesiastical History* and Eusebius' other writings[6] but also specifically in the use he makes of Acts as a source for the history of the early church, as the following close examination of his text will demonstrate. From this it will be seen that Eusebius knew well, and deeply respected, the book of Acts (and is, incidentally, a major authority for its Lukan authorship).[7]

Eusebius' first book deals with Jesus' lifetime, and so does not make extensive use of the book of Acts. Eusebius does however include in his discussion of the revolt of Judas the Galilean a comparison of the Acts account (Acts 5:37) with that of Josephus, in terms which show his familiarity with the book of Acts (H.E. 1.5.3).[8]

In the second book Eusebius begins with the life of the Apostles after the ascension of Christ. Though he makes use of Acts, it is not his only source and Clement, Philo, Tertullian and Josephus are named as major references. In the case of Philo and Josephus, comparison of particular points is made with Acts.

Eusebius' order of treatment of events is not identical with that of Acts, though the Acts sequence is broadly followed. Eusebius'

---

[4]*HE.* 1.1.3, 5, esp. the phrase ὅτι μηδένα πω εἰς δεῦρο τῶν ἐκκλησιαστικῶν συγγραφέων διέγνων περὶ τοῦτο τῆς γραφῆς σπουδὴν πεποιημένον τὸ μέρος.
[5]Eusebius attempted to reconcile the two groups, and in the process showed a certain sympathy towards Arianism.
[6]For a full list, see *Biblia Patristica* (n. 1).
[7]H.E. 3.4.6-7. Eusebius says too that Acts was an eyewitness account.
[8]ἧς καὶ παρ' ἡμῖν ὁ Λουκᾶς ἐν ταῖς πράξεσιν μνήμην ὧδέ πως λέγων πεποίηται.

history is no replica of any of his sources, but involves his making a judgement of his own about the various opinions, and selecting material according to the criteria set out in the preface.

There are many episodes in Eusebius' second book where Acts is either quoted or closely followed. The selection of Matthias to replace Judas (Acts 1:23-6) is related in the opening section (H.E. 1.12.3). There is less emphasis on Peter's role in the establishment of the church in Eusebius' account than in Acts. Eusebius follows Acts in noting Stephen's appointment to administer the common fund, and the manner and consequences of his death,[9] though the lengthy speech is omitted, in this instance as in others. Eusebius' attitude to speeches in his history in any case differed from that of Acts.[10]

The conversion of Paul in Eusebius' account does not go into any of the details about his vision. At H.E. 2.1.9, Paul's persecution of the Christians in the aftermath of Stephen's death is mentioned (Acts 8:3). Of his conversion, Eusebius simply says that he was chosen through the revelation of Jesus (H.E. 2.1.14). In the case of this and other significant events, where Eusebius' account is briefer than that of Acts, the reader really needs the Acts account to fill in the picture. Eusebius' intended audience would have been assumed to be familiar with the scriptural account, with which Eusebius is certainly not setting himself in conflict.

Other episodes from Acts which Eusebius elects to cover are Philip's visit to Samaria (H.E. 2.9-10; Acts 8:5-13) and the story of Philip and the Ethiopian eunuch (H.E. 2.1.13; Acts 8:26-38). Eusebius (H.E. 2.3.3) repeats the information given in Acts 11 that the name 'Christian' was first used in Antioch, and notes that both Acts and Philo comment on the way the early Christians shared their possessions (H.E. 2.17.6; Acts 2:4, 5).

The heresy of Simon Magus is significant for Eusebius, since the detection and punishment of heresy were important aspects of his theme (H.E. 2.1.12; 13.1-15.1; Acts 8:18-23). The tale of Simon Magus is taken up twice by Eusebius and related in considerably more detail than in Acts, with additional reference to the writings of Justin and Irenaeus.

Again, Eusebius goes into more detail than Acts over the retribution visited by God on Herod for the death of James. Eusebius quotes from Acts (H.E. 2.8.2; Acts 12:1, 2). He also adds information

---

[9]H.E. 2.1.1, 8; Acts 6:1-6; 7:58-59; 8:1; 11:19.
[10]See below, n. 17.

from Clement and Josephus, giving details of the king's death, though he has to explain the different name of the king in Josephus.

After this amplification of the Acts account of the death of Herod, Eusebius does not take up in such detail any of the Acts material, though he continues to refer to Acts, and to compare Josephus where possible. For instance at 2.11.1 he compares Josephus A.I. 20.197-8 with Acts 5:34-6 in relation to Theudas; he then notes (2.12.1) that Josephus (A.I. 20.101) agrees with the Acts account of the famine in Claudius' time, when food was sent via Barnabas and Paul from the Christian community in Antioch for the relief of Judaea (Acts 11:29-30).

Chapters 16-18 of Eusebius' Book 2 follow Philo's writings and relate them to the early church. Eusebius narrates how Aquila and Priscilla came to stay with Paul (H.E. 2.18-19; Acts 18:2, 18-19, 23). The account of Paul's arrest is filled out with discussion of Josephus' accounts of disputes among the Jews and does not repeat much of the Acts account (H.E. 2.21-23). Eusebius is in fact brief where Acts is detailed (H.E. 2.22.1; Acts 25:8-12; 27:1) and assumes that his reader is well acquainted with the ending of Acts (H.E. 2.22.1). Eusebius goes to lengths to add information from traditional stories about Paul's activities after the visit to Rome mentioned at the end of Acts. Eusebius indeed argues that Paul was not martyred on this occasion (H.E. 2.22.7).

Again, Eusebius fills out the Acts narrative considerably in his account of the death of James the brother of Jesus (H.E. 2.23; Acts 23:13-15; 25:3). This elaborated martyrdom is an important part of Eusebius' theme; hence the lengthy and literary treatment.

It would seem clear then that in relation to the form and conception of his work Eusebius does not acknowledge a debt to the first account of the development of the church, though he does make specific acknowledgement of matters of content. Clearly he knew Acts very well, so it is appropriate to seek for the influence of Acts upon Eusebius' conception and presentation of ecclesiastical history.

While the intervening period of nearly 300 years of course made for profound differences between the outlook of Eusebius and that of Acts, several of the major themes of Eusebius are already present, some in incipient fashion, in the book of Acts, and to that extent Acts should be seen to have contributed to defining the notion of ecclesiastical history. By taking Eusebius' declared themes individually, as enumerated above, we can see how each of them has a precursor in Acts.

(i)   the succession of apostles: one of the earliest concerns of Acts;

(ii)   transactions recorded in the history of the church: almost all of the events fall into this category;

(iii) those distinguished as leaders of the church: Acts focuses particularly on the leadership rôle first of Peter, then of Paul;

(iv)   ambassadors of God, in speech or writing: Peter, Stephen and Paul fall into this category in Acts;

(v)   heretics: Simon Magus;

(vi)   the fate of the Jewish nation: the destruction of Jerusalem is outside the time frame of Acts but there are references to concern for the fate of the Jews;

(vii) persecution and martyrdom: several accounts in Acts including the imprisonment of Peter and Paul and the martyrdom of James the brother of John.

These various themes are given a different weighting in the two works, largely because of the different times in which they were written. For instance, there is understandably more emphasis on the spreading of the gospel in Acts, though Eusebius treats it under his heading of ambassadors. The apostolic succession is of particular concern to Eusebius because of the need to prove doctrinal continuity through the apostolic succession.

On a more fundamental level, the view taken of the nature of history in Acts resembles closely that of Eusebius in his *Ecclesiastical History*. There is similarity in the ending and underlying message of the two works. Both end on a note of optimism. In the case of Acts, the final verse leaves Paul's ministry in Rome in full flight.[11] In the case of Eusebius, the church is triumphant over its former persecutors. The hand of God is responsible for the ultimate triumph of Constantine over Licinius and thus of the Church over its enemies. Throughout the book of Acts God is clearly in control. The work of the Holy Spirit permeates the Acts account. The theme of God's providence is fundamental. The hand of God is seen in both works expressed through miracles. These similar views of the purpose of history need not be, and indeed very probably are not, due to the direct influence of Acts on Eusebius, but rather to influences common to both authors. Both were influenced in their conception of history

---

[11]While the ending of Acts has seemed unsatisfactorily indecisive to many modern commentators, the ancient reader would be left with an air of optimism which accords well with the theme of the book. One might compare the open ending of 2 Chronicles.

by the Old Testament and by Hellenistic conceptions of history writing.

The debt of the Book of Acts to the Old Testament is readily apparent especially in the citations in the speeches.[12] A theocratic interpretation of history is fundamental, for example, to 1 and 2 Kings where retribution strikes those such as Omri, who turned from the way of the Lord. Such a view of history was inherent in the Jewish scriptures so it is not surprising to find divine retribution exacted from Herod in Acts.[13] Throughout his tenth Book, Eusebius presents the triumph of Constantine over Licinius as the triumph of God over evil.

God's guiding hand in all human history is the focus both of the book of Acts and Eusebius' *Ecclesiastical History*. This makes for a consistent view point, unlike the at times capricious interventions of fate or fortune found extensively though not universally, in the Graeco-Roman historiographical tradition.[14]

If we now turn to a comparison between the form of Acts and that of Eusebius we see a similarity initially in that both, after the manner common to Graeco-Roman historians, begin with a preface.[15] There is however an important difference in form in relation to a literary feature of Greek historiography. A major departure of Eusebius' *Ecclesiastical History* from classical histories lies in the extensive use made by Eusebius of the verbatim citation of documents, especially letters.[16] Greek and Roman historians generally paraphrased speeches with greater or less rhetorical flourish, to ensure stylistic consistency. In the polemical circumstances under which Eusebius was writing, absolute accuracy was necessary for his arguments to be convincing. In two instances, the accuracy of Eusebius' citation of a document has been confirmed by the discovery of an inscription or a papyrus.[17] Eusebius' successors, Socrates, Sozomen and in particular Theodoret in the fifth

---

[12]E. Earle Ellis, *Paul's Use of the Old Testament* (Grand Rapids, 1957); *idem*, *The Old Testament in Early Christianity* (Tübingen, 1991) 64 and references cited in n. 67.

[13]Colin J. Hemer, *The Book of Acts in the Setting of Hellenistic History* (Tübingen, 1990) 79-85.

[14]John T. Squires, *The Plan of God in Luke-Acts* (Cambridge, 1993) 38-46.

[15]Loveday Alexander, *The Preface to Luke's Gospel* (SNTSMS 78; Cambridge: Cambridge University Press, 1993).

[16]See Momigliano, n. 2 above.

[17]A.H.M. Jones in P.A. Brunt (ed.), *The Roman Economy* (Oxford, 1974) 257ff.; Stephen Mitchell, 'Maximinus and the Christians in A.D. 312: a new Latin inscription', *Journal of Roman Studies* 78 (1988) 105-124.

century continued this practice.[18] It is generally, though not without continuing controversy, agreed that the speeches of Acts, while retaining the substance of what was said, are to some degree adapted (and abbreviated).[19] In the speeches of Acts, appeal is frequently made to Scripture to argue the point and to convince the hearers. Such is the case for instance with Peter's speech (Acts 2:14-40) and Stephen's speech (Acts 7:1-53). This is the same kind of appeal to specific sources which underlies the Eusebian departure from the mainstream of historiographical tradition. It was, too, a feature of Christian apologetic. It is not the case that Graeco-Roman historians never quoted documents verbatim, but they did so rarely. To present an over-sharp contrast between ecclesiastical and classicizing or secular historians on this point can be misleading. For instance, the traditional historian Ammianus Marcellinus, writing in Latin at the end of the fourth century, quoted in Greek the inscriptions on an obelisk which had been brought to Rome.[20]

Conclusion

There are indeed similarities between the way the history of the early church is written up in the book of Acts and the way the history of the church over three hundred years was written up by Eusebius. Some of these are due to the authors' common experience of the way history was presented in the Old Testament and with Greek traditions of history writing. Nevertheless, Eusebius' familiarity with Acts and his use of it as a major source influences his presentation of episodes in the life of the early church. Eusebius' use of Philo and Josephus to corroborate the evidence of Acts shows his desire to convince others of its veracity. On a deeper level, Acts as scripture (along with the rest of the New Testament) moulded his view of the working of God in history. The result is that for both writers God is fully in control of events; miraculous interventions are evidence of this.

Acts does provide us with a connected and literary narrative of the early days of the Christian church, of a kind which Eusebius claimed that his predecessors had not given. We should not fail to

---

[18]Glenn F. Chesnut, *The First Christian Histories* (Paris, 1977) chs. III & VII.
[19]See chapter 10 below.
[20]Ammianus Marcellinus, *Res Gestae* 17.4.18-23.

consider Acts as ecclesiastical history simply because it does not lay claim to it whereas Eusebius does claim to be setting out on a new path.[21] But then nor should we immediately censure Eusebius for failing to acknowledge that he had in some respects his predecessor in the field. It is no doubt the case that since Acts was scripture, he did not see his own work in a similar category. It was important for Eusebius to define his new approach to his genre because he was departing from the classical historical tradition and also from the writings of his more immediate Christian predecessors. His preface was particularly directed at those who would be expecting one or other of these kinds of writing about the past. The definition of his task which Eusebius gives in his preface is appropriate to his projected audience and linked with his (conventional) disclaimer abut his own abilities.

The ancients did sharply differentiate chronicle from history, and it was primarily this distinction that Eusebius had in mind when he claimed his path was untrodden. His confidence in his approach was (we can see with hindsight) justified since he inspired several later historians to continue his ecclesiastical history after a similar fashion to his own, and citing documents. Yet he had covered his chosen ground so thoroughly that none of his successors has left us an attempt to relate the history of the church in the first three centuries. (Sozomen alludes to such an earlier version of his history, now lost.)[22]

The major extant fifth century ecclesiastical histories began from the reign of Constantine. Socrates, Sozomen and Theodoret all were primarily concerned with the development of the Arian controversy during Constantine's reign. This falls outside the scope of Eusebius' *Ecclesiastical History* though not of his later *Life of Constantine*. Philostorgius, the Eunomian historian whose work is preserved only in fragmentary form, also began with Constantine and refers approvingly to Eusebius.[23] Extant ecclesiastical historians subsequent to Eusebius, while modifying some elements of his treatment, in particular the balance between ecclesiastical and secular events, did not go afresh to the early church and rework its history

---

[21]F.F. Bruce, 'The First Church Historian', in James E. Bradley and Richard A. Muller (eds.), *Church, Word and Spirit* (Michigan, 1987) 1-3; cf. n. 10, drawing attention to the judgement of Eduard Meyer.

[22]Sozomen, *H.E. Introd.* (eds. Bidez/Hansen; G.C.S. series; Berlin, 1960).

[23]A.M. Nobbs, 'Philostorgius' History: an "alternative ideology"', *Tyndale Bulletin* 42 (1991) 280-1.

directly from Acts and other sources as Eusebius had done. Their affinities with Acts, apart from their general familiarity with Scripture, are mediated through those features which Eusebius had adopted, consciously and unconsciously.

One persistent feature, common to all ecclesiastical historiography from Acts onwards, is the theme of God's direction of history. His intervention sometimes takes place through miracles, sometimes through natural events such as earthquakes. In the case of orthodox writers, it is the Arians who are visited with divine retribution.[24] For the neo-Arian or Eunomian Philostorgius, God's favour is withdrawn from emperors who persecute the Arians.[25] All of these fifth century ecclesiastical historians join in condemnation of Julian the Apostate, and see the hand of God in his unexpected death during his Persian campaign. This common thread, traceable to the Old Testament before Acts, is interpreted according to the historian's individual views. Philostorgius has a gloomier apocalyptic tone to his view of God's judgement in history. Adherents of the Arian cause were not, by the time he was writing in the late 430s, faring well in the secular world and in imperial favour.

The subject matter of the genre of ecclesiastical history, as defined in Eusebius' preface, but following in several respects closely, as we have argued, the subject matter of Acts, remained the substance of the genre until the sixth century. By the time of Evagrius, writing at the end of the reign of Justinian, it had become impossible to separate ecclesiastical from imperial policy, as they had become fused in the person of the emperor. It is at this point that the particular type of ecclesiastical history pioneered by Eusebius, and influenced in the manner we have seen, by the book of Acts, becomes no longer an appropriate vehicle for the history of the church in later antiquity.[26]

[24]E.g. Socrates, H.E. 1.38; Sozomen, H.E. 2.30.
[25]Philostorgius, H.E. 12.9 (eds. Bidez/Winkelmann; G.C.S. series; Berlin, 1981.)
[26]P. Allen, *Evagrius Scholasticus, the Church Historian* (Louvain, 1981); B. Croke and E. Emmett, 'Historiography in late Antiquity: An Overview', in *idem* (eds.), *History and Historians in Late Antiquity* (Sydney, 1983) 7.

CHAPTER 7

ACTS AND THE 'FORMER TREATISE'

I. Howard Marshall

Summary

The literary relationship between the Gospel of Luke and the Acts of the Apostles has been variously assessed: are they separate works or parts of an integrated whole? After a survey of scholarship the essay argues that the prologues to the two books indicate that they are to be read as one connected story, that various small features in the narratives point in the same direction and that the ending of the Gospel points forward to a sequel. This hypothesis raises fruitful questions about the relevance of the prologue to the Gospel for understanding Acts, the possible genre of the work as a whole, and the structural relationship of the two books.

Our task in this essay is yet another aspect of putting the Book of Acts in its literary setting. That setting manifestly includes the fact that, as we have it, Acts is presented as the second 'treatise' by its author in relation to his earlier work, the Gospel. What precisely is the relationship between these two treatises, and how does it affect our understanding of the second of them?

I. Theories of the Relationship between
the Gospel and Acts

The relationship between the Book of Acts and the Gospel of Luke has been understood in various different ways, and there is a large set of possibilities with significant implications for our understanding. Perhaps a majority of scholars today assume that we are dealing with a single literary work, conveniently designated 'Luke-Acts'; typical of the current approach is the work of R.C. Tannehill whose two-volume work is intended to 'emphasize the unity of Luke-Acts' by showing how it is a narrative unity.[1] Tannehill is aware of objections that might be raised to this assumption, but part of his aim is to defend it by drawing attention to a whole corpus of cross-links, parallels and other literary phenomena which tend to confirm it. His thesis might be summed up as 'See how much fresh light is shed on the narrative in the Gospel and Acts when we treat the two books as a literary unity'.

But is the assumption really justified? It is the complaint of M.C. Parsons and R.I. Pervo that it is no more than an assumption, and that scholars have not tested it adequately; they proceed to produce some arguments which in their view suggest that it is not as well-founded as people think, although they hesitate to say that they have knocked it skyhigh.[2] In fact, there has been a number of different theories regarding the relationship between the Gospel and Acts.

---

[1] R.C. Tannehill, *The Narrative Unity of Luke-Acts; A Literary Interpretation* (Minneapolis: Fortress, Vol. 1, 1986; Vol. 2, 1990). See also W.S. Kurz, *Reading Luke-Acts: Dynamics of Biblical Narrative* (Louisville: Westminster/John Knox, 1993) who likewise assumes 'a unified two-volume narrative' and proceeds to explore the role and activity of the narrator; his findings about the different roles and procedures adopted in different parts of the story confirm the belief that one author is responsible throughout, even though some of them are found in only one of the two volumes.

[2] M.C. Parsons and R.I. Pervo, *Rethinking the Unity of Luke and Acts* (Minneapolis: Fortress, 1993). (I am indebted to Dr. Parsons for the opportunity to see the galleys of this book in advance of the date of publication.) This book brings together the fruits of their earlier studies listed in its bibliography.

1. Separate works by two different authors

The two books are separate works by two different authors, the latter presumably deliberately emulating the style and theology of the first. Although J.C. Hawkins offered a defence of the linguistic unity of the two books by listing their common features, he also noted some interesting differences between them.[3] These differences were exploited by A.C. Clark in 1933 to develop a case against common authorship on the basis of linguistic evidence,[4] but he found no immediate followers.[5] The question was reopened by A.W. Argyle in 1974,[6] who gave a full list of linguistic differences between the two works and appears to have concluded that Acts was an anonymous work; 'the author, being too diffident to write under his own name, took shelter under a better-known name'. The strength of Argyle's case was that he showed how the author of Acts used other words as synonyms for items in the vocabulary of the Gospel. The argument was subjected to devastating criticism by B.E. Beck, who showed (a) that the pairs of words cited by Argyle are often not precise synonyms, (b) that some of the differences in vocabulary may be due to the use of sources, and (c) that within both the Gospel and Acts taken individually the use of synonyms is common.[7] Nevertheless, Beck did not tackle the problem of the significance of the other, undeniable linguistic differences. That such differences can be established between the two works is clear. We may refer in particular to the high relative frequency of τε in Acts compared with the Gospel (9:145), to the variations in the use of the impersonal ἐγένετο construction,[8] and to the relative frequencies of μετά + genitive (51:36) and σύν (23:51).[9] These differences in style may be

---

[3] J.C. Hawkins, *Horae Synopticae* (ed 2; Oxford, 1902) 174-82. Hawkins also discussed the language of the 'we'-sections of Acts and argued that they were written by the main author of Acts and of the Gospel (*Ibid.*, 182-9).

[4] A.C. Clark, *The Acts of the Apostles* (Oxford, 1933) 393-408.

[5] See the reply by W.L. Knox, *The Acts of the Apostles* (Cambridge, 1948) 1-15.

[6] A.W. Argyle, 'The Greek of Luke and Acts', *NTS* 20 (1973-4) 441-5.

[7] B.E. Beck, 'The common authorship of Luke and Acts', *NTS* 23 (1976-7) 346-52. An unpublished paper by D. Deeks advances arguments for separate authorship of Luke and Acts, but unfortunately I have not been able to take it into consideration.

[8] According to Argyle the ratio is 38:17. The usage falls into 3 categories: (a) with accusative and infinitive, 6:17; (B) followed by a finite verb, 22:0; (C) followed by καί and a finite verb, 11:0.

thought sufficiently significant to demand some explanation even on the hypothesis of common authorship. Some would argue that they are fatal to that hypothesis.[10]

2. Separate works by the same author

Beck notes that J.C. Hawkins suggested a gap in time between the composing of the two works.[11] We would then have a basis for the hypothesis that the Gospel and Acts are separate works by the same author.

It has occasionally been suggested that Acts was written before the Gospel. G. Bouwmann finds it strange that Acts does not refer back to the Gospel and argues that its theology is more primitive.[12] Neither point is convincing.[13]

The other, more realistic possibility is that Luke wrote the Gospel first without any thought of a sequel, and then wrote Acts *much later*.[14] On this view, it would surely be inevitable that the author would regard Acts as a sequel to the Gospel. If so, questions arise as to whether the Gospel underwent any revision in the light of

---

[9]The statistics are taken from R. Morgenthaler, *Statistik des neutestamentlichen Wortschatzes* (Zürich/Frankfurt, 1958) with corrections to the Nestle-Aland Greek text of the NT given in his *Beiheft zur 3. and 4. Auflage* (1982). In each case the figures separated by : are for the Gospel and Acts respectively.

[10]In his Fernley-Hartley lecture (1980) on 'The Lukan School in Ephesus', David G. Deeks has put forward the hypothesis that the Gospel and Acts were composed by different authors within the same school. He develops his argument in terms of differences in architecture, theology, style and historical usage and offers a wealth of acute comments in support of it. It is much to be hoped that this study with its fresh and innovative approach will be published. It would be improper of me to enter into discussion of it in advance of the author's definitive presentation of it, and I must allow him to remain poised in ambush on my flank.

[11]J.C. Hawkins, *op. cit.*

[12]G. Bouwmann, *Das dritte Evangelium. Einübung in die formgeschichtliche Methode* (Düsseldorf: Patmos, 1968) 62-7.

[13]This hypothesis is to be distinguished from C.H. Talbert's view that 'Acts has the logical priority in the Lucan scheme' ('The Redaction Critical Quest for Luke the Theologian', in D.G. Miller [ed.], *Jesus and Man's Hope* I [Pittsburgh Theological Seminary, 1970] 171-222, quotation from 202). He argues that Luke's purpose was to present the theme of succession and show how the life of Jesus was lived out in the lives of his successors. On this view Acts was part of Luke's scheme right from the beginning, and it should not be thought of as in any way an afterthought to the Gospel. We shall return to these points later.

[14]G. Schneider, *Die Apostelgeschichte* I (Freiburg: Herder, 1980) 76-82.

the composition of Acts. These revisions might be in any of three areas:

(i) First, there is *the prologue* to the Gospel. Do we have the original prologue, or has it been altered in view of the sequel? Or is the prologue to be understood in any case as applying only to the Gospel? It can be said immediately that there is no textual or other evidence which would enable us to reconstruct an earlier form of the prologue. Opinions differ considerably on whether the prologue, as we now have it, is to be understood as referring only to the Gospel[15] or to the two treatises regarded as a single composition.[16]

(ii) Did the author make any changes in *the general contents* of the Gospel? For example, are there features in the Gospel which point forward to Acts, whether hints taken up later or material left out from his sources to which he supplies an equivalent in Acts?

(iii) Did the author make any changes to *the conclusion* of the Gospel so that it became the ending to a part of the story and in effect an invitation to read further, rather than a final ending?

If we make affirmative replies to any of these three questions, then we are in effect saying that, although the two treatises were composed at an interval, nevertheless in the final intention of the author they were to be regarded as belonging together in some kind of unity.

This view, then, offers a spectrum of possibilities from what we shall call view (2a), that the two books were substantially independent of each other, to what we may call view (2b), that,

---

[15]H. Schürmann, *Das Lukas-Evangelium* (ed 2: Freiburg: Herder, 1982) 4; E. Schweizer, *The Good News according to Luke* (London: SPCK, 1984) 11. E. Haenchen, *Die Apostelgeschichte* (ed 12: Göttingen: Vandenhoeck und Ruprecht, 1959) 105 n. 3 (without argument); H. Conzelmann, *Die Mitte der Zeit* (ed 5; Tübingen: J.C.B. Mohr, 1964) 7 n. 1. See especially G. Schneider, *op. cit.* I, 79-82; also J. Nolland, *Luke 1-9:20* (Waco: Word, 1989) 11f.

[16]I defended this view in 'Luke and His "Gospel"', in P. Stuhlmacher (ed.), *The Gospel and the Gospels* (Grand Rapids: Eerdmans, 1991) 273-92, esp. 278-80. For this view see also, H.J. Cadbury, in *BC* I:2, 492; R. Maddox, *The Purpose of Luke-Acts* (Edinburgh: T. & T. Clark, 1981) 1-6; J.A. Fitzmyer, *The Gospel according to Luke I-IX* (New York: Doubleday, 1981) 289; C.F. Evans, *Saint Luke* (London: SCM Press, 1990) 120f.; F. Bovon, *Das Evangelium nach Lukas (Lk 1,1-9,50)* (Zürich: Benziger/Neukirchen: Neukirchener, 1989) 41f.

however long elapsed between their composition, they were assimilated to each other so as to become in effect a two-part work.

One specific proposal that has been offered in connection with a lengthened time scale for the composition of Luke-Acts is that of C.S.C. Williams who proposed that Luke originally produced a shorter Gospel composed of material from Q and his own special sources ('Proto-Luke') followed by Acts, and then proceeded to make a revised version of the Gospel by the inclusion of material from Mark. The significance of this theory was that it enabled Williams to do justice to the evidence which in his view pointed to a date of composition for Acts before the death of Paul and to a date of composition for the Gospel as we have it after the publication of Mark which was to be dated around A.D. 70.[17] The Proto-Luke hypothesis has not found acceptance among subsequent scholars— with the notable exception of G.B. Caird[18]—and Williams' theory clearly hangs or falls with that hypothesis. Nevertheless, there are in my opinion good grounds for believing that the material in the Gospel which is drawn from the traditions used in common with Matthew (Q) and from Luke's special sources (L) was put together before being combined with the material from Mark. If this was done by Luke himself, this strengthens the view for a lengthier period of composition for the Gospel and hence for the view that Luke could have been working on Acts at the same time.

A somewhat different approach to the problem has been taken by M.C. Parsons and R.I. Pervo.[19] These two scholars argue that, ever since H.J. Cadbury argued for the unity of the Gospel and Acts as a single work, scholars have tended to treat this as an untested assumption and basis for further study. They plead that it should be regarded more as an open question, and they point to various differences between the two works which prevent a simple answer. In particular, they list three areas of difference: a. The varying genres of the two works. Attempts to find a single genre to cover the two-part work have so far not been successful, and the two works appear to vary in genre from one another. b. differences in the narrative. A distinction is drawn between the narrative (the story) and the

---

[17]'The Date of Luke-Acts', *Exp. T* 64 (1952-3) 283f.; *The Acts of the Apostles* (London: Black, 1957) 13-15. See further the authors listed by G. Schneider, *op. cit.*, 79 n. 20.
[18]G.B. Caird, *St Luke* (Harmondsworth: Penguin, 1963).
[19]See n. 2.

discourse (the way in which it is told), and it is argued that the forms of discourse show some subtle variations which are greater than the variations within either of the component parts. c. differences in theology. Arguing that studies of the theology of Luke-Acts have tended to concentrate attention on the Gospel, they begin with Acts and consider its anthropology. They find a continuity between the gods, and humankind and a unity within the human race. To be sure, it is not immediately clear whether they find significant differences between the Gospel and Acts at this point. Rather, their point is that a different picture may emerge if we begin with Acts and see whether the Gospel fits in with it.

The work of Pervo and Parsons, however tentatively it is presented, expresses the main contemporary advocacy of a view that would insist that unity must be argued rather than assumed and that there is prima facie evidence for viewing the Gospel and Acts as two separate, though related works.

3. A two-part work composed as a whole

A third possibility is that we have a two-part work which was composed as a whole, divided into two parts from its inception, and carefully planned accordingly. This view is strongly advanced by R. Pesch over against the possibilities that either part was composed before and independently of the other.[20]

In this case we would have to ask how this unity of composition manifests itself as regards both unconscious factors (the common style of writing) and conscious aims. We should want to know whether the author intended and achieved structural unity, and, if so, of what kind. Such unity might appear in the form of similar types of structure, or one structure covering the whole work, or deliberate parallelisms between the two parts.

4. One continuous work, later separated into two parts

A fourth possibility is that the two books which we now have were originally written as one continuous work which was then separated

---

[20]R. Pesch, *Die Apostelgeschichte* I (Zürich: Benziger/Neukirchen: Neukirchener, 1986) 24f.

into two parts and Luke 24:50-3 and Acts 1:1-5 added to conclude the first part and introduce the second part respectively.[21] This theory has rightly not found favour with contemporary scholars.[22]

If we set aside views 1 and 4 as not commanding serious support among contemporary scholars, the two possibilities listed as 2a and 3 represent the two extremes in a spectrum of possibilities. So far as view 2b is concerned, it can be argued that there is not much difference between two books composed at a longer interval but with the first revised in view of the fact that it now had a sequel, and two books composed from the start as parts of a single work. Again, it could be that Luke wrote the Gospel without thinking of a sequel, but then decided in the course of composition—or perhaps after it was concluded (a request from Theophilus?)—to write a second volume. Thus view 2b is almost indistinguishable, so far as the final result is concerned, from view 3. The real difference is then between two separate works by the same author and a two-part work (whatever the time scale involved and the changes of plan on the way).

In this connection a word needs to be said on 'publication'. It could be claimed that there is no firm evidence for the separate publication of the Gospel apart from and before Acts, but we should then have to ask whether it is meaningful to speak of 'publication'. 'Publication' in the modern sense broadly covers the production of a document and its becoming available to readers whether in one or multiple copies. No doubt once the Gospel (unaccompanied by Acts?) reached Theophilus it could be said to be in the public domain. There is, however, no reason why a revised copy or copies could not be made by the author. What we do not know is whether the Gospel circulated by itself for a time and/or whether it circulated separately from Acts once the latter was written: the introduction to Acts suggests that it was meant to be read as a sequel whether or not it was accompanied by 'Part 1'.

The main evidence for separate circulation is the claim that Marcion's canon apparently consisted of the Gospel and the Pauline Epistles but without Acts. J. Knox asked why Marcion should have omitted Acts if he knew of it, and concluded that Acts did not exist at

---

[21]For this view see the authors listed by G. Schneider, *Die Apostelgeschichte* I, 77 n. 7, especially E. Trocmé, *Le Livre des Actes et l'histoire* (Paris: Presses universitaires de France, 1957) 30-4.
[22]See W.G. Kümmel, *Introduction to the New Testament* (London: SCM Press, 1966) 109-12, 114-39.

this point.[23] His extremely later dating of Acts has rightly not found favour among scholars generally.[24] The question is bound up with that of the canonisation of the two books. Thus B.S. Childs holds that 'Luke was first assigned a canonical sanctity and only subsequently did Acts acquire a similar status'.[25] However, this prior canonisation of the Gospel will have happened because it had been separated from Acts and formed part of the four-gospel collection, and it says nothing about the compositional relationship of the two books.

We thus have in effect two main options before us. The one is that the Gospel was written before and independently of Acts. The other is that Luke produced the two books as two parts of the one work, with some shaping and adaptation of each in a process which cannot now be reconstructed in detail. On the former of these views, we may ask what relationship Acts bears to the previous work, both intended and non-intended; in the case of the Gospel any relationship that exists to its sequel would be entirely due to the effect of creating a subsequent work, just as an object painted in one particular colour may look different when a fresh background is painted in round it, whereas in the case of Acts there would inevitably have been some deliberate attempt to relate it to what went before. If, however, the two works were created as part of one enterprise, then each would have been shaped to some extent in the light of the other. C.K. Barrett has posed the question which volume is of primary importance: there is 'the view that the gospel is primary and Acts serves the gospel by confirming it; the counterpart of this is that Acts is primary, and the gospel serves Acts by introducing it'. He thinks that these two propositions are both correct and they are complementary.[26]

On the one hand, then, our choice between these options affects the question of how we approach and understand the Gospel. If we have a unified work, then the Gospel is not to be understood purely on its own. It is to be seen as an unfinished story at least to some extent, in that it leads on into a sequel. Therefore, it is not enough to

---

[23]J. Knox, *Marcion and the New Testament* (Chicago: University of Chicago Press, 1942) 114-39.

[24]Subsequent commentators have held to the view that Tertullian's evidence is that Marcion deliberately excluded Acts; G. Schneider, *op. cit.*, I, 171.

[25]B.S. Childs, *The New Testament as Canon: An Introduction* (London: SCM Press, 1984) 238.

[26]C.K. Barrett, 'The Third Gospel as a Preface to Acts?' in F. van Segbroek (*et al.*), *The Four Gospels: Festschrift Frans Neirynck* (Leuven: Leuven University Press, 1992) Vol. II, 1451-66.

get at the meaning of the Gospel simply by comparing it with its synoptic companions; it must also be seen in comparison with Acts. Questions must be asked to what extent it does contain a story and message of its own as compared with containing part of a story and message.

On the other hand, the same questions also arise with our understanding of Acts—is it to be understood on its own and is it a complete work in itself? Or does one need to understand the Gospel in order to understand it? Clearly, the writer presupposes some knowledge of what preceded—and deliberately points his readers backwards—but is this the same thing as to say that the readers must have a knowledge of the actual Gospel? Again, is a 'theology of Acts' a meaningful exercise as opposed to a 'theology of Luke-Acts'? Do we fail to do justice to either the Gospel or Acts by treating them together? Are we right to stick to the principle that the Gospel and Acts must be regarded as components of a two-part work with all that this implies for understanding them?

II. The Unity of Luke-Acts

In our opinion the view that the Gospel and Acts are intended to be read as two parts of the one, unified work is to be preferred for such reasons as the following:

1. The evidence of the prologues to the two books

The prologue to Acts, reminiscent in language of the prologue to the Gospel, establishes that in their present form we have two parts of one work. In her study of the preface(s) L. Alexander states that the use of the re-capitulatory preface does not demand that the two treatises are necessarily closely linked together: the evidence from ancient prefaces indicates that we could have two works which 'while complementing each other, are none the less very different in conception'.[27] Against Alexander, however, it is to be observed that more often than not the recapitulation is used where the works are closely linked, and further that the similarity in theme between the

---

[27]L. Alexander, *The preface to Luke's Gospel: Literary convention and social context in Luke 1.1-14 and Acts 1.1* (Cambridge: CUP, 1993) 146.

Gospel and Acts as well as the close chronological relationship make it extremely likely that Luke saw Acts as being tied closely to the Gospel, and that Alexander is carrying a proper scholarly caution to excess.

This would make it surprising if the prologue to the gospel was not conceived as referring to the whole work, although it has to be allowed that a prologue could refer to only the first volume of a series. Alexander again notes that the preface to the Gospel 'applies much more directly to the Gospel than to Acts'. But the crucial phrase here is 'much more', and hence the vital question is whether there are any aspects of the prologue which require a reference to Acts or which find a better and fuller explanation if they include a reference to Acts.[28]

It is, then significant that Luke refers to the 'things' which have 'come to fulfilment' among 'us'. Granted that the 'us' refers to Christians generally, the phrase is more easily explained if it refers to what happened in the experience of the readers and therefore includes the growth and establishment of the Christian churches.[29] The use of 'things' in the plural is an odd way of referring simply to the life-story of one person. And the use of 'fulfil' may also suggest more than simply the life of Jesus, the more especially since Jesus himself spoke of things that were yet to be fulfilled in the activity of his followers (Lk. 24:47-9).

Verse 2 of course refers to activity in the church. However, the question arises as to why the phrase 'from the beginning' had to be included. Does this time reference not imply that the events in question carried on 'from the beginning' to an unspecified point. Alexander's note that Paul himself is described in Acts 26:16 in almost identical terms as 'a witness and servant' may suggest that Luke saw him as one of the group on whose evidence he relied, and she herself allows this conclusion.[30]

Then in verse 3 there is the celebrated problem of the participle which may be translated 'being thoroughly familiar with' or perhaps 'having followed [them] all, sc. as sources'.[31] This again is open to the

---

[28]Cf. M. Korn, *Die Geschichte Jesu in veränderter Zeit* (Tübingen: J.C.B. Mohr, 1993) 6-32.

[29]C.F. Evans, *op. cit.*, 124.

[30]L. Alexander, *op. cit.*, 124.

[31]*Ibid.*, 128-30.

interpretation that Luke himself had a personal familiarity with what had happened, but this is somewhat weaker.

Finally, there is the point in verse 4 that Christian instruction is likely to have covered far more than the contents of the Gospels and to have included something of the apostolic preaching—and conceivably of its working and effects.

These points cumulatively suggest that the prologue is not only broad enough to include Acts but also is better understood against this wider background.[32] We can certainly say at the least that there is nothing in Acts which is inconsistent with the description of the whole work given here. Alexander holds that there would be a problem if we were unable 'to show that Acts too is an account of traditional material'.[33] Recent study indicates that there is a substantial traditional basis to Acts.[34]

2. The evidence of material in the Gospel as a whole

This falls into a number of categories.

a. We are able to demonstrate that in a number of places material in the Gospel which has been taken over from sources appears to have been redacted in the light of what was to follow in Acts.[35]

R. Pesch suggests that the change from 'clouds' in Mark 13:26 to 'cloud' in Luke 21:27 is to suit the 'cloud' (sing.) in Acts 1:9-11 which prefigures the parousia. He also notes that the addition of 'prison' to the prophecy in Luke 21:12 reflects the events in Acts. He

---

[32]Cf. C.K. Barrett, op. cit., 1463f., who argues that some ambiguities in the prologue are due to Luke's intention that it should apply to both parts of his work.

[33]L. Alexander, op. cit., 206. For the view that traditions about the early church existed and were used in Acts see J. Jervell, Luke and the people of God (Minneapolis: Augsburg, 1972) 19-39

[34]See G. Lüdemann, Early Christianity according to the Traditions in Acts: A Commentary (London: SCM Press, 1989). My own view is that Lüdemann does not go far enough in recognising the degree of reliable tradition in Acts (I.H. Marshall, The Acts of the Apostles [Sheffield: JSOT Press, 1992] 82-99). R. Pesch holds that the corrections made in the Gospel which reflect knowledge of situations in Acts (he is thinking of sanhedrin procedures) show that Luke was dependent on traditions. This leads him to the significant inference that Luke used traditions in Acts which have influenced the Gospel as well (op. cit. I, 25).

[35]For what follows see especially R. Pesch, op. cit. I, 24f. Cf. Bruce, The Acts of the Apostles, 102, 249, 282.

might also have noted the corresponding change in Luke 22:33 which points forward to the story in Acts 12.

b. There are instances where Luke has not taken over material from his sources in the Gospel but there is an equivalent in Acts.

Here we may note the omission of the material in Mark 7 on purity and the healing of a Gentile—a theme which is reserved for Acts 10-11.

Luke has no parallel in the Gospel to Mark 13:32, but there is an equivalent in Acts 1:7.

Luke omits the 'temple saying' in the trial of Jesus—which is reserved for the trial of Stephen.

c. There is some material in the Gospel which is prophetic of what is to happen in Acts (this category overlaps with category a). C.K. Barrett offers a list of possible instances of this kind and makes a cautious selection of those which are most plausible. His selection includes Luke 3:6; 3:15; 11:49; 14:15-24; 21:12-19; 22:31-34.[36]

Here we note especially the instructions regarding the mission of the disciples after Easter in Luke 24. The detail given here is significant, and above all the fact that it comes at the end of the book and prepares the way for what is to follow.

d. There are alterations in the Gospel which reflect knowledge of traditions attested in Acts. Pesch claims that the setting of the sanhedrin trial by day and not by night shows the knowledge of procedure from traditions found in Acts 4-5. Similarly Luke 21:15 differs from Mark 13:11 in the light of trial procedure, and Luke 22:54 differs from Mark 14:53 in its reference to Jesus being 'arrested' in agreement with Acts 1:16.

3. The ending of the Gospel

There is the question whether the ending of the Gospel shows signs of adaptation from an earlier form to allow for a sequel and whether in any case the ending does prepare for a sequel. (The question is complicated by the possibility that scribes may have altered the wording of both the end of the Gospel and the beginning of Acts

---

[36]Op. cit., 1453-61.

when the two works were separated from each other by inclusion in a canon which interposed John as the fourth Gospel before Acts.)[37]

The end of the Gospel and the beginning of Acts have been thoroughly discussed by M.C. Parsons. He rightly argued that there is no evidence for interpolation in either passage, and he shows how Luke has used the ascension story to provide the closure for the Gospel and the narrative beginning for Acts; the repetition serves to tie the two volumes together. Where Parsons, however, is not so clear is on whether the ending is an 'incomplete closure', encouraging the reader to believe that he has reached a temporary terminus and there is yet more to come. On the whole, he appears to accept this view:

> . . .conflict is resolved only to be reopened in Acts—the fate of Israel still undecided by the end of Luke. Many prophecies and predictions do *not* find fulfilment within the narrative time of the Gospel. The journey of Jesus is finished; but his *analempsis* is 'to be continued' in Book II.[38]

At this point we have to take into account the prophetic elements in the Gospel which point forward to Acts, and which are especially found in the concluding sections. There is no doubt that this feature is strongly emphasised in Luke. Luke 24:49 in particular stands in tension with verse 53 and invites resolution. The story is not finished—but is the narrative? After all, the other Gospels each conclude with commands whose fulfilment is not recorded, and we have no grounds to suspect a second volume in any of these cases. At best, then, this point is in the nature of a step in a cumulative argument.

The weight of these considerations points strongly in our opinion to the hypothesis that the Gospel was published as the first part of a two-volume composition, whatever be the process by which it came to its present form. Elsewhere I have argued the case that Luke's justification for his fresh attempt to give an account of 'the things that have taken place among us' was in the fact that his

---

[37]F.F. Bruce, *The Acts of the Apostles* (Leicester: Apollos, 1990) 98f., refers to this suggestion to which he had originally given some support in the first edition of his commentary, but he had by then abandoned it. B.M. Metzger, *A Textual Commentary on the Greek New Testament* (London: United Bible Societies, 1971) 273-7. See E. Haenchen, *op. cit.*, 107 n. 3. H. Conzelmann, *Die Mitte der Zeit*, 7 n. 1, 86 n. 3, 189 n. 4, argued that Lk. 24:50-3 was an interpolation.

[38]M.C. Parsons, *The Departure of Jesus in Luke-Acts* (Sheffield: JSOT Press, 1987) 113.

predecessors had treated only the material contained in the Gospel and not gone on to present other, comparably important material about the spread of the gospel. Their story was incomplete. Luke rightly saw that a story which told merely what Jesus *began* to say and do needed to be taken further if the church was to understand its beginnings and its marching orders aright.[39]

III. The Consequences for understanding Acts:

1. The applicability of the prologue

If the prologue to the gospel covers both parts of the work, what follows?

a. The material in Acts belongs in the category of 'the things accomplished among us' and 'us' refers to the author and a broad group of people. This point is significant—1. the story of the early church is part of what was prophesied and has been brought to fulfilment; 2. there may be a sense of completion in that the coming of salvation has been fully accomplished.

b. The material in Acts as well as that in the Gospel was handed down by the witnesses and servants of the word. This need not apply to all of the material; it leaves scope for the author's personal knowledge.

c. Luke's claim to careful composition extends to Acts. This is not to say that Acts is necessarily a reliable narrative. It is to say that Luke makes the same claims for reliable composition in Acts as for the Gospel, and his work should be assessed in terms of what he was aiming to do.

d. The material in which Theophilus had been instructed would include at least some aspects of the post-Easter story. This fits in with the view that the proclamation of the gospel included some reference to the development of the church.

---

[39]I.H. Marshall, 'Luke and his "Gospel"' (see n. 13 above).

2. The genre of Luke-Acts

If the Gospel and Acts are regarded as independent works, then the question of genre arises in a different form from when they are parts of the same work.

On its first view, the genre of the Gospel is a matter to be considered on its own, and the most probable conclusion is that the Gospel is a work of the same kind as its one known predecessor, the Gospel of Mark. The similarities in structure and content are fairly obvious.[40] Equally, the genre of Acts is a matter to be considered on its own.

If, however, we see the Gospel and Acts as two parts of one work, then the question is that of the genre of Luke-Acts as a whole. We should still have to ask whether one can have a whole which contains two different kinds of part (in which case we are back with the previous way of asking the question).

Scholars who take the view that Luke-Acts is a unified piece or who have discussed the genre of Acts by itself have tended to think in terms of a historical monograph—a useful category that can be distinguished from a universal history. This view has been developed especially by D.E. Aune who gives a valuable survey of the different types of ancient history and finds that Luke-Acts as a whole fits into this category.[41] This agrees in essentials with the view of D. Palmer elsewhere in this volume, although he does not tie the Gospel and Acts too tightly together as two volumes of a single work but rather as two related works by a single author.[42] Another view is that Acts is a historical romance or historical fiction.[43] This last view can be dismissed for a number of reasons; here it is appropriate simply to

---

[40]One possibility is that the Gospel is a biography, although this genre is inappropriate for Acts. For a nuanced discussion see A. Dihle, 'The Gospels and Greek Biography', in P. Stuhlmacher (ed.), *The Gospel and the Gospels* (Grand Rapids: Eerdmans, 1991) 361-86.

[41]D.E. Aune, *The New Testament in Its Literary Environment* (Philadelphia: Westminster, 1987). See further E. Plümacher, 'Die Missionsreden der Apostelgeschichte und Dionys von Halikarnass', *NTS* 39 (1993) 161-77, who continues to maintain that Acts falls into the category of history and not of biography or romance.

[42]See D. Palmer, 'Acts and the Historical Monograph', above.

[43]R.I. Pervo, *Profit with Delight: The Literary Genre of the Acts of the Apostles* (Philadelphia: Fortress, 1987). Cf. R. Kany, 'Der Lukanische Bericht von Tod und Auferstehung Jesu aus der Sicht eines hellenistischen Romanlesers', *Nov. T* 28 (1986) 75-90, who extends the question to the Gospel.

comment that it is an improbable characterisation of the sequel to a Gospel which is demonstrably based in large measure on sources which have been redacted but not revamped. A third possibility, that Acts is an aretalogy, has not commanded any following.

Here we need to take account of the theory of C.H. Talbert that Luke-Acts resembles the Hellenistic type of 'succession narrative', a biography or *bios* which deals with the life of a philosopher and his subsequent influence.[44] Both Aune and Alexander have noted a number of difficulties with this proposal.[45] D.L. Barr and J.L. Wentling have likewise pointed to problems in Talbert's approach. They concede that the Gospel shows some biographical features, but do not think that Acts can be satisfactorily accounted for in this way.[46] Nevertheless Alexander notes that the place of biography within the school tradition needs further investigation.

L. Alexander's own thesis is that Luke's work belongs in the category of the scientific treatise—and this is argued primarily from the prologue to the Gospel (which may or may not cover both parts of the work; however, it would seem that the author would regard the description as also fitting Acts even if the prologue is intended simply to introduce the Gospel). If so, we would need to ask in more detail what kind of works fell into the category of such treatises—the list of types is quite extensive and does not include anything of quite this kind. Alexander's work does not really get beyond arguing that the prologue falls into a specific genre: the implications for the genre of the work as a whole are not raised. In particular, the question of those characteristics of the work which are typical of the historical genre is not discussed. In this connection one thinks particularly of the speeches. It may be, of course, that scholars in the past have been off target in evaluating the speeches by comparison with the historians. Their function is partly to exemplify the church's preaching and partly to offer defence of the apostles and their task. Proclamation and defence sum up their functions.

It would seem so far that no proposal to account for Luke-Acts in terms of known genres has been successful. Even within the

---

[44]C.H. Talbert, *Literary patterns, theological themes and the genre of Luke-Acts* (Missoula: Scholars Press, 1974) 125-40.
[45]D.E. Aune, *op. cit.*, 781; L. Alexander, *op. cit.*, 202-4.
[46]D.L. Barr & J.L. Wentling, 'The conventions of classical biography and the genre of Luke-Acts, a preliminary study', in C.H. Talbert (ed.), *Luke-Acts: new perspectives from the Society of Biblical Literature Seminar* (New York: Crossroad, 1984) 63-88.

Christian context there is nothing corresponding to it: Christians produced apocryphal Gospels and apocryphal Acts, but not apocryphal Gospels-cum-Acts. The whole work demonstrates affinities both to historical monographs and to biographies, but it appears to represent a new type of work, of which it is the only example, in which under the shape of a 'scientific treatise' Luke has produced a work which deals with 'the beginnings of Christianity'. One can, of course, argue with Parsons and Pervo that the difficulty of coming up with a genre for 'Luke-Acts' is an indication that we are really dealing with two separate works each with its own genre, but this ignores the possibility that a new phenomenon required a new genre to give it adequate expression.

3. The structure of Luke-Acts

If Acts is regarded as the sequel to the Gospel, important questions arise regarding the way in which the contents of the two books are related. A number of scholars have seen a general similarity between the structure of the two books. Earlier proposals were brought together in a comprehensive list of parallels by C.H. Talbert who argued for 'a loose correspondence of content and sequence between persons and events in the Third Gospel and those of the Acts'.[47] Talbert lists some 32 general correspondences that occur in the same order in both books, and then notes some correspondences between Luke 24 and Acts 1 and between Luke 9:1-34 and Acts 1:1-12. It is not too difficult to find such echoes and resemblances. Indeed, we may expect them to occur since the experiences and teaching of Jesus and his followers would inevitably show resemblances.

One particular aspect has been developed in great detail by W. Radl, who traces detailed resemblances between the pictures of Jesus and Paul, particularly in regard to their sufferings and the theological understanding of these events. This resemblance has been developed redactionally by Luke at the cost of fidelity to the traditions which he used—and therefore at the cost of historicity.[48] Radl claims that much

---

[47]C.H. Talbert, op. cit., 22.
[48]W. Radl, Paulus und Jesus im lukanischen Doppelwerk: Untersuchungen zu Parallelmotiven im Lukasevangelium und in der Apostelgeschichte (Bern: H. Lang/Frankfurt: P. Lang, 1975). See also Radl's parallels are:
1. The prediction				Acts 9:15f./Lk. 2:32, 34b.
2. The beginning				Acts 13:14-52/Lk. 4:16-30.

of what Luke writes is free invention with little or no historical basis, and thus he had the freedom to mould the account to bring out a parallel between Paul and Jesus.

For Radl, then, the unity of Luke-Acts is tied up with a verdict of non-historicity on certain sections of Acts. However, Radl's negative attitude to historicity is not dependent upon his view of the unity of the two works. Rather the judgement that a section of the narrative is not based squarely on history or tradition but shows signs of free Lukan creation or modification is what allows him to go on to look for a particular *Tendenz* in it, namely the shaping of the narrative to give a parallel with the Gospel. It would still be fair to claim that Luke saw parallels between the stories of Jesus and Paul and drew attention to them without working on the presupposition of non-historicity, although we might wish to assess the extent of the *Tendenz* somewhat differently. We can question one of Radl's presuppositions without necessarily denying totally the validity of a hypothesis partly built on dubious foundations.

The Gospel thus to some extent constitutes the matrix for Acts in that it establishes the first part of the story and sets the programme for what is to follow, namely the way in which good news spread and embraced the Gentiles. Acts tells the story of how the followers of Jesus bore witness to him and of the obstacles which they had to overcome in so doing. And it brings out the way in which their task and the way in which they fulfilled it followed a pattern similar to that of Jesus himself.

But are the two stories told in the same kind of way? Here we must interact briefly with the consideration brought forward by Parsons and Pervo in claiming that the stories are told differently and so perhaps are different stories. There are, to be sure, some manifest differences between the Gospel and Acts which can be largely accounted for in terms of the fact that Luke had at least one existing model for the Gospel and was dependent on a set of traditions which had a peculiar status within the early churches whereas the source

---

3.	Turning towards to Jerusalem	Acts 19:21/Lk. 22:21-38.
4.	The farewell discourse	Acts 20:18-35/Lk. 22:21-38.
5.	Prophecies of suffering	Acts 20:22-25; 21:4, 10-12/Lk. 9:22,44f.; 12:50; 13:32f.; 17:25; 18:31-34.
6.	Face to face with death	Acts 20:36-8; 21:5f., 13f./Lk. 22:39-46.
7.	Suffering	Acts 21:27-26:32/Lk. 22:47-23:25.
8.	Paul's journey to Rome—a parallel to Jesus' death and resurrection.	
9.	Acts 28:17-19 and the Lukan passion.	

situation for Acts was somewhat different. There is also the fact that Luke presents himself as having participated personally in some of the episodes in Acts, whereas he makes no such claim for the Gospel. Parsons and Pervo draw attention to the fact that the characters in Acts do not imitate the teaching of Jesus, but there is ample evidence that the early kerygma was not in fact an attempt to repeat what Jesus had said, and therefore a literary explanation of the point is inappropriate. Other points which they make are not particularly compelling. On the whole, it appears that they have not paid sufficient regard to the peculiar place that the Jesus-tradition occupied in the early church.

Conclusion

Our study has been confined to the literary relationship between the Gospel and Acts. It lies beyond the scope of this volume to discuss in any detail the theology of Acts. Accordingly, such questions as that raised above by G. Bouwmann concerning the allegedly more primitive character of the theology of Acts or the question of Luke's anthropology raised by Parsons and Pervo must be set aside for possible treatment elsewhere.[49] For the moment it must suffice to have stated our view that the Acts is to be seen in close literary association with the Gospel. They form two parts of one work, conceived in its final form as a unity, whether or not the original composition of the Gospel took place independently of the plan to produce the two-part work. Although there are other examples of literary compositions in two parts (Josephus, *Contra Apionem*, is one of the nearest parallels to Luke-Acts in time and cultural context), Luke's work appears to be unique among Christian writings and to have no close secular precedents in its combination of the stories of a religious leader and of his followers.

---

[49]W. Radl, *Paulus und Jesus im lukanischen Doppelwerk: Untersuchungen zu Parallel-motiven im Lukasevangelium und in der Apostelgeschichte* (Bern: H. Lang/Frankfurt/M., 1975).

CHAPTER 8

ACTS AND THE PAULINE CORPUS I: ANCIENT LITERARY PARALLELS

T. Hillard, A. Nobbs and B. Winter

Summary

The purpose of this composite chapter is to present case studies on Cicero, Favorinus and Julian, some of whose literary remains we possess in addition to biographical material by their contemporaries or near contemporaries. These are being examined in order to test the implications for the study of the relationship between Acts and the Pauline corpus. Placing the latter in this wider literary perspective helps to clarify issues concerning the treatment of Paul in Acts.

I. Introduction

In a mere handful of instances from Graeco-Roman antiquity does the ancient historian have first-hand documents (e.g. letters or speeches) written by a particular figure together with a near-contemporary historical account of that same figure. Such a combination of sources provides a rare insight into our understanding of the past.

It is even rarer for the documents written by the figure concerned to be accompanied by a historical account written by a historian who was personally involved in the events related and who was with him on some of the major expeditions. At least three instances exist—one from the Roman Republic, another from the early Roman empire and one from the late Roman empire.[1]

The first concerns Cicero and the Catilinarian conspiracy in which Cicero was a leading player and later recorded speeches made during the tumultuous events of 63 B.C. in Rome. Sallust, a contemporary historian, was to write of it in his *Bellum Catilinae* after the death of the major participants in it.

The second, Favorinus, was a leading sophist of the early second century A.D. whose extant remains consist of three orations and on whom there is information and speeches in the work of Gellius. As his student and friend he was a companion of Favorinus and heard some of his speeches which he translated into Latin. A short biographical entry on Favorinus is to be found in Philostratus' *Lives of the Sophists* which was written some eighty years after his death.

Lastly there was the emperor Julian the Apostate many of whose orations and letters are extant and whom the historian Ammianus Marcellinus writes of in his *Res Gestae*. The latter gives eyewitness accounts of some events from A.D. 353 onwards.

These case studies will be dealt with in chronological order by the three authors and conclusions drawn at the end of the chapter will help place Acts and the Pauline corpus in the setting of these ancient literary parallels.

---

[1] D.W.J. Gill has drawn attention to another helpful parallel in Marcus Aurelius. His own correspondence and his *Meditations* are extant and there is biographical material in Dio Cassius' *Roman History* and the later *Historia Augusta*. For an outstanding biography see A. Birley, *Marcus Aurelius: A Biography* (London: B.T. Batsford, 1987) esp. 226-31 for discussion of sources.

II. Cicero and Sallust (T. Hillard)

The year 64 B.C. had seen unprecedented pressure at Rome for debt relief.[2] Marcus Tullius Cicero whose election to Rome's chief executive office dismayed Rome's ruling élite, was a staunch champion of the propertied classes. In the following year's election campaign for consuls, the patrician Lucius Sergius Catilina (Catiline) emerged as a champion of the debtors. His election speech was sufficient excuse for Cicero, as the presiding officer, to postpone them.[3] Catiline's defence of it before the Senate[4] was enough in itself to ensure that Catiline lost the election (when it was at last held). Catiline had now been thwarted in a number of quests for the consulship and he had also lost the elections of the preceding year (when in competition with Cicero).

Discontent in various parts of Italy continued (no doubt exacerbated by Catiline's defeat at the polls). The Senate passed an emergency decree and offered a reward for information relating to any sedition.[5] When news reached Rome of an insurrection in Tuscany, Cicero delivered a blistering attack on Catiline at the Senate, claiming secret intelligence of a conspiracy and that he (i.e. Catiline) lay behind all the unrest and a foiled assassination attempt on Cicero's life the morning before. Catiline left Rome to command the rebels at Faesulae (Fiesole). Messengers were arrested carrying letters which implicated a number of prominent citizens in sedition and collaboration with Catiline. Cicero addressed the people, claiming that the 'conspirators' had planned to set fire to the city of Rome. According to Sallust, supporters of those imprisoned now scoured the streets seeking to stir up a following and secure their release. The Senate duly executed those implicated (Cicero was the chief executive officer) that evening. In early January of the next year (62), Catiline died in battle against the consular Roman forces. The rights and wrongs of the case (and including some details outlined above) instantly became a matter of intense public debate.

These tumultuous events of 63 B.C. are recorded by one of the principal participants, Cicero, in his speeches and by the historian

---

[2]Cicero writing two decades afterwards: *de Officiis*.

[3]Cicero, *pro Murena* 51.

[4]*Ibid.*, 52. 'The crowded Senate groaned', says Cicero: *congemuit senatus frequens*.

[5]A *senatus consultum ultimum*, ultimate senate resolution, traditionally giving sweeping powers to the executive for the purpose of securing order.

Sallust. For the year 63, Cicero left speeches in abundance.[6] They were not, strictly speaking, the primary documents which they might at first sight appear to be. Like so many ancient speeches published by the author, they were re-worked; in this case, a good three years after the event. Cicero himself provides some background on the context (see pp. 188ff.).

Two decades later Gaius Sallustius Crispus (Sallust), looking back on a misspent public career,[7] had turned to the writing of history as a way of making amends, to himself—and to the public.[8] He chose to begin by publishing an account of the events of 63 as a focus which might provide edification for a lost generation:

> It is my intention to give a brief account, as accurate as I can make it, of the conspiracy of Catiline, a criminal enterprise which I consider specially memorable as being unprecedented in itself and fraught with unprecedented dangers to Rome.[9]

Sallust thus makes it clear from the outset on which side of the fence he stands. If there were debates as to the merits of Catiline's stand (or as to the exact nature of his plans) and over the propriety of executive action in 63, they did not sway Sallust. Catiline was an evil; those who suppressed him had served Rome. In broader historical terms, his account will not differ from Cicero's.

1. Cicero

Cicero left behind his version of events in a multiplicity of forms. Numerous references to the events crop up in his personal correspondence. Relevant speeches (which purport to be speeches delivered both during and after the crisis) are extant. He also wrote a poem *de Consulatu Suo* (of which only fragments survive), verse

---

[6] And clearly did not subsequently feel any embarrassment about their circulation.

[7] *Catiline* 3.3 (Penguin trans.).

[8] 'You must work hard to find words worthy of your subject. And if you censure misdeeds, most people will accuse you of envy and malice. When you write of the outstanding merit and glory of good men [*not* a common feature of Sallustian historiography], people are quite ready to accept what they think they could easily do themselves; but anything beyond that is dismissed as an improbable fiction': Sallust, *Catiline* 1-2 (Penguin trans.).

[9] *Ibid.*, 4.3f.

eulogies of his consular actions in both Greek and Latin, a poem *de Temporibus Suis* ('On His Times') and a secret history that was either so honest or so defamatory that he left instructions for it not to be published during his lifetime. It was later circulating amongst historians. (The last may or may not have been available to Sallust.) Certainly there was no dearth.[10]

All this material was available to Sallust if he sought to achieve the fullest possible understanding of events—and the designs of one of the historical principals. The writings of others of the chief historical actors were also available. In the same way, it might be expected that a chronicler of Paul's missions would avail himself of Paul's own compositions if they were available.

a. Letters

Letter-writing in Rome might well have been an art (even by the age of Cicero), epideictic by intention,[11] and by the time of Pliny the Younger (the other great letter-writer of pagan Rome whose output has been preserved) the letter as literary genre had come into its own. The letters give every impression of being polished essays.[12] This is

---

[10]For a convenient survey of the Ciceronian material (and other evidence) see P. McGushin, *C. Sallustius Crispus: Bellum Catilinae. A Commentary* (Mnemosyne; Leiden: E J Brill, 1977) 7-9. On the 'secret history', see the discussion of B.A. Marshall, *A Historical Commentary on Asconius* (Columbia: University of Missouri Press, 1985) 44-45.

[11]Letters of condolence or consolation may well have been such in republican Rome. Cicero refers to this on the death of Atticus' grandmother: *ad Atticum* 1.3. Compare the famous letter of Cornelia. Genuine or not, Cornelia is seen as addressing her son, as one scholar puts it, 'as if he were a public meeting'.

[12]'To understand Pliny's significance as letter writer it is necessary to observe what an *epistula* from his hand meant. We have nothing quite like it earlier. . .' (J. Wight Duff, *A Literary History of Rome in the Silver Age*, 541). This need not mean that Pliny was the pioneer. 'Classical Greece presents in this field relatively slight remains. . .As travel and separation greatly predispose to letter writing, it is natural to think that the breadth of interest which furnishes the best epistolary equipment came more easily to a Rome in the days of a world empire. . .The letter, as published by Pliny, goes far beyond the scope of the simplest private form written to make a request or give information. . .the epistle has overstepped the rigid bounds of a letter; it has become a *causerie* on paper. . .The recipient really represents the great public, while Pliny ranges at will anywhere through the width of human life among themes likely to provide interesting material. . .' (*ibid.*, 541-3).

not so with Cicero's correspondence which seems very much of the moment and frequently offers intimate revelations.[13]

But as regards the crisis of 63, the correspondence serves us little: there are a few letters to Titus Pomponius Atticus, his closest confidante, *before* 63, none in 62 but six in 61 (when Cicero often casts the odd backward glance on those events),[14] an exchange of letters with the proconsul of Cisalpine Gaul in January 62, a letter to Rome's much celebrated homecoming general Pompey in April of the same year, a letter to a certain Sestius in mid or late 62 and a letter to his former consular colleague, Gaius Antonius in December.[15] There is precious little here.

b. Speeches

Cicero's published speeches deal much more fully (not to say colourfully) with events. They were intended for public consumption. How should they be approached? When it comes to their use as historical evidence, it is the question of their original purpose which first springs to the historian's mind. Was the author's intention likely to lead to a distortion of the facts?

One recent school of thought would see the speeches as published for school use; as case studies for oratorical training; as textbooks in public speaking (and Cicero's satisfaction as derived

---

[13]Some of Cicero's correspondence was composed as public statement. After the crisis of 63 had been resolved (to Cicero's satisfaction), he wrote a letter (unfortunately not extant) to the general Pompey, absent in the East on military campaign. It was clearly not intended for the recipient's eyes alone. Nor was that its fate. In the following year, its contents were cited in open court as if public knowledge and Cicero did not feign embarrassment at their revelation. Cicero, *pro Sulla* 67. Other correspondence (surely the bulk of that which is today available) was surely not intended at the time for public perusal. Some of it is abrupt, other parts routine. It is ephemeral. The style is often allusive, sometimes cryptic. Concern for the security of communication is expressed, and a form of code sometimes introduced to thwart prying attentions. A letter such as that wherein Cicero discusses with his intimate friend Atticus the rights and wrongs, as he sees them, in the troubled marriage of their respective siblings, should convince any reader that we are reading genuine communication rather than an essay on marriage. Indeed the revelations of Cicero's letters have led to one extreme hypothesis that they were posthumously published to discredit the author, see J. Carcopino, *Les secrets de la correspondence de Cicéron* (Paris, 1974).
[14]Atticus, whom Cicero trusted and to whom he willingly opened his mind (which makes the correspondence between them so valuable), had been urgently summoned to his side in 63 itself, to share the danger and offer wisdom in the more immediate context.
[15]Cicero, *ad Familiares* (To his Friends) 5.1-2; 7; 6 and 5.

from association with masterpieces of persuasive discourse).[16] On the other hand, modern scholarship has had a tendency to see them as political pamphlets.[17] The implications of either classification for the modern scholar will be clear. If didactic, they might *seem* to be less problematic for the modern investigator (though this need not be the case); if political, caution must prevail. And each item of the contents must be weighed against the possible political advantage to be gained by the author.

Of course, they might be both. One purpose could be nominal, the other obvious. That is to say, particular examples might be released for the relatively 'innocent' purpose of education, but only if it was at the author's political convenience and certainly not if it was likely to prove to his disadvantage.[18] Even if the didactic purpose *was* the primary one, the historical use of the speeches is not plain sailing for they may indeed be closer to uncontaminated documents of a historical moment—but they may also have been 'improved' (in the interests, of course, of providing the best possible samples for

---

[16]W. Stroh, *Taxis und Taktik* (Stuttgart, 1975) 50-52

[17]For a recent discussion of the reasons for publication, see J.W. Crawford, *M. Tullius Cicero: The Lost and Unpublished Orations* (Hypomnemata 80; Göttingen: Vandenhoeck and Ruprecht, 1984) 3ff.

[18]There can be no question that Cicero was clearly aware of the political ramifications of publication. On one particularly painful occasion, we find him embarrassed by the untimely and undesirable circulation of a piece of history: 'Then you have given me a blow about the circulation of that speech. Try, as you say, to patch up the damage if you can. I did write it long ago in a fit of annoyance with him because *he* had written against me, but I suppressed it and never expected it to leak out. How it did get out I don't know. However, as I have never exchanged a contentious word with him in my life and as it seems to me more carelessly written than my other compositions, I think it may be passed off on internal evidence as a forgery. Would you please see to that, if you think my case is curable?' (*ad Atticum* 3.12.2, Penguin trans.).

We may observe there a note of professional pride, suggesting that standards of oratory provided the criteria by which a piece was judged worthy of publication, though clearly the composition and limited circulation originally intended were politically inspired, just as the present embarrassment was politically governed.

A similar discussion, however, seems to confirm the dual purpose of publication, and particularly the importance of the secondary (i.e. the political) while affirming the nominal (i.e. the educational). It sits in a letter to his brother Quintus and refers to a speech against Cicero published by one of his enemies whom he had previously attacked in a well-circulated speech of his own: 'I am surprised that you think I should write a reply to that, especially as nobody will read it if I don't reply, whereas all schoolchildren learn mine against him as though by dictation' (*ad Quintum fratrem* 3.1.11).

students!) and, even if not modified, they carried with them the political slant or tendentious argument that may have marked the original. This original in the case of either a forensic or political speech, was never intended to tell the *whole* story, but to be persuasive.[19]

In 60 B.C. politics was warming up and there were clouds on Cicero's horizon in that criticism of the severity of executive action in 63 was threatening to become more of a political issue than Cicero might have wished. When he wrote to Atticus in early June of that year he announced:

> I'll send my little speeches, both those you ask for and some more besides, since it appears that you too find pleasure in these performances which the enthusiasm of my young admirers prompts me to put on paper. Remembering what a brilliant show your countryman Demosthenes made in his so-called *Philippics* and how he turned away from this argumentative, forensic type of oratory to appear in the more elevated role of statesman, I thought it would be a good thing for me too to have some speeches to my name which might be called 'Consular'. They are: (1) delivered in the Senate on the Kalends of January; (2) to the Assembly, on the agrarian law; (3) on Otho; (4) in defence of Rabirius; (5) on the children of persons proscribed; (6) delivered when I publicly resigned my province; (7) when I sent Catiline out of Rome; (8) to the Assembly the day following Catiline's flight; (9) at a public meeting the day the Allobroges turned informers; (10) in the Senate on the Nones of December. [Seven of those survive.] There are two further short pieces, chips, one might say, from the agrarian law. I shall see you get the whole *corpus*, and since you like my writings as well as my doings, the same compositions will show you both what I did and what I said. Otherwise you shouldn't have asked—I was not forcing myself upon you.[20]

These are useful sources for any historian wishing subsequently to reconstruct events. Clearly any historical protagonist would wish that this documentary material generously provided would be of assistance to later chroniclers. Caesar is said to have provided his *commentarii* as the raw material from which later historians would

---

[19]Cicero, we know, prided himself on his powers of obfuscation; Quintilian, *Institutes of Oratory* 2.17.21; cf. R. Nisbet, in T.A. Dorey (ed.), *Cicero* (London: Routledge and Kegan Paul, 1964) 59-60.
[20]*ad Att.* 2.1.6.

draw. The apparently unpretentious elegance of his own composition dissuaded reworkings.[21]

So it was with Cicero. In the same letter cited above, he acknowledges receipt of a draft of Atticus' celebration of his achievements, a sketch in Greek. He professes pleasure in it, but between the lines there is a strong hint that he was disappointed with its understatedness. 'Now *my* book has used up Isocrates' entire perfume cabinet along with all the other little scent boxes of his pupils, and some of Aristotle's rouge as well.' (Here Cicero is talking of 'Clio's cosmetics', the touch-ups applied to History—to give the muse colour.)[22] '. . .Poseidonius has already written from Rhodes that when he read this *ébauche* of mine, which I had sent him with the idea that he might compose something more elaborate on the same theme, so far was he from being stimulated to composition, he was frightened away. The fact is, I have dumbfounded the whole Greek community so that folk who were pressing me on all sides to give them something to dress up are pestering me no longer. If you like the book, please see that it is made available at Athens and other Greek towns. I think it may add some lustre to my achievements.'

Cicero had been anxious to stamp his understanding of the way things had happened on the record[23] but seems to have had difficulty inducing chroniclers to lay the foundations for him to enjoy during his life.[24]

2. Sallust

The historical account which would do most to immortalise the events of 63, that of Sallust, appeared after Cicero's death. Sallust had no known close bond with the events of 63, but wrote within a

---

[21]Suetonius, *Divus Iulius* 5.

[22]On which subject, see T.P. Wiseman, *Clio's Cosmetics: Three Studies in Greco-Roman Literature* (Leicester: Leicester University Press, 1979).

[23]On Cicero's anxiety on the score of posterity's judgement, *ad Att.* 2.5.1. (It is a common refrain of his.)

[24]He had, as we saw above, (inadvertently) scared them off, he liked to think, with his eloquence. Possibly other literary artists simply felt that Cicero had done the topic to death. He tried to interest the historian Lucceius in the project (and the letter he wrote to the historian, *ad Familiares* 5.12, is well worth reading for its views on the manner in which the hard facts might be 'improved' by a warm treatment) but any success in that regard is unknown. It is significant, then, that Sallust felt he had something worthwhile to offer here, something new to add.

generation of the event (which had occurred during his lifetime). He may be styled, therefore, as contemporary; but his account may not. It was written around 43 when all the major protagonists were dead. All the same, Sallust's approach to the task may usefully be analysed.

How did he go about researching the topic—or remembering? He had been twenty-three years old in 63.[25] Cicero's material was available. He *may* have used it. (It is usually assumed that he *was* familiar with it since he refers to it.)[26] Other letters were also available. He *did* use those. He cites, and quotes, letters by Catiline and other 'conspirators'. Other speeches and documents were available. Cicero had cautiously ensured that the interrogation and responses of witnesses who came forward to denounce the 'conspirators' (and possibly all the speeches delivered on those fateful days of December 4th-5th) were taken down by four specially selected senatorial 'stenographers';[27] this was no common occurrence as senatorial deliberations were not regularly reported until 59 B.C. Cicero claimed that he had this evidence broadcast throughout Italy, and indeed to all the provinces.[28] The pivotal speech in the final debate of Cato the Younger was, it seems, published and available to later researchers.[29] A speech against Catiline by the orator Lucceius survived to be put to later academic use.[30]

One thing is certain: 'documents' (Ciceronian or otherwise) in no way provided the core of his research. Nor is the Ciceronian material used in any dramatic way such that it seems, to the modern eye, tailor-made. To take one obvious example, Cicero's 'First Catilinarian' speech of November 8th was by any account a pivotal moment in the unfolding drama. It opens pungently and to the point: 'For just how long, Catiline, will you abuse our patience? For how long will your insanity make fools of us?' Other memorable rhetorical moments follow. *O tempora, o mores* opens the next paragraph. Sallust eschews the opportunity to borrow eloquence, or to compete by providing his *own* version of the speech (such as was

---

[25]On the evidence for Sallust's birthdate, see Ramsey, *op. cit.,* 1.
[26]It is sometimes argued that he was particularly influenced by Cicero's *pro Sulla* delivered in 62.
[27]Cicero, *pro Sulla* 41-42.
[28]*Ibid.,* 43: 'And so I say that there is no place in the world where the name of the Roman people is known to which this transcribed evidence has not come'.
[29]Plutarch, *Cato minor* 23
[30]It is referred to by Asconius in his commentary on Cicero's *in Toga Candida* (Clark, 92)

the custom of some historians). 'Cicero', Sallust says, 'either fearing Catiline's continued presence or from rage', made 'a substantial speech of service to the state, which he afterwards wrote down and published.' That is all. There follows a lengthy gloss of Catiline's futile response to Cicero's *tour-de-force*, culminating with the report that the hapless Catiline was howled down when he would have continued his protest. One might almost suspect, as it has been suggested, that Sallust (for diverse reasons speculated) intentionally sets out to downgrade the role of Cicero. Overall, the work is a defence of Cicero's stand. Cicero is called *optimus consul* ('excellent consul').[31] But there is not as much here as Cicero hoped for in his lifetime. It is Catiline, the anti-hero, who is centre stage.

Sallust prefers his own, more general sources of information: word of mouth, general report, and rumour. The general memory found a place in his information gathering. That he placed great store by it is indicated by his withholding his authority from specific beliefs. 'Some, I know, have believed that young men who resorted to Catiline's house practised unnatural lewdness; but this rumour was credited rather because the rest of their conduct made it seem a likely inference than because anyone knew it to be so.'[32] On other occasions too,[33] his report of what was generally believed at the time indicates that he personally declines to vouchsafe the particular story. Elsewhere,[34] he offers variant rumours.[35] He could fall back on the memories of some of the major players and his personal acquaintance (at what degree of familiarity we cannot know) with those men. At 48.9 he reports his own hearing of an assertion by Marcus Licinius Crassus, one of Rome's most influential men at the time, who had been implicated by informers in the 'conspiracy': 'Afterwards, I actually heard Crassus declare that this great contumely had been made against him by Cicero'. Sallust would, then, seek confirmation of items which stretched his credulity or on which he was aware of

---

[31]Faint praise, perhaps, in view of Cicero's hopes.

[32]14.7 (Penguin trans.).

[33]For example at 17.1.

[34]For example at 19.4 and at 48.7-8.

[35]At section 22, he prefaces a report that Catiline forced his confederates into horrendous rites (oaths taken over human blood etc.) with 'There were those at the time who said. . .' This is followed by the statement that 'others' thought this a fabrication and concluded with the disclaimer, 'For my own part, I have too little evidence for pronouncing upon a matter of such weight'.

(or admitted) controversy. Documentary analysis does not seem to have offered itself as a solution.

Here we might briefly note the almost decorative use to which the correspondence of Catiline was put. How much of it was available? We cannot know. This one item was preserved and made public by the recipient. Sallust introduces his one example by reporting that Catiline, on the eve of his final departure from Rome, wrote to a number of the city's leading men, vindicating his position and asserting his innocence and victimisation. Sallust's announcement of its quotation seems formally to decree its authenticity. *Earum exemplum infra scriptum est.* 'Below is written a copy of the letter' (34.3). It is worth reading in full. It has all the hallmarks of a genuine document and is generally accepted by scholars to be so.[36] The style of the letter is not Sallustian, and a number of words and phrases which are not found elsewhere in Sallust's distinctive prose occur here.

What is remarkable about this letter is the image of Catiline which emerges. We hear the man himself. And the picture, not surprisingly perhaps, is very different to that offered by Sallust (and Catiline's other detractors in antiquity, who otherwise have the ear of history). The point is that Sallust seems to have felt no constraint to mould it more smoothly into his narrative. It seems to have been presented as a relic rather than as a piece of evidence and it has played no appreciable part in the formation of Sallust's view of Catiline; nor does Sallust feel any obligation to explain its paradoxical impact. Taste or design, then, took Sallust's composition away from the documentary evidence.

The ancient historian, Ronald Syme's assessment of Sallust's account judges Sallust to be credulous in his use particularly of Cicero. Writing recent history was, of course difficult, because of the 'plethora of evidence'.[37] Sallust, says Syme, was aware of the bias in Cicero's speeches, yet in fact accepted their version of Catiline as villain (and worse). Nevertheless, Sallust claimed not to be writing in a partisan manner (Sallust, *Cat.* 4.2). As a particular case, Syme argues that Sallust has given credence to an alleged, but dubious 'first Catiliniarian conspiracy'.[38]

---

[36]See, for example, Syme, *op. cit.*, 71-77; McGushin, *op. cit.*, 195-196; Ramsey, *op. cit.*, 159-162.
[37]Syme, *op. cit.*, 83.
[38]Syme, *op. cit.*, 93-4.

The Catiliniarian conspiracy of 63 has been overestimated by posterity, because of its importance to Cicero and the emphasis he laid on it in his speeches. Syme judges Sallust's prime defect as a historian to be the way he accepted Cicero's conception of the affair.[39] The result for historians has been grave difficulty in reconstructing the pro-Catilinarian (or even neutral) version of events from such partisan material.

Conclusions

What options do ancient historians have in dealing with these sources? Broadly speaking there are four options: (1) to mesh the two accounts (traditionally the favoured approach), using Sallust's narrative as a base and inserting details from Cicero's extant material, all the time rationalising discrepancies; (2) to choose Sallust as the favoured guide because of the greater coherence of his account (*not* a particularly defensible line of thought in source criticism) and (more defensible) because of a reluctance to trust Cicero's manifest partisanship and because of warning bells sounded *within* Cicero's evidence; (3) to give preference to Cicero's evidence wherever it conflicts with Sallust as 'documentary evidence'; or (4) to distrust *both* accounts because of discrepancies and internal contradictions.

Approach (3) might be divided into an approach which reposes trust in Cicero's information and, to go further, sees it as endorsed, at least as something which must have seemed credible at the time, by its public reception (which cannot be assumed); and the more critical approach which would treat Cicero's evidence as documentary but with caution, regarding public reception as thin validation.

This third approach is often fed or fuelled by a line of thinking which demonstrates little faith in the veracity of the 'Ciceronian version'; namely, to distrust Sallust precisely because, independent of Cicero though he might be (and though he hints at a certain critical independence, almost inadvertently, with his retail of stories told against Catiline), he shares the same basic view, i.e. some received interpretation or 'line' of the Catilinarian affair, and shows little appreciation of the deep divisions of opinion in contemporary society regarding the events. Sallust accepted a certain interpretation of

---

[39]Syme, *op. cit.*, 136.

events and then applied his skills to the most effective presentation of that picture. His was not a critical analysis.

The fourth approach seems the best advised to me given the proven degree to which ancient writers can play fast and loose with fact if it improves presentation. This leaves the ancient historian with the need to work with both Cicero *and* Sallust (who remain the chief sources) and to devise a working strategy if any attempt to reconstruct events is to be made. It would be sheer foolishness to discard either one or the other, even if manifestations of inaccuracy or mendacity are described (and proven to a historian's satisfaction). As with daily affairs, there is no one view of reality—a neat version of history may be satisfying, but is unlikely to be beyond challenge. Indeed, the discrepancies are valuable precisely because they sound warning bells, bells that would not have been sounded had we possessed only one account. They raise questions which would never have been asked if we had possessed only one or other of the sources.

III. Favorinus, Gellius and Philostratus (B. Winter)

The extant orations of Favorinus (A.D. c. 90 – mid second century) and of Gellius (A.D. c. 125-8 – c. 180) provide an important literary parallel to Acts and the Pauline corpus. Favorinus is referred to by Gellius as his teacher and friend. Gellius's work contains references to shared experiences as well as reported speeches of Favorinus from occasions when both dined together;[40] there is also a relatively short biographical entry on him in the extended work on *Lives of the Sophists* 489–92 by Philostratus (A.D. c. 170 – c. 249) which was written c. 230. This is interesting evidence which provides an opportunity to evaluate autobiographical information with the contemporary profile by Gellius and a short biography by Philostratus written some eighty years after his death.

---

[40]There are differences as well. Unlike the Pauline corpus where there are only fragmentary negative comments on him which provide biographical data (2 Cor. 10:10, 11:6 and 12:14ff.) we do possess criticisms of Favorinus by Polemo who engaged in a bitter and highly personal attack on him (for the text see G. Hoffmann, *Scriptores physiognomonici* 1.93-294 and Galen who devoted a work on the best education in which he is critical of the teaching method of Favorinus, Περὶ ἀρίστης διδασκαλίας).

1. Favorinus[41]

Of the literary works of Favorinus we possess an oration delivered by him to the Corinthians on the occasion of his third visit to that Roman colony c. A.D. 110.[42] He takes them to task because of their unjust move in relation to a bronze statue they erected as no small honour to his great rhetorical abilities as the complete Hellenophile in this highly prestigious and powerful Roman colony in which wealthy Greeks themselves jockeyed for civic honours. He presents his case against the Corinthians in a very skilful oration complaining that they 'banished it [the statue] not only without holding any trial, but also without having any charge at all to bring against it' (16). His impact on Roman Greece is reflected in portions of the wording of the inscription on the pedestal which was resolved by the Council and the People who authorised the erection of the statue, preserved in the oration. He was 'noblest among the Greeks' and had operated for 'the good of the city and for all the Greeks' (22-23). He provides a short autobiographical account informing the Corinthians that he was:

> a Roman, not one of the masses but of the equestrian order, one who has affected, not merely the language, but also the thought and manners and dress of the Greeks, and that too with such mastery and manifest success as no one among either the Romans of earlier days or the Greeks of his own time, I must say, has achieved. . .he inclines toward the Greek [as against the Greek orators who have gone to Rome to seek their fortune] and to that end is sacrificing both his property and his political standing and absolutely everything, aiming to achieve one thing at the cost of all else, namely, not only to seem Greek but to be Greek too. . . (25).

---

[41]He was a virtuoso orator of the Second Sophistic who was born c. A.D. 90 in Arles and died in the middle of the next century. He was among the élite of Rome who moved in the imperial circle until sent into exile to the East by Hadrian and was attacked by another significant orator, Polemo. He was restored to imperial favour by Antonius Pius and was to secure his status and influence in the capital where he remained until his death.

[42]Or. 37 in Dio Chrysostom's corpus. For the arguments attributing this and Or. 64 to Favorinus see A. Barigazzi, *Favorino di Arelate: Opera Introduzione, Testo Critico e Commento* (Florence: Lelice Le Monnier, 1966) 245, 298ff.

Even allowing for overstatement Favorinus made an enormous impact not only on Rome and the Celts (he was born in Arelate) but in Greece where he has revived 'hellenism' among the Greeks—'all look to this man' (27).

He alludes to the slander to which he has been subjected and argues in his defence that this is not uncommon as men in the public arena in the past have been subjected to similar unfounded accusations. He calls them to remember that in the midst of the lax morals of the Greeks he had 'lived a decent life' as they knew, and what would cause him to change his behaviour when living under the nose of the emperor in Rome. An unnamed informer is responsible for this unjust accusation (31-35). Of this accusation Philostratus points out the paradox and irony of the charge that although a eunuch he was 'tried for adultery' (*Lives of the Sophists* 489).

Favorinus informs the audience of the requests made for his services by various cities. Sophists in the early empire filled an important political role in local politics and on embassies to governors on behalf of cities. He was sent 'here and there' and his success results in the erection of statues in various cities in appreciation for his services (37). He concludes with a moving *peroratio* where he speaks 'words of comfort to my friend, my statue' and after citing Hesiod affirms that he will be resurrected and placed in the precinct of the goddess, presumably of Fame, where none will be able to tear him down '—not earthquake or wind or snow or rain or jealousy or foe' (47). This is a very polished oration with literary allusions, historical precedents which were very skilfully presented for the purposes of playing on the emotions, mounting a 'legal' case against them in order to shame them into restoring his honour by re-erecting his statue. It yields autobiographical details within the context of the oration in much the same way Paul does in his letters to the Corinthians in particular as he seeks to persuade them concerning the attitude some have adopted towards him.

His second work on *Fortune* reveals his religious convictions as he argues for the providential role of this goddess, Τύχη, over the affairs of men and women (*Or.* 64). He sees the goddess reproached for all the calamities that occur and the problems that humanity experiences—emotional weaknesses and physical dangers on land and sea. Fortune also controls what is allotted '—to orator or to general, to rich or poor, to old or young' (26), and gives the good things of life (7). He takes Diogenes, the Cynic, to task for railing against Fortune. He claimed that although 'she had shot many shafts against him as her target, she could not hit him' (18). Fortune would hit him if she wished, Favorinus asserts. He then enumerates the shafts that have hit Diogenes. 'She made you an exile; she brought you to Athens. . .if staff and wallet and a meagre, simple mode of living serve you as a cloak of affection, you have Fortune to thank even for these things, for it is by grace of Fortune that you practise philosophy' (18). Here and elsewhere in the oration there is a feeling of a personal witness of how he himself coped with the fortunes and misfortunes of his own life, especially during the period of his relegation from Rome.

His third extant oration is on this very theme of exile, *De Exilio*, which uses various Stoic and Cynic motifs.[43] The work has a fourfold structure which discusses how exile brings about the loss of fatherland, relatives, reputation and riches and finally freedom which he regards as the most important.[44] Some modern authors have doubted that Favorinus actually underwent exile.[45] However the actual references scattered throughout the extensive work would suggest otherwise—'For me, even before my enforced exile, ἐμοὶ δὲ ᾧ καὶ πρὸ τῆς ἀναγκαίας φυγῆς, the majority of my life was spent throughout many parts of land and sea, in the company of foreign people, away from home' (11:8ff.). 'Missing one's family and friends, on top of loving one's country, is set out as a second battle in addition to that one, as it recalls one's origin and one's common nurture, going to school together and spending time in the same ways in the gymnasiums, good times with one's contemporaries and close friends, these are like a spell, a bait alluring the soul' (12:39ff.). The place of his 'relegation', rather than 'exile' was apparently Chios

---

[43]L. Holford–Strevens, *Aulus Gellius* (London: Duckworth, 1988) 78.
[44]This is a more recently discovered treatise which provides this autobiographical details. *P.Vat.Gr.* II (early 3rd century A.D.). For a critical edition see A. Barigazzi, *op. cit.*, 375-409.
[45]For those in favour of exile see C.P. Jones, *Roman World of Dio Chrysostom* (Loeb Classical Monographs; Cambridge, Mass. and London: Harvard University Press, 1978) 46 and 48, *contra* G.W. Bowersock, *op. cit.*, 36 who holds that the exile is by no means a secure fact. Bowersock discusses this in relation to the immunities granted by emperors and the reasons for exile generally and appears to have overlooked some comments by Favorinus himself cited above.

(14:39ff.). It was by means of Stoic and Cynic sentiments that something of the pain and difficulty of exile are dealt with by Favorinus who is both a philosopher and a sophist. That he raises the issues in the way he does reveals the personal experience of this period in the wilderness before his restoration to Rome under Antonius Pius where he continues to function in imperial circles until his death. Another personal detail that emerges from this work is his personal devotion to his sister who is mentioned in a reference to his parents (11:22-24).

Although none of the orations was intended as autobiographical work yet they yield substantial information on Favorinus. While the Corinthian oration was written to shame and persuade the hearers because the personal honour of Favorinus was at stake, it provided great insights into the life and character of this second-century virtuoso orator. The other two orations reveal much concerning his testimony as to how as a philosopher he coped with personal adversity.[46]

2. Gellius on Favorinus

Holford–Strevens begins his chapter on Favorinus in his recent book on Gellius with the observation 'Of no contemporary does Gellius speak so often or so warmly as of Favorinus. . .Gellius attached himself on leaving the schools of rhetoric; even afterwards he loved him as a friend, and revered him as a teacher'.[47] What biographical portrait emerges from his pen?

Gellius *Attic Nights* records a number of occasions when they dined or discussed issues with others. Gellius himself relishes such occasions—'His delightful conversation held my mind enthralled, and I attended him wherever he went, as if actually taken prisoner by

---

[46]Criticisms are to be found in the work of Polemo who mounts a bitter personal attack on one with whom he debated both in Asia Minor and Rome. Galen is critical of the teaching method of Favorinus who appears to have presented both sides of the argument to his pupils without drawing conclusions. These works are cited in n. 41.

[47]L. Holford–Strevens, *op. cit.*, 72. B. Baldwin, *Studies in Aulus Gellius* (Lawrence, Kansas: Coronado Press, 1975) has counted some 27 appearances and quotations and allusions to him on 6 more occasions.

his eloquence; to such a degree did he constantly delight me with his most agreeable discourse' (16.3.1). While Philostratus casts him in the sophist's mould of engaging in strife with other orators (*Lives of the Sophists* 490-91), Favorinus emerges from Gellius' pages as a perceptive observer of the problem when friends do not take side where reconciliation is needed.

> The philosopher Favorinus thought that this same course ought to be adopted also with brothers, or friends at odds. . .that those who are neutral and kindly disposed towards both parties, if they have had little influence in bringing about reconciliation because they have not made their friendly feelings evident, should then take sides, some one and some the other, and through this manifestation of devotion pave the way for restoring harmony. 'But as it is,' said he, 'most of the friends of both parties make a merit of abandoning the two disputants leaving them to the tender mercies of ill-disposed or greedy advisers, who, animated by hatred or by avarice, add fuel to their strife and inflame their passions' (2.12.5).

In public he is cast as arbiter in a discussion between a Stoic and a Peripatetic on the role of virtue in determining the happy life and whether happiness was dependent on external circumstances (18.1). 'That Favorinus, with his personal charm, his rhetor's invention, and his polyhistor's stock of themes and information, could take charge of the proceedings is entirely credible', concludes Holford-Strevens commenting on 4.18.[48] His discussion for example of the winds reveals his semantic interests as well as his knowledge of ancient authors whose works are regularly cited throughout his works, as one would expect of a man of his education. On the meaning of a passage from Sallust's *Catiline* we find him seeking the views of others, offering a suggestion and commenting negatively on the view of another because it misrepresented the work of an ancient author (3.1.6, 14). His custom was to have a slave standing at the table reading either from Greek or Latin literature while he was dining with friends (3.19). He emerges as one who belonged to a lively literary circle.[49] When he read a passage from a history his mind was stirred and affected by no less emotion and excitement than if he were himself an eye-witness of their contest (9.13.5).

---

[48]L. Holford–Strevens, *op. cit.*, 88.
[49]C.P. Jones, *Plutarch and Rome* (Oxford, 1971) 35 on his friendship with Plutarch.

The report of the visit by Favorinus who was accompanied by Gellius to the famous Fronto shows something of the measure of our philosopher. In a debate on colour words in Greek and Latin Favorinus concedes defeat and does so acknowledging the erudition of Fronto (2.26.20).

On recorded speeches interesting features emerge. Only one is a monologue. Most arise out of the context of meals in the convention of the *symposium*. There is a discourse by Favorinus in which he urges that a woman of rank must feed her children herself and not allow a wet nurse to do it (12.1). The context is the visit to a friend to rejoice in the birth of a child and the view impressed by the grandmother present that her daughter should not be restricted by having to feed the baby. At the end Gellius writes 'I heard Favorinus make this address in the Greek language. I have reproduced his sentiments, so far as I was able, for the sake of their general utility, but the elegance, copiousness and richness of his words hardly any power of Latin eloquence could equal, least of all my humble attainments' (12.1.24). As Baldwin notes 'Gellius normally presents, with suitable modesty about his style, a Latin paraphrase'.[50] At the end of one dinner discussion Gellius writes 'This is what Favorinus recounted to us at his own table. . .with extreme elegance of diction and in a delightful style throughout' (2.22.27). He adds a comment on the discussion which Favorinus may have added with hindsight. There is a further observation not attributed to Favorinus (2.22.31). On the latter the editor observes 'Gellius, as he sometimes does elsewhere, refers to Favorinus' statement as if it were his own'.[51]

Favorinus in discussing a syllogism that either you marry a beautiful or an ugly woman indicates that there is a third possibility i.e. to marry a 'normal' woman i.e. one with moderate and modest beauty which he called 'conjugal' (5.11.8-13). Sections 1-7 cite an ancient author and commentary by Gellius. There follows both direct and indirect speech ascribed to Favorinus where the latter is presented in summary form.[52] What conclusions can be drawn about the verbatim speeches and summaries of speeches by Gellius? He

---

[50]B. Baldwin, *op. cit.*, 28.

[51]J.C. Rolfe, *Aulus Gellius*, LCL, 1.191 n. 5.

[52]L. Holford–Strevens, *op. cit.*, 87 postulates 'we may believe that he [Favorinus] repeated orally in Latin, what he also included in a Greek treatise on marriage. . .but not that Gellius worked from such a text'.

aimed to report them carefully, sometimes in direct speech and on other occasions as summaries in indirect speech.

In conclusion, Gellius produces a portrait of Favorinus which endorses the *Suda's* entry lauding his learning and his list of publications only three of which are extant. 'His constant lecturettes on linguistic points and fund of recondite knowledge befit the polymath author of an encyclopaedia.'[53] He is a philosopher and regularly introduced as such and is not portrayed as a sophist by Gellius.

3. *Philostratus on Favorinus*

The personal details about the nature and activities of Favorinus which arise from personal friendship and contact which are found in Gellius stands in sharp contrast to the biographical entry by Philostratus who writes about him some eighty years after his death. What can be said of this short biography and the role which it plays in this extended work on the *Lives of the Sophists* and his sources?

Philostratus discusses three aspects of the life of Favorinus whom he calls 'the philosopher' and introduces him with the accolade that he was proclaimed a sophist by reason of 'the charm and beauty of his eloquence'. His public conflict with another noted sophist, Polemo, in Asia and then Rome where it caught the public imagination. It is discussed in one sentence and then follows general observations about human nature and rivalry especially among the sophists. His declamations were such that in Rome even those who did not understand Greek crowded to listen because of his captivating delivery and the rhythm of his speeches. He 'sang' the *peroratio* of his orations which was a new fad in his day. The mention of his relationship with Herodes Atticus who is the central figure in the *Lives of the Sophists* is made, for he epitomised the sophist in their heyday known as the Second Sophistic.

He repeats the well-known comment of Favorinus that though he was a Gaul he lived the life of a Hellene, a eunuch, he was accused of adultery, and though he quarrelled with an emperor he lived. His

---

[53]B. Baldwin, 'Friends and Enemies', *op. cit.*, 29. For a discussion of major entries on Favorinus see his ch. 2 esp. 21-31.

high status is revealed with the reference to his appointment as 'high priest' i.e. president of the games and required to sponsor them at his own expense. The throwing down of his statue in Athens 'as if he were the emperor's bitterest enemy' is referred to but not the similar incident in Corinth. His eirenic comment in the face of the former incident reflects his patient character. If his style of eloquence was careless in construction, it was both 'learned and pleasing' (491). Philostratus concludes that Favorinus was one of those who pursued philosophy but acquired the reputation of a sophist (492).

Favorinus has a role in that he provides Philostratus with the opportunity to herald his pupil, Herodes Atticus. The portrait is incomplete, if not distorted. It reflects a lack of information, for after some comments relating to his life Philostratus proceeds with generalisations.

Conclusions

How have ancient historians evaluated this autobiographical and biographical material on Favorinus?

The most recent biography on Philostratus makes the following observations about his treatment of Favorinus in a chapter taken up with Philostratus' shorter discussion of sophists before reaching the central figure in the *Lives*, Herodes Atticus.[54] Anderson feels that his treatment is 'just as eclectic' as it was with Dio Chrysostom. The presentation of the quarrel with Polemo is considered to be 'equally ill-digested'. In other matters the biographer is occupied with 'trivia'. Anderson speculates as to why this is so. He asks whether it was reluctance on the part of Philostratus to mention certain matters or ignorance on his part.[55] C.P. Jones suggests that the omission of any reference to his exile may be accounted for with Philostratus who does not record either the exile of Dio Chrysostom or Favorinus, his pupil, for 'this is a blemish that Philostratus does not like to admit in his heroes'.[56]

---

[54]G. Anderson, 'Brief Lives: Some Philostratean Portraits', *Philostratus* (London: Croom Helm, 1986) ch. 6.
[55]G. Anderson, *op. cit.*, 102, 103, 104.
[56]C.P. Jones, *Roman World, op. cit.*, 48.

Anderson forms the opinion that Philostratus 'may have known only enough about his subject [Favorinus] to be able to include the most colourful material; and his choice of that may have again been determined by his own interest as a biographer'. He shows that Philostratus 'falls short on another count: Favorinus represents a much fuller share in the intellectual life of the second century than Philostratus is willing or able to give him'.[57] This is a very substantial deficiency given the dual description of philosopher and sophist by Philostratus himself.

'As in the cases of Dio and Favorinus, Philostratus seems to submerge substantial problems beneath a series of scintillating encounters.' Anderson concludes his discussion with the comment that 'too much of. . .Favorinus is nevertheless unmentioned and we can accordingly have no confidence about the nature and extent of his omissions, purposeful or otherwise, in the short notices'.[58]

In a passing comparison with the biographical entry of Philostratus G. Anderson comments on Gellius,

> Even on a random sample of material preserved in the naive and indiscriminate Gellius [sic.], he can sometimes emerge as a sensitive and responsible scholar rather than an archaising pedant. . .Gellius affords a staggering impression of Favorinus' bilingual erudition and his professional philosophic and religious interests.[59]

The self 'portrait' of Favorinus is transformed into a statue by the lively comment of Gellius and insights into his personality and thought recorded in his speeches and dialogues. If the biographical entry of Philostratus was all that was extant on this important figure in the East and the imperial circle as is the case with other sophists, even the rough sketch would leave us with an imprecise impression on details of this second-century figure.

---

[57]G. Anderson, *op. cit.*, 104.
[58]G. Anderson, *op. cit.*, 105, 115.
[59]G. Anderson, *op. cit.*, 104.

IV. Julian and Ammianus Marcellinus (Alanna Nobbs)

Few figures from antiquity are as well documented as the emperor Julian and numerous biographies have been written as a result.[60] Of the major contemporary sources, we first have the writings of the emperor himself. These comprise eight orations, two major letters (to Themistius and to the Senate and People of Athens), two satires (*Misopogon* and *The Caesars*) and over seventy pieces of correspondence together with some shorter fragments, a variety of epigrams and a treatise against the Galileans, accompanied by miscellanea.[61]

Other contemporary sources include speeches by the sophist Libanius (favourable to Julian), an invective against him by Gregory of Nazianzus, a panegyric by Claudius Mamertinus and evidence from inscriptions and coins.

The historian Ammianus Marcellinus' *Res Gestae* is a narrative, analytical history in the classical manner recounting events from the reign of Nerva (A.D. 96) to the death of Valens (A.D. 378). For events from 353 onwards (where the surviving books begin) he gave a partially eyewitness account, and had in fact served in the army while Julian was in Gaul as Caesar and also on the Persian expedition. The history was not written immediately, however. Ammianus later lived in Rome where he published his work in c. 392.[62]

For this brief study, we will first focus on two case studies related to problems of Julian's career,[63] using his own letters and the

---

[60]E.g. Robert Browning, *The Emperor Julian* (London, 1975); G.W. Bowersock, *Julian the Apostate* (London, 1978).

[61]These are available in the Loeb series. A useful translation of some less accessible material pertaining to him is to be found in S.N.C. Lieu, *The Emperor Julian* (Translated Texts for Historians 2; 2nd ed.; Liverpool: Liverpool University Press, 1986).

[62]John Matthews, *The Roman Empire of Ammianus* (London, 1989), ch. 2 *passim*.

[63]He was born in 332, a child by the second marriage of the emperor Constantine's younger half brother. His mother died soon after his birth, and shortly after the death of Constantine in 337 his father and other male members of his family (except for his younger half brother, Gallus) were murdered by the army, whether or not at the direct instigation of one of Constantine's sons, Constantius II. Julian spent a secluded youth at Nicomedia and later at Macellum under close supervision. He received an education both classical and Christian, though he was later to repudiate the latter. Gallus was made Caesar (i.e. junior emperor) by Constantius, but was beheaded by him in 354; the military problems of empire made necessary a second ruler, so Julian was summoned from his

history of Ammianus, and set aside the other sources, both contemporary and later, to make a close parallel with the case of Paul in his letters and in Acts.

1. Julian's appointment as Caesar in Gaul

In the mid-fourth century, the frontiers of the Roman Empire were under threat in several areas. The Persian frontier was unstable and Constantius had inherited a war there from his father Constantine. Both the Danube and Rhine frontiers were under threat and there had, in 353, been an attempted usurpation. Julian's task as Caesar was primarily to defend Gaul and prevent barbarian raids, while Constantius as Augustus (senior emperor) concentrated on the East. Historians debate the precise nature of the task entrusted to Julian and the degree of trust reposed in him by Constantius.

The two sources we will be looking at closely give essentially the same version, but (naturally) their own slant. As Julian marched eastwards to confront Constantius, having been proclaimed Augustus by the troops, he wrote a series of public letters (really manifestos) to Rome, Sparta, Corinth and Athens, explaining and justifying the course of action he was taking. Only the letter to the Senate and People of Athens survives. Athens was particularly significant to Julian because of his education there and his passion for Greek culture, so he would have made every effort to present his cause in a favourable light.

Ammianus, by the time he wrote at Rome in the late 380s, was writing at this point about events of his own lifetime and which, in some cases, he had personally experienced. As well as his own notes and memories, he by then had access to written accounts including, among many others, Julian's own writings and probably the work of his near-contemporary, the Greek historian Europius. Nevertheless, Ammianus offers his own distinctive, well thought out and largely

---

studies in Athens to the rank of Caesar in Gaul. Despite his civilian background, he was very successful as a soldier and popular with his troops. He won a great victory at Argentoratum (Strasbourg), but relations worsened with Constantius. Julian's troops proclaimed him as Augustus and while he was marching to fight Constantius, the latter died (361). As sole emperor, Julian openly declared his adherence to the old gods, favoured paganism and discouraged Christianity. In 363, while on a massive and unsuccessful campaign in Persia, he was killed, and his pagan revival came to naught.

sober judgement of events, despite his admiration for Julian the man and what his reign stood for.

From both these sources we can see that, despite the difficulties he faced, Julian fulfilled his mission in Gaul successfully. Julian's account (*Ep. Ath.*, A.D. 279-289), though tendentious in complaining that he was denied a triumph, since it was standard procedure for the Roman emperor to claim the victories of his generals, shows that he had succeeded in securing the frontiers by his victory. Ammianus puts a speech into the mouth of Constantius (15.8.5-8) in which it is stated that the raids of the barbarians have made it necessary to protect their frontiers, and hence Julian's appointment. Julian further claims that his acceptance of the dangerous appointment was the result of his own obedience to the gods (*Ep. ad. Ath.* 277A). In his public letter, Julian stresses his belief in, and submission to, the old gods. Ammianus is more subtle and circumspect.[64] While he subscribed to the overall view that all changes in human fortune are the work of Fortuna (or Nemesis to the Greeks, 14.11.29-34), he does not emphasise a religious motif in his account of Julian's elevation in Gaul. Instead he writes obliquely of Julian quietly quoting Homer during the imperial ceremony: 'By purple death I'm seized and fate supreme' (15.8.7). This chapter portentously ends with a prophecy from an old blind woman that Julian would be the one to repair the temple of the gods (15.8.22).

Thus from these two different sources we arrive, in this case, at a coherent picture of events. Julian, sent to Gaul to defeat the raiders and secure the frontiers, achieved Constantius' stated purpose, while believing himself to be guided by the gods. However the different motives and presentation of the sources have to be uncovered first.

2. Julian's proclamation as Augustus

Upon Constantius' demand that Julian send troops to him in the East, Julian was reluctant to send the barbarian volunteer soldiers, who had been told they would not have to serve beyond the Alps (Ammianus, 20.4.4). Both Ammianus and Julian in his *Letter to the Athenians* refer to the decision to send the men, but only Ammianus records the dinner party given for the leading nobles, after which a

---

[64]E.D. Hunt, 'Christians and Christianity in Ammianus Mancillimis', *Classical Quarterly* no. 9. 35 (1985) 186-200.

'spontaneous' revolt broke out, as a result of which Julian was persuaded by the troops to accept the title of senior emperor (Augustus).

Julian's failure to mention this gathering (although he calls Zeus, Hermes, Ares, Athena and all the other gods to witness that he had no suspicion of the plan to declare him Augustus until that evening [*Ep. ad. Ath.* 284A]) is surely 'disingenuous'.[65] Ammianus, on the surface at least, goes to pains to stress Julian's lack of initiative in the matter, and his eventual reluctant compliance with the will of the troops (20.4.17-18). In other respects, Ammianus and Julian are in broad agreement concerning the event, the reaction of Constantius and the subsequent negotiations.

In other words, Ammianus appears to confirm the version given by Julian and, indeed, the version of Julian's other supporters such as Libanius (who also emphasises Julian's reluctance but is even more emphatic about the role of the gods). Yet Ammianus had been a professional soldier (14.9.1; 31.16.9) and had, moreover, been sent on an earlier mission under Constantius' general Ursicinus to put down the usurpation of Silvanus in Gaul (15.5.1-35). While in general conceding that a legitimate emperor had the right to protect his imperial power, since as a solider he was well aware that anarchy would result otherwise, he does censure Constantius for holding on to his power with such cruelty (21.16.12). A hint of the degree of subtlety in Ammianus' presentation of the Julianic version of his proclamation may be discovered in his later obituary of Julian, where among other admirable qualities he stresses Julian's ability to control his soldiers, even without pay (25.4.12). Ammianus surely asked himself, though it is suppressed in his narrative, what happened to the control on the night of the proclamation. For Ammianus too, while the will of the gods was not emphasised in the actual narrative, their leading had to be taken into account.[66]

Conclusion

In these two case studies, we have the considered judgement of a favourable contemporary, writing later as an analytical historian and

---

[65]So described by Matthews, *op. cit.*, 98.
[66]Cf. *Am.* 21.1.6, where Julian learns by divination of Constantius' impending death.

Julian's own version of affairs written as an *apologia* for his own conduct. A more extended analysis, stretching throughout Julian's career, would give a far better picture. Nevertheless, from a modern perspective, we are able to form a picture of Julian's character and motives as he himself wished them to be seen and as another judged them. The two versions are complementary, and reveal that the onlooker, the historian, was able to make subtle judgements based on his first hand knowledge of the figure concerned and of his life and times.

V. Conclusions

What are some of the conclusions which can be drawn from the three disparate case studies presented in this chapter?

In the case of Cicero, a major player in the Catilinarian rebellion, the knowledge of when and why he published his speeches provides an important perspective in evaluating them. The fact that he does participate in those events does not mean that his written record does not have a particular *Tendenz* or that the significance of 'saving' Rome would not be judged even by some of his contemporaries as political exaggeration. But no written material is without its bias. Where that emerges from explicit comments by the author it is easier for ancient historians to make judgements and evaluate both ancient as well as modern interpretations. Participation in events does not imply impartiality in recording them in written form. A disclosure of purpose in recording the events subsequently provides a perspective for the ancient historian to enable him to appreciate the author's *Tendenz*.

The Sallust account is particularly interesting for it highlights the fact that access to 'primary' sources such as Cicero's does not mean that he used them in his treatment of the conspiracy, or that in the case of the letter of Catiline he drew from it the judgements that an ancient historian of the present century feels it is possible to make. This case study has alerted New Testament scholars to the fact that they have perhaps been too ready to assume that there is a single enterprise with agreed rules called 'ancient historiography'. They can be more diverse in approaches and the use and non-use of sources. That Sallust composed his history after the death of the major players does not of itself allow the conclusion to be drawn that the work is *ipso facto* less credible in what it sets out to do.

Cicero and Sallust raise the issue of sources and the question of the dependence of the history on the letters and the speeches. Some 200 years ago Dr. William Paley raised this question in a similar project on Acts and the Pauline corpus. Noting the possibilities that 'the letters' of Paul were invented from 'the history' of Acts, or 'the history' was invented from 'the letters' or that they were independent of one another, Paley coined a phrase from the vocabulary of his interests in the category of 'design' from his apologetics—'the undesignedness of the evidence'. It is not Paley's 'proof' of 'undesignedness' that is pertinent here, but rather the stimulus that his insight provides in weighing up the alternatives in the discussion of any ancient literary parallel.[67]

The autobiographical details of Favorinus, and the biographical data recorded by Gellius and Philostratus presented above provide another yardstick for the discussion of Acts and the Pauline corpus. What use is made of the parallel may depend on judgements made as to whether Luke was for a time part of the Pauline mission.[68] If Luke was a Pauline associate then the former may have much more in common with Gellius than Philostratus. Those who hold that position would recognise that the portrait of Paul in Acts has been painted from a particular angle. All portraits are of necessity painted from a certain standpoint. The signature on the particular presentation of Paul in Acts is of course that of the author.

If it could be demonstrated from the extant evidence that Luke was not a travel companion or that his work belongs to a *genre* which an ancient audience would automatically assume to be a novel, then the judgement on the relationship between Acts and Paul may be that

---

[67]W. Paley, *Horae Paulinae: or the Truth of the Scripture History of St. Paul Evinced by a Comparison of the Epistles which Bear his Name with the Acts of the Apostles, and with One Another* (ed. 9; London, 1816) 7. For his conclusions see his p. 360
[68]The discussion of this issue will be evaluated in the next volume in this series, *The Book of Acts in its Graeco-Roman Setting*—it should not be concluded that the matter has been resolved in favour of Luke's travel narrative.

Luke has more in common with the succinct and therefore 'incomplete' presentation of the shorter biographical entries of Philostratus' *Lives of the Sophists*. But all presentations are incomplete and if part of a larger work, they are clearly crafted for a particular purpose as is the case in Acts.

The careful reporting by Gellius of Favorinus' speeches either *verbatim* or in indirect speech should alert us to the fact that it may not always be apposite to evaluate all or some of the speeches of Acts in what New Testament scholars popularly perceive to be the 'Thucydidean' tradition.

The use of the term 'Lukan Paul' may be seen by some to be more appropriate if the Philostratus literary parallel is used because they conclude that the author had no relationship with one of the central players in the spread of early Christianity.[69] However, on reflection, 'Lukan Paul' is a misleading term and, it might be added, not a device that ancient historians would use when discussing an ancient person. L. Holford–Strevens has produced a chapter drawn from extant sources on Favorinus and while evaluative in his use of primary material nowhere does he speak of the 'Philostratean Favorinus'.[70] New Testament studies operate from a small amount of primary material compared with that available from other authors of the same period. The restriction imposed by some Lukan and Pauline scholars on what they judge to be the illegitimate use of the Pauline corpus is not one which an ancient historian would feel the need to operate under even if writing on Paul.

In the two examples cited, in the case study of Julian and Ammianus, it was seen that we have the considered judgement of a favourable contemporary, writing later as an analytical historian and Julian's own version of affairs written as an *apologia* for his own conduct. The two versions were concluded to be complementary, and to reveal that the onlooker, the historian, was able to make subtle

---

[69]Ancient historians might well devote a monograph to the presentation of a particular ancient author's treatment of a person or an event. It is unlikely that the reasoning behind the recent publication by R.I. Pervo, *Luke's Story of Paul* (Minneapolis: Fortress, 1990) which excludes all references to the Pauline corpus would commend itself to ancient historians on the grounds that Acts is judged to be a novel.

[70]L. Holford–Strevens, *op. cit.*, ch. 6.

judgements based on his first hand knowledge of the figure concerned and of his life and times.

For some the question of Acts and the Pauline corpus is seen as a vexed question for Acts scholarship. Many ancient historians would welcome the sort of evidence presented by Acts and the Pauline corpus. Where there are uncertainties on certain aspects between the accounts they would see them providing the stimulus to look at the subject from angles that may well have not occurred to them had there not been only a biographical or autobiographical perspective. It is hoped that when scholars turn to Acts and the Pauline corpus the contours of that discussion may well appear different as a result of the three case studies which constitute ancient literary parallels. When Jerome asked *Quid facit cum apostolo Cicero?* 'What has Cicero to do with Paul?' he little realised how stimulating that question could be for this important aspect of Acts scholarship.[71]

---

[71]Jerome, *Epist.* 22.29.

CHAPTER 9

ACTS AND THE PAULINE CORPUS
II. THE EVIDENCE OF PARALLELS

David Wenham

Summary

Over half of the book of Acts is devoted to describing the ministry of Paul. For the student of Acts, therefore, the Pauline letters, being a first-hand expression and reflection of that ministry, are an immensely important resource. This chapter examines the parallels between Acts and the letters in order, starting from the background to Paul's conversion and paying particular attention to the relationship of Galatians 2 to Acts 11 and 15. The chapter does not reach definitive conclusions, but describes the evidence and explains the widely differing scholarly assessments of the evidence. The comparison of the two traditions is seen to hold great potential for illuminating particular texts and for the evaluation of Acts as a literary and historical work.

Introduction

Any scholar wishing to evaluate the book of Acts as a literary and historical work has an extraordinarily important resource in the letters of Paul. But what precisely do the letters tell us? Is the Paul of the letters recognisably the same person as the Paul of Acts? Or does Acts offer a tendentious and historically misleading account? Or is the truth somewhere inbetween? The answer to these questions will obviously have a bearing on other important questions related to Acts, both historical questions (e.g. was the author of Acts a companion of Paul, and/or did he know Paul's letters?) and literary questions (e.g. is Acts a historical romance or monograph?).[1]

In comparing Acts and the Pauline letters it is possible, on the one hand, to ask broad questions about the portrayal of Paul and his theology in the two traditions. The danger with this approach is that it can be relatively subjective: Luke's portrayal of Paul and Paul's own portrayal of himself can both be construed in all sorts of different ways, and have been so construed. It is possible, on the other hand, to attempt a more detailed historical examination of possible parallels of points of contact and points of tension. This approach also has its dangers, since the details must ultimately be seen not in isolation but in their broad context, and yet it may be preferable to start with some of the detailed groundwork before proceeding to more ambitious analyses. This chapter attempts to do some of that groundwork, going through the Acts narrative, examining possible points of contact and conflict with the Pauline letters, and setting out some of the evidence, issues and options that face the scholar.

I. Paul's Early Life and Conversion and its Immediate Aftermath

1. Before conversion

In the book of Acts Paul first appears on the scene as a 'young man' at the killing of Stephen (Acts 7:58). Acts gives us very little information about his background; but we gather that he had a Hebrew and a Roman name (Saul and Paul respectively). Born in Tarsus he was a citizen of that city (21:39; 22:3), and also a Roman

---

[1]In this chapter I will use 'Luke' to refer to the author of Acts, without intending to prejudge the authorship issue. For a useful survey of different positions on Acts and the Pauline letters see A.J. Mattill Jr., 'The Value of Acts as a Source for the Study of Paul', in C.H. Talbert (ed.), *Perspectives on Luke-Acts* (Edinburgh: Clark, 1978) 76-98.

citizen by birth (16:38; 22:26, 27). By trade he was a tent-maker (or leather-worker) (18:3). A 'Pharisee and son of Pharisees', he trained in Jerusalem under Gamaliel, 'educated strictly according to our ancestral law, being zealous for God' (22:3; 23:6). He was fluent in Hebrew/Aramaic (22:2) but apparently associated with the Greek-speaking synagogues of Jerusalem (to judge from his involvement with Stephen, cf. 6:9 and also 9:29).

The information to be gleaned from Paul's own letters on this period is modest. But in Philippians 3:5, 6 Paul speaks of his orthodox Jewish background, 'circumcised the eighth day, of the tribe of Benjamin, a Hebrew of Hebrews, according to law a Pharisee. . .as to righteousness under the law blameless'. In Galatians 1:14 he describes how 'I advanced in Judaism beyond many among my people of the same age, for I was far more zealous for the traditions of my ancestors'. Paul does not refer specifically to his tent-making trade in his letters, but he does describe how he worked so as not to burden his congregations (1 Thes. 4:11; 1 Cor. 9). His bi-lingualism is clear enough from his letters.

The evidence of Acts and the epistles on this period is thoroughly compatible. The epistles do not mention Paul's Hebrew name 'Saul', but it is a likely enough name for a Jew from the tribe of king Saul. They do not mention his Tarsan origin, but do refer to his extensive missionary work in Asia Minor, including the Tarsus area ('Cilicia' in Gal. 1:21).

Questions have been raised about the reference in Acts to Paul training in Jerusalem under Gamaliel, on the grounds that Paul speaks in Galatians 1:22 of being 'unknown by sight' to the churches of Judea after his conversion. The same text has been used to contradict Acts' description of Paul persecuting the church in Jerusalem.[2] But this is probably to press Galatians 1:22—a comment of Paul about his *post*-conversion contact with Jerusalem—too far.[3] Paul certainly does not mean that no one in the churches of Jerusalem or Judea knew him: he could very well have trained under Gamaliel and even have been a leading persecutor of the Jerusalem church in its earliest days without being a familiar face to the large majority of the members of the fast-growing Judean churches a few years later.

---

[2] So E. Haenchen, *The Acts of the Apostles* (Oxford: Blackwells, 1971) 625; F. Watson, *Paul, Judaism and the Gentiles* (London: SCM, 1986) 27; E.P. Sanders, *Paul* (Oxford: OUP, 1991) 9.
[3] On this verse see also pp. 221-25 below.

Positively it is highly likely that the enthusiastic Pharisee from Tarsus would have studied in Jerusalem under a leading rabbi such as Gamaliel, and that his persecution of Christians started in Jerusalem.[4]

Questions have also been raised as to whether Paul is likely to have been both a strict Jew, a 'Pharisee son of Pharisees', and also one of the social élite in Tarsus as a citizen of the city and a Roman citizen.[5] Such a combination of qualifications may have been unusual, but that Paul was unusual in his background and 'qualifications' is not difficult to believe.[6]

2. Paul's conversion

Acts has three accounts of Paul's conversion, the first being Luke's own description (ch. 9), the other two being on Paul's own lips, one before the Jewish crowd (ch. 22), the second before king Agrippa (ch. 26). The three accounts are broadly similar, describing Paul's vitriolic campaign against the Christians, his journey (authorised by the Jerusalem authorities) to Damascus to imprison Christians, his

---

[4]See M. Hengel, *The Pre-Christian Paul* (Philadelphia: Trinity/London: SCM, 1991) 23-29, noting that Jerusalem was quite big enough for people not to know Paul. G. Lüdemann, *Early Christianity according to the Traditions in Acts* (London: SCM, 1989) 240, claims that there is no evidence of Pharisees training outside Jerusalem. Scholars have discussed whether Paul's exegetical method is what might be expected in a pupil of Gamaliel; F.F. Bruce in *Paul Apostle of the Free Spirit* (Exeter: Paternoster, 1977) 51, concludes: 'In most matters. . .Paul was probably an apt pupil and faithful follower of his teacher'. That Paul's persecution is likely to have started where the church started, i.e. in Jerusalem, is argued by Bruce in 'Galatian Problems 1. Autobiographical Data', *BJRL* 51 (1968-9) 297, noting that Paul in Gal. 1:23 refers to the Christians in Judea referring to him as the one who persecuted 'us'.

[5]So J.C. Lentz, *Luke's Portrait of Paul* (Cambridge: CUP, 1993), arguing that Luke's portrayal of his hero as a man of social standing and virtue is not historical (e.g. p. 56).

[6]It is not hard to believe that Paul, who moved so freely through the Roman world, was a man of some social standing, as well as a trained Pharisee. See the thorough discussion (and response to Lenz) by Brian M. Rapske, *Pauline Imprisonment and the Lukan Defense of the Missionary Prisoner Paul in the light of Greco-Roman Sources* (PhD thesis of Aberdeen University, 1992) 119-68. Also arguing for Paul's Roman citizenship see Hengel, *Pre-Christian Paul*, 1-17, and Lüdemann, *Early Christianity*, 240-41. Whether 'son of Pharisees' in Acts 23:6 means literally that Paul came from a family of Pharisees and, if so, whether they were Pharisees when in the Diaspora or only after moving to Jerusalem, is debatable. See Rapske, *op. cit.*, 151-2.

experience near Damascus of being struck down by a bright light and then of speaking with the risen Christ ('Saul, Saul, why are you persecuting me?' etc.), and his entry into Damascus a converted man.

There are certain differences between the accounts, with Acts 9 being much fuller than the others and Acts 26 being the briefest. In 9:7 Paul's travelling companions are said to hear the heavenly voice but to see no one; in 22:9 they see the light, but don't hear the voice 'of the one who was speaking to me'. In Acts 26 Paul is told actually on the Damascus Road that he is to have a mission to the Gentiles; in chapters 9 and 22 he is simply told to go into Damascus where he will receive his instructions. In Acts 9 it is Ananias who has a vision about Paul's future ministry to Gentiles; nothing is said about Paul receiving this information, but Acts 22 has Ananias tell Paul that 'you will be my witness to all people'.

Luke was apparently not worried by such minor divergences. This could be seen as evidence of Lukan lack of interest in historical precision. On the other hand, it could be that Luke had different sources, and that he prefers to allow the slightly divergent accounts to stand than to harmonise them. And/or it could be that Luke would have explained or harmonised the narratives in some of the ways suggested by modern scholars.[7] Our concern, however, is with how the Lukan accounts compare with Paul's own references to his conversion.

Paul in his letters does not retell the story of his conversion, but he does refer to it. In the first place, he speaks on several occasions of his experience of having 'seen the Lord' in a way that puts him on a par with the apostles (1 Cor. 9:1; 15:8). Luke agrees that Paul's experience was one of 'seeing the Lord'.[8] But then, secondly, Paul refers in

---

[7]Haenchen, *Acts*, 322, notes that Luke believes that Paul saw Jesus (Acts 9:7; 22:14; 26:16) and comments on 9:7: 'Presumably Luke imagined the occurrence in such a way that Saul's companions saw only a formless glare where he himself saw in it the figure of Jesus'. Lüdemann, *Early Christianity*, 110, suggests that in 22:9 Luke is wishing to make it clear that the companions of Paul were not party to a revelatory experience, as the reference to them 'hearing the voice' in the pre-Lukan tradition of 9:7 might have suggested. As for Paul being given a commission to go to the Gentiles on the Damascus Road, it seems most likely that Acts 26 is a compressed account of what is more fully narrated in Acts 9 and 22. (Compare Luke 24 and Acts 1:3 on the resurrection appearances.)

[8]See fn. 7 above. Luke only uses the word 'apostle' of Paul (with Barnabas) in 14:4, 14, and his reticence has been seen as evidence that Luke was not close to Paul (so Haenchen, *Acts*, 114-15). But the argument is uncertain: Paul emphasises his apostleship in polemical contexts when he is being compared unfavourably

more detail to his conversion in Galatians 1:13-17: he tells of how 'I was violently persecuting the church of God and was trying to destroy it' (a point confirmed in Phil. 3:5). Then he describes how God through his grace 'was pleased to reveal his Son to me', God's purpose being 'so that I might proclaim him among the Gentiles' (1:15, 16).[9] Paul does not specifically refer to the Damascus locality as the place of his conversion, but this is implied when he speaks of going away to Arabia and then 'afterwards I returned to Damascus' (1:17).

There is nothing here to contradict the Acts accounts, and several points fit in well with them. An exception might be his comment that 'I did not confer with any human being (flesh and blood)' (1:16), since Acts makes it clear that Ananias was an important player in the drama of Paul's conversion.[10] However, it would be absurd literalism to take Paul's remark in Galatians 1:16 to mean that he had nothing to do with any Christians in Damascus when he was converted. The remark must be seen in the context of a polemical discussion of Paul's relationship to the Jerusalem apostles, where Paul is responding to the accusation that he is a second-class apostle with a second-hand message. He replies that his 'gospel was not of human origin; for I did not receive it from a human source, nor was I taught it, but I received it through a revelation of Jesus Christ' (1:11, 12). He goes on to emphasise his lack of contact with the Jerusalem apostles immediately after his conversion. In this context the likely meaning of his remark about not conferring with flesh and blood is that he did not at that point have an official consultation with any apostle or representative of the apostles.[11]

---

with the original apostles; Luke may have preferred to keep the term mostly for the 'originals' (perhaps because it was a sensitive issue), but 14:4, 14 show that he felt no great antipathy for the usage. (The point would be unaffected, even if the speculation that Luke is using a source in chapter 14 and/or that 'apostle' here means delegate of the Antioch church were to be accepted; see Bruce, *Acts*, 318-19.) Indeed Luke sets Paul up in his narrative alongside Peter in a rather Pauline manner. See also I.H. Marshall, 'Luke's View of Paul', *Southwestern Journal of Theology* 33 (1990) 46-7, citing K. Haacker, 'Verwendung und Vermeidung des Apostelbegriffs im Lukanischen Werk', *NovT* 30 (1988) 9-38.
[9]Watson, *Paul*, 30, considers that Paul had no call to Gentile mission at the time of his conversion and that Gal. 1:16 represents a reading back of his later convictions. Luke agrees with Paul's account, but Watson is even more sceptical about Luke's account of Paul's early activity than about Paul's.
[10]H.D. Betz, *Galatians* (Philadelphia: Fortress, 1979) 73, sees Paul as countering the sort of story that Acts tells about Ananias.
[11]We might suspect Paul of rhetorical exaggeration rather than Luke of inaccuracy; but either way involves an unnecessarily literal interpretation of

3. The aftermath of his conversion

It is in the description of what followed his conversion that there is significant divergence between Acts and Paul. In Acts 9 it is said that Paul after his conversion and baptism was with the disciples there 'some days' (ἡμέρας τινάς), and that he immediately began to proclaim Jesus in the synagogues, saying 'He is the Son of God' (v. 21). It goes on to speak of his ministry in Damascus becoming increasingly more powerful. Then it continues: 'When many days were completed' (ὡς δὲ ἐπληροῦντο ἡμέραι ἱκαναί) the Jews plotted to kill him. . .but his disciples let him down through the wall in a basket' (vv. 23-25). It then refers to his coming to Jerusalem and to Barnabas introducing him to 'the apostles'. He then goes in and out of Jerusalem 'being bold in the name of the Lord' and speaking and arguing with the Hellenists. Then in the face of another plot on his life, the brothers take him to Caesarea and ship him off to Tarsus (vv. 26-29). The Acts 22 and 26 accounts do not significantly add to this picture: they agree that Paul went from Damascus to Jerusalem, and Acts 26 speaks of him ministering in Jerusalem and 'throughout the countryside of Judea'.

Galatians 1 tells a different story. After saying that he conferred with no one following his conversion, Paul goes on 'nor did I go up to Jerusalem to those who were apostles before me, but I went away at once into Arabia, and afterwards I returned to Damascus. Then after three years, I did go up to Jerusalem to visit Cephas and stayed with him fifteen days, but I did not see any other apostle except James the Lord's brother. In what I am writing to you, before God, I do not lie! Then I went into the regions of Syria and Cilicia, and I was (still) unknown by sight to the churches of Judea; they only heard it said, "The one who formerly was persecuting us is now proclaiming the faith he once tried to destroy. . ."'.

The differences between the Lukan and the Pauline accounts include: (a) Acts shows no knowledge at all of Paul's post-conversion visit to Arabia. (b) The impression we get from Acts is that Paul went

---

Paul's rhetoric. Cf. R.Y.K. Fung, *The Epistle to the Galatians* (Grand Rapids: Eerdmans, 1988) 62-71. Paul's general insistence that his gospel came by revelation not through human agents should not be seen as a denial that he learnt any Christian tradition from other Christians (cf. 1 Cor. 11:23, 15:3), but as testimony to the fact that in his Damascus Road experience he learned first-hand the gospel truths for which he was fighting in Galatians—about salvation in Christ, about grace and the law.

to Jerusalem quite shortly after his conversion, whereas Galatians allows for a three year lapse of time. (c) Acts describes Barnabas introducing Paul to 'the apostles', whereas Paul says that on his first post-conversion visit to Jerusalem he met only Peter and James the Lord's brother. (d) Acts describes Paul having a bold ministry in Jerusalem (and in ch. 22 in Judea); in Galatians Paul claims that he remained unknown to the churches of Judea.

As well as Galatians 1, 2 Corinthians 11:32, 33 is a probable parallel to the Acts narrative, since Paul writes: 'In Damascus, the governor under King Aretas guarded the city of Damascus in order to seize me, but I was let down in a basket through a window in the wall, and escaped from his hands'. This reference may lend some support to the Acts account, but it also presents us with a new discrepancy between Acts and Paul in that Paul blames King Aretas's governor for the plot rather than the Jews, who are blamed by Luke.

The disparities between the account of Paul's post-conversion experiences in Galatians 1 and Acts 9 are such as to convince many critics that Luke is seriously misinformed and significantly misleading at this point in his narrative. Luke, it is suggested, was ignorant of Paul's post-conversion visit and mission to Arabia. As a result he gets various things wrong. First, he ascribes the plot against Paul in Damascus (of which Luke knows) to his Jewish opponents because of his ministry to Jews in Damascus, rather than to King Aretas because of his ministry in Arabia. Then, instead of sending him to Arabia, Luke makes Paul do the obvious thing straight after his conversion, i.e. go up to Jerusalem to establish his credentials with the 'apostles'. Because Paul is going to Jerusalem soon after his conversion, Luke can portray Barnabas (Paul's later colleague) as introducing Paul to the suspicious apostles, something that would hardly be necessary if the visit to Jerusalem was several years after Paul's conversion (as it was!). Luke's idea of Paul having a powerful, public ministry in Jerusalem is pure Lukan assumption about what would have happened, clearly contrary to what actually happened (Gal. 1:22, 'I was still unknown. . .to the churches of Judea').[12]

It is hard to avoid the conclusion that Luke's account of what followed Paul's conversion is historically inaccurate in various

---

[12]For these arguments see, e.g., Haenchen, *Acts*, 331-36.

respects.[13] And yet the arguments are not all as strong or clear-cut as they may seem at first. The following further points are worth noting:

(a) Luke gets some of the salient facts about the first post-conversion visit of Paul correct. He knows that Paul has been in Damascus; he knows that Paul left Damascus ignominiously via a basket;[14] he knows that Paul came from Damascus to Jerusalem; he knows that Paul went from Jerusalem to Tarsus.[15] So if Luke is inaccurate in this section, he still is working within a historical framework.[16]

(b) The references in Acts 9 to Paul's stay in Damascus do not necessarily imply that his stay in the city was very short: Acts refers to his staying 'some days', then to 'many days being completed'. It would be unwise to argue that Luke presupposes the Arabia visit between the 'some days' and the 'many days', since Luke gives no direct hint of this. But the Lukan wording and his reference to Paul being let down from the Damascus walls by 'his disciples' at least allow for a longer stay and ministry in Damascus than we might at first glance infer. It may be that Paul's visit to Arabia was quite short-lived, and that in fact most of the 'three years' between his conversion and his first visit to Jerusalem was spent in Damascus.[17]

(c) The Lukan explanation that Paul escaped from Damascus by basket to avoid the Jews could be Luke's theological construction or uninformed assumption. But it is entirely possible—even probable—that the converted Paul will have witnessed to Jews in Damascus on his return from Arabia (if not also while in Arabia), and it is quite likely that they will have responded with hostility. To postulate some collaboration between the ethnarch of Aretas and the Jewish

---

[13]So F.F. Bruce, 'The Acts of the Apostles: Historical Record or Theological Reconstruction' in *Aufstieg und Niedergang der Römischen Welt* 25/3 (Berlin: de Gruyter, 1985) 2580.

[14]He could have known 2 Cor. 11:32, 33 (so Lüdemann, *Early Christianity*, 118), guessing that the incident happened at this time.

[15]Acts says he went to Tarsus (in Cilicia), then was called to help Barnabas in Antioch (in Syria); in Galatians Paul says he went to the regions of Syria and Cilicia.

[16]Lüdemann, *Early Christianity*, 116, compares Acts 9:20 on Paul proclaiming Jesus as Son of God with Gal. 1:16, where Paul describes his conversion as a revelation of God's Son.

[17]See M. Hengel, *Acts and the History of Earliest Christianity* (London: SCM, 1979) 84.

community of Damascus is in no way fanciful: they could well have made common cause.[18]

(d) It is certainly true that we would naturally take 'the apostles' to whom Barnabas introduces Paul in Acts 9 as more than just Peter and James, but it is a generalising statement, and Luke need not have intended us to have imagined a gathering of the whole apostolic college.[19]

(e) As for Barnabas, it is true that the Acts account of Barnabas introducing Paul and explaining his conversion to the disciples who 'did not believe that he was a disciple' makes good sense if the visit took place soon after the conversion event. However, it is quite possible that extreme suspicion of the arch-enemy, who had been supposedly converted and who was now setting himself up as a Christian leader (as it seemed), might have persisted among the Christians of Jerusalem; his failure to report back to Jerusalem after his conversion and his disappearance into Arabia for a time could have fuelled suspicions.[20] It is also quite possible that someone with the generous spirit traditionally associated with Barnabas might have taken a lead in welcoming the former persecutor. Galatians has no mention of Barnabas being involved in this visit,[21] and Luke might have brought him into the story because he knows of their later collaboration. However, that later collaboration must have begun somewhere and somehow, and the account of Acts that they met in Jerusalem at this point and that Barnabas then later called Paul to assist him at Antioch is not implausible.

(f) As for Paul's comment that he was unknown by face to the 'churches of Judea' (Gal. 1:22), this does seem to conflict with the

---

[18]Lüdemann, *Early Christianity*, 119, unnecessarily dismisses the idea.

[19]See Betz, *Galatians*, 78, on doubts about James being one of the apostles in Gal. 1:19, but see Fung, *Galatians*, 78.

[20]It is one thing to hear second-hand reports and another to meet up face to face with someone who has been greatly feared. See Betz, *Galatians*, 78. Hengel, *Acts*, 86, sees the fear portrayed in Acts 9:26 as incredible, arguing (curiously in view of the chronological sequence in Gal. 1) that Gal. 1:23 shows that Jerusalem knew plenty about Paul's conversion. He admits that Barnabas could have been a useful middle man, given divergences between Paul and Jerusalem over missionary policy.

[21]Paul's failure to mention Barnabas is hardly surprising in a summary account, but is in any case explicable in the context of Galatians if relations between Paul and Barnabas are still strained because of the Antioch incident (2:13). See R. Bauckham's persuasive reconstruction 'Barnabas in Galatians', *JSNT* 2 (1979) 61-70.

account of his ministry in Jerusalem on his post-conversion visit.[22] However, the statement is a generalisation on Paul's part, probably about the period after his visit, rather than a comment about the visit.[23] Paul probably means that he remained a relatively unfamiliar figure on the Judean Christian scene (contrast the apostles and others), not that no Judean Christians got to know him during (or before) his post-conversion visit to Jerusalem. Although his visit was short and specifically to get to know Peter, there is no hint in Galatians that the visit was secret and no likelihood that the only Christians he met were Peter and James;[24] the implication is, if anything, the opposite—i.e. that he met people other than apostles.

The suggestion in Acts that he got embroiled in discussion with Jews during his visit, though not confirmed by Galatians, is likely enough. It is hard to see how he could have avoided such discussions on his first return visit to Jerusalem, unless his visit was deliberately secret. Martin Hengel observes that in Romans 15:19 Paul refers to having preached the gospel 'from Jerusalem' and as far round as Illyricum, and concludes that: 'Paul seems to be referring to missionary proclamation in Jerusalem itself, however brief that may have been'.[25] It is quite possible that the occasion in mind was his post-conversion visit.

Acts' description of the resulting plot against Paul is not unlikely. There is a possible reference to it in 1 Thessalonians 2:15 where Paul speaks of the Jews who 'killed the Lord Jesus and the prophets and drove us out. . .' Paul may here be referring to the Jews driving him out of Thessalonica; but (a) he has been speaking in the immediately preceding context of the Jews of Judea, and (b) he may well be echoing a saying of Jesus that was associated (at least in tradition) with Jesus' Judean opponents (compare Mt. 23:29-36/Lk. 11:45-54).[26]

---

[22]Also with Acts 26:20. Hengel, *Pre-Christian Paul*, 73, notes that 'Judea' connotes the whole of Palestine.

[23]It follows Gal. 1:21.

[24]Betz, *Galatians*, 77, infers that there were other apostles in Jerusalem whom Paul chose not to meet. But Hengel, *Pre-Christian Paul*, 78, comments: 'these earliest Jewish missionaries will not have been in Jerusalem at that time'.

[25]Hengel, *Acts*, 87.

[26]Note the use of two aorist tenses 'who killed the Lord. . .and drove us out. . .' followed by the present tenses 'and do not please God. . .etc.' On the use of tradition here see my *Gospel Perspectives IV: The Rediscovery of Jesus' Eschatological Discourse* (Sheffield: JSOT, 1984) 351, 352.

A further point in favour of the Acts story of a plot against Paul may be the long gap between Paul's first and second post-conversion visits (Gal. 2:1 'after fourteen years): was it the life-threatening hostility which Paul encountered on the first visit that kept him away from Jerusalem for so long?[27]

What may we conclude about Acts' account of Paul immediately after his conversion? (1) It may well be the case that Luke did not know all the details of what followed Paul's conversion, and yet he does have a significant amount of information that agrees with what Paul tells us. (2) Luke's account is compressed: in Acts 9 he simply describes the conversion itself and then Paul's reception back in Jerusalem; he does not start to tell the story of Paul in any detail until the coming of Paul to Antioch in his chapter 11. (3) The Lukan account may be historically misleading in certain respects (e.g. in the reference to Paul meeting 'the apostles' and perhaps in the suggestion that the Jerusalem church needed informing by Barnabas about Paul's conversion). (4) But there is no significant, proved discrepancy between Acts and the Pauline epistles, and Luke's additions to the Galatians account are historically possible.

II. Paul's Second and Third Visits to Jerusalem

It is Luke's account of Paul's second and third visits to Jerusalem that raises the most complicated questions vis-à-vis the evidence of Paul's letters.

In this case it will be helpful to start with Galatians. In Galatians 2 Paul describes how 'after fourteen years' he made another visit to Jerusalem. He went with Barnabas and Titus, in response to a revelation of some sort. There in a private meeting he put before 'the acknowledged leaders'—Peter, John and James the Lord's brother—the gospel that he preached to Gentiles—'in order to make sure that I was not running, or had not run, in vain' (v. 2). The discussion evidently had some bearing on the question of the Gentiles being circumcised (vv. 3-5). The upshot was the recognition of Paul's ministry to the Gentiles, the three leaders in Jerusalem giving Paul and Barnabas the right hand of fellowship, only asking them 'to remember the poor, which was actually what I was eager to do' (v. 10). Despite this recognition of Gentile freedom and of the

---

[27]So Hengel, *Acts*, 86, 87.

ministry of Paul and Barnabas, the problems did not all go away, since Paul describes how later in Antioch he had to confront Peter, when under pressure from people from James he and even Barnabas withdrew from eating with Gentiles, 'for fear of the circumcision faction' (vv. 11-13). Also the letter of Galatians itself is testimony to the fact that the Judaizing problem had not gone away.

In Acts the second post-conversion visit to Jerusalem is the so-called 'famine-relief' visit of Acts 11:27-30. Acts has described the influx of 'Hellenists', evidently including Gentiles, into the Antioch church; Barnabas was sent there from Jerusalem presumably to supervise the new situation, and he brings Paul from Tarsus to assist him. Paul and Barnabas met with the church 'for an entire year' and 'taught a great many people, and it was in Antioch that the disciples were first called "Christians"' (11:26). Acts then goes on to refer to prophets coming from Jerusalem to Antioch and to one Agabus predicting that there would be a severe famine over all the world, and tells us that 'this took place during the reign of Claudius'; in response to this prediction the disciples decided to send relief to the believers in Judea, and 'this they did, sending it to the elders by Barnabas and Saul' (11:29). Acts then proceeds in the following chapter to refer to Herod Agrippa's execution of James the apostle, to Peter's imprisonment and subsequent escape 'to another place' and then to Herod's death; the chapter concludes with the comment that 'after completing their mission Barnabas and Saul returned to Jerusalem and brought with them, John, whose other name was Mark' (12:24).

It is immediately obvious that the Galatians account of Paul's second visit with its description of consultations in Jerusalem about the Gentile mission is quite different from the Acts account of the famine relief mission. However, Acts goes on in chapter 15 to describe a consultation about the Gentiles.

In Acts 15 Paul and Barnabas have returned to Syrian Antioch after their so-called 'first missionary journey', in which they have had notable success among Gentiles and encountered significant opposition from Jews. Then 'certain individuals came down from Judea and were teaching the brothers, "Unless you are circumcised according to the custom of Moses, you cannot be saved"' (15:1). The controversy is sharp, and Paul and Barnabas are appointed to go to Jerusalem to discuss the matter with the apostles and elders. They receive a warm welcome except from some Pharisaic Christians who insist on the need for the Gentiles to keep the law. There is a long debate among the apostles and elders, in which Peter refers to his experience with Cornelius and firmly affirms Gentile freedom; then Paul and Barnabas report on what God had done among the Gentiles, and finally James sums up and gives his judgement 'that we should not trouble those Gentiles who are turning to God, but we should write to them to abstain only from things polluted by idols and from fornication and from whatever has been strangled and from blood. For in every city, for generations past, Moses has had those who proclaim him. . .' This decision is agreed by the whole church and is conveyed to the church in Antioch by Paul, Barnabas and two appointees of the Jerusalem church, Judas and Silas. The news is cause for great rejoicing; Paul and Barnabas continue in Antioch, but split up for their next missionary journeys, Barnabas taking Mark (whom Paul does not trust) and Paul taking Silas.

There are a whole range of differing views about how Galatians 2 relates to the two Acts passages. Probably the majority of scholars identify the second visit of Galatians (Gal. 2:1-10) with the Council of Acts 15; but a significant minority argue that the visit of Galatians 2:1-10 is the famine relief visit of Acts 11 and 12. We will describe the case for and against each view.

1. Galatians 2:1-10=Acts 15

(a) *Arguments in favour.* The principal arguments in favour are the correspondences between the visits as described in Galatians 2 and Acts 15.

(i) *Agreement in subject matter.* The question of Paul's mission and of Gentiles and the Jewish law is on the agenda in Galatians 2 and Acts 15, whereas in Acts 11 the purpose of the visit is famine relief.

(ii) *Agreement over the participants involved.* The participants in the discussion in both Galatians 2 and Acts 15 are Barnabas and Paul from Antioch, and Peter and James the Lord's brother from Jerusalem. Acts says that Paul and Barnabas went from Antioch; Galatians does not specify this, though it may be presupposed, as there is mention of Paul being in Syria and Cilicia before the visit and of him and Barnabas being in Antioch afterwards (1:21; 2:11-13).

Galatians also mentions Titus as accompanying Paul and Barnabas and the apostle John involved in the consultation: Acts 15 doesn't mention either of these, but it does refer to Paul and Barnabas being accompanied by 'some of the others' (v. 2) and to 'the apostles' in general being involved in the discussions (vv. 2, 6). Acts 11 on the other hand only mentions Paul and Barnabas going to Jerusalem and to them meeting 'the elders'; it gives no hint that Paul and Barnabas met Peter or John or James (unless James is included in the 'elders').

Not only does Acts 15 have the same people involved as Galatians 2, but the respective roles of the people seem to correspond: James is mentioned first in Galatians 2:9 ahead of Peter and John, though Peter is obviously a key figure (2:7, 9); similarly in Acts 15 James is the one who finally sums up and expresses the conclusion of the meeting, but Peter is an important contributor to the debate. Peter sides with Paul and Barnabas in Acts 15 and would do so in Galatians except for pressure from 'the men from James'. James in Acts 15 goes with Paul and others on the circumcision issue, but proposes dietary arrangements to meet some Jewish concerns; similarly in Galatians he gives the right hand of fellowship to Paul and Barnabas, but has some connection with the Judaizers.

(iii) *Agreement over the outcome.* The outcome of the discussions is broadly similar with Paul's gospel being recognised and with agreement on the fundamental principle that the Gentiles need not be circumcised.

(b) *Problems with the identification.* The case seems quite strong. However, there are problems.

(i) *Acts 11:30 needing to be explained.* If Galatians 2=Acts 15, what is to be made of the famine relief visit of Acts 11? There are two possibilities: either Paul failed to mention it in Galatians 2. This seems a little unlikely since he is very carefully and specifically detailing his contacts with Jerusalem, in order to rebut accusations (1:18, 20; 2:1); but it is just possible that, if on the famine relief visit he and Barnabas only met 'the elders' referred to by Acts and none of the apostles, then he might have deemed the visit unimportant for his argument in Galatians 2.[28]

The alternative explanation is that Luke is inaccurate: either he could be wholly mistaken about Paul's involvement in the famine relief visit, or he could have confused various of Paul's visits. One view is that Acts 11:30 and Acts 15 are in fact the same visit, and that

---

[28]So J.B. Lightfoot, *Saint Paul's Epistle to the Galatians* (London: Macmillan, 1881) 127.

Luke has misleadingly separated them, no doubt because of confusion over his sources of information.[29]

(ii) *Private or public meeting*. The description of the visits in Galatians 2 and Acts 15 differs. Paul specifically says that his meeting was a private consultation (Gal. 2:2) with only the so-called 'pillars' of the Jerusalem church, James, Peter and John, whereas Acts 15 describes an official, plenary gathering of the leadership of the Jerusalem church ('the apostles and elders').

Two observations diminish the force of this argument. (1) Despite Paul's reference to privacy, the meeting as described in Galatians was a meeting with top people discussing important policy issues, which led to a significant agreement; it was not just an informal chat.[30] (2) Luke portrays Paul's first post-conversion meeting with Peter and James as a meeting with the 'apostles' in general (see above). It may be that in Acts 15 he again makes a bigger, more formal gathering out of what was a consultation with a few leaders.[31]

(iii) *The decrees*. Not unrelated to the previous point is the problem that Acts has the meeting agree a final declaration which is then enshrined in an official letter, affirming that Gentiles need not be circumcised, but requiring them to respect at least some of the Jewish dietary scruples. The letter was taken to Antioch and subsequently elsewhere (Acts 16:4). Paul does not refer to such a decree at all, though it might have been thought to have been pertinent to his argument in Galatians, and he gives no hint that there was any decision taken about questions of diet and table-fellowship between Gentile and Jewish Christians. Indeed he suggests that no demands were made at all, except the request for aid for the poor.

Various explanations of this discrepancy between Acts 15 and Galatians 2 have been proposed. One possibility is that Paul did

---

[29]W.O. Walker, 'Why Paul Went to Jerusalem: The Interpretation of Galatians 2:1-5', *CBQ* 54 (1992) 503-10, offers a complicated explanation of Acts 11:27-30 as constructed from three different traditions (a) about Agabus, (b) about Paul and Barnabas going to Jerusalem 'by revelation', (c) about Paul's collection for Jerusalem.

[30]See J.D.G. Dunn, *Jesus, Paul and the Law* (London: SPCK, 1990) 173. Betz, *Galatians*, 86, and others rather implausibly find two meetings in Gal. 2:2, a public meeting with 'them' (i.e. the church at large) and a private meeting with 'the acknowledged leaders' (Gal. 2:2); Betz also sees significance in the verb 'I laid before them'. But see Hengel, *Acts*, 115.

[31]See D.R. Catchpole, 'Paul, James and the Apostolic Decree', *NTS* 23 (1977) 428-44, esp. 434.

know of the decrees, but refrained from mentioning them, either because he was unhappy about them—he refers to them nowhere in any of his letters, though they might have been relevant to his discussions of eating and not eating certain foods (e.g. in Romans and 1 Corinthians)—or because he did not see them as relevant to the Galatians.[32] This suggestion is not entirely satisfactory: Paul's careful defence of his position in Galatians 2 would be undermined by any blatant inaccuracy or pertinent omission.

An alternative explanation is that there were two separate consultations which Luke has conflated in Acts: the first (as also described in Galatians) at which Paul was present, the second at which the decrees were agreed at which Paul was not present.[33] One suggestion is that the first meeting failed to clarify the issue of table fellowship, which then came to the fore in the Antioch incident (of Gal. 2:11-14) and so had to be addressed at a second meeting.[34]

The theory of two meetings solves a problem perceived by several authors in Luke's suggestion in Acts 15 that Paul agreed to the decrees as described in Acts and even delivered them to churches that he had found (16:4). It is argued that the decrees with their restrictions on Gentiles (e.g. on the matter of food offered to idols) do not represent Paul's views;[35] he ignores them and maybe specifically

---

[32]Lüdemann, *Paul Apostle to the Gentiles* (Philadelphia: Fortress; London: SCM, 1984) 70, suggests that the decrees were for mixed Jew-Gentile churches such as Antioch and for Barnabas as leader of that church, not for Paul and his largely Gentile churches. This remarkable speculation divides Paul and Barnabas in a way that neither Acts nor Galatians does, and goes against the evidence of Acts (our source of information about the decrees), which describes Paul and Silas conveying them to the churches of South Galatia (16:4).

[33]So, among others, Haenchen, *Acts*, 468; Dunn, *Jesus Paul and the Law*, 160 (though he also offers the alternative explanation that the decrees only described what was Pauline practice anyway and so did not merit mention, 177). Acts 21:25 has sometimes been cited as evidence that Paul was not party to the Council that formulated the decrees, but Luke clearly does not intend this.

[34]So Hengel, *Acts*, 115-17. *Contra* Lüdemann, *Paul*, 73, who doubts if the Council could have discussed the Gentile issue without addressing the issue of table fellowship.

[35]Catchpole, 'Paul, James and the Apostolic Decree', suggests that the decrees represent the views of Judaizers and provoked Peter's separation from the Gentiles and the Antioch incident. C.K. Barrett, *Freedom and Obligation* (Philadelphia: Westminster, 1985) 97-101, associates the decrees with the Hellenists. F.F. Bruce, 'The apostolic decree of Acts 15' in W. Schrage (ed.), *Studien zum Text und zur Ethik des Neuen Testaments* (Berlin: de Gruyter, 1986) 115-24, suggests that the decrees were a response to the Antioch incident and that they represent Peter's view, making it possible for him to have table-

rejects them in a letter like 1 Corinthians, and so cannot have been party to them.[36]

The Acts account of the Council is, on this view, significantly misleading, whether because of Lukan ignorance of the events and/or because of his desire to paint a more harmonious picture of Paul's relationship to Jerusalem than was actually the case.

(iv) *The point at issue.* A further related problem about identifying Acts 15 and Galatians 2 is that, whereas Acts 15 unambiguously describes a consultation discussing the circumcision of Gentile converts and also, by inference from the decrees, table fellowship between Jewish and Gentile Christians, Galatians 2 suggests that the topic of discussion was Paul himself and his gospel. It is implied that this had a bearing on the circumcision question (vv. 3-5), but, when Paul directly refers both to the topic of their discussions and the outcome of their discussions, it is not circumcision or table fellowship that he mentions, but the question of his own recognition by the Jerusalem apostles (vv. 2, 7-9).

These differences, which are often overlooked by commentators, are striking. However, (a) Paul makes it clear that the discussion of his gospel which he describes in Galatians 2 did have some relevance to the question of the Gentiles and circumcision. He specifically refers to Titus not being circumcised (v. 3) and then to false brethren 'to whom we did not submit for a moment' (vv. 4, 5).[37]

---

fellowship with Gentiles. (He also suggests that the Cephas party may have been advocating observance of the decree in Corinth.)

[36]The argument is inconclusive. Although Paul does not cite the decrees in his discussion of food offered to idols—he is cautious about referring to the authority of Jerusalem because of his critics—he argues on the basis of his own first principles both for Gentile freedom, but also for accommodation to the scruples of others, including Jewish Christians. It is thus not clear that he would have refused a compromise solution to a critical situation (in which his own ministry and the unity of the church were threatened) which was based on those two principles. Acts 16:4 is not incredible, even if Paul had some reservations about the decrees. (See F.F. Bruce, *The Acts of the Apostles* [ed 3: Leicester: Apollos; Grand Rapids: Eerdmans, 1990] 353, for suggested textual corruption in Acts 16:4.) P. Carrington, *The Primitive Christian Catechism* (Cambridge: CUP, 1940) 16-17, and M. Newton, *The Concept of Purity at Qumran and in the Letters of Paul* (Cambridge: CUP, 1985) 103-4, find possible echoes of the apostolic decree in 1 Thes. 4:1-9, e.g. in the 'abstain from immorality'; I am grateful to Dr W.A. Strange for this reference.

[37]It is possible to read these verses as indicating that the meeting with the pillar apostles was in response to pressure from the false brethren—thus very like the situation described in Acts 15:1, 2—and even that Titus was brought to Jerusalem

(b) Paul's focus on the question of his own position and status may reflect the context of Galatians: if Paul is writing to defend himself at a time when even Barnabas has gone over to the Judaizing side, then it is not surprising that he emphasises the recognition given to him and his gospel, relegating Barnabas and other issues to the sidelines.[38] It is, however, still very curious that he describes the outcome of the meeting so egocentrically, not mentioning any decision about the circumcision issue, which is after all of importance in Galatians.

Lüdemann offers a quite different solution: noting the stylistic peculiarities of vv. 7, 8 (including the unusual use of the Greek name Peter, not Paul's usual Cephas), he suggests that it is not describing what happened at the Council but is referring back to an earlier agreement reached between himself and Peter on his first post-conversion visit to Jerusalem (Gal. 1:18). This ingenious explanation involves detaching vv. 7 and 8 from their context in an unnatural way, and also ignores the fact that most of the rest of Galatians 2:1-10 is 'first personal'.[39]

(v) *The outcome of the council.* Galatians 2 makes it clear that the consultations in Jerusalem did not solve anything very much. The issue of circumcising Gentile converts did not go away: the Galatians are being pressed on precisely this point, hence Paul's letter to them. And the issue of table fellowship was not solved: even Peter and

---

as a test case. (Compare Walker, 'Why Paul Went to Jerusalem', 503-10.) However, it is just as possible to see Gal. 2:4, 5 (about the false brethren) as a parenthesis in Paul's narrative describing how the issue blew up acutely *subsequently* to the meeting and to see Titus not as a test-case, but on the contrary as someone whose non-circumcision showed that Gentile circumcision was a non-issue at the time of that visit to Jerusalem. See F.F. Bruce, *The Epistle to the Galatians* (Exeter: Paternoster; Grand Rapids: Eerdmans, 1982) 116, Fung, *Galatians*, 91-93.

[38]See Dunn, *Jesus, Paul and the Law*, 121, and also, though not identifying Acts 15 and Gal. 2, Bauckham 'Barnabas in Galatians'.

[39]Lüdemann himself recognises, that the arguments from the style of vv. 7 and 8 are not strong. Paul's unusual use of 'Peter' could be because Paul has in mind the tradition of Peter's commissioning as 'Peter, the rock', and so uses the Greek word; see among others my 'Paul's Use of the Jesus Tradition' in *Gospel Perspectives 5* (Sheffield: JSOT, 1984) 24-28. See also A. Schmidt, 'Das Missionsdekret in Galater 2.7-8 als Vereinbarung vom ersten Besuch Pauli in Jerusalem', *NTS* 38 (1992) 149-52, supporting Lüdemann's view; but B.H. McLean, 'Galatians 2.7-9 and the Recognition of Paul's Apostolic Status at the Jerusalem Conference', *NTS* 37 (1991) 71-74, A. Suhl, 'Der Beginn der Selbständigen Mission des Paulus', *NTS* 38 (1992) 430-47, both disagreeing.

Barnabas are embarrassingly confused about it according to Galatians 2:11-14. None of this makes very good sense given a simple identification of Galatians 2 with Acts 15, since the official nature of the council in Acts 15 addressing precisely the issues of circumcision and table fellowship should at least have resolved matters for a time.[40]

The matter is slightly alleviated—at least so far as the issue of table fellowship goes—by the hypothesis that the decrees were not formulated at the Council (despite Luke) but subsequently, perhaps in response to the Antioch incident. But that does not explain the continuing pressure to have the Galatian Christians circumcised. Lüdemann doubts if the circumcision matter could have been tackled apart from the matter of table fellowship. His solution, therefore, is to propose that the Antioch incident happened before the Jerusalem Council and led to the Council, and that it has been transposed by Paul for rhetorical effect.

(c) *Concluding observation.* Lüdemann's is perhaps the most brilliant defence of the identification of Acts 15 and Galatians 2, but he has to resort to some complex reasoning in order to maintain the identification. Thus (a) Galatians 2:7, 8 refers back to Paul's first visit to Peter; (b) Galatians 2:11-14 is chronologically misplaced as preceding the events of Galatians 2:1-10; (c) Paul knew of the Acts decrees, but saw them as inapplicable to himself and his Gentile churches. Like others who identify Acts 15 and Galatians 2 he finds both Galatians and Acts to be significantly misleading. Whether this is a correct and necessary conclusion may depend on whether there are preferable explanations of the data.

2. Galatians 2:1-10=Acts 11:30

(a) *Preliminary observations in favour.* The case for identifying the visit of Galatians 2 with that of Acts 11 (rather than with that of Acts 15) is a serious one, though it has often been neglected by scholars. The following considerations, some of more weight than others, may support the identification:

---

[40]Suhl, 'Der Beginn', 439, thinks that Peter's eating with Gentiles (as in Gal. 2:12) shows that table fellowship had been discussed at the Council. Acts suggests that Peter learned to eat with Gentiles through the Cornelius incident (Acts 10).

(i) *Acts 11:30 accounted for.* Galatians 2 is the second post-conversion visit described in Galatians, Acts 11 is the second such visit in Acts. Other things being equal we might expect them to be the same. To identify them means, obviously, that we do not have the problem of explaining Acts 11 which the Acts 15 identification entails.

(ii) *The parties involved.* In both Galatians 2 and Acts 11 Paul goes up to Jerusalem with Barnabas.[41] Acts says they went from Antioch; Galatians, as we saw, probably assumes this too.

(iii) *A revelation.* Paul says that he went up to Jerusalem 'by revelation' (Gal. 2:2). In Acts Paul and Barnabas go up to Jerusalem at the behest of the Antioch church after a group of prophets have come down to Antioch from Jerusalem and specifically in response to a prophecy of famine from Agabus. We would not assume from Galatians that the 'revelation' was a prediction of famine, but it is striking that Acts and Galatians both put the visit in the context of some sort of prophetic activity.[42]

(iv) *A situation of material need.* Paul says that the Jerusalem apostles gave himself and Barnabas the right hand of fellowship, accepting their mission to the Gentiles; 'they only asked one thing, that we remember the poor, which was actually what I was eager to do' (Gal. 2:10). This last remark suggests that material hardship was on the minds of the Jerusalem apostles, which fits the context of actual or threatened famine referred to by Acts.[43] The present tense 'that we remember' (μνημονεύωμεν) can very well be construed to mean 'that we go on remembering' and the aorist 'I was eager to do' (ἐσπούδασα) may be construed as pluperfect in sense, i.e. 'I had been eager to do'.[44] We may thus have an oblique reference to the official purpose of the visit as described by Acts.

---

[41]No one else is mentioned in Acts 11; Galatians refers to Titus, and Acts 15 to 'some others'.

[42]C. Hemer, 'Acts and Galatians reconsidered', *Themelios* 2 (1977) 81-88, identifies the revelation and Agabus' prophecy, 87.

[43]Even if the 'poor' were understood in the religious sense of the 'pious poor', the request presupposes a situation of need (cf. Rom. 15:26), perhaps caused by persecution as well as famine.

[44]Cf. Lüdemann, *Paul*, 77-79. His argument that Gal. 2:10 cannot refer to the famine relief visit of Acts 11, since Paul does not say that he visited Jerusalem between his first visit to Peter and his next visit for the conference collapses if the identification of Galatians 2 with Acts 15 is questioned. Against his denial that the aorist ἐσπούδασα could refer to something already started by Paul (so also Haenchen, *Acts*, 377) see D.R. Hall, 'St. Paul and Famine Relief: A Study in

(b) *Problems*. There are, of course, various possible objections to the identification of Acts 11:3 with Galatians 2.

(i) *No Gentile controversy in Acts 11:3*. Acts does not refer to any discussion of the Gentile issue during the visit, which seems to some to make any correlation with Galatians 2 unlikely. However, this is an argument from silence, and there are various possible responses.

First, the immediately preceding context of the passage in Acts is a description of what Acts seems to see as a pioneering (and highly successful) ministry by Paul and Barnabas among Gentiles in Antioch. It is unthinkable, given this context as Luke portrays it, that the question of the Gentiles would not have been arisen in the course of the visit, even if the primary business was something different. The presence of the uncircumcised Titus with Paul and Barnabas would have made such discussion the more likely.

Second, the impression we get from Galatians 2 is that the main issue discussed with the pillars was not circumcision in particular, but rather Paul himself, his gospel and his apostleship. Barnabas is involved, but he is somewhat in the background, and Paul seems to be the issue. The result of the consultation is recognition of Paul and Barnabas and of the validity of their mission to Gentiles.

This description of what happened could, as we have seen, be Paul's one-sided reading of a much broader consultation, such as is described in Acts 15. But Galatians 2 makes a great deal of sense in the context of Acts 11. Two observations are relevant:

(1) Acts 11 suggests that it was in Antioch that Paul emerged as a missionary whom the Jerusalem church had to reckon with. Whereas Barnabas was the trusted delegate of the Jerusalem church who had been sent to look after the church (and the Gentile mission) in Antioch,[45] Paul by contrast had been a relatively unknown quantity: ever since his conversion he had been working as a freelance missionary (not under the direction of Jerusalem), and he had not been seen in Jerusalem for many years (Gal. 2:1). He had perhaps been out of the limelight for some years,[46] but then he was

---

Galatians 2:10', *ExpT* 82 (1970-71) 309-11, R.N. Longenecker, *Word Biblical Commentary 42: Galatians* (Dallas: Word, 1990) 59-61, Suhl, 'Der Beginn', 445.

[45]Hengel, *Acts*, 101, sees no reason to question the tradition about Barnabas.

[46]Neither Paul nor Acts give any clue about what Paul did in the years between his first and second visits to Jerusalem. Was he a relatively unknown and uncontroversial figure—until Barnabas brought him to Antioch to work with him among the Gentiles? Did he minister mainly 'to the Jew first' before coming to Antioch? (Note Acts 9:20-22, 28-29; 2 Cor. 11:24 and the not always persuasive

brought by Barnabas into the provincial capital city of Antioch and into a church that was very much Jerusalem's mission field. Under their combined leadership, with Paul perhaps taking an increasingly prominent role, the church of Jews and (significantly) Gentiles became increasingly large and influential. It is natural that these developments would have been discussed when Paul and Barnabas brought gifts from the Antioch church to Jerusalem and natural too that the question of Paul's authority and of his relationship to Jerusalem might have needed clarification, not least if some were questioning aspects of his teaching.

(2) The famine relief visit in Acts 11:27-30 follows on directly from the account of Peter's controversial ministry to the Gentile Cornelius and his family (10:1-11:18). If Paul and Barnabas came from Antioch while that event was still in the minds of people in Jerusalem,[47] then it is all the more obvious that they would have discussed the question of the Gentile mission with the 'pillars', including Peter. In particular it makes excellent sense that the question of responsibility for the Gentile mission would have been addressed: was Peter or Paul (with Barnabas) to take the lead? Galatians 2:1-10 presupposes precisely such a discussion, the decision being that Peter would concentrate on the circumcised and Paul on the Gentiles.[48] It makes sense that after this top-level recognition of

---

arguments in Watson's *Paul, Judaism and the Gentiles*.) Or was it precisely because he had been working with Gentiles that made him look a suitable colleague to Barnabas (perhaps the more natural inference from Gal. 1:16 and from Acts)? In either case, were his experiences in the important Jew-Gentile church of Antioch formative in the development of his thought about Jew, Gentile, law and apostleship? (Cf. Bauckham, 'Barnabas in Galatians', 67, Dunn, *Jesus, Paul and the Law*, 162.)

[47]It would be unwise to press arguments depending on the precise chronology of events in Acts 11, but Luke at least intends a broadly chronological sequence in Acts and the argument remains that, given the Lukan context, Gal. 2:1-10 makes sense.

[48]It can be argued that the Cornelius episode should have (a) led to Peter not Paul being seen as apostle to the Gentiles, (b) solved in advance the question of table fellowship that surfaced in the Antioch incident (so P.F. Esler, *Community and Gospel in Luke-Acts* [Cambridge: CUP, 1987] 95-6, raising doubts about the Acts narrative). However, it is just as arguable that (a) the experiences of Peter and Paul/Barnabas with Gentiles made a discussion of responsibilities (as described in Galatians 2 desirable. (b) The decision made practical and theological sense, with Paul being at home in the Greek-speaking world and having a sense of call to Gentiles, and Peter having been commissioned by Jesus for Jewish mission (if Mt. 10:5 is to be believed). In practice the division of

Paul's and Barnabas's apostleship or authority the two apostles to the Gentiles go off together on further missionary outreach (Acts 12-14).[49]

(ii) *No apostles in Acts 11:30.* Acts 11:30 mentions no meeting of Paul with the apostles, whereas in Galatians 2 Paul only describes his meeting with James, Peter and John, the 'pillar apostles'. Acts 15 clearly scores more highly here than Acts 11, since it specifically mentions Peter, James and 'the apostles' meeting Paul and Barnabas.

The importance of this evidence should not be minimised, but it is again an argument from silence and not decisive against the identification of Acts 11 and Galatians 2. It could be that the delivery of the aid was to the elders, because they were now responsible for church administration (compare the later 21:18), but that Peter and John were still in Jerusalem and that Paul and Barnabas naturally discussed the bigger questions about the Antioch mission with these 'pillars'.

Two things at least may tell in favour of this proposal.[50] First, Paul describes the consultation with the pillars as a private meeting (Gal. 2:2). This seems a little odd if in fact the visit was explicitly and openly to do with the Gentile issue, but makes sense if the 'official' business was the delivery of the famine relief, with the discussions about Paul's ministry being, officially speaking, a side-issue, even if ultimately of very great importance.

Second, there is the evidence of Acts 12, where Luke describes Herod Agrippa's attack on the church in which James was martyred and Peter imprisoned before his miraculous escape. It is interesting that Acts encloses this description of Herod's murderous activities within the story of the famine-relief visit—describing the visit immediately before telling us about Herod (11:27-30), but then finishing it off after telling us about Herod (12:25). The implication of this arrangement must be that the Herod story somehow relates to the famine relief visit. Perhaps the most likely clue to the relationship

---

responsibilities was probably not interpreted rigidly by either Paul or Peter. (c) The Cornelius incident explains Peter's initial openness to eating with Gentiles in Antioch; his wavering under pressure may have been because he was conscious that his 'apostleship to the circumcision' was his agreed priority.

[49]Some on the basis of Gal. 2:8 have doubted if the pillars recognised Paul actually as an 'apostle', but see Fung, *Galatians*, 99, and McLean, 'Galatians 2.7-9'.

[50]K. Lake, *The Earlier Epistles of St. Paul* (London: Rivingtons, 1930) 285-6, in his useful discussion of the alternative Galatians 2/Acts correlations, notes how Acts 6 has the apostles delegate relief work to others.

lies in the reference to the 'elders' in 11:30, since chapter 12 arguably functions in Acts precisely as an explanation of the transfer of power within the Jerusalem church from the apostles to the elders. Having described Barnabas and Saul bringing the relief to 'the elders', Luke goes on to explain how it is that elders are now in active leadership in Jerusalem instead of the apostles: he explains that Herod's persecution led to the demise of the apostles from the scene and to the rise of James, the Lord's brother.[51]

This explanation is historically plausible,[52] and, if we are right in seeing Acts 12 as an explanation of the transition, then Luke is probably implying that the famine relief visit took place after— relatively soon after, maybe—the transition, with James and the elders now in power.[53]

The relevance of this to our argument is that Galatians 2 would fit well into this situation: we note first that James the Lord's brother is listed ahead of Peter and is seemingly now number one in Jerusalem; second, that Peter and John are still important figures in the church, being known as 'the reputed ones' and 'the pillars'. We might deduce from this Pauline evidence that we are in a transitional period, with the old apostolic leadership, in which Peter, John and his brother James may have been the key leaders, beginning to give way to the leadership of James the Lord's brother.[54] It is in precisely such a context that Luke locates the famine visit.

A plausible reconstruction of events on the basis of the Lukan and Pauline evidence is that Herod's attack on the church brought to an end the old leadership, the apostle James being dead and Peter for

---

[51]See R. Wall, 'Successors to "the Twelve" According to Acts 12:1-17', *CBQ* 53 (1991) 628-43.

[52]See Hengel, *Acts*, 95-7, and Lüdemann, *Earliest Christianity*, 142-6.

[53]Paul describes the meeting of Gal. 2 as taking place 'after 14 years'. It is hard to evaluate Paul's chronological statements, and in this case to decide whether the 14 years are from Paul's conversion or from his first visit to Jerusalem. Acts links the visit to the reign of Claudius (A.D. 41-54) and to the brief period of Herod Agrippa's rule in Jerusalem (A.D. 41-44). The period 45-49 was a period of significant famines in the Palestine region. On Pauline chronology see, e.g., C. Hemer, *The Book of Acts in the Setting of Hellenistic History* (Tübingen: Mohr/ Winona Lake: Eisenbrauns, 1989) 261-270; R. Riesner, *Die Frühzeit des Paulus* (Tübingen: Mohr).

[54]Note their prominence in the gospel tradition. Bruce, *Galatians*, 123, speculates that 'the pillars' were originally Peter and the two sons of Zebedee. See also D. Wenham and A.D.A. Moses, '"There are some standing here. . .": did they become the "reputed pillars" of the Jerusalem church? Some reflections on Mark 9:1, Galatians 2:9 and the transfiguration' (*NovT*, forthcoming).

a time being forced out of Jerusalem. But after Herod's death Peter and John were able to return, forming some sort of new triumvirate of 'reputed' ones or 'pillars' along with James the Lord's brother, but with the day to day business of the church remaining in the hands of James and the elders. Things may have continued dangerous for Peter and perhaps for John, making it wise for the 'pillars' to operate privately, leaving the public business at this stage to the elders.[55]

(c) *The outcome of the meeting.* A final argument for Acts 11:30=Galatians 2:1-10 relates to the Antioch incident of Galatians 2:11-14, since this arguably makes sense after Acts 11:30 and before Acts 15.

(i) *The Antioch incident makes sense after Acts 11:30 not after Acts 15.* Galatians makes it clear that the discussions described in that chapter with 'the pillars' (2:1-10) did not resolve the question of circumcision (if indeed they addressed it at all directly). The context of the whole letter is a campaign by Judaizers (including men from James, Gal. 2:12?) to get Gentiles in Galatia circumcised. This is odd if Galatians 2:1-10=Acts 15 and if the circumcision issue had been officially discussed and apparently resolved (under the leadership of James); but it makes perfectly good sense if Galatians 2:1-10=Acts 11:30, the public business being the delivery of relief and the private talks being about Paul's ministry and the division of responsibility.[56]

Galatians also makes it clear that the discussions with the pillars did not resolve the question of table fellowship, since the crisis in Antioch was all to do with uncertainty on that issue, affecting even Peter and Barnabas. This is odd if Galatians 2:1-10=Acts 15, since the decrees address precisely that issue, but it makes good sense if Galatians 2:1-10=Acts 11:30.[57]

---

[55]See Fung, *Galatians*, 89. If Herod's persecution of the Christians was prompted by Jewish irritation about the church's Gentile mission and if James the Lord's brother was more traditional and more acceptable to the Jews than Peter, then (a) Peter may have had to be secretive after his return, (b) it may have been prudent to discuss the Gentile mission in private.

[56]Dunn fails to see this when he finds it puzzling that circumcision is still a debated issue if Gal. 2 preceded Acts 15 (*Jesus, Paul and the Law*, 159).

[57]For the idea that the decrees derived from a different meeting see previous discussion. On the quite technical Jewish background to the table fellowship issue see Esler, *Community*, 71-109, Dunn, *Jesus, Paul and the Law*, 130-159. It may be that matters were relatively *ad hoc* before the Antioch incident, with Gentile and Jewish Christians eating together, often on Jewish terms (in Jewish and God-fearing homes), but occasionally and increasingly, as the numbers of Gentiles

(ii) *Acts 15 makes sense as a response to the Antioch incident.*

(1) According to Galatians the incident happened (a) after Paul's second post-conversion visit to Jerusalem (the consultation with the pillars), (b) after his mission to Galatia.[58] Similarly the council of Acts 15 happens (a) after Paul's second post-conversion visit to Jerusalem (the famine relief visit), (b) after the mission of Paul and Barnabas to South Galatia.

(2) According to Galatians the incident arose in Antioch, when certain people of the 'circumcision faction' came down from James (2:12). It is presumably the same party who have been in Galatia disturbing the church there and insisting on circumcision. Similarly the council of Acts 15 was provoked by the arrival in Antioch of 'certain individuals' who came down from Judea and were teaching 'Unless you are circumcised according to the law of Moses, you cannot be saved'.[59]

(3) According to Galatians the incident came to a head over the issue of table fellowship: Peter and Barnabas had been eating freely with Gentiles, but, under pressure, withdrew from such table fellowship. Paul had a public show-down with Peter over the issue (though it is clear for Paul that it is the circumcision issue and the whole status of Gentile Christians that is at stake and even more fundamental than table fellowship). Acts 15 does not mention the specific issue of table fellowship being discussed at the Council, nor the division between Paul and his colleagues.

However, (a) Acts 15 does refer to 'no small dissension and debate'. (b) The parties to the debate in Antioch as described in Galatians 2:11-14 are precisely the same as feature in the account of the council of Acts 15 (the Judaizers, James, Peter, Barnabas and Paul), and they represent the same sort of positions on the 'conservative/liberal' spectrum in Galatians and Acts, as we will see.[60] (c) The fact that the council decrees (Acts 15:19-21) include regulations to facilitate table fellowship suggests that the problem

---

increased, on Gentile terms (in Gentile homes). This increasing trend came to the attention of Jerusalem, hence the pressure on Jewish-Christians like Peter not to compromise their Jewishness and on Gentile Christians to accept circumcision.

[58]It is plausibly argued that Galatians was written soon after the incident, when the matter was still unresolved, hence Paul's failure to mention any definite outcome.

[59]The phraseology 'certain people came down from' is intriguingly similar in Gal. 2:12, Acts 15:1.

[60]On James see comments above on the Galatians 2=Acts 15 view.

was important at the council. (d) Acts 10 and 11, the Cornelius story, suggest that Peter's position before the Council was to eat freely with the uncircumcised (11:2-10); the Council represents a change to a more restrictive policy, presumably because of Jewish-Christian pressure. (e) Although Peter's troubles at Antioch aren't mentioned, the figure of Peter and his experience (with Cornelius) are central to the discussions of Acts 15. He is portrayed as essentially on Paul's side of the debate, which is where Paul in Galatians suggests that he was by conviction. (f) Although there is no suggestion of tension between Barnabas and Paul in Luke's description of the Council, they do in fact split up in Acts 15:36: the division of opinion is over Mark, but it is entirely plausible that the Antioch incident was a catalyst to the parting of the ways.[61]

3. Concluding remarks on Acts 11:30=Galatians 2:1-10

The case for the Acts 11:30=Galatians 2:1-10 identification is a much weightier one than is sometimes realised. If it is correct, it has significant implications for the understanding of Galatians, making a South Galatian destination and a date for Galatians before the Jerusalem council of Acts 15 likely. Both positions are rejected by many critics, who date Galatians to the same general period as Romans, i.e. rather late in Paul's career, and who identify the 'Galatians' with the ethnic Galatians of so-called 'North Galatia'. Others, however, argue forcibly for the early date and South Galatian destination of the letter; it is not possible in this chapter on Acts to go into those specifically Galatian problems.[62]

---

[61]The idea that Paul 'lost' in the controversy at Antioch, failing to persuade Peter, Barnabas and others and so severing his relationships with Jerusalem and Antioch, is mainly an inference from Paul's failure to mention the resolution of the Antioch crisis. But this is explained if Galatians was written between the crisis and the subsequent Jerusalem council. It is possible, even on this view, to see the Jerusalem council of Acts 15 as representing a compromise, not reflecting Paul's views in their entirety and thus perhaps as a catalyst to the development of Paul's independent ministry. But there is no evidence of a drastic breakdown of relationships.

[62]On Galatia and Galatians see the commentaries and also Hemer, *Acts*, 277-307. On the issue of date, two considerations not always noted may be mentioned: (a) the thematic similarity of Galatians and Romans may reflect not closeness of date, but similarity of situation, with Galatians being written after the Antioch incident when the Jew-Gentile issue and questions of Paul's relationship with

The argument for identifying Acts 11:30 and Galatians 2:1-10, if correct, would enhance the argument for Luke's historical accuracy considerably, and yet indicate that Luke's account is very partial (e.g. his failure to mention the meeting with the 'pillars' in the famine relief visit). His silence on the controversy between Paul, Peter and Barnabas at Antioch might be because the event cast a rather unhappy light on three of the heroes of his story (Peter, Paul and Barnabas), but might be because he is writing after the event when that difference, which mattered so much to Paul at the time, was past history and rather unimportant.

III. The 'First Missionary Journey'

Acts 13 and 14 describe Paul's so-called first missionary journey with Barnabas. A few things only need be noted.

1. New mission

We have already observed that this new missionary initiative makes good sense if Galatians 2:1-10 is identified with the Acts 11:30 view, since Galatians describes the apostles encouraging Paul and Barnabas in their Gentile mission.

2. The Jew first

In each place that they visit Paul and Barnabas go first to the synagogue and to the Jewish community and only then to the Gentiles. This has been seen as in tension with the agreement of Galatians 2:10 that they 'should go to the Gentiles',[63] but (i) it is doubtful if that agreement was ever understood to mean that Paul

---

Jerusalem were dominating his mind, and with the rather less heated Romans being written when Paul was again heading for Jerusalem facing some of the same issues and hostility (cf. Rom. 15:30-32, Acts 21). (b) It is arguable that the emphasis we find in Galatians on freedom in the Spirit and on male/female equality could have given rise to some of the problems that Paul faced in the Corinthian church, but is unlikely to have been Paul's emphasis after his Corinthian experiences.

[63]So Sanders, *Paul*, 9.

would never minister to Jews, (ii) the Jewish community formed a natural way into a city community for Paul and his colleagues,[64] (iii) the policy is entirely in accord with Paul's statement of divine priorities in the book of Romans, i.e. 'to the Jew first, and then to the Greek'.

Acts describes considerable opposition to the mission, spearheaded almost exclusively by 'unbelieving Jews'. This makes historical sense, if the Jews and their sympathisers were the evangelistic starting-point for these two men who themselves had come from Judaism. If hostile Jewish reports of Paul's and Barnabas's mission (and especially of their open-doors policy to Gentiles) got back to Jerusalem, this might have prompted the Judaizers' pro-circumcision campaign in Antioch and Galatia.[65]

3. Appointing elders

Acts' description in 14:23 of Paul and Barnabas appointing elders in each church has been seen as an anachronism on the part of the author of Acts.[66] However, even if the term is anachronistic, there is evidence of structured leadership in the earliest Pauline churches. Whether Galatians is the first Pauline letter or 1 Thessalonians, both refer to leaders, even, in the case of Galatians, to paid teachers (Gal. 6:6; 1 Thes. 5:12, 13; cf. Phil. 1:1). In 1 Thessalonians Paul is writing to a church that he has just left and founded and there are already recognised leaders in place.[67]

---

[64]So F.F. Bruce, 'Is the Paul of Acts the Real Paul', *BJRL* 58 (1975/76) 293

[65]See also K.P. Donfried, '1 Thessalonians, Acts and the Early Paul', in R.F. Collins, *The Thessalonian Correspondence* (Leuven: Leuven University Press, 1990) 3-36. He accepts Lüdemann's early dating of 1 Thessalonians and notes various parallels between 1 Thessalonians and the Acts accounts of Paul's first and second missionary journeys (e.g. 1 Thes. 1:6/Acts 13:52, 1 Thes 3:2/Acts 14:22).

[66]There is widespread agreement that Luke here describes an 'unPauline form of polity', so H. Conzelmann, *Acts of the Apostles* (Philadelphia: Fortress, 1987) 112; cf. Haenchen, *Acts*, 436, Lüdemann, *Early Christianity*, 163.

[67]The church of 1 Cor. may look like an unstructured, charismatic church, but it was founded shortly after that in Thessalonica, and is likely also to have had leaders. There are one or two hints of their existence (1 Cor. 12:28, 16:16); it may be that Paul does not appeal to their leadership, because they were at sixes and sevens among themselves.

IV. The 'Second Missionary Journey'

The aftermath of the Acts 15 council was the parting of the ways between Paul and Barnabas, with Paul taking Silas on his so-called 'second missionary journey' which took them (and Timothy whom they recruited in Lystra) through Turkey and then on through Greece: Neapolis - Philippi - Thessalonica - Athens - Corinth, where they stayed for 'a considerable time' (at least 18 months) (18:11, 18).

How does the Acts picture fit in with what we can gather from the epistles? We note a few points.

1. Silas and Timothy

The involvement of Silas and Timothy with Paul in his mission to Greece is attested directly in 2 Corinthians 1:19, which refers to Silas and Timothy preaching the gospel with Paul in Corinth, and by implication in 1 and 2 Thessalonians, since both are written as from Paul, Silvanus and Timothy. (It is probably rightly inferred that 1 Thessalonians, if not 2 Thessalonians, was written in Corinth, though it could have been in Athens.)

2. The journey

Various stages of the journey, as described by Acts, are reflected in Paul's letters: thus 1 Thessalonians 2:2 and Philippians 4:15, 16 refer to Paul going from Philippi to Thessalonica and on out of Macedonia. 1 Thessalonians 3:1 indicates that Paul went from Thessalonica to Athens, and 2 Corinthians 1:9, as we saw, refers to Paul, Silas and Timothy working in Corinth.

3. Circumcising Timothy

The description in Acts of Paul circumcising Timothy 'because of the Jews' (Acts 16:3), which is often seen as historically quite implausible, will be discussed in section V below.[68]

---

[68]The Acts comment about Timothy's Jewish mother does find an echo within the Pauline corpus in 2 Tim. 1:5; 3:15.

4. Philippi

Acts describes Paul and Silas having some success in their mission at Philippi,[69] though it ended with the imprisonment of Paul and Silas and their expulsion from the city (16:16-40). Philippians confirms that the mission was successful, and Paul speaks in 1 Thessalonians 2:2 of having 'suffered and been shamefully mistreated at Philippi'.

5. Thessalonica

Acts portrays Paul's visit to Thessalonica also as meeting with some success (17:1-9), but Jewish agitation against Paul leads to a town-wide uproar and to Paul and Silas moving on to Berea. The opposition spreads here, and Paul is sent off by the believers to Athens, Silas and Timothy being left behind and only rejoining Paul after he had moved on to Corinth (18:5). 1 Thessalonians gives a similar picture: Paul writes to an established church, but one which he had had to leave and about which he was anxious. He compares the sufferings of the Thessalonians to those of the Judean churches, quite probably implying that the opposition in Thessalonica had been Jewish in inspiration (2:13-3:13). He refers to being left alone in Athens and of sending Timothy to find out about the faith of the Thessalonians, but then he reports (writing from Corinth) that 'Timothy has just now come to us from you' (3:6).

There are two points of tension between the accounts. First, whereas Acts refers to Paul arguing in the synagogue for three weeks, 1 Thessalonians may imply a significantly longer visit and Philippians speaks of the Philippian Christians sending Paul help 'more than once' (4:16).[70] Luke may be poorly informed at this point; on the other hand Acts need not mean that Paul stayed in Thessalonica for only those weeks when he ministered in the

---

[69]Lüdemann, *Early Christianity*, 183, comments on the Acts account of Paul's miracle-working in Philippi, and notes that Paul himself alludes to that aspect of his ministry in Rom. 15:18f.; 2 Cor. 12:12. Haenchen, *Acts*, 113, 114, sees Luke's enthusiastic accounts of Paul's miracles as significantly at odds with the evidence of Paul himself. But the difference is at best one of emphasis. See J. Jervell, 'Paul in the Acts of the Apostles' in J. Kremer (ed.), *Les Actes des Apôtres* (Leuven: Leuven University Press, 1979) 299, on the 'charismatic, miracle-believing, visionary and ecstatic Paul'.

[70]See Conzelmann, *Acts*, 135; Lüdemann, *Early Christianity*, 188.

synagogue, and 1 Thessalonians need not imply a long ministry on Paul's part—the Thessalonians' worries over the death of some of their number may suggest that Paul was not there long enough to face with them the problem of Christians dying.

The second point of tension is that Acts suggests that Paul left Silas and Timothy in Berea, whereas 1 Thessalonians suggests that Paul sent Timothy from Athens back to Thessalonica. Luke may have given a simplified version of events here.[71]

6. Athens

Acts describes Paul in Athens and speaking to the Areopagus court. It says that some believed, but there is no suggestion of a substantial ministry having taken place. Paul's stay in Athens is referred to in 1 Thessalonians 3:1, but there is no reference anywhere in the Pauline corpus to an established church in Athens.[72]

There has been a great deal of debate about Paul's speech in Athens, as it is described by Luke.[73] Some have seen the appeal to the Athenians' innate knowledge of God and the lack of emphasis on the cross to be seriously at variance with Paul's pessimistic verdict on the guilt of the pagan world and his consistent emphasis on the cross (e.g. Rom. 1; 1 Cor. 1). Others have argued that the conciliatory approach of the speech is perfectly plausible, given Paul's evangelistic purpose;[74] specifically it has been observed that the speech is thematically similar to 1 Thessalonians 1:9, 10, where Paul's description of the conversion of the Thessalonians may be a clue as to his evangelistic priorities during his mission to Greece (including Athens).[75]

---

[71]Cf. Conzelmann, Acts, 136; Lüdemann, Early Christianity, 188, argues with excessive subtlety that Luke wishes to leave the stage in Athens clear for Paul.

[72]We should probably not make too much of Paul's observation in 1 Cor. 2:3 about coming to Corinth 'in fear and much trembling' as evidence that he felt a failure after Athens.

[73]We cannot go into the question of ancient speech-writing conventions here, nor into a full discussion of the theology of the Pauline speeches in Acts. One of the most influential treatments of the Paulinism of Acts has been P. Vielhauer's 'On the "Paulinism" of Acts', in L.E. Keck and J.L. Martyn (eds.), Studies in Luke-Acts (London: SPCK, 1968) 33-50. See also W.W. Gasque, A History of the Interpretation of the Acts of the Apostles (ed 2; Peabody: Hendrickson, 1989) 201-305.

[74]Cf. 1 Cor. 9:19-23; contrast the pastoral purpose of his letters.

[75]1 Thes. is usually thought to have been written from Corinth very shortly after Paul's visit to Athens.

7. Corinth

Acts describes an extended and fruitful stay of Paul in Corinth, working first among Jews then among Gentiles. That Paul did have such a ministry in Corinth is confirmed (a) by 1 and 2 Corinthians, which testify to Paul's closeness to the Corinthians as well as to his frustration over their development as a church, (b) by the writing of 1 Thessalonians: Paul is settled enough to write to Thessalonica.

Acts describes Paul meeting up with Aquila and Priscilla in Corinth and working with them tent-making. It may be no accident that in 1 Thessalonians (written from Corinth) he refers to how in Thessalonica he 'worked night and day, so that we might not burden any of you while we proclaimed the gospel of God' (2:9, cf. also 2 Thes. 3:6-12), and that in 1 Corinthians he discusses at some length his policy of not accepting payment for his gospel ministry preferring to earn his own way (1 Cor. 9).

Paul's close association with Aquila and Priscilla is confirmed in Paul's letters: thus Paul sends their greetings to the Corinthians in 1 Corinthians 16:19. This makes sense (a) if they have lived in Corinth as Acts reports and (b) if they then left Corinth and came to Ephesus (from where 1 Corinthians was probably written), as Acts also reports (18:18, 26). Paul also sends them greetings in Romans 16:3, referring warmly to their collaboration with him in his ministry: their presence in Rome also makes sense given the account of Acts that they came to Corinth 'because Claudius had expelled all the Jews to leave Rome' (18:2). It is likely enough that they would have returned to Rome after the edict had lapsed.

Suetonius, the Roman historian, refers to this expulsion as due to Jewish rioting in Rome 'at the instigation of Chrestus (*impulsore Chresto*)',[76] and it is a plausible hypothesis that the trouble in the Jewish community in Rome was caused by the arrival of the gospel of Christus. (Compare the Acts accounts of Jewish-Christian clashes in Asia Minor and Greece.) If Aquila and Priscilla were expelled in such circumstances, it is quite possible that they were Christians (i.e. Christian Jews) before they met Paul, and this may be implied by the absence of any reference to their conversion in Acts.[77]

---

[76]Suet. *Cl.* 25, 4.
[77]So Conzelmann, *Acts*, 151, noting their absence from Paul's account of his early ministry in Corinth in 1 Cor. 1. *Contra* Lüdemann, *Early Christianity*, 201.

There are two points at which this hypothesis may converge with the evidence of the epistles:[78] first, it is an attractive theory that Paul may have written Romans to address a church experiencing some tensions between Gentile Christians and Jewish Christians, hence the focus on the Jew-Gentile theme and the pleas for unity. If the Roman church had originally been a largely Jewish-Christian body, which lost its Jewish-Christian leadership (like Aquila and Priscilla?) due to Claudius's edict, there could have been significant tensions when those Jewish Christians were able to return.[79]

Second, one of the most mysterious passages in 1 Thessalonians is 2:13-16, where Paul speaks with unusual bitterness of the Jews but then comments that 'God's wrath has overtaken them at last'.[80] The fierceness of the passage makes some sense given (a) the destination of the letter, i.e. Thessalonica, if Acts is correct in describing the acute Jewish harassment of Paul's mission there (17:1-15), (b) the place from which the letter was sent, probably Corinth, if there too there were violent clashes between Jews and Paul and his companions (so Acts 18:1-17), (c) the time of writing, i.e. during Paul's stay in Corinth after the expulsion of the Jews from Rome. The expulsion would inevitably have been of great importance in the household of Aquila and Priscilla, where Acts has Paul staying, and, if the expulsion was in the context of violent opposition to the Christian mission, then Paul had yet one more reason for denouncing the Jews 'who displease God and oppose everyone by hindering us from speaking to the Gentiles that they may be saved' (1 Thes. 2:16).

As for Paul's puzzling phrase 'the wrath has come upon them at the last', one serious possibility is that it refers to the Claudian expulsion.[81] Paul could have seen it as God's wrath on the Jews for

---

[78]Note also Crispus in Acts 18:8 and 1 Cor. 1:14.

[79]See recently A.J.M. Wedderburn, *The Reasons for Romans* (Edinburgh: Clark, 1988) 54-59; but see the rather different approach of Watson, *Paul, Judaism and the Gentiles*, 91-105.

[80]There is no decisive reason for viewing the passage as a non-Pauline interpolation; see, e.g., J.W. Simpson, 'The Problems Posed by 1 Thessalonians 2:15-16 and a Solution', *Horizons in Biblical Theology* 12 (1990) 42-72; J.A. Weatherley, 'The Authenticity of 1 Thessalonians 2.13-16: Additional Evidence', *JSNT* 42 (1991) 79-98.

[81]See E. Bammel's useful article, 'Judenverfolgung und Naherwartung. Zur Eschatologie des ersten Thessalonicherbriefs', *ZTK* 56 (1959) 294-315. The identification of Paul's wrath with Suetonius' expulsion would still be possible if the expulsion were of key Jewish and Jewish Christian leaders, as some have speculated. See E. Schürer, *The History of the Jewish People in the Age of Jesus Christ*

their opposition to the gospel,[82] or at least as one evidence of that wrath, along with the recent disastrous massacre of Jews in Jerusalem at the hands of the Roman governor,[83] especially so if he and his readers were familiar with those Jesus-traditions which spoke of judgement to come on the Jews.[84]

V. The 'Third Missionary Journey' and Paul's Final Journey to Jerusalem

1. The Ephesian period

Paul's 'third missionary journey' is focused on Ephesus. Acts speaks of Paul having an extraordinarily effective ministry there over two years or more and comments that 'all the residents of Asia, both Jews and Greeks, heard the word of the Lord' (19:10).

III.1 (Edinburgh: Clark, 1986) 77-78; E.M. Smallwood, *The Jews Under Roman Rule From Pompey to Diocletian* (Leiden: Brill, 1981) 210-16.

[82]Admittedly Jewish-Christians, as well as non-Christian Jews, felt the force of Claudius's wrath, but his action was still directed to Jews as a group (according to Suetonius and Acts). It is interesting, though possibly nothing more, that Paul can speak of the Roman authorities as agents of God's 'wrath' on the evildoer (Rom. 13:4, 5).

[83]Jos. *War* 2.223-31, *Ant* 20,105-117, refer to 20,000 or 30,000 people being killed by Cumanus. See R. Jewett, 'The Agitators and the Galatian Congregation', *NTS* 17 (1970-71) 204-5, who associates the zealot activity in Jerusalem at the time with opposition to Christianity. The word 'wrath' in 1 Thes. 2:16 has seemed to some commentators an inappropriate word for such mundane events, but historical events are regularly given eschatological significance in Jewish apocalyptic.

[84]For evidence of such knowledge see my *Rediscovery of Jesus Eschatological Discourse*. Whether it goes back substantially to Jesus or whether it had its origin in the crisis situation provoked by the emperor Caligula in A.D. 39, as some suppose, the discourse envisages a disaster in Jerusalem akin to the attack of Antiochus Epiphanes in 167 B.C., with the Romans now the likely perpetrators. Paul could well have seen the events of A.D. 49 as the start of such 'wrath' on the Jews—and not without some reason, given the way things developed into the war of A.D. 66 (cf. A. Kasher, *Jews and Hellenistic Cities in Eretz-Israel* [Tübingen: Mohr, 1990] 253). It is interesting that Luke's version of the eschatological discourse (with which Paul may show some familiarity elsewhere, e.g. Rom. 11:25) refers to the coming disaster in Jerusalem as 'wrath on this people', ὀργὴ τῷ λαῷ τούτῳ (21:23). It is possible that Paul's reference to the 'wrath' having come on the Jews in 1 Thes. 2:16 was understood by some Thessalonians to mean that the eschaton promised by Jesus was indeed at hand, so that Paul has to calm their excitement in 2 Thes. 2.

This impression is confirmed by 1 Corinthians, where Paul comments that 'I will stay in Ephesus until Pentecost, for a wide door for effective work has opened to me' (16:8, 9), and also probably by Colossians, which implies that the church in Colosse was founded by Epaphras, quite likely during this fruitful period of ministry in Ephesus (1:7; 4:12, 13).

1 and also 2 Corinthians suggest that a lot happened in this Ephesian period which Acts does not describe, especially in connection with Corinth. It is clear that all sorts of problems arose between Paul and the church that he founded, leading to a vigorous correspondence between Paul and the Corinthian church (with two of Paul's letters being lost to us, cf. 1 Cor. 5:9; 2 Cor. 2, etc.) and also to a 'painful visit' by Paul to Corinth, of which Acts tells us nothing (2 Cor. 2:1). In 1 Corinthians 15:32 and 2 Corinthians 1:8, 9 Paul also describes some massive personal crises that he experienced in Asia (possibly compare Rom. 16:4), which some have identified with the riot of Acts 19:21-41 but which may be something not recorded at all by Acts. We are reminded of the selective nature of Luke's narration.

One point at which 1 Corinthians and Acts converge is in the references to Apollos. Acts describes his meeting in Ephesus with Priscilla and Aquila (18:24-28): he is described as an Alexandrian, 'an eloquent man, well versed in the Scriptures' who spoke 'boiling in spirit' (ζέων τῷ πνεύματι). His theology was defective according to Acts, since he only knew John's baptism, but he was instructed by Aquila and Priscilla, and in due course went to 'Achaia' with the encouragement of the Ephesian Christians and proved a great help there to the believers.

1 Corinthians dovetails with this account in several ways. First, as we have seen, 1 Corinthians 16:19 attests the presence of Aquila and Priscilla in Ephesus at about the right time. Second, 1 Corinthians makes it clear how influential Apollos had been in Corinth, with some of the Corinthians apparently preferring his style to that of Paul. Third, both Acts and Paul describe Apollos in a way that hints that he was in basic agreement with Paul, and yet independent of Paul and someone about whom some had doubts (note Acts 18:27; 1 Cor. 16:12).

One other possibility is worth mentioning. A possible reading of the situation described in 1 Corinthians 1-4 is that Paul is contending (among others) with people who were setting Apollos on a pinnacle and putting him down. Two of the things that the Corinthians seem to have prized especially were (a) wisdom/

knowledge/eloquence, hence Paul's polemic in 1 Corinthians 1 and 2, (b) charismatic manifestations of spiritual power, hence 1 Corinthians 12-14. It is possible that both of these things were associated by the Corinthians with Apollos, since he is described in Acts both as someone of unusual eloquence, but also as 'boiling in spirit', an expression that could hint at his charismatic emphasis.[85]

Acts describes Paul in Ephesus resolving to go through Macedonia and Achaia, then on to Jerusalem and finally to Rome. Accordingly he sent 'Timothy and Erastus to Macedonia, while he himself stayed for some time longer in Asia' (19:21, 22). Compare 1 Corinthians 16:5-11 where Paul speaks of his intention to travel to Macedonia and Corinth, but says that 'I will stay in Ephesus until Pentecost. . .' and then goes on to tell them to welcome Timothy if he comes. 2 Corinthians 1 and 2 have Paul coming into Macedonia *en route* for Corinth, but it is clear that a lot of troubled water has passed under the bridge since 1 Corinthians. It looks as though Paul did leave Ephesus for Macedonia (as he proposed in 1 Cor. 16), but that he went to Corinth first, intending to go from Corinth to Macedonia, then back to Corinth and on to Jerusalem (see 2 Cor. 1:16). But things were disastrously unhappy when he came to Corinth, and so he changed his plans and instead of returning from Macedonia to Corinth (where the church seemed unlikely to welcome him or to support his collection for the saints in Jerusalem) he went back to Asia Minor. From here he sent Titus to gauge and repair the situation, and then he followed, hoping this time to proceed with his planned journey to Jerusalem via Macedonia and Achaia and writing 2 Corinthians *en route* to prepare for his visit to Corinth, among other things explaining his changed itinerary (2 Cor. 1:15-22).[86]

Luke does not make clear the complexity of the comings and goings during the Ephesus period, but he finally has Paul come to Achaia (i.e. Corinth), staying there for three months (Acts 20:3), before proceeding on his journey towards Jerusalem.[87]

---

[85]Compare Rom. 12:11. See Lüdemann, *Early Christianity*, 209, and especially P. Richardson in 'The Thunderbolt in Q and the Wise Man in Corinth' (in Richardson and J.C. Hurd, *From Jesus to Paul* (Waterloo: Laurier, 1984) 101-107, who also thinks that the remarks about baptism in 1 Cor. may reflect the baptist connections of Apollos suggested by Acts.

[86]On Paul's itinerary compare R.P. Martin, *Word Biblical Commentary 40 2 Corinthians* (Waco: Word, 1986) xxxiv.

[87]Hemer, *Acts*, 259, comments that Acts' abbreviated description of Paul's ministry in Ephesus reflects his desire to take the story on to Rome.

2. *The journey to Jerusalem*

Acts describes Paul journeying from Corinth to Jerusalem by land and sea, with a group of companions, visiting various places *en route*, including Miletus, where he addresses the Ephesian elders. There is a sense of finality about the journey, with Paul and his hearers sensing that he is leaving them for the last time and that he faces acute trouble in Jerusalem. On arriving in Jerusalem he faces suspicion on the part of the Jewish Christians and violent hostility from non-Christian Jews. He is arrested, and after an extended imprisonment and a series of trials he is taken by ship to Rome for trial before the emperor.

There are a number of possible links with the epistles.

(1) *Romans 15, 16.* The letter to the Romans seems to have been written from Corinth (see 16:1), very probably in the visit described in Acts 20:3. In Romans Paul speaks of his plan to go to Jerusalem and then on to Rome and even Spain (15:22-25). This fits in with his planned itinerary, described in Acts 19:21. Paul's explanation that he is now taking leave of his former mission fields, having completed his work there (15:23), fits with the picture in Acts of Paul bidding a final farewell to people on his route (Acts 20:38). In Romans Paul is apprehensive of the reception he will receive in Jerusalem from both Jews and Jewish Christians (15:31); Acts 21 makes it clear that his fears were in the event well founded.

(2) *The Miletus speech.* Paul's speech to the Ephesian elders in Acts 20:17-35 is the only example in Acts of Paul's teaching for Christians, the other speeches being evangelistic, and is therefore the only speech which is really comparable to Paul's letters. Scholars have noted a number of ideas and phrases reminiscent of the letters, most significantly the reference to redemption through the blood of Christ (Acts 20:28). Whether this reflects Lukan artistry or the use of authentic Pauline tradition is debated.

(3) *The collection.* A notable divergence between Acts and the Pauline letters is that Acts does not make clear that Paul's visit to Jerusalem was in order to bring his collection for the 'poor among the saints in Jerusalem' (Rom. 15:25-28). For Paul this was clearly a very important and significant initiative (see also 1 Cor. 16:1-4 and 2 Cor. 8 and 9). Luke has Paul explaining to Festus that 'I came to bring alms to my

nation' (Acts 24:17), but this is the nearest we come to any direct reference to the collection,[88] though it is possible to see a very indirect allusion to it in Luke's listing of the companions of Paul on his last journey to Jerusalem (20:4), if they were the representatives of their respective churches bearing (or accompanying) the gifts sent by their churches (cf. 1 Cor. 16:4; 2 Cor. 8:19).[89]

Luke's failure to mention the collection directly suggests that at the time of writing he did not see the collection as having the significance which Paul attached to it in the period leading up to his final visit to Jerusalem. It may be that its symbolic importance for Paul was overshadowed for Luke by the way things turned out—i.e. by Paul's dramatic arrest and subsequent trials and journey to Rome. It is possible that it was a sensitive subject for Luke when writing and that one of the accusations against Paul had to do with his money-raising project.[90]

(4) *Paul and Jewish observances.* Acts portrays Paul as someone who respects Jewish customs and scruples, accepting the requirement of the Jerusalem council that Gentile converts should respect Jewish dietary practices, circumcising Timothy 'because of the Jews', himself observing a vow and the Jewish festivals of unleavened bread and Pentecost (ch. 15; 16:3; 18:18; 20:6, 16). This picture of Paul comes most sharply into focus in Acts 21:20-25, where Paul is told by James that the Christians of Jerusalem 'have been told about you that you teach all the Jews living among the Gentiles to forsake Moses, and that you tell them not to circumcise their children or observe the customs'. Paul is then invited by James to undertake a vow: 'thus all will know that there is nothing in what they have been told about you, but that you yourself observe and guard the law. But as for the Gentiles. . .' Paul according to Acts accepts the suggestion of James.

Luke's rather Jewish Paul has been regarded by many scholars as seriously at odds with the radical Paul of the epistles who

---

[88]Hemer, *Acts*, 189, dismisses Haenchen's 'disingenuously hypercritical' claim that Luke is misleading in speaking of 'alms for my nation' rather than as for the church.
[89]Lüdemann, *Early Christianity*, 225, finds a problem with this view in that no representatives of Corinth or Philippi are mentioned. Luke by using 'we' does imply that others went with Paul than just those mentioned.
[90]So F.F. Bruce, *Aufstieg*, 2581. Other less persuasive suggestions have been made, e.g. about the collection not being accepted or actually delivered, e.g. Lüdemann, *Early Christianity*, 237; Haenchen, *Acts*, 611-14.

denounces the Jewish-Christian moves to have Gentiles circumcised as 'another gospel', who sides with 'the strong' in their insistence that they are free to eat anything rather than with the weak, even though he advocates charity towards the weak, and who says openly that 'to those outside the law I became outside the law' (1 Cor. 9:21).[91]

Other scholars have been unpersuaded that there is a serious discrepancy. In the first place, although Acts does describe Paul observing certain Jewish practices, he is at the same time portrayed as a controversial missionary to the Gentiles, whom zealous Jews crossed repeatedly and suspected intensely, not least because of his attitude to the law (see 15:5; ch. 21, etc.). It is at least implied that he was a liberal so far as the law and eating with Gentiles was concerned (cf. Peter's words 15:10 and 10:1-11:18; 13:38; 20:7).

In the second place, Paul's letters make clear his uncompromising commitment to Gentile freedom, but also (a) his respect for 'weak' Jewish Christians who maintain their dietary customs, (b) his deep concern for and involvement with Jerusalem and Jewish Christians,[92] and (c) his willingness to identify with Jewish customs.[93] Thus in 1 Corinthians 9:19-23 he not only speaks of his freedom not to keep the Jewish law, but equally of his freedom to keep that law: 'To the Jews I became as a Jew in order to win the Jews. . .'[94] It is argued that this Paul could well have circumcised the half-Jewish Timothy in order to facilitate his ministry among Jews, and that he might have gone a long way towards appeasing his Jewish critics in Jerusalem at a time of considerable personal danger.[95]

---

[91]E.g. Vielhauer, '"Paulinism"', 40, 41.

[92]2 Cor. 11:24 suggests considerable, painful involvement.

[93]His remark in 1 Cor. 16:8 about staying in Ephesus until Pentecost may suggest, like Acts 20:6, 16, that the Jewish festivals had some continuing significance for Paul.

[94]The flexibility of 1 Cor. 9:19-23 would of course have been complicated at times, not least in relationships with Jews. But we know that those relationships were complicated. It is arguable that Paul himself was a more complex person than many critics allow.

[95]Paul comments that he was perceived as being more moderate in person than in his letters (2 Cor. 10:1, 10), which may be significant in any comparison of Acts and the letters. On the Jewishness of Paul see especially Jervell, 'Paul in the Acts', 297-306, arguing vigorously that Luke brings out a side of Paul that is in shadow in the epistles.

(5) *Paul the speech-maker.* Luke has Paul, when he is under arrest, making various speeches in his own defence, and portrays Paul as no mean orator.[96] Paul, however, speaks of his incompetence as a speaker (e.g. in 2 Cor. 10:10). Some see a significant tension here;[97] but this may be to take Paul's self-deprecating remarks too literally: it is clear from his letters that he was a competent speaker in terms of theological content and an effective one in terms of results. It may be that Luke is more enthusiastic about Paul's preaching than Paul was, but even Luke does not suggest that Paul was always effective (e.g. in Athens).

(6) *Paul the prisoner.* The concluding chapters of Acts describe Paul as in prison for extensive periods, first in Caesarea and then in Rome. The Roman imprisonment is specifically described as house arrest. The so-called prison epistles of Paul (including Philippians, Colossians, Philemon and Ephesians) by their very existence confirm that Paul was imprisoned in circumstances that allowed him some freedom (e.g. to write letters), though whether the traditional association of all the prison epistles with the Roman imprisonment is correct, or whether some of them were written in Caesarea or in Ephesus (during an imprisonment not described in Acts) is debated by scholars.

VI. Concluding Observations

It is not the intention of this chapter to present any ambitious conclusions about what the comparison of the Paul in Acts with the Paul of the epistles proves for the study of the book of Acts. But we have gathered a significant amount of the relevant evidence, and it is possible to make a few general remarks about what has emerged.

First, it is clear that Acts and the Pauline letters do very frequently intersect.[98] The author of Acts is not vaguely familiar with the story of Paul, but has a considerable amount of detailed knowledge, about Paul's journeys, the churches that he founded and the people that he worked with.

---

[96]See B. Winter's chapter in this volume.
[97]So Haenchen, *Acts*, 114.
[98]Cf. Hemer, *Acts*, 181-90 for a list of possible links. Marshall, 'Luke's View', 45-46, finds Paul's missionary vision and his decision-making (through prayer, revelation and common-sense) similarly portrayed in Acts and the epistles.

Second, some of this information Luke could have gleaned from the letters, if he was familiar with them, but much of the story of Paul in Acts has no basis in the letters and some of the strongly emphasised features of the letters are not in Acts (e.g. the collection), so that it is highly probable that Luke had other sources of information about Paul (as may in any case be inferred from the 'we' sections of Acts).

Third, the comparison of Acts and Paul's letters is often illuminating for the study of both texts: Acts 18:1-3, for example, with its reference to Paul staying with fellow-tent-makers Aquila and Priscilla after their expulsion from Rome, throws all sorts of light on the letters. The letters with their description of the collection for the saints illuminate the Acts account of Paul's last journey to Jerusalem. The Acts narrative suggests a chronological and geographical context for the letters.

Fourth, although there are many points of contact, Luke offers a different perspective on Paul's ministry than the one we get from the Pauline letters. He treats some periods quite selectively and briefly (e.g. the period immediately following Paul's conversion before his first visit to Jerusalem and the period of his ministry in Ephesus) and fails or almost fails to mention things that were important to Paul (e.g. the Antioch incident and the collection).

Fifth, this different perspective may indicate that Luke was significantly misinformed or deliberately misleading. Thus his silence about some of the controversies that are referred to in Paul's letters (e.g. in Corinth) may reflect a desire on his part to portray his hero as a more irenic and acceptable statesman than he actually was. On the other hand, the explanation may be that Paul's letters were typically problem-shooting letters written in situations of controversy, whereas Luke is interested in Paul's part in taking the gospel from 'Jerusalem. . .to the ends of the earth' and so offers a less problem-dominated view of Paul's ministry. Luke (like any historian) offers his own perspective on what he describes, but whether his perspective is historically misleading or whether it complements the picture we get from Paul's occasional letters is open to question.[99]

---

[99]We have touched on the question of Luke's understanding of Paul's theology, when considering the Areopagus speech and the Jewishness of Paul in Acts. It is not possible in this chapter to explore these theological issues, but it is worth emphasising the occasional nature of Paul's letters and the limited scope of Luke's description of Paul. (Cf. W.W. Gasque, 'The Book of Acts and History' in R.A. Guelich [ed.], *Unity and Diversity in New Testament Theology* [Grand Rapids:

Sixth, scholars have detected various specific contradictions between Acts and Paul's letters, but in very few cases is the evidence weighty. If Galatians 2:1-10 is identified with Acts 15, then there is a significant question-mark over the Acts account at that point; but the identification is insecure. Those scholars who consider the picture of Paul in Acts to be historically misleading must appeal to general impressions rather than to proven discrepancies with the epistles. Other scholars will judge that the cumulative evidence suggests that Acts is a well-informed historical narrative.[100]

Eerdmans, 1978] 67, 68.) It is likely enough that Luke had a less sharp sense of the failure of the law than Paul the Jewish convert, but whether he misunderstood Paul is another question.

[100]Jervell, 'Paul in the Acts of the Apostles', 302, comments: 'I do not for a moment doubt that the author of Acts knew Paul well, if not personally'.

CHAPTER 10

PUBLIC SPEAKING AND PUBLISHED ACCOUNTS

Conrad Gempf

Summary

In the ancient world, rhetoric was power and speech was a type of action. Ancient historians, in their recording speeches in their works, were giving records of events rather than transcripts of words. Their statements of method indicate that they took this task seriously. The modern categories of 'accurate' versus 'invention' for these accounts are the wrong conceptual tools, judging the account as a transcript. These accounts should be regarded as either 'faithful' or 'unfaithful' to the historical event. A public speech included in an ancient history should be seen as having a two-pronged goal: being appropriate to the historical event and being appropriate to the historical work as a whole. These goals were pursued in tandem by the best of the historians, and probably also by the author of Luke-Acts.

I. Word *as* Action

1. The General and the Rhetor

'The Romans regarded rhetorical training as the basis of all literary and intellectual activity.'[1] There are two ways to make a group of people do as you wish. You must either force them, or convince them. A person successful with either method is a person of power, and the ancient world gave recognition to both the great general and to the great rhetor.

The word 'rhetoric' itself to the modern ear carries the implication of 'empty, if nice-sounding, words'. For us, a speech is something boring that happens before a bill is passed in Parliament or before everyone can leave the graduation ceremony. But values and attitudes were very different in the first-century world. At the time that the New Testament was being written, the Greek ideal of educating for a sound mind and body had given way to the primacy of rhetoric. The subjects of mathematics and science were pushed aside, taught only if the pupils' vocational interests demanded. Even music was taught and valued chiefly for those facets which could also be useful in public speaking: an understanding of metre, learned modulation of the voice, and grace in gesture.[2]

Rhetoric was, to the ancients, *power*, whether for good or for ill. In the Graeco-Roman world, *speaking* was central to success. It was not that speech was more important than action but rather that oratory and rhetoric *were* action—perhaps the most excellent form of action—as Isocrates wrote:

> In most of our abilities we differ not at all from the animals; we are in fact behind many in swiftness and strength and other resources. But because there is born in us the power to persuade each other and to show ourselves whatever we wish, we not only have escaped from living as brutes, but also by coming together have founded cities and set up laws and invented arts, and speech has helped us attain practically all of the things we have devised. . .Nothing done

---

[1]Ronald Mellor, *Tacitus* (London: Routledge, 1993) 113-114.
[2]E.B. Castle, *Ancient Education and Today* (Harmondsworth: Penguin, 1965) 128-129.

> with intelligence is done without speech, but speech is the marshal of all actions and of thoughts. . .[3]

Similarly, the Roman orator, Cicero:

> . . .there is to my mind no more excellent thing than the power, by means of oratory, to get a hold on assemblies of men, win their good will, direct their inclinations wherever the speaker wishes, or divert them from whatever he wishes. . .the wise control of the complete orator is that which chiefly upholds not only his own dignity, but the safety of countless individuals and of the entire State.[4]

Speeches are not mere commentary on events nor accompaniment to events: speeches must be seen *as* events in their own right. Ancient historians tended to focus on battles *and* speeches as the events that shaped history.[5] Modern socio-linguistics has re-discovered the 'event' character in some types of contemporary utterances, using the titles of 'performative speech acts' and 'performative language' for these related concepts.[6]

It is no accident then, that so much of the ancient histories focus on not only battles within a war, but the speeches that led directly to the wars or policy changes within the wars. The prime example of

---

[3]Isocrates, 'Antidosis', 253-256.

[4]Cicero, De Oratore 1.8.30, 34, trans. E. Sutton and H. Rackham, LCL, although the next section of the dialogue discusses and raises hypothetical objections to these assertions. This 'power over people' is perhaps what the Apostle Paul wished to avoid. See Bruce Winter, 'The Entries and Ethics of Orators and Paul (1 Thessalonians 2:1-12)', *TynB* 44 (1993) 55-74, esp. 73-74. On the abuse of power see Plato, 'Gorgias', 456, 457, in *Gorgias*, trans. T. Irwin (Oxford: Clarendon Press, 1979) 24, 25.

[5]Recently there have been further studies of 'performative language' in other ancient contexts. See for example, David C. Mirhady, 'The Oath-Challenge in Athens', *Classical Quarterly* 41 (1991) 78-83, Virginia Hunter, 'Gossip and the Politics of Reputation in Classical Athens', *Phoenix* 44 (1990) 299-325 and Stephen Halliwell, 'Comic Satire and Freedom of Speech in Classical Athens', *Journal of Hellenic Studies* 101 (1991) 48-70.

[6]Probably the most often cited examples are the 'I pronounce you husband and wife' of the marriage ceremony and the 'I declare this place open' of official opening ceremonies. See John Lyons, *Semantics* (Cambridge: Cambridge University Press, 1977) 484, 511 and 726-727, where the concept is described as '. . .the distinction between saying something and doing something by means of language'. See also R. Wardhaugh, *An Introduction to Sociolinguistics* (Oxford: Basil Blackwell, 1986) 274-281; and A. Thistleton, *New Horizons in Hermeneutics* (London: Harper-Collins, 1992) 16-19.

this, of course is Thucydides' account of the Peloponnesian War(s).[7] The closest modern analogy is perhaps our ability to speak of, for example, 'summit talks' or 'the Geneva Talks', phrases that we use to refer to an event, rather than the actual words of the dialogue. The art of negotiation, like rhetoric, uses the medium of words. But the core and significance of a piece of negotiation, like a piece of rhetoric, lies in its nature as event, and the results of that event.[8]

A failure to appreciate the ancient 'power' or 'art' of rhetoric and the centrality of oratory in the culture in which early Christianity grew up would be disastrous for the student of the New Testament.

2. Battle, Speech and Reporter

Given this importance, it is hardly surprising to find that many ancient authors wrote theoretical and practical works about rhetoric.[9] At first glance, however, we might have expected more *examples* of oratory to have survived. We do have 'written speeches' from some of the famed orators, such as Cicero and Isocrates, but in the main written speeches seem to have been frowned upon,[10] and not without some rationale. Transcripts of orations are deficient. An important part of a rhetor's training concerned the actual presentation, down to details such as breathing properly. The transcript of a speech is even worse than a modern musical score as a document of a performance, as the score will have *some* indications of volume and speed of delivery. Orators won respect for their delivery technique as well as the content of their speeches, and a speech that could be enjoyed as a dead written document was the exception rather than the rule—not an unheard of phenomenon, but not the norm.

---

[7]Thucydides, *The History of the Peloponnesian War*, trans. C. Forster Smith, LCL, *passim*, but see perhaps especially the debates and speeches of Alcibiades. Cf. Hunter R. Rawlings, *The Structure of Thucydides' History* (Princeton University Press, 1981) 25-42, esp. 37-38. See also Plümacher's reading of Dionysius in Eckhard Plümacher, 'Die Missionsreden der Apostelgeschichte und Dionys von Halikarnass', *NTS* 39 (1993) esp. 166-168.

[8]Another modern example might be Anwar Sadat's address before the Israeli Knesset in 1977. The words pale into insignificance compared with the actual fact of such an address taking place!

[9]Examples are the Platonic dialogues *Gorgias* and *Phaedrus*, Aristotle's *Rhetoric*, Cicero's *De inventione* and *De oratore*, and Quintilian's *Institutio oratoria*.

[10]See G. Kennedy, *The Art of Persuasion in Greece* (Princeton University Press, 1963) 5 for a brief discussion of the apparent bias against the written word.

Furthermore, an important part of rhetoric concerned tailoring the delivery *and* the content to the situation and mood of the audience. A written document cannot afford the rhetor this degree of flexibility and adaptation. Our earlier analogy of 'negotiation' is instructive here. We can more easily recognise the difficulty of isolating a 'successful piece of negotiation' out from a particular situation and audience.

Yet it is a fact that the major historians of the ancient world liberally sprinkled accounts of speeches in their narratives. These accounts, although very often presented in the form of direct speech, are not transcripts of the speeches presented at the occasion. This will be clear to all but the most naïve reader, as the accounts are almost always absurdly short for a real speech. Closer readings of the works in which the speeches are found generally reveal that the speeches are presented more or less in the vocabulary and style of the author of the book rather than of the alleged speaker. The question is, then, if they were not records of the words as spoken, what are the speeches doing there?

The superficial answer that presents itself to the modern mind is that the speeches are most likely to be fabrications of the author—a device to allow the author to express his own point of view. Such an evaluation cannot stand more than a moment's scrutiny, however, for most writers are fond of placing the speeches in opposing pairs. The historian cannot be construed to be on *both* sides of the argument, and it is not unusual for both arguments to be presented with equal strength.[11]

It is rather that the speeches are included not to form a transcript of the words spoken on the occasion as much as to document the *event* that was the speech. Just as the write-up of a battle is impressionistic rather than choreographic in nature, yet might faithfully preserve something of the strategy and tactics of the event, so the record of a speech is not a transcript, yet should preserve faithfully the strategies behind the speech viewed thus as *event*.[12] Given the political value of rhetoric, it is not surprising that

---

[11]In Luke-Acts, too, it is not unheard of for opponents to give speeches that are meant to be convincing: Gamaliel (Acts 5), the Ephesian town clerk (19), and to some degree Tertullus (24).

[12]See Paula E. Arnold, 'The Persuasive Style of Debates in Direct Speech in Thucydides', *Hermes* 120 (1992) 44-57, especially 46, 57. She has argued that even the style used by the historian is intended to re-create the experience of the debates rather than record the exact words.

conventional Greek historiography regarded history as a matter of both πράξεις καὶ λόγοι.[13]

Critics of the speeches may bring in the statements of ancient authors such as Isocrates or Dionysius which seemingly indicate that the historian is to invent speeches out of thin air just to make an impression on the audience.[14] In fact, the write-up of a speech in an ancient history *does call* for rhetorical skill simply because the author must, while being faithful to the main lines of the historical 'speech-event', adapt the speech to make it 'speak to' a new audience in a different situation. Delivery and adapting to the mood and situation of the audience is, as we have seen, an important part of rhetoric. Thus, to say that in presenting a speech, the historian has an opportunity to show rhetorical skill is a bit like saying that the write-up of a battle is an occasion for the author to write colourfully. 'Colourfully' and 'rhetorically' need not mean 'unfaithfully'. The ancient writers themselves are very clear on this point. A recorded speech is not a transcript,[15] but woe betide the historian if the speech is not *faithful* to the alleged situation and speaker.

Just as a writer was expected to represent faithfully the strategies, tactics and results of a battle, but not necessarily all the fine movements of each combatant, so a writer was expected to represent faithfully the strategies, tactics and results of a speech, without necessarily recording the exact words used on the day.

---

[13]F.W. Walbank, *Speeches in the Greek Historians* (Oxford: Basil Blackwell, 1965) 1; see also P. Hohti, *The Interrelation of Speech and Action in the Histories of Herodotus* (Helsinki: Societas Scientiarum Fennica, 1976).

[14]'Indeed, an important part of history is the oratory it contains. In the speeches of the actor the artist can more fully show his skill. . .from Thucydides downwards, speeches reported by the historians are confessedly pure imagination.' So H. Cadbury (and the editors) in 'Greek and Jewish Traditions', in *The Beginnings of Christianity: Vol. II Prolegomena II, Criticism* (London: Macmillan, 1922) 12-13, citing both Dionysius and Lucian in support.

[15]So, for example Mellor writes of Tacitus: 'Any modern desire for a verbal exactitude would have seemed to him pedantic and unworthy of the literary artistry expected in serious historical writing', Mellor, *Tacitus*, 116.

II. Historians and Speeches

1. *Graeco-Roman Method*

The ancient historians' task is defined in the tension between 'history as an account of the particular and history as individualisation of the general'.[16] The first clause demands vigorous investigation, the second, artistic excellence. Every historian of merit had to attempt both. For this dual aim, a single word could be used: τὸ πρέπον (appropriateness).[17] Although I know of no modern author who deliberately does so, it seems useful for modern students of historiography to consider this appropriateness as being two-sided: artistic or literary appropriateness on the one hand and historical appropriateness on the other.

On this hypothesis, the historians quite obviously considered themselves to be artists, and aimed to produce works which were unified and harmonious wholes.[18] The speeches too had to 'fit'. This is the reason why virtually all of the historians presented the speeches of their characters using vocabulary, phraseology, and style that is primarily the author's own. On the other hand, if this thesis is correct, the speech had not only to fit in stylistically and thematically into the whole of the work, but it also had to fit the speaker and the reported historical situation; it had to be historically appropriate as well. Thus, no matter how well a speech might fit into the historian's work, it would be judged inappropriate if it was not what the speaker would have said, or if it displayed anachronistic knowledge or was otherwise unsuitable to the situation. If the Greek and Roman historians are considered to be merely interested in telling a good story (literary appropriateness), then nothing that they tell us need be true. But it is possible that appropriateness for them meant more—

---

[16]B. Gentili and G. Cerri, 'Written and Oral Communication in Greek Historiographical Thought', in E.A. Havestock and J.P. Hershbel (eds.), *Communication Arts in the Ancient World* (New York: Hastings House, 1978) 143.

[17]According to Callisthenus of Olynthus, it is the duty of all who write μή ἀστοχεῖν τοῦ προσώπου, ἀλλ' οἰκείως αὐτῷ τε καὶ τοῦς πράγμασι τοῦς λόγους θεῖναι. F. Jacoby, *Die Fragmente der Griechischen Historiker: Zweiter Teil A-B* (Berlin: Weidmannsche Buchhandlung, 1929) number 124, fragment 44, 654. Cf. Walbank, *Speeches*, 5, 18.

[18]Herodotus, if truly considered a historian, is the only possible exception, but even he had some sense for the whole of his piece, despite the digressions.

that under this heading can fit, albeit in creative tension, two seemingly separate excellences: style and faithfulness.

The historians are here being considered as possible methodological models for the author of Luke-Acts, and it seems probable that explicit statements about method will be more influential to an aspiring historian than his or her guesses about the consistency with which the method was executed. Our primary question is not: how accurate was historian X?, but: what impression about speeches and accuracy would X's statements and practice leave upon the literate ancient?[19]

a. Thucydides

While Herodotus is generally regarded as the 'Father of History', it is Thucydides who brought to the discipline the focus and 'scientific' self-consciousness we expect of serious history-writing. Concerning the speeches, he wrote:

> With reference to the speeches in this history, some were delivered before the war began, others while it was going on; some I heard myself, others I got from various quarters; it was in all cases difficult to carry them word for word in one's memory, so my habit has been to make the speakers say what was in my opinion demanded of them by the various occasions, of course adhering as closely as possible to the general sense of what they really said.[20]

However, while this passage appears to make plain the historian's method, it still leaves a great deal of scope for interpretation.[21]

It is possible to interpret Thucydides' statement in such a way as to understand there being a 'contradiction' between two criteria the historian wishes to hold at once: suitability on the one hand, and

---

[19]Thus to some extent I disagree with Stan Porter's otherwise excellent study. Stanley Porter 'Thucydides 1.22.1 and Speeches in Acts: Is there a Thucydidean View?', *NovT* 32 (1990) 141, his point 3.

[20]Thucydides, 1.22.1, trans. R. Crawley, *The History of the Peloponnesian War* (London: Longman, Green and Co., 1874) 14: Καὶ ὅσα μὲν λόγῳ εἶπον ἕκαστοι ἢ ἐν μέλλοντες πολεμήσειν ἢ ἐν αυτῷ ἤδη ὄντες, χαλεπὸν τὴν ἀκρίβειαν αὐτὴν τῶν λεχθέντων διαμνημονεῦσαι ἦν ἐμοί τε ὧν αὐτὸς ἤκουσα καὶ τοῖς ἄλλοθέν ποθεν ἐμοὶ ἀπαγγέλλουσιν ὡς δ' ἂν ἐδόκουν μοι ἕκαστοι περὶ τῶν αἰεὶ παρόντων τὰ δέοντα μάλιστ' εἰπεῖν, ἐχομένῳ ὅτι ἐγγύτατα τῆς ξυμπάσης γνώμης τῶν ἀληθῶς λεχθέντων, οὕτως εἴρηται·

[21]So also Porter, 'Thucydides 1.22.1 and the Speeches in Acts', 128: 'An examination. . .reveals that it is anything but straightforward'.

the truth on the other.[22] It seems wiser to take these to be poles or boundaries on a continuum rather than as contradictions. Adcock has called them 'limiting factors'.[23]

The first of these factors is the clause 'what was in my opinion demanded of them by the various occasions'. This is clear indication that Thucydides allowed himself some freedom in reproducing the speeches. A.W. Gomme is one of the few who have argued that the constraints of these 'various occasions' actually gave Thucydides very little room to improvise. Hence, he translated the phrase: '. . .the speeches have been composed as I thought the speakers would express what they *had* to express. . .'[24] or 'what the speaker needed to say (and therefore, in default of evidence to the contrary, may be presumed to have said) in order to get his way with a particular audience in particular circumstances'.[25] This is too extreme a position, for Gomme must all but ignore Thucydides' phrase 'in my opinion' and its implications. It seems better to say that the historians strove for historical as well as artistic appropriateness, therefore their aims need not be antithetical to accuracy, but Gomme's assertion that appropriateness *must* lead to an approximate accuracy is too extreme and can only be rejected.

The second clause, 'adhering as closely as possible to the general sense of what they really said', is the 'limiting factor' in the other direction. Within this clause, the two crucial phrases are τῆς ξυμπάσης γνώμης and τῶν ἀληθῶς λεχθέντων. Despite Eduard Schwartz's attempt to interpret the latter as meaning 'nicht den authentischen Wordlaut, sondern dass die Redner nur in solchen Situationen auftreten sollten, in denen sie wirklich gesprochen hatten',[26] it seems doubtful that the phrase means anything other than 'what in truth was said'. It must, however, be conceded that this phrase is only a modifier; the substantive in the clause is τῆς ξυμπάσης

---

[22]So, for example, Walbank, *Speeches*, 4. See also N.G.L. Hammond, 'The Particular and the Universal in the Speeches of Thucydides', in H.F. Harding (ed.), *The Speeches of Thucydides* (Lawrence, Kansas: Coronado Press, 1973) 49-50.
[23]F.E. Adcock, *Thucydides and his Histories* (Cambridge: Cambridge University Press, 1963) 28.
[24]A.W. Gomme, 'The Speeches in Thucydides', in A.W. Gomme (ed.), *Essays in Greek History and Literature* (Oxford: Basil Blackwell, 1937) 160.
[25]A.W. Gomme, A. Andrewes and K.J. Dover, *A Historical Commentary on Thucydides: Vol. V* (Oxford: The Clarendon Press, 1981) 395.
[26]E. Schwartz, Book review of Taeger's *Thucydides*, *Gnomon* 2 (1926) 79-80, as cited by Gomme, 'Speeches', 156ff. See also D. Kagan, 'The Speeches in Thucydides and the Mytilene Debate', *Yale Classical Studies* 24 (1975) 73.

γνώμης 'the general sense'. On this phrase, too, there is a variety of opinion.[27] Based on the uses of τὸ ξυμπᾶν and γνώμη in other places in Thucydides' history, the most likely interpretation is that the historian means by it not merely the main purpose, but what amounts to an outline comprising purpose, reasons and proposals. This is the 'essence' of the speech.[28]

Having explored the possible meanings of these two clauses, we return to the notion of a continuum between the two poles. Thucydides tells us that, on the one hand, he will never go so far toward making the speakers say what *he* thinks appropriate that he completely loses track of what was actually said; on the other hand, neither will he supply the speaker's exact words. The most accurate account we may expect is something akin to a point-by-point summary, and that only when the points seem to him relevant to the occasion, for the clause: 'the general sense of what was actually said' has a secondary force, serving to limit the historian's reconstruction, as implied by the word order of the preface.[29] In terms of his research, Thucydides wrote that it was hard to remember every word; in terms of the principles behind his practice, he said that he kept as closely to the truth as possible; but about the practice itself, the way he perceived the actual recording of the speeches is 'I have made the speakers say what was in *my* opinion appropriate'. We must conclude that he was more interested in suitability than accuracy, strictly speaking, although he adhered to the latter 'as closely as possible', and, as stated above, we must not underestimate what was possible.

His interest in accuracy, albeit secondary, is genuine, and historiographers, in the past decade or two, have begun to re-emphasise this. Griffith writes in a survey of Classical scholarship that he finds encouraging the 'revival' of the view that Thucydides' statement at I.22.1 was intended 'to enlighten his readers and not to

---

[27]This ranges from Schwartz's idea of a vague 'Willingsrichtung im ganzen' or 'praktische Zweck der Rede' (Schwartz, Book review of Taeger's *Thucydides*, 79-80), to Dover's suggestion that it means something similar to the English phrase 'the line taken by the speaker'—or 'some point of the scale between the base imperative for which the speaker argues and the total sequence of argument which he employs' (K.J. Dover, *Thucydides* [New Surveys in the Classics, 7; Oxford: Clarendon Press, 1973] 22).

[28]Gomme, *et. al.*, *Historical Commentary: Vol. V*, 394ff. Cf. the assessment made by Kagan, 'The Speeches in Thucydides and the Mytilene Debate', 71-72.

[29]See also J.H. Finley, *Thucydides* (Cambridge, Massachusetts: Harvard University Press, 1942) 95.

bamboozle them'.[30] In the past, detailed study of the components of Thucydides' statement tended to obscure the reason for its presence in the first place. As Cogan[31] and others[32] have noticed, the fact that Thucydides has brought the original speakers and speeches into the discussion at all is very suggestive. It may be that the *substance* of Thucydides' statement is capable of being interpreted in such a way as to seem to support the idea that the speeches were purely inventions, but the *presence* of the statement militates against that understanding.

b. Isocrates and his Followers

Only a few works and fragments survive from the period between Thucydides and Polybius. What texts and references we do have seem to show that the emphasis in writing history took a turn from exactness of record to eloquence of style. This was due in part to the influence that the writer and orator Isocrates exerted on the Greek world at that time. Although he was not an historian, and has left no statements of method that relate directly to speeches in histories, it is not difficult to imagine what method he would have taught to his historian pupils.

Isocrates, who lived from approximately 436-338 B.C., is sometimes credited with being the chief creator of rhetoric as a

---

[30]G.T. Griffith, 'The Greek Historians', in M. Platnauer (ed.), *Fifty Years (and twelve) of Classical Scholarship* (Oxford: Basil Blackwell, 1968) 225-226.

[31]'There can be no grounds, in this statement, for concluding that he here apologizes for inventing the speeches. Thucydides does not apologize for the *inclusion* of speeches, he apologizes for any errors of fact. The problem is [exactness in the speeches, not whether they were ever really given]. If one were inventing speeches and their occasions, one would not trouble about the exactness of the record of what was spoken', [Emphasis mine]; M. Cogan, *The Human Thing: Speeches and Principles of Thucydides' History* (University of Chicago Press, 1981) xiii.

[32]Cf. Fornara, who writes: 'One should observe that Thucydides takes it as understood that the procedure [of including speeches] is appropriate, indeed mandatory, and justifies not the inclusion of speeches but his method of presenting them (1.22.1), actually apologizing for not providing the exact words of the speakers. . .Thucydides, in other words, not only accepted the premise that speeches and deeds were the integral elements of "the memorable actions" that comprise history. . .but held, in theory, at least, that verbatim speeches would have been best'. C.W. Fornara, *The Nature of History In Ancient Greece and Rome* (Berkeley and Los Angeles: University of California Press, 1983) 143. See also: A. Andrewes, 'The Mytilene Debate', *Phoenix* 16 (1962) 65-66, and Kagan, 'The Speeches in Thucydides and the Mytilene Debate', 72.

distinct science. He is best remembered for speeches written for others and for his educational system. Most details of this system are lost to us, but doubtless training in rhetoric played an important part. Isocrates and his students felt very strongly that prose should have just as great an ability to emotionally 'move' people as poetry and that it should be as much of an art form. Although writing as a eulogiser rather than a historian, Isocrates suggests: '. . .someone should assemble [a person's] achievements, giving them verbal adornment (τῷ λόγῳ κοσμήσας), and submitting them. . .that [others], emulating those who are eulogized, may desire to adopt the same pursuits. . .'[33]

He had many students on whom he had a direct influence. Among those pupils were the historians Theopompus,[34] and Ephorus.[35] Only fragments of these authors' books remain, but the fact that the first-century historian Diodorus used Ephorus extensively has helped us to reconstruct his writing. Xenophon was probably also a student of Isocrates,[36] although once again, only fragments of his master-work, the *Hellenica*, a continuation of Thucydides' *History*, survive.

c. Polybius

If, by some quirk of fate, the Histories of Theopompus had survived and those of Polybius were lost instead, our picture of the development of the science of historiography would be very different. It would then be possible to argue that the evidence available shows that history writing in Greece became less and less attentive to exactness and never recovered from the dip it took after Thucydides. Instead, it is the remarkable work of Polybius that has been saved, at least in part, making it impossible to write off completely zeal for historical reliability in the recording of speeches. Whether there were others whose methods were like Polybius', but whose works were in fact lost, we have no way of knowing.

---

[33]Isocrates, 'Evagoras', 76.
[34]Jacoby, 'Theopompos von Chios', number 115, in *FGH*, 526-617. He was widely used by other ancient writers and *FGH* has about 400 fragments.
[35]Jacoby, 'Ephoros von Kyme', number 70, in *FGH*, 2a, 37-109.
[36]We have no firm evidence that Xenophon was one of Isocrates' pupils, but there are indications of influence, such as the fact that Isocrates' 'Evagoras' is the first biography we possess, and the 'Agesilaus' of Xenophon is the second, seemingly using Isocrates as a model. Cf. J.B. Bury, *The Ancient Greek Historians* (London: Macmillan, 1909) 153.

In the first of four extant sections which discuss the use of speeches in a historical work, Polybius argues that since the purposes of a historian are different from those of a tragic poet, the methods they employ in recording discourse will necessarily also be different.

> [The historian should] simply record what really happened and what really was said, however commonplace. . .[For the poet,] it is the probable that takes precedence, even if it be untrue, the purpose being to create illusion in the spectators. . .[while for the historian,] it is the truth, the purpose being to confer benefit on learners.[37]

It is a practical and moral didacticism that is at stake: the practice of including invented speeches is opposed on the grounds that it is an obstacle to this central purpose of history writing.[38]

The second section on speeches, found in the fragments of chapter 25 of book 12, really consists of three loosely connected criticisms of the historian Timaeus. Again appealing to the usefulness of history, Polybius writes:

> The peculiar function of history is to discover, in the first place, the words actually spoken, whatever they were, and next to ascertain the reason why what was done or spoken led to failure or success. For the mere statement of a fact may interest us but is no benefit to us: but when we add the cause of it, study of history becomes fruitful. . .a writer who passes over in silence the speeches made and the causes of events and in their place introduces false rhetorical exercises and discursive speeches, destroys the peculiar virtue of history. And Timaeus especially is guilty. . .[39]

In this book, Polybius also accuses Timaeus of composing speeches for his own purposes:

---

[37]Polybius, 2.56.10-13, trans. Paton.

[38]On Polybius 12.25b: '"Ότι τῆς ἱστορίας ἰδίωμα τοῦτ' ἐστὶ τὸ πρῶτον μὲν αὐτοὺς τοὺς κατ' ἀλήθειαν εἰρημένους, οἱοί ποτ' ἂν ὧσι, γνῶναι λόγους. . .', see below. See also Walbank, *Speeches*, 7.

[39]Polybius, 12.25b, trans. Paton. The question is, of course, how did Polybius know what was said? The speeches which he criticises most heavily are those delivered by Hermocrates at Gela in 424. For these at least, it is probably that there was an 'approved' version, available in Thucydides or another source, from which later historians should not be expected to diverge radically. In other words, this passage seems to indicate that historians took seriously the tradition of faithful, if somewhat rhetorical, reporting of speeches in historical works. See 12.25a.

When we find one or two false statements in a book and they prove
to be deliberate ones, it is evident that not a word written by such an
author is any longer certain and reliable. But to convince those also
who are disposed to champion him [i.e. Timaeus] I must speak of
the principle on which he composes public speeches. . .Can anyone
who reads them help noticing that Timaeus has untruthfully
reported them in his work and has done so of set purpose? For he
has not set down the words spoken nor the sense of what was really
said, but having made up his mind as to what ought to have been
said, he recounts all these speeches and all else that follows upon
events like a man in a school of rhetoric attempting to speak on a
given subject, and shows off his oratorical power, but gives no
report of what was actually spoken.[40]

Polybius appears also to expect his *readers* to be outraged at
Timaeus' methods. Those 19th and 20th century historiographers
who believe that the insertion of invented speeches into historical
works was a 'normal, perfectly acceptable and universally
understood literary convention' need to explain how it is that
Polybius, well-educated, widely-travelled statesman and author of
several books, not only rebels against the convention (that may be
explainable), but appears neither to know such a practice was
acceptable for historians, nor expect that his readers would know.
For if the convention *was* currently in practice, it would be flattery to
compare Timaeus with a rhetorician showing 'oratorical power'. It
seems unlikely that such a statement would have been placed in an
argument aimed at convincing any 'who are disposed to champion
him'.[41] Polybius is unusual, even unique in terms of the surviving
literature, for the extreme position he takes on this question, but this
passage in particular makes it very difficult to maintain that the
opposite extreme was in vogue even 150 years after Isocrates.

This section, book 12, also contains a stumbling block in the
attempt to understand Polybius' ideas. It is difficult to follow the
flow of his argument, as only pieces of the chapter are extant, but it
seems as though he criticises Timaeus for lacking the knowledge
needed to decide which of the 'possible arguments' (τοὶς ἐνόντας
λόγους) are suitable for a particular occasion '. . .since the needs of the
case vary, we have need of special practice and principle in judging
how many and which of the possible arguments we should

---

[40]Polybius, 12.25a.
[41]Polybius, 12.25a, trans. Paton.

employ. . .'[42] Polybius is probably saying that even when the main thrust of the speech is recorded correctly, the arguments by which Timaeus makes the speakers arrive at these conclusions are objectionable.[43] The competent historian should be able to fill the logical gaps based on the other historical evidence available from the source. Even here, Polybius assumes some kernel of the actual speech must be present for the historian to expand upon.

> For the present, the best way of conveying my meaning is as follows. If writers [i.e. the sources], after indicating to us [i.e. the historians] the situation and the motives and inclinations of the people who are discussing it report in the next place what was actually said and then make clear to us the reasons why the speakers either succeeded or failed, we shall arrive at some true notion of the actual facts, and we shall be able. . .to treat any situation. . .[44]

Thus we must take issue with Walbank's words: 'Polybius' position then is clear and uncompromising. Thucydides, on the other hand. . .left an unresolvable antithesis. . .',[45] for Polybius here, in apparent contrast to his earlier statements, allows additions to the actual words, if they are rooted securely enough in the historical situation. The passage does not, however, treat the inclusion of speeches for which the historian does not have a source to begin with.[46]

The third of the sections on speeches is found in the fragment of book 29, chapter 12. Again the theme of deliberate error surfaces:

> In all these [reports of battles, speeches, etc.]. . .I may be justly pardoned if I am found to be using the same style, or the same disposition and treatment, or even actually the same words as on a

---

[42]Polybius, 12.25i.

[43]Schuckburg translates λόγους as 'language', so that the historian needs to choose the 'proper and appropriate language'. Schuckburg translation, quoted by K. Sacks, *Polybius on the Writing of History*, University of California Publications: Classical Studies, Vol. 24 (Berkeley and Los Angeles: University of California Press, 1981) 79-80. It is difficult, though, to imagine what sort of practice Timaeus would have been engaged in that might elicit the complaint that he recites 'all the possible *language*'. The most natural interpretation remains 'arguments'.

[44]Polybius, 12.25i, trans. Paton.

[45]Walbank, *Speeches*, 11. Sacks, *Polybius on the Writing of History*, 79-81, disagrees as well.

[46]So also Sacks, *Polybius on the Writing of History*, 89.

previous occasion. . .in all such matters the large scale of my work is sufficient excuse. It is only if I am found guilty of deliberate mendacity or if it be for the sake of some profit, that I do not ask to be excused. . .[47]

This passage, too, leads us away from the notion of complete verbatim accuracy and closer to the ideals of Thucydides. A historian may use his own words, and these may be identical at different times.

Polybius mentions the topic of speeches again at the beginning of book 36, where he writes:

Perhaps some may ask themselves why I do not. . .display my talent and report the particular speeches after the fashion of most authors who lay before us all that is possible to say on either side. That I do not disapprove of such a practice is evident from various passages of this work in which I have quoted both the speeches and the writings of politicians, but it will now be made clear that it is not my principle to do this on any and every pretext. . .nor is it the proper part of a historian to practise on his readers and make a display of his ability to them, but rather to find out by the most diligent inquiry and report to them what was actually said, and even of this only what was most vital and effectual.[48]

There may have been more to this passage, but the rest of the chapter has been lost. The κατὰ in τὰ κατ' ἀλήθειαν ῥηθέντα here serves to soften the phrase to something very similar to the Thucydidean ἡ ξυμπᾶσα γνώμη τῶν ἀληθῶς λεχθέντων. In any case, the need for the historian to select is again mentioned only in the context of 'diligent inquiry' and faithfulness to the truth.[49]

In his principles, Polybius, like Thucydides, balanced the historian's opinion with the things actually said. Polybius was perhaps more interested in fidelity, although our last passage shows that even if truth is the chief criterion for the *inclusion* of a speech, suitability and 'literary appropriateness' were the chief criteria for the speech's final form.

---

[47]Polybius, 29.12, trans. Paton.
[48]Polybius, 36.1.
[49]Walbank, *A Historical Commentary on Polybius: Vol. III* (Oxford: Clarendon Press, 1979) 651ff. See also Walbank, *Speeches*, 8.

d. Dionysius of Halicarnassus

Dionysius lived from about 50 B.C. to approximately 10 years into the first century A.D. His concept of speeches in a historical work is more readily discernible from his letter, 'On Thucydides' than from his own attempt at history writing, *Roman Antiquities*. He conceived of history basically as an art form—as merely a branch of rhetoric, the very characterisation that Diodorus (perhaps following Ephorus) made of some of his contemporaries.[50] Dionysius comments upon the speeches in Thucydides almost exclusively from the point of view of contemporary rhetoric. Dionysius' critique of Pericles' last speech does not concern the question of whether Pericles made such a speech or whether the address was rooted in the historical situation.[51] The placement of the Funeral Speech of Pericles so early in the book is a rhetorical, not a historical, problem for Dionysius: 'What possible reason can he have for including it at this point rather than at another!'[52] For Dionysius, the fashioning of speeches is taken to be the test of a real historian's ability, that ability being reckoned in terms of rhetorical style and skill. At times this emphasis comes very close to rationalising the sacrifice of truth to style and 'literary appropriateness', as shown by Dionysius' remark 'that Thucydides sinned against good taste in making his own countrymen responsible for the war. . .'[53]

---

[50]'. . .Some writers, by excessive use of rhetorical passages have made the whole art of history into an appendage of oratory.' Diodorus, 20.1.2, in *Diodorus of Sicily: Vol. X*, trans. R.M. Geer, LCL (London: Heinemann, 1954) 144-145. He is not entirely against the use of speeches, however, and where Polybius regards the creation of speeches as 'destroying the peculiar virtue' of history, Diodorus seems to regard the practice as part of the historian's duty: 'Nevertheless, in disapproving rhetorical speeches, we do not ban them wholly from historical works; for since history needs to be adorned with variety,. . .whenever the situation requires either a public address from an ambassador or a statesman, or some such thing from the other characters, whoever does not boldly enter the contest of words would himself be blameworthy', Diodorus, 20.2.1.

[51]Dionysius, *On Thucydides*, 18. See also 44, where it may seem at first that Dionysius is judging on the grounds of suitability, but in fact his criticisms are in terms of rhetorical practice, i.e. saying, ironically, 'Pericles, of all people would have known. . .'

[52]Dionysius, *On Thucydides*, 18.

[53]Dionysius, *On Thucydides*, 41, in the guise of an argument about appropriateness and factuality, but apparently going against the facts. See S. Usher's introductory essay, *Dionysius of Halicarnassus: The Critical Essays* Vol. 1, LCL, trans. and ed. by S. Usher (London: Heinemann, 1974) 459 and W.K.

Yet even Dionysius recognised there should be some attempt at 'historical appropriateness'. Of the speeches in Xenophon's *Hellenica*, Dionysius writes '[Xenophon] will put philosophic speeches into the mouths of ordinary people, "amateurs" and barbarians: and will use phraseology better suited to a debating society than to soldiers and the circumstances of war'.[54] Or, of Thucydides' speeches: 'I for my part do not believe that such words were appropriate for [these particular speakers]. . .and I should say that it ill befitted [them]. I believe that even if any other people attempted to say such things. . .[the audience] would have been indignant'.[55] In this case again, he imagines the hypothetical audience objecting to the arguments and language more than to the content. There is, however, at least one passage in which Dionysius seems to acknowledge clearly the desirability of recollection rather than invention:

> That the historian was not present on that occasion at the meeting, and that he did not hear these speeches from the Athenians or the Melians who recited them, may be readily seen [from what the author writes of his own experiences]. . .So it remains to be examined whether he has made the dialogue appropriate to the circumstances and befitting the persons who came together at the conference. . .[56]

For Dionysius, then, artistry was most important, even at the expense of faithfulness. The surest way of securing his praise was not by recording a speech accurately, but by penning one which, like one of the few of Thucydides' which meet with his approval, 'makes use of language that is pure and clear and containing no figure [of speech] that has been twisted on the rack'.[57]

e. Cicero

The Roman orator Cicero gives us the only elaborations we have from the Romans on the art of writing Histories, and they are chiefly

---

Pritchett, *Dionysius of Halicarnassus: On Thucydides* (Berkeley and Los Angeles: University of California Press, 1975) xxviii.

[54] . . .περιτιθεὶς ἀνδράσιν ἰδιώταις καὶ βαρβάροις ἔσθ' ὅτε λόγους φιλοσόφους, λέξει χρώμενος λόγοις πρεπούσῃ μᾶλλον, ἢ στρατιωτικοῖς κατορθώμασι. Dionysius of Halicarnassus, *De Vet. Script. cens.*, 3.2.

[55] Dionysius, 'On Thucydides', 41 in Pritchett, *Dionysius of Halicarnassus: On Thucydides*, 34.

[56] *Ibid.*, 33.

[57] Dionysius, 'On Thucydides', in Pritchett, *Dionysius of Halicarnassus: On Thucydides*, 34.

in the form of commendations and criticisms of historians of the past. He sees rhetorical adornment as important, 'mere facts' are undesirable. He disparaged those who 'did not embellish their facts, but were chroniclers and nothing more'.[58] It should come as no surprise that the great arch-enemy of Polybius, Timaeus, is judged by Cicero to be among the best of the Greek historians.[59]

Interestingly, Cicero mentions Thucydides in various writings. He clearly prefers the truthfulness of Thucydides compared with the imaginative excesses of the reporting of others.[60] While he praises Thucydides' faithfulness in the telling of deeds, he has backhanded compliments for the speeches: 'I have always praised them; but. . .I could not [imitate them] if I wished, nor should I wish to, I imagine, if I could'.[61]

f. Lucian of Samosata

Lucian is another writer who did not, as far as we know, ever write a history. Rather, he was known as a satirist. His essay on 'How History Ought to be Written' is worth noting, however, even though it is a second-century A.D. document. Like Dionysius, Lucian is considerably more interested in history as a form of art: 'Then having put it [the history] in order, let him [the aspiring historian] bestow beauty on it, add colouring to the diction, and suit the language to the subject, and study a correct composition'.[62] Overall, he has a high regard for truth: '[as opposed to *encomium*]. . .history cannot admit a lie, even a tiny one. . .' and '. . .show nothing distorted, of different colour or different shape. . .historians do not write for teachers of oratory;. . .they have not to seek what they are to say, but how they ought to say it'.[63]

Surprisingly, where speeches are concerned, Lucian is clearly of a different opinion:

> Ἢν δέ ποτε καὶ λόγους ἐροῦντά τινα δεήσῃ εἰσάγειν, μάλιστα μὲν ἐοικότα τῷ προσώπῳ καὶ τῷ πράγματι οἰκεῖα λεγέσθω, ἔπειτα ὡς

---

[58]Cicero, *De Oratore* 2.12.53-54, trans. E. Sutton and H. Rackham, LCL (London: Heinemann, 1942) 236, 237.
[59]Cicero, *De Oratore* 2.14.58.
[60]Cicero, *Brutus* 11.43.
[61]Cicero, *Brutus* 83.287.
[62]Lucian, 'How History Ought to be Written', 48, in *Stock's Lucian*, trans. D.B. Hickie (Dublin: P. Byrne, 1818) 103.
[63]Lucian, 'How History Ought to be Written', trans. Hickie, 7, 50.

σαφέστατα καὶ ταῦτα πλὴν. ἐφεῖταί σοι τότε καὶ ῥητορεῦσαι καὶ ἐπιδεῖξαι τὴν τῶν λόγων διενότητα.[64]

This is significant in that it shows speeches were regarded as a separate category, at least for Lucian, probably for others as well. It also shows, however, that there is a type of historical appropriateness to which at least some historians felt themselves bound; according to Lucian, the writer is only to 'play the rhetorician' once the speech is suited to the alleged speaker and the alleged situation. Although Lucian places these criteria alongside, perhaps even above, clarity and eloquence, his advice falls short of the 'accuracy' that he seems to advocate in the reporting of actions.

2. Graeco-Roman Practice

Assessing the practice of the historians is considerably more difficult than examining their statements of method. In fact, it is probably impossible to evaluate their practice with much certainty, except in those places where the practice is particularly unhistorical and poorly done. In either case, any convincing attempt must be based upon thorough investigation into the background, language and culture of the historian in question and his alleged speaker[65]—in other words, to say anything about the practice of a historian would require a major article in itself to be of any genuine value. Within the bounds of the present study, little more can be done than to give an introduction to the various trends and types of material, as well as a critical look at the conclusions of scholars who *have* thoroughly studied the various historians.[66]

Herodotus was the first writer that could be called a historian in the modern sense of the term. He consciously adopted a more

---

[64]'If a person has to be introduced to make a speech, above all let his language suit his person and his subject, and next let these also be as clear as possible. (It is then, however, that you can play the orator and show your eloquence.)' Lucian, 'How to Write History', 58, trans. Kilburn, LCL (London: Heinemann, 1959) 70-71.

[65]In fact, the classicist has much less hope of evaluating the accuracy of speeches as recorded by historians than has the student of the speeches in Acts (with one major exception, as we shall see below), since we have so much of Paul's own writing.

[66]As has been argued above, the actual practice of the historians is of less concern for the purposes of this article.

critical methodology in his handling of sources than one would expect from a teller of tales or a composer of epics.[67] Although Herodotus is not a sophisticated historical scholar, neither is he always a naïve myth-teller.

Herodotus has left no introductory statement concerning his method in preserving or inventing the speeches we find in his work. These addresses share certain features which link them all to the pen of Herodotus himself rather than the presumed speaker, notably a consistent outlook and morality, shared by speakers of different ages and countries.[68] Some of the speeches, perhaps most, are imaginary, as are a great many of the recorded conversations. But for at least some the speaker is portrayed as a historical character speaking on subjects that are historically valid.[69]

With Thucydides comes not only the first explicit statement of method, but also an important shift in focus that allows the possibility of more accurate recording of speeches. Thucydides wrote about events in his own time, whereas Herodotus wrote about events far removed and for which he probably had no reliable sources. The tendency to write recent histories, based on personal experience and eyewitness reports, becomes the norm after Thucydides, with later attempts at 'Universal Histories' in the minority.[70]

Although Thucydides specifically claims to have heard some, and to have interviewed eyewitnesses of others, it is possible to find the same range of complaints about the reliability of his accounts as we find of Acts: there are possible anachronisms,[71] some speeches appear to be interdependent,[72] and some again seem more suitable as asides to the readers than as addresses to an alleged audience.[73]

---

[67]Herodotus, *Histories* 2.117, trans. A.D. Godley, LCL (London: Heinemann, 1921) in which Herodotus notes discrepancies in his sources. See also 2.118, and 2.120.

[68]M.L. Lang, *Herodotean Narrative and Discourse* (Cambridge, MA, and London: Harvard University Press, 1984) 19-20.

[69]K.H. Waters, 'The Purpose of Dramatisation in Herodotos', *Historia* 15 (1966) 167.

[70]Ephorus wrote a 'universal history'. Polybius broke the mould, too, to some extent, though his writings do not take him too far outside his own lifetime. Then, of course, there are the 'Antiquities' of Dionysius and Josephus.

[71]Bury, *The Ancient Greek Historians*, 262ff.

[72]M. Grant, *The Ancient Historians* (London: Weidenfield and Nicholson, 1970) 91.

[73]Grant, *The Ancient Historians*, 90. Also Malcolm Heath, 'Justice in Thucydides' Athenian Speeches', *Historia* 39 (1990) 385-400, and Bury, *The Ancient Greek Historians*, 137.

None of the specific occasions for these complaints, when considered individually, is conclusive, but seen as a whole the effect is forceful. It appears very much as though Thucydides is responsible for the speeches. In the past, scholars have often felt justified in taking the speeches as simply the work of the historian. They were considered the 'mouthpieces of the author'. There are, however, serious problems with the 'mouthpiece' theory, the most obvious being that Thucydides quite regularly places 'sound' remarks on the lips of even those characters with whom we know he did not agree.[74] Even when the speaker is Thucydides' hero, the 'mouthpiece' theory falters. When Thucydides wishes to give his own views on a particular matter, he does not need the device of speeches behind which to hide, he makes comments freely, such as his undisguised disregard for Cleon's 'vain talk' and 'mad promises'.[75]

One of the cornerstones of the 'mouthpiece' theory is the fact that the speeches are all in Thucydides' style and diction rather than the various styles of the individual speakers. For years, scholars had taken this to mean that there is little or no individualisation between speakers.[76] Recently more detailed studies have shown this to be in error. D.P. Tompkins has identified far more differentiation than had been thought was present.[77] Still further, it is plain that there exists some individualisation of *content* as well. The final speech of Pericles (2.60-64), for example, is his own self-defence,[78] whereas, once again, Thucydides is willing to make his own comments on the subject after

---

[74]See, for example, the speech of Cleon 3.37-40, which is followed by a counter-speech by Diodotus 3.42-48, both of which are soundly composed, and after the two, Thucydides writes that the 'opinions had been maintained with equal force', (3.49). Cf. also G.B. Grundy, *Thucydides and the History of His Age: Vol. I* (Oxford: Blackwell, 1948) 19ff., and Bury, *The Ancient Greek Historians*, 134.

[75]Thucydides, 4.30 and 4.39, respectively. Other examples may be found in Gomme, 'Speeches', 179-180.

[76]Cf. Grant, *The Ancient Historians*, 90, and Bury, *The Ancient Greek Historians*, 146f., although the latter is more generous, see esp. 108-116.

[77]D.P. Tompkins, 'Stylistic Characterization in Thucydides: Nicias and Alcibiades', *Yale Classical Studies* 22 (1972) *passim*. See also H.P. Stahl, 'Speeches and the Course of Events in Books 6 and 7 of Thucydides', in P.A. Stadter (ed.), *The Speeches in Thucydides* (Chapel Hill, N. Carolina: University of North Carolina Press, 1973) 61.

[78]'. . .he surely intended [Perikles' last speech] to illustrate what Perikles, and not any other man, was like, and what he was like just on that occasion, in that situation and not on other occasions. . .nor, as it seems to me, is the speech at all what he would have said had he been able to view the whole course of events. . .' Gomme, *Historical Commentary: Vol. II*, 181.

the speech.[79] None of these things proves that Thucydides did not compose the speeches himself, and none of the modern scholars quoted advocates a view that Thucydides was completely 'objective' or 'accurate'. Many, however, are voicing strong opposition to the once popular hyper-critical use of terms such as 'inventions' or 'free compositions' to describe Thucydides' speeches.[80]

It is without a doubt the case that Thucydides' *History* is a single work of art and that Thucydides used the speeches to express that which *he* thought should be expressed. But, rather than fabricating them, it is more likely that he accomplished these aims through placing emphases and choosing those speeches which should be included.[81]

Not all historians, of course, were as concerned with what was really said, especially after the Isocratean era of rhetorical interest. Xenophon, who wrote a continuation of Thucydides,[82] the *Hellenica*, is important to our survey for what he has *not done* with the speeches in his Histories. Since he continued Thucydides' work, he must have known of his methodological statement about speeches. Yet it seems clear that he did not follow that method himself.[83] There are numerous possibilities as to why this might have been the case: the influence of Isocrates, Xenophon's own natural gift for story-telling, or his ability to be original and innovative.[84] For whatever reason, the fact that it was possible for a historian to be interested enough in a predecessor's work actually to continue it without also taking up the

---

[79]See 2.65, in which Thucydides writes, essentially, that he concurs with the judgements in Pericles' speech: 'he appears to have made a far-sighted estimate of [Athens'] strength'. He then goes on with more of his personal (though not unusual) estimates of Pericles' wisdom and worth to the city.

[80]Thus Stahl writes concerning the 'mouthpiece' theory: 'Such a concept is as simple as it is false, and it does not contribute to the reputation of our guild that it was held. . .' Stahl, 'Speeches and the Course of Events in Books 6 and 7 of Thucydides', 60-61.

[81]Kagan, 'The Speeches in Thucydides and the Mytilene Debate', 78f. argues this particularly well. See, however, the questions raised about the extent of these authorial emphases raised by Heath 'Justice in Thucydides' Athenian Speeches', 385-400.

[82]Xenophon was not the only historian to attempt a completion of Thucydides— although he and Theopompus were among the most famous.

[83]Nor, however, does he include his own introductory statement, allowing us to question whether he accepted Thucydides' method or not.

[84]D.J. Mosley, 'Xenophon', in N.G.L. Hammond and H.H. Scullard (eds.), *The Oxford Classical Dictionary* (Oxford: Oxford University Press, 1970) 1143.

method should make us very cautious about assigning importance to the methodological precedents of any particular author.

Dionysius of Halicarnassus was not a student of Isocrates, but belonged in the same rhetorically-centred camp. We have already discussed his ideas on speech recording in the section on statements of method above. There can be no doubt that Dionysius composed the speeches he presents in his own books in a stereotyped rhetorical fashion.[85]

On the other hand, reliability in the recording of speeches was not abandoned altogether in later writers. Polybius would have trouble living up to all that he wrote about truthfulness,[86] but for the most part the speeches are such that we can believe that Polybius had access to information about them, although we may not trust that information as much as he appears to have done.[87]

The accounts written by Julius Caesar seem to forsake rhetorical adornment and composition, despite the author's record as a public speaker. The speeches therein are bare and to-the-point.[88] The impression is that he takes up a position directly opposed to the Isocratean principles.[89] It seems a fair conclusion that Caesar purposely wrote as an adherent of an established school of historiographical thought, namely the tradition of Thucydides and Polybius.[90] The speeches were used as a method of filling in backgrounds and motivations, and of clarifying Caesar's opponents' ideas and aims, and not to display the author's rhetorical ability. More interested in the rhetorical 'Isocratean' histories, Cicero, a contemporary of Caesar, regarded the future emperor's work as little

---

[85]Pritchett, *Dionysius of Halicarnassus: On Thucydides*, 128.

[86]The important speeches in 9.28-39, for example seem to have been at least 'improved' for the sake of the history. Some of the paired speeches of Hannibal and Publius Scipio might also be looked upon sceptically.

[87]Walbank allows that Polybius may sometimes have preserved fictitious speeches because he was deceived by his source, and therefore was a bit less critical than we would like, but he still 'cannot fairly be accused of inventing', Walbank, *Speeches*, 18.

[88]They are, in fact, often reported in indirect speech.

[89]T.A. Dorey, *The Latin Historians* (London: Routledge and Kegan Paul, 1966) 68.

[90]Perhaps deliberately rejecting the alternatives. See Dorey, *The Latin Historians*, 69.

more than 'a source book for real history'.[91] There is no evidence that Caesar thought of his work as other than a finished product.[92]

Although the Roman historian Sallust put the speeches he recorded into his own style, it is clear that his purpose was *not* to display his own rhetorical ability. Laistner has pointed out a few passages which show Isocratean influence,[93] and has argued that the composition of the speeches in pairs is 'conformable' to, though not necessarily stemming directly from, the rhetorical schools.[94] In the main, however, Sallust, like Caesar before him, seems to have deliberately chosen Thucydides as a model, to the exclusion of the more dramatical and rhetorical historians.[95] Sallust reproduces certain characteristics of Philippus' oratory, as described independently by Cicero in the *Brutus*, but the Sallustian authorship is never in doubt.[96]

In the speeches recorded in the work of the historian Livy, we have a rare opportunity to compare the final product with their source, in this case the speeches he found in Polybius:

Polybius	3.62ff.	Livy 21.42f.
Polybius	11.28ff.	Livy 28.27ff.
Polybius	15.6,4ff.	Livy 30.30
Polybius	21.19ff.	Livy 37.53f.[97]

Livy treats the speeches in his sources with some respect, reproducing the content while changing the form, and almost always adding to the length of the speech considerably, without thereby adding fictitious topics, and what additions are there can often be chalked up to the attempt to give a convincing character study. Even ancient authors seem aware of this; according to Quintilian: 'all will admit that the counsel given is in accordance with the speakers'

---

[91]Cicero, 'Brutus', 75.262, trans. Hendrickson.

[92]Contra G. Kennedy, *The Art of Rhetoric in the Ancient World* (Princeton University Press, 1972) 287-288, who sides with Cicero.

[93]M.L.W. Laistner, *The Greater Roman Historians* (Sather Classical Lectures, Vol. 21; Berkeley and Los Angeles: University of California Press, 1947) 47.

[94]Laistner, *The Greater Roman Historians*, 62.

[95]R. Syme, *Sallust* (Berkeley and Los Angeles: University of California Press, 1964) 244-248, 260ff.

[96]See K. Büchner, *Sallust* (Heidelberg: Carl Winter Universitätsverlag, 1960) 161. Compare Sallust, 1.55 with the description in Cicero, *Brutus*, 173.

[97]Examples as cited in P.G. Walsh, *Livy: Historical Aims and Methods* (Cambridge: Cambridge University Press, 1961) 231.

characters'.[98] Cato's speech on the Oppian Law (34.2-4) even contains some of the characteristics of that orator's style, apparently deliberately introduced by Livy.[99]

One more Roman example must be mentioned. A bronze tablet found in Lyons in the early sixteenth century preserves a portion of a speech given by the Emperor Claudius, which most likely contains the original text of a speech also recorded in the work of the Roman historian Tacitus—a unique opportunity to compare one historian's account of a speech with the *ipsissima verba*.[100]

At first glance, Tacitus' version bears very little resemblance to the original; in fact, until one examines the two more closely, it is difficult to even recognise them as the same speech. Tacitus' version is much shorter, the order in which topics are addressed is drastically altered and the style is much more polished. Since the Lyons tablet is not complete, it is difficult to be sure if any substance has been added to the original by the historian.[101] Much in the original, however, has been condensed and even left out entirely in the published account. Tacitus' text is a better organised and more cogent version of the same arguments; or, to paraphrase Thucydides, it is the general sense of what was really said, phrased in a way that the historian felt was most appropriate.[102] And, although many of the peculiarities of the original are omitted or remedied, there remain some indications of Claudius' pedantic manner.[103]

Overall, we may say that although the historian used considerable freedom in reporting the text of the speech, it is yet

---

[98]Quintilian, 3.8.13, as quoted by Walsh, *Livy: Historical Aims and Methods*, 223.

[99]Laistner, *The Greater Roman Historians*, 96.

[100]The published version of the speech is in Tacitus, *Annals* 11.24, and the text of the tablet may be found in H. Furneaux, 'Appendix I: The Fragments of the Actual Speech of Claudius, and their Relation to the Version Given by Tacitus', in *The Annals of Tacitus: Vol. I*, introduced and edited by H. Furneaux (Oxford: Clarendon Press, 1891) 208ff. (N.B. The first appendix in this book is given on pages 208-214, rather than at the end of the volume.)

[101]Contra Laistner, *The Greater Roman Historians*, 129.

[102]So, too, Walker, who writes: 'The essentials are recognizably the same; Tacitus has included all Claudius' main points and expressed faithfully the speaker's general intention', B. Walker, *The Annals of Tacitus* (University of Manchester Press, 1952) 147.

[103]Furneaux puts it most expressively: 'The style and expression is thus his [Tacitus'] own, and the tedious antiquarian pedantry of Claudius is just sufficiently suggested to make the speech characteristic without being wearisome'; Furneaux, *The Annals of Tacitus: Vol. I*, 209. See also Fornara, *The Nature of History in Ancient Greece and Rome*, 154, and Mellor, *Tacitus*, 115-116.

evident that quite a lot of effort must have been put in to understand Claudius' original and reproduce its main points in an orderly fashion.[104] Tacitus conveyed the general sense of the original speech and something of the character of the speaker. Certainly liberties were taken with the original; the speech is not 'accurate' in the 20th century sense. It does, however, seem to be faithful to the event. It is of course difficult to know how typical this single example of Tacitus' method might be, and in any case, it is too late to be considered as a precedent for Acts.

3. Jewish Practice and Precedents

We have considered mainly the Greek and Roman historians, which some critics have thought an odd background against which to study a piece of religious literature such as Acts. Gärtner, for example, argues that the background of the speeches in Acts is not the Greek and Roman historians but rather the Old Testament and Apocrypha. His argument, it must be admitted, has some appeal. It has proved impossible to find any definite links with any of the particular secular historians the way, for example, that we may be fairly certain that Josephus imitated Dionysius of Halicarnassus or, indirectly, Thucydides. Gärtner would seem to be on very firm ground in asking why the New Testament scholar should seek after vague clues in literature that Luke may well not have known when it is perfectly clear that the author of Acts knew the Old Testament, and there are speeches to be found there which closely parallel the speeches in Luke's work. Gärtner writes of Luke: 'His method of filling the Acts with speeches much resembles the way in which the Greek and Roman historians similarly embellished their works. But despite this superficial likeness, there are essential differences. . .'[105]

The problem with Gärtner's view is that it is not quite so clear which is the superficial resemblance and which the significant one. Certainly the outward forms of many of the speeches are like the Old Testament, indeed, many authors have written about the

---

[104]It is an overstatement for den Boer to complain that Tacitus 'took the wildest liberties when reporting speeches. . .' W. den Boer, 'Some Remarks on the Beginnings of Christian Historiography', *Studia Patristica IV, Texte und Untersuchungen* 79 (1961) 350.

[105]Bertil Gärtner, *The Areopagus Speech and Natural Revelation*, trans. C.H. King (Acta Seminarii Neotestamentici Upsaliensis XXI; Uppsala: Gleerup, 1955) 7.

'Septuagintisms', but Luke's methodological concerns and his self-consciousness as researcher and writer point to a deeper undercurrent that is more like that of the Greek and Roman historians.[106] In his efforts to distance Acts from the Gentile background, Gärtner allows only a small number of pagan writers to be eligible for close comparison, namely, ones closest in time to Luke, a questionable decision.   °

Gärtner's statement: 'In the light of the then rhetorical taste and the licence shown in composing speeches, in conjunction with the uncritical approach to history of Luke's time, the Acts of the Apostles stands out as a work which differs considerably from *the style then most in favour'*[107] [emphasis mine] clearly betrays an important conceptual over-simplification. Gärtner believes that there were clear trends in historiographical methodology—that it moved, generally, from the historical realism of Thucydides and Polybius to become more and more dominated by rhetoric.[108] Gärtner's remarks to the effect that Acts is different from the Greek and Roman writings are based on the two assumptions that 1. there was a somewhat unified historiographical practice in Luke's time, and since, on this assumption, historiography was constantly progressing, 2. the consensus at the time of Luke was the most important. This latter point is in fact spelled out explicitly: 'When comparing Luke and the Classical historians, therefore, we must have before us the historiographical ideals that arose during the first year A.D. and not, as has hitherto been the practice, those of an earlier period'.[109] Neither of these assumptions can be maintained.

First, it is not true that there was a flow and smooth progression in historical method. Polybius and Thucydides, champions of the more 'accurate' speeches, were not contemporaries at the start of the genre whose ideals thereafter eroded. Perhaps the single most significant rhetorical influence, Isocrates, stands, in fact, *between* the times of Polybius and Thucydides. Nor is it possible to speak of one style as being most in favour during a particular period.

---

[106]The criticisms of Evans are particularly germane: C.F. Evans, 'The Speeches in Acts', in A. Descamps and André de Halleux (eds.), *Mélanges Bibliques* (Festschrift for B. Rigaux; Gembloux: Duc·lot, 1970) 289-290, 291ff.

[107]Gärtner, *The Areopagus Speech and Natural Revelation*, 17-18.

[108]Although when writing of individual historians, he allows individuality, notice the abundance of progression-oriented language in his survey: Gärtner, *The Areopagus Speech and Natural Revelation*, 15-18.

[109]Gärtner, *The Areopagus Speech and Natural Revelation*, 17.

Not enough of the writings of the ancients has survived to speak confidently of the style of a particular age. It is clear, however, from the writings we do have, that the most vigorous debates regarding 'accuracy' versus 'stylistic' perfection were not always between writers separated by time, like Dionysius and Thucydides, but were frequently between contemporaries: Polybius and Timaeus or Caesar and Cicero.[110]

Second, even if there had been a sweeping development in methodology it still would not be possible to argue that the contemporary influences are the most significant. This evaluation not only demands that the author of Luke-Acts be on the 'cutting edge' of historiography, and up-to-date with current trends, but it owes too much to modern culture in which great works are published and distributed in a matter of months and in which 'new' frequently is equated with 'improved', and 'old-fashioned' is often a derogatory term. The situation in antiquity was quite different; 'old' was more likely to hold positive connotations like 'firmly rooted' than negative ones like 'outdated'. Far from being disregarded, the oldest traditions in historiography should be highly regarded in the comparison of Graeco-Roman practice with Acts.[111] Thus, while Gärtner is right in emphasising the importance of the Jewish tradition in Acts, especially as regards the *finished* form and style of the speeches,[112] the lack of any clear methodological statements in these works make it much more likely that Luke took his understandings of method from the secular culture around him.[113]

The argument that the speeches in Acts are indebted to ancient religious literature is similarly valid primarily in the sphere of the style of the finished product. Even if *Joseph and Asenath* is dated early

---

[110]As Laistner writes, of a period not remote from Luke's own: 'There was great variety in taste. If a good proportion of the literature composed in that age had survived, we should almost certainly find a far greater variety and gradation. . .than can be deduced from the ancient critics that are extant. . .' Laistner, *The Greater Roman Historians*, 17.

[111]See, for example, Lucian, who, though writing *after* Acts, refers to the works of Thucydides and Xenophon as models in his 'How to Write History'. Cf. A. Momigliano, 'Greek Historiography', *History and Theory* 17 (1978) 15, on the survival of Thucydidean method.

[112]See especially such speeches as those of Paul at Pisidian Antioch and Miletus.

[113]This conclusion can only be strengthened by the recent findings of Mealand concerning stylistic parallels between Acts and the Hellenistic Historians, as cautiously as those findings must be taken. D.L. Mealand, 'Hellenistic Historians and the Style of Acts', *ZNW* 82 (1991) 42-66.

enough to be a possible influence, it is not truly comparable. Acts deals with historical and contemporary (or near contemporary) characters who give speeches that can be considered as 'land-marks' for the historical communities to which they were addressed. The only bodies of literature which give any statements of method for reporting on such events are histories and biographies.[114]

The obvious parallel of the work of the Jewish historian Josephus is a dangerous one. Josephus lived and wrote from approximately 39 to 100 A.D. It is, therefore, theoretically possible that the author of Acts knew his writings, but the evidence seems to point against it, for even though the writings of the two authors occasionally overlap, they rarely agree.[115]

In the first and second books of Maccabees, it is clear that the works were in the Jewish tradition, but were influenced to various degrees by the Greek models of historical writing. In the work of Josephus, the Greek influence dominates the Jewish content to such an extent that even Gärtner, who is interested in showing the Jewish aspects of the works he covers, is forced to admit that Josephus 'adheres wholly to the Greek tradition of historical writing'.[116] There have been various suggestions for Josephus' historiographical precedent. He can easily be fitted into the Isocratean tradition,[117] his imitation of Dionysius of Halicarnassus is obvious even from the titles of the works,[118] and there are numerous references and allusions to other Greek and even Roman writers in *The Jewish War*,

---

[114]The obvious *religious* parallel is 2 Maccabees, which however, clearly draws on secular models for its method. For more on the Jewish literature see my arguments elsewhere, C. Gempf, *Historical and Literary Appropriateness in the Mission Speeches of Paul in Acts,* unpublished PhD dissertation (University of Aberdeen, 1989) 115ff.

[115]Perhaps most convincing is H. Schreckenburg, 'Flavius Josephus und die Lukanischen Schriften', in W. Haubeck and M. Bachmann (eds.), *Wort in der Zeit* (Festgabe für Rengstorf; Leiden: Brill, 1980). See also A. Plummer, *A Critical and Exegetical Commentary on the Gospel According to St. Luke,* ICC (Edinburgh: T. & T. Clark, 1901) xxix-xxx; F. Jackson, *Josephus and the Jews* (London: SPCK, 1930) esp. 273-274; and G.A. Williamson, *The World of Josephus* (London: Secker and Warburg, 1964) esp. 19-22.

[116]Gärtner, *The Areopagus Speech and Natural Revelation,* 29.

[117]Jackson, *Josephus,* 257.

[118]Josephus' is called Ἰουδαικά Ἀρχαιολογία in twenty books, while Dionysius' was titled Ῥωμαικά Ἀρχαιολογία. For other likenesses see Momigliano, 'Greek Historiography', 16.

supplied either by Josephus or by his assistant translators.[119] There can be no doubt that Josephus is to be placed squarely in the Greek tradition.[120]

When, in the *Jewish War* Josephus writes: 'Let historical truth be held in honour by us, since by the Greeks it is neglected',[121] he may well be more concerned with the content of the Greeks' writing (about the Jews in particular) than, strictly speaking, with their reliability as a matter of methodology. Josephus was not able to provide accuracy, and especially not in 'precise details', despite these programmatic statements, but Williamson's almost humorously cautious endorsement contains a serious truth:

> Apart from such liberties as these [invention of speeches, elaboration or omission of incidents, etc.], taken in the interest of 'fine writing', impressiveness and dramatic effect, and apart from the frequent exaggeration. . .can we regard Josephus as in essentials a trustworthy historian? With certain qualifications, I think we can.[122]

There are two areas which prove the major exceptions to this general, if qualified, assessment: detail and speeches. In his attempts to relate matters of detail such as names or numbers, Josephus' method ranges from what is called by Cohen 'arbitrary reproduction',[123] to inflation and obvious exaggeration.[124] It is in presenting speeches, however, that Josephus departs most radically from any basis in historical fact or his sources.

Thackeray, in his classic study, divides the speeches into three general categories: 1. a few that seem to approximate what was actually said; 2. speeches that were so linked with the occasion in which they were given that we can reasonably hope to get the gist of the historical message; and 3. the great 'set' speeches inserted and

---

[119]Thucydides, Sallust, and Livy are among the most prominent. Grant, *The Ancient Historians*, 254.
[120]S.J. Cohen, *Josephus in Galilee and in Rome* (Columbia Studies in the Classical Tradition, Vol. 8; Leiden: Brill, 1979) 31.
[121]Josephus, 'Jewish War', 1.16, in *Josephus: Vol. II: War I-III*, trans. H. Thackeray, LCL (London: Heinemann, 1927) 10,11.
[122]Williamson, *The World of Josephus*, 292.
[123]Cohen, *Josephus in Galilee and in Rome*, 47.
[124]This can be seen perhaps most clearly by comparing figures in the *Jewish War* with those in the *Antiquities*: e.g. *War* 2.6.3.97 = *Antiquities* 17.11.4.320 and *War* 2.6.3.100 = *Antiquities* 17.11.5.323.

invented for the turning points in the literary piece.[125] Often the
speeches are not only invented, but quite inappropriate and even
tedious. Vespasian's son Titus, for whom Josephus was a translator/
intermediary during the siege of Jerusalem, is given a speech
intended to encourage his men which included the words:

> For our reverses are but the outcome of the Jews' desperation, while
> their sufferings are increased by your valiant exploits and the
> constant co-operation of the Deity. For faction, famine, siege, the fall
> of ramparts without the impact of engines—what can these things
> mean but that God is wroth with them and extending His aid to us?
> Surely, then, to allow ourselves not merely to be surpassed by
> inferiors but to betray a divine Ally would be beneath our
> dignity. . .[126]

It is difficult to believe that a Roman soldier would ever speak this
way about the Jewish God in *private*, much less openly to his men.
Even more well known is the speech of Herod, fighting against the
Arabs, which the historian records first in *The Jewish War* 1.373ff. and
then again in *The Jewish Antiquities*, in book 15.126ff.[127] The two are
without a doubt wholly different speeches. The obvious conclusion is
that Josephus has merely 'scrapped' the speeches from the old
history and replaced them with new ones.

Donald Jones suggests in his 1966 doctoral thesis that it is
logical to compare the speeches in Acts with Josephus because of the
'fact that he was a typical historian of the period'.[128] This seems to the
present author a very misleading statement. Perhaps what Jones
means is that Josephus differs in his method and style from the Old
Testament in directions that are typically Greek. It is clear that none
of the other Greek or Roman historians or critics mentioned here
would have praised or endorsed the clumsy and inappropriate
speeches of Josephus, even though a few would agree with the
principle that allowed more freedom in presenting orations than is

---

[125]H.St.J. Thackeray, *Josephus: The Man and the Historian* (New York: Jewish
Institute of Religion Press, 1929) 42f.
[126]Josephus, 'Jewish War', 6.39-41, trans. H. Thackeray, LCL (London:
Heinemann, 1928) 388, 389.
[127]Josephus, *Josephus: Vol. II: War I-III*, and *Josephus: Vol. VIII: Antiquities XV-
XVII*, trans. R. Marcus and A. Wikgren, LCL (London: Heinemann, 1963).
[128]D.L. Jones, *The Christology of the Missionary Speeches in the Acts of the Apostles*
(Ann Arbor, MI: University Microfilms, 1966) 31.

allowed with the narrative.[129] Considered as a whole, Josephus' work is an attempt to defend and explain the Jewish history and traditions in Greek and Roman idioms, but it cannot be regarded as typical of even that particular task, much less as typical of contemporary historiography in general.[130]

III. Implications for Acts Scholarship

The first significant modern comparison of Luke's speeches with the Greek and Roman historians was made by Henry Cadbury. In two articles in the *Beginnings of Christianity* collection[131] and in his book *The Making of Luke-Acts*,[132] he set forth the view that the ancients were chiefly interested in form as opposed to accuracy.[133] He allowed for some variety in the practices of individuals, but in general regarded the convention as uniform. Thus, he wrote of '. . .the custom prevalent in the ancient world of adorning historical works with imaginative speeches. . .'[134] Cadbury alluded to the concept we have called historical appropriateness: 'Aside from rhetorical style, the chief requisite of these speeches was appropriateness to the speaker and to the occasion'.[135] But in his desire to stress the difference between this and accuracy, he usually calls this tendency 'dramatic imagination' or 'historical imagination'. Far from seeing it as held in tension with literary appropriateness, this 'historical imagination' is for him always clearly secondary to the artistic aims of the historian.[136]

---

[129]We think particularly of Lucian of Samosata's 'How History Ought to be Written', which was probably later than Josephus, and is quoted above.

[130]It would be better to say, with Sterling, 'The author of Luke-Acts thus shares command historical and historiographical traditions with Josephos', Gregory E. Sterling, *Historiography and Self-Definition: Josephos, Luke-Acts & Apologetic Historiography* (Leiden: Brill, 1992) 369.

[131]H. Cadbury, *et al.*, 'The Greek and Jewish Traditions of Writing History', in *BC, Vol. II*, and H. Cadbury, 'The Speeches in Acts', in *BC, Vol. V*.

[132]H. Cadbury, *The Making of Luke-Acts* (London: SPCK, 1968). (First published in 1927.)

[133]Cadbury, 'Greek and Jewish Traditions', 11.

[134]Cadbury, 'Speeches', 402.

[135]Cadbury, *Making*, 185.

[136]Even in an otherwise balanced statement such as that found in Cadbury, 'Speeches', 426-427.

In the first of the three works, Cadbury made the bold generalisation: 'From Thucydides downwards, speeches reported by the historians are *confessedly pure imagination*'.[137] The last of the three, 'The Speeches in Acts', in *BC, Vol. V*, presented a slightly more balanced view. After writing that there are 'rare' exceptions in the genre, like Polybius, he continued '. . .even they prevent our assuming a general rule of pure invention. . .'[138] His conclusion is that there is little hope of reliability, but in some cases we may wish to give the same benefit of doubt we might grant to a historian such as Tacitus.[139]

For one reason or another it was not Cadbury's articles on the speeches that came to be seen as the starting point for discussion, but the later work of the form-critic Martin Dibelius. Like Cadbury, he recognised the important point that ancient historians had literary aims in presenting the speeches and that accuracy was by no means the guiding concern.[140] Also like Cadbury, he regarded as most important the question of the artistic relevance or appropriateness of the speeches.[141] Dibelius however had even less respect than Cadbury for the historical dimension in the speeches, limiting the concept of appropriateness to the single facet which we have called 'literary appropriateness'. He even went so far as to claim that one of the possible reasons for an ancient historian to present a given speech was to give his readers

---

[137]Cadbury, 'Greek and Jewish Traditions', 13. He gives the Thucydidean reference (1.22), but does not give the text in this essay.
[138]Cadbury, 'Speeches', 405-406.
[139]Cadbury, 'Speeches', 406.
[140]M. Dibelius, 'The Speeches in Acts and Ancient Historiography', in H. Greeven (ed.), *Studies in the Acts of the Apostles* (London: SCM Press, 1956) 144f. (essay first published in 1944). Dibelius wants to exclude the missionary speeches from those that rely on historiographical convention, as they relay some of the traditional kerygma (which would have otherwise been troublesome for his view of the convention). Dibelius, '. . .Ancient Historiography', 166. Modern followers of Dibelius, however, nearly all part company with him on this point. Cf. U. Wilckens, *Die Missionsreden der Apostelgeschichte*, Vol. 5 Wissenschaftliche Monographien zum Alten und Neuen Testament, G. Bornkamm and G. Von Rad (eds.) (3rd edition; Neukirchen: Neukirchener Verlag, 1974), Eckhard Plümacher, *Lukas als hellenistischer Schriftsteller* (Göttingen: Vandenhoeck und Ruprecht, 1972) and most recently, Plümacher, 'Die Missionsreden der Apostelgeschichte und Dionys von Halikarnass', *NTS* 39 (1993).
[141]Dibelius, '. . .Ancient Historiography', 144f. See now also Tannehill, 'The Functions of Peter's Mission Speeches in the Narrative of Acts', *NTS* 37 (1991) 400-414.

> an insight into the meaning of the historical movement concerned, but one which goes beyond the facts of history. Even though this insight may not have been revealed to the historical character at the moment when he is making the speech, the writer nevertheless lets him supply it.[142]

From a detailed survey of the ancient historians, one would have trouble proving that this was *tolerable* in a history, much less that it was a possible 'aim' of the historians. Dibelius did not allow that historians' works might have an appropriateness guided by historical rather than pure literary concerns, nor did he write about the possibility that something admittedly included for reasons that are literary might also (even if accidentally) have historical value. He seems to see these goals as mutually exclusive, a tendency which Classicists have recognised as undesirable in their studies. Gomme described it as: '. . .a sub-conscious belief that Thucydides' skill as an artist is in some way incompatible, in the speeches, with his truthfulness as a historian. . .'[143]

Dibelius was very clear in his writing that he felt that the speeches in Acts were totally different from the real St. Paul.[144] More recent writers have seen in his work the basis for denying the traditional view of the authorship of Luke-Acts. It is not uncommon for this branch of scholarship to endorse Dibelius' study of ancient historiography without realising that that *invalidates* any negative argument on the authorship question based on the speeches. For if, as Dibelius envisaged, the speeches are essentially a-historical inventions, then the lack of similarities to the real Paul can be explained by artistic license rather than by lack of genuine knowledge. Similarly, it cannot be argued that since Josephus places such a different speech in the mouth of Abraham at the sacrificing of Isaac from that found in Genesis, he could not have known the Old Testament text himself. Yet, for example, Kümmel, after explicitly endorsing Dibelius' findings, follows the endorsement by arguing that Luke did not reproduce even 'the most significant features of the historical Paul', and concludes that 'from these facts it is sufficiently clear that the author of Acts was not a missionary companion of

---

[142]Dibelius, '. . .Ancient Historiography', 140.

[143]Gomme, 'Speeches', 179.

[144]Dibelius, 'Paul on the Areopagus', in *Studies in the Acts of the Apostles*, 61, 62, 71.

Paul'.[145] Would he then also argue that it is sufficiently clear that Josephus was not familiar with the Isaac story?

Dibelius himself never fell into this fallacious way of thinking, believing as he did that the author of Acts was Luke. Indeed he anticipates some of his followers when he criticises some of his predecessors:

> [There is a 'critical' view which holds that] the Acts of the Apostles could not have been written by Luke, Paul's companion, because it contained more errors than could have been made by one who was so close to Paul. This theory somewhat exaggerates both the proximity to Paul and the number of errors. But especially, however, the ancient historian does not wish to present life with photographic accuracy. . .[146]

Regardless of the decision about the identity of the author, Dibelius' influence concerning speeches as the 'creations' of the author persists in New Testament studies to the present day. This can be seen in the recent article of Plümacher, in which he writes of the matter as if it had been solved long ago: 'Bei den Reden der Apostelgeschichte handelt es sich bekanntlich nicht um Referate wirklich gehaltener Ansprachan, sondern um Produkte aus der Feder des Actenverfassers selbst'.[147]

A somewhat more conservative estimate of the overall trustworthiness of the ancient historians is urged by A.W. Mosley.[148] This review has the advantage of being a systematic study of each of the major Greek and Roman writers in chronological order, rather than merely an elaborate hypothesis corroborated by occasional quotations from various ancient sources. Unfortunately, Mosley's focus is rather wide and his article is short. Although he notes that he has not paid as careful attention as he might to the use of speeches in the historians,[149] it seems odd that he manages to incorporate the more positive statements of Thucydides and Polybius on speeches

---

[145]W.G. Kümmel, *Introduction to the New Testament*, trans. A.J. Matill Jr. (London: SCM Press, 1966) 129-130. Note, however, that 'these facts' include other arguments as well as those about the speeches.

[146]Dibelius, 'The First Christian Historian', in *Studies in the Acts of the Apostles*, 136f.

[147]Plümacher, 'Die Missionsreden' (1993) 161-177.

[148]A.W. Mosley, 'Historical Reporting in the Ancient World', *NTS* 12 (1965-66) 10-26.

[149]Mosley, 'Historical Reporting', 25.

into his work,[150] but does not discuss the more problematic or negative statements, like those of Lucian.[151] Despite his selectivity, however, the survey approach keeps him from over-simplifying and his conclusions are modest.[152] Similarly, T.F. Glasson concluded that the statement in Thucydides should not be used to build a case that historians in antiquity were not concerned with what was actually said.[153]

In the early 1970's, Ward Gasque wrote an article more directly attacking Dibelius *et al.*, and more positive in its conclusions than either Glasson or Mosley.[154] One of his basic points is that Dibelius misunderstands or misrepresents the ancient historians. To correct this, Gasque reviews the statements on them in Dibelius' work. It is unfortunate that he is content to refute the use of the examples found in Dibelius' essay, rather than, like Mosley, investigating all of the historians. Gasque is forced to admit that Josephus composed unhistorical speeches, and even that such invention was a widespread (but not universal) practice.[155] But in most of Dibelius' examples—Polybius, Thucydides and Tacitus' Claudius speech— Gasque finds fruitful ground for criticising his opponent's interpretation.[156] Gasque does not, however, treat the awkward Polybian passage 12.25, in which Polybius appears to allow elaborations by the historian.

Even more misleading is Gasque's citation of Lucian's *How History Should Be Written*. Gasque attempts to cast Lucian as being against the inclusion of invented rhetorical speeches: 'Thucydides and Polybius were in principle opposed to the practice, as were men of letters such as Lucian'.[157] But Lucian is, in reality, no ally. Gasque quotes only part of Lucian's advice about speeches, writing: '. . .and

---

[150]Mosley, 'Historical Reporting', 12f. and 14ff., respectively.
[151]Lucian, 'How History Ought to be Written', 58, 70-71. In his section on Jewish writers, however, Mosley does mention the obviously invented speeches of Josephus.
[152]Mosley, 'Historical Reporting', 26.
[153]T.F. Glasson, 'The Speeches in Acts and Thucydides', *Expository Times* 76 (1964-1965) 165.
[154]W.W. Gasque, 'The Speeches of Acts: Dibelius Reconsidered', in R. Longenecker and M. Tenney (eds.), *New Dimensions in New Testament Study* (Grand Rapids: Zondervan, 1974).
[155]Gasque, '. . .Dibelius Reconsidered', 242-243.
[156]Gasque, '. . .Dibelius Reconsidered', 244-245. He does make it clear however that the latter is only a loose paraphrase and abridgement.
[157]Gasque, '. . .Dibelius Reconsidered', 246.

although he recognizes the fact that speeches have rhetorical value even in historical narrative he argues that "what is said must be above all appropriate to the character and suitable to the occasion"'.[158] But in the original the sentence which follows goes beyond 'recognition that speeches have rhetorical value'! Lucian writes: 'It is then, however, that you can play the orator ($\dot{\rho}\tau o\rho\epsilon\hat{u}\sigma\alpha\iota$) and show your eloquence'.[159] Similarly, Gasque writes: 'Lucian criticizes one "historian" for composing a funeral oration to a fallen general which had no basis in fact'.[160] Although it is true that this account fits into a larger context of mistakes which Lucian has found in historians, it is by no means clear that Lucian regards this particular example as an error *because* of its lack of factual basis. What Lucian actually writes is: 'So, after burying Severianus in magnificent style he [the historian] makes a centurion, an Africanus Silo, mount the tomb as a rival to Pericles [who delivered the famous funeral oration in Thucydides]; his rhetoric was so strange and so exaggerated that by the Graces I just cried and cried with laughing. . .'[161] The objection is not that the event had no basis in reality, but rather that the speech was *unrealistic* in content and in style.

In an article written a few years later, Gasque reproduces much of his argument in an abbreviated fashion, only mentioning Lucian once, and that parenthetically.[162] He acknowledges in this later article that 'an imposing number of counter-examples could also be adduced'.[163] Again, though, he does not specify what it is we can expect from historians who do not invent; the implication is a sort of accurate paraphrase.

Kistemaker is one who does not shy away from the word 'accurate'. Writing about the Thucydidean prologue, he says 'The apparent intention of this ancient writer is to state that the speeches he wrote were historically accurate and not based on his own

---

[158]Gasque, '. . .Dibelius Reconsidered', 245-246. Lucian, 'How History Ought to be Written', 58.
[159]Lucian, 'How History Ought to be Written', 58.
[160]Gasque, '. . .Dibelius Reconsidered', 245. The reference in Gasque is to Lucian, 24-26, but he focuses on the story of Severianus in 26.
[161]Lucian, 26.
[162]W.W. Gasque, 'The Book of Acts and History', in R. Guelich (ed.), *Unity and Diversity in New Testament Theology* (Festschrift for G.E. Ladd; Grand Rapids: Eerdmans, 1978).
[163]Gasque, 'The Book of Acts and History', 61.

imagination'.[164] And on Luke the verdict seems similarly clear: 'The speeches in Acts accurately portray the speakers and their individual traits'.[165] In fact, however, Kistemaker's view is a bit more complex than those simple statements appear. 'Although Luke is the writer of the speeches in Acts, he is not their composer. That is he does not create discourses which he places in the mouths of speakers.'[166] He allows that the speech accounts are shorter than real speeches would be, but is concerned to stress what he calls 'accuracy'.

F.F. Bruce has written extensively on the book of Acts, notably two works dealing specifically with the speeches.[167] It is surprising that, although a Classics scholar himself (at the time the first article was published he was in fact a teacher of classical Greek), he deals with the question of the historical convention only briefly, to refute the use of Thucydides' preface as proof of a universal practice of invention. What is characteristic of his approach is 1. the observation that there are many ways in which the ancient writers used speeches; 2. his contention that a close study of the actual practice in Acts reveals Luke's difference from the more rhetorical historians, which suggests reliability of speech material in Acts; and 3. his insistence that theological purpose in Luke need not necessarily be inversely proportional to historical trustworthiness.[168] This way of regarding the speeches is correct in affirming the variety in ancient practice and the need to evaluate Luke's work on its own merits rather than assuming either that all historians invented or that all historians were careful (except Josephus). But Bruce seems content to leave the ancients to one side once he has refuted any notion of an easily transferable parallel.

---

[164]Simon Kistemaker, *Acts* (Grand Rapids: Baker Book House, 1990) 9.
[165]Kistemaker, 'The Speeches in Acts', *Criswell Theological Review* 5 (1990) 41.
[166]Kistemaker, 'Speeches', 41.
[167]F.F. Bruce, *The Speeches in the Acts of the Apostles*, Tyndale New Testament Lecture, 1942 (London: The Tyndale Press, 1944) and F.F. Bruce, 'The Speeches in Acts—Thirty Years After', in R. Banks (ed.), *Reconciliation and Hope* (Festschrift for L. Morris; Grand Rapids: Eerdmans, 1974).
[168]In these points, he is followed to a large extent by most of the more conservative scholars; see for example: I.H. Marshall, 'The Resurrection in the Acts of the Apostles', in W.W. Gasque and R.P. Martin (eds.), *Apostolic History and the Gospel* (Festschrift for F.F. Bruce; Exeter: Paternoster Press, 1970) 92-95; M.B. Dudley, 'The Speeches in Acts', *Evangelical Quarterly* 50 (1978) 147-155; and to some extent Gasque, 'The Book of Acts and History', and Gärtner, *The Areopagus Speech and Natural Revelation*.

Colin Hemer, like Bruce, rejects any attempt to 'tidy the ancient evidence into too neat a pattern'[169] and writes: 'There are two basic things to stress: that ancient historiography is an extremely complicated business and that it is not easy to specify exactly how Luke relates to it'.[170] Hemer is optimistic about the speeches in Acts, however. He notes that Luke's method in the matter of recording speeches in the Gospel, in those places where we can check his report with the source, show him to be a careful and conservative reporter.[171] In separate articles on the Athens and Miletus speeches, Hemer further demonstrates Luke's faithfulness, without denying his editorial activity.[172]

IV. Conclusions

We have maintained that the most important foci for the study of the ancient historians are the statements of method that are to be found in their writings, since this is as close as we can come to understanding how an ancient reader/hearer would have understood the practices.[173] So, for example, it might be well for us to conclude, in the light of our 20th century investigations, that the speeches in historian X are completely unreliable, but we have no guarantees that a first-century reader would have known that to be the case, even presuming we are correct.

This consideration has led to the in-depth study primarily of Greek historians and literary critics, since they were more inclined to discuss matters of method. The Romans seem to have simply adopted the various types of Greek practice, and with them inherited the squabbles as well.[174] In the case of the Jewish literature, the Old

---

[169]C. Hemer, 'Luke the Historian', *Bulletin of the John Rylands Library* 60 (1977-1978) 29.

[170]Hemer, 'Luke the Historian', 29.

[171]C. Hemer, *The Book of Acts in the Setting of Hellenistic History* (WUNT 49; Tübingen: Mohr, 1989) 427.

[172]C. Hemer, 'The Speeches of Acts: I. The Ephesian Elders at Miletus', *TynB* 40 (1989) 77-85, and C. Hemer, 'The Speeches of Acts: II. The Areopagus Address', *TynB* 40 (1989) 239-259. See especially 'Miletus' 85.

[173]We include in 'statements of method', besides the methodological introductions of the historians themselves, the criticisms of peers or near peers, such as Lucian and Dionysius of Halicarnassus.

[174]Thus, Caesar and Cicero in some ways parallel Polybius and Timaeus, only this time the more rhetorically-minded is doing the criticising.

Testament presents no discernible clues as to the methodology employed, and the Jewish historical works that we possess which are nearly contemporary with Luke-Acts, Maccabees and Josephus, show considerable hellenistic influence.

Perhaps the most striking feature of the statements of method is their self-contradictory nature, or rather, their nature which seems to us self-contradictory. Most writers are in favour of truthfulness, but all also seem agreed that the historian may (indeed, *should*) take what we would call 'liberties' with the text of the speech even when that is known. Explicit and implicit in their statements is the important role that the historian is to play in the utilising of speeches in his history. What is contradictory for us does not appear to have been thought of as paradoxical or unusual by them, or else we would expect more elaboration on the point from the historians and certainly more criticisms from the sharp-mouthed critics like Lucian, who delighted in showing places where other writers contradicted themselves.

Where historians can be checked against the sources of the speeches, they seem to reflect well the balance that we have concluded to be present in the statements of method. The speeches are the compositions of the author, but at their best are representative of the speaker, the situation and of the contents of the original. The exception is Josephus, who also shows himself to be somewhat deficient in areas of historical writing other than the recording of speeches.

When we turn to the book of Acts, knowledge of the variety to be found in the ancient authors, coupled with the awareness that much of the ancient literature is lost, should keep us from saying glibly that 'Luke *could not* have done x' on the one hand or 'Luke *must* have done y' on the other. Haenchen greeted the suggestion of F.F. Bruce that the author of Acts may have taken short-hand notes of speeches with astonishment,[175] yet we know of the practice from Quintilian, who mentions it, but advocates memory to take in the points of an oration at which one is present.[176] Similarly, some modern authors assume that all writers fabricated their material, since 'the Greeks always invented speeches'. The evidence for this

---

[175]Commenting only with an exclamation mark in parentheses, as if the idea was too hopelessly preposterous for words, Haenchen, *Acts*, 590. See p. 307 below.

[176]Cf. Quintilian, 11.2.2, on remembering the speeches of others (usually opponents), not merely in the order that they were presented, but in an order useful to your own line of thought. On short-hand systems see the same chapter in Quintilian, 11.2.25.

position is largely 20th century presuppositions disguised as common sense, as in this quote from Bartlett: 'Like other ancient authors, the author of I Maccabees was not in a position to give us the actual words of any speaker; he had no tape-recorder and relied heavily upon the memories of men who were probably not all first-hand witnesses'.[177] Aside from the obvious lack of respect for the ancients' abilities to remember, Bartlett here shows a more subtle bias toward thinking of all historians as 'armchair historians'. The ancients considered involvement in the events as a prime qualification for historians, but Bartlett clearly thinks more along the line of: 'what aids could this *scholar* have had at his disposal?' We can no more disregard the achievements of the ancient writers because of their lack of tape recorders than we can dismiss the pyramids on the basis of the patent dates of the bulldozer and crane.

It seems clear that unless they are very heavily qualified, our terms ('accuracy' or 'invention') for describing the speeches are misleading. And even when properly qualified, to try and fit the speeches of Acts into these categories is the wrong way to look at them.[178] We must ask not 'how close is this account to what was said?', but rather 'how close is this account to what happened?' Now, obviously, the two are related, but the change in emphasis is truer to the nature of the data under observation and has some important consequences.

The first consequence is that we will no longer be in the least surprised that, despite the implication for the modern reader of the speech being in the first person, the form of the speech that we have has been composed by the author.[179] It is only because of expectations alien to first-century practice that we tend to think that the most natural explanation is that the speech did not happen or at least did not happen as the author records it, although we will graciously allow that there might possibly be another explanation.

We will also be disabused of a similar notion. When a speaker in a narrative gives a speech, the content of which is in line with what

---

[177]J.R. Bartlett, *The First and Second Books of the Maccabees* (Cambridge Bible Commentary 61; Cambridge: Cambridge University Press, 1973) 17. Note the wording: 'probably not all first-hand witnesses'.

[178]The implication of this constant need for qualifications is that the phenomena and the categories do not really fit each other.

[179]We should expect this to be the case in rhetorical situations, where the speech is regarded as 'act', although not necessarily when it is 'teaching' material, preserved for its own sake, as in the Gospel passages.

the author is known to believe, this can no longer be taken as good evidence for branding the account as an unfaithful witness to an event. For whether it is a faithful witness or not, we should expect the author of the book to so select facets of the event and write the matter up in a way that suits the purposes and aims of the book. Coherence of the speech with the author's own purposes are not sufficient grounds for dismissing the record of a speech as invention.[180]

An examination of the author's purposes and beliefs *can* be useful in a negative way however. If the speech as recorded, or a feature thereof, *does not* fit in with the author's own views or vocabulary, then there is reason to investigate whether such features might, in fact, be due to their being 'historical faithful' or even what we might call 'accurate'.[181]

In determining historical *faithfulness*, the most important clues are likely to come in weighing whether a speech shows 1. traces of the alleged situation into which it was purported to have been delivered and 2. traces of the personality and traits of the alleged speaker. If discontinuities appear, then there is reason for questioning the faithfulness of the speech to the event. Thus, for example, when the Roman historian Livy records a long and stirring speech of an army commander to his men as they attempt to sneak quietly over a hill in the dead of night,[182] or when Josephus has the Roman general Titus encourage his Roman soldiers against the Jews with a speech that asks the soldiers '. . .what can these things mean but that God is wroth with them and extending His aid to us?'[183] we have cause to wonder how likely such events might be. It is not their likeness to the authors' point of view but rather their lack of regard for the alleged situation and speaker that are the problem.

---

[180]See also for example Rawlings, who questions the 'assumption that because Thucydides can be shown to have great artistic control over his material, he must therefore be guilty of manipulating or distorting that material', Rawlings, *Structure of Thucydides' History*, 267-272, citing from 268.

[181]The fact that the ancients were not aiming towards this goal does not mean that they did not on occasion fulfil it. Occasionally first-century practice and our 20th century expectations do overlap.

[182]Wisely, however, the 'speaker' urges his men not to applaud! 'You must preserve the silence, soldiers, as you listen to me, omitting all soldier-like acclaim', Livy, 7.35.1-12. Translation from the Loeb edition.

[183]Not, I suggest, the interpretation that would suggest itself to the Roman mind when facing an opponent who insisted that Roman gods did not exist and theirs was the only true God. Josephus, *Jewish War* 6.39-41.

In terms of Acts, then, it is true that in the Book of Acts, several different speakers make reference to a particular argument about David and appear to do so in such a way that each speech relates a complementary part of the whole argument. But this is insufficient evidence to be used as a positive indicator of Lukan invention.[184] Given the fact that the speakers are all Jews and the importance of the promises to David relating to the Davidic Kingdom, it is likely that the speakers would have touched upon such arguments and understandable that Luke would have selected and fashioned the accounts in a way that they would work together. There is nothing, in this evidence alone, to allow us to choose either for or against faithfulness.

A more helpful criticism of the speeches in Acts would be *if* it could be shown, in the account of Paul's visit to Athens, that either the altar mentioned by Paul could not have existed (thus suggesting that the speech was unsuitable for the alleged situation) or that the speech goes against Paul's own theology (thus suggesting that the speech was unsuitable for the alleged speaker).[185]

Space does not permit us to continue to this further step of evaluating the faithfulness of Acts.[186] This essay only suggests the categories which such an exploration must use. For whatever our view of their historical worth, we must stop approaching the speeches in Acts with a 20th century preconception and learn instead to view them in the setting of first-century literary conventions. This *does not* mean, as Dibelius thought, setting aside any connection between recorded speeches and historical referents.[187] That is to

---

[184]The reference to Ps. 16:10 is used in a speech of Peter in 2:25ff. as well as in Paul's speech in 13:35. The interpretation given is the conclusion of, for example, Dibelius: 'It is a literary-theological, not an historical task which he wants to fulfil here. . .' M. Dibelius, *Studies in the Acts of the Apostles*, 111. See also Tannehill, 'Functions of Peter's Mission Speeches', 414.

[185]Both have been suggested; see, for example, Haenchen, *The Acts of the Apostles* (Oxford: Basil Blackwell, 1971) 521ff.

[186]See, however, Gärtner, *The Areopagus Speech and Natural Revelation*; C. Hemer, 'The Speeches of Acts II. The Areopagus Address'; and chapter 4 of C. Gempf, 'Historical and Literary Appropriateness in the Mission Speeches of Paul in Acts', unpublished Ph.D. thesis (University of Aberdeen, 1989) summarised in C. Gempf 'Athens' in *Dictionary of Paul and His Letters* (IVP: forthcoming), regarding the allegations against the Athens speech mentioned above.

[187]Dibelius, '. . .Ancient Historiography', 184: 'The very admission that the author worked historically [i.e. with the conventions of ancient historiography] prevents the speeches in Acts from being used as sources for the ideas and words of the speakers themselves'.

misunderstand the first-century authors. We have suggested thinking of the speeches in terms of the two-pronged concept of *literary and historical appropriateness*: the historians were interested in including speeches that were appropriate to their book and also appropriate to the alleged speaker and situation. We must learn to think of the public speeches not as (accurate or falsified) transcript/summaries of the words of famous people, but rather as records (faithful or unfaithful) of historical *events*.

CHAPTER 11

OFFICIAL PROCEEDINGS AND THE FORENSIC SPEECHES IN ACTS 24-26

Bruce W. Winter

Summary

Extant non-literary forensic speeches made in Roman courts in the early empire, similar to those made in Acts 24-26, enable us to better place those official proceedings in that particular ancient literary genre by a form critical analysis. It is proposed to do this (I) by discussing non-literary legal documents and the protocol surrounding the recording of forensic proceedings, (II) by subjecting specific non-literary forensic sources which were composed according to the form laid out in the rhetorical handbooks to a form critical examination, (III) by applying the fruits of these to the speeches of Tertullus and Paul, and (IV) by providing a comparable literary example.

I. The Protocol on Official Proceedings[1]

1. *Evidence*

There is extensive evidence of forensic speeches in the early empire. Over 250 extant papyri of official court proceedings in the early Roman empire similar to those recorded in Acts 24ff. have been published to date. The number continues to grow with the on-going publication of collections of non-literary sources.[2] These official documents are the recorded presentations of legal cases, and an analysis of them reflects the advocacy of professional rhetoricians. Some papyri preserve the case for both the prosecution and the defence.[3]

---

[1]In recent times attention has been given to both its Roman legal background—A.N. Sherwin-White, *Roman Society and Roman Law in the New Testament* (Oxford: Clarendon Press, 1963); M. Black, 'Paul and Roman Law in Acts', *RQ* 24 (1981) 209-18; H.W. Tajra, *The Trial of Paul* (Tübingen: J.C.B. Mohr [Paul Siebeck], 1989); and the forensic speeches in Acts—J. Dupont, *Études sur les Actes des Apôtres* (Paris, 1967) 527-52; F. Veltman, 'The Defence Speeches of Paul in Acts', in C.H. Talbert (ed.), *Perspectives on Luke-Acts* (Edinburgh, 1978) 243-256; W.R. Long, *The Trial of Paul in the Book of Acts: Historical, Literary and Theological Considerations* (Ph.D. dissertation; Brown University, 1982); and 'The *Paulusbild* in the Trial of Paul in Acts', *SBL 1983 Seminar Papers* 22 (Chico, 1983) 87-105; J. Neyrey, 'The Forensic Defence Speech and Paul's Trial Speeches in Acts 22-26: Form and Function', in Talbert (ed.), *Luke-Acts: New Perspectives from the Society of Biblical Literature Seminar* (New York: Crossroad, 1984) 210-24. My own 'The Importance of the *Captatio Benevolentiae* in the Speeches of Tertullus and Paul in Acts 24:1-21', *JTS* n.s. 42 (1991) 505-31 forms the basis of part of this chapter.
[2]The list of papyri recorded in R.A. Coles, *Reports of Proceedings in Papyri* (Papyrologia Bruscellensia 4; Brussels, 1966) 55-63 and for additional forensic papyri edited subsequent to Coles' publication in 1966 see for example *P. Oxy. Hels.* 18 (A.D. 124), 19 (A.D. 138); *P. Oxy.* 2852 (A.D. 104/5), 2853 (A.D. 245/6), 2955 (A.D. 218?), 3015 (2nd century A.D.), 3117 (3rd century A.D.); *P. Wisconsin* 7 (2nd century A.D.); *P. Lond.* 2910 (A.D. 176?); *P. Mich.* 602 (3rd century A.D.); and *P. Lips.* 41 (4th century A.D.).
[3]For examples of extracts of official proceedings of the Christian era in which both the accusers and defendant are recorded see *P. Flor.* 61 (A.D. 86-8); *P. Hamb.* 29 (A.D. 4); *P. Fam. Teb.* 19 (A.D. 118); *P. Mil. Volg.* 25 (A.D. 126-7); *BGU* 969 (A.D. c. 142); *P. Tebt.* 287 (A.D. 161-9); and *BGU* 15 (A.D. 194).

2. Recording Proceedings

How do we know that the official extant court speeches are what they purport to be, *i.e.* official records of speeches of actual proceedings? In the Roman period these were recorded as *oratio recta* by an official. As the speech was being presented in court it was taken down in shorthand.[4] Although there is some uncertainty as to precisely when shorthand was actually introduced into court, it is known that these proceedings were being thus recorded no later than c. A.D. 50.[5] They were summarised by the scribe as *oratio recta*, after the proceedings had ended. Although presented in the form of a précis, they were regarded as *verbatim* accounts of the argument.[6] This explains the fairly standard length of the official proceedings.[7] When measured against the lengthy 'N' documents which are briefs,[8] they are clearly summaries. The reason the courts did not reproduce the whole of the speech may well be related to the tendency of orators to speak at great length. The promise of brevity by Tertullus reflects the known loquacity of orators—'But in order not to weary you further, I would request that you be kind enough to hear us briefly' (Acts 24:4).[9] The somewhat similar length of the speeches further substantiates the conclusion that all official proceedings are summaries. For all that, they were nevertheless regarded as accurate representations of what was said in court. These official documents were placed in government archives, for Rome attached great importance to the storage and preservation of all official documents, not least all those relating to legal proceedings.[10]

---

[4]R.A. Coles, *op. cit.*, 13ff. They were re-produced as *oratio recta*, whereas in a previous period they were recorded *oratio obliqua*.

[5]R.A. Coles, *op. cit.*, 13.

[6]R.A. Coles, *op. cit.*, 19. For examples of actual speeches composed for presentation in court see *P. Princ.* 119 (c. A.D. 325) and *P. Col.* 174 (c. A.D. 325-350).

[7]The length of many of the official proceedings approximates to that of the speeches in Acts 24ff., although it is clear that those of Tertullus and Paul are summaries as were all records of such proceedings, *contra* E. Haenchen, *op. cit.*, 656, 'The speeches of Tertullus and Paul do not offer any text—they are much too short for that'.

[8]For discussion of 'N' documents see pp. 311-2.

[9]A.E. Hanson, 'Memorandum and Speech of an Advocate', *ZPE* 8 (1971) 18 on unnecessary repetition in a case.

[10]See *P. Fam. Tebt.* 15 (c. A.D. 114-15) for a lengthy inquiry into the deterioration and loss of official documents through carelessness and poor storage and the

3. Copying Proceedings

Certified copies of official documents relating to judicial proceedings were available to a defendant, as was the forensic petition which initiated the judicial action.[11] *P. Oxy.* 2131 (A.D. 207) *ll.* 3-4, which will be examined later, is an example of an attested copy of a petition. It was extracted from 'the roll of conjoined petitions', copied and certified by six witnesses which the editor of the papyrus notes was the usual number of witnesses used to certify documents.[12] So too was other evidence such as petitions, letters and memoranda related to the legal cases. Therefore, a certified copy of any legal document was regarded in its day as genuine and there was no discrimination against a certified copy in favour of the original.

4. Incorporation of documentary evidence

Official papers, including records of the proceedings which had been resumed are also extant. As an example, there is a collection of legal documents connected with a case which contains a report of a trial, a petition, and an ordinance of a prefect *P. Fam. Tebt.* 15 (A.D. 114-5). Another collection has official proceedings of a trial with annexed documents containing pleading on behalf of three participants, the reading of a petition, a report of a first session presided over by the *strategus*, a second session, the verdict, and a supplementary verdict, *P. Fam. Tebt.* 24 (A.D. 124). Certified copies of these documents were made available to the defendant.

5. Official Documents in Acts

Do the narratives of Acts surrounding the forensic speeches suggest the use of official documents? There are two pieces of evidence. Firstly, prior to Paul's trials before Felix and Festus, the narrative in Acts records what is said to be the text of the official letter of

---

steps taken to have damaged papers pasted together again at the expense of those who had been neglectful.

[11]See R. Coles, *op. cit.*, 29-30 on the use of the term μεθ' ἕτερα for 'certified copies'.

[12]A.S. Hunt, *The Oxyrhynchus Papyri*, Vol. 17, 235.

Claudius Lysias in which nine legal terms have been located (Acts 23:25-30).[13] E.A. Judge, after an analysis of an official petition where τύπος was also used, concludes that the author of Acts meant his readers to regard 23:25-30 as 'the direct citation' of a copy available to him—γράψας ἐπιστολὴν ἔχουσαν τὸν τύπον τοῦτον (v. 25). He argues,

> the term surely prevents us treating the letter on the same basis as the speeches. . .written speeches will often have arisen only as retrospective stocktaking by their authors. . .while letters passed at once into the possession of their recipients and would be preserved by them as proof of the point they documented.[14]

Such a document would have been available to the defendant.[15]

Secondly, soon after Festus assumed office from Felix he had to forward legal proceedings and documents to Rome following Paul's successful move to have his case heard in the highest court of appeal. Acts notes the concern of Festus about producing *litterae dimissoriae* of the proceedings to date which had to accompany the prisoner—'of whom I have no certain thing to write to my Lord' (Acts 25:26)[16]—because he must forward to the emperor a covering memorandum explaining the legal aspects of the case. The requisite documentation was being gathered for Rome.

It should be noted in passing that Luke also records a fundamental principle of Roman law to which Festus finds it necessary to draw attention—'it is not the custom of the Romans to sentence any man, before the accused have accusers face to face, and to have had the opportunity to make his defence' (Acts 25:16).[17]

---

[13]For evidence see H. Conzelmann, *Die Apostelgeschichte* (Tübingen, 1963) 131; E.T., *The Acts of the Apostles* (Philadelphia, 1987) 195.

[14]E.A. Judge, *New Docs*. I. 77-8 who cited Goppelt, *TDNT* 8, 248 states that τύπος must mean the 'text of the letter' basing this on its use in 3 Macc. 3:12-29 and *P. Coll. Youtie* 66 *ll*. 28, 32 which also uses the term.

[15]See *P. Oxy*. 237 (A.D. 186) which is an extremely long petition by a woman quoting official correspondence, official proceedings and decrees between the prefect of Egypt and the *strategos*, and *P. Oxy*. 1204 (A.D. 299) where the petitioner cites the official proceedings in his possession of a court case involving himself (*ll*. 10-22) and an instruction for the issuing of minutes by an official notary (*l*. 26).

[16]ἀσθαλής, cf. Lk. 1:4.

[17]This statement from Acts is used as an example by N. Lewis and M. Reinhold, *Roman Civilization Sourcebook II: The Empire* (New York, 1955) 550 of a crucial principle of Roman law undergirding legal procedure.

II. Forensic Speeches and Official Petitions

1. Advice on composition

Do the handbooks on rhetoric advise on the composition of a forensic speech? Quintilian, for example, explains how skilful the orator had to be in preparing his speech because of the expectations of the judge.

> But to avoid all display of art in itself requires consummate art: this admirable canon has been insisted on by all writers. . .the judges themselves demand the most finished and elaborate speeches, thinking themselves insulted, unless the orator shows signs of having exercised the utmost diligence in the preparation of his speech, and desire not merely to be instructed but to be charmed.[18]

It was therefore not an inconsiderable challenge for the forensic orator to show 'unobtrusiveness' (ἀνεπίφατος) as the Greeks called it according to Quintilian, in 'making no vain display' in the presentation of his case. He instructs forensic orators 'to speak with care but without elaborate design. . .that no unusual word, nor overbold metaphor, no phrase derived from the lumber–rooms of antiquity or from poetic license should be detected in the *exordium*'.[19] Nowhere was this more important than in its introduction. Antonius (late 2nd century to 1st century B.C.) indicates the difficulty in structuring the *exordium*. 'It was my practice to think last of what is to be spoken first, what *exordium* should I employ. For when I have been inclined to plan it first, nothing has occurred but what is bald, trifling, shapeless, or ordinary'.[20] Quintilian sees the difficulty in composing the *exordium* of a forensic speech. In this he agrees with Antonius, although he himself is keen to see the *exordium* finally written down in the right order.[21]

> I cannot however approve the view of those who think that the *exordium* should actually be written last. For though we must collect all our material and determine the proper place for each portion of

---

[18]Quintilian, 5.1.57.
[19]Quintilian, 4.1.58-60.
[20]Cicero, *De oratore* 2.77.315.
[21]D.L. Clark, *Rhetoric in Greco-Roman Education* (New York: Columbia University Press, 1957) 115 draws attention to the fact that Quintilian's concern is with faulty presentations of forensic cases in the schools as these instructions are directed mainly to students.

it, before we begin to speak or write, we must commence with what actually comes first. . .We must therefore review the subject matter in the order laid down, but write our speech in the order in which we shall deliver it.[22]

Nowhere was this seen more clearly than in the skill required for the composition of the *captatio benevolentiae*, which aims to further the subsequent arguments. Nowhere is this better demonstrated than in a petition where a teacher struggles with it by writing two drafts.[23]

2. 'N' Documents

There are also extant 'N' documents which were actual briefs prepared for a case.[24] They would be prepared after due research by a νομικός who was a legal assistant to a rhetor.[25] All the 'N' documents contain a wide left–hand margin. Some have a summary of the facts of the case preceded by the name of the clients written in it for the benefit of the rhetor presenting his client's case.[26] In some cases they comprise not only the *narratio* but also the *confirmatio* and *peroratio* of a forensic speech but not the *captatio benevolentiae* in the *exordium*. Its absence suggests that this was composed by the rhetor

---

[22]3.9.8-9.

[23]See *P. Coll. Youtie* 66 where the teacher produces a second version of it.

[24]For the 'N' documents see *P. Thead* 16 (c. 332); *P. Princ.* 119 (c. 325) re-edited by A.E. Hanson, *op. cit.*, 15-27; *P. Col. 174* 'Memorandum and Notes for an Advocate' (c. 325-350); *P. Lips* 4 (late 4th century); *P. Panop.* 31 (329); and *P. Vindob. Gr.* inv. no. 39, 757 edited by P.J. Sijpesteijn and R.A. Worp, 'A sixth "Narratio" Document', *ASP Bulletin* 15 (1978) 115-23. *P. Thead* 16 has a blank left-hand margin nine cm. wide. The 'N' documents contain a summary of the facts of the case in the left margin.

[25]On the meaning of the term, νομικός, see Epictetus 2.13.6-7; cf. also *Encyclopedic Dictionary of Roman Law*, TAPS 43.2 (1953).

[26]For a history of the discussion about the meaning of 'N' see H.C. Youtie, 'Πράγματα μετέωρα: Unfinished Business', *Scriptiunclae posteriores* (Bonn, 1981) I, 1-15 where he examines the views that 'N' = νομικός and *narratio* and seeks to argue the extremely unlikely suggestion that it refers to 'Victory' (Νίκη). The view that 'N' stands for *narratio* is also unlikely because some briefs clearly contain more than that with the *peroratio*, e.g. *P. Col.* 174. In *P. Thead.* 16 the opening sentence states 'You are speaking on behalf. . .' These are clearly instructions to another who is presenting the case, cf. *P. Princ.* 119, 'If he offers the plea. . .we shall say. . .' After these instructions the brief is presented by the rhetor as if his clients were actually speaking. Neither 'Victory' nor *narratio* fits the evidence but νομικός does.

himself.[27] A comparison between the length of official proceedings and actual speeches in 'N' documents further indicates that the former were summaries.

3. Petitions as summaries of speeches

Petitions which aimed at instituting legal proceedings are often the work of rhetors acting on behalf of clients.[28] Those discussed below follow the normal divisions of a court room speech recommended in the handbooks and have an *exordium*, a *narratio*, *confirmatio* and *peroratio*.[29] They can therefore be treated as summaries of the intended speech to be delivered in court. In fact they compare favourably in length with the official proceedings.

   P. Fouad 26 (A.D. 157-9) is a petition which follows the literary conventions for it comprises an *exordium* in *ll.* 30-5, a *narratio* which begins with τὸ δὲ πρᾶγμα τίθημι (*ll.* 35-43), the *confirmatio* which is introduced with καίτοι, 'and indeed' (*ll.* 43-5) and the *peroratio* which commences with ὅθεν, 'for which reason' (*ll.* 49-56). The presentation of his cause also reflects the same succinctness of the *narratio* section of actual court presentations made in the Christian era by other rhetors. The *narratio* is put forward with a degree of contrived

---

[27]E.g. *P. Ryl.* 114 where the rhetor is also the author of the petition which initiates the case with the petition *P. Thead.* 16. See n. 91.

[28]In defence of the use of Egyptian sources for discussing Paul's case which was conducted in Caesarea, given the alleged peculiarity of Egypt, see N. Lewis, 'Greco-Roman Egypt: Fact or Fiction?', *Proceedings of the 12th International Congress of Papyrologists* (Toronto, 1970) 3-14 esp. 5-6, 'that the more our studies bring to the fore the Roman elements in the organisation of Roman Egypt (including the law), the less unique Egypt appears and the more it represents other eastern provinces of the Roman Empire', *ibid.*, 14, *contra* J.J. O'Rourke, 'Roman Law and the Early Church', in S. Benko and J.J. O'Rourke (eds.), *Early Church History: The Roman Empire as the Setting of Primitive Christianity* (London: Oliphants, 1972) 165, 'in Egypt the legal situation was especially unlike that which existed elsewhere'. Cf. R. Taubenschlag, *The Law of Greco-Roman Egypt in the Light of Papyri 332 BC - AD 640* (Warsaw, 1955) where the conclusion of Lewis can certainly be demonstrated in the area of the legal procedures involving litigation.

[29]J.L. White, *The Form and Structure of the Official Petition: A Study in Greek Epistolography* (SBL Dissertation Series 5; Missoula, 1972) does not address the issue of the ancient rhetorical forms here or later in his 'Epistolary Formulas and Clichés in Greek Papyrus Letters', *SBL Seminar Papers* 2 (1978) 289-319 although he concedes possible 'rhetorical influences', 310.

sophistication, carefully worded on behalf of one 'in manifold ways oppressed and wronged'. This aimed to incite the prefect into action against the defendant's contempt for the judicial processes and also to evoke pathos for his own cause. Aspects of the *peroratio* reinforce the *captatio benevolentiae* of the *exordium* (*l*. 49).[30] The subsequent petitions to be examined use the same device of skilful repetition of sentiments from the *captatio benevolentiae* at the beginning of the petition in the *peroratio*. The *exordium* itself concludes with the petition—καὶ αὐτὸς πολλωταπῶς βιαζόμενος καὶ ἀδικούμενος ἔσπευσα ἐπὶ σὲ καταφυγὼν τῶν διακαίων τυχεῖν (*ll*. 32-5), a point which was commended in forensic debate.[31] It reflects the sentiments in the *captatio benevolentiae* as the petitioner hastens to appeal for justice. The original petition was framed within the conventions of a forensic speech and is a 'pre-trial' document, prepared by a rhetor.[32]

P. Oxy. 2131 (A.D. 207) is a certified copy of a petition to a prefect, in which a petitioner complains of 'unjust and lawless deeds of daring' against him (*ll*. 6, 17). The petition contains the *exordium ll*. 7-8, the *narratio ll*. 8b-13a, the *confirmatio ll*. 13b-16a, and the *peroratio ll*. 16b-18 introduced by ἀξιῶ. An analysis of the petition under these prescribed divisions of forensic speech substantiates the claim that this is the work of a skilled rhetor.[33] The *peroratio* catches up, with an economy of words, the statements in the *exordium*.[34] It does so with perhaps more finesse than *P. Fouad* 26.

---

[30]In addition to 'the saviour of all', *l*. 25 and 'ever anticipated all needs', *ll*. 49-50, there is the appeal for the prefect to act so the petitioner may be 'able to obtain his rights through your benevolence' (δυνηθῶ διὰ τῆς σῆς εὐεργεσίας τυχεῖν) *l*. 5. which is a repetition of the thought 'your innate benevolence' in *ll*. 30-1.

[31]See D.L. Clark, *op. cit.*, 115 and the rhetorical handbook sources cited on this issue.

[32]Pharion did not draft this petition for he claims no status which was the mark of an educated person. He was 'forced to borrow "small" sums of money' for which he was charged twice the current interest, which is another mark of his lack of status. In contrast, his opponent had undertaken duties as a magistrate. To have qualified for that office he would have had to have been certified as 'well-to-do', cf. *BGU* 18 (A.D. 169) *ll*. 12-3.

[33]The petitioner says of himself that he 'is entirely without means', *l*. 13. When cognisance is taken of the petition one would not expect Totoes to be its author, for it is presented in a cogent fashion with an economy of words, and reflects the protocol of a legal case prepared by a forensic rhetor.

[34]ἀξιῶ ἐὰν σοῦ τῇ εὐμενέστατῃ τύχῃ δόξῃ διακοῦσαί μου πρὸς αὐτόν. . .ὅπως τυχὼν τῶν δικαίων where δικαία is a synonym for ἐδικία (*ll*. 16-17). ἡ τύχη δόξῃ is again used. Cf. *P. Fouad.* 26 *ll*. 50-1, except here εὐμενεστατη, 'your most gracious

P. Ryl. 114 (c. A.D. 280) commences with the customary *exordium* (*ll.* 1-6), the *narratio* is introduced clearly with τὸ δὲ πρᾶγμα οὕτως ἔχει (*ll.* 6-7), the *confirmatio* with ἐπεὶ δέ (*l.* 18), followed by the *refutatio* with ὥστε in *l.* 27 and the *peroratio* with ὅπως in *l.* 29.

An examination of these three sample petitions has provided confirmation that they are the work of professional forensic rhetors and give clear evidence of having been skilfully constructed and highly apposite to the needs of the particular petitioner. The case of each of the petitioners was presented with an *exordium, narratio, confirmatio* and *peroratio*.[35] They also followed the recommendations of the text books, *viz* that which comes last in the *exordium* should be that which most readily links itself with the *narratio* and is clearly seen to do so. That *dictum* of Quintilian is clearly seen in the petitions that '. . .it is important [as the means of winning the favour of the judge] that the points which seem most likely to serve our purpose should be selected for introduction into the *exordium*' (4.1.23).

These official petitions are invaluable for literary comparison with Acts because none of the official proceedings contains an *exordium* with the traditional *captatio benevolentiae* which is found in the speeches of Tertullus and Paul. That part of the speech was not recorded in the official court proceedings.[36] Along with the official proceedings they provide a setting for the forensic speeches of Acts.

---

eminence', is chosen. Totoes also adds 'for it appertains to your power to punish' (*l.* 17).

[35]The accusative and not the genitive absolute in *P. Ryl.* 114 by no means overthrows the case because the use of the latter in the official proceedings has been well established. The *exordium* of Paul also begins the former construction.

[36]None of the official proceedings cited by Coles or published subsequently contains an *exordium*. It is reasonable to assume from the considerable number of extant official proceedings that it was never recorded. Why this is so was never declared although its exclusion is explicable. From the Greek and Roman rhetorical handbooks an *exordium* of which the *captatio benevolentiae* had long been considered crucial in the presentation of such speeches. Cf. the customary praise of a city in the entry speeches of orators on their first visit to a city discussed in my 'The Entries and Ethics of Orators and Paul (1 Thessalonians 2)', *Tyn. B.* 44 (1993) 55-74. Self-deprecatory periphrasis was used in opposition to laudatory titles for one's superiors, e.g. 'My mediocrity', *P. Col.* 175 (339) *l.* 67 and a measure of self-effacement would have demanded the exclusion of the *captatio benevolentiae* being recorded in official proceedings lest it be thought that it had interfered with the so-called 'impartiality' of Roman law.

III. Forensic Speeches in Acts[37]

1. Tertullus (Acts 24:1-8)

An analysis of the speech of the professional orator, Tertullus, recorded in Acts 24 gives evidence of a standard length *exordium* while the *narratio* to be found in vv. 2b-3 and 4–5 and the *confirmatio* reflected in v. 6ff. are summaries.

a. The *exordium*. The similarities between the *exordia* of the petitions discussed above and the *exordium* of Tertullus are quite striking and deserve detailed examination and comparison.

The *captatio benevolentiae* of *P. Fouad* 26 reads 'Since your innate benevolence, My Lord Prefect, has ever anticipated all needs, (τῆς ἐνφύτου σου εὐεργείας, ἡγεμὼν κύριε, εἰς πάντα ἐφθακυίης) being myself in manifold ways oppressed and wronged, I hasten to appeal to you in order to obtain justice' (*ll.* 31-5).[38] His *captatio benevolentiae* is not dissimilar in grammatical construction, form, language and intent to that of other petitioners or Tertullus in his *exordium* (Acts 24:2). The original petition of *P. Fouad* 26 begins with the customary genitive absolute, which in trial documents is used as an introductory verb form to begin the recording of proceedings.[39] There is also the use of laudatory titles as in the speech of Tertullus (24:2) for Pharion addressed the prefect as ὁ πάντων σωτήρ in the *peroratio* (*ll.* 49-50), having already used the title 'the saviour of Egypt' in his introductory petition (*l.* 25).[40] Finally, and most importantly, are the

---

[37]Acts 22:1-2 is excluded from the discussion although included by W.R. Long, 'The *Paulusbild*', 97-102. That of Festus in Acts 25:14-21 is not strictly a forensic speech.

[38]The petition which is an original one and not a copy was registered with a number. It was addressed to the prefect and contains a copy of a petition which had already been presented to the prefect. He now urges that his case be heard by the prefect and not a lesser official to whom it has been referred because he knows that he would not obtain justice if his case went before a jury, 'I shall be unable to oppose him before a jury of this kind i.e. local, for he, the defendant is very influential' (*ll.* 14-16).

[39]R.A. Coles, *op. cit.*, 40. See H.W. Tajra, *The Trial of St. Paul* (WUNT 2.35; Tübingen: J.C.B. Mohr [Paul Siebeck], 1989) 119-20, who, while noting an example of the use of the genitive absolute in commencing official proceedings, is unaware that this was a normal literary practice.

[40]Cf. Germanicus Caesar, son of Augustus, who in an edict deprecates the use of 'acclamations' addressed to himself, stressing its appropriateness only to the gods who include his father, to whom alone the title 'saviour and benefactor of

statements concerning the competence of the governor to hear the case for, like the prefect who possessed 'innate benevolence',[41] and 'has ever anticipated all needs', Felix possesses the same attribute expressed by the synonymous πρόνοια (24:2). The petitioner appeals to the prefect's providential role with the use of the verb φθάνειντο, implying that he is a true benefactor and ruler who, in his judicial role, anticipates the needs of the citizens through the promulgation of laws as a means of sustaining justice and peace.

The *captatio benevolentiae* of the *exordium* in *P. Oxy.* 2131 reads, 'Since your ingrained justice, my Lord Prefect, is extended to all men' (τῆς ἐμφύτος σου ἡγεμὼν δέσποτα δικαιοδοσίας διηκούσης εἰς πάντας διηκούσης ἀνθρώπους) I myself having suffered injustices fall back on you, expecting to receive a legal remedy' (*l.* 7). In contrast to *P. Fouad* 26 the attribute referred to is δικαιοδοσία, *viz* the administration of judicial processes. The prefect is said to have such ability that he hears through to the end all who present their case to him.[42] What is being stated is that the prefect gives a fair hearing to all men who appear before him, that he discriminates against none, and that he gives prompt legal decisions.[43] The request of the plaintiff draws attention not only to the injustices he suffered, but also to his expectations of receiving justice at the hands of this legally competent prefect. The *exordium* is skilfully contrived with the use of δικαιοδοσία which is 'innate' in the prefect. This results in all receiving a hearing, διακούειν, with expectations of receiving ἐκδικία in the face of the ἀδικία suffered by the petitioner. It begins with the genitive absolute as in the previous petition and Acts 24:2, and its conclusion is clearly marked with the commencement of the *narratio*, ἔχει δὲ οὕτως (*l.* 8) (cf. Acts 24:4).[44] It also deals with 'ingrained justice' just as Tertullus is commended executing his 'providential' role in jurisprudence 24:2.

---

the whole human race' should be used, *S. P.* II, no. 211 (*ll.* 38-40). For honorific benefaction titles see e.g. 'benefactor' *P. Flor.* 61 (A.D. 86-88) *l.* 14 used by a rhetor, also *P. Oxy.* 486 (A.D. 131) *l.* 27, and *P. Graux* 2 (A.D. 58-9) *ll.* 15-16 'the saviour and benefactor of all'.

[41]ἔμφυτος means 'inborn', 'natural'.

[42]διακούειν means 'to hear out' or 'to hear to the end'.

[43]This was certainly not the case with all, for there is abundant evidence of the adjourning of proceedings, the referral for advice to legal officials, and general delays in obtaining a decision.

[44]Cf. *P. Fouad.* 26 (*ll.* 30-5) and *P. Ryl.* 114 (*ll.* 6-7).

The *captatio benevolentiae* in the *exordium* in *P. Ryl.* 114 reads 'Conscious of your love of equity, my lord prefect, and your solicitude of all, especially the women [wives] and widows' (τὸ μετριοφιλές σου αἰσθομένη δέσποτά μου ἡγεμών καὶ περὶ πάντας κηδεμονίαν μάλιστα περὶ γυμαῖκας καὶ χήρας) (*ll.* 3-5). The use of τὸ μετριοφιλές αἰσθομαι is apposite for it implies the prefect's record of judicial decision-making was marked by love of fairness which has been perceived.[45] It can be compared with what Tertullus says of Felix's 'law reform' in Acts 24:2, for κηδεμονία is synonymous with πρόνοια, conveying the idea of 'providence' or 'care' for all including 'especially women and widows'. In the *peroratio* the petitioner again reflects the same sentiment which he expressed in the *captatio benevolentiae* ὅπως τά ἴδια ἐκ τῆς σῆς τοῦ κυρίου καὶ πάντων εὐεργέτου φιλανθρώπου (*ll.* 29-30). The remainder of the *exordium* is a simple appeal, 'I make my approach to you begging you to come to my aid'. The whole *exordium* aims to evoke for this widow what the textbooks recommended *viz pathos*.

Like the *captatio benevolentiae* in the petitions, the *exordium* of Tertullus plays an important role in presenting the charges brought against Paul. It deals with law and order and legal reform, and will be seen to be not unconnected with the charges outlined in the *narratio*. Tertullus commences with the traditional convention of 'seeking the good will' of Felix, declaring that the governor has exercised his *imperium* by stating πολλῆς εἰρήνης τυγχάνοντες διὰ σοῦ.

Firstly, it should be noted that all three papyri use τυγχανεῖν, 'to gain one's end'. In *P. Oxy.* 2131 *ll.* 8, 17-8 it is used in the *exordium* to beg for justice and in the *peroratio* to obtain rights so that the requisite liturgy will be fulfilled. The request in *P. Ryl.* 114 *l.* 6 is likewise in the *exordium*. It begs the prefect to come to the aid of the widow and her children. In *P. Fouad* 26 *ll.* 55-6 it is used in the *peroratio* asking that the petitioner might obtain his rights through the benevolence of the prefect.[46] Unlike the three forensic papyri which use the verb in the

---

[45]αἴσθομαι = αἰσθάνομαι 'perceive', 'apprehend'; μετριοφιλές = 'love of equity'.

[46]It is usual at this point for commentators to draw attention to Felix's poor record of keeping the peace since he became procurator of Judaea and accuse Tertullus of 'excessive courtesy' or 'flattery'. F.F. Bruce, *The Book of Acts* (London, 1962) 464, and E. Haenchen, *op. cit.*, 657, '. . .Roman governors in general prided themselves on having maintained peace and public order in their provinces'. While the overall conduct of Felix invited well-earned criticism, the rhetor is alluding to his maintenance of law and order. This is the issue in the case against Paul, for Tertullus will portray him in the *narratio* as one of the disturbers of

active form, it is expressed in the passive by Tertullus to indicate to Felix that the petitioners have already enjoyed much peace through his administration.

Secondly, Felix had very recently restored law and order by quelling the rebellion of an Egyptian prophet as mentioned by Claudius Lysias in Acts and recorded elsewhere.[47] Tertullus commends Felix in the *exordium* for exercising his *imperium* to maintain public order i.e. 'much peace'.[48] His comment is then a statement of fact demonstrated by a recent event and judiciously chosen because it relates to the case in hand. Paul in the *narratio* is declared to be the disturber of the public order in the Diaspora and in Jerusalem (v. 5). The implication is clear that Felix needs to punish this defendant in order, as governor, to continue his task of maintaining the peace.

There is also a link between the *captatio benevolentiae* and the *narratio* in Acts 24. In *P. Fouad* 26 it is stated that because 'innate benevolence. . .has ever anticipated all needs being myself in manifold ways oppressed and wronged, I hasten to appeal. . .to obtain justice' (*ll.* 31-5). This has a bearing on the issues raised in the *narratio* which indicates interference in judicial processes and exorbitant interest rates (*ll.* 35-49); *P. Oxy.* 2131 records the reputation of the prefect for the impartial administration of judicial procedures to all (*ll.* 7-8) which is linked to the unjust imposition of a liturgy; *P. Ryl.* 114 describes the judge's love of equity and providential care for all (*ll.* 3-4) which has a bearing on the illegal sequestration of the widow's sheep (*ll.* 7-20). In Acts 24 it needs to be noted firstly, that

---

peace in world-wide Jewry, epitomised by his recent actions in the temple in Jerusalem. For discussion see my 'The importance of the *captatio*. . .', *op. cit.*, 515-8 and the view that it re-enforces the serious charges against Paul, 521.

[47]Acts 21:38, and further details on Felix's actions, see Josephus, *Bellum Judaicum* 2.261-3 and a summary in I.H. Marshall, *op. cit.*, 351.

[48]A.N. Sherwin-White, *Roman Society and Roman Law in the New Testament* (Oxford: Clarendon Press, 1963) 2ff. See 2 Macc. 4:6 for the 'seeking of peace' (τυχεῖν εἰρήνης) in public affairs through the king. S. Lösch, 'Die Dankesrede de Tertullus: Apg. 24.1-4', *Theologische Quartalschrift* 112 (1931) 307 uses literary and non-literary sources to demonstrate the importance of the use of πολλὴ εἰρήνη citing Plutarch, *Alcibiades* 14.2, Josephus, *Antiquities* 7.20, BGU 226, *P. Giss* 61. Cf. H.W. Tajra, *op. cit.*, 120 who feels that the phrase has a hollow ring and suggests 'Tertullus made the statement merely to flatter Felix as Roman governors in general prided themselves on maintaining peace and public order in their provinces'. The granting of the *imperium* to the governor was for the maintenance of the *Pax Romana* and was executed through the enforcing of law and order.

reference is made to 'the reforms introduced on behalf of the nation', and secondly, that this was done by means of Felix exercising his 'providence' (v. 2c). διόρθωμα is used of periodic revision of legal ordinances.[49] Certainly it came within the responsibilities of Felix to effect such changes to the law. It is not clear what these revisions were. They may have had to do with matters relating to the procedures of the Sanhedrin or temple administration.[50] There is a reference to the judicial competence which Felix brings to this case, and that comment was not without justification.[51]

Felix is told that it has also been through 'your providence' (διὰ τῆς σῆς προνοίας) that this revision has come to pass. The theme of 'providence' was used in two of the three forensic papyri,[52] and the introductory formula of the edicts of the Egyptian prefects shows the traditional nexus between πρόνοια and the revision of law.[53] It is only natural that any *captatio benevolentiae* in which the revision of law and its administration was mentioned should feature the idea of providence as the summary *narratio* will show.

Thus the two virtues of peace and providence through legal reform in the *captatio benevolentiae* are said by Tertullus to be the source of true thanksgiving by the Jewish authorities for the procuratorship of Felix (v. 3). They are at the heart of the case brought against Paul.

The *exordium* concludes with the promise of brevity in v. 4. In proceeding quickly to the *narratio* in v. 5 Tertullus follows a wise convention on which Quintilian, 4.1.34. was later to write, 'We shall also find it a useful device to create the impression that we shall not

---

[49]S. Lösch, *op. cit.*, 307-10 suggests that this term, or the variant reading, points to the 're-establishment' of law and order. See R. Taubenschlag, *op. cit.*, 15, n. 36a for its use to indicate the revision of law.

[50]For the possibilities see A. Deissmann, *Light from the Ancient East* (rept.; Grand Rapids, 1978) 79–80 and E. Schürer, *The History of the Jewish People in the Age of Jesus Christ* (ed. 2; Edinburgh, 1979) II, 220–22.

[51]Prior to his appointment to Judaea, Quadratus appointed Felix as one of the judges to assist the emperor Claudius in deciding a legal matter. It was this which impressed the Jewish delegation headed by Jonathan and resulted in their request for his appointment to his present position, Tacitus, *Annals* 12.54.

[52]In *P. Fouad.* 26 the prefect is spoken of as having 'ever anticipated all our needs', *l.* 32, and there is the 'care of all' by the prefect in *P. Ryl.* 114, *l.* 5.

[53]A.A. Trites, 'The Importance of Legal Scenes and Language in the Book of Acts', *Nov T* 16 (1974) 277-84 makes no reference to this important legal term.

keep them long and intend to stick closely to the point'.[54] The 'N' documents reveal how discursive some orators could be.

b. The *narratio, confirmatio* and peroratio. According to the rhetorical handbooks, agitation or sedition, στάσις, was the right charge to bring against an opponent in criminal proceedings.[55] Happily for the prosecution it was 'precisely the one to bring against a Jew during the Principate of Claudius and the early years of Nero'.[56] The essence of the charge is spelled out in the *narratio.* It was that Paul was 'an agitator among all the Jews throughout the world' (v. 5a) and a ring-leader of the Nazarenes αἵρεσις who were apparently known to Felix. The linking of the two together implied that membership of it constituted a known breach of the law (v. 5b).

The *confirmatio* would appear to be reflected in v. 6ff., being stated by means of three relative pronouns presenting the proof—ὄς καί, ὄν καί, παρ' οὖ. As with the *narratio,* the writer of Acts is summarising. The proof of the charge against Paul is supported by the fact that he profaned the temple. What he had been doing 'throughout the world' as a ringleader of the Nazarenes, he has done in Jerusalem. If proved, it invited serious punishment, *viz* the summary execution which the Jews had attempted, cf. Acts 23:27 and 24:7, as well as imperial wrath with which Claudius had threatened the Alexandrian Jews. The *peroratio* calls on Felix to examine Paul in order that he may learn the truth about the charge brought against him (v. 8). Tertullus' case, which was backed up by his clients' own testimony, was a formidable one to answer (v. 9).

The question arises as to why the *exordium,* which is comparable in length to those found in the forensic petitions examined above, is presented in such detail and the remainder of the case in what has rightly been seen as a highly summarised form.[57] The significant role of the *captatio benevolentiae* in forensic speeches examined in the non-literary sources helps us to see how Felix and any first-century reader would have been alerted to the seriousness

---

[54]He also noted that where it was necessary to give a lengthy introduction because of the complexity of the case the lawyer should apologise, 4.1.79. Cf. H.W. Tajra, *op. cit.,* 120 who suggests 'detain/weary you no further' was standard vocabulary used in the *exordium.*

[55]*Ad Herennium* 2.3.3-3.4, Cicero, *De inventione* 2.5.16-8.28 cited by J. Neyrey, *op. cit.,* 211 and n. 35.

[56]A.N. Sherwin-White, *op. cit.,* 51.

[57]I.H. Marshall, *op. cit.,* 374.

of the charges brought against Paul. The inclusion of the *captatio benevolentiae* in some detail was, therefore, highly apposite to Luke's purpose. It is misleading to conclude that Tertullus engaged in 'irrelevant flattery' which made for 'an ineffectual *exordium*'.[58] Its prominence cannot be explained, as Hemer does, in terms of 'Luke's artistry' with his 'richly entertaining irony'.[59] Dibelius was incorrect when he concluded that 'the orator's courtly phrases [i.e. the Latin and Greek official language parallels acknowledged from Lösch's important essay] in vv. 2 and 3. . .are of no importance as far as the subject matter is concerned'.[60] The use of form criticism has enabled us to understand the function of the *exordium* in non-literary forensic cases and in particular, the reason for including it in the edited version of the speech in Acts.

Tertullus has been declared an orator of fairly insignificant ability when contrasted with that of ancient authors.[61] He is also judged to have produced a clever piece of oratory.[62] and his work described as 'a very weak, ill-constructed speech',[63] while Haenchen sees it as a Lukan invention in which the abilities of Tertullus are played down because the author is 'too clever to show the adroitness of the lawyer in the handling of the actual case'.[64] Within the speech itself, Bruce suggested that there was a 'striking contrast between the very lame and impotent conclusion and the rhetorical flourish of the *exordium*'.[65] It has also been suggested that 'The speech is almost a humorous caricature, like the account of the behaviour of the mob in the temple at Ephesus'.[66] By placing this summary of the speech in a comparable literary setting and evaluating it with the use of form critical tools, Tertullus is presented as an able professional rhetor whose *captatio benevolentiae* was carefully linked to his accusations in

---

[58]W.R. Long, *The Trial of Paul*, 230.

[59]C.J. Hemer, *The Book of Acts in the Setting of Hellenistic History* (Tübingen, 1989) 207.

[60]M. Dibelius, *Studies in the Acts of the Apostles* (London, 1956) 171

[61]A. Sizoo, 'De Rede van Tertullus', *Gereformeerd Theologische Tijdschrift* 49 (1949) 67 although he cites no ancient authors nor secondary literature in support of his conclusion.

[62]S. Lösch, *op. cit.*, 317 rightly refers to this as a masterpiece of rhetorical composition.

[63]I.H. Marshall, *op. cit.*, 374.

[64]E. Haenchen, *op. cit.*, 657 who concludes that Luke placed this ineffectual *exordium* in the mouth of Tertullus to work by contrast to Paul's advantage.

[65]F.F. Bruce, *The Book of Acts* (1962) 467.

[66]R.P.C. Hanson, *op. cit.*, 227.

the hope of mounting a formidable case against Paul.[67] He portrayed
Paul as an agitator in Jerusalem and an insurrectionist in world-wide
Jewry.[68] It was a presentation calculated to excite the intense interest
of Felix and the emperor against a Jew. 'Luke allows us to detect that
Tertullus knows his trade and is a dangerous opponent.'[69]

2. Paul (Acts 24:10b-21)[70]

It has been suggested by Long that the defence begins with a short
exordium in v. 10b, is followed by three proofs in vv. 11–20, and
concludes in v. 21 with the *peroratio*. The first proof consists of
arguments against the charge (v. 5a) that he is a pestilent fellow and a
revolutionary (vv. 11-13). The second answers the religious
accusations in v. 5b in vv. 14-16 concerning the sect. In the third proof
in vv. 17-20 Paul shows that he came as a benefactor to the city of
Jerusalem and to the temple, and thereby refutes the serious charge
that he profaned the temple (v. 6). The *peroratio* is to be found in vv.
20-21. While Long's division is attractive it does not readily accord
with the text of Acts. He argues,

> At first glance v. 11 seems to function as a *narratio*, but upon closer
> inspection, one sees that it goes quite well with vv. 12-13 to form a
> first proof. There is no reason for a *narratio* to be present in every

---

[67]On this speech of Tertullus, G.A. Kennedy, *New Testament Interpretation through
Rhetorical Criticism* (Chapel Hill, 1984) 135 comments 'In a conventional classical
proem he flatters the governor (24:2-4), alleges that Paul is a Nazarene agitator
who has profaned the temple, and asks the governor to interrogate him'. His
discussion in the light of the preceding analysis in this section is somewhat
incomplete and he does not attempt to analyse the form of this forensic speech,
although that form has been discussed elsewhere by G.A. Kennedy, *Classical
Rhetoric and Its Christian and Secular Tradition from Ancient to Modern Times*
(London and New York: Croom Helm, 1980) 93ff.
[68]Paul was being charged not with endangering public security, but with treason,
W. Kunkel, *An Introduction to Roman and Legal Constitutional History* (ed. 2;
Oxford: Clarendon Press, 1973) 66.
[69]E. Haenchen, *op. cit.*, 657.
[70]See F. Veltman, *op. cit.*, 254 where he argues that Paul's defence 'has all the
earmarks of a typical apology'. By 'apology' he means the usual rhetorical
divisions in a forensic speech, and the conventions which he summarises on 252.

example of forensic oratory, especially when the case is so brief as to permit an immediate response to the charges.[71]

Quintilian is cited in support of his conclusion (4.2.4-8). However, Quintilian goes on to specify that this happens only with the *narratio* 'where there is no necessity for explanation or where the facts are admitted and the whole question turns on a point of law' (4.2.5). This is certainly not the case for Paul as his defence shows.[72]

Most authorities, according to Quintilian, divide the defence speech into five parts, *prooemium* or *exordium*, *narratio*, *probatio*, *refutatio* and *peroratio*,[73] and Paul's defence as it appears in this very summary form seems to have followed this division. The *prooemium* or *exordium* is found in v. 10b, and the brief *narratio* in v. 11. The *probatio* or *confirmatio* was clearly stated, the essence of which was that his accusers lacked proof (vv. 12-13). The *refutatio* in vv. 14-18 shows that the only difference between Paul and his accusers hinged on the means by which they and he worshipped the God of their fathers (vv. 14-15); that Paul acted according to these common convictions before God and men, refuting any suggestion of being a 'pestilent fellow' (v. 16); his coming to Jerusalem was solely for the purpose of bringing alms and offerings to his nations (v. 17), and the allegation of his creating a στάσις in the temple could not stand because he was there without crowd or tumult (v. 18). In the *peroratio* he drew attention to the fact that those who brought this charge were absent, contrary to the rule of law (vv. 18-19), and that there were no possible charges which members of the Sanhedrin could have brought against him, except in relation to the one sentence he had uttered concerning the resurrection (vv. 20-21).[74]

---

[71]W.R. Long, *The Trial of Paul*, 231.

[72]*Ibid.*, 231 n. 250.

[73]Quintilian, 3.9.1. *P. Ryl.* 114 although a petition seeking to initiate proceedings contains a *refutatio* with ὥστε in *l.* 27-8 along with the customary *exordium*, *narratio*, *confirmatio* and the *peroratio*. The inclusion of the *refutatio* can be accounted for because the petitioner answers a charge, either anticipated or actually made by an official who is accused of stealing from her, *viz.* that her deceased husband owed money to the Treasury which would justify the sequestration of the sheep immediately after his death.

[74]G.A. Kennedy, *New Testament Interpretation*, 136 suggests that v. 11 is a *propositio* or a *probatio* i.e. *confirmatio*. Quintilian, 4.4.1 argues that at the beginning of every *confirmatio* is a *propositio*, which was a moot point in his day as he himself notes. The present writer believes that v. 11 should be treated as *narratio*, see p. 324.

a. The *Exordium*. The *captatio benevolentiae*, like that of Tertullus, made reference to Felix's expertise to hear this case. Paul specified that this expertise was with respect to the *Jewish nation*, and for this reason he is confident about making his defence before him. The issue for Paul is a very Jewish matter indeed, *viz* the resurrection, and although a Roman, Felix possesses the competence to hear the case by reason of his experience in Jewish affairs. Paul reflected the confidence that a rhetor was encouraged to display.[75] Luke confirms Felix's knowledge of Christianity (24:22).

b. The *narratio* and *probatio* or *confirmatio*. The *narratio* simply declares that the purpose for which Paul came was to worship (v. 11).[76] Paul's proof was that he was not involved in disputing with anyone nor will the charge in v. 5a of στάσις hold, for he was not involved in ἐπιστάσις (v. 12). That this was the case was emphasised by the fact that he had not engaged in disputing with anyone nor had he stirred up the crowd either in the temple, the synagogue or in the city (v. 12). It has been suggested that here we see the use of 'lawyer-like speech'.[77] As it had only been approximately twelve days since he arrived in Jerusalem, this matter could be verified by witnesses.[78] Paul promptly added that the evidence which had been given in court did not substantiate this charge of στάσις (v. 13).[79] There was no

---

[75]Quintilian, 5.21.51 citing Cicero in support of his contention that 'our orator must therefore adopt a confident manner'. W.R. Long, *The Trial of Paul*, 231-32 notes, Paul, 'following the advice of Quintilian, links his case with the ability and interest of the judge. The presence of εὐθύμως ("cheerfully", "confidently") expresses his confidence in the rectitude of the judgment to be rendered. The presence of ἀπολογοῦμαι to summarise the important point of the speech, appearing as it does in the last word of the *exordium*, follows the advice of Aristotle'. Quintilian did not write his work until the closing years of the first century.

[76]Quintilian, 4.2.4 mentions that only a brief summary of the facts, *narratio*, may be needed which is the case in v. 11.

[77]F.F. Bruce, *The Acts of the Apostles* (London, 1952) 424, commenting on the use of οὔτε three times by Paul.

[78]As W.R. Long, *The Trial of Paul*, 233 notes 'the fact that no one, even among his accusers, was able to prove or even bring a shred of evidence against Paul's conduct (except for an attempted desecration of the temple, a charge that Paul will answer later) gives the reader the impression that the charges are groundless'.

[79]5.3 'neither can they prove to you what they now bring up against me'. παραστῆσαι can mean 'to substantiate the argument with the proof' or 'produce in court', *BGU* 759, *ll.* 22.

πίστις—proof. This restriction of evidence to Jerusalem would, in Paul's subsequent argument, focus attention on the location in which his accusers alone were competent to bring charges and Felix could assess them.[80]

c. The *refutatio*. In this portion of the speech Paul specifically answers the charges brought against him. If Tertullus had hoped to gain any mileage from the fact that Paul was a ring-leader of the Nazarenes (v. 5b), he failed to do so. In his *refutatio* Paul readily admitted his association with them. He worshipped the God of 'our fathers' according to 'the Way' which was called a party, αἵρεσις, but believed both the scriptures and the resurrection of the just and the unjust, *even as his accusers did* (vv. 14-15).[81] Showing fidelity to the religion of his forefathers could hardly constitute a criminal offence.

He can thus refute any charge of profaning the temple (v. 6). Paul argued that he had taken great pains to have a clear conscience both before God and man as he had always done (v. 16).[82] His purpose in coming to Jerusalem was a commendable one and endorsed by Rome who provided an armed escort for Jewish collections (v. 17).[83] In the temple he was οὐ μεθ' ὄχλου οὐδὲ μετὰ θορύβου (v. 18).[84] No crowd accompanied him, and at the most there may have been four men with him whose expenses he paid to undergo the rite of purification. His presence in the temple was entirely legitimate (Acts 21:23).

d. The *peroratio*. Paul begins his conclusion by drawing attention to an important issue upon which much in the case legally stands or falls, *viz* the absence of the accusers, the Asian Jews. With two *anacolutha* the weakness of Tertullus' case concerning Paul's alleged world-wide subversive activities is exposed. He correctly argued 'but

---

[80]It is 'a good classical Greek periodic sentence', for it was 'short and respectful', G.A. Kennedy, *New Testament Interpretation*, 136.

[81]'Even as they themselves receive' is taken to refer to both participial construction πιστεύων and ἔχων.

[82]W.R. Long, *The Trial of Paul*, 233 'It is the appearance of the word "conscience" that makes his confession a real proof, for the word means that he has a conscious record of his past acts, his awareness of having done good or bad'. See also E. Haenchen, *op. cit.*, 655 and *BDF* # 219, 'If I were not true to my ancestral religion, my conscience would witness against me'.

[83]On the Roman protection of the delivery of such funds see K.F. Nickle, *The Collection: A Study in Paul's Strategy* (SBT 1/48; London, 1966) 83-4.

[84]As in v. 12 Paul's phrases are carefully balanced.

there were certain Jews—' and 'if they had anything against me—' (vv. 18b-19a).[85] The absence of his accusers 'may mean the withdrawal of the charge with which they were particularly associated' as Sherwin-White points out.[86] Paul had put forward a sound technical objection.[87] That aspect of the case could not stand.[88]

His prosecutors had to produce evidence and on this note Paul concludes his *peroratio*. His defence refuted all the charges they have laid to date. He invites them at that moment to bring a sustainable charge of a criminal act which he had committed in Jerusalem, throwing down the gauntlet to the Jews present, including the High Priest, '. . .let these men themselves say what wrong-doing they found, when I stood before the Council' (v. 20). The only location where they could operate as witnesses according to the law was Jerusalem. Paul actually proffers the only charge his opponents could bring because he informs the governor that there was only one sentence he uttered. 'With respect to the resurrection I am on trial before you this day' (v. 21b).

The implication was that their competence to act as witnesses or accusers was restricted to that examination which Claudius Lysias had permitted (v. 21a, cf. v. 9 and 23:28). Paul's argument was right, for he not only had pressed that the accusation of the Asian Jews should be dropped, but also had drawn the parameters for the Jews present, including the high priest, to act in a legal way before Felix and bring a criminal charge which could be sustained in a court of law.

Sherwin-White observed that Tertullus' charges were in effect political but the supporting evidence was theological.[89] The above examination of this forensic speech has established the skilful way in which Paul reduced those charges to a theological one. He showed

---

[85]The previous part of the sentence is left unfinished, v. 18 and 'certain Jews from Asia. . .bring whatever accusation they had against me', v. 19 is the other anacoluthon.

[86]He cites evidence of the reigning emperor's great concern about what was known as *destitutio*, for which a legal remedy was sought by his successor, A.N. Sherwin-White, *op. cit.*, 52, and adds 'The Roman law was very strong against accusers who abandoned their charges'.

[87]ἔδει ἐπὶ σοῦ παρεῖναι καὶ κατηγορεῖν εἴ τι ἔχοιεν πρὸς ἐμέ, v. 19. R. Taubenschlag, *op. cit.*, 499ff. and A.N. Sherwin-White, *op. cit.*, 53.

[88]W.R. Long, *The Trial of Paul*, 234, suggests that '. . .rather than his [Paul] causing a disturbance it was the Jews of Asia, who placed the accusation, who were responsible for the disturbance, v. 19'.

[89]A.N. Sherwin-White, *op. cit.*, 51.

that he was on trial before the Sanhedrin and Felix for affirming 'the resurrection'. The governor would have been aware that this was an issue upon which the members of that august body were deeply divided. The relationship between the *captatio benevolentiae* and the *refutatio* is clear, for the case rests on a theological issue that has to do with 'this [Jewish] nation'.

The use of *proemium* or *exordium, narratio, probatio, refutatio* and *peroratio* in this form-critical analysis of Paul's defence helps us to understand more precisely the way in which he refuted the serious charges brought against him. The author of Acts intended his readers to see Paul handling his defence with great dexterity, and refuting these charges. He had done this by prescribing the limits of evidence based on Roman law, proscribing the charges of absent accusers, using forensic terminology, and, not least of all, presenting a well argued defence, even if preserved in a summary form. Paul conducted his own defence in an able manner against a professional forensic orator.[90]

3. Paul (Acts 26:1-23)

Although we have no extant examples of the official proceedings recording both the first and subsequent hearings as in the case of Paul, there is evidence of a petition and a resumed hearing of the same case. Given that the official petitions outlined the case presented in the official proceedings, this combined evidence warrants examination before we proceed to investigate subsequent hearings.

The petition has already been examined, *viz P. Ryl.* 114, with the customary *exordium* (*ll.* 1-6), the *narratio* introduced clearly with τὸ δὲ πρᾶγμα οὕτως ἔχει (*ll.* 6-7), the *confirmatio* with ἐπεὶ δέ (*l.* 18), followed by the *refutatio* with ὥστε in *l.* 27 and the *peroratio* with ὅπως in *l.* 29. The official proceedings of the second hearing are recorded in *P. Thead.* 15 and the latter follows the outline of the *narratio* (*ll.* 3-13), *confirmatio* (*ll.* 13-15a), and the *peroratio* (*ll.* 15b-16). The same orator

---

[90]See A.M. Vitta, 'L'eloquenza di Paolo colta al vivo da S. Luca negli Atti', *Biblica* 22 (1941) 159-97 although he makes no specific reference to Paul's speech in 24:10–21 and only a passing comment on 24:5-6 on p. 192. For an examination of Paul's ability in and use of oratory see my *Philo and Paul among the Sophists: A Hellenistic Jewish and a Christian Response* (forthcoming SNTSM; Cambridge: CUP).

presented both.[91] One of the interesting features is a slight change of emphasis in the way the same case was presented at the resumption of the hearing. While use is made of the pathos of the widow in both documents, in the petition she lays emphasis on the power of her opponent, an official, who is accused not only of taking sheep which her deceased husband has grazed, with permission, on the defendant's land, but also taking corn dues from her without issuing a receipt. Her children feature in it only in a minor way being linked with her losses at the hand of the defendant. The petition is annotated by the prefect instructing that the case is to be investigated 'with the utmost equity' (*l*. 35).[92] At the hearing which was resumed some two months later, the children who are now present at the proceedings are the ones on whose behalf the rhetor pleads that the sheep be returned to them both at the end of the *narratio* and the *peroratio*. Much is made at the resumption of the failure of the defendant to appear. His representative pleads absence on Treasury business but relates a promise to reply to the charges against him. It is the same case, but the rhetor, sensing the non-attendance of the defendant, strengthens his client's position and also seeks an injunction against him should he 'flee from justice' (*l*. 19). Comparisons can be drawn between the different emphases at the two hearings of this case. These can also be detected in the presentations of Paul's defences before Felix and Festus in the presence of Agrippa. This will be noted at the end of the analysis of the structure of Acts 26:2-23.

J. Neyrey confines his analysis of this speech to the *exordium*, *narratio* and *confirmatio*. He proposes that the *exordium* is to be found in vv. 2-5 with an appeal to the judge and a reference to the 'ethos of the speaker'; the *narratio* covers the 'main question' (vv. 6-7), the 'justifying motive' (vv. 16-20), and the 'point for the judge's decision' (vv. 6-8); the *confirmatio* consists of the 'witness' (v. 16), the proof (vv.

---

[91]Both papyri use ὅπως to introduce the *peroratio*, and in addition both documents refer to the case as πρᾶγμα. More noticeable is the immediate repetition of the same word or a synonym used for effect in both papyri e.g. ἐμοῦ τῆς χήρας, 'the property of. . .myself, the widow' *P. Ryl.* 114 *l*. 22; ἐμὲ τὴν χήραν *l*. 26; οἱ παῖδες οἱ ἀφήλικες *P. Thead.* 15 *l*. 3, τὴν βίαν κωλύσης τὴν δὲ Βίαν πολλάκις *l*. 6, and αὐτῷ τῷ Συρίωνι *l*. 11. Of the other petitions examined, *viz. P. Oxy.* 2131 and *P. Fouad.* 26, such peculiarities of style are not present. This would tend to re-enforce common authorship of *P. Ryl.* 114 and *P. Thead.* 15, *viz.* Isadorus the rhetor mentioned in the latter.

[92]The *captatio benevolentiae* which emphasised his love of equity had apparently done its work.

12-18), the sign (v. 13), the corroborating witnesses (v. 5, 12-13) and the probabilities (vv. 14-18). While his essay provides some important insights into details of the speech in Acts 26, his comparison with Acts 22:1-21 predetermines much of his analysis of the form, even though Luke does not present the latter strictly as a forensic speech. When he draws comparisons with the speech before Felix in Acts 24:10b-23a he sees no *exordium* in Paul's speech, simply the 'main question' (vv. 10-20 with vv. 14-15 and 21) the 'point for the judge's decision'.[93] In the main he has restricted his analysis of Acts 26 to Cicero's *De Inventione* from which nine topics are enunciated for the development of the *confirmatio* of a speech, although Neyrey invokes them for the *narratio* and not the section he designates the *confirmatio*.[94] His intention in the essay to discuss in part the 'form' fails because of this. He also appears not to have appreciated sufficiently the distinction between the conventional form of a speech and its contents.[95] An alternative division of Luke's summary of Paul's speech is offered based on the form criticism of the petitions which reflect the discussion of rhetorical handbooks. This does not necessitate the dislocation of the text.

a. The *exordium*. This is to be found in vv. 2-3 with the *captatio benevolentiae* of Agrippa expressing pleasure that he can make his 'defence' before one who is an expert in 'all the customs and questions' of the Jews, cf. a similar succinct statement in 24:10b. Paul follows the convention that the role of the *captatio benevolentiae* is to stress the competence of the judge to hear the case and to connect it with the *narratio* where Jewish customs and questions form the essence of the case. The *exordium* ends with a plea for a patient hearing on the part of the king.

b. The *narratio*. In vv. 4-18 Paul explains his upbringing from his youth—as a Jew in Jerusalem and his life as a Pharisee. He states that he stands before the judgement seat of this Roman court because of

---

[93]*Op. cit.*, 210-11. He acknowledges the presence of the *refutatio* and *peroratio* in the forensic handbooks in such speeches, he does not defend this restriction without explaining why.

[94]Cicero, *De Inventione* 1.24.34.

[95]F. Veltman, *op. cit.*, 255 argues that the speech has a short 'introduction' with a brief *captatio benevolentiae*, and move into 'the body of the speech' which he suggests may end at v. 21 and the 'conclusion' follows with what he regards as a repetition of his role as a witness.

'the hope of the promise made by God to the fathers'. This promise was made to the twelve tribes who are earnestly serving God in the expectation of attaining the hope. It is concerning this hope that Paul stands at the judgement seat.[96] Paul relates it to the resurrection which he once thought to be absolutely impossible—a reference to the resurrection of Jesus as subsequent discussion reveals as he unfolds his original opposition to it and the circumstances surrounding his ultimate conversion and commissioning.

c. The *confirmatio*: This commences with ὅθεν in v. 19 as it also does in *P. Oxy.* 2131 of *P. Fouad* 26.[97] Here Paul attests that he was not disobedient to his commission for he began in Damascus, moved to Jerusalem and Judaea and finally to the Gentiles calling for genuine repentance.

d. The *refutatio*. In v. 21 there is the refutation of the charge originally brought against Paul by the Jews under Felix that they sought to arrest him because of the alleged criminal conduct in the temple (Acts 24:6). He states that he had only sought to fulfil his commission from God, and in doing so the Jews sought to apprehend and assassinate him.

e. The *peroratio*: This is signalled with the statement ἐπικουρίας οὖν τυχὼν.[98] Any forensic speech contains a plea for help, for which the use of the verb τυγχανεῖν is standard. Paul acknowledges God's help in contrast to that sought of the official by the petitioners whether the prefects of Egypt or a governor of Judaea.[99] His *peroratio* affirms that he continues to this very moment testifying only to what Moses and the prophets taught concerning the coming Messiah, *viz* his death and resurrection, the latter having resulted in the proclamation of light for the Jews and Gentiles (vv. 22-23).

The differences between the speeches in Acts 24 and 26 can be readily accounted for. In Acts 24 Paul is fighting for his life and his

---

[96] I follow in part the outline of J. Neyrey, *op. cit.*, 211-12 from Cicero but not his summary on p. 221 or his dislocation of the speech.

[97] l. 13. The papyrus addresses the governor at the point in the same way Paul addresses the king.

[98] On the connection of ἐπικουρία with τυγχανεῖν in literary sources see F.F. Bruce, *The Acts of the Apostles* (ed. 3; Grand Rapids and Leicester, 1990) 504.

[99] See its use in the *exordium* and in the *peroratio* in *P. Oxy.* 2131 *ll.* 8, 17-8 and in the *peroratio* in *P. Fouad.* 26 *ll.* 55-6. In Acts 24:2 an acknowledgement of help having been given accounts for this passive voice in the *exordium*.

defence aimed at reducing the charge of a capital offence to simply a theological issue, *viz* the matter of the resurrection which he affirmed before the Sanhedrin (23:6, cf. 24:2). The theme of the latter speech is still the promised resurrection (Acts 26:6-8, 22-23), although the context in which it is delivered is different. Festus, in the presence of Agrippa, the chief captains and principal men of the city of Caesarea Philippi, has declared Paul's innocence of any capital offence (25:24-5), and here he is seeking assistance in formulating the requisite memorandum to be forwarded to Rome for the appeal. The speech in Acts 26 is primarily recorded by Luke because it is the fulfilment of God's promise that Paul would bear witness before kings (Acts 9:15). This last substantial speech is addressed to king Agrippa (26:2ff.)[100] The differences in emphasis in Acts 24 and 26 are as explicable as they are in the case of the widow and her children in *P. Ryl.* 114 and *P. Thead.* 15. While intervening circumstances moulded the subsequent presentation, the essence of the cases remained unchanged.

IV. Forensic Speeches in Literary Compositions

The genre and structure of the forensic speeches in Acts have been subjected to a form critical analysis and have been found to be comparable to official proceedings. Unlike the latter, those in Acts belong in a literary setting, being part of a much wider work. Do we find forensic speeches in comparable settings in ancient literature in this period?

There is the example of Servius Servilius' defence at his trial for a capital offence which is part of the recorded events of a particular year in *The Roman Antiquities* of an ancient historian of the early empire, Dionysius of Halicarnassus (9.28-32).[101] It is a very skilfully constructed and presented *oratio recta*. There is a lengthy *exordium* in which he had to secure the good will of his hearers, for his accusers had mounted a powerful but unjust case against him (29.1-3a). In the *narratio* the facts of his consulship, and the *confirmatio*, are succinctly

---

[100]F.J. Foakes-Jackson, *The Acts of the Apostles* (London, 1931) 224, 'It was intended to be the most important, as it is the last of all the speeches of Acts and resulted in his acquittal by Agrippa II, the chief personage of the Jewish nation'. Cf. P. Schubert, 'The Final Cycle of Speeches in the Book of Acts', *JBL* 87 (1968) 10ff.

[101]This is one of a number of examples provided by Feltman, *op. cit.*, 244ff.

laid out 29.3b-4a and 4b, as they are in the Tertullus' speech. The *refutatio* which begins with οὖν 29.5 tackles three issues crucial to the defence, *viz* whether a general is responsible for the death of his soldiers even if he finally wins the battle, whether it is right to charge him with inexperience and imprudence and not treachery and cowardice, ἐπειδὴ δέ (31.1), and whether it is right to express their hatred of him for a matter external to the case, *viz* the allocation of land which relates to the duties of the senate, περὶ δέ (32.1). The *peroratio* is briefly made (32.7). If found guilty, it would mean that in the face of any defeat in battle a general could be put to death. It was seen that such a verdict 'would do great harm to the commonwealth if they punished their generals for being unfortunate', i.e. the gods do not guarantee victory. Two points emerge from it. The speech for the prosecution is produced *oratio obliqua* and that of the defendant *oratio recta*. His accusers' could well reflect the official proceedings which were recorded thus in the early first century, and because of its length, his speech may well have been the defence reflecting the essence or the actual speech. This was also a very important trial and was realised to be so because of the undesirable and far-reaching precedent it would establish in the army (28.3).[102] Its inclusion in the events of that year is explicable.[103]

Speeches such as these play an important role in literary works in the same way the forensic speeches did for Luke. Acts 24–26 was crucial to his theme of Paul's innocence, and the reason for his appeal to Caesar. They also show how Paul fulfilled his commission to bear witness to the resurrection of Jesus before kings i.e. the emperor's vice-gerents and Agrippa. They are part of a larger segment in Acts beginning in chapter 21 and concluding with Paul in Rome. He has been delivered from the Jews in Jerusalem and Caesarea, from the shipwreck in the storm and from the serpent bite in Malta. It was a sign of providential protection when the Maltese pagan assumptions that 'Justice did not permit him to live' (Acts 28:4) were proved wrong. Paul arrives in Rome to bear witness there to the lordship of Jesus Christ without let or hindrance (Acts 28:31).

---

[102]This division of the speech disagrees with the brief analysis of Feltman who divides speeches into the *exordium*, the *narratio* and the *peroratio*, *op. cit.*, 245, 252.
[103]Livy (57 B.C. - A.D. 17) records a large number of trials including a number of defence speeches. For a brief discussion see Feltman, *op. cit.*, 246-7.

V. Conclusions

A form–critical analysis of legal petitions written by rhetors who
sought to initiate judicial proceedings on behalf of clients and official
proceedings when compared with major speeches in Acts 24–26
clarifies our understanding of the rhetorical divisions in the latter.
Reading them in the light of the advice given in the handbooks on
forensic speeches, especially the works of Cicero and Quintilian,
shows that those in Acts 24–26 follows the conventions
recommended in the handbooks.[104] This analysis assists in recovering
something of the import of these speeches.[105]

Luke's redactional hand is also extremely important for
understanding the legal issues in these passages. His knowledge of
the importance of the *exordia* in forensic speeches was a key factor
influencing his careful redaction of relevant parts of his sources. He
was able to craft them in the helpful way he did for his readers
precisely because of his knowledge of the important function which
the *captatio benevolentiae* exercised within the *exordium* in highlighting
the respective cases to be outlined in the *narratio* etc.[106] In recent
studies emphasis has rightly been placed on Luke's literary abilities
as the author of Acts. In acknowledging them,[107] it does not
necessarily follow that in the forensic speeches the hand of Luke
must automatically be seen as the composer. That he undertook the
task of editing forensic sources would make his literary efforts no less
significant.

The conclusion in the last paragraph presupposes the possible
use of official sources. In any narrative in the first century A.D.
purporting to be summary forensic speeches before a Roman court,

---

[104]They followed the customary outline of forensic speeches, E. Preuschen, *Die Apostelgeschichte Handbuch zum Neuen Testament* (Tübingen, 1912) 4/1, 137.

[105]*Contra* the unlikely suggestion of C.J. Hemer, *op. cit.*, 207 on the inclusion of Acts 23:26-30 and 24:2-8 that 'their prominence in this brief narrative might be questioned. . .It might be quite unconventional, but completely plausible, to see the genesis of this passage in the hilarious and memorable manner of Paul's telling the story'.

[106]As was observed by Quintilian, 4.1.23 'it is important that the points which seem most likely to serve our purpose should be selected for introduction into the *exordium*'.

[107]See P. Satterthwaite chapter 12 in this volume; R.C. Tannehill, *The Narrative Unity of Luke–Acts: A Literary Interpretation* (Minneapolis: Fortress Press, 1990) and L.T. Johnson, *The Acts of the Apostles* (Sacra Pagina; Collegeville, Minnesota: The Liturgical Press, 1992).

the use of legal sources would not be dismissed out of hand by the contemporary reader. The possibility then cannot be ruled out that in Acts 23:26-26:23 legal documents and official proceedings might be behind the narratives. That sources were used by Luke has long been maintained by some and denied by others.[108] For example, Cadbury suggested, 'It is doubtful whether the writer had access to any official records such as are known to us from the Egyptian papyri'[109] and E. Haenchen states categorically that 'The speeches of Tertullus and Paul do not offer any original text'.[110] However, not all have drawn this conclusion. One hundred years ago Blass argued on the basis of the words used in Acts 26:2-23, that it was the work of Paul and not Luke.[111] In the 1930's two scholars submitted the speech of Tertullus to detailed examination. Lösch argued that it was the work of that orator and not Luke,[112] and Sizoo felt that notes had been made in court of the speech of the Jews' advocate.[113] More recently Bruce states without elaboration, 'It is conceivable. . .Luke had at his disposal some document which played a part at Paul's trial'.[114] Maddox believed that 'Luke is composing freely' in chapter 24 although in chapters 24 and 26 he is controlled by a tradition going back to Paul himself.[115] Lüdemann has argued that 'Luke had an account of Paul's trial in Caesarea before Festus.'[116] Comments such

---

[108]For a summary of views both for and against see Haenchen, *op. cit.*, 656.

[109]E.g. H.J. Cadbury, 'Roman Law and the Trial of Paul', in F.J. Foakes Jackson and Kirsopp Lake (eds.), *The Beginnings of Christianity* (London: Macmillan, 1933) V, 298.

[110]E. Haenchen, *op. cit.*, 657 bases his conclusions on 'detailed exposition' and believes that 'references to sources in this section are either entirely questionable or simply do not remove the real difficulties because of what they assumed. On the other hand all our troubles are removed, if. . .we resolutely interpret the speeches as Lucan compositions'. It is hard to see how Haenchen's discussion in vv. 6-8, 17 and 22 which he cites as the source of the problem raises 'the real difficulties' especially the matter of the collection for Jerusalem in v. 17. C.J. Hemer, *op. cit.*, 189 accuses Haenchen's comments on this point of being 'disingenuously hypercritical'.

[111]F. Blass, *op. cit.*, 264ff.

[112]S. Lösch, *op. cit.*, 316-19 remains the most thorough examination to date of the linguistic background of this speech.

[113]A. Sizoo, *op. cit.*, 72 believed that Luke has captured the most important elements of the original submission of Tertullus' case. He did not suggest that this was done by an official shorthand writer but by some friend of Paul's.

[114]F.F. Bruce, 'Paul's Apologetic and the Purpose of Acts', *BJRL* 69 (1987) 392.

[115]R. Maddox, *The Purpose of Luke–Acts* (Edinburgh, 1982) 35.

as 'Most scholars of today, under the influence of Haenchen, consider the investigation of Luke's sources to be a dead–end enterprise' give the impression that such an investigation is fruitless.[117] Accessibility to official material would suggest that it is not necessarily so. It is also sometimes overlooked that the text of Acts itself may not be without its own clue that use was made of forensic sources. By including a copy of the official letter (Acts 23:26-30), did Luke intend to signal to his first readers, among other things, that he would now be drawing on primary sources in reporting the judicial proceedings before governors (Acts 24-26)?[118]

When the forensic speeches in other literary works of first-century writers such as Dionysius of Halicarnassus are compared with those in Acts 24ff., the latter adds an important case study on litigation for the ancient historian. Luke's narrative is a cameo of some of the complexities of criminal litigation in the first century as it proceeds through three hearings before two Roman governors in the East.[119] Acts records the initial hearing of a case, its suspension for a very lengthy period, and its resumption under another governor when the prisoner appealed to the emperor because of the danger of being assassinated or found guilty because the course of justice could be corrupted if transferred to another assize centre. In addition, there is the declaration of the prisoner's innocence by the trial judge and a subject king when the hearing was resumed in the presence of leading civic officials as the requisite legal memorandum was being drawn up to accompany the prisoner to Rome. The forensic speeches in Acts are then useful to the ancient historians in the same way that the second century novel of Apuleius, *Metamorphoses* or *The Golden Ass* has proved to be a valuable source for ancient historians who are

---

[116]G. Lüdemann, *Early Christianity according to the Traditions of Acts: A Commentary* (ET; London, 1989) 22, 250, 254, although he cites Festus as the presiding judge in Acts 24 and not Felix.

[117]W.R. Long, '*Paulusbild*', 90 n. 15.

[118]If the letter of Claudius Lysias was not what it purported to be, then it was a forgery and therefore illegal in the light of Roman forensic conventions. Roman authorities severely punished those who tampered with documents or forged them. See for example the decree of Quintus Veranius of A.D. 43-4 where the death penalty was threatened for the alteration of official documents in R.K. Sherk, *The Roman Empire: Augustus to Hadrian* (Translated Documents of Greece and Rome; Cambridge: CUP, 1988) Vol. 6, no. 48.

[119]For a discussion of similar difficulties in civil litigation see evidence cited in my 'Civil Litigation in Secular Corinth and the Church: The Forensic Background to 1 Corinthians 6:1-8', *NTS* 37 (1991) 559-72.

interested in understanding forensic activities in Corinth and the East in general.[120]

Finally this investigation has shown that the discussion of speeches in Acts by scholars needs to be nuanced. The importance of evaluating the public speeches in Acts within the setting of a particular genre has been argued in the previous chapter. This chapter has sought to demonstrate that conclusions about the forensic speeches in Acts 24ff. can be drawn more confidently when analysed alongside comparable material with the use of the form critical tools which are provided by the rhetorical handbooks.

---

[120]F. Millar, 'The World of the Golden Ass', *JRS* 71 (1981) 63-75.

CHAPTER 12

ACTS AGAINST THE BACKGROUND OF CLASSICAL RHETORIC

Philip E. Satterthwaite

Summary

The chapter argues that the literary techniques of Acts have been heavily influenced by classical rhetorical conventions. Luke, like most educated men of his day, writes as one trained in these conventions. The chapter draws many comparisons between Acts and classical literature, especially classical rhetorical treatises. It begins with (1) a brief survey of classical rhetoric and compares Acts and Classical Rhetoric under the headings of (2) 'Invention/Arrangement' and (3) 'Style'. It is concluded that such a study helps us to understand Luke's purposes in writing Acts, and to form a clearer picture about how Acts might have been received by an audience aware of rhetorical conventions.

A number of recent studies have examined books of the New Testament in the light of classical rhetoric.[1] This chapter will offer a

---

[1]See, for example, the survey in B.L. Mack, *Rhetoric and the New Testament* (Minneapolis: Fortress, 1990). G.A. Kennedy, *New Testament Interpretation through*

similar study of Acts; not concentrating on one specific rhetorical genre and attempting to understand Acts in the light of that genre (an aspect covered by some of the other chapters in this volume) but regarding rhetoric in a more general manner, as a pervasive phenomenon in the Graeco-Roman world, which appears to have influenced Luke's presentation of his material in Acts in a number of ways. The general approach adopted, therefore, is similar to that of Morgenthaler's recent study of Luke-Acts in the light of Quintilian's *Institutio Oratoria;*[2] though the detailed conclusions reached are often rather different.

I. Classical Rhetoric: A Brief Survey

Rhetoric has to do with persuasion, specifically the persuasive powers of words, spoken or written. That is clearly how classical writers on the subject thought of it.[3] It is helpful, following Kennedy, to distinguish between 'primary' rhetoric, the art of persuasive public speaking as part of social and civil life, and 'secondary' rhetoric, the use of the techniques of 'primary' rhetoric in literature whose main focus is not a public speech; for example, historical accounts,

---

Rhetorical Criticism (Chapel Hill and London: University of North Carolina Press, 1984) offers a brief treatment of a number of NT books. More detailed studies include the essays collected in D.F. Watson (ed.), *Persuasive Artistry: Studies in New Testament Rhetoric in Honor of George A. Kennedy* (JSNTS 50; Sheffield: JSOT Press, 1991); F.W. Hughes, *Early Christian Rhetoric and 2 Thessalonians* (JSNTS 30; Sheffield: JSOT Press, 1989); D.A. Campbell, *The Rhetoric of Righteousness in Romans 3.21-26* (JSNTS 65; Sheffield: JSOT Press, 1992).

[2]R. Morgenthaler, *Lukas und Quintilian. Rhetorik als Erzählkunst* (Zurich: Gotthelf, 1993). See also the second section of W.S. Kurz, 'Hellenistic Rhetoric in the Christological Proof of Luke-Acts' (*CBQ* 42 [1980] 171-95) entitled 'The Likelihood of Luke's Familiarity with Greek Rhetoric' (pp. 184-95).

[3]The definition of rhetoric as πειθοῦς δημιουργός is attributed to one of the earliest known teachers of rhetoric, the Sicilian Gorgias, in Plato, *Gorgias,* 453a. Aristotle, *The Art of Rhetoric,* 1.2.2, has the definition: Ἔστω δὴ ἡ ῥητορικὴ δύναμις περὶ ἕκαστον τοῦ θεωρῆσαι τὸ ἐνδεχόμενον πιθανόν. Quintilian's definition of rhetoric as *bene dicendi scientiam* (*Institutio Oratoria* 2.14.5, 2.15.38) only differs superficially from these definitions: as his discussion of the nature of rhetoric in 2.15-21 shows, he is well aware of the importance of persuasion in any attempt to define rhetoric. G.A. Kennedy's books provide helpful surveys of Greek and Roman Rhetoric: *The Art of Persuasion in Greece* (Princeton: Princeton University Press, 1963); *The Art of Rhetoric in the Roman World* (Princeton: Princeton University Press, 1972); *Classical Rhetoric in its Christian and Secular Tradition from Ancient to Modern Times* (London: Croom Helm, 1980).

philosophical treatises, drama, and poetry.[4] Just like 'primary' rhetoric, 'secondary' rhetoric aims to persuade the reader or hearer, and will, ideally, display many of the same virtues (e.g., clarity, the ability to maintain the audience's interest); but the setting is different, and the aim is usually not to influence the intended audience towards a particular policy decision or verdict in law, but to commend a certain view of life or interpretation of past events. As the aims of both types of rhetoric may on occasions overlap, this distinction is not absolute.

Certainly rhetoric, both 'primary' and 'secondary', was an important feature of Graeco-Roman cultural, civic and political life, and we can trace its influence from the speeches uttered by the characters in Homer's *Iliad* and *Odyssey* (commonly dated to the 8th century B.C.) down to the 1st centuries B.C. and A.D. (which will be our main focus) and well beyond. The main indications of the importance of rhetoric for the Greeks and the Romans are to be found not only in the many political, legal, and panegyric speeches written by Greeks and Romans, and in the large amount of Graeco-Roman literature which displays 'secondary' rhetoric (including epic poetry, drama, lyric poetry, historiography, and philosophical dialogue) but also in the numerous theoretical treatments of rhetoric which have come down to us, among them Aristotle's *The Art of Rhetoric* (c. 330 B.C.), Cicero's *De Oratore* (55 B.C.), *Brutus* (c. 46 B.C.), and *Orator* (46 B.C.) and Quintilian's *Institutio Oratoria* (c. 95 A.D.). In what follows I will concentrate on the 1st century B.C. and the 1st century A.D. One should bear in mind, however, that the rhetorical practice and theory of these centuries has roots stretching far back into the past. Much in the rhetorical treatises of this period, for example, goes back to Aristotle. Later writers were conscious of standing in a long tradition of theoretical discussion.[5]

The theoretical treatises are mainly (though not exclusively) concerned with public speaking,[6] and contain detailed discussion of a

---

[4]*Classical Rhetoric in its Christian and Secular Tradition from Ancient to Modern Times*, 4-6.

[5]E.g., Cicero, *de Oratore* 3.16.59-18.68 and Quintilian's discussion of the definition of rhetoric in 2.15-21, which shows a wide familiarity with previous writers on the topic.

[6]More than once in the literature the wise statesman who is also an accomplished orator, able to sway national fortunes by his persuasive words, is put forward as an ideal: Cicero, *de Oratore* 2.9.35; Tacitus, *Dialogus* 5-10 (though seemingly ironically); see also Virgil, *Aeneid* 1.147-153.

wide range of matters relevant to public speaking: the various types of public speaking (forensic, deliberative, epideictic);[7] the aims of the speaker (to present a clear argument, to please his hearers, to move his hearers);[8] the five parts of oratory, or the five tasks of an orator as he prepares to speak in public, summed up under the words Invention, Arrangement, Style, Memory, and Delivery;[9] the training which is appropriate for an orator from boyhood onwards.[10]

The treatises also contain interesting surveys of past and present public speakers,[11] and also of the literature of previous generations.[12] Much of this discussion reflects an abiding interest in the question of style, and in the question of which writers are appropriate models for orators to imitate.[13] Reading these treatises leaves one with a clear impression of how central rhetoric was to literary endeavour in the Graeco-Roman world in the 1st centuries B.C. and A.D.[14]

This aspect also emerges when we consider Greek and Roman education.[15] The teaching of rhetoric, linked by tradition to the rise of democracy in Greek city-states in the 5th century,[16] spread widely over the Mediterranean world with the spread of Hellenistic

---

[7]See the section on Speech Structure below.

[8]Cicero, *Orator* 21.69; cf. Aristotle, *Rhetoric* 1.2.3.

[9]See the introductory comments on Invention/Arrangement below.

[10]Much of Cicero's *de Oratore* discusses the question of what one should study if one wishes to be an orator, and what practical training one should undergo; e.g., Crassus' statement (1.32.144-61.262). Quintilian devotes most of Books 1-2 of *Institutio Oratoria* to the topic. See also Tacitus, *Dialogus* 28-35.

[11]Cicero, *Brutus*; Tacitus, *Dialogus* 16-26.

[12]Quintilian's survey, *Institutio Oratoria* 12.1.1-131, deals with a large number of Greek and Roman writers in most of the major genres: epic, tragedy, history, and so on. See also the comments on previous writers in Aristotle, *Poetics*; Lucian, *On How to Write History* (c. 170 A.D.) and Longinus, *On the Sublime* (c. 100 A.D.?).

[13]Thus Cicero's *Brutus* was written as a contribution to a contemporary controversy as to whether a pure ('Atticist') or fuller ('Asianist') style was the better. Demetrius' *On Style* (? 50-100 A.D.) is a more technical discussion of many aspects of style.

[14]Also interesting in this regard are Suetonius' *de Grammaticis* and *de Rhetoribus* (c. 110 A.D.) which offer brief accounts of famous *grammatici* and *rhetores* from the middle of the 2nd century B.C. onwards.

[15]For general surveys of this field, see H.I. Marrou, *A History of Education in Antiquity* (ET; London: Sheed & Ward, 1956) and D.L. Clark, *Rhetoric in Greco-Roman Education* (New York and London: Columbia University Press, 1957).

[16]See Cicero, *Brutus* 12.45-46, who cites a work of Aristotle no longer extant as his authority; Marrou, *A History of Education*, 47-49.

civilisation at the end of the 4th century.[17] The Hellenistic style of education was in due course adopted at Rome,[18] to the extent that Roman education, particularly the higher levels of education, was basically an education in rhetoric.[19] Cicero's accounts of his own early training and that of his contemporary Hortensius are interesting primary evidence for the 1st century B.C.[20] However, the most extensive ancient theoretical statement on education (based on much practical experience of teaching) is that of Quintilian, *Institutio Oratoria* , Books 1-2, which deals with every stage of the upbringing and education of boys. Simply listing some of the topics he covers gives an idea of the importance of rhetoric at Rome: the need for care in choosing nurse and *paedagogus* for the infant (1.1.4-11); teaching the child to read and pronounce words (1.1.12-37); the need for care in choosing the first teacher (*praeceptor*) (1.2); teaching boys to read and write (1.3); the next stage of education, under a *grammaticus*, encompassing the beginnings of the study of literature, grammar (particularly morphology) (1.4), style, correct usage and pronunciation (1.5-6), correct spelling (1.7), reading out loud and elements of literary criticism (1.8), various forms of literary composition (1.9), as well as the ancillary study of other subjects such as music, geometry, and mathematics (1.10) and physical exercise (1.11); the need for care in the choice of a *rhetor*, the teacher who will oversee the final stage of education (2.1-2); matters to be dealt with by the *rhetor*, including longer written compositions (narratives, proofs and refutations, panegyrics and denunciations, arguments for and against various positions) (2.4), declamation (2.6) and memory work (2.7). Obviously, Quintilian's guidelines represent an ideal which was not always attained; yet they still give an idea of how rhetoric dominated education at Rome.[21]

---

[17]See Cicero, *Brutus* 13.51 for a brief statement. A more detailed account is to be found in Marrou, *A History of Education,* 95-226; see particularly his chapters on 'primary' education (pp. 142-159) 'secondary' education (pp. 160-175) and on the place of rhetoric in more advanced stages of education (pp. 194-205).

[18]Marrou, *A History of Education,* 242-264.

[19]See on this S.F. Bonner, *Education in Ancient Rome. From the Elder Cato to the Younger Pliny* (London: Methuen, 1977).

[20]See Cicero, *Brutus* 88.301-93.322; also his remarks on his own and Marcus Caelius' upbringing in *Pro Caelio* 1.1-4.9.

[21]See also the treatment of the various stages of stages of education, and what was taught at each stage, in Bonner, *Education in Ancient Rome,* 163-327.

What was true at Rome came to be increasingly true throughout the Roman Empire.[22] Palestine had been affected at an earlier stage by the spread of Hellenistic culture across the Eastern Mediterranean;[23] there were men of repute in Greek literature who came from Palestine from the 3rd century B.C. onwards.[24]

In view of the value that was placed on rhetoric in the Graeco-Roman world, it is not surprising that works of literature other than speeches written for public delivery were affected by rhetorical ideals and methods;[25] 'primary' rhetoric naturally generates 'secondary' rhetoric. Thus rhetorical treatises approach poetry or historiography in basically the same way they approach public speaking. We find, for instance, Antonius in Cicero's *de Oratore* advocating a view of rhetoric as an art of speaking which will equip one for any eventuality (he specifies panegyric, the composition of official dispatches, history-writing, and talking on a whole range of abstract topics).[26] Lucian (*On How to Write History*) makes stylistic comments in connection with history-writing similar to those made by Cicero about public speaking: the need for truthfulness, faithfulness to facts (24-32, 37-42, 47-51; cf. *de Oratore* 2.24.99-27.102); the desirability of avoiding a style weighed down with dialectic and syllogisms (17; cf. *de Oratore* 1.51.219-54.233; 2.38.157-161); the need to cultivate a natural style, which avoids extremes of style and over-use of 'purple passages' (43-46; cf. *de Oratore* 3.25-26).[27]

In a similar way, the rhetorical treatises recommend the reading of literature as a way of developing a speaking style, and on occasions include stylistic evaluations of epic, tragedy,

---

[22]See Marrou, *A History of Education*, 292-98, dealing mainly with Gaul, the Danubian provinces, and Africa.

[23]See the survey of Jewish attitudes to Hellenistic culture in this period in J. Goldstein, 'Jewish Acceptance and Rejection of Hellenism' in E.P. Sanders, A.I. Baumgarten, A. Mendelson (eds.), *Jewish and Christian Self-Definition, Vol. 2: Aspects of Judaism in the Graeco-Roman Period* (London: SCM, 1981) 64-87. Goldstein concludes that with some exceptions in Judaea itself, attitudes were largely positive.

[24]M. Hengel, *Judaism and Hellenism*, Vol. I (ET; London: SCM Press, 1974) and G. Ogg in E. Schürer, *The History of the Jewish People in the Age of Jesus Christ*, revised and edited by G. Vermes, F. Millar, and M. Black, Vol. II (Edinburgh: T. & T. Clark, 1979) 49-50.

[25]See, for example, the treatment of rhetorical elements in Augustan literature in Kennedy, *The Art of Rhetoric in the Roman World*, 378-427.

[26]*De Oratore* 2.10.40-16.70.

[27]A.J. Woodman, *Rhetoric in Classical Historiography* (London and Sydney: Croom Helm, 1988) emphasises the strongly rhetorical nature of ancient historiography.

historiography, and so on. Two of the most extended such passages are in Quintilian, *Institutio Oratoria* 1.8.1-21 (dealing with material suitable for use in the elementary stages of education) and 10.1-130 (with reference to a more advanced stage). Quintilian's long survey in 10.1.1-130 moves freely between orators, writers of epic, tragedians, and historians, with no suggestion that drastically different categories must apply to each genre.[28]

In the light of these considerations, it seems legitimate to use the material in the treatises which relates to public speaking as a standard of comparison for 'secondary rhetoric'. It seems particularly appropriate to study Acts against the background of classical rhetoric, in view of the prefaces to Luke and Acts (Lk. 1:1-4; Acts 1:1-2) which, whatever the precise generic niche to which they lay claim,[29] seem show an awareness of recognisably classical rhetorical conventions.

In what follows many links will be drawn between the book of Acts and classical rhetorical treatises. However, there are two aspects in which these treatises are limited. Firstly, they must by nature generalise from (at most) a small number of examples, and do not cover all possible uses even of the literary techniques they do discuss. Secondly, there are some literary techniques which seem not to be suited to public speeches,[30] which one would not expect to occur in the rhetorical treatises. For these reasons, it will be appropriate on occasions to refer to Greek and Roman works which display 'secondary rhetoric', especially epic and historiography.

According to a standard presentation, oratory may be divided up into five parts, corresponding to five tasks of the orator as he prepares a speech.[31] These are: invention (*inventio*), the selection of facts and devising of arguments for use in the speech; arrangement (*dispositio*), the structuring of these facts and arguments into a coherent and persuasive structure; style (*elocutio*), the casting of the speech into a form aesthetically pleasing in all its details; memory

---

[28]See also Cicero's briefer survey at *Orator* 11.36-13.42, and his comments on the stylistic excellence of Herodotus and Thucydides (*de Oratore* 2.13.54-57).

[29]See L.C. Alexander, *The Preface to Luke's Gospel. Literary convention and social context in Luke 1.1-4 and Acts 1.1* (SNTS Monographs 78, Cambridge: Cambridge University Press, 1993); also Palmer's chapter in the present volume.

[30]See particularly the section on 'Implicit Commentary' below.

[31]See, for example, the summary statements in Cicero, *de Inventione* 1.7.9 and Quintilian, *Institutio Oratoria* 6.4.1; *Institutio Oratoria* 3.3.1-15 provides a longer discussion of this division of the topic.

(*memoria*), learning the speech by heart in preparation for delivery; delivery (*pronuntiatio*), to do with voice control, appropriate gestures, and so on. While memory and delivery are not relevant here, invention, arrangement and style do provide useful categories under which to treat the book of Acts. We shall first of all consider Acts from the point of view of invention and arrangement, treating these two aspects as closely related, and then from the point of view of style.

The coverage of Acts will be selective: some passages will be discussed at length, and others more briefly, with a reference to more detailed discussion elsewhere. Some passages will be cited more than once.

II. Invention/Arrangement

Rhetorical treatises have much to say both on choice of material and on the arrangement of that material: one must select one's arguments carefully, and one must be equally careful in presenting them effectively.[32] Most of what is said on this topic has speeches in view, but similar statements can be found in respect of other literary genres; for example, Lucian's description of the historian carefully seeking out witnesses, evaluating conflicting accounts, assembling facts, and then arranging them into a narrative which will present these facts in the clearest and most coherent way.[33]

In speaking of selection and arrangement, the writers of the treatises are by no means solely concerned with the content and logical structure of speeches: one of their chief emphases is how to construct a speech that will be persuasive. Choice of material is governed by the question of what will lend itself to an effective and convincing presentation.[34] Similarly, much of what is said about

---

[32]See also the section on Speech Structure below. The question of the types of arguments an orator may use is systematically treated by Books 1 and 2 of Aristotle's *Rhetoric*. Cicero, *de Oratore* 2.145-173, deals with various possible types of proof, and this is followed in Sections 291-350 of the same book with a discussion of arrangement. Quintilian devotes Book 5 of his *Institutio Oratoria* to discussing the materials an orator may use (legal precedents, evidence of various types, witnesses, various types of argument one may devise) and Book 7 to the question of how these materials are to be arranged.

[33]Lucian, *On How to Write History*, 47-51.

[34]Thus Cicero's discussion of choice of argument in *De Oratore* 2.34.145-40.173 leads into a discussion in the sections following of how to secure the audience's

arrangement deals with it as a means of enhancing the persuasive power of a speech:[35] typically, statements of the importance of arranging one's ideas well will be set in the context of an extensive treatment of what types of arguments will be most convincing in particular circumstances, when one should bring forward one's strongest arguments, how to handle arguments or facts potentially damaging to one's own case, and so on.[36]

An important aspect of both speeches and narratives is the question of proportions, which involves both choice and arrangement of material. The most immediately relevant passage for our purposes is Lucian, *On How to Write History* 56-57 (cf. chs. 27-8) in which Lucian states that a writer must take care not to waste words on inessential matters, but must pass over them quickly in order to concentrate on what is most important for his purposes. Cicero, Quintilian, and Longinus have somewhat similar comments about 'amplification' or 'embellishment':[37] at times it will be appropriate to dwell on a point, at times one will want to pass over several points quickly. However, 'amplification' as treated by these writers is not simply a matter of how long one spends on a point, but also of employing various forms of heightened diction, and developing additional lines of argument that will support one's main point.[38] Cicero notes that it is most effectively employed in trying to convince an audience or to win their support.[39] The question of proportions, in other words, is (again) one of persuasive strategy.

Finally, the speech or narrative should flow well. One aims to secure one's audience's interest at the start, and then lead them on,

---

favour and arouse their emotions in one's support (2.41.174-49.201). It is important, for instance, to avoid monotony in presenting proofs (177) and to present one's client in the best possible light (182-184).

[35]Cicero, *de Oratore* 1.31.142 notes that one is not merely concerned with the orderly presentation of arguments, but with marshalling them according to their relative weight.

[36]Thus, the statement of Cicero, *de Oratore* 2.76.307-309 is part of a much larger treatment of how to present an effective case. The Preface to the Book 7 of Quintilian's *Institutio Oratoria* briefly states the importance of arrangement, and the remainder of the book discusses at length various types of arguments that may be used under different circumstances.

[37]Cicero, *de Oratore* 3.27.104-5, 53.202-203; Quintilian, *Institutio Oratoria* 8.4; Longinus, *On the Sublime* 11-12.

[38]Thus Cicero's treatment of 'amplification' in *de Oratore* 3.53.202-203 is quoted in full by Quintilian in the course of a discussion of figures of thought and speech (*Institutio Oratoria* 9.1).

[39]*De Oratore* 3.27.104-5.

stage by stage. One should briefly define the central issue of the case or state one's topic, and then move naturally into the main body of what one has to say, going on from point to point with smooth transitions between each point.[40]

With this preamble, we turn to a consideration of more specific aspects of invention and arrangement in Acts, under the following heads: (1) choice of material; (2) large-scale arrangement; (3) narrative proportions; (4) small-scale arrangement; (5) speeches; (6) speech structure; (7) implicit commentary.

1. Choice of Material

A discussion of Luke's choice of material in Acts is linked with the question of Luke's purposes in writing the book (and its companion volume the Gospel of Luke): what was he choosing his material for? Different answers have been given to this question, many of which have something to be said for them, and which are not necessarily mutually exclusive.[41] Clearly Luke and Acts together are presented by the writer as an accurate and authoritative account of the life and ministry of Jesus and of the spread of the church which bore witness to him as risen Lord (see Lk. 1:1-4 and Acts 1:1-2); and this aim in itself explains the presence of much of the material which we find in Acts: there were some events which simply had to be included in order to create an intelligible and coherent narrative, key moments in the history of the church, and key figures who had to be included in the account. But, as Marshall notes, this approach will only take us so

---

[40]Cicero, *de Oratore* 2.79.320-81.331, a discussion of how one should organise the opening sections of a speech, more than once stresses the need for clarity, pleasing presentation, and a smooth narrative flow. Quintilian, *Institutio Oratoria* 4.1.76-79, discussing the transition from the *exordium* to the next section of the speech, states that transitions should be noticeable (in order that the structure of the speech should be clear) but simple and natural. For discussions relating specifically to history-writing see Lucian, *On How to Write History* 52-54, on the need for an introductory statement; also Cicero, *de Oratore* 2.15.63-64, and Lucian, *On How to Write History* 55, on the need for historical writing to be clear and well arranged, presented in a flowing and easy style, with each new topic carefully linked to what precedes. Note also the claim at the beginning of Luke that what follows will be an 'orderly' account (καθεξῆς, Lk. 1:3).

[41]See R. Maddox, *The Purpose of Luke-Acts* (Edinburgh: T. & T. Clark, 1982); also I.H. Marshall, *The Acts of the Apostles* (New Testament Guides; Sheffield: JSOT Press, 1992) 31-46.

far:[42] Acts, while coherent, becomes increasingly selective. This leads onto the suggestion that Luke has a more focused, apologetic intent.

According to Maddox and Johnson, Luke-Acts attempts to show that Jesus and the church he founded were God's fulfilment of his promises to Israel, thereby assuring both Jewish and Gentile believers of the reliability of the message they have heard, and of God's faithfulness.[43] This accounts well for much of the material in Acts: the great number of Old Testament quotations and allusions in Acts; the passages in Acts which speak of fulfilment (e.g., Peter's speeches at 2:14-39 and 3:12-26, Paul's speech at 13:16-41, cf. 26:19-23); the insistence that Christ's death was foretold in Scripture (2:22-35; 8:32-35; 13:26-37; 26:23); and (by no means the least important aspect) the considerable space given in Acts to explaining the rejection of the Christian message by many Jews and its acceptance by many Gentiles, both also seen as a fulfilment of Scripture (see respectively ch. 7; 13:40-41; 28:25-28; and 13:46-48; 15:15-18).

Within this basic framework, there are further refinements we may introduce. We can note, with Squires, that a presentation of Christianity as a religion with roots stretching into antiquity would perhaps commend it to interested pagans suspicious of novelty in religion.[44] For Squires the theme of 'the plan of God' is an important strand running through Acts, and particularly emphasised in the speeches.[45]

We may note an emphasis on Christians as law-abiding citizens who will not threaten the political stability of the Roman Empire. This emerges most clearly in the portrait of Paul in the last third of the book as a Roman citizen able to secure good treatment at the hands of a succession of Roman magistrates (e.g. 16:37-40; 18:12-17; 22:24-29; 23:23-35) and to defend himself before them (24:1-23; 26:1-32). It is also implicit in the fact that on two occasions a contrast is drawn between apostles and individuals known to have been involved in sedition (5:35-37; 21:37-40), and in the fact that all disorderly assemblies and incidents of riotous or criminal behaviour

---

[42]I.H. Marshall, *The Acts of the Apostles*, 31-32.

[43]Maddox, *The Purpose of Luke-Acts*, 31-56, 182-7; L.T. Johnson, *The Writings of the New Testament* (Philadelphia: Fortress, 1986) 200-4; *idem, The Acts of the Apostles* (Sacra Pagina 5; Minnesota: Liturgical Press, 1992) 7-9. See also the essays of Peterson and Rosner in the present volume.

[44]J.T. Squires, *The Plan of God in Luke-Acts* (SNTS Monograph Series 76; Cambridge: Cambridge University Press, 1993).

[45]*The Plan of God*, 58-77.

in Acts are caused by opponents of the gospel, besides whom the
Christians emerge as peaceable individuals (6:10-14; 13:50-52; 14:5-7,
19; 16:19-24; 17:5-9; 19:23-40; 21:27-34; 23:12-15; 25:1-3). Certainly we
can imagine Luke wishing to defend Christianity against the charge
of being intrinsically seditious.[46]

This has not been an entirely circular argument (deducing
Luke's purposes from his selection of material, and then using these
purposes to explain why material has been selected). The issues we
have mentioned are such as we can in general imagine to have been,
in different ways, pressing for the early church.[47] When we approach
Acts with these issues in mind, we find that the material Luke
presents is indeed well-calculated to address such issues.

2. Arrangement: Large-scale

It is often noted that there are patterns and themes which run
through Acts and unify it.[48] The most obvious of these is the spread
of the message of Christ throughout the Mediterranean world,
starting in Jerusalem and moving further and further away from its
starting-point until by the end of the book the Apostle Paul is
preaching Christ in Rome, the capital of the Gentile world.[49] Acts falls
into four sections, each of them roughly equal in length, and each of
which sees a further stage in this spread: 1:1-7:60, which concentrates
on events in Jerusalem; 8:1-14:28, in which the gospel reaches
Samaritans, 'God-fearers' and Gentiles, and the church in Antioch
becomes a base for Paul and Barnabas' missionary journey; 15:1-
21:17, in which the Jerusalem council places Jews and Gentiles on an
equal footing in the church, and Paul's further missionary journeys

---

[46]Marshall, *The Acts of the Apostles*, 33, 46, accepts that Acts has secondary
apologetic purpose of this sort. Maddox, *The Purpose of Luke-Acts*, 181, is more
sceptical.

[47]For this approach, cf. Johnson, *The Writings of the New Testament*, 110-11; C.F.D.
Moule, *The Birth of the New Testament* (3rd ed; San Francisco: Harper & Row,
1982).

[48]See, for example, I.H. Marshall, *Acts* (Leicester: IVP, 1980) 23-34; Johnson, *The
Acts of the Apostles*, 10-12.

[49]Johnson (*The Writings of the New Testament*, 204-5) argues that this is part of a
larger structure running through Luke-Acts: the Gospel of Luke begins in Judaea
and Jerusalem, Acts ends in Rome; the middle section (Lk. 19 - Acts 7) details the
rejection of Jesus and of his Apostles by the Jerusalem establishment.
Morgenthaler (*Lukas und Quintilian*, 351-353) takes a similar view.

take him further afield in the Gentile world, until he returns to Jerusalem with the further aim of going to Rome; 21:18-28:31, describing Paul's arrest and the long delays before he finally reaches Rome.[50]

There are summary statements which come roughly at the beginning and end of each of these sections, and further clarify the presentation: 1:6-8, which maps out much what follows; 8:1-4, which notes how the gospel spread outside Jerusalem as a result of persecution (picked up by 11:19-20, which is followed by the founding of the church in Antioch); 14:27, concluding Paul's and Barnabas' first missionary journey with a statement of how God has been at work among the Gentiles; 21:29, a similar statement at the end of Paul's further missionary journeys; 28:31, which concludes the book with a picture of Paul preaching without restrictions in Rome. There are other such statements throughout the book, which similarly summarise events so far, or indicate the direction the narrative is taking: see 9:31, 12:24, 19:21 and the more detailed comments on chapters 1-7 below.

---

[50]This analysis is substantially the same as that of Morgenthaler, *Lukas und Quintilian*, 321-323, the only difference being that Morgenthaler begins the fourth section at 21:27. However, surely the break between 21:17 and 18 is more obvious than that between 21:26 and 27: verses 15-17 mark Paul's arrival in Jerusalem (to which everything since 19:21 has been pointing forward) and verse 18 begins the account of what happened to Paul in Jerusalem; whereas to make a break between verse 26 and verse 27 splits the account of Paul's temple vow unnaturally in two. Morgenthaler argues that Paul's journeys in the third section do not come to an end until Paul actually enters the temple (p. 322). However, though Paul has been anxious to reach Jerusalem since 19:21, nowhere is it stated that he specifically wished to visit the temple; rather he goes to the temple at the request of elders in the Jerusalem church (21:20-26) this being presented as a fresh development in the narrative. It is hard, therefore, to see Paul's visit to the temple as the logical conclusion of the third section of Acts. One of the factors which seems to have led Morgenthaler towards his proposed division is his fascination with statistics, and particularly with making observations based on fairly exact numerical correspondences (see, for example, pp. 219-224; 229-234; 258-260): following his division the four sections of Acts all have roughly equal word-counts (4690, 4731, 4400, 4561); whereas to make the break at 21:17 produces more sharply divergent figures for the third and fourth sections (4690, 4731, 4205, 4746). But surely these figures are close enough to allow us to speak of Acts falling into four 'roughly equal' sections? This is not the only occasion we shall have to question Morgenthaler's statistical approach.

There are, of course, other theological themes running through Acts, for example: the fulfilment of God's promises to Israel;[51] the kingdom of God (which often finds expression in the references to the risen Jesus as the promised king of David's line); the rejection of Jesus as Messiah by many Jews, and his acceptance by many Gentiles. These three linked themes are carefully underscored at key points in Acts. As they are treated at length in Peterson's chapter, it is unnecessary to go into detail here. We may note, however, that Acts begins and ends with a reference to the kingdom (1:6; 28:31, in the latter case explicitly called the kingdom of God and linked to Jesus as Lord). Similarly, the pattern of the gospel being preached first to Jews and then to Gentiles is pointedly maintained right up to the end of Acts (see, e.g., 1:8; 11:19; 13:46-48; 14:1; 18:1-5; 28:17-28), thereby emphasising the paradoxical result, that it is increasingly Gentiles rather than Jews who come to believe.[52] The treatment of these and other themes are further examples of Luke's careful arrangement of his material.[53]

---

[51]Johnson sees the pattern prophecy-fulfilment as the most fundamental structural element in Acts (and Luke): see *The Writings of the New Testament*, 205-7; *The Acts of the Apostles*, 11-14.

[52]For a similar treatment, see Morgenthaler, *Lukas und Quintilian*, 342-344, who sees the gradual turning from Jews to Gentiles as one of the major theological themes of Acts. For a defence of the ending of Acts as forming a perfectly intelligible conclusion to the prophecy-fulfilment structure of the book, see Johnson, *Acts of the Apostles*, 473-7, and the literature cited there.

[53]Morgenthaler (*Lukas und Quintilian*, 334-40) again attempts to trace this careful arrangement in the detailed statistics of Acts, and again seems to push basically reasonable observations to implausible lengths. Thus he notes that if we divide Acts into the four sections suggested above the figures for Peter's and Paul's speeches in these sections are the exact opposite of each other: for Peter the figures are 4-2-1-0, for Paul 0-1-2-4 (pp. 334-5). A more moderate form of this argument, to the effect that Peter, generally linked with Jerusalem in Acts, gradually recedes, while Paul, the apostle to the Gentiles, gradually takes centre-stage seems acceptable, and fits with the movement in Acts from Jerusalem to Rome. But it is hard to imagine the average reader, having divided Acts into four, carefully counting speeches in each section to arrive at Morgenthaler's mathematically exact pattern. It is still harder to see how this reader would refine their understanding of this move from Jerusalem to Rome by noting that only one of Peter's seven speeches is *not* in Jerusalem, while only one of Paul's speeches *is* in Jerusalem (335); or by noting that the total word-counts for Peter's speeches (*c.* 1500) and Paul's speeches (*c.* 2000) stand in the proportions 3:4 (335). That there is an intentional pattern in Acts is not in question: but that Luke should have deliberately created such exact numerical correspondences (and expected his readers to perform the calculations necessary to reveal them!)

3. Narrative Proportions

We noted above that the question of proportions is one which combines aspects of selection and arrangement. Turning to Acts, it seems that, if Luke dwells on an incident, it is because it is thematically and structurally significant; and, equally, because it has an important part to play in the persuasive strategy of Acts. Such an approach helps to explain the enormous length of Stephen's speech in Acts 7, and particularly its lengthy treatment of Moses: the theme of Jesus as a second Moses (a 'prophet like Moses': 3:22; 7:37) who like Moses is twice rejected by Israel, which can be traced back into the gospel of Luke, comes to its head in the death of Stephen.[54] The speech, and the decisive rejection of its message by those listening, marks the end of a period in which the gospel is preached only in Jerusalem and only to Jews. The great length of the speech, therefore, turns out to be Luke's way of giving this turning-point in his narrative appropriate emphasis.

Similarly, Peter's vision in 10:10-16 is substantially repeated at 11:5-10, when he relates in Jerusalem how Gentiles have come to accept the word of God. Luke's point in presenting this striking vision in full twice seems to be to emphasise that it is at God's leading that the word has been proclaimed to Gentiles.[55] Repetition (which is, of course, another way of dwelling on an incident) gives appropriate weight to a significant development.

The last third of Acts is dominated by the theme of Paul's desire to go to Rome, which is obviously linked to the theme of the spread of the gospel through the Gentile world. The theme is first raised at

---

strains credulity. Similar comments may be made about Morgenthaler's statistico-geographical treatment of Paul's journeys in Acts, in which the figure of 500 kilometres frequently recurs, along with the observation that Athens stands approximately 1000 kilometres in a straight line from Jerusalem, and Rome 1000 kilometres from Athens (339). Again, one accepts the point that Paul's journeys take him further and further afield; but what do all these numbers add to our understanding?

[54]On this, see Johnson, *The Writings of the New Testament*, 207-211; *The Acts of the Apostles*, 12-14.

[55]Note that though Peter's account in 11:11-17 recapitulates 10:17-48 (the events subsequent to the vision) in a much more abbreviated form, the points which he emphasises in this part of the account are again those which indicate that God has been at work: Peter's leading by the Spirit (v. 12); the original vision of the angel to Cornelius; the coming of the Spirit on Cornelius and his household (v. 15) seen as a gift of God in fulfilment of Jesus' promise (vv. 16-17).

19:21, which in fact outlines the shape of the remainder of the book: Paul goes first to Jerusalem, and on to Rome. However, Paul does not arrive until almost the end of the book (28:14). Luke describes many of the intervening incidents in considerable detail: hearings and other official procedures (21:40-22:21; 22:30-23:10; 23:23-35; 24:1-22; 25:1-12; 25:23-26:31); threats to Paul's life (23:12-22; 25:3-5; see also 27:30-32, 42-43); delays (24:23-27); the storm and shipwreck (27:13-44). One of Luke's purposes in dwelling on these incidents seems to have been to show Paul, the Apostle to the Gentiles, defending himself and preaching the gospel before both Jew and Gentile (see especially his own words, 26:19-23), and to stress Paul's innocence of the charges laid against him. His journey also has great symbolic significance: here is a man born and raised a Jew, who yet goes to the capital of the Gentile world in his obedience to God's purposes.[56] This is surely one of the reasons why Paul's speeches in this section twice recount in detail how he was dramatically converted (22:6-21; 26:9-23, both recapitulating the account in 9:1-19), setting this in the context of his strict upbringing in the traditions of his fathers (22:3-5; 26:4-5); in a metaphorical as well as a literal sense, he has 'come a long way', and the journey he has made is an index of a new development in God's purposes, recapitulating on an individual level a pattern running through the whole of Acts.[57] Yet perhaps Luke has a more fundamental purpose: to show that the various obstacles to Paul's arriving in Rome are, with God's help, overcome, and that Paul's journey to Rome is part of God's purposes: 23:11 and 27:23-24, where Paul receives divine assurance that he will reach Rome, are significant in this regard. The obstacles, and the length at which they are narrated, create a suspense in the narrative, and reinforce our sense of God's purposes reaching fulfilment when Paul finally does arrive in Rome.

In these ways, then, Luke arranges the proportions of his narrative so as to underscore his theological themes. Note also the vividness and passion of many of these sections on which Luke dwells: the forcefulness and variety of many of the speeches,[58] the

---

[56]Note the presence of 'Roman' elements in the narrative before Paul reaches Rome: Paul's Roman citizenship (22:25-9); the legal procedures, which become increasingly Roman (chs. 22, 24, 26).

[57]Note also Paul's explicit statements that he preaches Jesus as Christ because of his commitment to God and his belief in God's promises to Israel (23:1, 7; 24:14-15; 26:6-8).

[58]See the discussion of Speeches below; also the section on Style.

vividness of the visions related, the drama of the storm and shipwreck. In a way entirely in line with classical rhetorical ideals, Luke's 'amplifications' are not simply a matter of multiplying words, but involve heightened diction and striking presentation of events. Luke's 'amplifications' hold the attention and, also in line with classical ideals, give his narrative great persuasive power.[59]

4. Arrangement: Small-scale

The last aspect mentioned in the preamble to Section I was that the discourse should flow naturally from point to point, with transitions marked, but not so prominent as to disrupt the narrative. Space does not permit an analysis of the whole of Acts along these lines, so we will confine ourselves to the first section of the book, 1:1-8:3.

Acts begins with a reference to a previous volume, whose contents are briefly summarised (1:1-2); it is thus a 'secondary preface'.[60] It does not state directly what subjects will be dealt with, but slides into a description of Jesus' last days with his disciples and, particularly, of his final words with them (vv. 3-8);[61] this in turn leads into an account of Jesus' ascension, the words of the angels, and the return of the disciples to Jerusalem (vv. 9-14); by which time the narrative of Acts is fully launched. However, though Acts does not begin with a formal statement of the topics to be covered, Jesus' final words outline themes which are to run through Acts: the reign of God (v. 3); the giving of the promised Holy Spirit (vv. 4-5); the question of what is to happen to Israel's hopes of national restoration (vv. 6-7); the spreading witness to Jesus following the coming of the

---

[59]Cf. Longinus, *On the Sublime* 15 and 25-7 for a discussion of vividness in prose and poetic texts. There are numerous examples in classical literature where the writer dwells on incidents, presenting them in a heightened style. Two famous examples are the description in Thucydides 7.79-87 of the end of the Sicilian expedition, emphasising the comprehensiveness of the defeat inflicted on the Athenians, and Virgil's description of the death of Turnus at the end of *Aeneid* 12, which concludes the whole *Aeneid* in a remarkably ambivalent way.

[60]For a detailed treatment of Acts 1:1 and the preface to the Gospel, see L.C. Alexander, *The Preface to Luke's Gospel*, 142-6.

[61]Verse 3 simply begins with a relative pronoun (οἵς) referring to τοῖς ἀποστόλοις. . .οὓς ἐξελέξατο (v. 2). It is anything but an emphatic, new beginning.

Spirit (v. 8). They are, thus, programmatic in character, and have the function, if not the form, of an opening statement.[62]

It can be seen how Luke is at pains to link successive sections of the narrative that follows.[63] The description in 1:12-14 of the disciples in Jerusalem, expectantly praying, forms the background for the following incident, in which a twelfth disciple is chosen to take Judas' place (1:15-26);[64] it also leads into chapter 2, describing the coming of the Spirit at Pentecost.

In chapters 2-7 there is a logical progression in the events narrated: the miraculous event of speaking in tongues, followed by Peter's preaching (2:1-40); the response to the preaching, and the unity of spirit among those who believed, expressed in the sharing of possessions (2:41-47); the miraculous event of the healing of the lame man, followed by Peter's preaching (3:1-26);[65] the response to the preaching (4:1-4) which this time includes opposition; confrontation between Peter and John and the temple authorities (4:5-22); prayers for boldness in facing opposition, answered by another outpouring of the Spirit (4:23-31); description of the unity of the believers, expressed in the sharing of possessions (4:32-35);[66] the contrasting examples of Barnabas, who wholeheartedly sells his possessions, and Ananias and Sapphira, who dissimulate in this matter (4:36-5:11); the miracles performed by the apostles, attracting people from cities around Jerusalem (5:12-16);[67] further confrontation with the temple authorities, who are filled with jealousy at this popularity (5:17-40),

---

[62]On this, see R.C. Tannehill, *The Narrative Unity of Luke-Acts, Vol. 2: the Acts of the Apostles* (Minneapolis: Fortress, 1990) (hereafter 'Acts') 11-18.

[63]Which is not to say that events in these chapters merely form a linear succession: they also display recurring patterns (see the section on Implicit Commentary).

[64]Note how the list of disciples in verse 13, in which there are only eleven names, also prepares for this incident.

[65]Note how the comment in 2:46 that those who believed worshipped in the temple sets the scene for what follows, explaining how Peter and John came to be going up to the temple in 3:1.

[66]These verses are part of a general presentation of the early believers as a united community (see 2:41-47 and 6:1-6, especially 6:5) and so are not inappropriate to their broader context; but care is taken to link them to what immediately precedes by the common theme of the continued preaching of the message of Jesus (compare 4:31 and 33).

[67]Once again, these verses both fit in the broader context of chapters 1-7 (see especially 3:1-11, also describing miracles wrought by the apostles) and are tied to what immediately precedes by the common theme of awe at the power at work among the believers (compare 5:5, 11 with 5:13).

concluding with a note that the apostles nonetheless continue their public preaching (5:41-42); the growth in the numbers of the believers leads to dissent between 'Hellenists' and 'Hebrews', which leads to the appointment of men to oversee the daily distribution, among them Stephen (6:1-7); Stephen is the main figure in the confrontation which follows (6:8-7:60); into the account of Stephen's stoning is introduced the significant figure of Saul (7:58) who then takes the lead in the persecution which follows (8:1-3) and who is, of course, to play such a large part in the subsequent narrative.

The above will have to suffice to demonstrate the care Luke takes to link the events described. It is also worth noting how summary statements alternate with episodes treated in more detail, and serve to articulate the narrative by charting the progress of events (2:42-47; 4:4; 4:32-35; 5:11; 5:12-26; 6:7).[68]

5. Speeches

The speeches in Acts are treated separately in this and the following section. They could be dealt with under several headings (e.g., style, persuasion); but they are also a clear example of arrangement in Acts. Here it is appropriate to bring classical historiography and epic into the discussion: as they are both narrative genres, they provide us with the closest parallels for the use of speeches in Acts.

Classical historiography and epic, in spite of their basically narrative structures, contain many speeches; and the material in the speeches is almost always of especial significance in its context. Thucydides' famous programmatic statement (1.22.1) that he will use speeches at those points in his narrative where he knows negotiations or policy debates took place, as a way of defining and discussing important issues,[69] can apply, *mutatis mutandis*, across the board: in

---

[68]Morgenthaler attempts to demonstrate a different kind of small-scale arrangement, by arguing that the successive episodes of Acts are structured so as to observe certain proportions (*Lukas und Quintilian*, 324-7): thus Acts 1:3-11 falls into two sections, 3-8 (123 words) and 9-11 (63 words) yielding the proportions 2:1; Acts 1:12-26 yields the proportions 1:3; Acts 2:1-13 yields the proportions 1:2; Acts 2:13-36 yields the proportions 1:1:1; and so on. Once again, it is hard to imagine a reader noting these proportions (particularly as the proportions vary in the case of each episode); and still harder to see what he or she would gain by doing so.

[69]This text is, of course, notoriously difficult to interpret exactly: see the recent detailed discussion of S.E. Porter, 'Thucydides 1.22.1 and the Speeches in Acts: Is

Homer, Herodotus, Thucydides, Livy, and Tacitus (among others) speeches are significant events, and very often important for interpretation.[70] Though all these writers also have many passages of dramatic descriptive narrative, spoken words provide a naturally more vivid and direct way of highlighting matters of significance.[71]

The same is true in Acts. Acts does contain passages of dramatic or vivid narrative (e.g. chs. 2, 9, 10, 12, 16, the storm in ch. 27) but it is in the speeches that the important theological themes of Acts are stated at greatest length: the theme of Jesus as the promised Christ, now exalted and ruling at God's right hand (2:22-36; 3:12-26; 13:23-37); the theme of Jesus as a 'prophet like Moses' (3:22; 7:22-43); the offer of salvation to Gentiles as well as to Jews (10:34-43; 11:5-17; 17:22-31); the question of whether Gentile converts should be made to keep the Jewish law (15:7-20).[72] Similarly, it is often the speeches which interpret events taking place at the time: thus Peter in 2:14-21 interprets the gift of tongues as the fulfilment of Joel's prophecy; Stephen in chapter 7 interprets Jewish opposition to Christian preaching as part of a wider tendency of Israel to disobey God; Paul in 13:46-47 states the pattern which is to be programmatic in the chapters following, that Christ will be preached first to the Jews, but then to the Gentiles.

---

there a Thucydidean View?', *NovT* 32 (1990) 121-42. The summary offered above is deliberately stated loosely in order to allow for various interpretative options.

[70]On Homer, see, M.W. Edwards, *Homer, Poet of the Iliad* (Baltimore and London: John Hopkins University Press, 1987) 88-97. On Herodotus, see M.L. Lang, *Herodotean Narrative and Discourse* (Cambridge, Mass. and London: Harvard University Press, 1984) especially pp. 18-36; P. Hohti, *The Interrelation of Speech and Action in the Histories of Herodotus* (Helsinki: Societas Scientarum Fennica, 1976) especially pp. 130-42. On Thucydides, see H.R. Immerwahr, 'Pathology of Power and the Speeches in Thucydides', in P.A. Stadter (ed.), *The Speeches in Thucydides* (University of N. Carolina Press, Chapel Hill, 1973) 16-31; H.-P. Stahl, 'Speeches and Course of Events in Books Six and Seven of Thucydides', *ibid.*, 60-77. On Livy, see P.G. Walsh, *Livy: His Historical Aims and Method* (Cambridge: Cambridge University Press, 1961) 219-44; T.J. Luce, *Livy: the Composition of his History* (Princeton: Princeton University Press, 1977) 27-8, 115-6, 190-1. On Tacitus, see E. Keitel, 'Speeches in Tacitus' Histories I-III', *ANRW* 2.33.4 (Berlin: de Gruyter, 1991) 2772-2794; *idem*, 'Speech and Narrative in Histories 4', in T.J. Luce and A.J. Woodman (eds.), *Tacitus and the Tacitean Tradition* (Princeton: Princeton University Press, 1993) 39-58.

[71]See also Lucian, *How to Write History* 58 on speeches as an appropriate form for a historian to use, and also an occasion on which a writer may allow himself some eloquence.

[72]11:5-17 and 15:7-20 are also examples of important policy questions being debated in speeches.

Care is taken to integrate these speeches into the narrative. Introductions set the scene for the speeches. Sometimes they simply indicate where the speech took place and to whom it was addressed (e.g., 21:40-22:2; 24:1-2) but on other occasions they lead more directly into what follows. They may indicate some circumstance which serves as the point of departure for the speech (e.g., the accusation of drunkenness in 2:13 which Peter picks up in v. 15; the note of amazement in 3:10-11, similarly picked up in v. 12). They may touch on issues relevant to the speech to follow (e.g., the double reference to Moses in 6:11 and 14 preceding Stephen's speech, which also has much to say about Moses, though from a radically different perspective; the accusation made against Peter in 11:2-3 of eating with uncircumcised men, which he answers in vv. 5-17; 15:1-5, describing sharp dissent over this same issue, and leading into the Jerusalem council, where this issue is resolved). Or they may characterise the hearers in some way (e.g., 17:19-21, offering a thumbnail sketch of Paul's Athenian hearers). In a similar way, Luke notes the responses to speeches (e.g., 2:37-41; 7:54-8:1; 13:42-45; 17:32-34; 22:22). The introductions and conclusions Luke provides for the speeches could also be cited as another example of orderly presentation.[73]

6. Speech Structure

Another aspect of arrangement deserving separate treatment is the structure of the speeches in Acts. The classical treatises commonly divide oratory into three main types: forensic (typically relating to past events, and concerned with truth or justice), deliberative (typically relating to the future, and concerned with self-interest or benefit), and epideictic (typically relating to the present and involving praise or blame).[74] For each of these three types there is an

---

[73]For a fuller discussion of the appropriateness of the speeches in Acts to their contexts and to the characters of the speakers, which is also an aspect touched on by, for example, by Lucian (*On How to Write History*, 58) see Gempf's chapter in the present volume.

[74]Aristotle, *Rhetoric* 1.3.4-6; Cicero, *de Inventione* 2.4.12-13, 2.51.155-52.158; *Rhetorica ad Herennium* 1.2.2; 3.2.2-3, 3.6.10-11; Quintilian, *Institutio Oratoria* 3.4.12-16; 3.7.1-28; 3.8.1-6; 3.9.1.

appropriate structure.[75] Forensic speeches take the form: proem (*exordium*), a narration of the facts of the case (*narratio*); the division of the argument of the speech into a series of propositions to be demonstrated (*partitio*); the demonstration itself (*confirmatio*); refutation of opposing viewpoints (*reprehensio*); epilogue (*conclusio*).[76] Deliberative speeches omit the refutation, giving the form: proem, narration, division, demonstration, and epilogue. Epideictic speeches have a yet simpler form: proem; amplified topics (e.g., a setting forth of the life of the person commemorated under various heads); epilogue.

In a recent article, Black has argued that the speeches in Acts in general conform well to the requirements of classical writers in this regard, provided it is recognised that classical writers show considerable flexibility both in defining the three types of speech and in setting out the structures of the three types: that is, they were willing to allow that the distinction between the three types was not absolute, and that in certain cases the three types of speech structure could be modified.[77]

---

[75]Aristotle's discussion of structure (*Rhetoric* 3.13-19) covers all three types of oratory: see also, on forensic oratory Cicero, *de Inventione*. 1.14.19-61.109; *Rhetorica ad Herennium* 1.3.4-2.31.50, Quintilian, *Institutio Oratoria*, 3.9.1-5 (expanded at massive length in Books 4-6 following); on deliberative oratory, *Rhetorica ad Herennium* 3.2.2-5.9, Quintilian, *Institutio Oratoria* 3.8.6-13; on epideictic oratory, *Rhetorica ad Herennium* 3.6.10-8.15, Quintilian, *Institutio Oratoria* 3.7.1-6 (a discussion of the kind of topics that may be covered which seems to assume that a formal beginning and ending will be supplied). As well as setting out the structures of the three types of speech, these treatments discuss questions relating to the underlying aims of the three types and (often in great technical detail) the types of argument one may employ at various points in the speech.

[76]The Latin terms given above are taken from Cicero's *de Inventione* 1.14.19. There is some variation in the terminology; *ad Herennium* 1.3.4 has *exordium, narratio, divisio, confirmatio, confutatio, conclusio*; Quintilian, *Institutio Oratoria* 3.9.1-5, does not regard the *partitio* as a separate section, but argues for the five-fold division *proemium, narratio, probatio, refutatio, peroratio*.

[77]C.C. Black II, 'The Rhetorical Form of the Hellenistic Jewish and Early Christian Sermon: A Response to Lawrence Wills', *HTR* 81 (1988) 1-18. The article by Wills to which he was responding was L. Wills, 'The Form of the Sermon in Hellenistic Judaism and Early Christianity', *HTR* 77 (1984) 277-299. Wills had argued that the speeches in Acts and other examples of sermons in the early Christian writings were composed according to a threefold pattern (Exempla, Conclusion, Exhortation) which could not be fitted into any schema derived from classical rhetoric. Black argues for a more flexible approach, citing Quintilian's point (*Institutio Oratoria* 3.4.16; cf. 3.7.1-4) that the three types of speech may in practice

Against this general background, Black examines Paul's speech at Pisidian Antioch (13:16-41), and concludes that it may be divided into the following sections: narration (vv. 17-25, a review of Israelite history, leading up to the coming of Jesus as saviour); division (v. 26, in this case simply a single proposition, that the message of salvation is now being proclaimed to Jews and God-fearers); demonstration of the proposition (vv. 27-37, arguing that God has vindicated Jesus by raising him from the dead, and that therefore salvation can be preached to Israel); conclusion (vv. 38-41, urging acceptance of this salvation on his hearers).[78] This speech may not fit any of the three patterns listed above exactly; but, as noted, these were not applied rigidly by the classical theorists. The speech could be said to accord in broad outline with the requirements of the theorists.

It is interesting to apply Black's approach to Peter's speech at Acts 3:12-26 and Paul's at 17:22-31. Peter's speech emerges as a somewhat anomalous composition in which the constituent parts can all be classified according to classical rhetorical categories, but the structure is unusual: proem (v. 12); proposition (God has glorified his Son, v. 13a); demonstration (vv. 13b-16); peroration (vv. 17-21), of which the concluding words form another proposition (the reference in vv. 20b-21 to Jesus as the fulfilment of prophecy) which leads into a further demonstration (vv. 22-24) and a further peroration (vv. 25-26). The structure is not unintelligible, however, and we should bear in mind that Luke, in view of the setting of the speech (an impromptu sermon given in the aftermath of a spectacular healing) may have intended this speech to give an impression of something exuberant, spontaneous, and impassioned, which would naturally tend towards a loose structure.[79]

---

overlap considerably in their subject matter (p. 5, n. 17) and the same writer's frequent statements to the effect that an orator needs to be flexible, adapting his approach to the requirements of a specific case: see especially *Institutio Oratoria* 7.10.11-13, relating specifically to speech structure (p. 7, n. 21).

[78]Black explains the absence of a proem on the grounds that the sole purpose of a proem was to secure audience favour (Quintilian, *Institutio Oratoria* 4.1.5); Paul, speaking to fellow-Jews, could presuppose an initially favourable disposition, and needed only the briefest of appeals for attention (v. 16).

[79]Cf. Kennedy, *New Testament Interpretation through Rhetorical Criticism*, 118-9, part of a chapter ('The Speeches in Acts', pp. 114-40) which provides brief structural analyses of twenty-seven speeches in Acts. He concludes that the speeches in Acts portray the early Christians as resourceful in preaching the gospel on any occasion that presented itself (p. 140).

Paul's speech in 17:22-31 emerges as a textbook example of a deliberative speech: proem (v. 22, seeking to secure audience goodwill) narration (v. 23a, giving background); division (again a single proposition: I will tell you of this God you worship as unknown, v. 23b); demonstration (God as incomparably greater than idols, vv. 24-29); peroration (vv. 30-31). As Morgenthaler notes, this is a speech appropriate to one of the rhetorical centres of the Graeco-Roman world.[80]

For further examples of speeches in Acts whose structure follows Graeco-Roman rhetorical conventions, see Winter's chapter on the forensic speeches in Acts 24-26; note particularly his argument that Luke seems to display knowledge of specific forensic conventions; also Watson's analysis of Paul's Miletus address (20:17-38) as an example of epideictic rhetoric.[81]

7. Implicit Commentary

Though Acts contains many explicit interpretative statements (e.g., the summarising comments noted in the discussion of narrative flow in chs. 1-7), and on occasions offers open evaluations of characters (e.g., 10:2; 11:24; 17:11) and events (12:23; 13:48; 16:14), it also contains a number of indirect interpretations and evaluations, which may be designated by the general term 'implicit commentary'.[82] It is interesting to compare these narrative techniques of Acts with similar

---

[80]*Lukas und Quintilian*, 331-332. Morgenthaler analyses the speech as: proem (vv. 22-23); narration (24-29); peroration (30-31) (333). Kennedy (*New Testament Interpretation through Rhetorical Criticism*, 129-31) has the analysis: refutation of the charge that Paul is preaching a foreign deity (vv. 22b-28); refutation of religious errors of the Athenians (vv. 29-31). But the analysis offered above seems to fit the details more closely.

[81]D.F. Watson, 'Paul's Speech to the Ephesian Elders (Acts 20.17-38): Epideictic Rhetoric of Farewell', in D.F. Watson (ed.), *Persuasive Artistry*, 185-208.

[82]Tannehill, *Acts*, discusses many such examples, some of them noted in what follows. Tannehill sets out his general approach on pp. 1-9 of the companion volume on Luke (*The Narrative Unity of Luke-Acts: a Literary Interpretation, Volume 1: The Gospel According to Luke* [Philadelphia: Fortress, 1986]). The third section of W.S. Kurz, *Reading Luke-Acts: Dynamics of Biblical Narrative* (Louisville: Westminster/John Knox, 1993) entitled 'Implicit Commentary' (pp. 135-55) uses the term in a somewhat different sense from that in which it is used above, to denote cases where the narrator's perspective differs from that of a character.

techniques in Old Testament narrative.[83] As will emerge, there is some overlap, which might suggest that the Old Testament has been the major influence on Acts in this regard. Clearly it is appropriate to see the Old Testament as a possible influence, in view of the numerous Old Testament citations in Acts (see the chapter by Rosner in the present volume); however, it will be argued below that classical literature also contains many examples of such techniques, and so also provides us with a framework against which we may understand these aspects of Acts.

In this section, comparisons will first be drawn between Acts and Old Testament narrative techniques; and then similar techniques in classical writers will be noted (as in the discussion of speeches, comparison will be made with classical historiography and epic, rather than with rhetorical treatises).

(1) Simple Juxtaposition. Sentences in Old Testament narrative are with few exceptions linked by (various forms of) one conjunction, ‏ו‎ (*we*, 'and'). When we contrast this feature with, for example, the rich variety of conjunctions and particles in Greek, which make it possible for Greek writers to specify with some precision the nature of the link between two events (logical, temporal, and so on), Old Testament narrative may seem limited in its reliance on one highly imprecise conjunction. But in fact Old Testament writers are able to exploit the very inexplicitness of the conjunction ‏ו‎ for artistic gain; for they are able simply to juxtapose two sentences, or two incidents and thus to lead the reader to ponder on possible links between what has been simply juxtaposed. A gap is created in the narrative, perhaps leaving unclear the motives of one of the characters or the connection between two events, and the reader has to try to fill this gap in order to make sense of the narrative.[84] Such techniques of juxtaposition are,

---

[83]See particularly, R. Alter, *The Art of Biblical Narrative* (New York: Basic Books, 1980); *idem, The World of Biblical Narrative* (London: SPCK, 1992); A. Berlin, *Poetics and Interpretation of Biblical Narrative* (Bible and Literature Series 9; Sheffield: Almond, 1983,); M. Sternberg, *The Poetics of Biblical Narrative: Ideological Literature and the Drama of Reading* (Bloomington: Indiana University Press, 1985); S. Bar-Efrat, *Narrative Art in the Bible* (JSOTS 70; Sheffield: Almond, 1989). Tannehill himself refers at a number of points to the work of Sternberg.

[84]On the inexplicitness of conjunctions in OT narrative, see Bar-Efrat, *Narrative Art in the Bible*, 132-3; for examples of the uses to which this inexplicitness can be put, see, for example, Alter, *The Art of Biblical Narrative*, 5; Sternberg, *Poetics of Biblical Narrative*, 193-8, 213-4, 242-7.

of course, also possible in languages which have a greater variety of conjunction. There seem to be a number of such examples in Acts.

Thus in chapter 5, Peter and John, who have been arrested by the temple authorities, are miraculously released from prison, and resume their preaching in the temple (vv. 17-21a). The temple authorities send an order to the prison for Peter and John to be brought before them, and are baffled by the news that Peter and John are no longer in prison. Finally the captain of the temple has to bring them before the temple authorities without force (vv. 21b-26). There follows a confrontation between the apostles and the temple authorities (vv. 27-32), a private discussion in which Gamaliel gives his opinion (vv. 33-9), and the apostles are flogged and released. Luke gives no explicit comment during this chapter; but by juxtaposing the attempts of the temple authorities to arrest the apostles with the incident describing the apostles' miraculous release, he suggests that the temple authorities are increasingly resisting God, which is the danger Gamaliel warns of in verse 39 (μήποτε καὶ θεομάχοι εὑρεθῆτε); he also suggests the ineffectiveness of their efforts to muzzle the apostles.[85]

This theme occurs in a yet more dramatic form in chapter 12. Herod has James put to death, and Peter arrested and elaborately guarded (vv. 1-5). Peter is miraculously released (vv. 6-17), and Herod has to be content with punishing the guards (vv. 18-19). There follows the curious incident of Herod's death as a punishment for his arrogance before God (vv. 20-23), and the chapter concludes with two notes concerning the spread of the word of God (v. 24) and Barnabas' and Saul's successful completion of their appointed task. No explicit connections are drawn between verses 20-23 and the incidents on either side; but the reader is left to draw the twin conclusions that Herod's death comes as a punishment for his opposition to the church and that such opposition is ultimately vain.[86]

A further example of significant juxtaposition is found in Acts 23. In 23:11 Paul while under arrest has a word from the Lord assuring him that he will reach Rome. This influences our interpretation of the following incident, where Paul escapes a plot against his life (23:12-35); though God is at no point said to have intervened to thwart the plot, we are surely meant to see God at work in the fact that Paul's nephew happens to overhear the plot (23:16).

---

[85]Cf. Tannehill, *Acts*, 64, 74.
[86]Cf. Johnson, *The Acts of the Apostles*, 217-8.

(2) **Analogical Patterning.** It has been noted that in Old Testament narrative incidents are often analogically patterned; that is to say, two or more incidents show a number of significant structural or thematic similarities.[87] Whereas scholarship of previous generations tended to explain many of these cases as doublets due to the combination of two or more sources, a more recent tendency has been to see such similar patterning as a deliberate authorial strategy which invites the reader to read one incident in the light of the other.[88] When one does this, one notes both similarities and significant differences, which seem to lead one towards a particular interpretation or evaluation.

The same seems to hold good for Acts. In Acts 2-7 there is a repeated pattern of miracle or preaching (or both), response to the miracle/preaching, and some description of the communal life of the church. Into this pattern incidents of increasing opposition gradually introduce themselves. Thus:

Miracle/Preaching	2:1-39	3:1-26	5:12, 15	6:8
Response (positive)	2:40-41	(4:4)	5:13-14, 16	(-----)
Opposition	(-----)	4:1-23	5:17-42	6:9-8:3
Community Life	2:42-47	4:32-5:11	6:1-6	

The pattern is not altogether neat, in that elements which correspond to each other in the pattern are often of unequal length. Yet it seems legitimate to regard chapters 2-7 as a 'structure of intensification' in which each subsequent cycle in the pattern develops elements in the previous cycle. Most notably, the positive response which has been present in the first three cycles is absent in the fourth, and opposition, which has been absent in the first cycle, intensifies in the next three: in chapter 4 Peter and John, are dismissed by the temple authorities with threats (4:21); in chapter 5 they are dismissed after having been flogged (5:40); as the culmination of the last cycle, Stephen is killed, and a period of severe persecution comes upon the church (7:58-8:3).

---

[87]E.g., the three incidents in which a matriarch is in danger in Genesis (chs. 12, 20, and 26); the crossing of the Red Sea in Exodus 14 and the crossing of the Jordan in Joshua 3-4.

[88]It is instructive, for example, to compare Alter's treatment of Genesis 37 and 38 (*The Art of Biblical Narrative*, 3-10) R.P. Gordon's treatment of 1 Samuel 24, 25, and 26 ('David's Rise and Saul's Demise: Narrative Analogy in 1 Samuel 24-26', *Tyndale Bulletin* 31 [1980] 37-64) and Sternberg's treatment of 1 Samuel 15 (*The Poetics of Biblical Narrative*, 482-515) with treatments of the same passages in most commentaries written before the 1980s.

By presenting chapters 2-7 according to a similar pattern, Luke draws attention to a growing opposition to the church's preaching.[89]

More briefly, the accounts of Paul's conversion (9:1-19) and of Cornelius and Peter (10:1-48), while not similar in every respect, have significant similarities of pattern:[90]

Vision to person to be converted	9:3-6	10:1-6
Response	9:7-9	10:7-8
Vision to person who aids conversion	9:10-12	10:9-13
Initial Doubt answered by God	9:13-16	10:14-16
Arrival of Messengers	(-----)	10:17-22
Response (journey)	9:17a	10:23-24
Welcome	(-----)	10:25-33
Response (giving of message)	9:17b	10:34-43
Conversion	9:18-19	10:44-48

Luke seems to invite us to compare the two accounts, and to reflect on the fact that the conversions of the man who is to be the apostle to the Gentiles and of the first Gentile convert mentioned in Acts are both part of God's purpose that the gospel should be preached to the Gentiles.[91]

In a similar way, Acts at various points seems to recall events from the Gospel of Luke.[92] The narrative of Stephen's death (7:55-60) recalls both the trial and crucifixion of Jesus: his vision of the Son of Man sitting at the right hand of God (vv. 55-56) recalls Jesus' words at his trial (Lk. 22:69); and his final prayers for Jesus to receive his soul (v. 59) and for the forgiveness of those responsible for his death (v. 60) recall similar prayers of Jesus at his death (Lk. 23:46 and 23:34).[93]

---

[89]Cf. Tannehill, *Acts*, 74, 84.

[90]Cf. Morgenthaler, *Quintilian und Lukas*, 329.

[91]Cf. Squires, *The Plan of God*, 60-61. This is one aspect of a careful interleaving of the accounts of Peter and Paul in chapters 8-14; see Johnson, *The Writings of the New Testament*, 229. In his commentary Johnson notes other parallels between Peter and Paul in Acts (*The Acts of the Apostles*, 10): they perform similar wonders (compare Acts 3:1-10 with 14:8-11 and 9:36-40 with 20:7-12) and have similar miraculous escapes from prison (compare Acts 12:6-17 with 16:25-34).

[92]Many of the observation in this and the preceding paragraphs are already to be found in H.J. Cadbury, *The Making of Luke-Acts* (London: Macmillan, 1927) 231-2. An exhaustive (and not entirely convincing) list of such parallels internal to Acts and between Acts and Luke is to be found in C.H. Talbert, *Literary Patterns, Theological Themes and the Genre of Luke-Acts* (Missoula: Scholars Press, 1974) 15-26. See also Tannehill, *Acts*, 68-77.

[93]Though some mss. omit these words from Lk. 23:34.

The narrative of Peter's arrest echoes the narrative of Jesus' arrest in Luke.[94] In the same way that Jesus sets his face to go to Jerusalem (Lk. 9:51), Paul 'resolves in the Spirit' to go to Jerusalem and then on to Rome (Acts 19:21). In each case Luke seems implicitly to suggest that following Jesus faithfully may mean, as it did for Jesus, facing arrest and even death.

(3) Narration and Dialogue. Recent interpreters of Old Testament narrative have made much of the subtle play that can occur between the spoken words of the characters and the narrative framework in which these spoken words are set.[95] The Old Testament writers, it seems, expected their readers to notice both similarities and differences between the narrator's and the characters' presentations of the same events. Where a character's words agree with the narrator's, this tends to indicate that the character is telling the truth, or shares the narrator's perspective. Where there is a divergence, this tends to indicate that the character is lying, in error, or under some misunderstanding, or has a different perspective from that of the narrator.

In Acts we do find such plays of perspective, particularly in dialogue spoken by those opposed to, or not committed to, the gospel. There are the words of those Jews who accuse Stephen in Jerusalem (6:11, 14), and Paul in Corinth (18:13) and in Jerusalem (21:28), full of certainty that those preaching Christ have broken the Mosaic law; the more detached view of Claudius Lysias' letter (23:26-30, not strictly dialogue, of course, but still expressive of his viewpoint), who does not feel competent to pass judgement in such matters; and there is the frank puzzlement (or scepticism?) of Festus' reference to 'a certain Jesus who was dead and whom Paul claimed was alive' (25:19). We may also note the rapidly changing attitudes of the inhabitants of Malta, at first convinced that Paul is a murderer whom the gods are not allowing to escape, then 'changing their opinion' when they see that the snake has not killed him, and declaring him to be a god (28:3-6). There is an irony in all these differing statements, of course, as none of them represent what Luke

---

[94]For this, see Tannehill, *Acts*, 152-3; the references to Passover in 12:3-4 are particularly suggestive. Johnson, interestingly, finds echoes of Luke's resurrection narrative in the account of Peter's release (*The Acts of the Apostles*, 218-9).

[95]See the suggestive treatments in Alter, *Art*, 63-87 and Sternberg, *Poetics*, 365-440.

believes to be the truth about Jesus or the gospel; in their different ways, they are all misunderstandings. Yet the narrative gains both in complexity and realism by their inclusion. In a similar category, perhaps, is the Apostles' question about the restoration of the kingdom to Israel in 1:6; which may represent an overly nationalistic view of God's purposes for the future, and which is seemingly corrected by Jesus in 1:7-8.[96]

At other points too the narrative clashes with spoken words, and presents those who speak them in a different light from that in which they wish to appear. Thus in chapter 16 the owners of the girl with the spirit of prophecy in Philippi, when they bring Paul and Silas before the magistrates, accuse them of causing a disturbance and of trying to induce the citizens of Philippi to behave in un-Roman ways (vv. 20-21). But Luke has undercut their plausible and dignified-sounding accusation by stating that the real cause of their indignation is that the girl will no longer be able to earn them any money, now that Paul has cast the spirit out of her (v. 19; the commercial value of the girl is also stressed in v. 16). The total effect is to portray them as devious and hypocritical.[97]

Examples of this sort are rarer in Acts than they are in the Old Testament. One explanation for this might be that many of the spoken words in Acts occur in the speeches, and in the speeches of Acts the speakers' and the narrator's viewpoints coincide. Here we would not expect the subtle plays that occur in the Old Testament; these speeches ought rather to be compared to speeches in the Old Testament where the speaker's and the narrator's viewpoints again coincide (e.g., Jos. 24, 1 Sam. 12; most of Deuteronomy).

Turning now to classical literature, we can find in both epic and historiography examples of literary techniques similar to those we have noted in Old Testament narrative and in Acts. Similes in Homer and Virgil, for example, are recognised not to be purely ornamental, but to offer implicit commentary on the situations to which they refer.[98] Immerwahr's large-scale treatment of Herodotus draws attention to analogical patterns and examples of ring composition in Herodotus, whose effect is to bring out both similarities and

---

[96]Tannehill, *Acts*, 14-17.
[97]Cf. Tannehill, *Acts*, 198.
[98]See W.A. Camps, *An Introduction to Homer* (Oxford: Oxford University Press, 1980) 55-60; M.W. Edwards, *Homer, Poet of the Iliad*, 102-110; R.O.A.M. Lyne, *Words and the Poet: Characteristic Techniques of Style in Vergil's Aeneid* (Oxford: Clarendon, 1989) 63-99, 135-148.

dissimilarities between events.[99] Recent studies of Thucydides have found examples of analogous patterning of incidents and of play between narration and dialogue.[100] A recent treatment of the portrayal of Germanicus in Tacitus' *Annals* has drawn attention to a number of subtle literary techniques, including allusions to other episodes, and ironic play between speeches and their context.[101]

To conclude this section, implicit commentary in Acts seems to be another area where Luke's techniques overlap with those of classical writers; though, because the Old Testament has also possibly influenced Luke at this point, one cannot say more than this. It is worth mentioning that techniques of implicit commentary can be very effective, simply because the reader has to put some work into the interpretative process: the insights and interpretations that the reader gains by noting narrative patterns or comparing narration and dialogue, though they may be those intended by the writer, are in another sense, the reader's 'own work'. Because they involve the reader in the interpretative process, they can be particularly persuasive, more persuasive, perhaps, than an explicit interpretation or evaluation on the part of the writer (though, as noted above, these are not lacking in Acts either).[102]

III. Style

Classical rhetorical treatises have much to say on matters which may be loosely grouped under the heading 'Style'. Thus we find in Cicero's *de Oratore* discussion of the following topics: choice of words; metaphors; sentence structure and cadences; clausulae, rhythm, articulation of discourse, variation of short and long sentences; particular importance of sentence ends (3.37.148-51.198;

---

[99]H.R. Immerwahr, *Form and Thought in Herodotus* (Cleveland: American Philological Association, 1966) 148-237.
[100]W.R. Connor, *Thucydides* (Princeton: Princeton University Press, 1984) especially 231-6; C.W. Macleod, *Collected Essays* (ed. O. Taplin; Oxford: Oxford University Press, 1983) 52-122.
[101]C.B.R. Pelling, 'Tacitus and Germanicus' in Luce and Woodman (eds.), *Tacitus and the Tacitean Tradition*, 59-78.
[102]Cf. Connor's similar treatment of Thucydides, countering the view that Thucydides' general avoidance of explicit comment or evaluation is a sign of his objectivity: '. . .part of the technique is to draw the reader in, to awaken our critical and evaluative faculties, and to make the energy of our response contribute to the power of the text' (*Thucydides*, 17).

see also the summary list at 3.54.206-8 of numerous figures of speech, including uses of repetition, patterning, variation, antithesis, asyndeton, and differing groupings of words). The same writer's *Orator* adds to this list literary embellishments (39-40), the arrangement of words in a sentence, euphony, sentence symmetry, cadences (44-48), choice of words, the use of balanced clauses to end a sentence, the use of antithesis (49-51), the use of rhythmic effects, the use of periodic sentences as an effective way of creating a climax; and concludes by stating that artistry of this sort must be unobtrusive in order to be effective (52-68). Longinus, *On the Sublime* discusses many of the same topics: images; figures of speech; the use of short phrases; inversion of the expected order; accumulation, variation, climax; the importance of choosing the right word; the way in which a striking metaphor can form an effective climax; rhythm, pacing; the need to avoid fragmentation.

There are also discussions of the larger-scale aspects of style, for which we can again cite Cicero: *de Oratore* 3.25.96-26.103 notes that one's style must generally be elegant and pleasing, and must not contain too many grandiloquent or impassioned passages, as this tends to undermine the intended effect; *de Oratore* 3.53.202-5 notes numerous ways in which the texture of the discourse may be varied (asides, direct addressing of the audience, now dwelling on points, now passing on quickly, etc.); the more extended discussion of *Orator* 5.20-9.33; 21.69-31.112 distinguishes between three types of style: one which is full and rounded, one which is plain and vigorous, and a middle style which combines features of both the other two, each of which has its own rules, and each of which is particularly appropriate for certain sections of a speech.

Many other similar treatments could be referred to.[103] It is possible to use these sections of the treatises as a 'check-list' against which portions of Acts may be evaluated. Cadbury's chapters on 'The Common Language' and on 'Language and Style' bring together much material relevant to this section.[104] Among the features of Luke's style in Acts he notes are: Luke's knowledge of idiomatic

---

[103]See, for example: Quintilian, *Institutio Oratoria,* Book 8 on style and Book 9 on figures of thought and speech. Cicero's *Brutus* is an extended review of Roman orators from the beginnings of oratory at Rome down to Cicero's own day, in which many aspects of style are discussed (cf. also Marcus Aper's briefer and much less complimentary review in Tacitus, *Dialogus* 17-23). Cicero, *de Oratore* 2.13.54-15.64 discusses style specifically in relation to history-writing.
[104]*The Making of Luke-Acts,* 113-126 and 213-38.

Greek words and phrases; distinctive forms of emphasis (the repeated use of πᾶς and αὐτός); variations of style (on the whole, the further Luke's narrative takes him from Palestine, the fewer Semitic idioms he employs); the dramatic quality of Acts, especially evident in the way Luke can create suspense; the pathos of Paul's farewell in 20:17-38.

Morgenthaler has a similar study of Paul's speech in Athens (Acts 17:22-31) which he finds to display the following features also mentioned in the treatises: words paired together or grouped in threes; the use of key-words as a means of unifying the argument, especially the repeated use of the adjective πᾶς (vv. 22, 24, 25, 26, 30, 31); alliteration; hyperbaton; litotes; a number of sentences ending with recognised clausulae; he also notes a carefully-ordered periodic structure. As we noted above, Morgenthaler finds this carefully-constructed speech appropriate to its setting in one of the centres of rhetoric in the classical world.[105]

The question of appropriateness, which runs through the treatises, is important in comparative approaches of this sort.[106] It is not enough merely to point to features of style in Acts which are also listed in the treatises. One must also ask whether individual features are stylistically appropriate to a given passage. Decisions on this question will depend on the specifics of that passage and our view of the writer's purposes in that passage; and these are matters which by their very nature lie beyond the scope of the theoretical statements in the treatises (which are often, in fact, little more than lists of stylistic features).

The section following will analyse Peter's speech in Acts 3:12-26 and the whole of Acts 16 from the point of view of style. As well as drawing attention to details of style, the aim will be to assess the way in which these details are organised into an over-arching narrative or rhetorical 'economy'. Particular attention will be paid to what may be classified as 'verbal artistry' and 'variety of texture'. The different passages examined (a speech and a chapter which contains narrative summaries, more detailed scenes, and some dialogue) should give a fair sample of the various types of material in Acts.

---

[105]Morgenthaler, *op. cit.*, 331-4.

[106]Indeed, a good deal of what the treatises have to say on every topic relating to rhetoric could be summed up in the word 'appropriateness'.

Acts 3:11-26

The context of Peter's speech is dramatic: Peter and John have just healed a man lame from birth, and an amazed crowd has gathered around them (v. 11). Peter responds with an eloquent and emotionally-charged address.[107] Addressing his hearers as ἄνδρες Ἰσραηλῖται, an appropriate beginning for a speech which is to lay great weight on God's fulfilment of his promises to Israel (see vv. 25-6), he picks up the crowd's amazement with the words τί θαυμάζετε ἐπὶ τούτῳ (v. 12), suggesting that, properly understood, what has happened is not at all startling. The longer question following, ἢ ἡμῖν τί ἀτενίζετε ὡς ἰδίᾳ δυνάμει ἢ εὐσεβείᾳ πεποιηκόσιν τοῦ περιπατεῖν αὐτόν, makes it plain that the explanation for what has happened is not to be found in any powers or qualities possessed by Peter and John (note the emphatic position of ἡμῖν). This striking opening sentence (the phrase ὡς...πεποιηκόσιν, expanded by the word-pair ἰδίᾳ δυνάμει ἢ εὐσεβείᾳ, is particularly impressive) thus leads into the affirmation of verse 13. The opening words of this verse, ὁ θεὸς Ἀβραὰμ καὶ ὁ θεὸς Ἰσαὰκ καὶ ὁ θεὸς Ἰακώβ, ὁ θεὸς τῶν πατέρων ἡμῶν, with their massive emphasis, might seem to be introducing a statement that the God of Israel is the one who has healed the lame man, but instead introduce a specifically Christian element, ἐδόξασεν τὸν παῖδα αὐτοῦ Ἰησοῦν, which is developed until the end of verse 15. Verses 13b-15 repeatedly and forcefully stress that the crucifixion of Jesus was a wicked act for which those listening bear blame. Virtually every element in these verses underscores this point: the word-pair ὑμεῖς μὲν παρεδώκατε καὶ ἠρνήσασθε (v. 13); κρίναντος ἐκείνου ἀπολύειν (v. 13) making it plain that Pilate did not wish to crucify Jesus; τὸν ἅγιον καὶ δίκαιον ἠρνήσασθε (v. 14) another word-pair, further emphasising Jesus' innocence; καὶ ᾐτήσασθε ἄνδρα φονέα (v. 14) noting the guilt of the man whose release was requested; τὸν δὲ ἀρχηγὸν τῆς ζωῆς ἀπεκτείνατε (v. 15) a striking title which suggests that Jesus of all people did not deserve to die. The final mention of God raising Jesus from the dead, and of the witness of the apostles (v. 15b), picks up and explains the statement in verse 13 that God has glorified Jesus.

  Having returned to the theme of God's vindication of Jesus, Peter in verse 16 relates the lame man's healing to it. The construction

---

[107]Marshall comments that the address 'certainly catches the spirit of the occasion' (*Acts*, 90).

of verse 16 is awkward: the nouns which seem to be the subject of the main verbs in the sentence (ἐστερέωσεν τὸ ὄνομα, ἡ πίστις. . .ἔδωκεν) are also used in a clause which seems to indicate the basis on which these actions have taken place (ἐπὶ τῇ πίστει τοῦ ὀνόματος αὐτοῦ).[108] But however the sentence is to be taken, the double use of πίστις and ὄνομα, along with the triple use of αὐτοῦ, referring to Jesus (cf. v. 6), emphatically state that the man's healing is a sign of Jesus' vindication. The crowd know the state the man had been in (ὃν θεωρεῖτε καὶ οἴδατε), and now he has been healed before their eyes (ἀπέναντι πάντων ὑμῶν).

These verses are not, perhaps, particularly subtle or elegant: most of their force lies in the use of emotionally loaded language, and of lengthy sentences (vv. 12, 13, 14-5, and 16 are each one sentence) which heap up repetitive phrases. They do, however, lead convincingly into the subsequent appeal. A particularly effective feature is the way in which verse 16 directs the hearers' attention once again to the miraculously healed lame man from whom the speech took its starting-point.

The main appeal (whose beginning is marked by ἀδελφοί in v. 17) starts with two shorter and less weighty sentences (vv. 17 and 18), appropriate as Peter explains in more measured tones that his main purpose is not to condemn his hearers, but to proclaim that God's purposes were fulfilled in the death of Jesus. In verse 18 the unusual order, with the subject (ὁ δὲ θεός) and the main verb (ἐπλήρωσεν οὕτως) separated by a clause stating that God had foretold the sufferings of the Christ through the prophets, seems to throw emphasis both on what had been foretold and on the fact of its fulfilment. The rest of the speech is both an extended call to respond and a fuller statement of the theme of Jesus as the climax of God's plan of salvation. Its construction is ingenious and intricate.

Verses 19-21 form one long sentence, a huge eloquent appeal beginning with the command to repent (μετανοήσατε οὖν καὶ ἐπιστρέψατε), and followed by a chain of clauses: an offer of forgiveness of sins (v. 19b); the promise of times of refreshing and of the sending of the appointed Christ (v. 20); a statement that the Christ

---

[108]Some mss. omit ἐπί. See F.F. Bruce, *The Acts of the Apostles: the Greek Text with Introduction and Commentary* (3rd ed; Grand Rapids: Eerdmans, 1990) 142 for some possible solutions. Perhaps one could mark a break after ἐστερέωσεν and take ὁ θεός, the subject of the previous sentence, as the subject of this verb as well; but could ὄνομα and πίστις both be taken along with the singular ἔδωκεν?

must reign in heaven until the time for the restoration of all things as previously prophesied (v. 21). The notes sounded here (forgiveness, refreshing, restoration) are all positive.

The reference to the prophets at the end of verse 21 (picking up v. 18, and also the reference in v. 20 to Jesus as the one appointed by God) is now developed: Jesus is the prophet like Moses spoken of in Deuteronomy (vv. 22-23; cf. Dt. 18:15-20); further, all the Old Testament prophets foretold the events now taking place (v. 24). Note that as the Old Testament citation is extended through verse 23, it becomes a demand for obedience to the prophet. Verses 25-6 conclude by stating that those listening are the natural inheritors of the blessings foretold through the prophets, and of the covenant made to Abraham; and so they will be the first to be blessed through Jesus—if (a further implicit appeal) they turn from their wicked deeds.

One is struck by the inventiveness of this swift-moving address. The structure, as noted in the section on Speech Structure, is anomalous, and conveys a sense of spontaneity: statements of how God has raised Jesus from dead and of how this is in accordance with what was foretold are intermingled with condemnation of the wickedness of those who put Jesus to death and appeals to repent. Yet though the discourse seems simply to expand by an 'additive' process, one idea suggesting the next, there is a logic controlling the flow of ideas, and the themes introduced develop with each successive occurrence. Note particularly how the reference to God as the God of the patriarchs in verse 13 returns at the end of the address in the reference to the promise to Abraham (v. 25), but now with a distinctively Christian focus (v. 26): this double reference brackets and unifies the whole address. These verses give the impression of a writer in control of his material.

Acts 16

A similar picture emerges from a consideration of Acts 16, in which Luke skilfully varies summary, sometimes extremely brief, with more detailed narration of selected incidents.

Verses 1-5 look back as well as forward: verses 1-3 introduce Timothy, who is to accompany Paul on the journeys described in chapter 16; at the same time his circumcision is linked to the debate in chapter 15 about how far Gentile converts are to be made to observe the law of Moses. Paul, who has argued in chapter 15 that Gentile converts should not be circumcised (15:2, 12), here has Timothy circumcised in order to avoid causing offence to Jewish believers, in the spirit of the Jerusalem decree (15:24-9, esp. 28-9). Verses 4-5 note how Paul and those with him made this decree known in many cities and strengthened the churches in those cities. Both the detailed incident of verses 1-3 and the summary of verses 4-5 show Paul acting as directed by the Jerusalem apostles (15:25-7).

In a similar way, verses 6-8 briefly summarise a considerable journey, twice noting (without giving details) that Paul and those with him were prevented by the Spirit from evangelising;[109] these two comments prepare for the decisive incident described in verses 9-10, in which Paul sees a Macedonian man in a vision imploring him, in words of dramatic brevity, to come to Macedonia: διαβὰς εἰς Μακεδονίαν βοήθησον ἡμῖν (v. 9). The negative leading is followed by the positive (v. 10)

In verses 11-12 Paul and those with him arrive in Philippi, which Luke carefully marks out as a Macedonian city (v. 12), making it plain that they are following the leading of the vision. The narrative then focuses on the conversion of Lydia (vv. 13-15): the reference to the Lord 'opening her heart to respond to Paul's words' (v. 14), as well as continuing the theme of God taking the lead in this new evangelistic venture, seem to mark her out as the first convert. Events move quickly in these verses: no sooner is Lydia introduced than she is responding to Paul's words (v. 14) and being baptised, along with her household (v. 15). Her offer of hospitality verse 15, the only words she says, mark her out as committed to God and to the spreading of the message of Christ. Note how her words contain a reference to the Lord (πιστὴν τῷ κυρίῳ) which picks up verse 14 (ἧς ὁ κύριος διήνοιξεν τὴν καρδίαν), suggesting that what she does is a response to the Lord who has intervened in her life. Luke can cover events efficiently, conveying much with a few words.

The narrative now broadens out to deal with the central incident of Luke's account, the arrest of Paul and Silas and the conversion of the Philippian gaoler (vv. 16-34). Paul, increasingly irritated by the girl with a prophetic spirit who follows him around, commands the spirit to leave her (ἐξελθεῖν ἀπ᾽ αὐτῆς), which it does (ἐξῆλθεν) (v. 18). The girl's owners, far from being impressed by this

---

[109]Note the varied phraseology: κωλυθέντες ὑπὸ τοῦ ἁγίου πνεύματος (v. 6) καὶ οὐκ εἴασεν αὐτοὺς τὸ πνεῦμα Ἰησοῦ (v. 7).

sign of God's power, note only that their hope of income has also departed (ἐξῆλθεν, v. 19, the repetition of the verb emphasising the difference of perception). Their words to the magistrates, as noted previously, are full of (hypocritical) civic self-righteousness.[110] The crowd joins in the protest, Paul and Silas are flogged, and then they are handed over to the gaoler, who carefully carries out his charge to 'guard them safely' (ἀσφαλῶς τηρεῖν αὐτούς, v. 23, picked up by τοὺς πόδας ἠσφαλίσατο, v. 24). God's power, at work in the earlier part of this chapter and in the casting out of the spirit from the girl, seems temporarily absent; but this merely prepares for the startling reversal to come.

Paul and Silas are praying and singing, a scene vividly evoked by the description of the other prisoners listening to them (v. 25), when there is a sudden earthquake which brings about an immediate and total reversal of the situation, an idea underscored by many of the words and phrases used (v. 26): ἄφνω δὲ σεισμὸς; μέγας, ὥστε σαλευθῆναι τὰ θεμέλια; παραχρῆμα; αἱ θύραι πᾶσαι καὶ πάντων τὰ δεσμὰ (note the chiasmus which throws emphasis on πᾶσαι, πάντων). Startled from sleep, the gaoler sees the doors are open, draws his sword, and is about to kill himself (v. 27: the three participles γενόμενος, ἰδών, and σπασάμενος throw the emphasis on the main verb ἤμελλεν ἑαυτὸν ἀναιρεῖν, on which the narrative then lingers with the explanatory participial phrase νομίζων ἐκπεφευγέναι τοὺς δεσμίους). Paul's shout halts him (v. 28), and the gaoler, recognising his authority, casts himself trembling at Paul and Silas' feet (v. 29).

The description of the gaoler's conversion and that of his household is in some ways similar to that of Lydia earlier in the chapter, but it is a longer and more dramatic presentation (note the stark question and response of vv. 30-31). Luke emphasises the gaoler's change of attitude: he washes Paul and Silas' weals, even though it is the middle of the night, and only then are he and his household baptised (v. 33); he offers Paul and Silas hospitality and rejoices in his new-found faith, along with his household (v. 34). This is a striking and moving climax to the account.

The concluding verses (35-40) further underline the authority of Paul and Silas, and also make it clear that they had been arbitrarily and wrongfully arrested. The magistrates, seemingly having decided that there is no reason to detain them, send a brief order for their

---

[110]Their last words ('Ρωμαίοις οὖσιν, v. 21) prepare for Paul's subsequent insistence on being treated as a Roman citizen should be (v. 37).

release (ἀπόλυσον τοὺς ἀνθρώπους ἐκείνους, v. 35). The gaoler substantially repeats this in v. 36, adding (by a fine touch of characterisation) the more friendly words νῦν οὖν ἐξελθόντες πορεύεσθε ἐν εἰρήνῃ. Paul rejects this order, to which the repetition has drawn our attention, in the most rhetorically imposing spoken words in the whole chapter (v. 37): note the heaping-up of words and phrases which describe the indignity and illegality of the treatment to which Paul and Silas have been subjected (δείραντες ἡμᾶς δημοσίᾳ ἀκατακρίτους, ἀνθρώπους Ῥωμαίους ὑπάρχοντας, ἔβαλαν εἰς φυλακὴν); the scornful question in which νῦν and λάθρᾳ (contrasted with δημοσίᾳ) point out how differently the magistrates are now behaving; and the rejection of the proposal by the emphatic words οὐ γάρ, ἀλλὰ and the demand that the leaders should come and take them out of custody personally (αὐτοί). The magistrates, now fearful, duly come and lead them out of the prison (vv. 38-9), and the narrative of events in Philippi comes to a close with Paul and his companions firmly in control, encouraging the believers (v. 40).

In this chapter again, we can note the carefully-observed proportions of the narrative, the way in which Luke skilfully builds towards the concluding scenes, and the use of vivid, powerful language at key moments. Examples of verbal artistry, for example, word-play and effective sentence-structure, were also noted. A narrative such as Acts 16, which includes a number of diverse episodes, could easily have become fragmented: that it has not testifies to Luke's skill as a narrator, and shows the extent to which his narrative, here as elsewhere in Acts, conforms to classical requirements concerning style.

IV. Conclusions

1. Persuasive Qualities of Acts

Rhetoric, as has been noted previously, and as the rhetorical treatises constantly stress, is not a matter of mere surface decoration, but of persuasion.[111] The previous discussion has often drawn attention to the persuasive qualities of Luke's discourse, but some aspects of the

---

[111]This point is emphasised by W. Wuellner, 'Where is Rhetorical Criticism Taking Us?' (*CBQ* 49 [1987] 448-63).

topic remain to be dealt with. How, then, does Luke seek to persuade his readers of the things of which he speaks?

Overt Persuasion. In some parts of Acts the persuasive intent is overt. The speeches again and again set out in powerful and dramatic language a clear view of Jesus as the promised Christ, raised from the dead and thus vindicated by God, as foretold in the Scriptures. Luke generally underscores these presentations by noting the responses, both positive and negative, and leaves the reader in little doubt as to what is in his view the proper response to the message of Christ.

No less clear are the recurring summaries (see the discussion of Arrangement above) which trace the spread of the gospel. Luke presents the gospel as spreading irresistibly further and further afield, with God guiding the believers through every successive stage. We have also noted a number of explicit evaluative or interpretative comments (10:2; 11:24; 12:23; 13:48; 16:14; 17:11); sometimes a brief phrase is enough to influence our reading of a section of narrative (for example, the description of Gamaliel in 5:34 as a 'teacher of the law held in honour by the people', or the description of Sergius Paulus in 13:7 as a 'discerning man').

Covert Persuasion. There are, however, other means of persuasion, less obvious, and for that reason perhaps more effective. Quintilian, for example, more than once states, in a variety of connections, that it is better not to be seen to be using techniques of persuasion.[112] All the varieties of implicit commentary noted above come into the category of covert persuasion. One could, indeed, also cite most of the features discussed under choice of material and arrangement: Luke at all points gives the impression of being well in control of his material, and this supports his claim to be giving an authoritative account of the early church.[113]

Luke's portrayal of the apostles and the believers gives implicit support to his presentation of the message of Christ in the speeches: they are obedient to God (4:19; 5:29; 9:10-17; 26:19-20); responsive to God's leading (8:26; 11:17; 13:2-3; 16:9-10; 19:21); eager to seize any opportunity to preach Christ that presents itself (3:11-26; 7:1-53; 8:4-6, 27-40; 17:16-31; 18:9-11; 19:8-10; 26:27-9; 28:17-22); willing to endure

---

[112]*Institutio Oratoria* 4.1.57; 4.2.58-9; 4.5.5; 9.4.147.
[113]See S.M. Sheeley, *Narrative Asides in Luke-Acts* (JSNTS 72; Sheffield: JSOT Press, 1992) for a treatment of the narrative asides as contributing to our impression of Luke as a reliable narrator.

opposition, physical violence, imprisonment and death (4:18-21; 5:41-2; 7:54-60; 12:1-5; 14:10-20; 16:22-6; 20:22-4). Those who oppose them often emerge in a less favourable light: as trying to suppress the message of Christ because it threatens their own interests (4:15-21; 5:27-28, 40; 16:16-21; 19:23-7); as misguided (21:27-9), ridiculous (19:28-34) and irrationally opposed to the gospel (5:33; 6:10-11; 7:54; 9:1); as devious (23:12-15; 25:1-3) and law-breakers (13:50-52; 19:23-40).[114]

Treatment of Opposing Viewpoints. Luke, however, does not present an over-simplified picture of responses to the gospel. He at least twice notes that people who accept the gospel are capable of duplicity or self-seeking (5:1-11; 8:18-24). And on the other hand there are those who, while not accepting the gospel, urge caution (5:34-9) or restraint (19:35-40), hover on the verge of commitment (17:32; 24:22-26, though v. 26 portrays Felix's motives as at least mixed; 26:28), or at least do not offer violence (28:25). As noted in the discussion of Narration and Dialogue, Acts contains a number of different voices, and thereby gains in depth, complexity, and plausibility.[115]

Luke also appears to anticipate possible counter-arguments: for example, that Jesus' death argues against his being the Christ; or that the rejection of the message of Jesus by many Jews invalidates it. Old Testament citations and allusions are repeatedly used to suggest that both Jesus' death and his rejection by many Jews were foretold in Scripture.[116] As noted in the discussion of choice of material, this might also serve to answer the objection that Christianity was a religious 'novelty'.

It is true that the opponents of the gospel do not in general speak at length in Acts: the longest such speech is that of Tertullus in 24:2-8, which is not much to set against the twenty or so sermons and speeches by Christians, many of them much longer than seven verses.[117] Further, as noted above, such opponents are often

---

[114]Other references were noted above, under Choice of Material.

[115]In a similar way, Luke is on occasions prepared to allow that there were disagreements or tensions among the believers (Acts 6:1; 11:1-3; 15:1-5; 15:36-41; 21:20-21).

[116]This could be treated as an example of interpreting written evidence differently from one's opponents; see Cicero, *de Oratore* 2.26.110.

[117]In contrast, opposing pairs of speeches are a recurring feature of classical epic and historiography: see, for example, Homer, *Iliad* 9; Thucydides, 1.66-88; 5.85-113.

presented unfavourably. Yet the objections which are at various points made are not straw men. Rather, they identify serious issues, and attempt to answer objections which we can imagine would have been raised against preaching such as we find in Acts: that it encouraged transgression of the Old Testament law (6:13-14; 18:12-13; 21:18; the debates in chs. 11 and 15 also deal with this question); and that it encouraged sedition (16:19-21; 17:6-7; 24:5-8).

Mack distinguishes between discourses which live in a world of their own, and those which genuinely engage with different viewpoints.[118] On the basis of the above considerations, Acts appears to belong to the latter category: it focuses on serious objections to the gospel (the death of Jesus, the rejection of Jesus by many Jews, the charge of breaking Old Testament law, the charge of sedition, and the linked charge of religious 'novelty'), and presents carefully thought-out answers.

2. Luke's Indebtedness to Classical Rhetoric

This chapter has examined many aspects of Luke's literary techniques in Acts, and shown that there is a large overlap between them and those of classical literature. At point after point Acts can be shown to operate according to conventions similar to those outlined in classical rhetorical treatises. There are some aspects which it is hard to explain other than by concluding that Luke was aware of rhetorical conventions: the preface; the layout of some of the speeches; and the presentation of legal proceedings in chapters 24-26.[119] The preface, in particular, seems to make an implicit claim to be operating within classical conventions.[120] That is not to say that other influences have not been at work. The Old Testament has obviously exerted considerable influence on Acts; and this may have extended to narrative techniques (as noted in the section on Implicit Commentary). Yet even in this case classical parallels can also be adduced. In general it seems fair to speak of a considerable indebtedness to classical rhetoric; that is, he gives clear indication of having received the kind of (rhetorical) education one would expect in a Graeco-Roman writer of this period who embarked on a work of

---

118*Rhetoric and the New Testament*, 96.
119See Winter's chapter in the present volume.
120See Palmer's chapter in the present volume.

this sort. Luke, however, is not a slave to classical conventions: it is hard, for example, to see Cicero or Quintilian approving of his frequent citations of the Old Testament as a testimony in the speeches. This, rather than indicating incompetence in Luke, suggests Luke's freedom in regard to the conventions in which he had been educated, which implies a considerable mastery of those conventions.

A study such as this also provides insight into how Acts might have been read by one with some rhetorical education.[121] Such a person might have been alert to the importance of speeches in the structure of the narrative, and to techniques of implicit commentary (one result of this study is to show that 'modern literary' approaches to Acts, such as those discussed in Spencer's chapter have a venerable pedigree). He/she might have appreciated the artistry of certain sections, and the generally clear arrangement. Though a positive response to Acts depends on much more than appreciation of literary skill, such a reader might have been impressed by the care with which Luke presents his account, and the seriousness with which he takes possible objections.

This chapter necessarily leaves some questions unanswered. It has not sought to determine the genre of Acts, nor to answer the linked question of its social register. However, a consideration of Acts against the background of classical rhetoric leads us to the heart of the book, uncovering Luke's literary techniques, helping us to see what his purposes were in writing, and demonstrating how effectively he carried out those purposes; and this, to use a litotes similar to those which periodically occur throughout Acts, is a not inconsiderable gain.

---

[121]This does not necessarily imply that Acts would only have been accessible to such people. See F.G. Downing, 'A Bas les Aristos: the Relevance of Higher Literature for the Understanding of the Earliest Christian Writings' (*NovT* 30 [1988] 210-30) who argues for the presence in the Graeco-Roman world of 'a very pervasive oral culture sharing much common content with the refined literature of the aristocracy'.

CHAPTER 13

ACTS AND MODERN LITERARY APPROACHES

F. Scott Spencer

Summary

This chapter examines recent literary approaches to Acts (typically as a constituent of Luke-Acts), charting the moves from redaction criticism to composition criticism to narrative-critical and reader-response methods dependent on secular literary theory. Particular attention is paid to the place of traditional historical analysis within these newer literary studies. This survey demonstrates that modern literary investigations of Acts typically maintain some interest in the book's ancient historical and cultural setting, while at the same time they promote a significant shift in interpretive focus from author and event (major concerns of historical criticism) to text and reader.

The 1970s and 1980s have witnessed an explosion of interest in literary investigations of the Bible in general (both Old and New Testaments) and the book of Acts in particular (typically as a constituent of Luke-Acts). A recent bibliographic survey[1] catalogues

---

[1]M.A. Powell, C.G. Gray and M.C. Curtis (eds.), *The Bible and Modern Literary Criticism: A Critical Assessment and Annotated Bibliography* (Bibliographies and

close to 1,000 modern literary-critical studies of the Bible up to 1992, and the trend towards such publications promises to continue and even accelerate towards the turn of the century.[2]

At first glance, the impact of this new literary movement may appear minimal, easily assimilated within the established historical-critical paradigm governing biblical scholarship. Since the Enlightenment, 'scientific' criticism of ancient sacred texts has consistently utilised literary analysis in conjunction with historical inquiry. Any competent historical critic interpreting a book like Acts attends to literary matters of structure, sources, themes, motifs, poetic devices, and so on; and likewise, virtually all modern literary critics of the Bible still read their texts in the original languages of Hebrew, Aramaic and Greek and realise they are examining ancient Mediterranean documents from no later than the second century A.D. and not yesterday's news or a best-selling novel.

Still, whatever the apparent fit between literary and historical approaches to biblical interpretation, in fact the relationship between these methods has become increasingly uncertain, uneasy and at times antagonistic. At the extremes, some literary enthusiasts in the biblical guild give the impression of crusading for a total paradigm shift away from supposedly defunct historical methods, while certain historical-critical stalwarts seem to dismiss the current preoccupation with literary theory—particularly that derived from secular critics— as a passing fad and needless distraction.

Of course there is plenty of room between these poles for more balanced and nuanced assessments of the biblical-critical landscape. For example, literary-oriented interpreters might (a) bracket out external, historical information when focusing on the final form of a particular narrative without necessarily debunking such information as irrelevant or misleading; (b) modify or challenge a standard historical reading of a specific text—but, again, without impugning the value of all historical exegesis; or (c) incorporate selected dimensions of historical analysis into an eclectic 'interdisciplinary' model of interpretation. In short, modern literary study of the Bible

---

Indexes in Religious Studies 22; New York/Westport, CT/London: Greenwood, 1993).
[2]E.g. three presses have recently launched new commentary series which will utilise newer literary methods: Crossroad, ('Readings the New Testament Series'); Sheffield Academic Press ('Readings: A New Biblical Commentary'); and Polebridge ('The Narrative New Testament Series').

can supplement historical criticism in various ways without supplanting it.

The purpose of this final chapter is to map recent trends in the literary criticism of Acts with a particular eye on the ways in which such criticism both complements and challenges historical approaches to Acts as a first-century historical narrative. No attempt will be made to provide an exhaustive survey of modern literary-critical scholarship on Acts. The focus will be limited to major works: mainly, commentaries, volumes of collected essays, and monographs treating significant portions of Acts.[3]

I. Shifting Sands[4]

The post-war era was marked by a decisive methodological shift in biblical scholarship toward 'redaction-historical' (*redaktions-geschichtlich*) or simply 'redaction' criticism. This new critical tool proved to be especially useful in the study of Luke-Acts by leading German scholars such as Hans Conzelmann, Ernst Haenchen and Ernst Käsemann.[5] These interpreters began to appreciate that the literary achievement of the writer of Luke and Acts ('Luke') involved more than a 'scissors-and-paste' compilation of discrete written sources and oral units of tradition. Rather they viewed Luke as a creative author, a hands-on *redactor* freely adapting, supplementing and arranging received materials into an overarching narrative vehicle for his theological agenda. In this approach, the critic's main task was to uncover this theological purpose (*Tendenz*) by isolating the ideas and motives behind Luke's editorial operations on his sources or, in other words, by separating redaction and tradition. In the case of the Third Gospel this demanded a close examination of Lukan alterations of Mark and the hypothetical sayings source (Q) shared with Matthew. With regard to Acts where synoptic material is

---

[3]For a survey of key articles on Luke-Acts in periodicals, see Powell, Gray and Curtis (eds.), *Bible and Modern Literary Criticism*, 308-24.

[4]Title taken from C.H. Talbert, 'Shifting Sands: The Recent Study of the Gospel of Luke', *Int* 30 (1976) 381-95. I have previously discussed some of the material in this section in F.S. Spencer, *The Portrait of Philip in Acts: A Study of Roles and Relations* (JSNT Sup 67; Sheffield: Sheffield Academic Press, 1992) 18-22.

[5]See the overview of Lukan studies in W.C. van Unnik, 'Luke-Acts: A Storm Center in Contemporary Scholarship', in L.E. Keck and J.L. Martyn (eds.), *Studies in Luke-Acts* (Nashville: Abingdon, 1966; reprinted, London: SPCK, 1976) 15-32.

lacking, underlying sources were hypothesised and redactional interests pinpointed on the basis of perceived 'breaks' or 'seams' in the text and comparisons with other sketches of early Christian history and theology drawn chiefly from Paul's letters (presumed to be more reliable than Acts).

Although the focus had extended beyond individual pericopes to the whole of Luke's two-volume work, the basic aim of German redaction criticism remained consistent with form-critical concerns: to peer *through* the window (or *behind* the curtain) of the Lukan text to glimpse the social and historical situation(s) (*Sitz im Leben*) which produced it. As for the situation prompting Luke to write a sequel to his Gospel, there was basic agreement that the delay of Christ's parousia (*Parousieversörgerung*) played a critical role. It was thought that in some way the book of Acts reflected Luke's explanation of the church's continued existence in the world a generation beyond the ministry of Jesus. Conzelmann credited Luke with devising a comprehensive scheme of salvation history (*Heilsgeschichte*) comprised of three successive, distinct epochs: the bygone age of Israel up through John the Baptist, the 'centre of time' during the ministry of Jesus, and the current period of the church stretching from Jesus' ascension to his parousia at some indefinite future point. This final stage, in which the book of Acts falls, is marked by increased temptation and persecution of Jesus' followers, demanding the virtue of patient endurance.[6] Haenchen laid more stress on Luke's interests in the ongoing kerygmatic and apologetic mission of the church in the era following Jesus' departure. In Acts the church maintains ties with the ministry of Jesus by proclaiming the 'Word of God' (= the message of the Lukan Jesus) throughout the Roman empire and guarantees its survival by proving not to be a political threat to Roman authorities.[7] Käsemann exposed Luke's overriding ecclesiastical agenda in which 'the church itself more and more becomes the content of theology'.[8] Specifically, Käsemann viewed Acts as a sample of 'early Catholicism' (*Frühkatholizismus*) similar to

---

[6]H. Conzelmann, *The Theology of St. Luke* (London: Faber & Faber, 1960; reprinted, London: SCM, 1982) 9-17.
[7]E. Haenchen, *The Acts of the Apostles: A Commentary* (Philadelphia: Westminster, 1971) 90-110; *idem*, 'The Book of Acts as Source Material for the History of Early Christianity', in L.E. Keck and J.L. Martyn (eds.), *Studies in Luke-Acts* (Nashville: Abingdon, 1966; reprinted, London: SPCK, 1976) 258-78.
[8]E. Käsemann, 'Ephesians and Acts', in L.E. Keck and J.L. Martyn (eds.), *Studies in Luke-Acts* (Nashville: Abingdon, 1966; reprinted, London: SPCK, 1976) 290.

that found in Ephesians and the Pastorals, in which the unity and purity of the developing church was safeguarded by institutionalised succession to apostolic office (*una sancta apostolica*) and preservation of apostolic doctrine.[9]

Although a number of their interpretive conclusions have been challenged, these groundbreaking studies remain starting-points for many Lukan scholars who continue to utilise redaction-critical methodology. In the 1970s, however, a small but significant group of biblical critics, mostly from North America, began to question certain aspects of redactional analysis from a literary standpoint. Lukan scholars within this movement perceived several problems with standard redaction-critical practice:[10]

1. Lukan deviations from sources such as Mark may not be as ideologically motivated as redaction critics tend to think. Editorial changes may reflect simply linguistic and stylistic preferences and have more to do with Luke as literary artist than tendentious theologian.

2. Redaction criticism tends to ignore the significance of received materials which Luke incorporates *unchanged* into his narrative. In appropriating certain traditions, Luke adopts them as his own and fits them into his overall presentation. Hence, they may be just as revealing of Luke's theological interests as revised materials.

3. Identifying the sources which Luke has supposedly redacted is a speculative enterprise. The dominant two-source model based on Mark and Q has been vigorously challenged by proponents of alternative paradigms and remains at best a working *hypothesis*, not an assured result of Gospel analysis.[11] Even less assured are reconstructions of the sources behind Acts, given the absence of other contemporary narratives of apostolic acts with which to compare and contrast Luke's account.

4. Luke's competence as a literary craftsman argues in favour of his close weaving of tradition and redaction into a seamless whole. Thus

---

[9]Käsemann, 'Ephesians and Acts', 288-97; *idem*, 'Paul and Early Catholicism', *New Testament Questions of Today* (Philadelphia: Fortress, 1969) 236-51; *idem*, 'The Problem of the Historical Jesus', *Essays on New Testament Themes* (London: SCM, 1964; reprinted, Philadelphia: Fortress, 1982) 28-9.
[10]See Talbert, 'Shifting Sands', 392-95.
[11]See e.g., M.D. Goulder, *Luke: A New Paradigm* (2 vols.; JSNT Sup 20; Sheffield: Sheffield Academic Press, 1989).

the effort of redaction critics to unravel this tapestry seems largely an exercise in futility at odds with Luke's compositional purpose.

5. For all their insistence on viewing Luke-Acts as a literary whole, redaction critics' continuing preoccupation with backstage historical developments deflects the focus away from the final (canonical) presentation of the Lukan text. As long as the text is treated primarily as a window into areas of interest outside the text, important dimensions of the Lukan message will remain uncharted.

6. The quest for a single, overarching theological scheme—such as 'redemptive history' or 'early Catholicism'—controlling Lukan redaction runs the risk of reducing Luke's message to a monotone and muffling the symphony of multiple literary themes and patterns echoing throughout Luke's work.

In the face of these concerns, some Lukan interpreters began to advocate a modified form of redaction criticism in which the emphasis on Luke's shaping of his total narrative was maximised and the attention to Luke's revising of various putative sources was minimised. The emerging new method, which some have dubbed 'composition criticism',[12] remained oriented toward elucidating Luke's theological message in the classic areas of soteriology, christology, eschatology and ecclesiology, but sought to find these ideas exclusively within the close-knit framework of Luke's final composition. External materials were still consulted for broad comparative purposes but not to determine Luke's sources or decipher the editorial process leading up to the finished narrative product. In this approach, the finished product of Luke-Acts was judged to be its own best commentary.

Charles Talbert, a keen inside analyst of contemporary Lukan scholarship, singles out a series of lectures by Paul Minear in 1974 as a key turning-point away from established redactional approaches to Luke-Acts.[13] In these lectures, later published under the title, *To Heal and Reveal: The Prophetic Vocation according to Luke*,[14] Minear clearly set forth the distinctives of his method of interpreting Luke-Acts:

---

[12]See R.F. O'Toole, *The Unity of Luke's Theology: An Analysis of Luke-Acts* (Good News Studies 9; Wilmington, DE: Michael Glazier, 1984) 11-14; S.D. Moore, *Literary Criticism and the Gospels: The Theoretical Challenge* (New Haven/London: Yale University, 1989) 4-7.

[13]Talbert, review of J.A. Fitzmyer, *The Gospel according to Luke (X-XXIV)*, *CBQ* 48 (1986) 337.

[14]New York: Seabury, 1976.

> A comparative study of this kind (using Mark and Q) has many merits, but I believe that in his own mind when Luke was writing the Gospel he was not so much revising earlier documents to conform to his own theological notions as composing the first of two volumes which would be read together by the same readers. The interdependence of these two volumes is such that the purposes of volume one can be most clearly discerned by observing the contents and sequences of volume two.[15]

Actually, Minear argued for this perspective several years earlier in an essay on the Lukan birth narratives appearing in an important collection of Lukan studies which also included contributions from Conzelmann, Haenchen and Käsemann.[16]

Resisting the tendency to read the birth stories in Luke 1-2 as a patchwork of traditional materials prefixed to the beginning of Luke's corpus with little relation to what follows, Minear traced a number of terms, motifs, and literary patterns within these narratives which in fact bear a heavy Lukan imprint and set the stage for Luke's entire work. He particularly took Conzelmann to task for lopping off the nativity narratives as inauthentic due to their contradiction of Luke's alleged periodisation of salvation history. For example, the obvious parallels between the ministries of John the Baptist and Jesus forecast in the stories surrounding their births do not fit the Lukan program, which Conzelmann derived from Luke 16:16, of strictly separating these two figures and their participation in God's kingdom (John is excluded from this realm; Jesus is central). In Conzelmann's opinion, this clash with Luke 16:16 was reason enough to discount the birth narratives. In Minear's view, however, the problem was not with the alien character of Luke's birth stories but with Conzelmann's faulty schema based on a forced reading of a single text: 'It must be said that rarely has a scholar placed so much weight on so dubious an interpretation of so difficult a logion (16:16)'.[17] Minear also thought that other isolated units which Luke added to Mark, even down to terms and phrases such as 'today' (σήμερον) in Luke 4:21 and 'but now' (ἀλλὰ νῦν) in 22:36, played a disproportionately pivotal role in Conzelmann's analysis, leading to a distorted understanding of Lukan theology. A clearer view of Luke's message would result from less 'exaggeration, particularization, and

---

[15]Minear, *To Heal*, 83.
[16]Minear, 'Luke's Use of the Birth Stories', in L.E. Keck and J.L. Martyn (eds.), *Studies in Luke-Acts* (Nashville: Abingdon, 1966; reprinted, London: SPCK, 1976) 111-30.
[17]*Ibid.*, 122.

schematization' of selected Lukan elements and more careful attention to the 'subtle sense in which each prophetic message (including those in the birth narratives) opens the way to the *whole* sequence of events which follows, each message a programmatic announcement of God's *whole* design' (emphasis added).[18]

Although Talbert rightly points to Minear as a catalyst of the literary-holistic 'new look' in Lukan studies, Talbert himself has been the more prolific and influential pioneer in this direction.[19] In the same year as Minear's lectures, Talbert published *Literary Patterns, Theological Themes, and the Genre of Luke-Acts*[20] and inaugurated his role as chairman of the newly established Luke-Acts Seminar in the Society of Biblical Literature.[21] In his monograph, while Talbert continued to employ redaction criticism based on the two-source hypothesis to verify distinctive Lukan emphases, he sought to balance this approach with a technique called 'architecture analysis', in which the

> primary concern. . .is to detect the formal patterns, rhythms, architectonic designs, or architecture of a writing. That is, this approach is concerned with style insofar as it shapes the final product by the arrangement of the larger units of material, especially the whole.[22]

Among the large structural patterns delineated by Talbert were numerous parallels between the Peter and Paul sections of Acts in chapters 1-12 and 13-28 respectively, elaborate chiastic arrangements of the material in Luke 10:21-18:30 and Acts 15:1-21:26, and extensive intervolume links between portions of Luke and Acts, such as those between Luke 9, 24 and Acts 1.

This exposure of intricate stylistic designs shaping the whole of Luke-Acts had been attempted by other scholars before Talbert,

---

[18]*Ibid.*, 125.

[19]See M.C. Parsons and J.B. Tyson (eds.), *Cadbury, Knox, and Talbert: American Contributions to the Study of Acts* (SBL Biblical Scholarship in North America 18; Atlanta: Scholars, 1992) 131-251.

[20]SBLMS 20; Missoula, MT: Scholars, 1974.

[21]Many of this seminar's studies over the ensuing decade reflected Talbert's concerns. See the published findings in two collections edited by Talbert: *Perspectives on Luke-Acts* (Danville, VA: Association of Baptist Professors of Religion; Edinburgh: T. & T. Clark, 1978), *Luke-Acts: New Perspectives from the Society of Biblical Literature Seminar* (New York: Crossroad, 1984).

[22]Talbert, *Literary Patterns*, 7.

notably Henry Cadbury[23] and Martin Dibelius,[24] on a limited basis, and Robert Morgenthaler[25] and Michael Goulder,[26] on a larger scale. What distinguished Talbert's work from the latter two scholars, however, was 'their failure to use comparative materials from the wider Mediterranean world of Luke's time'.[27] By contrast, Talbert associated his method of architecture analysis with the work of classical scholars in interpreting the writings of Homer, Herodotus and Vergil. Moreover, Talbert blended his architectural approach with 'genre criticism', which aimed to correlate Luke's patterning techniques with the formal characteristics of a certain type of literature in Mediterranean antiquity. Talbert found his analogue in ancient biographical accounts of philosophers, exemplified in such works as Diogenes Laertius' *Lives*. These works followed the typical pattern of, first, recounting the life of an eminent founder of a philosophical movement and, then, demonstrating how the founder's teachings and practices were perpetuated and legitimated by a group of faithful successors. As for the Lukan corpus, the Gospel portrayed the life of the church's religious founder, Jesus, and Acts depicted the *parallel* lives and ministries of Jesus' 'true' followers.

From this venture in genre criticism informed by architecture analysis, Talbert moved back finally to familiar redaction-critical ground to clarify the historical occasion which produced Luke-Acts. Why did Luke write a carefully designed, multi-paralleled, two-volume work in the framework of an ancient biography?

> . . .the Lucan writings have their *Sitz im Leben* in the struggle against heresy. Their *function* is to present the authentically Christian picture of Jesus and of Christian faith just as Laertius intended to present the true way of the various successions.[28]

In later commentaries on Luke (1982) and Acts (1984),[29] Talbert continued to exhibit a strong interest in broad *literary* patterns pertaining to style and structure, a variety of *theological* themes related to the dominant motive of legitimation, and *historical* ties to

---

[23]*The Making of Luke-Acts* (London: Macmillan, 1927).
[24]H. Greeven (ed.), *Studies in the Acts of the Apostles* (London: SCM, 1956).
[25]*Die lukanische Geschichtsschreibung als Zeugnis: Gestalt und Gehalt der Kunst des Lukas* (2 vols.; ATANT 14-15; Zürich: Zwingli, 1949).
[26]*Type and History in Acts* (London: A. & C. Black, 1964).
[27]Talbert, *Literary Patterns*, 3.
[28]*Ibid.*, 130.
[29]Talbert, *Reading Luke: A Literary and Theological Commentary on the Third Gospel* (New York: Crossroad, 1982); *Acts* (Knox Preaching Guides; Atlanta: John Knox, 1984).

the wider milieu of ancient Mediterranean culture. These studies also marked a notable change in Talbert's method: he now explicitly jettisoned all source-dependent redactional analysis (based on the two-source or any other theory) as unnecessary baggage. Luke and Acts were deemed to be the primary sources for interpreting each other and the two-volume work as a whole.

Outside Luke-Acts, Talbert persisted in casting his net widely for illuminating parallels from ancient Graeco-Roman, Jewish and Christian literature (one reviewer counted 29 references to 15 ancient extracanonical sources in the first 11 pages of *Reading Luke!*),[30] but he stopped short of tracing any *direct* appropriation of these materials by Luke. At this point Talbert's work resembles various 'rhetorical' analyses of Acts, in particular, which examine Luke's handling of ancient literary conventions—rather than his redacting of specific documentary sources—in the composition of speeches, conversion accounts, 'we'-sections, seafaring tales and other units of discourse.[31]

Obviously, the shift away from redaction criticism outlined thus far toward a more comprehensive, holistic literary reading of the final form of Luke's two-volume work has *not* been accompanied by a radical departure from redaction criticism's basic theological and historical orientation. The concern to interpret Luke's writings within their first-century religious and cultural environment remains paramount for New Testament literary critics like Talbert.

But Talbert's is not the only literary approach to Luke-Acts in recent years challenging the venerable paradigm of Conzelmann, Haenchen and Käsemann. Beginning in the late 1970s and gathering steam in the 1980s and 90s has been a trend toward applying modern, secular literary theory to the practice of biblical interpretation. Despite his claim to be 'heavily influenced by nonbiblical literary criticism',[32] Talbert makes virtually no reference to secular literary critics or their theories; his main partners in dialogue remain traditional Lukan scholars.[33] Other biblical interpreters, however,

---

[30]Parsons, 'Reading Talbert: New Perspectives on Luke and Acts', in M.C. Parsons and J.B. Tyson (eds.), *Cadbury, Knox, and Talbert: American Contributions to the Study of Acts* (SBL Biblical Scholarship in North America 18; Atlanta: Scholars, 1992) 165.

[31]For a brief survey of selected rhetorical studies of Acts, see Talbert, 'Luke-Acts', in E.J. Epp and G.W. MacRae (eds.), *The New Testament and its Modern Interpreters* (Philadelphia: Fortress; Atlanta: Scholars, 1989) 309-310; and M.A. Powell, *What Are They Saying About Acts?* (New York/Mahwah, NJ: Paulist, 1991) 96-9.

[32]Talbert, *Reading Luke*, 2.

[33]See Moore, *Literary Criticism*, 4, 18; Parsons, 'Reading Talbert', 164-66.

have more boldly waded into and even immersed themselves in the strange and exotic waters of modern literary theory. Potentially emerging from this baptism is a different breed of biblical scholars with different ways of conceptualising the critical enterprise, not least with respect to the use of historical analysis. We now turn to investigate the effects of this new methodology on recent studies of Luke-Acts.

II. New Literary Currents[34]

In tracking the post redaction-critical trajectory of Lukan scholarship directly informed by secular literary theory, we will once again focus first on an early watershed study, by Norman Petersen in this case, and then examine later contributions from the most productive and salient figure in this movement, Robert Tannehill.

In 1978 Petersen published a pioneering work on *Literary Criticism for New Testament Critics*,[35] which concluded with a substantial chapter on Luke-Acts. Initially, Petersen laid a theoretical foundation for his project by exposing various 'Literary Problems in the Historical-Critical Paradigm' (ch. 1) and proposing a particular 'Literary-Critical Model for Historical Critics' (ch. 2). In his view, historical criticism was particularly flawed in the way it tended to judge the 'evidential value' of people and events referred to in a given text on the basis of some predetermined, external situations or traditions out of which the text supposedly evolved. As a *literary* document, 'the text itself must be comprehended in its own terms before we can ask of what it is evidence, whether in relation to the time of writing or in relation to the events referred to in it'.[36] And Petersen further contended that achieving this interpretive aim required a comprehensive model of literary analysis which biblical historical critics have lacked.

Petersen sought to fill this void with the verbal communications model propounded by the Russian linguist and literary theorist, Roman Jakobson. Among the various components of this model, two

---

[34]Title drawn from the new 'Literary Currents in Biblical Interpretation' series published by Westminster/John Knox Press, Louisville, KY.
[35]N.R. Petersen, *Literary Criticism for New Testament Critics* (Guides to Biblical Scholarship; Philadelphia: Fortress, 1978).
[36]*Ibid.*, 20.

functional elements controlling the flow of information between 'addresser' and 'addressee' were especially important for Petersen's analysis of Luke-Acts:

(a) The *referential* function has to do with *what* is being communicated or referred to, the 'propositional content' of the narrated message. Such content is a direct reflection of the narrative itself and should not be construed as a representation of some set of concepts or objects existing in the 'real world' outside the world implied by the narrative ('referential fallacy').

(b) The *poetic* function is concerned with *how* a message is narrated, specifically, how various elements from the narrative world combine into linear sequences and repetitive cycles to form the narrative's *plot*.[37]

With respect to Luke-Acts, Petersen was interested in determining how these *literary* perspectives might impinge upon the *historical* task of reconstructing the events surrounding the 'authentic' ('real') Jesus and primitive Christian church. As a test case, Petersen assessed the historical value of Paul's distinctive pattern in Acts (not apparent from Paul's letters) of preaching to the Gentiles and establishing separate Christian communities only after being rejected in synagogues by hostile Jewish audiences.

Following Jakobson's model, Petersen gave priority to understanding 'the plotting [= poetic function] of Luke's narrative world in order to avoid confusing it with the real world [= referential fallacy]'.[38] What he perceived was that Acts' presentation of the Pauline mission was inextricably linked to Luke's 'principal plot device of repeated confrontation and rejection incidents'[39] strategically deployed throughout his two-volume narrative (cf. Lk. 4:16-30; 20:1-19; Acts 3-4; 5:12-42; 13:13-52; 18:1-11). From this poetic analysis of Lukan composition, Petersen moved to a referential conclusion: since Acts' portrait of Paul is so completely wrapped up (emplotted) in Luke's narrative world, its value as a signifier of the historical Paul's actions in the real world is severely limited. Accordingly, in this case literary criticism serves to strengthen historical criticism's tendency to privilege earlier evidence of Paul's career from his own letters. But it is important to recognise methodologically that such confirmation stems from primary *literary*

---

[37]*Ibid.*, 33-48.
[38]*Ibid.*, 82.
[39]*Ibid.*, 91.

analysis of the entire Lukan narrative, not from *a priori* judgements regarding the greater authenticity of Paul's autobiographical accounts.

Petersen's work was a harbinger of numerous applications of modern literary criticism to New Testament study over the next fifteen years up to the present date. In the field of Lukan scholarship during this period, Tannehill's efforts have been the most prodigious, culminating in his two-volume commentary on *The Narrative Unity of Luke-Acts*.[40]

Tannehill practices what is commonly called 'narrative criticism', which approaches a biblical narrative as a complex yet coherent literary unit, 'an interactive whole, with harmonies and tensions that develop in the course of narration'.[41] In tracing these developments, narrative critics pay special attention to plot lines, gaps and redundancies, character roles, points of view, foreshadowing, irony and other literary features associated with the study of modern novels, short stories and films. As the most extensive and elaborate narrative in the New Testament, 'written by an author of literary skill and rich imagination who had a complex vision of the significance of Jesus Christ and of the mission in which he is the central figure', Luke-Acts, as Tannehill sees it, is particularly amenable to narrative-critical analysis.[42]

Although his commentary is by and large free of technical literary jargon and he avows 'not [to be] concerned with developing narrative theory',[43] Tannehill's dependence upon the insights of secular narratologists is transparent at a number of points.[44] For example, he draws on (a) Wayne Booth's distinctions among a literary work's 'real' author (composer of the text with identity separate from the text—*not* a factor in Tannehill's commentary), 'implied' author (whose profile is wholly contained with the text) and 'narrator' (a 'reliable' voice in Luke-Acts with a perspective virtually indistinguishable from the 'implied' author); (b) Gérard Genette's classification of techniques for managing narrative time, such as

---

[40]Philadelphia: Fortress, 1986-90.
[41]Tannehill, 'Narrative Criticism', in R.J. Coggins and J.L. Houlden (eds.), *Dictionary of Biblical Interpretation* (London: SCM; Philadelphia: TPI, 1990) 488.
[42]Tannehill, *Narrative Unity*, 1. 1.
[43]*Ibid*.
[44]In secular literary studies the method is called 'narratology'; biblical scholars have coined the designation, 'narrative criticism', probably as a counterpoint to source, form and redaction criticism.

'prolepses' and 'analepses' (which Tannehill labels 'previews' and 'reviews'); (c) Shlomith Rimmon-Kenan's discussion of 'focalising' characters from whose viewpoint a story is narrated (cf. Peter's role in recounting the Cornelius narrative in Acts 11:1-18); and (d) Marianna Torgovnick's functional analysis of narrative closure (applied to the problematic ending of Acts). In each case, Tannehill clearly explains his borrowed concepts and terminology and demonstrates their usefulness in interpreting the Lukan narrative.[45]

Tannehill's dominant interest in the unfolding *story* of Luke-Acts does not preclude a corresponding quest for the *theology* conveyed through this narrative. Indeed, Tannehill perceives the 'purpose of God' (βουλή τοῦ θεοῦ) as the pulsing energy controlling the entire narrative and holding it together. In unpacking specific ideas and values contained within this overriding theological purpose, however, Tannehill insists that these messages not be wrenched from the narrative context in which they are embedded and reduced to a set of abstract, dogmatic propositions. Stated positively, Tannehill finds the evidence for Lukan theology especially wedded to four types of narrative material: (1) previews of ensuing events (e.g. birth stories) and reviews of past action (e.g. Acts summaries and speeches); (2) repeated or accentuated scriptural citations or allusions (e.g. key Isaianic references); (3) commissioning instructions (e.g. Lk. 24; Acts 9-11); and (4) interpretive comments by trustworthy characters (e.g. Jesus, Peter, Stephen, Paul). Through the course of these and other materials in the plotted story of Luke-Acts, the divine purpose moves as a dynamic force instead of a static concept, adjusting to recurrent conflicts (e.g. opposition from certain Jewish and Roman leaders) and fresh opportunities (e.g. receptivity of Samaritans and Gentiles) that arise along the way.[46]

However much Tannehill has continued to engage in theological inquiry as part of his literary investigation, he has not demonstrated a correspondingly high degree of interest in *historical* analysis. This is not to say he has been hostile to such analysis or ignored it altogether but simply that for the most part he has bracketed out historical queries (see discussion above) from his narrative-centred method. In the first volume of his commentary dealing with the Gospel of Luke, Tannehill disregards virtually all

---

[45]Tannehill, *Narrative Unity*, 1. 7-8, 11-12, 18-23; 2. 6, 16-17, 43, 143-45, 283, 353-56.
[46]*Ibid.*, 1. 2-12, 2-23; cf. Tannehill, 'Israel in Luke-Acts: A Tragic Story', *JBL* 104 (1985) 69-85.

extratextual information, with two limited exceptions: he explores a number of links between the Lukan narrative and various Septuagintal stories, and he draws on comparative linguistic data to elucidate the meaning of several Greek terms. In both cases Tannehill peeks beyond the bounds of Luke's narrative world into the wider domain of ancient Greek literature; but on the whole his critical eye remains fixed on the textual data and story line of Luke-Acts.

In his second volume on Acts, Tannehill ventures a little further into historical-critical territory, although again without ever losing sight of the narrative borders of Luke-Acts. The main example of Tannehill's blending of literary and historical analysis comes in his treatment of the Stephen speech in Acts 7.[47] Stephen's closing emphasis on the universality of God's presence beyond the confines of 'houses [= temples] made with human hands' (7:44-50) was, in Tannehill's opinion, 'a point of acute relevance in the author's *historical setting*, in which memory of the [Jerusalem] temple's destruction was still painful for any who honored Israel's tradition and respected the devout men and women who worshipped in its temple' (emphasis added).[48] Explicit recurring references to the razing of Jerusalem and its temple in Luke's Gospel (13:32-5; 19:41-4; 21:5-6, 20-4; 23:27-31) confirm that this historical event was a part of the stock of images influencing both the author's composition and reader's interpretation of the Stephen speech.

Anticipating that some narrative-critical purists might object to his appeal to any extratextual information, Tannehill defends (in a footnote) his use of historical data on the grounds that 'all communication, including narrative communication, rests on a bed of presupposed knowledge that is not explicitly cited'.[49] In a similar vein, in introducing his volume on Acts Tannehill flatly announces his belief 'that study of first-century Mediterranean literature and society may illuminate unspoken assumptions behind the narrative and may also suggest specific reasons for emphases in the text'.[50] Significantly, with this perspective, Tannehill forges closer ties with genre and rhetorical critics (such as Talbert) and prepares the way for other narrative critics to engage in more extensive research than he

---

[47]Tannehill, *Narrative Unity*, 2. 92-6.
[48]*Ibid.*, 2. 93.
[49]*Ibid.*, 2. 95 n. 45.
[50]*Ibid.*, 2. 5; cf. pp. 3-5.

has elected to pursue into the intersection between the literary and historical worlds of Luke-Acts.

In fact some recent studies of Luke-Acts have already taken some important first steps beyond Tannehill in blending narrative criticism and historical analysis, although no study as yet has approached the comprehensive scope of Tannehill's two-volume, 650-page commentary on the entire Lukan narrative. Among the most significant of these innovative, 'interdisciplinary' projects are the following five monographs. In this section a primarily descriptive sketch of key historical and narrative components of these studies is presented, setting the stage for a more evaluative critique in the final section.

1. In *The Departure of Jesus in Luke-Acts*, Mikeal Parsons examines the ascension narratives which close Luke's Gospel (24:50-3) and open the book of Acts (1:1-11) through both diachronic and synchronic lenses, aiming to give 'just treatment' to these narratives 'both as ancient writings of the first century and as timeless literary structures'.[51] On the *historical* side, Parsons utilises conventional source and form analysis in comparing the ascension accounts with ancient Jewish and Graeco-Roman 'farewell scenes' (Lk. 24) and 'assumption stories' (Acts 1). He also engages in extensive text-critical analysis, not merely as a technical 'filler' for footnotes, but as an essential foundation for all types of biblical interpretation. Motivating this serious pursuit of textual criticism is Parson's conviction

> that all forms of High Criticism, particularly redaction studies, narrative criticism, and structuralism, are severely crippled (if not totally incapacitated) if the theology and literary style reflected in the document are that of a third-century scribe and not that of the author(s).[52]

From a *narrative* perspective, Parsons probes various contexts for understanding the ascension stories, paying special attention to how these stories function *independently* as the climax of one plot segment (Luke) and commencement of another (Acts) and *together* as the hinge connecting the two-part series (Luke-Acts). As models for this

---

[51]M. Parsons, *The Departure of Jesus in Luke-Acts: The Ascension Narratives in Context* (JSNT Sup 21; Sheffield: Sheffield Academic Press, 1987) 199. Cf. my review of this work in *WJT* 52 (1990) 376-78.
[52]Parsons, *Departure*, 125.

analysis, Parsons draws chiefly on Torgovnick's classification of closural strategies (circularity, parallelism, linkage); Boris Uspensky's outline of various 'framing' techniques (psychological, spatial, temporal, phraseological, ideological) which usher the reader in and out of the story's point of view; and information theory's examination of 'redundant' patterns of communication, concentrating on both verbatim and variegated repetitions at various levels of discourse (word, phrase, thought unit, story, etc.)[53] Parsons' discussion of these and other theoretical models is more extensive than Tannehill's, but it still remains clear and to the point, never losing sight of the goal of establishing the proper contexts for understanding the Lukan ascension scenes.

2. In a wide-ranging investigation of *Method and Message in Luke-Acts*, Robert Brawley draws eclectically on selected insights from a variety of literary theorists. But in the main he structures his study around Roland Barthes' analysis of five 'voices' which define the contours of literary texts.[54] Four of these voices function strictly within the bounds of the text, expressing 'what is true in the hermetically sealed universe of the literary work without recourse to the external worlds',[55] and, as it happens, these four all bear rather confusing, esoteric designations which, despite Brawley's generally helpful explanations, tend to limit their usefulness for the average biblical scholar. A brief sketch of the main emphases of these voices in relation to the study of Acts will suffice.

(a) The 'hermeneutic' voice focuses on key questions raised by the text—such as those related to 'the promise of the Father' announced by Jesus in Acts 1:4 (What promise? How and when is it fulfilled?)—and possible resolutions intimated throughout the course of the text (in material both preceding and succeeding the point of inquiry).

(b) The voice of the 'semes' is principally concerned with the significance (= signifying function) of characters in the text or, more specifically, with how various bits of descriptive information and assessments of personal actions, attitudes and emotions work together to shape distinctive characters (Brawley emphasises the role

---

[53]*Ibid.*, 65-113, 151-86 (chs. 3, 5).
[54]R.L. Brawley, *Centering on God: Method and Message in Luke-Acts* (Literary Currents in Biblical Interpretation; Louisville, KY: Westminster/John Knox, 1990) 17-20.
[55]*Ibid.*, 40.

of *God* as the most important character in Luke-Acts, followed by Jesus, Peter and Paul).

(c) The 'proairetic' voice identifies segments of a plot which are tightly linked in a cause-and-effect sequence (as opposed to an 'episodic' jumble of discrete incidents), such as the series of events in Acts 3-5 triggered by Peter and John's healing of the lame beggar.

(d) The 'symbolic' voice traces the boundaries and explores the tensions between two opposing realms of thought, such as the spatial (present/absent, down/up, earth/heaven) and temporal (present/future, go/will come) antitheses configuring the ascension scene in Acts 1:1-11.

Barthes' *fifth* voice, however—(e) the 'cultural' voice—stands out from the others as less abstruse in its label (although he also calls it the 'voice of science') and more interested in the interpretive influence of the (cultural-historical) world *outside* the text. Indeed, this voice takes into account all of the implicit, 'unformulated' knowledge necessary for a reader to comprehend the text fully. And as Brawley sees it, the extent of this assumed knowledge is virtually immeasurable: 'the text is but the proverbial iceberg compared with what remains unexplained'.[56] For an *ancient* text, the cultural literacy required of an informed reader pertains to a vast array of concepts, events, people and institutions from the *historical* milieu in which the text was produced. In the case of Luke-Acts, a conservative (not exhaustive) checklist of the 'repertoire' of information necessary for understanding would include such topics as:[57]

> popular medicine, magic, soothsaying, the Roman military, the Olympian gods and their priesthood, Epicurean and Stoic philosophy, judicial and political systems, every biblical citation and allusion, Jewish eschatological expectations, commandments, purity laws, feasts, marriage customs, the nature and meaning of table fellowship, the functions and significance of the temple, and the social status of women, shepherds, priests, Sadducees, Pharisees, and toll collectors.[58]

To elaborate on one example, the enigma to modern readers of the punishment spectacle in Acts 5 involving Ananias and Sapphira is

---

[56]*Ibid.*, 160; cf. pp. 159-81 (ch. 7).
[57]Brawley derives this term from W. Iser, *The Act of Reading: A Theory of Aesthetic Response* (Baltimore: Johns Hopkins University, 1978) 69.
[58]Brawley, *Centering on God*, 162.

elucidated by comparable scenes from ancient Jewish and Graeco-Roman literature which comprise part of the unformulated textual background to the Lukan narrative. The book of Joshua reports the stoning of Achan and his family as a consequence of Achan's pilfering of forbidden war booty and incurring of divine judgement on the entire Israelite community;[59] Diodorus of Sicily relates the Vaccaei policy of executing any farmers who hoard part of their harvest instead of surrendering all of it to the community storehouse (5.34.3). Both accounts illustrate in a social and economic context similar to that reflected in the Ananias and Sapphira incident 'a far-reaching standard in antiquity that communal norms take precedence over individual life'.[60] Thus modern dissonance over strange values espoused in ancient literature (in this case regarding standards of justice and fairness) may be overcome in some measure when unspoken cultural voices underlying one text (Acts) are heard through the medium of other texts (Joshua; Diodorus) from the same environment.

3. In his analysis of the Pharisees' portrayal in Luke-Acts, David Gowler approaches the Lukan narrative from a 'socio-narratological' perspective both as a literary composition which artfully presents a plotted sequence of characters and events and as a 'socially symbolic act' which 'assumes, utilizes, or controverts elements of the cultural milieu in which it was created'.[61] From this perspective, Gowler utilises theoretical studies of characterisation techniques in modern literature to identify the roles and characteristics of the Pharisees in Luke-Acts. But he first takes pains to apply and adapt these modern techniques to a broad sample of *ancient* narratives (Jewish/Greek/Roman; tragedy/biography/history/romance) and to supplement and correlate these literary traits with *cultural* scripts (or codes) of human behaviour which permeated ancient Mediterranean society (honour/shame; patron/client; purity/pollution; kinship/house-

---

[59]νοσφίζομαι ('pilfer, embezzle'), a rare verb in biblical literature, appears in both Josh 7:1 (LXX) and Acts 5:2 as an indicator of the close links between the Achan and Ananias/Sapphira stories (*Ibid.*, 177).

[60]*Ibid.*, 177.

[61]D.B. Gowler, *Host, Guest, Enemy, and Friend: Portraits of the Pharisees in Luke and Acts* (Emory Studies in Early Christianity; New York: Peter Lang, 1991) 9. The notion of narrative as a 'socially symbolic act' is drawn from F. Jameson, *The Political Unconscious: Narrative as a Socially Symbolic Act* (Ithaca: Cornell University, 1981). Cf. Gowler, 'Characterization in Luke: A Socio-Narratological Approach', *BTB* 19 (1989) 57-62.

hold).[62] Underlying these efforts are critical *historical* assumptions that 'characters in ancient literature speak and act in ways foreign to modern readers' and that 'a reader should be aware, as much as possible, of the culturally-bound connotations of what happens in the narrative world'.[63]

The fruits of Gowler's labours may be sampled in his handling of the first episode in Acts involving the Pharisees. This scene features the Pharisaic teacher, Gamaliel, advocating a tolerant, 'wait-and-see' policy regarding the early Christian mission (5:34-40). The narrator characterises Gamaliel by way of both 'direct definition' and 'indirect presentation'. In the former case, a string of epithets in 5:34 *directly* establishes Gamaliel's position not only as Pharisee and rabbi, but also as prominent council-member commanding the respect of 'all the people' (note the comparable respect accorded to the *apostles* in 5:13). *Indirectly*, the form and content of Gamaliel's speech are especially revealing: his 'I tell you' (λέγω ὑμῖν) formula (unique in Acts) recalls the authoritative pronouncements of the Lukan Jesus (Lk. 7:9; 15:7; 19:40), and his insistence that the apostles be allowed to continue their work pits him against the ideological stance of the Sadducees on the council and aligns him with the point of view of the narrator.

This *literary* profile is sharpened against the backdrop of two implied *cultural* scenarios: (1) *honour/shame*: having himself attained superior social honour, Gamaliel is in a position to legitimate the honourable status of the apostles and further shame the resistant high priest and council cohorts in the eyes of the people; (2) *patron/client*: similarly, as a respected teacher of the law or 'broker' of spiritual blessings between God (patron) and Israel (client), Gamaliel reminds the council that it is ultimately the Heavenly Patron's responsibility to vindicate or discredit ministers such as the apostles who claim to be channels of divine favour.[64]

Although correlating the Acts portrait of Gamaliel with these ancient Mediterranean codes of conduct, Gowler's historical analysis does *not* extend to comparing external data on the 'real' Pharisees or Gamaliel from Josephus' writings or rabbinic literature. This lacuna

---

[62]In this area of ancient Mediterranean cultural scripts, Gowler is heavily indebted to the groundbreaking work of B. Malina, *New Testament World: Insights from Cultural Anthropology* (Atlanta: John Knox, 1981).
[63]Gowler, *Host*, 74; cf. pp. 9-27, 70-5.
[64]*Ibid.*, 274-80.

results from Gowler's conception of the accessible historical world overlapping Luke's narrative world as a general-symbolic social environment instead of a particular-referential set of individuals and events which he regards as 'unrepeatable and unrecoverable', too dependent for analysis on 'tentative and more-or-less probable reconstructions of what may have been'.[65] The possibility that Gowler carries such historical scepticism too far will be considered below.

4. In his examination of the 'dynamics' of the two-volume Lukan narrative, William Kurz primarily explores the literary functions of multiple narrators. Specifically, he targets for analysis *four* types of narrators in Luke-Acts which, even with their distinctive perspectives, still operate with 'solidarity and close teamwork. . .to produce one unified narrative':[66] (a) the 'I' narrator of the prologues (Lk. 1:3; Acts 1:1); (b) the dominant third person omniscient narrator; (c) the 'we' narrator; and (d) various character narrators. The first two narrators share a common omniscient, 'extradiegetic' (outside the narrative) point of view, while the latter two both reflect a limited, 'intradiegetic' (within the narrative) stance. The last two narrators are also distinguished by the fact that they emerge only in certain segments of the book of Acts, thus demonstrating in Kurz's view the high degree of narrative freedom and artistry in Acts in contrast to the more episodic and source-dependent texture of Luke's Gospel.

    Among the conclusions which Kurz reaches regarding the role of the 'we' narrator in Acts is its representation of qualified, partial support for Paul, much like that which the 'twelve' provide Jesus in Luke's Gospel. Appearing only a few times at intermittent stages in the narrative, the 'we' party grasps part of but not the full significance of the Pauline mission; and at a critical juncture (between Acts 21 and 27) the 'we' group disappears completely, leaving Paul to face his trials alone just as Jesus did at the end of the Gospel narrative.

    In addition to noting how the 'we' narrator helps to link the 'passions' of Jesus and Paul, Kurz claims that 'we' also suggests the voice of an eyewitness, a participant in the events being narrated. At this point, Kurz launches into a brief excursus on the *historical* implications of his narrative analysis. Unlike Petersen's negative

---

[65]*Ibid.*, 13-14.
[66]W.S. Kurz, *Reading Luke-Acts: Dynamics of Biblical Narrative* (Louisville, KY: Westminster/John Knox, 1993) 101.

verdict regarding the historical value of the Pauline material in Acts (see above), Kurz's appraisal based on the 'we' sections is more positive, although still allowing room for a creative hand in shaping the final report of witnessed events:

> On a merely narrative level, the implicit claims to participation made by the 'we' passages in those events are manifest. . .Whether or not one identifies the narrator in the 'we' passages with Luke, there seems genuine plausibility to the claims that the author of Acts was a companion of Paul and a peripheral participant during some of Paul's later journeys and experiences.[67]

The other type of 'intradiegetic' narrator in Acts is represented by certain key characters *within* the story who comment from their own personal vantage points on events and situations they have experienced. The classic examples appear in Peter's report to the Jerusalem church of his recent experiences in Cornelius' house (11:1-18) and Paul's testimonies before the Jerusalem crowd (22:1-21) and Agrippa (26:2-23) regarding his dramatic commission to preach to the Gentiles. Of course, in both cases there are other antecedent versions of these incidents (see 9:1-22; 10:1-48), and scholars have long been preoccupied with attempting to account for a number of discrepancies between the various stories. Rather than positing multiple underlying sources or careless Lukan redaction, Kurz explains the variations in terms of different narrative points of view (focalisations). The first accounts of the conversion episodes surrounding Saul (ch. 9) and Cornelius (ch. 10) are *shown* from the panoramic perspective of the omniscient, 'extradiegetic' narrator who reveals the thoughts and emotions (as well as actions) of *all* the characters involved (Jesus, Ananias, Cornelius, angel, household, alongside Paul and Peter), whereas the subsequent accounts are *told* to particular audiences from the more idiosyncratic standpoints of individual protagonists. The former give a more objective picture and thus carry more authority in the narrative, while the latter present more subjectively stylised and somewhat less 'official' sketches of the same incidents.[68]

Interestingly, Kurz finds some *historical* support for these narrative distinctions in the ancient Hellenistic rhetorical convention

---

[67]*Ibid.*, 123; see also *idem*, 'Narrative Approaches to Luke-Acts', *Bib* 68 (1987) 203-19; Spencer, *Portrait of Philip*, 246-50.
[68]Kurz, *Reading Luke-Acts*, 125-31.

of *prosopopoieia*, which he defines as 'the practice of. . .creating speeches suited to particular speakers, occasions, and audiences'.[69] At other points in his study, Kurz makes further claims that the Lukan narrative 'can best be understood within the tradition of Greek rhetoric, with which the implied author. . .has demonstrated his familiarity'.[70] For example, he detects the use of Greek friendship terminology (as well as Deuteronomic language) in the summary passage regarding communal sharing of goods in Acts 4:32-5, closely followed by *exempla* stories providing both positive (Barnabas) and negative (Ananias and Sapphira) illustrations of the situation. Also, Kurz notes that in speeches before the Athenian intellectuals (17:22-31) and Roman governor (24:10-21), Paul opens with the common oratorical device of *captatio benevolentiae*, issuing flattering statements to garner the favour of his audience.[71]

5. In his study of *Characterization in Luke-Acts*, focusing on the figures of John the Baptist, the Pharisees, and King Herod, John Darr employs 'a reader-response (or pragmatic) model attuned to the Graeco-Roman literary culture of the first century'.[72] Reader-response criticism (closely allied with narrative criticism in biblical studies) is a modern literary method which emphasises the role of the reader in eliciting meaning from a text. It endeavours to trace the various moves a reader makes in the process of interpretation, paying special attention—more than other approaches—to the effects of *sequential* reading, that is, the ways in which a first-time reader progressively 'builds' characters and events over the course of the narrative.

In Darr's view, examining Lukan characters from this linear, reader-oriented perspective provides a more accurate profile than composite images pieced together from bits of data scattered throughout the two-volume work. The Pharisees represent a key case in point. Whereas many scholars perceive the Lukan narrative to be somewhat tolerant of or even favourably disposed toward this Jewish

---

[69]*Ibid.*, 125; cf. pp. 98-9, 125-31.

[70]*Ibid.*, 82.

[71]*Ibid.*, 81-2, 96, 104. For another recent study of Lukan narrators which utilises both modern narratology and rhetorical analysis of ancient literature, see S.M. Sheeley, *Narrative Asides in Luke-Acts* (JSNT Sup 72; Sheffield: Sheffield Academic Press, 1992).

[72]J.A. Darr, *On Character Building: The Reader and the Rhetoric of Characterization in Luke-Acts* (Literary Currents in Biblical Interpretation; Louisville, KY: Westminster/John Knox, 1992) 14.

group in light of the support they seem to offer the early Christian movement in Acts (5:33-39; 15:5; 23:6-9), Darr regards this as a distorted view 'based on a *reverse* reading' from Acts to Luke, from sequel to beginning volume. Proceeding in linear order, the sharply negative portraits of the Pharisees which accumulate in Luke's Gospel and impress themselves *first* on the reader's mind 'cast a cynical and ironic shadow' over all subsequent images which develop in Acts.[73]

While Darr's reader-response analysis of Lukan characters is firmly grounded in modern literary theory (derived from critics such as Iser, Fish, Kermode and Harvey), it is complemented by a clear *historical* orientation 'attuned to the Greco-Roman literary culture of the first century'.[74] Such attention to historical matters is in fact central to Darr's methodology and not a peripheral addendum to a purely formalist literary treatment (à la New Criticism) of Luke-Acts. To read this work in a temporal and cultural 'vacuum' is to misread it, in Darr's estimation.

> [W]e cannot ignore the distance between ourselves and the readers of this ancient narrative. Although we can never recover it in full, the intended (authorial) reader's cultural repertoire remains the optimal extratext for understanding Luke's story. *Those who fancy themselves literary critics but not historians cannot contribute much of value to our knowledge of Lukan character* (emphasis added).[75]

This 'cultural (or extratextual) repertoire' necessary for competent reading includes familiarity with at least five areas of knowledge concerning the ancient Mediterranean world: (a) Greek language; (b) common social and cultural values; (c) classical and scriptural writings; (d) rhetorical conventions; and (e) well-known 'current events' and geographical data.[76]

Above all, the literate interpreter of Luke-Acts must be 'steeped' in the language, stories, patterns and ideas of the Greek Jewish Bible (LXX).[77] For example, in evaluating the depiction of

---

[73]*Ibid.*, 43; cf. pp. 42-3, 85-126. For a sequential analysis of the role of the *Samaritans* in Luke-Acts, see Spencer, *Portrait of Philip*, 53-87.

[74]This historical dimension is *not* prominent in another recent reader-response analysis of Luke-Acts: J.B. Tyson, *Images of Judaism in Luke-Acts* (Columbia, SC: University of South Carolina, 1992).

[75]Darr, *Character Building*, 170: cf. pp. 13-14.

[76]*Ibid.*, 22; cf. pp. 20-3.

[77]*Ibid.*, 28.

Herod 'the fox' who opposes John and Jesus in Luke's Gospel (3:18-20; 13:32-5) and other 'Herods' appearing in Acts who harass Peter and Paul (cf. 12:1-11; 25:13-26:32), Darr draws from the LXX on (a) vital *linguistic information* (ἀλώπηξ, 'fox', typified destructive threats to Israel's security in Ct. 2:15a; Ezk. 13:4-5; Neh. 3:35b; Lam. 5:17-18) and (b) a prominent *relational schema* (faithful/suffering prophet vs. rebellious/hostile king in Deuteronomic History, e.g., Elijah vs. Ahab; Jeremiah vs. Jehoiakim) to fill in the gaps of the sketchy portraits presented in Luke-Acts. Illuminated by these extratextual images (and others like the classical model of philosopher vs. tyrant, e.g., Diogenes vs. Alexander), Herod clearly emerges as the quintessential royal villain who persecutes God's messengers but is ultimately frustrated by their faithfulness under fire and God's consequent vindication of their cause.[78] Although Darr readily incorporates insights from the broad literary culture of Mediterranean antiquity into his reading of the Herod material in Luke-Acts, he does not explore possible connections with any extratextual reports about the 'real' Herod. He is concerned with Herod strictly as a literary character in Luke's story, not as a historical figure affecting religious and political events in first-century Palestine.

These five studies cover a wide range of particular *literary* issues (significance of ascension scenes, function of 'we' narrator, depiction of Pharisees, Herod, Ananias and Sapphira) and *historical* concerns (authenticity of text, identity of 'real' author, influence of Mediterranean honour-shame code and Septuagintal rejected-prophet motif) pertaining to Luke's two-volume narrative, each meriting careful evaluation. The purpose of this essay, however, is not to settle specific interpretive debates (e.g., are the Pharisees in Luke-Acts portrayed in negative or positive terms or both?), but to explore the broad methodological implications of attempts to combine modern narrative and traditional historical modes of analysis. We now turn to a final assessment of these issues in relation to the study of (Luke-) Acts.

III. Testing the Waters

The sampling of recent narrative-critical and reader-response studies of Luke-Acts offered above should put to rest any lingering

---

[78]*Ibid.*, 127-68 (chs. 5-6).

suspicions that such modern literary approaches are 'essentially ahistorical' or antihistorical.[79] Mark Allan Powell has reached similar conclusions in his wider survey of biblical narrative criticism, focusing especially on its application to the synoptic Gospels. As he explains:

> In reality, nothing in the assumptions or presuppositions of narrative criticism calls into question the legitimacy of historical investigation. . .Narrative criticism demands that the modern reader have the historical information that the text assumes of its implied reader. . .In short, narrative criticism is certainly not an antihistorical discipline. In fact, a symbiotic relationship exists between narrative and historical approaches to texts.[80]

Still, for all this compatibility between modern literary and traditional historical analyses of biblical texts, it cannot be said that these newer literary investigations simply represent critical business as usual with a little innovative twist here or there. Although modern literary approaches have neither called for nor brought about the total collapse of the historical-critical paradigm, they have instigated a substantial shift in focus from *author* and *event* (major concerns of historical criticism) to *text* and *reader*. How each of these elements is evaluated carries important implications for interpreting a first-century historical narrative such as Acts.

1. Author

The tendency of historical criticism to base its interpretation of Acts on suppositions regarding the author's identity either, by name, as Luke the physician or some other early Christian figure, or, by function, as a creative redactor of received traditions has been thoughtfully challenged by recent literary analyses. The prologue in

---

[79]This phrase comes from K.R.R. Gros Louis, 'Some Methodological Considerations', in K.R.R. Gros Louis and J.S. Ackerman (eds.), *Literary Interpretations of Biblical Narrative II* (Nashville: Abingdon, 1982) 14-15, cited in M. Sternberg, *The Poetics of Biblical Narrative: Ideological Literature and the Drama of Reading* (Bloomington, IN: Indiana University, 1985) 6. Note Sternberg's vigorous refutation of this supposed ahistorical/antihistorical bias of modern literary criticism (pp. 6-23).
[80]Powell, *What Is Narrative Criticism?* (Guides to Biblical Scholarship; Minneapolis: Fortress, 1990) 96-8.

Luke 1:1-4 certainly suggests the strong hand of an individual writer gathering testimonies and traditions and shaping them into a persuasive narrative; but nowhere in this or any other text throughout Luke-Acts is there a clear disclosure of the author's name, occupation, provenance or particular traditions at his (or her?) disposal. This is not to deny that the narrative contains certain clues to the author's identity and function, but ultimately any conclusions deriving from these clues must be classified as hypothetical constructions, not historical facts.

Also, problems of intentionality and circularity continue to plague author-centred models of interpretation. Even if we knew precisely who the author of Acts was and how he wrote his work, we could not certify the extent to which these 'facts' directly determined the final literary product. (If 'Luke' was a physician, does this necessarily mean his history writing reflects a medical slant, even when describing healing incidents? If 'Luke' utilised Mark as part of his bibliography, does this mean that deviations from this source must always be explained as deliberate alterations?) The modern literary critic's answer to these difficulties is to let the canonical form of the text in its overall narrative context be the first and final arbiter of exegesis.

Nevertheless, narrative criticism's cautious approach to authorial issues need not imply total scepticism. As noted above, Kurz's literary study of the 'we' narrator supports the conclusion of various historical critics that the author of Acts was a 'peripheral participant' in some of Paul's later missionary efforts. (After sifting the relevant New Testament and patristic data, Fitzmyer identifies the author as Paul's 'sometime companion', plausibly Luke the physician, present with the apostle, A.D. 50, 58-61, and absent during the main epistolary years, A.D. 50-58).[81] This acquaintance with Paul, although limited, on the part of the writer of Acts invites the interpreter to consult other first-century writings by or about the renowned missionary. Certainly care must be taken not to force harmonisations or indulge in dubious speculations regarding the author's *direct* literary dependence on Paul's letters. But broad comparative analysis may still yield valuable insights. Similarly, the Lukan message may be illuminated by comparison and contrast with other Gospel traditions (including Johannine), without being tied to

---

[81]J.A. Fitzmyer, 'The Authorship of Luke-Acts Reconsidered', *Luke the Theologian: Aspects of His Teaching* (New York/Mahwah, NJ: Paulist, 1989) 1-26.

any particular diachronic scheme of Gospel origins and development.[82]

2. Event

Historical criticism's typical preoccupation with both antecedent events which spark the production of biblical texts and contemporary events to which these texts refer can foster problematic tendencies to evade the full impact of the text itself or to predetermine the text's meaning on the basis of prior constructions of the world outside the text.[83] Increasingly, we encounter not only proponents of newer literary approaches but established historical critics as well exposing and seeking to avoid these methodological pitfalls.

For example, in his introduction to the historical Jesus and the four Gospels for 'The Oxford Bible Series', Graham Stanton works from a cautionary premise: 'we do well to resist the temptation to by-pass the teaching of the evangelists in an over-anxious rush to reach the teachings and actions of Jesus'.[84] This is not because Stanton is highly sceptical about what may be gleaned from the Gospels regarding the historical Jesus; indeed, he presents a substantial body of evidence pertaining to Jesus' life and ministry in Part II of his book. What Stanton is concerned about is a proper contextual orientation: the need to *start* with a careful literary and theological analysis of each of the four Gospel narratives in which the traditions concerning Jesus of Nazareth are set (see Part I, and note the order reflected in the titles of the book [*The Gospels and Jesus*] and its first chapter ['From the Gospels to Jesus']).[85]

---

[82]Cf. Talbert, *Reading Luke*, 1-2; Tannehill, *Narrative Unity*, 1. 6.

[83]I am using 'event' in the broadest sense to refer not simply to what happened (situation), but also to who was involved (people) and where and when (place and time) the event occurred.

[84]G.N. Stanton, *The Gospels and Jesus* (Oxford Bible Series; Oxford/New York: Oxford University, 1989) 4-5.

[85]See Stanton, *Gospels*, 12-13; and note S. Freyne's similar method in his study of Jesus and Galilee, in which he 'allow[s] a literary approach to the gospels (Part One) to take precedence over the more usual historical investigation (Part Two), as the first step'. The purpose behind this approach is that '[h]opefully, a critical reading of the gospels may set a more realistic historical agenda than might otherwise be achieved' (*Galilee, Jesus and the Gospels: Literary Approaches and Historical Investigations* [Philadelphia: Fortress, 1988] 3).

While narrative critics have played a useful role in calling historical critics back to the priority of examining the immediately accessible event of the text itself before moving on to consider more elusive background events, unfortunately some have tended to overtip the balance in the opposite direction by being so absorbed in 'poetic' features that 'referential' matters are scarcely given their due even as secondary concerns. With respect to the study of Luke-Acts outlined above, Petersen's efforts to move from poetic to referential analysis yielded such negative conclusions about what can be known of the 'real' world as to offer little encouragement to continue this type of investigation. Other narrative critics made much of the contemporary reader's need to understand the cultural 'repertoire' which an intelligent first-century Mediterranean reader would have brought to the text, but they defined this knowledge more in terms of broad, symbolic codes and literary patterns than specific, historical persons and events. Both Gowler and Darr, for instance, conducted their examinations of certain individuals and groups in Luke-Acts (John the Baptist, Herod, Pharisees) with little attention to external Jewish and Graeco-Roman reports about these same figures.

Still, despite sharing reservations about being sufficiently able to reconstruct historical events as well as concerns about imposing extraneous information on the finished text, some narrative critics have resisted a thorough-going scepticism regarding the study of the referential world surrounding Luke-Acts. We may recall (a) Darr's acknowledgement in principle, if not in practice, that 'commonly-known historical and geographical facts' comprise part of the data necessary for informed reading;[86] (b) Brawley's long list of extratextual 'things-to-know' in interpreting Luke-Acts—which included particular events, people and institutions such as Jewish feasts like Pentecost, religious parties like the Pharisees and Stoics, and the Jerusalem temple and priesthood—and (c) Tannehill's fruitful exploration of the links between segments of the Lukan narrative and the watershed political events of A.D. 70. In some measure, each of these scholars supports the attempt to correlate analyses of the poetic and referential functions of the Lukan text. Although their own pursuits of this enterprise remain limited,[87] they

---

[86]Darr, *Character*, 22.
[87]Although see Brawley's earlier work (*Luke-Acts and the Jews: Conflict, Apology, and Conciliation* [SBLMS 33; Atlanta: Scholars, 1987] 84-132), which makes

have opened the door for others to carry out more extensive investigations.

3. Text

Ironically, for all its emphasis on close, holistic readings of the final Lukan text—which may be applauded for counterbalancing certain atomistic and reductionist tendencies of source-, form- and redaction-oriented approaches—narrative criticism has typically failed to address adequately important literary and historical questions surrounding *which text* and *what kind of text* is being interpreted. For convenience sake, narrative critics of Luke-Acts—with the significant exception of Parsons noted above—typically adopt the standard Greek text in the latest Nestle-Aland or United Bible Societies edition, with little concern for variant textual options. In so doing, they undermine to some extent their own agenda of treating first things first and elevating the text as the primary guide to its own interpretation. The text must first be critically *established* before it is examined, and, as is well-known, this is no simple matter with respect to the book of Acts. Needless to say, accepting a different narrative framework incorporating all or part of the 'western' text of Acts could lead to substantially different narrative-critical conclusions.

A larger issue pertaining to the textual history of Acts has to do with its connection to the Third Gospel. As we have seen, modern literary/narrative critics put great emphasis on treating Luke and Acts together as a single, continuous, unified story—'Luke-Acts'. But this is by no means an unassailable, self-evident presupposition on either historical or literary grounds.[88] The canonical order bears witness to an early tradition of classifying Luke and Acts into different categories (Luke as part of the four Gospels, Acts as an introduction to the apostle Paul), raising the issue of whether any premodern hearers or readers would have approached the two works

---

substantial use of external Jewish sources in clarifying the Lukan portraits of the Pharisees, Sadducees and Jerusalem temple in Luke-Acts.

[88]See M.C. Parsons, 'The Unity of the Lukan Writings: Rethinking the *Opinio Communis*', in N.H. Keathley (ed.), *With Steadfast Purpose: Essays on Acts in Honor of Henry Jackson Flanders, Jr.* (Waco, TX: Baylor University, 1990) 29-53; M.C. Parsons and R.I. Pervo, *Rethinking the Unity of Luke and Acts* (Minneapolis: Augsburg/Fortress, 1993).

as a unified package. Moreover, the different patterns of narrative rhetoric displayed in Luke (more episodic, shorter teaching units, e.g., parables and wisdom sayings) and Acts (tighter plot sequences, more extended dramatic scenes and speeches)—features acknowledged by Tannehill and reflected in the different arrangements of his commentary on the two narratives[89]—pose nagging questions which Tannehill and other narrative critics gloss over regarding the constraints of variable *source* materials and *generic* models on the final composition of each volume.[90]

Thus, even as we accept the consensus view that Luke and Acts come from the same hand and present a logical sequence of compatible events and ideas—in other words, a coherent story—their different means of telling the story should lead us to bridle an over-exuberant quest for literary parallels ('parallelomania')[91] and to consider 'loosening the narrative hyphen in Luke-Acts' to some degree.[92] Again, it is a matter of allowing a particular text fully to speak for itself before rushing to compare it with other writings, even closely related writings by the same author/editor(s) (e.g. Ezra and Nehemiah, 1 and 2 Corinthians). As an earlier work by the same author to the same addressee (Theophilus), the Gospel of Luke may be profitably explored for points of contact with the book of Acts, but it should not be treated as a procrustean framework into which every element of Acts must fit. Acts has a literary and historical life of its own which must be respected. And as we then proceed to investigate links with other texts, we must not ignore the LXX (direct ties) and Pauline literature (indirect associations) as well as the Lukan Gospel.

A final point at which modern narrative approaches can betray their own emphasis on textual analysis pertains to the use of literary theory. In reviewing Brawley's *Centering on God*, Beverly Gaventa commends the author for providing some insightful readings of

---

[89]Tannehill organises his commentary on Luke topically, focusing on the figure of 'Jesus as he interacts with groups which appear repeatedly in the narrative' (e.g., 'Jesus' Ministry to the Oppressed and Excluded' [ch. 4]; 'Jesus and the Disciples' [ch. 7]; in his volume on Acts, however, Tannehill comments on each scene consecutively from beginning to end (cf. *Narrative Unity*, 1. 1-6; 2. 5-8).

[90]See the critique of Tannehill's emphasis on narrative unity in Moore, *Literary Criticism*, 29-40.

[91]Cf. Minear's trenchant critique of Talbert's *Literary Patterns*: 'I find the study to be an excellent example of industrious and ingenious parallelomania. So many instances are cited of the architectural symmetries that I became more sceptical of them all' (from *JAAR* 45 [1977] 85-6, cited in Parsons, 'Reading Talbert', 145).

[92]Parsons, 'Unity', 45; cf. *idem*, *Departure*, 24.

various Lukan texts but also sharply criticises him when his 'enthusiasm for literary theory manifestly overwhelms his common sense', that is, when 'theory triumphs over the text'.[93] Modern literary theory has its own complex jargon and method of argumentation which can quickly weary even the most diligent student in search of practical aids to understanding the biblical text. The burden is on the biblical critic informed by secular literary theory to demonstrate clearly and succinctly how such theory enhances comprehension of the biblical message. It is frustrating to wade through some heavy discussion of literary methodology to arrive at a few pages of application to biblical study which reveal nothing that could not have also been deduced by more conventional means. Especially in chapters 3 and 4 where he draws on structuralist schemes and formulae, Brawley does drift into some rather obscure and arid critical territory. Fortunately, he does not follow this trend throughout his work, and the other narrative-critical studies of Luke-Acts discussed above generally strike a better balance between theory and text. Especially notable in this regard is Tannehill's beautifully lucid narrative commentary which consistently lives up to its promise of 'using selected aspects of narrative criticism' to shed fresh light on the text-story of Luke-Acts.[94]

4. Reader

The fact that biblical criticism is practised by readers involved in the act of reading the biblical text appears on the surface to be an obvious, self-explanatory observation scarcely worth discussing. On closer reflection, however, it must be acknowledged that the reader plays a vital role in shaping interpretation (all readers to some degree see what they are conditioned to see) and that the act of reading is a varied and complex process of correlating myriad units of information, large and small. Such a conscious focus on readers and their responses to texts has been one of the more useful dimensions of recent literary approaches to biblical study.

---

[93]B.R. Gaventa, Review of R.L. Brawley, *Centering on God: Method and Message in Luke-Acts*, in E.J. Epp (ed.), *Critical Review of Books in Religion* (Atlanta: Scholars, 1992) 184.
[94]Tannehill, *Narrative Unity*, 1. 1.

From the literary investigations of Luke-Acts surveyed above, we recall a recurring emphasis on defining the 'repertoire' of a competent or literate reader. Much is left unsaid in Luke's writings that would be assumed as common knowledge for a first-century Mediterranean audience. Thus, the modern western reader, ensconced in a very different cultural and symbolic environment, is compelled to acquire this presumed understanding of Luke's world through rigorous and wide-ranging *historical* study.[95]

However, in further considering the profile of a competent reader of Luke-Acts from a historical perspective, it is possible for modern scholars to become in effect *too* competent or literate. Redaction critics, for example, presuppose a professional scholar-reader like themselves poring over every detail of the Lukan narrative surrounded by Gospel parallel-texts, concordances and other lexical aids—a scenario scarcely conceivable to Luke's original audience. Narrative critics often fare no better at this point. Although concentrating on the text of Luke-Acts independent of synoptic comparisons, Tannehill's repeated movements backwards and forwards through the narrative in hopes of uncovering 'what might be said after reading a second, third, or fourth time'[96] again presume an individual reader privately meditating for years on a personal copy of Luke's work—a luxury beyond the grasp of most readers in Luke's day.[97]

In fact, the whole notion of silent, reflective reading of a printed text—so central to modern conceptions of literacy—is largely alien to first-century experience. The scene featuring Jesus in the synagogue at Nazareth (Lk. 4:16-22) and the episode involving the Ethiopian eunuch (Acts 8:26-33) illustrate that biblical texts were typically read *aloud* and in *public* assemblies, except for the very wealthy (like the Ethiopian official) who could afford their own copies. In all likelihood, then, the first 'readers' of Luke and Acts were really *hearers* in a *community* setting.

Since how a text is *received* inevitably affects how it is *perceived*, the mode of communally hearing—as opposed to individually read-ing—the primitive Lukan text implies a distinctive set of interpretive

---

[95]Cf. B.J. Malina, 'Reading Theory Perspective: Reading Luke-Acts', in J.H. Neyrey, *The Social World of Luke-Acts: Models of Interpretation* (Peabody, MA: Hendrickson, 1991) 3-23.

[96]Tannehill, *Narrative Unity*, 1. 6.

[97]Cf. Moore, *Literary Criticism*, 71-84; Darr, *Character Building*, 26-9.

responses. As Stephen Moore explains: 'the aural appropriation of a text (in a public reading, for example) fosters a markedly different way of conceptualizing it than the predominantly visual appropriation of a private, silent reading'.[98] In particular, the hearer typically encounters the text moving in a steady rhythm and sequential order from beginning to end, without the opportunity afforded to the reader-scholar for reflective pausing and cross-referencing back and forth through the text. Consequently, the hearer's responses to the text are likely to be more impressionistic than scientific, more dynamic than static, more like a participant in a communication event than an examiner of linguistic data. Interestingly, the type of reader-response criticism advocated by Darr, with its strict attention to following the linear order of the Lukan narrative and stress on understanding the implied cultural milieu of Mediterranean antiquity, comes closer than other literary methods to approximating a first-time, first-century, aural experience of the text.

These critical reflections on the interplay between traditional historical analysis and modern literary investigations of (Luke-) Acts have been more suggestive than definitive, appropriate to a period of great methodological flux in biblical studies. It seems unlikely that we will return any time soon to the halcyon days (if they were ever that) of a single, dominant critical paradigm. However, such a state of affairs need not be mourned as a tragedy. This is an exciting era in which, as Tannehill puts it, 'methodological pluralism is to be encouraged, for each method will have blind spots that can only be overcome through another approach'.[99] We have explored some of the complementary and corrective dimensions of historical and literary approaches to Acts. Further integration of these critical methods must be hammered out in additional multi-disciplinary studies of all or part of the text(s) of Acts, and the realisation of this goal will no doubt be contingent, as Parsons suggests, 'on our ability to work together in collaborative efforts, pooling our resources and expertise'.[100] The present volume of studies takes a promising step in this direction.

---

[98]Moore, *Literary Criticism*, 85; cf. pp. 84-8.
[99]Tannehill, *Narrative Unity*, 2. 4. Cf. Freyne's comments: 'Insights and methods from various disciplines are increasingly brought to bear on the New Testament writings, since today, with a heightened hermeneutical awareness, many scholars have come to recognise that no one perspective can exhaust the possibilities of our texts, or adequately uncover their varied fields of reference' (*Galilee*, 3).
[100]Parsons, 'Reading Talbert', 166.

APPENDIX

ACTS AND THE PROBLEM OF ITS TEXTS

Peter Head

Summary

This paper discusses the problems associated with the Western text of the book of Acts. A brief survey of the history of research on the subject suggests that the scholarly consensus until recent years is that the Western text should be regarded as secondary and non-Lukan. This position has been challenged by several scholars and the bulk of the paper is given over to an investigation of supposedly tendentious readings in the Western tradition (relating to Christology, the Holy Spirit, the status of the apostles, and the apostolic decree). The author concludes by suggesting that modern proponents of the originality of the Western text have not yet managed to account for the theological Tendenz *of that text-type, which appears more like a secondary form of a more primitive original.*

I. Introduction

The crucial textual problem facing both historians and exegetes in dealing with the book of Acts is the existence of two relatively distinct forms of the text. One such text-type is generally known as the *Western* text (common usage rather than accuracy demands that we continue to use this term).[1] The primary representative of this text is Codex Bezae, which contains over 800 more words than the commonly used NA[26]=UBS[3] text for the extant sections.[2]

The other form of the text might be described as the *Alexandrian* text, with Sinaiticus and Vaticanus as its primary representatives.[3] A commonly cited comparison suggests that the Western text is 8.5% longer than the Alexandrian text.[4]

A further indication of the magnitude of the problems posed by the texts of Acts is supplied by the observation that Metzger's *Textual Commentary* on the UBS[3] edition devotes one-third of its pages to consideration of Acts, mainly because of the complexities of the Western text.[5]

Textual critics have struggled to explain the origin and nature of the Western text of Acts since at least 1685 when Jean Leclerc suggested that Luke may have published two editions of Acts (a suggestion he subsequently rescinded).[6]

In this paper we shall, in section II, briefly survey the discussions which contributed to the modern consensus that the

---

[1]Griesbach suggested that 'Western' (*occidentalis*) was an appropriate term for this recension in view of its use 'subsequent to the time of Tertullian by the Africans, Italians and Gauls and other Western nations' ('Prolegomena' of *Novum Testamentum Graece. Textum ad fidem Codicum versionum et patrum recensuit et lectionis varietatem adjecit* [Second Edition; 2 vols; London & Halle, 1796 & 1806] vol. 1, LXXIV). This term has remained, despite the widespread recognition that numerous witnesses for this type of text are not from the West at all (something Griesbach was not unaware of).

[2]Bezae lacks the following passages: 8:29-10:14; 22:10-20; 22:29-end.

[3]For general information on the terminology and practice of NT textual criticism see B.M. Metzger, *The Text of the New Testament: Its Transmission, Corruption, and Restoration* (3rd ed; NY & Oxford: OUP, 1992) or B. & K. Aland, *The Text of the New Testament. An Introduction to the Critical Editions and to the Theory and Practice of Modern Textual Criticism* (ET E.F. Rhodes; Grand Rapids: Eerdmans & Leiden: Brill, 1987).

[4]Kenyon arrived at 8.5% by comparing the (Alexandrian) text of Westcott & Hort (18,401 words) with the (Western) text of A.C. Clark (19,983 words), see 'The Western Text in the Gospels and Acts', *Proceedings of the British Academy* 24 (1939) 287-315; p. 310.

[5]B.M. Metzger, *A Textual Commentary on the Greek New Testament* (London: UBS, 1975). The general discussion on pp. 259-272 is an excellent introduction to the problem.

[6]In a letter to R. Simon, see W.A. Strange, *The Problem of the Text of Acts* (SNTSMS 71; Cambridge: CUP, 1992) 3 & 205.

Western text represents a later form of the text which arose from paraphrasing interpolations to the shorter (Alexandrian) original. This consensus has been challenged by various scholars, and in section III we shall investigate several of these alternative positions, including: i) the position of Blass that Luke was responsible for both versions of the text of Acts; ii) the view that the Alexandrian text is the result of a later redactor having abbreviated Luke's original ('Western') text; and iii) the position of Strange which incorporates elements of all the other views.

It will emerge from this historical survey that there are several crucial categories of variants which provide the basis for the consensus argument that the Western text is a secondary (non-Lukan) revision of a shorter *Vorlage* (best represented in the Alexandrian tradition). Section IV of our paper discusses several of these categories, focussing especially on variants which are said to reflect a distinctive (or at least secondary) theological *Tendenz* in the Western tradition, i.e. passages concerning Jesus, the Holy Spirit, the status of the apostles and the apostolic decree. The conclusion (section V) will briefly summarise our findings and suggest areas that need further exploration.

II. The History of Research: Towards a Consensus[7]

It was, in several ways, the pioneering work of Johann Jakob Griesbach which spelled the beginning of the end for the *textus receptus*.[8] Developing the earlier family-recension theories of Bengel and Semler, Griesbach assigned the textual material extant at the time to three different recensions: Alexandrian, Western, and Constantinopolitan.[9] This last group he believed to be a compilation from the two ancient recensions: the Alexandrian and the Western, of

---

[7]For bibliographical information see A.F.J. Klijn, *A Survey of the Researches into the Western Text of the Gospels and Acts* (Utrecht: Kemink, 1949); *A Survey of the Researches into the Western Text of the Gospels and Acts: Part Two 1949-1969* (NovTSS 21; Leiden: Brill, 1969).

[8]Although Bengel (1687-1752) and others had doubted many of the readings of the *textus receptus*, it was Griesbach who first abandoned the *textus receptus* in print (see Metzger, *Text*, 121; W.G. Kümmel, *The New Testament: The History of the Investigation of its Problems* [London: SCM, 1973] 74).

[9]'Prolegomena', *NTG* (1796) LXXIVf.; also Metzger, *Text*, 119f.

which he gave preference to the Alexandrian recension.[10] Subsequent investigations in the nineteenth century, informed by a flow of new material from Tischendorf and others, gave supremacy to the Alexandrian text-type in general (especially, for example, in Westcott & Hort, whose liking for Sinaiticus and Vaticanus is well known).[11] The support which many early papyri gave to an Alexandrian text-type means that the general situation, although markedly more complex, has not changed a great deal in the twentieth century. Most scholars accept (with variously weighty reservations) that the Alexandrian text-type is to be preferred to the Western text.[12]

The Western text of the book of Acts, represented by variant readings found within codex Bezae (and others) has been regarded as essentially secondary to the shorter 'Alexandrian' text.[13] This was true in the era of Westcott & Hort,[14] and has been supported by, *inter*

---

[10]According to Griesbach, Western readings occured in D, the Latin versions and older Latin Fathers as well as in the Syriac and Arabic translations ('Prolegomena', *NTG* (1796) LXXIV; cf. his earlier comments in 'Praefatio' § 2.5, *Novum Testamentum Graece. Textum ad fidem Codicum, versionum et patrum emendavit et lectionis varietatem adjecit* [Halae: vol 1, 1777; vol 2, 1775] vol 1, iii-xxxii: this volume deals with the Gospels and Acts).

[11]In fact, of course, B.F. Westcott & F.J.A. Hort believed in four groups: Syrian, Western, Alexandrian and Neutral (see 'Introduction', *The New Testament in the Original Greek* (2 vols; London: Macmillan & Co. Ltd, 1881) II, 178f. for summary; for discussion see Metzger, *Text*, 129-137). But as modern critics regard Sinaiticus and Vaticanus as generally 'Alexandrian' the language used above is not untenable.

[12]Some Western readings have been accepted as genuine and original, but this is generally despite their 'Westernness' (e.g. Mk. 2:22; 11:6; Lk. 24:52, 53) or because they in fact vary from Western tendencies (e.g. non-interpolations).

[13]The main witnesses for the Western text are Codex Bezae (D), three small papyri ($\mathfrak{P}$29 $\mathfrak{P}$38 $\mathfrak{P}$48), a thirteenth century minuscule (614), a fifth century coptic manuscript in Middle Egyptian (mae), readings in the Harclean Syriac some of which are marked in that text by an asterisk (syr^h*) others stand in the margin (syr^hmg), an Old Latin manuscript h and citations in early Latin Fathers. See Aland, *Text* or Metzger, *Text* for descriptions of manuscripts and for fuller treatments of the main witnesses see M.-E. Boismard & A. Lamouille, *Le Texte Occidental des Actes des Apôtres: Reconstitution et Réhabilitation* (Synthèse 17; Paris: Editions Recherche sur les Civilisations, 1984; 2 vols) I, 11-95. Also available is B.M. Metzger, *The Early Versions of the New Testament: their origin, transmission and limitations* (Oxford: Clarendon, 1977).

[14]See their discussion in 'Introduction', 120-126, 172-175. A few years later E. Nestle was clearly aware that his position, favouring the Western text, was a minority position (*Introduction to the Textual Criticism of the Greek New Testament* [London: Williams & Norgate, 1901] 222, 226 = *Einführung in das Griechische Neue Testament* [ed 2; Göttingen: Vandenhoeck & Ruprecht, 1899] 185, 189f.).

alia, J.H. Ropes,[15] F.G. Kenyon,[16] M. Dibelius,[17] E.J. Epp,[18] R.P.C. Hanson,[19] and B. Aland.[20] This consensus is clearly reflected in the texts of the favoured modern editions of the Greek New Testament (NA[26], UBS[3]). Metzger reports that 'more often than not the shorter, Alexandrian text was preferred [by the editorial committee]'.[21]

The consensus position has also been upheld, during the course of the present century, by most commentators;[22] including C.S.C. Williams,[23] F.F. Bruce,[24] E. Haenchen,[25] R. Pesch,[26] H. Conzelmann,[27] and G. Schneider.[28] In this context it is also appropriate to mention the historical work of C.J. Hemer. Hemer handles the textual problem in an explicitly consensual manner: in general he prefers the 'Alexandrian' rather than the 'Western' text (clearly affirming his conviction that the Western text is not original), but he seeks to allow some flexibility, and regularly notes Western readings which impinge on historical questions. Despite his sympathy with the view

---

[15]*The Text of Acts* (Vol III; *The Beginnings of Christianity: Part I: The Acts of the Apostles* [London: MacMillan & Co., Ltd., 1926]) esp. ccxv-ccxlvi.

[16]'The Western Text in the Gospels and Acts' (see n. 4).

[17]'The Text of Acts: An Urgent Critical Task', *Journal of Religion* 21 (1941) 421-431, cited here from H. Greeven (ed.), *Studies in the Acts of the Apostles* (London: SCM, 1956) 84-92.

[18]*The Theological Tendency of Codex Bezae Cantabrigiensis in Acts* (SNTSMS 3; Cambridge: CUP, 1966).

[19]'The Provenance of the Interpolator in the 'Western' Text of Acts and of Acts Itself', *NTS* 12 (1965) 211-230.

[20]'Entstehung, Charakter, und Herkunft des sogenannt westlichen Texte: Untersucht an der Apostelgeschichte', *ETL* 62 (1986) 5-65.

[21]Metzger, *Textual Commentary*, 272.

[22]W.W. Gasque suggests that Ropes' discussion convinced 'most scholars' (*A History of the Criticism of the Acts of the Apostles* [Grand Rapids: Eerdmans, 1975] 98), unfortunately the textual problem receives little treatment in his work.

[23]*A Commentary on the Acts of the Apostles* (BNTC; London: Adam & Charles Black, 1957) 48-53; cf. also his *Alterations to the Text of the Synoptic Gospels and Acts* (Oxford: Blackwell, 1951) 54-82.

[24]*The Acts of the Apostles: The Greek Text with Introduction and Commentary* (Grand Rapids: Eerdmans, 1951, reprint of 1975) 43f.

[25]*The Acts of the Apostles: A Commentary* (Philadelphia: Westminster, 1971; ET from 14th German edition; Göttingen: Vandenhoeck & Ruprecht, 1965) 50-59; cf. also 'Zum Text der Apostelgeschichte', *ZTK* 54 (1957) 22-55; and (with P. Weigandt), 'The Original Text of Acts?', *NTS* 14 (1967) 469-481.

[26]*Die Apostelgeschichte 1. Teilband (Apg 1-12)* (EKK; Zürich: Benziger, 1986) 53-55.

[27]*A Commentary on the Acts of the Apostles* (Hermeneia; Philadelphia: Fortress, 1987) xxxv.

[28]*Die Apostelgeschichte. Erster Teil: Einleitung. Kommentar zu Kap. 1,1 - 8,40* (HTKzNT; Freiburg/Basel/Wien: Herder, 1980) 167f.

that Luke may have produced two editions,[29] Hemer could find no Western reading which commended itself as original.[30]

III. Challenging the Consensus: the originality of the Western Text

It is F. Blass who is most often associated with the view that Luke was responsible for both forms of the text of Acts (although the position continues to have its modern advocates, as we shall see).[31] Blass argued that the two recensions have such a similar style that they must have come from the same author; that additional information such as that found in 1:5; 14:2; 21:16 could only have come from someone with knowledge of the events, and that the vocabulary of the Western variants is generally 'Lukan'.[32] According to Blass, Luke wrote a rough draft of his history of the church while in Rome, and this was the full and longer version that is represented in the Western recension (β). Luke subsequently used this rough draft as the basis for his second edition, the version sent to Theophilus. This version was clearer, terser and more carefully composed (deleting superfluous phrases), and this is represented in the Alexandrian recension (α according to Blass).

---

[29]*The Book of Acts in the Setting of Hellenistic History* (ed C.H. Gempf; WUNT 49; Tübingen: J.C.B. Mohr, 1989) 55.

[30]On pp. 193-201 Hemer discusses a long list of passages where the Western and Alexandrian texts differ (1:23; 2:17-21; 3:11; 4:6; 5:18, 21; 7:43; 11:20; 11:28; 12:10; 12:25; 13:8; 13:14; 13:33; 14:13; 14:25; 15:20, 29; 15:34; 16:12; 18:7; 18:21; 19:9; 19:14, 16; 19:28; 20:4; 20:15; 21:1; 21:16; 27:5; 28:16), and where the Western variations 'involve additional or discrepant historical details', (p. 200). He did accept (like many scholars) that the western text might occasionally preserve a correct tradition or inference, and suggested that 'the reviser had some knowledge of Asia Minor, as passages touching Lystra, Ephesus, Trogyllium and elsewhere can show', (p. 200).

[31]F. Blass, 'Die Textüberlieferung in der Apostelgeschichte', *TSK* 67 (1894) 86-119 and *Acta Apostolorum sive Lucae ad Theophilum liber alter. Editio Philologica* (Göttingen: Vandenhoeck & Ruprecht, 1895). For an exposition in English see 'The Question of the Double Text in St. Luke's Gospel and in the Acts' and 'The Proofs for Two Distinct Text in the Acts', in *Philology of the Gospels* (London: Macmillan, 1898) 96-112 & 113-137. Cf. also W.M. Ramsay, 'Professor F. Blass on the Two Editions of Acts', *The Expositor*, Series 5, Vol 1 (1895) 129-142, 212-225.

[32]*Acta Apostolorum*, 31f. (cf. Strange, *Problem*, 5).

Blass won numerous and influential supporters, including T. Zahn,[33] E. Nestle,[34] F.C. Conybeare,[35] and J.M. Wilson.[36] While some critics attacked his reconstruction of Luke's situation in Rome,[37] most focussed on what were felt to be the two crucial weaknesses of the theory. The first of these was the so-called pietistic *Tendenz* of many of the Western variants, especially in the inclusion of christological titles, a heightened emphasis on the Holy Spirit, and an elevated view of the apostles.[38] Such critics argued that if the Western text differs from the Alexandrian in a pietistic direction, then it can most readily be understood along the lines of other theologically motivated alterations which textual critics have generally accepted as secondary.[39] The second weakness which was perceived in the Blass hypothesis was the problem of inconsistencies between the Western and Alexandrian text-types. Thus, it was argued, that if in fact the same author had been responsible for both text-types, we would expect neither distinctive theological approaches, nor historical or geographical contradictions. Many critics have claimed, however, that just such inconsistencies do exist. A particular focus of interest in this area has been the divergent forms of the apostolic decree of Acts 15.[40] Both of these two areas of disagreement have continued to be of great importance in more recent discussions.

---

[33]T. Zahn, *Introduction to the New Testament* (trans from 3rd German edition; M.W. Jacobus; Edinburgh: T. & T. Clark, 1909; 3 vols) vol. 3, 8-41.

[34]*Introduction*, 224. (See n. 14.)

[35]'Two Notes on Acts', ZNW 20 (1921) 41f.

[36]*The Acts of the Apostles Translated from the Codex Bezae with an Introduction on its Lucan Origin and Importance* (London: SPCK, 1923).

[37]Blass maintained that the reverse situation applied to the Gospel: the fuller first version was sent to Theophilus (and is Alexandrian) while the revised, shorter version was left in Rome (Western); this reversal attracted criticism from A. Jülicher (*An Introduction to the New Testament* [trans by J.P. Ward from 1900 2nd ed.; London: Smith, Elder & Co., 1904] 452-455); cf. also Kenyon, 'Western Text', 299-301.

[38]Especially T.E. Page, 'Blass' Edition of Acts', *Classical Review* 11 (1897) 317-320 (Metzger, *Textual Commentary*, 262f. has substantial quotations); Ramsay, 'Are There Two Lukan Texts of Acts?', 466-469; also B. Weiss, *Der Codex D in der Apostelgeschichte* (TUGaL 2.1; Leipzig: J.C. Hinrichs, 1897).

[39]So, e.g. Williams, *Alterations*, 54-82; following M.-J. Lagrange, *Introduction à l'étude du Nouveau Testament: II. Critique Textuelle; II: La critique rationnelle* (EBib; Paris: J. Gabalda, 1935, 2nd ed.) 390-393. For a sympathetic assessment of the broad principle see P.M. Head, 'Christology and Textual Transmission: Reverential Alterations in the Synoptic Gospels', *NovT* 35 (1993) 105-129.

[40]See, e.g. Ramsay, 'Are There Two Lukan Texts of Acts?', 462-464. Ramsay was favourable to the historical information contained at certain points in the

Indeed, to some extent, the modern debate concerning the Western text revolves around the same issues which were current almost a century ago. Three crucial questions are: i) to what extent is the style and vocabulary of the Western text recognisably 'Lukan'?; ii) can the Western text be explained as a secondary recension of a shorter original motivated by a theological *Tendenz*? and iii) do the differences between the Western text and the Alexandrian text constitute evidence against common authorship? However, recent discussions have added additional complexities in the area of identifying the western text and the related question of whether the evidence suggests an individual 'redactor' behind the original form of the Western text, or merely a loose collection of paraphrastic renderings.

Of course, we should not give the impression that Blass' position has been the only option for advocates of the Western text. Ramsay pointed out that although much of Blass' discussion about the Western text had value, he had not established, even on his own terms, that the Eastern (Alexandrian) form was 'equally original and good'.[41] A.C. Clark argued that Blass' hypothesis was fatally flawed by the presence of contradictions between the two forms of the text.[42] He maintained the position that the Alexandrian form was a later revision of Luke's original Western text.[43] Clark's discussion was based on the palaeographical principle that lines of text ($\sigma\tau\acute{\iota}\chi o\iota$) could be omitted by homoioarcton or homoioteleuton. The Bezan text is written in lines of sense (properly $\kappa\hat{\omega}\lambda\alpha$), as was the original

---

Western text; but he regarded it as generally secondary, suggesting 'the first beginnings of Pauline legend', *St. Paul the Traveller and the Roman Citizen* (London: Hodder & Stoughton, 1895; cited from 1903 seventh edition) 26. Also A. Harnack, *Das Aposteldecret (Act. 15:29) und die Blass'sche Hypothese* (Berlin: Reimer, 1899) = *Studien zur Geschichte des Neuen Testaments und der alten Kirche. I: Zur neutestamentlichen Textkritik* (AzK 19; Berlin/Leipzig: de Gruyter, 1931) 1-32. More recently Haenchen cites the divergent forms of the apostolic decree as refuting Blass (*Acts*, 51).

[41] 'Are There Two Lukan Texts of Acts?', 461.

[42] *The Acts of the Apostles. A Critical Edition with Introduction and Notes on Selected Passages* (Oxford: Clarendon, 1933) xxif, xlviii-l (following P. Corssen, 'Acta Apostolorum ed. F. Blass', *Göttingische gelehrte Anzeigen* 158 [1896] 425-448). He draws attention to the following passages: 1:2; 4:6; 13:19f.; 13:33; 15:1f.; 15:20, 29; 18:19; 18:26f.; 19:14-16, cf. 21:16; 20:4. Note that this is one of the few matters upon which Clark and Ropes were in agreement (cf. Ropes, *Text of Acts*, ccxxix).

[43] See also his earlier work: *The Primitive Text of the Gospels and Acts* (Oxford: Clarendon, 1914).

(according to Clark), and Clark argued that the Alexandrian text was formed by the omission of these whole sense-lines from the original:

> in Acts (*not* in the Gospels) Γ [i.e. the Alexandrian text-type] represents the work of an abbreviator who, having before him a MS. written in στίχοι similar to those found in D, frequently (not, of course, always) adopted the rough and ready method of striking out lines in his model, botching from time to time to produce a construction.[44]

Clark's approach has not won scholarly support,[45] and was severely criticised by Kenyon who showed that there was no evidence for the use of such sense-lines in the early period.[46] Overall, the plausibility of this position will depend upon the plausibility of the deliberate redactional activity envisaged by Clark's theory.

Several recent works on the Western text have sought to provide support for the initial premise of Blass' hypothesis: that in style and vocabulary the Western readings bear a remarkable similarity to undisputed Lukan style. R.S. MacKenzie noticed several 'genuine Lucanisms' in the Western variants to Acts 10:41; 13:31, 38, 41 and 17:26-28:[47]

> i) the presence of συστρέφειν in 10:41D (also in 11:28D; 16:39D; 17:5D corresponding to Lukan usage in 23:12 and 28:3);
>
> ii) the use of ἄχρι νῦν in 13:31D (cf. 20:26D which also uses ἄχρι to designate a period of time; as Luke does in undisputed passages);
>
> iii) the use of μετάνοια in 13:38D (cf. Luke 3:16D; generally favoured by Luke);
>
> iv) the use of καὶ ἐσιγήσαν in 13:41D (Luke regularly signals the silent reaction of listeners to speeches in Acts);

---

[44]Clark, *Acts*, viii; cf. xlv-lii for the methods of the abbreviator.

[45]B.H. Streeter's positive review is an exception, 'The Primitive Text of the Acts', *JTS* 34 (1933) 232-241.

[46]Kenyon, 'Western Text', 301-309.

[47]'The Western Text of Acts: some Lucanisms in selected sermons', *JBL* 104 (1985) 637-650. A 'genuine Lucanism' is defined as: '(1) a word or expression used only in Luke-Acts; (2) a word or expression used especially by the author of Luke-Acts when another word or expression might have been expected; or (3) a word or expression used in a manner we have come to regard as characteristically Lukan', (p. 637).

v) the use of αἷμα in 17:26D; μάλιστα in 17:27D and καθ᾽ ἡμέραν in 17:28D (all, he argues, are regularly Lukan terms).

These proposals were investigated by R.F. Hull, and found wanting in detail and in method.[48] For example, he noted that Acts 10:41D 'harmonizes the content of Peter's sermon with the preamble of Acts (namely, 1:4) and the Emmaus story of Luke 24'.[49] In addition, although MacKenzie had argued that 'the possibility of the Lucan character of some of the variant readings means, among other things, that they cannot be dismissed as simply the work of a particular reviser or of revisers';[50] Hull pointed out that even if the 'Lukan' character of the Bezan vocabulary could be established MacKenzie's conclusion would not follow. This has been reinforced by T.C. Geer in his critique of recent studies of the vocabulary of the Western text: 'the only sure conclusion. . .is that if the compiler of this "Western" text was one of the New Testament authors, he would most likely have been Luke'.[51]

The most wide ranging and thorough investigation of the vocabulary and style of the Western text is the combined work of M.-E. Boismard and A. Lamouille.[52] In an earlier study Boismard (aided by Lamouille) had argued that the Western variants of Acts 11:2 and 19:1 were Lukan both in vocabulary and style.[53] In their 1984 attempt to reconstruct and rehabilitate the Western text they took this further, suggesting that an original Western text (TO) and the Alexandrian text (TA) both reflect Lukan characteristics.[54] The original Western text-form gave rise to two derivative forms, one a pure form (TO[1]),

---

[48]'"Lucanisms" in the Western Text of Acts? A reappraisal', *JBL* 107 (1988) 695-707.

[49]'"Lucanisms" in the Western Text of Acts? A reappraisal', 698.

[50]'The Western Text of Acts: some Lucanisms in selected sermons', 650.

[51]'The Presence and Significance of Lucanisms in the 'Western' Text of Acts', *JSNT* 39 (1990) 74; see pp. 70-72 on MacKenzie.

[52]M.-E. Boismard & A. Lamouille, *Le Texte Occidental des Actes des Apôtres: Reconstitution et Réhabilitation* (Synthèse 17; Paris: Editions Recherche sur les Civilisations, 1984; 2 vols). Henceforth cited as B & L.

[53]See M.-E. Boismard, 'The Text of Acts: A Problem of Literary Criticism?', *New Testament Textual Criticism: Its Significance to Exegesis* (FS B.M. Metzger; ed. E.J. Epp & G.D. Fee; Oxford: Clarendon, 1981) 147-157.

[54]They list over 950 examples of Lukan style in B & L, II, 195-335, sorted by alphabet, frequency and verse order, comparing frequency with Acts, Luke and the rest of the NT; and into categories: A (100% of occurences are in Luke-Acts); B (>80% are in Luke-Acts); C (>60% are in Luke-Acts).

and the other less pure (TO[2]).[55] Thus the original (Lukan) Western text needs to be reconstructed from the extant sources. Their overall theory then involves the priority of the Western text and a subsequent Lukan redaction:

> Luke wrote a first redaction of Acts, of which we find an echo in the Western text. . .a certain number of years later he radically altered his initial work, not only from the stylistic point of view, as Blass had it, but also from the point of view of its content; that these two redactions were fused into one to give the present text of Acts, or more precisely, the Alexandrian text (in a purer form than that which we now have).[56]

In connection with the questions commonly posed to the Blass hypothesis, Boismard and Lamouille answer that there *are* clearly secondary elements in the Western text (they agree with Ropes that many elements are due to 'the paraphrastic re-writing of a second-century Christian'),[57] but that these are not integral to the original Western text which they reconstruct from various sources. They postulate some years between Luke's two editions in order to account for the change in content.[58]

The material contained within Boismard and Lamouille's two volumes is of importance for our study, as it is for the study of Luke-Acts in general, and we shall interact on some detailed points in what follows. Two issues of a general nature must be considered briefly here.[59] The first concerns the hypothetical nature of their

---

[55]B & L, I, 97-118.

[56]'Luc aurait écrit une première rédaction des Actes dont nous trouvons un écho dans le texte Occidental; il aurait, un certain nombre d'années plus tard, profondément remanié son oeuvre primitive, non seulement du point de vue stylistique, comme le voulait Blass, mais encore du point de vue du contenu. Ces deux rédactions auraient été ensuite fusionnées en une seule pour donner le texte actuel des Actes, plus exactement le texte Alexandrin (sous une forme plus pure que celle que nous avons maintenant)'. B & L, I, 9; ET from Strange, *Problem*, 31.

[57]B & L, I, 10 citing Ropes, *Text of Acts*, [no page given]; examples of such re-writing, attributed to TO[2], are discussed in B & L, I, 111-118.

[58]Boismard & Lamouille have recently argued that the Alexandrian text is the third edition of Acts (Acts III); the reconstructed Western text (Acts II) helps in unravelling Luke's sources (Acts I), M.-E. Boismard and A. Lamouille, *Les Actes des deux Apôtres* (3 vols; Études Bibliques NS 12-14; Paris: Gabalda, 1990). For a summary and sympathetic review see J. Taylor, 'The Making of Acts: A New Account', *RevBib* 97 (1990) 504-524.

[59]See further F. Neirynck & F. van Segbroeck, 'Le texte des Actes des Apôtres et les caractéristiques stylistiques lucaniennes', *ETL* 61 (1985) 304-339.

reconstructed text, which has been criticised by both J.N. Birdsall and, to a lesser degree, J.K. Elliott.[60] In particular it is questionable whether their assumption of an earlier 'pure' form of the Western text is justified in view of the evidence of early 'western' papyri such as $\mathfrak{P}$29, $\mathfrak{P}$38, $\mathfrak{P}$48.[61] Further, it often appears that the main reason for the choice of an original occidental reading is often its proximity to Lukan style; this creates a degree of circularity in the structure of the whole argument, as Geer comments: 'the Western text seems to be what Boismard makes it'.[62]

The second problem is the issue we noted above in connection with MacKenzie: by limiting the comparison with the style and vocabulary of the New Testament, Boismard and Lamouille establish only that of all the New Testament writers the Western variants most closely resemble Luke.[63] This is clearly significant, but in view of the widespread scribal tendencies of harmonisation and assimilation, it is intrinsically probable that a secondary recension will stylistically resemble the *Vorlage*.[64] This is especially true if, as seems likely, the Western text conforms various passages to programmatic (Lukan) statements:[65] a later revisor will automatically look as if he is using Lukan style. Arguments from vocabulary and style cannot establish common authorship if the presence of inconsistencies and explicable

---

[60]See Birdsall's review in *JTS* 39 (1988) 571-577; and Elliott's in *NovT* 29 (1987) 285-289. Elliott (p. 286) draws attention to readings supported only by the Ethiopic (e.g. 27:38-40; 28:11-16) or a single Old Latin MS (27:2 based on h) or other single sources, as well as readings supported only by conjecture (13:27; 19:14).

[61]See Birdsall's review (p. 576); and B. Aland, 'Entstehung, Charakter, und Herkunft des sogenannt westlichen Texte', who advocates a layered approach to the development of the Western text.

[62]'The Presence and Significance of Lucanisms in the 'Western' Text of Acts', 67.

[63]See especially Geer, 'The Presence and Significance of Lucanisms in the 'Western' Text of Acts', 70, 74; cf. also Birdsall's review (p. 575).

[64]This is denied by J. Murphy-O'Connor in his review of B & L (*RevBib* 93 [1986] 599) but examples and parallels can be found in second century redactions of gospel material. Thus, even in the new material, the *Secret Gospel of Mark* bears significant stylistic parallels with Mark's Gospel and *Papyrus Egerton 2* contains significant parallels with John's Gospel. Other examples of this type of situation would probably bear investigation (e.g. the various re-presentations of Matthew's Gospel in the Ebionite and Nazarene Gospels).

[65]See below for the influence of passages such as 3:6 or 4:8; and cf. G. Zuntz, 'On the Western Test of the Acts of the Apostles', *Opuscula Selecta: Classica, Hellenistica, Christiana* (Manchester: Manchester University Press, 1972; essay originally dated 1939) 189-215.

tendencies in the variant readings demand a different explanation.[66] This is particularly true since the Western tradition (and Bezae in particular) in the Gospels is particularly marked by harmonisation, and harmonisation will invariably entail a degree of stylistic imitation.[67]

The most recent attempt to address *The Problem of the Text of Acts* is the book of that name by W.A. Strange.[68] This book is now (in English) the most important challenge to the consensus position since Clark (1933), although, as he acknowledges, it is Boismard and Lamouille who have prepared the way for his argument. His general position can be summarised as follows: The Western version arose as a 'commentary-like' series of annotations (and is thus later and supplementary to the shorter text), but is 'Lukan' in style and vocabulary (following Boismard and Lamouille). The author of Acts left two separate rough drafts of Acts, one of which consisted of an annotated version of the other.[69] These two versions remained unused until they were eventually published separately some time between A.D. 150 and A.D. 175 in order to counter the Gnostic and Marcionite claims to Paul.[70]

We shall deal below with Strange's arguments concerning some of the key passages (particularly Acts 8:36-39 and the apostolic decree: 15:20, 29; 21:25). At this stage we should note that there are several weaknesses in Strange's approach to the dating of these two editions. Firstly, it depends fundamentally on a massive argument from silence: he argues that since there is no conclusive evidence of its citation Acts did not exist until the middle of the second century.[71]

---

[66]Cf. Geer, 'The Presence and Significance of Lucanisms in the 'Western' Text of Acts', 71f.

[67]Concerning Bezae see D.C. Parker, *Codex Bezae: An early Christian manuscript and its text* (Cambridge: CUP, 1992) 198-228 and his summary statments on pp. 247f and 279f. In general see T. Baarda, 'ΔΙΑΦΩΝΙΑ - ΣΥΜΦΩΝΙΑ: Factors in the Harmonization of the Gospels, Especially in the Diatessaron of Tatian', *Gospel Traditions in the Second Century: Origins, Recensions, Text, and Transmission* (ed. W.L. Peterson; Christianity & Judaism in Antiquity 3; London & New York: University of Notre Dame, 1989) 133-154.

[68]See n. 6.

[69]Thus 'the copy of Acts from which the Western text was derived was an autograph annotated by the author' (Strange, *Problem*, 175).

[70]For a general discussion see my review in *EvQ* (forthcoming).

[71]Evidence (admittedly inconclusive, although not mentioned by Strange) which suggests knowledge of Acts among the Apostolic Fathers and Justin Martyr is given by B. Weiss, *A Manual of Introduction to the New Testament* (ET A.J.K. Davidson; New York: Funk & Wagnalls, 1889; 2 vols) I, 39, 69; additional

Secondly, his position requires that two forms of Luke's notes were kept, quite independently, across over eighty years, but never published or referred to (this is rather strange: who kept it? where? why? how?) In addition, this scenario fails to account for the prefaces (to Luke and Acts), which suggest a connected 'published' form. Nevertheless Strange offers important discussions of many Western variants, some of which I shall deal with below.

IV. The Theological *Tendenz* in Western Variants

We have mentioned several times that one of the key arguments used against the originality of the Western text is the presence within this text-type of variants which seem to reflect a later revision.[72] It is notable that Ropes, a key defender of the originality of the Alexandrian text, suggested that 'of any special point of view, theological or other, on the part of the "Western" reviser, it is difficult to find any trace'.[73] Nevertheless, he did find some such traces, such as a hostile attitude to Judaism (14:5); a positive attitude to Gentile Christianity (24:5; cf. 2:17; 2:14); and a desire to emphasise the pre-conversion paganness of the devout (20:21; 26:15). Several other categories have also been suggested, and a large number of passages containing Western variants are involved.[74] In what follows we shall

---

material is discussed in Haenchen, *Acts*, 3-14. According to patristic sources Acts was known (but rejected) by second century groups including: Ebionites (acc. Epiph., *Haer.* 30.16); Marcionites (acc. Tert., *Adv. Marc.* V.2), Severians (acc. Euseb, *EH* IV.29), Manichaeans (acc. August., *De Util. Cred.* II.7). In view of this, and the much later testimony of Chrysostom: 'To many persons this Book is so little known, both it and its author, that they are not even aware that there is such a book in existence' (*Homilies on Acts*, NPNF I.XI. [1889] 1) it is dangerous to assume the non-existence of the document on the basis of its non-appearance in the literature of the period.

[72]It should not be supposed that all passages containing Western variants exhibit distinctive theological tendencies. Many involve historical, geographical or grammatical differences from the Alexandrian text. Most scholars have focussed on theological differences as signalling a pattern of secondary development in the Western tradition more clearly than other sorts of differences, hence we have chosen to focus on these passages in what follows.

[73]*Text of Acts*, ccxxxiii.

[74]See especially P.H. Menoud, 'The Western Text and the Theology of Acts', *SNTS Bull* 2 (1951) 19-32 (cited here from his *Jesus Christ and the Faith: A Collection of Studies* [PTMS 18; Pittsburgh: Pickwick, 1978] 61-83); Williams, *Alterations*, 54-75; Epp, *Tendency*. There are at least two categories that I have not dealt with in

group these under the following headings: Christology (this includes material used in baptismal and confessional contexts), the Holy Spirit, and the Status of the Apostles; a final section will discuss the texts of the Apostolic Decree.[75]

1. Christology

A commonly cited tendency of some Western variants is the addition and/or expansion of honorific titles of Jesus. The most obvious examples include the addition of christological terminology to relatively simple titles of Jesus:

i) χριστος added to κυριος Ιησους in:
  1:21 (Dd 876 1108 1611 1765 1838 *pc* syh eth6mss mae). [TO2]
  4:33 (Dd Ee 323 945 1739 2495 *al* r). [TO2][76]
  8:16 (Dd vg3mss mae eth4mss). [TO2][77]

---

this paper. The supposed anti-Jewish tendency (mentioned by Ropes, cited above; and discussed by Menoud, 'Western Text', 73f. and most emphatically by Epp, *Tendency*; and 'The "Ignorance Motif" in Acts and Anti-Judaic Tendencies in Codex Bezae', *HTR* 55 [1962] 51-62), the key passages include 3:17; 4:9; 13:45; 14:2-7; 18:12f. (reservations are voiced by C.K. Barrett, 'Is There a Theological Tendency in Codex Bezae', *Text and Interpretation: Studies in the New Testament Presented to Matthew Black* [ed. E. Best & R. McL. Wilson; Cambridge: CUP, 1979] 15-27). Secondly a possible anti-woman tendency (Ropes, *Text of Acts*, ccxxxiv; Menoud, 'Western Text', 76f.; B. Witherington, 'The Anti-Feminist Tendencies of the "Western" Text in Acts', *JBL* 103 (1984) 82-84), the key passages are 1:14; 17:4, 12, 34; 18:26.

[75]The lists of witnesses given in the following sections refers to divergences from NA26 and are derived from four sources: Clark, *Acts*; NA26; B & L, vol. two; Strange, *Problem*. In general I have followed B & L as the authoritative collection of manuscript and versional evidence (although I have used the sigla of NA26 except where citing directly from B & L). I have not cited all the patristic witnesses given in B & L and Strange. I have also noted B & L's classification of the variants [TO, TO2 etc.]. Plans exist for a major critical edition of Acts (see C.D. Osborn, 'The search for the original text of Acts; the international project on the text of Acts', *JSNT* 44 (1991) 39-55.

[76]Ιησου Χριστου του κυριου is read by S.01 A 36 1175 *pc* vg. B & L's TO lacks του κυριου (with 808 1522 1831 ethms).

[77]B & L's TO lacks κυριου: a(629) vg(D*). This is an example of the slim attestation available for B & L's TO: the Latin column of a fourteenth century minuscule (Gregory-Aland: 629) and the original of a ninth century manuscript of the vulgate.

11:20 (D 33vid *pc* w mae). [TA=TO][78]

15:11 (C Dd Ψ 33 36 431 453 467 522 876 945 1175 1739 1765 1891 2298 it syrP boPt eth10mss geo Irenlat). [TO2][79]

16:31 (C Dd E Ψ 0120 𝔐 syrP sa eth12mss). [TO2]

19:5 (Dd 257 383 614 1799 2412 2147 a(629) b gig syrP syrh* sa eth10mss geo). [TO2][80]

21:13 (C D gig syrP eth10mss CyrilAlex. Tert. Jer. Aug.). [TO2][81]

ii) κυριος added to Ιησους χριστος in:

2:38 (Dd Ee 522 614 876 945 1611 1739 1891 2138 2412 *pc* b c p r syrPh geo [sa mae: different order]; Cyp. Basil). [TO2][82]

5:42 (Dd 1898 gig h p syrP sa eth8mss).[83]

10:48 (Dd 383 81* 1311 *pm* p syrP geo). [TO2][84]

iii) κυριος added to Ιησους in:

7:55 (Dd h p samss mae). [TO2]

18:5 (Dd 383) [not TO]

iv) κυριος and χριστος added to Ιησους in 13:33 (D sa mae Amb. [κυριος without χριστος: 614 & syrh*]). [TO2]

v) Miscellaneous similar additions:

9:20: ο Χριστος before ο υιος του θεου (h l m sa mae Iren.). [TO2, TO=TA]

16:4: τον κυριον Ιησουν Χριστον in wider alteration (D [syrh*]).

20:25: του Ιησου to την βασιλειαν (D gig [+ κυριου] sa Lucifer). [TO]

A very characteristic alteration occurs in several confessional and baptismal contexts:

---

[78]B & L make no reference to this reading (II, 80).

[79]B & L's TO lacks κυριου: ndl.1 (i.e. Netherlands version, from Latin: BM MS Ad. 26663) Tert. NB no Greek witnesses, very weak attestation for this reading.

[80]B & L's TO lacks κυριου: Vg(S) Ps.-Vg(codd) Eth.7 Geo. N.b. 'b' = University of Michigan MS 164 (Beuron 63).

[81]Cf. Clark, *Acts*, 138.

[82]B & L's TO lacks χριστου: IrenLat PhilM Boh(FS).

[83]B & L's TO reads τον κυριον Ιησουν (with C 33 257 *pc* mae).

[84]B & L's TO lacks χριστου: (383) 1175 Eth3.10.

vi) 6:8: The addition of δια του ονοματος κυριου Ιησου Χριστου provides a source for Stephen's signs and wonders (Dd Ee 33 257 431 614 876 913 1611 1765 2138 2412 p t sa mae Aug. [syr[h]: lacks Ιησου χριστου]). [TO[2], TO=TA][85]

vii) 9:17: The addition of εν τω ονοματι Ιησου Χριστου after επιθεις επ αυτον τας χειρας in connection with Ananias restoring Paul's sight (h mae t.3 vg[ms] ps-Chrys.[86]). [TO[2], TO=TA]

viii) 9:40: The addition of εν τω ονοματι του κυριου ημων Ιησου Χριστου occurs in words of Peter to Tabitha (it syr[h*] sa mae geo Cyp. Amb. Spec). [TO[2], TO=TA][87]

ix) 14:10: The addition of σοι λεγω εν τω ονοματι του κυριου Ιησου Χριστου to Paul's healing command (C Dd Ee 242 255 257 323 383 431 467 522 614 876 945 1175 1739 1765 1799 1891 2147 2298 2412 *pm* h syr[phmg] mae sa[mss] boh[mss] eth[10mss] geo). [TO[2], TO=TA]

x) 18:4: An alternative rendering of the verse reads as follows: εισπορευομενος δε εις την συναγωγην κατα παν σαββατον διελεγετο, και εντιθεις το ονομα του κυριου Ιησου, και επιθεν δε ου μονον Ιουδαιους αλλα και Ελληνας is slightly awkward, and introduces 'the name of the Lord Jesus' as the subject of Paul's teaching (D h [a b c dem gig syr[hmg]][88]). [TO]

xi) 18:8: Two separate alterations have Western support: firstly the addition of δια του ονοματος του κυριου Ιησου Χριστου supplying the content of the Corinthian faith (257 383 614 1799 2147 2412 syr[h*]); and secondly (alternatively) the addition of πιστευοντες τω Θεω δια του ονοματος του κυριου ημων Ιησου Χριστου as a description of their baptismal faith (Dd h). [TO].

These variants are widely known, and reflect a general trend which is present in many christologically motivated scribal alterations found in other parts of the New Testament textual tradition.[89] Most scholars have regarded this type of variant as both

---

[85]Cf. Acts 4:30.

[86]Cf. Clark, *Acts*, 55.

[87]Bezae deficient here. Note also the addition of παραχρημα in Ee g m p r sa mae eth[12mss].

[88]This verse is attested in several different forms, and I have oversimplified the situation somewhat here.

[89]See Head, 'Christology and Textual Transmission' for discussion and examples.

typical of the Western textual tradition and 'a strong argument against the view that the Western text is prior to the non-Western'.[90] Boismard and Lamouille have argued that these christological alterations only secondarily infected the Western tradition (hence they are mostly regarded as TO[2]).

According to Boismard and Lamouille the pure TO is the primitive form with a tendency to suppress christological titles,[91] evidence of the multiplication of christological formulae is consistently attributed to the degenerate form TO[2].[92] Thus without disputing the principle (addition of christological titles is characteristic of secondary alterations) they use exactly this criteria to distinguish between TO and TO[2]. The success of their whole endeavour can therefore be measured by the plausibility with which they can reconstruct TO at these points. From this perspective, however, it must be noted that the evidence given in support of their reconstructed TO is very often limited to late versional and patristic sources (see above, especially re. 8:16; 15:11; 19:5; 2:38; 10:48). At other points there is only one Western variant, but this is attributed to TO[2] rather than TO (see above, especially re. 9:20; 6:8; 9:17, 40; 14:10). As Strange suggests, the argument is circular: 'copyists are more likely to add Christological titles, some Western witnesses do not have certain Christological titles, therefore these witnesses give the original Western readings, and therefore the Western text originally had fewer Christological titles'.[93] Although Boismard and Lamouille's position is not impossible, it is far from self-evident, especially considering the widespread Western support for many of these readings, and the paucity of support for their TO readings.[94]

---

[90]Strange, *Problem*, 48.

[91]B & L, I, 107: 'Le TO, au moins sous sa forme primitive (cf. *infra*), a tendance à supprimer les titres christologiques, alors que la tendance des copistes est manifestement à les multiplier'.

[92]B & L, I, 118: 'C'est à TO[2] qu'il faut attribuer la multiplication des formules «au nom de Jésus Christ», surtout à propos des miracles, comme aussi l'addition des titres «Christ» et «Signeur» dès que le nom de Jésus apparaît; à ce point de vue, le TO était beaucoup plus sobre que le TA'.

[93]Strange, *Problem*, 49 (see pp. 48-50 for further critical discussion).

[94]This is not to deny that some western variants may be secondary (or tertiary) developments; examples of this can be seen in various places, including readings unique to D (e.g. 3:13: χριστος added to Ιησουν; 16:40: κυριος in an added sentence); and readings attested among the more marginal western witnesses (e.g. at 11:17 a western addition has three forms, probably reflecting a continuous pattern of development, see below).

In my opinion this type of pietistic variant provides the proper context for the investigation of the Western reading at 8:37. Strange suggests that this variant 'is one of the most theologically significant in the entire work',[95] and argues that the Ethiopian Eunuch's confession of faith is original. The text is as follows:

ειπεν δε αυτω [+ ο Φιλιππος E] ει [εαν E] πιστευεις εξ ολης της καρδιας σου [- σου 323] εξεστιν [σωθησει E] αποκριθεις δε ειπεν πιστευω τον υιον του Θεου ειναι τον Ιησουν Χριστον [εις τον Χριστον τον υιον του Θεου E]

E 36 242 257 323 453 467 522 629 876 913 945 1522 1739 1765 1891 2298 it (i.e. a b c gig l m p r t w y dem) vg[cl] syr[h*] mae geo eth[ms] Iren. Cyp. Aug.). [TO][96]

One of the main features which distinguishes this from the other variants listed above is its much more widespread support. Its absence from 𝔓45 𝔓74 S.01 A B C 33 81 614 cop etc. has stood against it in the eyes of most editors, primarily because 'there is no reason why scribes should have omitted the material, if it had originally stood in the text'.[97] Strange finds a reason, arguing that the verse was omitted because of second century secrecy about Christian rites, as Celsus said: 'Christians perform their rites and teach their doctrines in secret'.[98] The evidence adduced by Strange hardly provides the motive for the omission of a christological confession of such clarity, when such confessions were explicitly part of the public teaching of the church.[99] The passage is not about baptismal rites, but the content of baptismal faith, something that the Western text has taken pains to emphasise at other points (Strange makes his case only by isolating this passage from those listed above). This variant can be profitably compared with other Western expansions to baptismal scenes:

---

[95]Strange, *Problem*, 69.
[96]Strange gives a full list of versional and patristic support, *Problem*, 69; cf. p. 199f. (cf. B & L, II.61). Bezae deficient. N.b. 'y' indicates readings from *Missale Mixtum* (Migne, Pl. LXXXV), cited from B & L.
[97]Metzger, *Textual Commentary*, 359.
[98]Origen, *Contra Celsum*, I.3; Strange cites other evidence from Pliny, Justin and Origen in support (*Problem*, 69f.).
[99]In addition, as Strange acknowledges, Irenaeus quotes the verse with enthusiastic approval (*Against Heresies*, III.12.8).

i) 2:41, which explains that those who *believed* Peter's message were baptised (reading πιστευσαντες either in place of [Dd] or in addition to αποδεξαμενοι [p r vg^{ms} syr^{phmg} mae = TO]);

ii) 18:8, which explains the content of the faith of the Corinthians (discussed above);

iii) 19:5, which adds an explanation of the purpose of baptism (εις αφεσιν αμαρτιων: 𝔓38 Dd 257 383 614 1799 2147 2412 syr^{h*} Chrys.) as well as an expanded christological appelation (mentioned above).

These examples support the argument of Zuntz that the narratives in Acts have been transformed in the western text into 'scenes of a paradigmatic ecclesiastical character'.[100] The passages we have listed here suggest that in terms of transcriptional probabilities, the western variations could be regarded as in line with a common tendency to highlight christological material.[101]

2. The Holy Spirit

The Western text also includes numerous additional references to the Holy Spirit, or explanatory comments:

i) 6:10: the addition of τω αγιω to πνευματι (Dd Ee gig h p t g² mae eth = TO²). This takes place within the context of a larger addition which emphasises the authority of Stephen (which we shall mention below).[102]

ii) 11:17: several western witnesses attest an addition to Peter's question (which takes three forms):

του μη δουναι αυτοις πνευμα αγιον (467 p vg^{ms} mae Aug. BarS.) [TO]

τ. μ. δ. α. π. α. πιστευσασιν επ αυτω (Dd)

---

[100]Zuntz, 'Western Text', 193.

[101]The addition to the final verse in Acts provides a fitting summary to this category of Western variant: *'dicens quia hic est Christus Jesus filius dei per quem incipiet totus mundus iudicari'* [m p dem vg^{mss} syr^h Ephraim Spec.] = οτι ουτος εστιν Ιησους ο υιος του Θεου, δι ου μελλει ολος ο κοσμος κρινεσθαι. [TO²]

[102]Cf. a similar addition of το αγιον at 8:18 (𝔓45 𝔓74 A C D E Ψ 𝔐 latt syr bo = TO²) in a wide range of both Westen and non-Western sources.

τ. μ. δ. α. π. α. π. επι τον κυριον Ιησουν Χριστον (b vg³ᵐˢˢ syrʰ* bhm ndl.2 prv tpl).[103]

iii) 15:7: the addition of εν πνευματι (Dd l Tert. = TO) or εν πνευματι αγιω (257 614 1799 2412 syrʰᵐᵍ Cass.) to the description of Peter: 'standing up in the [Holy] Spirit he said to them. . .'

iv) 15:29: the addition of φερομενοι εν τω αγιω πνευματι (Dd l IrenᴸᵃᵗTert. Ephr. = TO) to the closing statement of the letter from the Jerusalem council.

v) 15:32: the addition of πληρεις πνευματος αγιου (Dd alone) to the description of Judas and Silas.

vi) 19:1: an alternative reading for the verse in which the Spirit tells Paul to return to Asia: ειπεν αυτω το πνευμα υποστρεφειν εις την Ασιαν (𝔓38 Dd syrʰᵐᵍ Ephr. = TO).

vii) 20:3: an alternative reading in which the Spirit tells Paul to return through Macedonia: ειπεν δε το πνευμα αυτω (Dd gig syrʰᵐᵍ Ephr. = TO).

Although these references have been regarded by some scholars as strong evidence for the secondary nature of the Western text in emphasising the work of the Holy Spirit,[104] the alterations are basically either formal (adding το αγιον) or concerned with another subject altogether, that is, emphasising the Spirit's endowment of the apostles and prophets of the Christian church.[105] When the following passages are taken into account this will emerge as a more clear cut tendency of the Western tradition.[106]

---

[103]Cited from B & L, II, 79. bhm ndl.2 prv tpl are secondary versions (from the Latin). This provides clear evidence for a continued development of the western tradition.

[104]E.g. Lagrange, *Critique textuelle*, 389-394; Williams, *Alterations*, 56; Epp, *Tendency*, 116-118.

[105]So especially Zuntz, 'Western Text', 194f. [noting also 17:15D & Ephraem; 24:10; 26:1]. In a thorough study M. Black detects three categories where the Spirit: i) inspires utterance; ii) directs action; or iii) is the pre- (or post-) baptismal Spirit; 'The Holy Spirit in the Western Text of Acts', *New Testament Textual Criticism: Its Significance to Exegesis* (FS B.M. Metzger; ed. E.J. Epp & G.D. Fee; Oxford: Clarendon, 1981) 160-178.

[106]For similarly negative assessments of this argument see Menoud who said that 'there is no theology of the Spirit peculiar to the Western writer', 'The Western Text and the Theology of Acts', 75 [= p.30 *SNTS Bull*].

3. The Status of the Apostles

It has been a well recognised feature of the Western textual tradition that it tends 'to emphasise the wisdom, authority, and power of the apostolic figures'.[107] This feature seems to have been significant in several passages given above (e.g. 6:10; 11:17; 15:7, 32) concerning references to the Holy Spirit. Additional passages which might be listed under this heading include the following:

i) 5:15: The Western tradition has two alternative additions, emphasising the effect of Peter's healing ministry. Firstly: και ρυσθωσιν απο της ασθενειας αυτων ([Ee] a b w y vg^cl eth^ms Lucif. = TO). Secondly: απηλλασσοντο γαρ απο πασης ασθενειας ως ειχεν εκαστος αυτων (Dd [e p mae: και for γαρ] Chrom. = TO2); alternatively:[108]

ii) 6:10f.: An alternative rendering of this verse highlights the wisdom and boldness of Stephen: ουκ ισχυον αντιστηναι τη ουση εν αυτω και τω πνευματι τω αγιω ω ελαλει, δια το ελεγχεσθαι αυτους επ αυτου μετα πασης παρρησιας. μη δυναμενοι ουν αντοφθαλμειν τη αληθεια (D [E] e h t w [syr^hmg mae] = TO [except for τω αγιω]).[109]

iii) 9:22: Western witnesses add (εν) τω λογω to the statement of that Paul grew strong (C Ee 467 h l p mae = TO; Bezae deficient).

iv) 13:8: an additional statement emphasises the positive response of Sergius Paulus to the preaching of Paul: επειδη

---

[107]Strange, *Problem*, 53; cf. earlier Lagrange, *Critique textuelle*, 391; supplemented by Williams, *Alterations*, 57f. (noting also 2:47; 5:38f.; 14:25; 16:35). Other passages such as 14:10 (the addition of ευθεως [1838 mae eth^10mss] or παραχρημα [Ee] or ευθεως παραχρημα [D syr^hmg]) should also be noted.

[108]We might also note, in connection with the status of Peter, the following: 2:14, where Peter is described as lifting up his voice *first* (πρωτος: D* vg^mss mae; προτερον: E); 5:29, where mention of the apostles is deleted so that Peter answers the Council charge alone (D [h syr^P]); 8:24, where Simon Magus is reduced to tears (D* [syr^hmg] mae); 9:34, where the long addition concerning Peter's mission in 11:2 (D [p w mae], see Strange, *Problem*, 77f. for text and apparatus); 15:7 (see above).

[109]Strange, *Problem*, 53 has a full apparatus. Some Western witnesses also add εστωτος εν μεσω αυτων at the end of 6:15 (D h t mae), thus Corssen: 'Stephanus steht vor seinem Richtern, er ist der Mittelpunkt der ganzen Scene' ('Acta Apostolorum ed. F. Blass', 434; cited from Williams, *Alterations*, 57).

ηδιστα ηκουεν αυτων (D* syr^{h*} mae = TO^2; cf. Ee: οτι ηδεως αυτων ηκουεν = TO). This is matched by the addition, with a similar effect, in v. 12 of εθαυμασεν και (D E syr^P eth Ephr. = TO): 'the proconsul, when he saw what was done *marvelled, and* believed. . .'

v) 13:43: a long additional statement (in two forms), emphasising the impact of Paul and Barnabas: εγενετο δε κατα πασαν πολιν φημισθηναι τον λογον (Ee w vg$^{m\,s}$ mae = TO); alternatively: εγενετο δε καθ ολης της πολεως διελθειν τον λογον (του θεου) (Dd syr^{hmg} = TO^2).

vi) 14:7: the addition of και εκινηθη ολον το πληθος επι τη διδαχη αυτων. . .(D [lacks αυτων] h [b w] vg^{ms} mae = TO), emphasising the effect of the mission of Paul and Barnabas on the whole region (cf. ολην added to end of v. 6 in D E lat [mae]).

vii) 16:4: An alternative rendering of the verse: διερχομενοι δε τας πολεις εκηρυσσον και παρεδιδοσαν αυτοις μετα πασης παρρησιας τον κυριον Ιησουν Χριστον, αμα παραδιδοντες και τας εντολας (Dd syr^{hmg} Ephr. = TO). This emphasises the boldness of Paul and Timothy in much the same way as previously noted concerning Stephen.

viii) An additional feature is the emphasis on the apostolic obedience to the charge of preaching the gospel (1:2: add και εκελευσε κηρυσσειν το ευαγγελιον (D [gig t] syr^{hmg} mae sa = TO^2); 10:41: add και συνεστραφημεν [D it syr^h mae]; cf. also 8:4; 11:1f.) even in the face of difficulties (note the occurence of θλιψις και διωγμος in 8:1; 13:50).

This tendency seems to be a well established feature of the Western tradition (as Boismard and Lamouille's classifications indicate and as Strange also acknowledges).[110] In the instances surveyed this does not include the use of honorific titles for the apostles,[111] nor the

---

[110]Strange, *Problem*, 53-56. Also Zuntz: 'the Apostles never act, decide, or speak without their dependence on their Lord and Master being stressed by themselves, or by the narrator' ('Western Text', 194). This also helps explain the addition of 'in the name of the Lord' in 6:8; 9:14, 17; 14:10 etc.

[111]Strange notes the use of μακαριος and other titles in references to Paul in the Apostolic Fathers (e.g. 1 Clem 47:1; Ignatius, *Eph.* 12.2; Polycarp, *Phil.* 3.2), *Problem*, 214 (n. 53 to p. 54).

hagiography of the later non-canonical Acts. In view of this Strange argues:[112]

> there is a clear divide between the treatment of the apostles in the Western text of Acts and in the apocryphal *Acts*. In the latter, the *Acts of Paul* in particular, the apostles are brought firmly into the writers' own age: Paul refutes Gnostic heresy,[113] encourages martyrdom,[114] and teaches clearly the custom of delaying baptism.[115] The Western text does not exhibit the second-century tendency to use the apostles to legitimate contemporary practice.

Nevertheless, in the passages listed above there are indications that the apostolic presentation has been contemporised in a way that is characteristic of these non-canonical second century writings, most particularly in the rendering of the setting and decree of the council of Jerusalem (also 8:37). This is not done by way of inventing new material (which is not really open to a reviser of manuscript material), nevertheless the Western text might stand part-way along the road to the non-canonical Acts.[116]

4. The Apostolic Decree

There are complex and difficult problems associated with the events of the council of Jerusalem and the terms of the apostolic decree recorded in Acts 15.[117] In particular the exact wording of the decree

---

[112]*Problem*, 55.

[113]*Acts of Paul*, 7.

[114]*Acts of Paul, passim*.

[115]*Acts of Paul*, 25.

[116]See further D. MacDonald, 'Apocryphal and Canonical Narratives about Paul', in W.S. Babcock (ed), *Paul and the Legacies of Paul* (Dallas: SMU Press, 1990) 55-70 and C. M. Martini, 'La tradition textuelle des Actes des Apôtres et les tendances de l'Eglise ancienne', *Les Actes des Apôtres. Traditions, rédaction, théologie* (BETL xlviii; Gembloux: Duculot/Leuven: Leuven University Press, 1979) 21-35.

[117]See M. Simon, 'The Apostolic Decree and its Setting in the Ancient Church', *BJRL* 52 (1970) 437-460; D.R. Catchpole, 'Paul, James and the Apostolic Decree', *NTS* 23 (1977) 428-444; G. Zuntz, 'An Analysis of the report about the "Apostolic Council"', *Opuscula Selecta: Classica, Hellenistica, Christiana* (Manchester: Manchester University Press, 1972, essay from 1939) 216-251. Some of the historical and theological difficulties are addressed elsewhere in this collection (esp. D. Wenham). The language of Paul in Gal. 2:6 and his advice in 1 Cor. 8-10 do not seem (at least at first sight) congruent with his agreement to the decree in

(Acts 15:20, 29; 21:25) has been much debated in view of the textual difficulties at this point.[118] The most recent discussion is in Strange (who has a useful presentation of the different text-forms of the decree on 𝔓88). According to Strange the consensus position is the one that has been defended by Kümmel and others, that is, the original text of 15:20 contained four prohibitions:[119]

ἀλλὰ ἐπιστεῖλαι αὐτοῖς τοῦ ἀπέχεσθαι τῶν ἀλισγημάτων τῶν εἰδώλων καὶ τῆς πορνείας καὶ τοῦ πνικτοῦ καὶ τοῦ αἵματος
𝔓74 S.01 A B C E 𝔐 lat^mss bo

From this original form (according to Kümmel *et al*) three alterations were made:

i) καὶ της πορνειας was omitted by 𝔓45 (also arm eth^mss);[120]

ii) και του πνικτου was omitted by Western witnesses (D d gig Iren^Lat Ambrosiaster Ephr. Aug. = TO);

iii) a form of the golden rule (και οσα αν μη θελωσιν εαυτοις γινεσθαι ετεροις μη ποειν) was added, mainly in Western

---

its Alexandrian form. This has led some scholars to opt for the Western version, since it provides a neater solution.

[118]See E. Bammel, 'Der Text von Apostelgeschichte 15', *Les Actes des Apôtres. Traditions, rédaction, théologie* (BETL xlviii; Gembloux: Duculot/Leuven: Leuven University Press, 1979) 439-446; C.K. Barrett, 'The apostolic decree of Acts 15:29', *ABR* 35 (1987) 50-59; T. Boman, 'Das textkritische Problem des sogenannten Aposteldekrets', *NovT* 7 (1964) 26-36; W.G. Kümmel, 'Die älteste Form des Aposteldekrets', *Heilsgeschehen und Geschichte: Gesammelte Aufsätze 1933-1964. Marburger Theologische Studien* 3 (1965) 278-288 (originally published in *Spiritus et Veritas* [FS K. Kundsin; ASTUL; Eutin: Andres Ozolin, 1953] 83-98).

[119]Kümmel, 'Aposteldekrets', (cf. *Introduction*, 181); UBS³ = NA²⁶; Epp, *Tendency*, 109f.; Metzger, *Commentary*, 432.

[120]Menoud argued that this version represented the original ('Western Text', 65-71; following M.J. Lagrange, 'Le papyrus Beatty des Actes des Apôtres', *RevBib* 43 [1934] 168). This depended partly on the assumption that such a text would be enlarged rather than contracted, and partly on the assumption that the decree was only concerned with food laws. These assumptions cannot be maintained, so this position (dependent as it is upon very slim manuscript evidence) has been rejected by most scholars (including both Strange, *Problem*, 89 and Kümmel, 'Aposteldekrets', 282f.).

witnesses ([Dd] 242 323 522 536 945 1522 1739 1891 2298 it[61] [eth] sa Iren[Lat]).[121]

A somewhat similar situation arises in the two other places where the decree is cited (15:29 and 21:25, see Strange's chart for details).

Most scholars have argued that the longer reading reflects a 'ritual' understanding of the decree (εἰδωλόθυτον refers to eating of meat sacrificed to idols; αἷμα refers to eating of blood; πνικτόν refers to strangled things), formed under the influence of the Old Testament (whether Noachian commands or Lev. 17-18 need not detain us here). The Western readings have been regarded as an 'ethical' version of this original 'ritual' decision, designed to appropriate the decree in a later situation.[122] However, Strange argues (following Resch, Harnack, Ropes and others) that this distinction (between 'ethical' and 'ritual') cannot be maintained; that some elements of 'ritual' (particularly abstention from blood) were in any case widespread in the second century;[123] and that the form of the western text conforms with Luke's desire to 'make the Decree into a regulation having validity for Christians of all places and in all times'.[124]

Strange does not, however, deal with related Western readings not only in the decree texts but in the surrounding contexts (he tends to isolate the Western readings in the decree from the Western readings throughout Acts, cf. above on 8:37ff.). The broader context into which the terms of the decree are located begins at 15:1 where the original issue posed 'Unless you are circumcised according to the custom of Moses, you cannot be saved' is considerably broadened in the western tradition by the addition of καὶ. . .περιπατῆτε (D syr[hmg] sa mae: TO): 'Unless you are circumcised *and live* [*lit. 'walk'*] according to the custom of Moses, you cannot be saved'.[125] Thus the

---

[121]Several different forms of the golden rule are found in these manuscripts, for example D has οσα μη θελουσιν εαυτοις γινεσθαι ετεροις μη ποειτε. N.b. 'it[61]' = Codex Armachanus (Trinity College, Dublin 52), cited from Strange.

[122]E.g. Metzger, *Commentary*, 432; Haenchen, *Acts*, 449f.

[123]Strange, *Problem*, 91-96.

[124]Strange, *Problem*, 104.

[125]Some other witnesses add a phrase identifying those who come from Judea as των πεπιστευκοτων απο της αιρεσεως των Φαρισαιων (Ψ 614 *pc* syr[hmg] = TO[2]). This has a similar effect: by drawing v. 5 into closer relation with v. 1 the broader issue of Torah-observance is highlighted as the crucial matter for discussion.

issue is not limited to circumcision, but the broader question of Gentile Torah-observance.

This broader issue is highlighted in the large western addition to 15:2, which identifies the content of the 'discussion' between Paul and Barnabas and these men: ελεγεν γαρ ο Παυλος μενειν ουτως καθως επιστευσαν διισχυριζομενος (Dd b gig w vg^ms syr^hmg mae = TO). Thus in response to the claim that Gentiles should keep Torah, Paul asserts that *'they should remain just as they were when they believed'*.[126] This significantly shapes the context in which Peter's statement 'Now therefore why do you make trial of God by putting a yoke upon the neck of the disciples which neither our fathers nor we have been able to bear' (15:20).[127] Note that the Western text signals its agreement with Peter by the addition of τω πνευματι in 15:7 at the outset of his speech (cited above), and by recording a general agreement with Peter in v. 12: συγκατατιθεμενων δε των πρεσβυτερων τοις υπο του Πετρου ειρημενοις εσιγησεν (Dd [l] syr^h* Ephr. = TO). These alterations result in a presentation of the council as a discussion of the principle of Torah-keeping among Gentile Christians. The different form of the decree itself (especially the presence of the golden rule) is in conformity with this.

This agreement is clearly reinforced in the later passage about the decree (Acts 21:20-25). In this passage the decree (v. 25) is mentioned in the context of a report that many Jews had been concerned that Paul was teaching Jews to forsake Moses (see v. 20f.: 'they have been told about you that you teach the Jews who are among the Gentiles to forsake Moses, telling them not to circumcise their children or observe the customs'). Thus Paul must give witness that he himself remains Torah-observant (v. 24), but what about the Gentiles? In the Western tradition we find the following (at 21:25):

> But as for the Gentiles who have believed, *they have nothing to say against you*, for (ουδεν εχουσιν λεγειν προς σε ημεις γαρ: D gig sa =

---

[126]The Western texts also give the strong impression that these Pharisaic believers insisted on a judgement upon Paul's position in Jerusalem. Note the addition of οπως κριθωσιν επ αυτοις after Ιερουσαλημ in v. 2 (Dd 257 383 614 1799 2147 2412 syr^h* = TO) and the description of these men in v. 5: οι δε παραγγειλαντες αυτοις αναβαινειν προς τους πρεσβυτερους (Dd syr^hmg = TO²).

[127]There is no difference in the wording of the texts at this point. The difference arises from the changes previously made which focus attention on Torah-observance as a whole, thus inviting the understanding that the 'yoke' is the whole yoke of the Law (cf. Gal. 5:1-3: a passage which may in fact explain these alterations).

> TO) we have sent giving judgement *that they should observe nothing of the sort except* (κριναντες μηδεν τοιουτον τηρειν αυτους ει μη: Dd 𝔐 gig syrh [C E Ψ 1739 *pc*]= TO) that they should abstain from what has been sacrificed to idols and from blood and from unchastity.

It is clear that 'keeping nothing of the sort' in the Western witnesses here refers to observance of the Torah as a whole; rather Gentile believers should should merely assent to the three items given. The terms of the (Western) decree do not in any way enforce Torah observance upon Gentile Christians. This understanding is also reflected in the actual text of the decree, which in the Western version of 15.29 reads:

> that you abstain from what has been sacrificed to idols and from blood and from unchastity, *and whatever they do not wish to be done to them, do not do to others* (και οσα μη θελετε εαυτοις γινεσθαι ετερω μη ποειν: Dd 242 323 522 614 945 1739 1799 1891 2298 2412 b l p syrh* sa (eth) IrenLat Cyprian = TO). If you keep yourselves from such things you do well, *being sustained by the Holy Spirit* (φερομενοι εν τω αγιω πνευματι: Dd l IrenLat Tert. Ephr. = TO). Farewell.

The evidence adduced (classified as TO by Boismard and Lamouille) suggests that the Western text must be understood as a thoroughgoing attempt to address the question of Gentile Torah-observance in a more decisive manner than the Alexandrian text allows. The focus is not on table fellowship and food laws, but quite specifically upon the place of Torah in the life of believing Gentiles, and the answer given is negative.[128] The Western form of the decree emerges as a Christian, ethical document, plainly stating total freedom from Torah.

It seems more likely to this writer that this Western form would have arisen in reaction to the Alexandrian tradition rather than *vice versa*. The alternative would require an Alexandrian redaction in a legalistic or historicising direction for which there is no evidence. Nor do the differences between these two approaches to the circumstances and terms of the decree suggest two versions from a single author. More plausible is the view of Zuntz, who described this case as 'the extreme instance of. . .neglect of historical tradition in favour of moral ecclesiastical teaching'.[129]

---

[128]The importance of harmonising Paul's attitude to the law with that of Acts would be an important factor in this process.

[129]Zuntz, 'Western Text', 195; cf. also Bruce, *Acts*, 44.

V. Conclusions

The weaknesses perceived in Blass' original hypothesis remain obstacles to the modern revival of the theory that Luke wrote two versions of Acts. We have seen that the Western text tends to include, specify, and emphasise matters in a way that is paralleled in secondary textual traditions in other parts of the New Testament (and in the re-use of New Testament material in subsequent non-canonical works). Recent attempts to either minimise the differences between the text-types (Strange) or distinguish between a pure and a later form of the Western text (Boismard and Lamouille) do not adequately account for the evidence we have surveyed. The consensus position in favour of originality of the 'Alexandrian' form of the text is preferable (as giving a plausible account of the theological tendencies of the 'western' tradition). In our opinion, the stylistic and vocabulary similarities between the two text-types (emphasised in particular by Boismard and Lamouille) do not represent an insuperable objection to this position (such stylistic similarities are a predictable outcome of such a revisionary practice).

There remain significant problems which we have not addressed. Can the origin of the Western tradition be traced to one major revision with later accretions? Where might this activity have taken place? Was Acts affected to such an extent because it 'achieved' canonical status at a later date than, for example, the Gospels, and thus suffered more from 'free treatment'? Notwithstanding the general conclusion that the Western text is secondary, might it occasionally record authentic historical information?[130] Although this possibility cannot be excluded, my own impression is that this is unlikely, as Kenyon concluded: 'the attractive character of several of the δ readings in Acts is to a considerable extent offset by the questionable company in which they are found'.[131]

In many ways the Western form of Acts witnesses to a text of Acts put to use in the service of the church. Its expansions 'provide

---

[130]Kümmel: Western might be original at 12:10; 19:9; 20:4; 20:15; 27:5; Bruce: some Western additions may be original, at least a strong case could be made for their originality: 8:24 (Simon's tears); 10:25 (Cornelius' servant); 11:2, cf. 21:17; 12:10; 16:30; 18:4, 21; 19:9, 28; 28:16: 'some of these added details give the impression of local knowledge, though others may have been deduced from the narrative, or even invented by the expander (though it is often difficult to see why)' (p. 44).

[131]Kenyon, 'Western Text', 314; also Zuntz, 'Western Text'.

the preacher and the missionary with suitable examples from the life of his authoritative predecessors and. . .give concrete directions for Christian life as it was meant to be lived in early Christian communities'.[132] As such these variations can be of use to the exegete in offering the earliest commentary on Acts. The argument of this essay, however, points to the likelihood that the Alexandrian text provides the closer approximation to the original text of the author, and should therefore be the primary object of the exegete's attentions.[133]

---

[132]Zuntz, 'Western Text', 196.
[133]I would like to thank Dr S. Pickering (Sydney) for his detailed and helpful comments on an earlier draft and Dr P.E. Satterthwaite (Cambridge) for the translations from Griesbach (n. 1 and 10).

INDEX OF BIBLICAL
REFERENCES

OLD TESTAMENT

APOCRYPHA

NEW TESTAMENT

INDEX OF ANCIENT AUTHORS

TARGUMS

PAPYRI

EARLY CHRISTIAN LITERATURE

INDEX OF MODERN AUTHORS

INDEX OF SUBJECTS